Introduction to Learning Disabilities

Second Edition

DANIEL P. HALLAHAN

University of Virginia

JAMES M. KAUFFMAN

University of Virginia

JOHN WILLS LLOYD

University of Virginia

ALLYN AND BACON

Boston • London • Toronto • Sydney • Tokyo • Singapore

Senior Editor: Ray Short
Series Editorial Assistant: Karin Huang
Marketing Managers: Ellen Mann Dolberg, Brad Parkins
Composition Buyer: Linda Cox
Manufacturing Buyer: Megan Cochran
Cover Administrator: Linda Knowles
Production Administrator: Rosalie Briand
Editorial-Production Service: Trinity Publishers Services
Electronic Composition: Omegatype Typography, Inc.

A Viacom Company
160 Gould Street
Needham Heights, Massachusetts 02194

Internet: www.abacon.com

Library of Congress Cataloging-in-Publication Data
Hallahan, Daniel P., 1944–
Introduction to learning disabilities / Daniel P. Hallahan, James M. Kauffman, John Wills Lloyd. — 2nd ed.
p. cm.
Includes bibliographical references and indexes.
ISBN 0-205-29043-4
1. Learning disabilities. 2. Learning disabilities—United States. 3. Learning disabled—Education. 4. Learning disabled—Education—United States. I. Kauffman, James M. II. Lloyd, John, Ph.D. III. Title.
LC4704.H34 1999
371.92'6—dc21 98-20485
CIP

Printed in the United States of America
10 9 8 7 6 5 4 3 RRDV 03 02

Photo Credits: Brian Smith, pp. 1, 59, 154, 182, 206, 263; Will Hart, pp. 35, 127, 327, 413; Ralph C. Eagle Jr./Photo Researchers, p. 41; Warren Anatomical Museum, Harvard Medical School, p. 45; Will Faller, pp. 91, 233, 290, 368.

Contents

PART FOUR: STRATEGIES FOR HELPING STUDENTS WITH LEARNING DISABILITIES ADJUST AND ADAPT

PART FIVE: STRATEGIES FOR TEACHING STUDENTS WITH LEARNING DISABILITIES IN KEY CONTENT AREAS

Preface

This book is a thorough introduction to the field of learning disabilities across the life span from early childhood to adulthood, covering basic information pertaining to causes, characteristics, parent and family factors, and educational approaches (including early childhood and adult programs). We have written the text for the first course in learning disabilities at the undergraduate or graduate level. Our inclusion of strategies for teaching makes the text especially appropriate for instructors who like to blend coverage of teaching methods with information on characteristics of students with learning disabilities.

Our goal was to write a highly readable text that presents clear, concise, and practical information about a field characterized by challenges and contradictions. These challenges and contradictions, however, are the very reasons we continue to find the field of learning disabilities such an exhilarating area of study and practice. We hope this text conveys our enthusiasm for wrestling with the many issues pertaining to educating students with learning disabilities, and we invite you, the reader, to engage in building a better future for persons with learning disabilities and their families.

KEY REVISION POINTS

Reorganization of Chapters

We have condensed and combined material on history, trends, definitions, prevalence, and demographics from Chapters 1 and 2 of the first edition into one streamlined chapter, "Ongoing Issues and Themes." On the advice of several users, we have also reordered the chapters, placing those devoted to teaching at the end of the book. In this way, readers will have a broad foundation regarding characteristics of students with learning disabilities before turning to discussion of educational methods.

Expansion of Boxed Features

Instructors using the first edition have pointed to the utility of the boxes—"Tips for Practice," "Current Issues," "Human Perspectives," "Multicultural Perspectives," and "Technology." Therefore, we have increased the number of these and added a new feature—"Example"—that helps explain important concepts and procedures in greater detail. We have also provided "Questions to Ponder" at the end of some of the boxes to encourage students to reflect on what they are reading.

Major Headings as Questions

Also in keeping with the notion of reflective reading, we have turned the major chapter headings into questions. By posing questions to readers, we hope to stimulate their curiosity and encourage them to seek answers as they read.

Up-to-Date Information

In this edition, we present the most current information on a variety of contemporary topics. Some of the most important are:

- *The 1997 amendments to IDEA.* We cover the changes in the Individuals with Disabilities Education Act that affect programming for students with learning disabilities.
- *Inclusionary practices.* We present the most current research and practices on how to include students with learning disabilities in general education classrooms.
- *Latest research-based teaching methods.* We take pride in presenting the most up-to-date proven teaching methods for students with learning disabilities.
- *Technological advances.* We present the most recent technological innovations pertaining to identifying and teaching students with learning disabilities.
- *Recent trends in diagnosis.* We present the latest research on identification practices, such as authentic assessment.
- *Latest research on biological causes.* We cover the ever-expanding research on biological causes of learning disabilities.
- *Latest evidence on connections between learning disabilities and attention deficit hyperactivity disorder.* We detail the growing research base on the link between ADHD and learning disabilities.

1

Ongoing Issues and Themes

When confronted by the human differences we call disabilities, our natural tendency is to ask a series of questions. For any given individual who exhibits what we consider a disability, our first questions are likely to be: Why did this happen? What caused it? What is it like to be different in this way? How might it have been prevented? What can be done about it? How should I interact with this person? If the difference we observe is only in behavior, not in appearance, we may wonder whether the disability is real or imagined. Is this person faking? Is my ignorance or bias, rather than this person's behavior, the issue? Teachers and those preparing to be teachers are likely to have additional questions: What if I have a student like this in my class? What am I supposed to know about students like this one? What is the best way to teach him or her? What are my responsibilities in cases like this? Where can I turn for help? Because learning disabilities are by far the most prevalent disabilities, these questions are most likely to be prompted by an encounter with a student who has a learning disability.

Before we can answer such questions in a comprehensive way, we need to have a basic understanding of some of the underlying issues facing the field of learning disabilities. These are undoubtedly some of the most complex and challenging in all of special education. In this chapter, we discuss the basic issues and themes that bring some coherence to the complex field known as learning disabilities.

WHAT IS LEARNING DISABILITIES LIKE AS A FIELD OF STUDY?

Interdisciplinary, International, and Multicultural

Today there is much controversy about the professional group that should be most responsible for students with learning disabilities, the professional perspectives that are most helpful, and how various professionals can best work together to provide the most effective services. There is also growing concern for ensuring that the multicultural aspects of learning disabilities are understood. As Moats and Lyon (1993) point out:

> Learning disabilities are considered the proper and legitimate concern of many disciplines and professions, including education, psychology, neuropsychology, speech and language pathology, neurology, psychiatry, ophthalmology, optometry, and occupational therapy. Each of these professions has traditionally focused on different aspects of the child with LD, so that there are sometimes extremely divergent ideas, and sometimes contentious disagreements, about the importance of etiology, diagnostic methods, the importance of different characteristics, instructional content and teaching methodologies, and professional roles and responsibilities. (p. 287)

The questions growing out of these concerns are wide ranging and immediate: To what extent are regular classroom teachers in general education responsible for teaching these students? To what extent should special education teachers be involved? What is the role of physicians in diagnosing and treating learning disabilities, especially in cases involving attention deficit hyperactivity disorder (ADHD), for which medications might be prescribed? (ADHD is characterized by extreme inattentive behavior, impulsivity, and/or high motor activity. We discuss ADHD further in Chapter 10.) What do psychologists have to offer, and how can they be helpful in identifying and remediating learning, behavioral, and emotional problems? Where do reading specialists come into the picture in teaching children who have reading problems and who might be called "dyslexic"? How are speech-language pathologists best involved, given the observation that many students with learning disabilities have difficulty using language effectively? To what extent are cultural differences mistaken for learning disabilities? How can cultural bias in definition, assessment, and treatment be avoided?

Questions like these are best understood against the backdrop of the multidisciplinary and multicultural origins of the field. Over the last hundred years, the professional groups most involved and influential in the field of learning disabilities have changed, and the pace of these changes has increased since the early 1960s. Figure 1.1 depicts our estimation of the relative level of involvement and influence of several professional groups on the field during various periods of the 19th and 20th centuries, with darker shading indicating relatively more intense involvement. Before 1900, physicians and those interested in what we now call speech-language pathology were virtually the only professionals studying what are now known as learning disabilities. Not until the 1920s, which saw the rapid development of special education, were educators a

FIGURE 1.1 A Century of Learning Disabilities

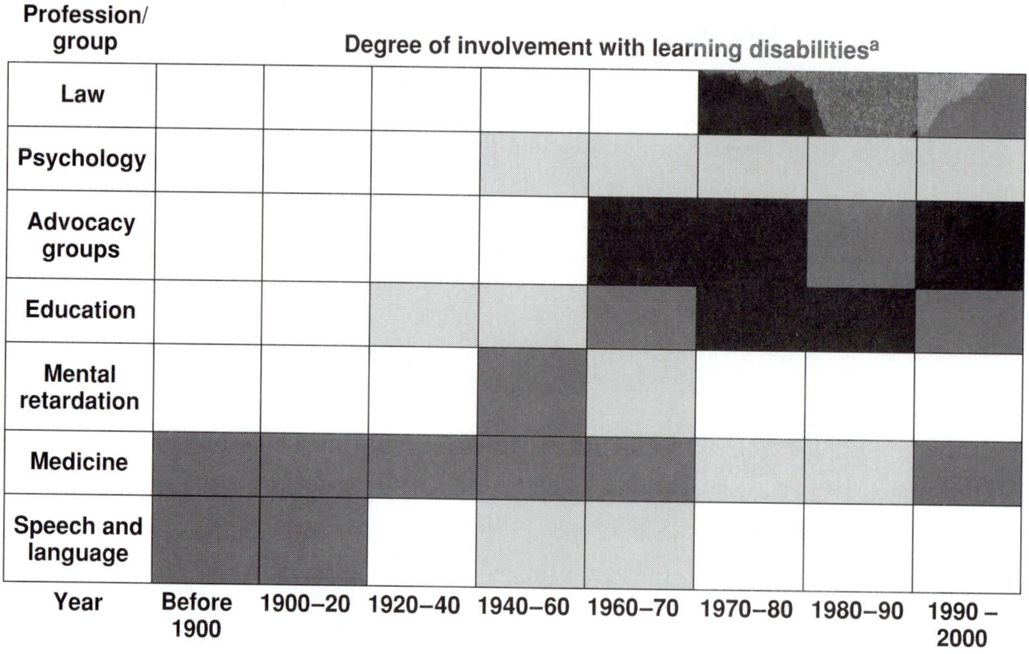

[a]Intensity of shading corresponds to amount of involvement, with darkest shading indicating highest involvement level.

significant part of the story of learning disabilities. By midcentury, psychology and specialists in mental retardation had begun making significant contributions to the development of the field. In the 1960s, the first major advocacy group was formed to work for the recognition of learning disabilities and improved services for children with such disabilities—the Association for Children with Learning Disabilities, now known as the Learning Disabilities Association of America. In the 1970s, lawyers became a particularly important force with the enactment of Public Law 94-142, which is now known as the Individuals with Disabilities Education Act (IDEA). This federal law and its regulations gave advocates a legal basis for pressing their claims to free and appropriate education for students with learning disabilities. In 1990, the enactment of the Americans with Disabilities Act (ADA) extended the legal rights of children and adults with learning disabilities to nondiscriminatory treatment in the larger society.

The historical roots of the field, as well as today's special education for students with learning disabilities, are international and multicultural as well as multidisciplinary (cf. Cruickshank & Hallahan, 1975a, 1975b; Fabbro & Masutto, 1994; Hallahan & Cruickshank, 1973; Opp, 1994; Richardson, 1992). However, the origins of the field as we know it are traced primarily to research conducted in various countries of Europe and in the United States. European neurologists and ophthalmologists, for example, provided many of the 19th-century and early 20th-century foundations of the field. The International Academy for Research in Learning Disabilities today provides a forum for sharing research findings, and in 1992, the *Journal of Learning Disabilities* began publishing a series of articles on international perspectives.

Although the bulk of descriptions of programs, practices, policies, and research has been published in the United States, learning disabilities are not an American phenomenon (Moats & Lyon, 1993). Comparisons of special education in various nations of the world, however, suggest that learning disabilities are seldom recognized in countries in which special education is just emerging (Artiles, Csapo, & deLorenzo, 1995; Artiles, Trent, & Hallahan, 1995). The recognition and treatment of learning disabilities are common only in countries having a well-developed system of universal public education and a heavy emphasis on academic achievement (see Mazurek & Winzer, 1994). Countries with less well developed education systems are more likely to concentrate their limited resources on disabilities that are more physically obvious, such as blindness, deafness, physical disabilities, and severe forms of mental retardation. There are several reasons why developing countries do not typically provide services for students with learning disabilities. The poverty in these countries results in a large segment of the population being relatively uneducated, which makes it difficult to distinguish between academic deficits due to a lack of educational opportunity and those due to a learning disability. Furthermore, the fact that the work force in these countries is less reliant on a high level of literacy and technological skill makes it easier for persons with learning disabilities to find a job and "fit in" with the rest of society.

Within various nations—especially those having a very diverse, multicultural composition of peoples—there is concern about the relationship between ethnic or cultural identity and identification and treatment of learning disabilities. Multicultural issues, such as cultural bias in assessment and instruction, will probably continue to stimulate controversy for decades to come.

Research Based: Both Basic and Applied and Quantitative and Qualitative

Advances in the field of learning disabilities have not come easily. Not unlike in other areas of scientific endeavor, discoveries and innovations in learning disabilities have depended on painstaking research. Much of this research has taken place in the laboratories of psychologists, neurologists, and other scientists interested in answering basic questions about the nature of learning disabilities. But the research has also taken place in the classrooms, homes, and workplaces in which persons with learning disabilities learn, live, and work. A learning disability is a condition that begs for answers to questions ranging from what biochemical reactions occur between neurons in the brain in persons with learning disabilities to how teachers can best present reading passages to students experiencing reading problems.

In the 1980s, psychologists and educators began raising new questions about the type of research appropriate for a science of human behavior and the practice of education. Today controversy rages regarding the use of quantitative versus qualitative methods of research. Quantitative research relies heavily on measurement of variables that are presumably controlled, objective, and valid. Qualitative research relies on variables that are not as easily measured, being obtained from personal experience, anecdote, and admittedly subjective reports. Most authorities now recognize the unique contributions that can be gained from quantitative as well as qualitative research methodologies. Both approaches have provided useful information for the learning disabilities field.

Historically, researchers and advocates for students with learning disabilities have been impatient for better methods of intervention, and the hope for the dramatic breakthrough springs eternal. Yet the history of the field shows that progress has been achieved only through patient, deliberate, meticulous research—little steps leading incrementally toward the goal of more effective instruction (cf. Kauffman, 1993a; Worrall & Carnine, 1994). A persistent theme throughout this book is that we must carefully examine the reliability of the evidence on which recommended practices are based, connect new evidence to the body of research that preceded it, and be cautious about claims of breakthroughs.

HOW HAS *LEARNING DISABILITY* BEEN DEFINED?

Learning disability is a term that was added to our language relatively recently, being formally introduced in the 1960s. In 1968, the label "specific learning disability" became a federally designated category of "handicapping conditions." The lengthy and complex story of how we deal with human differences is reflected in the evolution of this field, from the emergence of the concept of learning disability, the widespread acceptance of the term, and the rapid increase in the number of individuals said to have learning disabilities to the development of professional practices in response to learning disabilities and the continuing controversies surrounding virtually every aspect of them—concept, terminology, prevalence, and professional practices.

The learning disabilities story actually began long before 1963, when Samuel Kirk suggested the term at a meeting of parents advocating special educational services for their children who were having difficulty in school but who were not considered disabled by mental retardation or emotional disturbance. In the words of Kirk (1963):

> Recently I have used the term "learning disability" to describe a group of children who have disorders in development, in language, speech, reading, and associated communication skills needed for social interaction. In this group I do not include children who have sensory handicaps such as blindness or deafness, because we have methods of managing and training the deaf and the blind. I also exclude from this group children who have generalized mental retardation.

In earlier decades, these children's difficulties had been variously categorized as mild exogenous mental retardation (mild mental retardation caused by brain injury), **minimal brain dysfunction** (behavioral abnormalities similar to, but less severe than, those caused by brain injury, although brain damage cannot be verified), dyslexia (extreme difficulty in reading), perceptual impairment (persistent difficulty in making sense of sensory stimulation), hyperactivity (excessive motor behavior and inattention), and slow learning (a child whose intelligence is not far enough below average to indicate mental retardation) (Hallahan & Cruickshank, 1973; Hallahan & Kauffman, 1977; Mann, 1979; Wiederholt, 1974). The difficulties designated by these and other terms were eventually amalgamated into the concept of learning disabilities.

Today people from nearly every walk of life recognize the term *learning disability.* Learning disability is a separate category in the special education literature, a disability defined by federal and state laws, and a specialization for which teachers in many states must obtain special certification. The term has gained almost total acceptance among educators and the general public in the United States and many foreign countries (Mazurek & Winzer, 1994; Winzer, 1993). Although familiar, the concept is not yet completely formed. Like other complex but useful concepts, it requires perpetual refinement (see Kavale & Forness, 1985, 1992; Moats & Lyon, 1993; Torgesen, 1991).

To say that considerable debate has surrounded the issue of defining learning disabilities is an understatement. At least 11 definitions have enjoyed some degree of official status in the field (Hammill, 1990), and numerous professional and federal committees have convened to hammer out language acceptable to various constituencies.

A logical question is why so much professional energy has been expended on attempting to define this term. No less a philosopher than Socrates has pointed out the importance of definition while noting the futility of demanding a perfect definition:

> Socrates taught that real knowledge can be obtained only through absolute definition; if one cannot define something absolutely, then one does not really *know* what that something is (Stone, 1988). But Socrates also believed that people are inherently incapable of formulating ultimate definitions and therefore can never attain true and complete knowledge of anything. Yet, most of the Socratic dialogues recorded by Plato and Xenophon dealt with his efforts to define diverse terms. Obviously, even though they may be out of our reach, ultimate definitions are vital to pursue because they lead to better, if not total, knowledge of a particular subject. (Hammill, 1990, p. 74)

In addition to these lofty explanations are pragmatic considerations pertaining to questions of funding and legislation. In order to advocate for funds and legislation with lawmakers, it helps to be able to articulate clearly for whom the funds and legislation are intended.

Kirk's Definition (1962)

In the first edition of his very popular introductory text on exceptional children, Samuel Kirk defined learning disability as follows:

> A learning disability refers to a retardation, disorder, or delayed development in one or more of the processes of speech, language, reading, writing, arithmetic, or other school subject resulting from a psychological handicap caused by a possible cerebral

> dysfunction and/or emotional or behavioral disturbances. It is not the result of mental retardation, sensory deprivation, or cultural and instructional factors. (Kirk, 1962, p. 263)

Five components in Kirk's definition have appeared in many of the later definitions:

1. subaverage achievement (reading, writing, arithmetic) or achievement-related (speech or language) behavior
2. **intraindividual differences**—the possibility that the subaverage achievement or achievement-related behavior occurs in only some areas or one area, with average or above-average achievement in the other areas
3. reference to psychological handicaps (often referred to as psychological processes by Kirk and others) as causal factors
4. reference to cerebral dysfunction as a possible causal factor
5. exclusion of other disabling conditions (e.g., mental retardation) and environmental conditions as causal factors

Bateman's Definition (1965)

Barbara Bateman, a student of Kirk, offered the following definition:

> Children who have learning disorders are those who manifest an educationally significant discrepancy between their estimated intellectual potential and actual level of performance related to basic disorders in the learning process, which may or may not be accompanied by demonstrable central nervous system dysfunction, and which are not secondary to generalized mental retardation, educational or cultural deprivation, severe emotional disturbance, or sensory loss. (Bateman, 1965, p. 220)

Bateman's definition differs from Kirk's in at least two important respects. First, it does not include any reference to emotional factors as a cause of learning disabilities; in fact, it mentions severe emotional disturbance as one of the disabilities that does not cause learning disabilities. No major definitions since Bateman's have mentioned emotional disturbance as a possible causal factor. Second, and even more important, it includes reference to a discrepancy between intellectual potential and actual performance. As we discuss later, this discrepancy notion has been the focus of intense debate for several years.

Task Forces I and II Definitions (1966, 1969)

Beginning in 1963, the federal government and several national agencies began planning a series of three task forces to address various aspects of minimal brain dysfunction and/or learning disabilities. The title of the project, Minimal Brain Dysfunction: National Project on Learning Disabilities in Children, reflects the somewhat schizophrenic nature of the project. At this point in the history of the field, there were sharp disagreements concerning causal factors in learning disabilities. (See Chapter 2.) Some, primarily from medicine, subscribed to the idea of minimal brain dysfunction—relatively subtle neurological disorders that result in learning problems. Others, primarily from education, questioned the existence of minimal brain dysfunction and/or the educational value of looking to the brain for causal explanations of learning disabilities. The difference in orientation between the medical and educational professionals was also evidenced by the fact that Task Force I, composed primarily of medical personnel, formulated a definition of minimal brain dysfunction, whereas Task Force II, composed primarily of educators, chose to define learning disabilities.

Task Force I Definition (1966)

Task Force I defined minimal brain dysfunction as a disorder affecting

> children of near average, average, or above average general intelligence with certain learning or behavior disabilities ranging from mild to severe, which are associated with deviations of function of the central nervous system. These deviations may manifest themselves by various combinations of impairment in perception, conceptualization, language, memory, and control of attention, impulse, or motor function. . . .
>
> These aberrations may arise from genetic variations, biochemical irregularities, perinatal [occurring during the birth process] brain insults or other illnesses or injuries sustained during the years which are critical for the development and maturation of the central nervous system, or from unknown causes. (Clements, 1966, pp. 9–10)

Task Force II Definitions (1969)

Task Force II could not agree on one definition, so it offered two. The first emphasizes the idea of intraindividual differences contained in Kirk's definition. The second emphasizes the notion of discrepancy between estimated intellectual potential and actual level of performance introduced by Bateman's definition. The first definition reads:

> Children with learning disabilities are those (1) who have educationally significant discrepancies among their sensory-motor, perceptual, cognitive, academic, or related developmental levels which interfere with the performance of educational tasks; (2) who may or may not show demonstrable deviation in central nervous system functioning; and (3) whose disabilities are not secondary to general mental retardation, sensory deprivation or serious emotional disturbance. (Haring, 1969, pp. 2–3)

The second definition reads:

> Children with learning disabilities are those (1) who manifest an educationally significant discrepancy between estimated academic potential and actual level of academic functioning as related to dysfunctioning in the learning process; (2) may or may not show demonstrable deviation in central nervous system functioning; and (3) whose disabilities are not secondary to general mental retardation, cultural, sensory and/or educational deprivation or environmentally produced serious emotional disturbance. (Haring, 1969, p. 3)

These Task Force definitions are important because they were the first attempt to define learning disabilities at the national level and they highlighted some of the definitional arguments that still rage today—whether central nervous system dysfunction is a valid and important causal factor and whether a discrepancy between intellectual potential and academic achievement is a viable construct.

National Advisory Committee on Handicapped Children Definition (1968)

By the late 1960s, the U.S. Office of Education (USOE) was considering writing legislation for the funding of programs focused on learning disabilities. A committee was asked to formulate a definition of learning disabilities for this legislation. Headed by Samuel Kirk, the National Advisory Committee on Handicapped Children (NACHC) arrived at the following definition, which was then included in the Specific Learning Disabilities Act of 1969:

> Children with special (specific) learning disabilities exhibit a disorder in one or more of the basic psychological processes involved in understanding or in using spoken and written language. These may be manifested in disorders of listening, thinking, talking, reading, writing, spelling or arithmetic. They include conditions which have been referred to as perceptual handicaps, brain injury, minimal brain dysfunction, dyslexia, developmental aphasia, etc. They do not include learning problems that are due primarily to visual, hearing or motor handicaps, to mental retardation, emotional disturbance, or to environmental disadvantage. (U.S. Office of Education, 1968, p. 34)

Given that Kirk was the chair of this committee, it is not surprising that the NACHC definition was highly similar to Kirk's 1962 definition, with the following exceptions: The NACHC definition (1) refers specifically to children, (2) adds thinking disorders to the list of examples of learning disabilities, and (3) does not refer to emotional disturbance as a causal factor (Hammill, 1990).

The NACHC definition immediately became the most popular one among state departments of education (Mercer, Forgnone, & Wolking, 1976). And as Hammill has stated: "Without a doubt, this was the seminal definition of learning disabilities, for it was the basis for the 1977 USOE definition that was incorporated in Public Law 94–142" (Hammill, 1990, p. 75).

HOW IS *LEARNING DISABILITY* DEFINED TODAY?

U.S. Office of Education Definition (1977)

In wrestling with the formulation of a definition of learning disabilities for Public Law 94-142 (the single most important and comprehensive piece of legislation ever passed pertaining to education of students with disabilities), the USOE first considered the notion of relying on a formula for measuring the discrepancy between intellectual ability and achievement. In 1976, it floated a proposed formula that defined a severe discrepancy as "when achievement in one or more of the areas falls at or below 50% of the child's expected achievement level, when age and previous educational experiences are taken into account" (U.S. Office of Education, 1976, p. 52405).

The response to the idea of a formula was immediate and negative. We return to this topic later in the chapter, but suffice it to say that numerous authorities pointed out statistical as well as conceptual problems with the use of a formula. Based on overwhelmingly negative reactions from the field, the USOE dropped the formula from its final definition for P.L. 94-142:

> The term "specific learning disability" means a disorder in one or more of the basic psychological processes involved in understanding or in using language, spoken or written, which may manifest itself in an imperfect ability to listen, speak, read, write, spell, or to do mathematical calculations. The term includes such conditions as perceptual handicaps, brain injury, minimal brain dysfunction, dyslexia and developmental aphasia. The term does not include children who have learning disabilities which are primarily the result of visual, hearing, or motor handicaps, or mental retardation, or emotional disturbance, or of environmental, cultural, or economic disadvantage. (U.S. Office of Education, 1977, p. 65083)

Although it dropped the formula, the USOE did not give up on the idea of **ability-achievement discrepancy**—the discrepancy between intellectual potential and academic achievement. It was included in the P.L. 94-142 regulations as criteria for identification:

> *Section 121a.541 Criteria for determining the existence of a specific learning disability.*
>
> (a) A team may determine that a child has a specific learning disability if:
>
> (1) The child does not achieve commensurate with his or her age and ability levels in one or more of the areas listed in paragraph (a) (2) of this section, when provided with learning experiences appropriate for the child's age and ability levels; and
>
> (2) The team finds that a child has a severe discrepancy between achievement and intellectual ability in one or more of the following areas:
>
> (i) Oral expression;
> (ii) Listening comprehension;
> (iii) Written expression;
> (iv) Basic reading skill;
> (v) Reading comprehension;
> (vi) Mathematics calculation; or
> (vii) Mathematics reasoning.
>
> (U.S. Office of Education, 1977, p. 65083)

Thus, although the ability-achievement discrepancy was not included in the U.S. Office of Education's definition, its presence in the evaluation criteria has made it a de facto part of the definition. In fact, the vast majority of states now include some reference to ability-achievement discrepancy in their definitions and/or evaluation criteria (Mercer, Jordan, Allsopp, & Mercer, 1996). (We return to a discussion of ability-achievement discrepancy later in this chapter.)

National Joint Committee on Learning Disabilities Definition (1981)

In 1981, the National Joint Committee on Learning Disabilities (NJCLD), which consisted of representatives from virtually all major professional and parent organizations dealing with learning disabilities, issued yet another definition:

> Learning disabilities is a generic term that refers to a heterogeneous group of disorders manifested by significant difficulties in the acquisition and use of listening, speaking, reading, writing, reasoning or mathematical abilities. These disorders are intrinsic to the individual and presumed to be due to central nervous system dysfunction. Even though a learning disability may occur concomitantly with other handicapping conditions (e.g., sensory impairment, mental retardation, social and emotional disturbance) or environmental influences (e.g., cultural differences, insufficient-inappropriate instruction, psychogenic factors), it is not the direct result of those conditions or influences. (Hammill, Leigh, McNutt, & Larsen, 1981, p. 336)

One of the major concerns expressed by some members of the NJCLD was the emphasis given to **psychological processes** in the USOE definition. This was troubling because of its possible connection to the earlier treatment techniques of perceptual, perceptual-motor, and psycholinguistic training that had been so popular but had later been documented as ineffective. Proponents of these techniques claimed to remediate learning disabilities through exercises involving tracing geometric figures, finding figures embedded on a page within many distracting lines, discriminating among various figures that are similar in appearance, and so forth. (See Hallahan & Cruickshank, 1973, and Hammill & Larsen, 1974, for a discussion of these techniques and their demise.)

Learning Disabilities Association of America Definition (1986)

The Learning Disabilities Association of America (LDA) (formerly the Association of Children and Adults with Learning Disabilities, which was formerly the Association of Children with Learning Disabilities), the major parent organization devoted to learning disabilities, was the one organization belonging to the NJCLD that did not endorse the NJCLD definition. The LDA endorsed the following definition:

> Specific Learning Disabilities is a chronic condition of presumed neurological origin which selectively interferes with the development, integration, and/or demonstration of verbal and/or nonverbal abilities. Specific Learning Disabilities exists as a distinct handicapping condition and varies in its manifestations and in degree of severity. Throughout life, the condition can affect self-esteem, education, vocation, socializa-

> tion, and/or daily living activities. (Association for Children with Learning Disabilities, 1986, p. 15)

The LDA definition differs from the other two major definitions—USOE and NJCLD—in at least three respects: (1) It emphasizes the lifelong nature of learning disabilities. (2) It does not address the exclusion of other disabling conditions and environmental conditions as causal factors. (3) It mentions adaptive behaviors, such as vocational and daily living skills and social behaviors, as being potentially affected.

Interagency Committee on Learning Disabilities Definition (1987)

The Interagency Committee on Learning Disabilities (ICLD), consisting of representatives from several federal agencies, was charged by Congress to report on various issues pertaining to research on the cause, diagnosis, treatment, and prevention of learning disabilities and to make recommendations for research funding. Although not required to do so, the committee also took on the task of developing a definition of learning disabilities, as follows:

> Learning disabilities is a generic term that refers to a heterogeneous group of disorders manifested by significant difficulties in the acquisition and use of listening, speaking, reading, writing, reasoning, or mathematical abilities, or of social skills. These disorders are intrinsic to the individual and presumed to be due to central nervous system dysfunction. Even though a learning disability may occur concomitantly with other handicapping conditions (e.g., sensory impairment, mental retardation, social and emotional disturbance), with socioenvironmental influences (e.g., cultural differences, insufficient or inappropriate instruction, psychogenic factors), and especially with attention deficit disorder, all of which may cause learning problems, a learning disability is not the direct result of those conditions or influences. (Interagency Committee on Learning Disabilities, 1987, p. 222)

The ICLD essentially adopted the 1981 NJCLD definition with two important changes. First, it mentioned social skills deficits as a type of learning disability. Second, it added attention deficit disorder as a condition that may co-occur with learning disabilities but not cause them.

National Joint Committee on Learning Disabilities Revised Definition (1988)

In 1988, the NJCLD revised its earlier definition. The revised definition, in essence, was a response to the LDA definition's emphasis on the lifelong nature of learning disabilities and the ICLD definition's specification of social skills deficits as a type of learning disability. The revised NJCLD definition agrees with the former by noting that learning disabilities "may occur across the life span." But it disagrees with the latter by inserting a sentence stating that socialization problems may co-occur with learning disabilities but "do not by themselves constitute a learning disability." The 1988 NJCLD definition thus reads:

> Learning disabilities is a general term that refers to a heterogeneous group of disorders manifested by significant difficulties in the acquisition and use of listening, speaking, reading, writing, reasoning, or mathematical abilities. These disorders are intrinsic to the individual, presumed to be due to central nervous system dysfunction, and may occur across the life span. Problems in self-regulatory behaviors, social perception, and social interaction may exist with learning disabilities but do not by themselves constitute a learning disability. Although learning disabilities may occur concomitantly with other handicapping conditions (for example, sensory impairment, mental retardation, serious emotional disturbance) or with extrinsic influences (such as cultural differences, insufficient or inappropriate instruction), they are not the result of those conditions or influences. (National Joint Committee on Learning Disabilities, 1988, p. 1)

Individuals with Disabilities Education Act (IDEA) Reauthorized Definition (1997)

In 1997, the federal government signed into law a reauthorization of IDEA, Public Law 105-15. It includes a definition of learning disabilities that, except for a few minor wording changes, is essentially the same as the USOE definition of 1977. It reads:

> A. IN GENERAL.—The term "specific learning disability" means a disorder in one or more of the basic psychological processes involved in understanding or in using language, spoken or written, which disorder may manifest itself in imperfect ability to listen, think, speak, read, write, spell, or do mathematical calculations.
>
> B. DISORDERS INCLUDED.—Such term includes such conditions as perceptual disabilities, brain injury, minimal brain dysfunction, dyslexia, and developmental aphasia.
>
> C. DISORDERS NOT INCLUDED.—Such term does not include a learning problem that is primarily the result of visual, hearing, or motor disabilities, of mental retardation, of emotional disturbance, or of environmental, cultural, or economic disadvantage. (Individuals with Disabilities Education Act Amendments of 1997, Sec. 602(26), p. 13)

The Two Most Popular Definitions: USOE and NJCLD

Depending on how one defines popularity, a case can be made for either the USOE (or the slightly modified version of the 1997 reauthorization of IDEA) or NJCLD definition being more popular. If one defines popularity as actual use by state departments of education, the USOE is more popular. The majority of states use a definition based on it and the identification criteria pertaining to an ability-achievement discrepancy, and over the years, there has been an increase in the number of states using the USOE definition (Mercer et al., 1996). If one defines popularity as acceptance by professionals, one can make a case that the NJCLD definition is more popular because the NJCLD represents the vast majority of professionals working in the area of learning disabilities.

Some have made the case that the question of which is more popular—the USOE or NJCLD definition—is moot. Hammill (1990), for example, has noted that the two definitions, along with their contemporaries—the LDA and ICLD definitions—agree on most of the key points.

Similarities

Using some of the same criteria that Hammill (1990) used in his analysis, we can identify five ways in which the USOE and NJCLD definitions are similar. Both definitions:

1. point to central nervous system dysfunction as a potential cause of learning disabilities (with the NJCLD definition being more explicit in this regard)
2. allow for the fact that learning disabilities can be a lifelong condition (with the NJCLD definition being more explicit in this regard)
3. mention language as a potentially affected ability
4. mention the academic areas of reading, writing, and math as potentially affected
5. allow for the fact that learning disabilities can co-occur with other conditions (with the NJCLD definition being more explicit in this regard)

Differences

We already noted that the NJCLD definition differs from the USOE definition in that the former does not mention psychological processes. Another difference is that the USOE definition mentions spelling as a potentially affected academic ability, whereas the developers of the NJCLD definition did not specify spelling because they saw it as logically subsumed under "writing." Also, the NJCLD definition specifies reasoning as a potentially affected ability, whereas the USOE definition does not.

Perhaps the most important way that the USOE and NJCLD definitions differ with regard to their conceptualization of learning disabilities, however, has to do with the regulations pertaining to identification criteria. The USOE regulations refer to a severe discrepancy between intellectual ability and academic achievement. As we noted, most states have endorsed the notion of an ability-achievement discrepancy by including it in their definitions or evaluation criteria. The research community, however, has been divided on the wisdom of using such a discrepancy.

HOW WELL DO TEST SCORE DISCREPANCIES INDICATE LEARNING DISABILITIES?

The idea behind using ability-achievement discrepancy as a part of the definition of learning disabilities emanated from professionals' and especially parents' concerns about differentiating children with learning disabilities from those with mental retardation. When the learning disabilities field was first forming, parents of children with learning problems who did not score low enough on IQ tests to qualify for identification as mentally retarded (in many school districts, a score of 85 or below) were advocating for special education services for their children. The parents emphasized that their children were bright enough that they should be learning as well as their peers, yet they were having extreme academic problems. They stressed that these problems should not be expected, given their intelligence levels. In other words, their children were not living up to their potential.

At first glance, the idea of learning disabilities being defined, at least partially, as a discrepancy between intellectual potential and academic achievement appears straightforward and logical. Numerous authorities, however, have severely criticized the discrepancy concept. And still more have been critical of the use of formulas to measure ability-achievement discrepancies.

Objections to Ability-Achievement Discrepancy

Researchers have pointed to at least four problems inherent in the ability-achievement discrepancy concept. First, the concept of ability as measured by intelligence tests is fraught with problems. Disputes regarding the definition and measurement of intelligence have been characteristic of the field since Alfred Binet constructed the first IQ test at the beginning of the 20th century; and, if anything, issues surrounding the concept of intelligence have increased in intensity over the years. As one researcher put it, "the decision to base the definition of a reading disability on a discrepancy with measured IQ is . . . nothing short of astounding. Certainly one would be hard-pressed to find a concept more controversial than intelligence in all of psychology" (Stanovich, 1989, p. 487). And as others have stated:

> It seems unfortunate that the LD field has placed so much emphasis on intelligence in attempting to define LD. The concept of intelligence, itself, is fraught with difficulties, and they become magnified when applied to LD. Intelligence is not as fundamental to LD as has been believed. The LD concept needs to be examined in its own right, not built on another extant, but shaky, concept. Despite its longer history, and the comfort of its familiarity, intelligence is a relatively minor player in the complex amalgam of what is termed *LD*. It seems appropriate that the alliance be broken and the LD field begin to seek its own identity. (Kavale & Forness, 1995a, p. 186)

Just one of the problems with intelligence tests (and achievement tests, too) is that they focus on the end product of learning (Meltzer, 1994). They give the professional administering the test a score, but they provide little information on what processes and strategies the individual taking the test used or did not use to arrive at that score.

Second, some researchers have pointed out that the intelligence of students with learning disabilities may be underestimated by IQ tests because the latter depend on the former to a certain extent (Siegel, 1989; Stanovich, 1989). They have hypothesized that some type of **Matthew effect** may be in operation. (A Matthew effect refers to the idea of the rich getting richer and the poor getting poorer. It is derived from Matthew XXV:29 in the Bible: "For unto every one that hath shall be given, and he shall have abundance; but from him that hath not shall be taken away even that which he hath.") The line of logic with reference to intelligence dictates that students who are better readers are in a better position than poor readers to expand their vocabularies and increase their reading comprehension and thus learn about the world, resulting in better performance on intelligence tests (Stanovich, 1986a). The implication for learning disabilities is that poor reading skills may lead to poorer performance on intelligence tests, and this depressed IQ score reduces the discrepancy between IQ and achievement, making it more difficult to qualify as learning disabled.

Third, using a variety of information-processing and neuropsychological tasks, several researchers have found it difficult to distinguish between two groups of poor readers—those whose reading achievement is discrepant from IQ and those whose reading achievement is discrepant from their age but not their IQ (in other words, this group has IQs that are generally below average, but not low enough to be retarded—in the mid-70s to mid-80s) (Fletcher, Francis, Rourke, Shaywitz, & Shaywitz, 1992; Fletcher et al., 1994; Pennington, Gilger, Olson, & DeFries, 1992; Stanovich & Siegel, 1994). At best, results comparing the two groups are mixed. Furthermore, research on one of the most important skills (see Chapter 12) for learning to read—phonological awareness—has found the two groups to be more similar than different (Stanovich & Siegel, 1994).

Fourth, using a discrepancy makes it difficult to identify students as learning disabled in the early grades because they are not yet old enough to have demonstrated a discrepancy (Mather & Roberts, 1994). In the first grade, for example, the average child has only begun to master the rudiments of reading and math. In the case of a first-grader with academic problems and average intelligence, the narrow range between where he or she should be and actually is makes it difficult to distinguish this student from one who is achieving normally. Some teachers have complained that they were sure a student was learning disabled, but they had to wait until the next year in order for this child to score low enough in achievement.

Objections to Use of Formulas

Professionals have used a number of methods to determine a discrepancy between ability and achievement. For many years, they used a very simple method of comparing the mental age obtained from an IQ test to the grade-age equivalent taken from a standardized achievement test. A difference of two years between the two was frequently used as an indicator of a discrepancy. This method has largely been abandoned because there are statistical problems with grade-equivalent scores and two years below grade level is not equally serious at all grade levels. For example, a child who tests two years below grade 8 has a less severe deficit that one who tests two years below grade 4.

Starting in the late 1970s and early 1980s, many states and school divisions began to adopt different formulas for identifying IQ-achievement discrepancies. Most of these early formulas were statistically flawed, however. They did not take into account the strong statistical relationship between tested IQ and tested achievement. To take their place, some have advocated the use of formulas that do account for the relationship between IQ and achievement. These are referred to as *regression-based discrepancy formulas.*

Many have questioned the wisdom of using even statistically adequate formulas (Board of Trustees of the Council for Learning Disabilities, 1986). Among other things, they point out the following:

- The use of discrepancy formulas often creates a false sense of objectivity and precision among diagnosticians who feel that their decisions are statistically based when formulas are employed;
- In practice, discrepancy formulas are often used as the sole or primary criterion for determining legal eligibility for learning disability services;
- Although promoted as a procedure for increasing accuracy in decision-making, discrepancy formulas often represent a relatively simplistic attempt to reduce incidence rates of learning disabilities. (p. 245)

The last point refers to the fact that many school divisions are concerned with the growing numbers of students identified as having learning disabilities, and some see formulas as a way of setting cutoffs that would keep the numbers lower.

The Future of the Learning Disabilities Definition

As divisive as the issue of definition has been, the field of learning disabilities has operated under essentially the same definition since 1977, if you consider the USOE definition as "official." (And one can make the case that the time period is even longer because the USOE definition is essentially the same as the NACHC definition of 1968.) Whether the field will be able to continue to withstand critics who question the validity of the learning disabilities construct (see Franklin, 1987), however, may depend on the field's ability to remain united behind a single definition or, at the very least, key components of a few definitions. As Hammill (1990), a proponent of the NJCLD definition, has stated: "Political realities are such that the NJCLD definition may never replace the USOE definition in law. But this may not be important. What is important, however, is that professionals and parents unite around one definition so that we can say with assurance, 'This is what we mean when we say *learning disabilities*'" (p. 83). For now, that one definition appears to lie somewhere between that of the USOE and the NJCLD. And as Hammill notes, these two definitions are more alike than different. Furthermore, the definitions used by professionals are similar to those of people with learning disabilities themselves. (See Box 1.1)

BOX 1.1 ***HUMAN PERSPECTIVES***

How Successful Adults with Learning Disabilities Define Themselves

With all the controversy and debate concerning definitions of learning disabilities, one team of researchers thought it would be valuable to find out what adults with learning disabilities think a learning disability is. As part of an interview, they asked successful adults with learning disabilities to define this term (Reiff, Gerber, & Ginsberg, 1993).

The results followed relatively closely the most commonly accepted definitions of learning disabilities. For example, 16 out of 57 (28%) referred to psychological processing problems, but their descriptions of these problems tended to be as vague as professionals' attempts at description:

- "Brain is not programmed to process information like most people's brains are programmed."
- "Not a learning disability; it's a processing disability."
- "Probably a central nervous system condition that interferes with the person's ability to process information." (Reiff et al., 1993, p. 119)

Many described their problems as functional limitations, with a focus on academic concerns such as reading, writing, and math, and alluded to problems they had had in school. Very few mentioned social or vocational problems, although this may be because the sample chosen was based on their being vocationally successful. Interestingly, only six mentioned the issue of a discrepancy between achievement and potential.

The results of this study are provocative, although the study is limited in that the sample consisted only of adults, and it is impossible to tell how much the respondents were merely parrotting what they had read or heard from professionals. Further research in this area might lead to a clearer conceptualization of the phenomenon of learning disabilities.

Questions to Ponder

How do you think the results would have differed if the researchers had asked children, for example middle-schoolers, instead of adults to define learning disabilities?

Why do you think so few (28%) referred to psychological processing problems?

In what ways do you think those persons with learning disabilities who can articulate a clear definition of the term differ from those who cannot?

TO WHAT EXTENT IS LEARNING DISABILITY A SOCIAL CONSTRUCT?

Given all the controversy surrounding the definition of learning disability, it is not surprising that some have questioned its reality independent of social context. Many critics have asked whether it is a real phenomenon that exists within a person (e.g., has a neurological basis) or a **socially constructed phenomenon** that depends for existence on the demands, perceptions, values, and judgments of persons in positions of authority over students. One view is that students with learning disabilities are different from most people in ways that are relatively constant across social contexts. This view is associated with the assumption that the primary causes of learning disabilities are biological, that is, neurological. Another view is that learning disabilities are mostly created by social demands and expectations, that is, constructed by social contexts. This view is associated with the assumption that the primary causes of learning disabilities are social circumstances, including the demands of schooling and employment.

Few would suggest that the problems we call learning disabilities are wholly a function of either neurological dysfunction or environmental structure and expectations. All would acknowledge that learning disability is a concept constructed in the social context of the expectations and demands of school, employment, and other aspects of community life and that the concept serves important social and political purposes, whether they are benevolent or malicious. People differ substantially, however, in their attitudes toward the arbitrary social criteria chosen for defining learning disabilities. Some think that because the criteria for the definitions are arbitrary and can be changed at will, the social construction of the category is indefensible. Others have pointed out that the arbitrary criteria by which many categories (e.g., citizen, person of voting age, poor, at-risk) are socially constructed cannot be avoided if social justice is to be served (Kauffman, 1989).

The fact that social and cultural expectations and purposes have helped shape the definition of learning disabilities has led some to see learning disabilities as a socially constructed myth (e.g., Coles, 1987) or as a category designed to maintain school programs stratified by race and class (e.g., Sleeter, 1986; see Kavale & Forness, 1987a, for a critique). As Moats and Lyon (1993, p. 284) have noted, "LD in the United States appears to be a systemic problem: It is an educational category into which children are channeled when the learning-teaching interaction is no longer productive or rewarding for one or both parties." Although acknowledging that social and political forces are important in defining learning disabilities, others see the social construction of this special education category as overwhelmingly beneficial to the children who are identified because they can receive important special services with minimal stigma (e.g., Kavale & Forness, 1985; Moats & Lyon, 1993; Singer, 1988; Singer & Butler, 1987). Still others argue that using teacher requests for help with a specific child as the definition of the need for special education is both reasonable and humane (e.g., Gerber & Semmel, 1984). No doubt, controversy will continue to surround the extent to which learning disabilities are a function of social demands and expectations and the social, political, and educational interests that are served by identifying students as having these disabilities.

WHAT CHARACTERISTICS SHOULD BE INCLUDED IN THE CATEGORY OF LEARNING DISABILITIES?

The various definitions of learning disabilities provide strong clues regarding what characteristics make up this population. Perhaps first and foremost, as students, individuals with learning disabilities exhibit academic problems (e.g., reading, writing, or performing mathematical operations). Above and beyond these academic deficiencies are three other important characteristics of the learning disability category that need to be stressed. Persons with learning disabilities exhibit (1) wide **interindividual differences,** (2) wide intraindividual differences, and (3) a tendency to have other disabilities.

Wide Interindividual Differences

As a category, learning disabilities include an extremely varied group of individuals and problems. In any group of students with learning disabilities, some will have difficulties in reading, some in spelling; some will be inattentive; some will have obnoxious social behaviors. A term that is sometimes used to describe such variability among persons is *heterogeneity.* Although interindividual differences, or heterogeneity, are a hallmark of all categories of disability, this term is particularly applicable to persons with learning disabilities. The old adage "No two are exactly alike" is most appropriate for individuals with learning disabilities.

One of the frustrating realities for teachers and researchers alike is knowing that the term *learning disability* designates an extremely wide range of characteristics. Knowing that you will be teaching pupils with learning disabilities tells you only very generally about the behavioral characteristics you will encounter in specific students. And researchers are faced with the uncertainty of knowing whether variable results from one study to another are real or due to differences in the characteristics of the students selected for the studies.

Teams of researchers have been studying the problem of heterogeneity for some time (McKinney, 1987; McKinney, Short, & Feagans, 1985; McKinney & Speece, 1986; Moats & Lyon, 1993; Speece, McKinney, & Applebaum, 1985). These studies employ sophisticated statistical techniques to try to tease out subgroups, or subtypes, of learning disabilities. Thus far, the results are intriguing, but it is still too early to tell whether this search for subtypes will provide useful information for teachers and researchers.

Wide Intraindividual Differences

In addition to variation among one another, persons with learning disabilities usually display wide variability in their own ability profiles. For example, a student may be three years behind grade level in reading, at grade level in spelling, and a year above grade level in math. The tendency to exhibit wide intraindividual differences is the primary reason some professionals use the term *specific* learning disabilities when referring to this population. Some students with learning disabilities have deficits in just one area or a few areas of ability. This characteristic of uneven profiles is the reason that some students with learning disabilities are gifted.

The notion of intraindividual variation was introduced by Kirk in his 1962 definition of learning disabilities. In addition to his definition, Kirk helped establish the idea of intraindividual differences as a hallmark of learning disabilities with the publication of his *Illinois Test of Psycholinguistic Abilities* (Kirk & Kirk, 1971; Kirk & McCarthy, 1962). This test could purportedly be used to measure variation in processes important for learning to read. Although the test itself was later found to be an inadequate predictor of reading ability (Hallahan & Cruickshank, 1973; Hammill & Larsen, 1974a), the idea of intraindividual variation has withstood the test of time and is still very much associated with the population of persons who have learning disabilities.

Association with Other Disabilities

Once an individual is said to have a particular disability, the great temptation is to assume that the label we have chosen summarizes all of his or her difficulties or tells us what his or her problem *really* is. In fact, it is possible for people to have a combination of disabilities and special talents. Historically, every field of disability has sought diagnostic purity—clear distinctions between a particular disability and all other categories. But that diagnostic purity has always proven elusive.

Research on disabilities of all kinds, including learning disabilities, has shown that they often come in multiples; that is, some involve more than one disability. Some have estimated, for example, that about half of children who meet the criteria for one psychiatric diagnosis also meet those for one or more psychiatric disorders (de Mesquita & Gilliam, 1994, in Rosenberg, 1997). When one or more disabilities occur in the same person, they are referred to as **comorbid conditions.**

Comorbidity is often due to at least two factors. First, causal agents are frequently not particular about what part of the human organism they attack. For example, if a fetus does not have enough oxygen during birth (if the umbilical cord becomes wrapped around the neck and cuts off the oxygen supply), the result can be brain damage. It is virtually impossible to predict whether this damage will be localized or widespread. The more widespread, the more likely the child will have more than one disability. Second, the human organism is extremely complex and is made up of a seemingly infinite number of interrelated functions. When one function is affected, others are also likely to be altered. For example, when someone has a hearing impairment, speech is likely to be affected. When a student has an attention deficit hyperactivity disorder, his or her off-task behavior during instruction may result in a learning disability.

Learning disabilities can co-occur with virtually any other disability, as well as with giftedness. Two of the most common conditions that occur concomitantly with learning disabilities are attention deficit hyperactivity disorder and emotional disturbance, or behavior disorders. In each case, it is often difficult to determine whether one condition is causing the other or whether each occurs independently. Researchers are just beginning to address the many issues of comorbidity and learning disabilities. (A special issue of *Journal of Learning Disabilities* was devoted to this topic. See Rosenberg, 1997.)

CAN LEARNING DISABILITIES BE OVERCOME?

As much as we would like to be able to say that learning disabilities can be easily remediated, this is not the case. People naturally hope for a cure for any disability, or at least an intervention that will minimize it so they are not handicapped in ordinary life activities. If the disability involves academic learning and social behavior—things that seem to be under voluntary control and to the average person seem easily learned—then hope is redoubled that proper remedial training can make these difficulties temporary. Of all the various disabilities, therefore, learning disabilities are most vulnerable to the assumption that they will not be lifelong.

The early years of research and intervention in nearly every category of disability have been characterized by a search for and claims of a cure or something very near it. In fact, promoters of numerous interventions for almost every disability have claimed that they produce nearly miraculous effects, but these claims cannot be substantiated by careful scientific research. The strength of their appeal is in large measure a result of people's desire to avoid confronting a developmental disability that will persist over the individual's life span. The field of learning disabilities has had its share of excessive claims and quack treatments (Worrall, 1990).

There is increasing evidence that learning disabilities are truly developmental and not curable in the sense that a disease or unfortunate life circumstance might be. There is diminishing support for the assumption that, with proper intervention, learning disabilities can be reduced from a true developmental disability to a passing inconvenience. Nevertheless, the myth persists that most children with learning disabilities will outgrow these as adults. In fact, learning disabilities tend to endure into adulthood. Most successful adults who had learning disabilities as children continue to have specific difficulties, must learn strategies to cope with their problems, and must show extraordinary perseverance.

HOW CAN THE IMPACT OF A LEARNING DISABILITY BE LESSENED?

Although learning disabilities cannot be overcome in the sense of being cured, persons with them can learn strategies that greatly diminish their negative impact. Early in the history of learning disabilities, it became clear that students with these problems must have routines for approaching tasks (cf. Cruickshank, Bentzen, Ratzeburg, & Tannhauser, 1961; Strauss & Lehtinen, 1947; Werner & Strauss, 1941). Part of the problem that students with learning disabilities have is their unsystematic, disorganized ways of responding to academic work and the tasks of everyday living. Few would argue that organizational skills and task-approach skills are unimportant for individuals with learning disabilities. However, there is much room for debate about the exact skills that are most helpful and how systematic approaches to tasks are best taught.

Great strides have been made in instructional methods since the pioneering efforts of Cruickshank, Strauss, and their colleagues, whose interventions consisted largely of controlling extraneous stimuli and providing a reliable structure of routines. Researchers have been devising and refining instructional procedures that are more effective than earlier strategies. Among the major approaches we discuss in subsequent chapters are cognitive training (which includes procedures such as self-monitoring or self-instruction), mnemonics (which includes the use of key words and other ways of assisting memory), direct instruction (which includes careful sequences of instruction, rapid and frequent responding, and immediate feedback and correction of errors), metacomprehension training (which provides students with strategies for thinking about remembering the major points in the material being read), and scaffolded instruction (which includes gradual reduction of assistance and reciprocal teaching). Although they vary in the specific skills taught and how they are related to the curriculum areas being taught, these approaches are all systematic procedures for teaching task-approach skills to students with learning disabilities so they can apply these skills in their actual academic situations.

HOW MANY PEOPLE WITH LEARNING DISABILITIES ARE THERE?

According to figures kept by the federal government, the public schools have identified well over two million students 6 to 17 years of age as having learning disabilities, which represents 5.34% of those in this age range (U.S. Department of Education, 1996). Actually, this percentage is likely to be a slight underestimate of all cases of learning disabilities because the numerator consists of the number of students identified by the *public* schools, whereas the denominator includes *all* persons in the United States, including those in *private* schools. Because there are undoubtedly students in private schools who have learning disabilities but are not identified as such by the public schools, we can assume that the number in the numerator does not represent all students with learning disabilities.

Since the federal government started in 1976–1977 keeping data on students served in special education, the number of students ages 6 to 21 years identified as having learning disabilities has tripled. In addition, those with learning disabilities now represent over half of all students identified as disabled. Figure 1.2 shows the phenomenal growth in the proportion of students with learning disabilities relative to all students with disabilities.

Most authorities have expressed alarm at the rapid growth of students identified as having learning disabilities. Critics of the field have used this expansion as evidence that this is an ill-defined category consisting of many students who need nothing more than better instruction from general education teachers. Defenders of the field are also concerned that much of this growth is unwarranted and indicative of confusion over

FIGURE 1.2 Distribution of Different Categories of Disabilities for Students Ages 6 through 21 Years

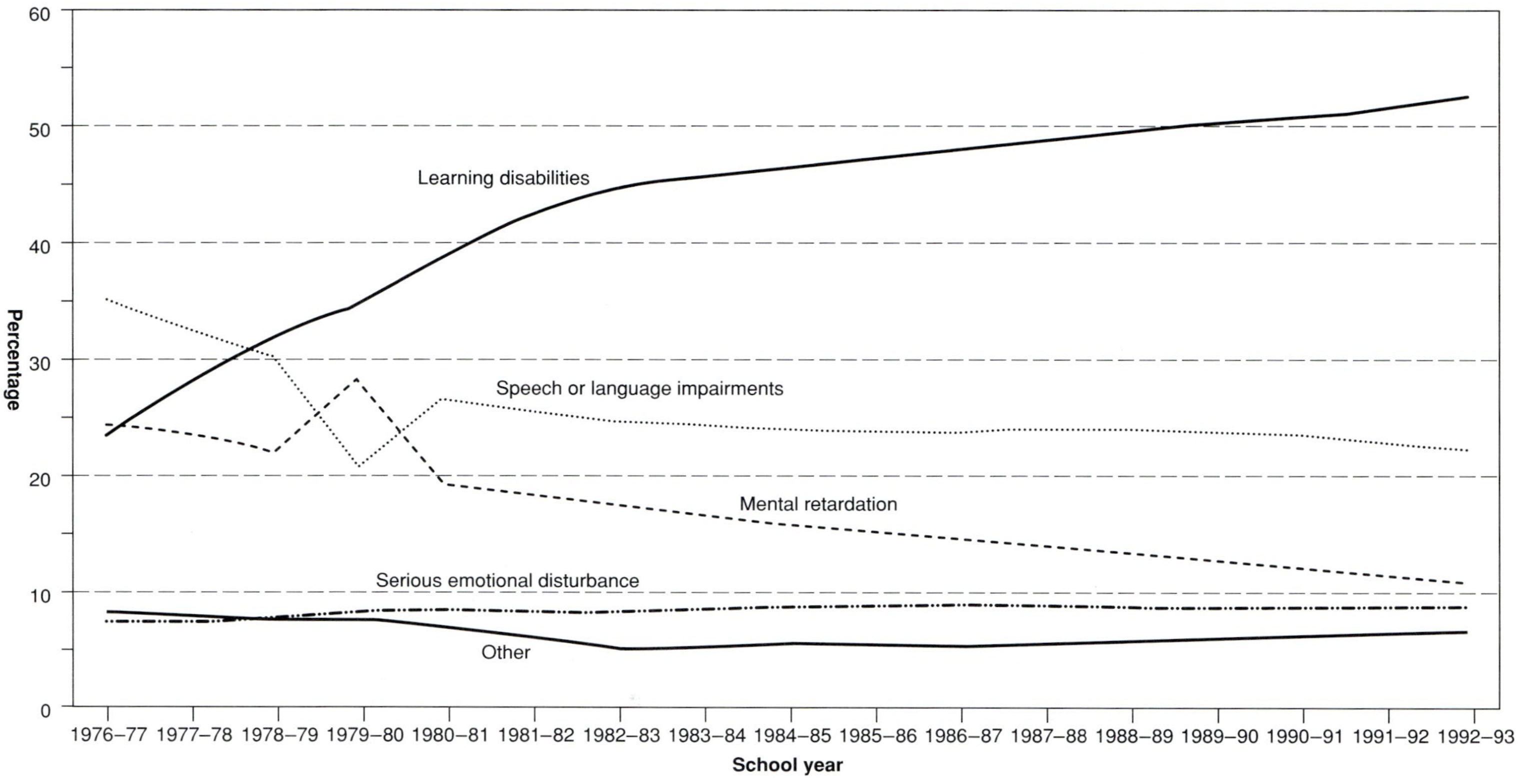

Source: From *Sixteenth Annual Report to Congress on the Implementation of the Individuals with Disabilities Education Act* (p. 11) by U.S. Department of Education, 1994, Washington, DC: Author.

definition and diagnostic criteria. They fear that many children are being misdiagnosed and that the increase has provided ammunition for critics, thereby jeopardizing services for students who truly have learning disabilities.

Some researchers have indicated that the idea of the learning disability definition being too loose is verified by the fact that it is virtually impossible to differentiate between low-achieving students and those classified as having learning disabilities (e.g., Algozzine & Ysseldyke, 1983; Ysseldyke, Algozzine, Shinn, & McGue, 1982). Others have analyzed the same data and concluded that this is a serious misstatement (Kavale, Fuchs, & Scruggs, 1994). They point out that a major part of the critics' case is based on the idea that the ability-achievement discrepancy should be used as the major criterion for classification as learning disabled. (See Box 1.2.)

Although misdiagnosis is the logical culprit causing the unbridled growth of learning disabilities, there is a paucity of research evidence on the subject. Some have noted that the increase in learning disabilities has occurred in almost direct proportion to the decrease in the number of students identified as mentally retarded. (See Figure 1.2.) They have hypothesized that political and social forces have resulted in a greater reluctance to identify children as mentally retarded, and many children who would formerly have been so labeled are now identified as learning disabled. Helping to bring about this shift in diagnosis was the American Association on Mental Retardation's 1973 decision to change its definition of mental retardation to include an IQ cutoff of about 70 to 75 rather than 85.

Not all professionals consider the increase in prevalence unwarranted. Hallahan (1992) has speculated that there may be valid reasons for some of the growth. First, he conjectures that, because the field of learning disabilities was relatively new when the federal government started keeping prevalence data in 1976, it may have taken professionals a few years to decide how to place children in this new category.

Second, he notes a number of social/cultural changes that have occurred since 1968 that have heightened children's vulnerability to developing learning disabilities. For example, an increase in poverty has placed more children at risk for biomedical problems, including central nervous system dysfunction (Baumeister, Kupstas, & Klindworth, 1990).

Social and cultural risks exist in addition to biological risks. Families, whether or not in poverty, are experiencing greater degrees of psychological stress. For example, a study of leisure arrived at the following conclusions:

> Americans are starved for time. Since 1969, the annual hours of work of employed Americans have risen markedly—by approximately 140 hours, or more than an additional three weeks. This increase includes both hours on the job and time spent working at home. As a result, leisure, or free time, has declined as well. Increasing numbers of people are finding themselves overworked, stressed out, and heavily taxed by the joint demands of work and family life. (Leete-Guy & Schor, 1992, p. 1)

Hallahan speculates that this stress on parents may result in their being less able to provide the social support necessary to help their children, who themselves are living

BOX 1.2 ***CURRENT ISSUES***

Are Learning Disabilities the Same as Low Achievement?

In the early 1980s, a team of researchers claimed to have found evidence that learning disabilities cannot be distinguished from low achievement (Epps, Ysseldyke, & Algozzine, 1983, 1985; Ysseldyke, Algozzine, & Epps, 1983; Ysseldyke, Algozzine, Shinn, & McGue, 1982). In a typical study (Ysseldyke et al., 1983), the researchers compared test scores for a group of students with learning disabilities with a group of low achievers using 17 different definitions of learning disabilities. They found that, using each definition, from 1% to 78% of the students who had learning disabilities and from none to 71% of the low-achieving students would be considered learning disabled, thus reflecting a great deal of overlap of these groups of students. They also found that 88% of the low-achieving group qualified as having learning disabilities using at least one of the definitions.

Kavale, Fuchs, and Scruggs (1994), however, took the same data used by the previously mentioned researchers and, performing what they considered more appropriate statistical operations, found only a 37% overlap between the group with learning disabilities and the group with low achievement. They also criticized the original studies because they relied on discrepancy for their various "definitions" of learning disabilities:

> Although the Minnesota studies provided up to 17 LD "definitions," each one described LD only within the limited and restricted confines of discrepancy. . . .
>
> Regardless of the combinations and permutations used to operationalize LD, the . . . studies based each definition on the notion of discrepancy. (p. 72)

Another team of researchers (Gresham, MacMillan, & Bocian, 1996), also using discrepancy as the criterion for learning disabilities, found an overlap of 39% between students identified as having learning disabilities and those having low achievement, which is more similar to that of Kavale et al.'s (1994) study than Ysseldyke et al.'s (1983). It is very difficult to compare all these studies, however, because they differ on several other variables, such as socioeconomic level and ethnicity.

Even if one accepts the criticisms of Kavale et al. (1994) concerning the use of a discrepancy to "define" the groups with learning disabilities, there is little doubt that the studies, by pointing out the difficulties in defining learning disabilities, have proved useful to the field:

> The . . . studies do, however, point out an important fact: LD diagnosis and classification is an imprecise and easily manipulated process. It is not correct, however, to draw the conclusion that the LD concept is indefensible. The proper conclusion is to acknowledge the complexity of LD and move toward more comprehensive diagnostic procedures that incorporate the complexity. The goal should be a complete description of LD that moves away from mindless statistical manipulations using a single problematic notion (i.e., discrepancy) that presumably "defines" LD. (Kavale et al., 1994, p. 72)

Questions to Ponder

What would be the ramifications of using only low achievement as a criterion for identifying students for learning disabilities services?

Ysseldyke et al. (1983) found 88% overlap between their low-achieving group and the group identified as learning disabled; Kavale et al. (1994) found a 37% overlap; and Gresham et al. (1996) found a 39% overlap. How much overlap would convince you that learning disabilities is too vaguely defined to be a useful category of learning disabilities?

Kavale et al. (1994) criticized others for relying solely on discrepancy as a criterion for identification as learning disabled. What other criteria might the researchers have used to identify the students as learning disabled?

under an increasing amount of stress. The result may be that children who in a previous time would have gotten by in their schoolwork with a less stressful lifestyle and more support are now experiencing failure.

WHO ARE PEOPLE WITH LEARNING DISABILITIES, AND WHAT IS THEIR REPRESENTATION?

Learning disabilities are found across an extremely wide spectrum of the population—among people of both genders, all ethnic groups, young and old, rich and poor, the socially prominent and the obscure, the academically successful and unsuccessful, those who are admired and those who are reviled, and among those of nearly every conceivable category of human being. As we have already discussed, individuals with learning disabilities are also a very diverse group in terms of the types and degrees of abilities and disabilities they have.

A persistent question about the diversity of students identified as learning disabled is whether certain groups are disproportionately represented. For example, are students of color, those who are poor, males, or those of some other description over- or underrepresented in the population of students with learning disabilities? Likewise, are students of one gender more likely to be identified as learning disabled? And if there is disproportionate representation by ethnicity or gender, is it due to bias, discrimination, or other unsavory causes? These questions are not trivial, for if disproportional representation is found to be the result of reprehensible practices that reflect bias or discrimination, then students are being mistreated, and these practices must be corrected. However, if disproportional representation is due to causal factors external to the school, such as poverty and its attendant disadvantages (in the case of ethnic disproportionality) or biological causes (in the case of gender disproportionality), then insisting on strictly proportional representation would be discriminatory in that it would deny appropriate services to students who would otherwise be qualified to receive them, which is another form of mistreatment (see Hallahan & Kauffman, 1997, for further discussion).

Ethnicity

Federal data are contradictory with regard to whether minority students are overrepresented among students with learning disabilities. In a survey of secondary students, the following ethnic breakdowns were found for the learning disabilities category: 67.2% are white, 21.6% are black, and 8.4% are Hispanic (U.S. Department of Education, 1992) (see Table 1.1). Comparing this to secondary-school students in general, who are 70% white, 12% black, and 13% Hispanic, demonstrates a disproportionately high prevalence of learning disabilities in African American students and a disproportionately low prevalence of learning disabilities in white and Hispanic students.

TABLE 1.1 Racial Characteristics of Secondary Students with Disabilities

	Race			
Disability	White	Black	Hispanic	Other
Specific learning disabilities	67.2%	21.6%	8.4%	2.8%
Speech or language impairment	54.2	38.0	25.3	3.6
Mental retardation	61.9	42.0	5.6	2.4
Serious emotional disturbance	67.1	25.1	6.0	1.8
Multiple disabilities	65.6	19.1	12.1	3.2
Hearing impairments	63.0	21.8	11.5	3.7
Orthopedic impairments	63.1	19.0	15.1	2.8
Other health impairments	54.2	20.3	22.5	3.0
Visual impairments	63.6	35.9	8.1	2.4
Deaf-blindness	67.0	25.0	5.8	2.2
All conditions	65.0	24.2	8.1	2.7
General population	**70**	**12**	**13**	**5**

Source: Adapted from *Fourteenth Annual Report to Congress on the Implementation of the Individuals with Disabilities Education Act* (p. 16) by U.S. Department of Education, 1992, Washington, DC: Author.

Whereas the 1992 report, which focused exclusively on secondary school students, indicated an overrepresentation of African American students in the learning disabilities category, a 1996 report, which used data on students between the ages of 6 and 17 years, did not indicate as strong an overrepresentation of African Americans or underrepresentation of Hispanics in the learning disabilities category. This survey found that the prevalence of learning disabilities in white students, African American students, and Hispanic students was 5.3%, 5.8%, and 5.3%, respectively (U.S. Department of Education, 1996).

Are minorities disproportionately represented among students with learning disabilities? Although the data are not clear-cut, we can probably conclude that there is suggestive evidence that African American students are disproportionately identified as learning disabled. There is also tentative evidence suggesting that Hispanic students may be underrepresented in the learning disability category.

What is more difficult to determine is why such disproportionality exists. Some have argued that racial discrimination is the culprit. Others have pointed out that professionals, such as school psychologists, are inadequately prepared to assess the capabilities of minority students. (See Box 1.3). These may indeed be factors, but why would Hispanic students be underrepresented in the learning disability category?

BOX 1.3 ***MULTICULTURAL PERSPECTIVES***

Are School Psychologists Adequately Trained to Assess Ethnically Diverse Students?

The school psychologist is often the most critical member of the team of professionals determining the eligibility of students for special education services. Scores obtained on standardized achievement and ability tests, administered and interpreted by a school psychologist, can often make the difference between a student being identified as learning disabled or not. Unfortunately, there is growing evidence that many school psychologists are not prepared to make valid assessments in the case of children from ethnically diverse backgrounds. For example, 83% of school psychologists surveyed described their training as less than adequate to assess culturally and linguistically diverse students (Ochoa, Rivera, & Ford, in press).

There is additional evidence that this lack of training leaves school psychologists at a loss considering cultural and linguistic issues in their testing. Researchers asked 671 school psychologists who had conducted assessments of bilingual children and children with limited English proficiency (LEP) the following open-ended question: "As a school psychologist, what criteria/standards do you use to rule out environmental, cultural, economic disadvantaged factors when determining LD eligibility when a LEP or bilingual student displays a severe discrepancy between intelligence and achievement or between grade levels?" (Ochoa, Rivera, & Powell, 1997). The results were extremely disappointing from a multicultural perspective. The school psychologists named very few factors that they use to interpret their results from a multicultural perspective. For example, only 25% referred to sociological information and family history, 15% considered the length of time or the number of years the student has lived in the United States, and none said he or she took into account the educational level of the parents or the level of literacy in the home. Only 6% considered the home language of the student, 5% considered the student's performance in comparison with other bilingual and LEP students from similar backgrounds, and 3% stated that they noted whether the child has received instruction in bilingual or English as a second language settings.

The open-ended nature of the questionnaire may have underestimated the actual degree to which school psychologists take into account cultural and linguistic factors when doing their assessments. Perhaps they were not able to recall all the variables they consider when interpreting their tests. If given a questionnaire listing a variety of factors, perhaps more of them would have stated that they use the factors listed. Even giving school psychologists this benefit of the doubt, however, it is perplexing that so few readily identified what should be obvious mitigating cultural and linguistic factors.

Questions to Ponder

Although very few of the school psychologists surveyed said they took into account cultural and linguistic factors, the group of 671 did come up with a total of 36 they said they used. What do you think some of these were?

Do you think teachers would be "guilty" of the same disregard for cultural and linguistic factors in their instructional practices?

Furthermore, if racial bias were the sole explanation, how could it account for the fact that African Americans are also overrepresented in categories such as visual impairment and hearing impairment? (See Table 1.1.) "[I]t is possible that black youth were more likely than their white counterparts to have experienced poor prenatal, perinatal, or postnatal health care and early childhood nutrition which may have resulted in actual disabilities" (U.S. Department of Education, 1992, p. 15).

Gender

Since the earliest days of the field of learning disabilities, researchers and practitioners have noted that a disproportionate number of boys is identified as having learning disabilities. Most studies have found that boys so identified outnumber girls by about 3 or 4 to 1. Data collected by the federal government are only for ages 13 to 21 years, but they are essentially in agreement with other studies in finding that 73% of students identified as having learning disabilities are males (U.S. Department of Education, 1992).

Some authorities have pointed to the possibility of greater biological vulnerability for boys as an explanation for this gender difference. Boys are at greater risk than girls for a variety of biological abnormalities, and their infant mortality rate is higher than that for girls.

Other authorities have raised the issue of possible bias in referral and assessment procedures, suggesting that boys might be more likely to be referred because they are more likely to exhibit behaviors that are bothersome to teachers, such as hyperactivity. Research results on gender bias are mixed. One team of investigators found no evidence of gender bias (Clarizio & Phillips, 1986). But researchers in two other studies did conclude that their data showed a bias toward identifying more males as having learning disabilities (Leinhardt, Seewald, & Zigmond, 1982; Shaywitz, Shaywitz, Fletcher, & Escobar, 1990).

Shaywitz et al. (1990) compared a sample of students identified by schools as reading disabled to an epidemiological sample on the discrepancies between IQ and reading achievement. The children in the latter sample were part of a longitudinal study in which virtually all children entering kindergarten in target schools were identified for testing. The ratio of boys to girls was about 4 to 1 in the school-identified sample, but it was about 1 to 1 in the epidemiological sample. Shawitz et al. also found that, in contrast to the epidemiological sample, the school-identified group exhibited more behavior problems than a control group of nondisabled students. One possible criticism of this study is that the researchers relied solely on a discrepancy between ability and achievement to arrive at a diagnosis of "true" reading disability.

More research is needed on the issue of whether the greater number of males identified for learning disabilities is due to bias. The findings of Shaywitz et al. (1990) are provocative, especially the data showing that school-identified students with reading disabilities show a greater degree of behavioral problems that might prompt teachers to refer them for testing in order to get them out of their classrooms. Our best guess at this point is that some bias does exist, but that the biological vulnerability of males also plays a role. For example, the federal government's figures indicate that all disabilities are more prevalent in males, including conditions that are difficult to imagine as resulting from referral or assessment bias, such as hearing impairment (53% are males), orthopedic impairment (54% are males), and visual impairment (56% are males) (U.S. Department of Education, 1992).

Summary

1. What is learning disabilities like as a field of study?
   a. Learning disabilities is an interdisciplinary field that is international and multicultural in scope. Professionals involved in the field include physicians, speech/language pathologists, educators, psychologists, specialists in mental retardation, and lawyers. Parents have also made major contributions through advocacy for their children. Although most work has been published in the United States, learning disabilities are a global concern, especially in developed countries.
   b. The field is based on and advanced by basic and applied, qualitative and quantitative research. No easy or quick solutions exist to the complex problems experienced by those with learning disabilities.
2. How has *learning disability* been defined?
   a. Samuel Kirk's 1962 definition contains five elements that appear in many later definitions: *subaverage achievement, intraindividual differences, psychological processing problems, cerebral dysfunction,* and *the exclusion of other conditions as causal factors.*
   b. Bateman's 1965 definition refers to an *ability-achievement discrepancy*—the difference between intellectual potential and actual academic performance.
   c. Definitions proposed by task forces organized by the federal government in 1966 emphasized medical explanations and in 1969 emphasized intraindividual differences and discrepancy between potential and performance.
   d. The 1968 National Advisory Committee on Handicapped Children definition refers specifically to children and added *thinking disorders* to the list of examples of learning disabilities.
   e. The USOE 1977 definition considers the notion of developing a *discrepancy formula;* this idea was met with a negative response. USOE did refer to an *ability-achievement discrepancy* in the regulations pertaining to identification.
   f. The NJCLD in 1981 reacted negatively to the USOE references to psychological processes.
   g. LDA, a major parent organization, did not endorse the NJCLD definition. Instead, in 1986, it emphasized the *lifelong nature* of learning disabilities, did not address other disabling conditions and environmental conditions as causal factors, and mentioned that adaptive behaviors (such as vocational and daily living skills) can be affected.

h. The ICLD 1987 definition was essentially the same as that of the NJCLD, but it added *social skills deficits* as a type of learning disability and *attention deficit disorder* as a potentially co-occurring condition.
i. In 1988, the NJCLD revised its definition to acknowledge the lifelong nature of learning disabilities and included socialization problems as potentially co-occurring, but not as a type of learning disability.
j. The definition of learning disabilities in the 1997 reauthorization of IDEA (Public Law 105-15), was essentially the same as the 1977 USOE definition.

3. Of these definitions, the two most popular are those of the USOE and NJCLD. These two definitions are similar in that they:
   a. point to central nervous system dysfunction as a potential cause
   b. recognize that learning disabilities can be a lifelong condition
   c. mention that language ability can be affected
   d. mention that academic performance can be affected
   e. allow that learning disabilities can co-occur with other conditions

   The definitions differ in the following ways:
   a. The NJCLD definition does not mention psychological processes.
   b. The USOE definition specifically mentions spelling as an academic area potentially affected.
   c. The NJCLD definition specifies reasoning as a potentially affected ability.
4. Although most states refer to a discrepancy between ability and achievement in identifying students with learning disabilities, many professionals have objected to the *ability-achievement discrepancy* concept and even more are opposed to the use of discrepancy formulas.
5. There has been considerable disagreement over definition of learning disabilities, but the field has operated under essentially the same definition since 1977 (the USOE definition).
6. To what extent is learning disability a social construct?
   Some have tried to dismiss the field, arguing that learning disability is not a condition that resides within individuals, but depends on society for its existence. Most professionals acknowledge that learning disability is shaped by societal demands of school and employment but do not see that this social construction rules out a biological basis. Proponents also think that designating persons as having learning disabilities serves the social purpose of providing needed services.
7. What characteristics should be included in the category of learning disabilities?
   The following characteristics fall into this category:
   a. Students with learning disabilities have academic problems.
   b. They exhibit wide interindividual differences.
   c. They exhibit wide intraindividual differences.
   d. Learning disabilities often coexist with other disabilities (*comorbidity*), and they sometimes coexist with giftedness.
8. Can learning disabilities be overcome?
   There is no easy cure for learning disabilities; they are a lifelong condition.

9. How can the impact of a learning disability be lessened?
   Students must learn systematic approaches to tasks.
10. How many people with learning disabilities are there?
    a. According to the U.S. Department of Education, there are over two million students 6 to 17 years of age who are learning disabled, which represents 5.34% of those in this age range.
    b. The numbers of students identified as having learning disabilities have tripled since 1977, when the federal government began keeping prevalence figures. Some think this indicates that the category is too ill defined to be useful. Others point to social and cultural changes that can explain at least some of the increase.
11. Who are the learning disabled, and are they disproportionately represented in certain groups?
    a. People with learning disabilities come from diverse backgrounds.
    b. There is contradictory evidence regarding whether minority students are overrepresented in the learning disabilities category. There is suggestive evidence that African American students are disproportionately identified as learning disabled and that Hispanic students are underrepresented. There are differing opinions about why such disproportionality might exist. Some think there is racial bias operating; others think that social conditions might account for disproportionality.
    c. There is also contradictory evidence regarding the prevalence of learning disabilities in males versus females. For many years, researchers consistently found a higher prevalence in males. Some recent research has questioned this finding. But this research itself has been criticized. More research is needed in this area.

2

Causes

One of the most frustrating things that has plagued the field of learning disabilities since its inception is the question of etiology, that is, what causes learning disabilities. The field was founded on the premise that there is a neurological basis to learning disabilities. But much of the early work was based on clinical guesswork because of the relatively unsophisticated techniques being used to measure neurological status back in the 1960s and 1970s. Much preliminary work in this area was speculative, so most professionals were skeptical about the validity of claims that learning disabilities were the result of neurological problems. In the late 1980s, this picture began to change as researchers developed computerized imaging techniques and other methods that could detect brain abnormalities with reasonable reliability. Today most professionals subscribe to the view that learning disabilities emanate from some kind of differences in brain structure or functioning, and the most widely used definitions suggest that the causes are neurological rather than environmental.

WHAT CAUSES LEARNING DISABILITIES?

Historical Context

One reason for a presumption of neurological dysfunction in learning disabilities is that there is often no other plausible explanation for the child's failure to learn. Another reason is that the field emerged gradually from the work of physicians who identified symptoms of known brain injury that were in many respects similar to the behavior of people who had learning disabilities but who did not have confirmed damage to their brains.

When neurology and ophthalmology were developing as medical specialties in the 19th and early 20th centuries, physicians began describing problems in understanding and using spoken and written language that were associated with damage to specific areas of the brain. Pierre Paul Broca and Carl Wernicke were 19th-century European physicians who identified particular areas of the brain that control speaking and understanding spoken language. Their work laid the foundation for understanding the speech and language problems termed *aphasia.* Other late 19th- and early 20th-century physicians researched reading disabilities that they called *dyslexia,* a term introduced by German ophthalmologist R. Berlin, or *word blindness,* a phrase invented by Scottish ophthalmologist James Hinshelwood.

Another neurologist who contributed much to the presumption of brain dysfunction in learning disabilities was Kurt Goldstein, who observed the behavior of soldiers who sustained serious head wounds during World War I. Goldstein's work with brain-injured soldiers in the 1920s and 1930s provided a backdrop for the work of two other German behavioral scientists who emigrated to the United States: Heinz Werner, a developmental psychologist, and Alfred Strauss, a neuropsychiatrist. Werner and Strauss extended Goldstein's work with soldiers to research with children (Strauss & Werner, 1942; Werner & Strauss, 1940, 1941). Their development of assessment and teaching procedures, in turn, influenced the thinking of a generation of scholars (e.g., Cruickshank, Bentzen, Ratzeburg, & Tannhauser, 1961; Cruickshank, Bice, & Wallen, 1957; Strauss & Kephart, 1955; Strauss & Lehtinen, 1947). Among those influenced by Strauss and Werner were Samuel Kirk, a psychologist and special educator who introduced the term *learning disability* in 1963, and a variety of early leaders in the field who emphasized perceptual-motor problems and training methods intended to overcome them (e.g., Ray Barsch, Marianne Frostig, Gerald Getman, and Newell Kephart; see Kauffman & Hallahan, 1976, for autobiographical statements of Barsch, Cruickshank, Frostig, Getman, and Kirk).

Another neurologist who had an important influence on the development of learning disabilities and the presumption of neurological dysfunction was Samuel Orton (Orton, 1937). He believed that reading disability was a result of mixed dominance of the cerebral hemispheres—meaning that neither side of the brain was clearly in control—which led to a breakdown in perceptual-motor abilities. He theorized that mixed dominance was inherited and led to perceptual reversals (e.g., reading "was" for "saw"). Orton's ideas led to the development of systematic instructional procedures in reading, spelling, and handwriting (Gillingham & Stillman, 1965), and his work lives on in the International Dyslexia Association. His theories also influenced speech-language and hearing specialists such as Katrina de Hirsch and Helmer Myklebust, whose methods were prominent in the 1960s and 1970s (de Hirsch, Jansky, & Langford, 1966; Johnson & Myklebust, 1967; Myklebust, 1973).

Reluctance to Accept Neurological Causes

Even though many of today's professionals believe that learning disabilities are neurologically based and even though the two most popular definitions of learning disabilities—those of the USOE and NJCLD, in existence since 1977 and 1981, respectively—both reflect a neurological basis for learning disabilities, the field was slow to embrace neurological dysfunction as a viable causal factor. There were at least two reasons why researchers and practitioners may have been skeptical about a neurological basis for learning disabilities: (1) the questionable accuracy of early neurological measures and (2) the emphasis on behaviorism and environmentalism.

Problems of Accuracy in the Measurement of Neurological Dysfunction

Many authorities rightfully questioned the reliability and validity of the standard tests neurologists used to diagnose neurological dysfunction in children with learning disabilities because in the 1960s and 1970s these tools were relatively crude. For example, in both research and clinical practice, neurologists still relied heavily upon the measurement of **soft neurological signs,** largely behavioral indices such as poor balance, poor visual-perceptual skills, poor fine motor coordination, distractibility, and clumsiness. Although these signs are prevalent in people with obvious cases of brain injury, they are not always accurate indicators of more subtle cases of brain dysfunction—the kind of cases that are likely to be learning disabled.

The research of Strauss and Werner was fresh in the memory of many who were working to establish the field of learning disabilities in the 1960s and 1970s. Strauss and Werner had conducted several studies comparing children who were mentally retarded and presumably brain-injured with children who were mentally retarded and non-brain-injured (Strauss & Werner, 1942; Werner & Strauss, 1940, 1941). They found that the group with brain injury performed more poorly than their non-brain-injured counterparts on visual and auditory tasks requiring the ability to distinguish figure from background. Their work was soundly and justly criticized, however, as having compared abilities that were highly similar to the behaviors used to differentiate the group with brain injury from the non-brain-injured group in the first place (Sarason, 1949). These criticisms underscored for learning disabilities professionals the weakness of using soft neurological signs as a means of determining subtle neurological dysfunction.

Emphasis on Behaviorism and Environmentalism

A second reason professionals were hesitant to look to neurology for answers to causal questions was the popularity of behaviorism and environmentalism in the social sciences in the 1960s and 1970s. **Behaviorism** is a philosophical orientation to psychology that stresses the study of observable behaviors instead of nonobservable mental events. It is closely linked to learning theory, which postulates that all behavior is learned and is shaped by rewards and punishments.

Intimately tied to behaviorism and learning theory, **environmentalism** holds that one's learning environment is crucial to psychological development. The 1960s was the heyday of the environmentalist position in child psychology relative to causes of learning and personality development. Several researchers contributed to the dominance of the environmentalist position. In 1961, J. McVicker Hunt published *Intelligence and Experience,* in which he reviewed several studies, many on lower animals, that demonstrated the devastating impact that lack of experiences could have on development. In this same vein, Rosenzweig (1966) published an influential study comparing rats placed in stimulus-"enriched" cages (e.g., numerous paraphernalia for exploratory activity) with those placed in cages devoid of stimuli. He found differential effects on brain structure and chemistry in that the former had thicker cortexes and more acetylcholine, a chemical important for learning.

With the optimism created by environmentalists, social scientists pushed for early intervention programs designed to reverse the negative effects of poverty on the intellectual development of young children. For example, Head Start, aimed at providing health and educational services for preschoolers from impoverished backgrounds, was instituted as part of President Lyndon Johnson's War on Poverty.

Some professionals used the behaviorists' and environmentalists' positions to point to another possible cause of learning disabilities in children—poor teaching, sometimes referred to as "dyspedagogia" (dys = poor, pedagogia = teaching) (Cohen, 1971). Researchers pointed out that teachers often spend an appallingly low percentage of their time actually engaged in reading instruction and that this and other poor instructional practices over a period of years can result in students developing learning disabilities.

Toward an Acceptance of Neurological Causes

Several factors have helped make professionals generally more favorably inclined toward neurological explanations of learning disabilities, chiefly the decrease in the popularity of behaviorism and environmentalism and the increase in the utility of neurological measures.

Decrease in Popularity of Behaviorism and Environmentalism

Although many authorities still think that behaviorism is an important theoretical position, several have swung to a more cognitive perspective (see Schulz, 1994). Cognitive psychologists recognize nonobservable thought processes as legitimate for scientific inquiry. And more and more cognitive psychologists are blending their work with that of neurologists, making connections between thought processes in the brain and their neurological underpinnings. Similarly, although environmentalism is still seen as a viable position by most working in the fields of education and psychology, some of the unbridled optimism of its early proponents has been tempered by the less than overwhelmingly positive results of early intervention programs. Intervening to remedy the devastating effects of poverty on child development has proved more difficult than was at first assumed. The disillusionment with behaviorism and environmentalism as causal explanations of learning problems has thus left a void that work in the neurological arena has started to fill.

Technological Advances in Neurological Research

Probably the major reason professionals are now more persuaded that neurological dysfunction is a viable causal factor in many cases of learning disabilities is the advances in neurological research. Starting in the late 1980s, neurological researchers began to make substantial progress in identifying neurological factors as underlying learning disabilities. Much of this progress has been due to advances in computerized neurological measures. Such techniques as **computerized axial tomography (CAT-scan), magnetic resonance imaging (MRI), positron emission tomography (PET-scan),** and **functional magnetic resonance imaging (fMRI)** have expanded the area of brain research. (See Box 2.1.) Although expense has thus far kept these techniques from being widely used to diagnose individual cases of learning disabilities in clinical practice, they have allowed researchers to begin to build a case for the importance of neurological dysfunction in many cases of learning disabilities. Before discussing the use of these procedures to determine neurological causes of learning disabilities, we present the basic anatomy of the brain and some of the functions performed by its major parts.

BOX 2.1 ***TECHNOLOGY***

Computerized Imaging and the Brain

A number of recent technological advances in x-ray techniques and computers allow researchers and clinicians to obtain better images of the living brain. Four such techniques are *computerized axial tomography, magnetic resonance imaging, positron emission tomography,* and *functional magnetic resonance imaging.*

Computerized Axial Tomography

In computerized axial tomography, often referred to as CAT-scans, the person's head is placed in a large ring containing on one side an x-ray tube that emits x-rays and on the other side an x-ray detector (Figure A). The x-rays pass through the person's head from the x-ray tube to the detector. The x-ray tube and detector rotate around the head, taking several measurements of the brain. The ring is then moved a few degrees in order to take measurements along a different plane. The computer takes the information obtained from these x-rays and plots a series of pictures of the brain.

Magnetic Resonance Imaging

Magnetic resonance imaging (MRI) (Figure B) provides an even more detailed picture of the brain than do CAT-scans. Instead of passing x-rays through a

FIGURE A Computerized Axial Tomography (CAT-Scan)

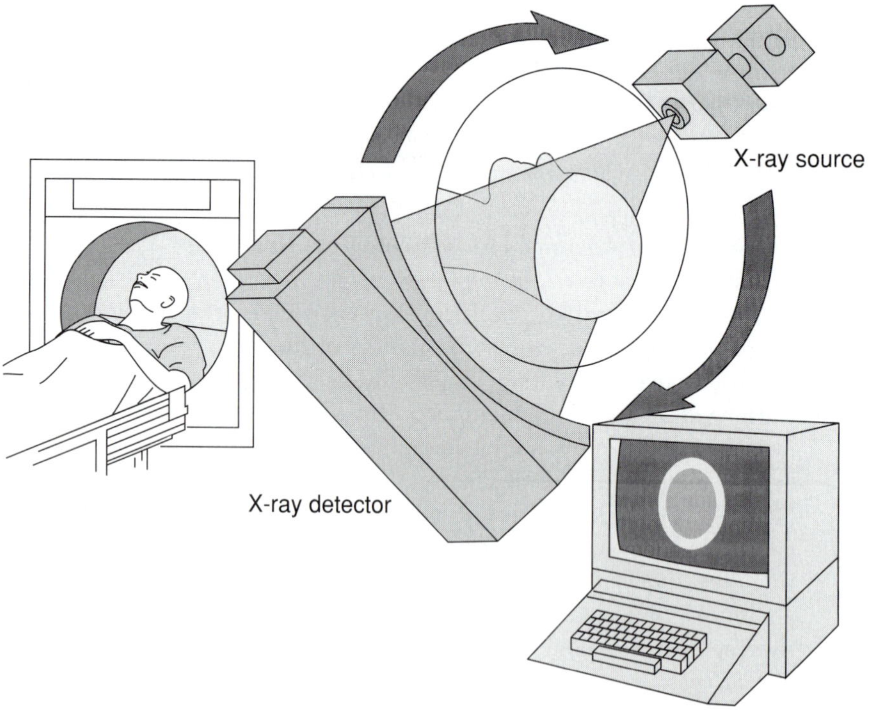

Source: From *Biopsychology,* 2nd ed. (p. 131, Fig. 5.2) by J. P. J. Pinel, 1993, Boston: Allyn & Bacon, Copyright 1993 by Allyn & Bacon. Reprinted by permission.

BOX 2.1 *continued*

FIGURE B An MRI Scan

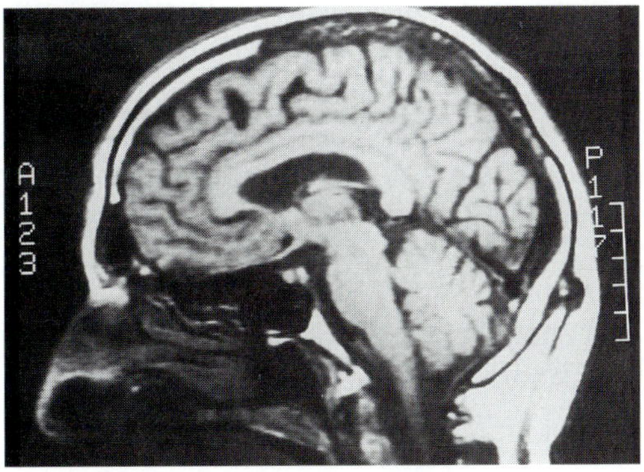

Source: Ralph C. Eagle Jr./Photo Researchers.

person's brain, the MRI scanner sends a strong magnetic field through the head. The magnetic field causes changes in the orientation of hydrogen atoms, which are detected by the scanner. Because various neural structures contain different amounts of hydrogen, the scanner detects these differences and uses these data to formulate photographs of slices of the brain.

Positron Emission Tomography

Whereas CAT-scans and MRI are usually used with people when they are at rest, positron emission tomography (PET-scan) can be used to take pictures of the brain while a person is engaged in various activities. It is thus a way of viewing the brain in an active state. PET-scans detect changes in metabolic activity in various parts of the brain. The person is usually injected with a substance of low radioactivity that is similar to glucose. Along with blood, the substance collects in active brain neurons and can be detected by a scanner. While the person performs a task, such as reading or memorizing, the PET-scan can detect which areas of the brain are activated because the radioactive substance is transported to them.

Functional Magnetic Resonance Imaging

Like the PET-scan, functional magnetic resonance imaging (fMRI) can be used to detect changes in the brain while it is in an active state. With the fMRI, one can record the metabolism of the brain as a person engages in a cognitive task. Unlike the PET-scan, the fMRI has the advantage of not involving the use of radioactive materials.

HOW DOES THE BRAIN FUNCTION?

Neurons Send and Receive Messages

Neurons are the most important cells in the human nervous system, being responsible for sending and receiving information in the brain. Most **neurons** consist of four structures: (1) the cell body or soma, (2) dendrites, (3) the axon, and (4) terminal buttons. These structures allow neurons to communicate with one another (Carlson, 1994; Haberlandt, 1994; Pinel, 1993).

The **soma** contains the nucleus and material that supports the functioning of the neuron. **Dendrites** are treelike projections that receive messages from the environment (e.g., sights, sounds, smells) or from other neurons. They receive messages from other neurons through the other neurons' axon and terminal buttons. The **axon** is a long, tubelike extension of the neuron that carries messages to the dendrites of other neurons. These electrical-chemical messages are transported from the axon to the dendrites via **terminal buttons**—buttonlike structures that secrete chemicals (**neurotransmitters**) into the **synapse,** a small gap between the axon and the dendrite. The particular neurotransmitter secreted helps determine whether a neuron will receive the message from another neuron and then send it to other neurons. Figure 2.1 presents an overview of how electrical-chemical messages are carried from one neuron to another over the synapse.

Our explanation of neuronal communication is brief and necessarily simplified. The fact that scientists have estimated that there are over 60 trillion synapses in the human brain makes the study of the structure and function of neurons extremely complicated (Shepard & Koch, 1990).

Different Parts of the Brain Have Different Functions

Neurologists have identified several areas of the brain they think are responsible for different functions (e.g., sensory, motor, language, cognition, and emotion). But because of the brain's complexity, neuroscientists do not always agree on the specificity

FIGURE 2.1 Overview of the Synaptic Connections between Neurons

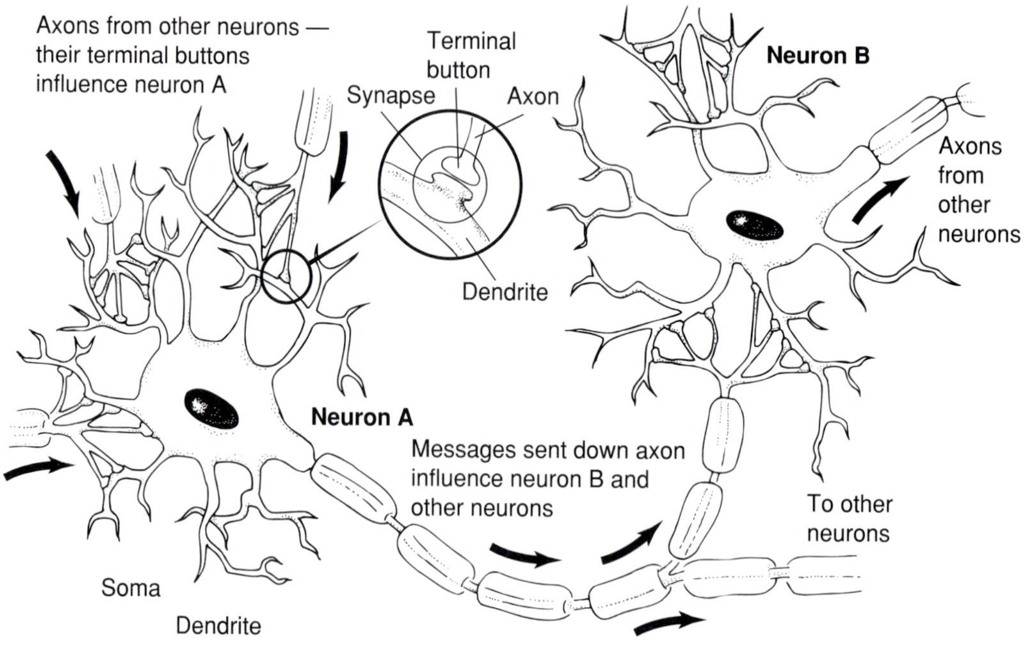

Source: Adapted from *Physiology of Behavior,* 5th ed. (p. 23, Fig. 2.3) by N. R. Carlson, 1994, Boston: Allyn & Bacon. Copyright 1994 by Allyn & Bacon. Reprinted by permission.

of some of these brain-behavior connections. Not only is there sometimes disagreement about whether a certain behavior is controlled by one or another part of the brain, but there can also be dispute about whether one or several parts of the brain are implicated. Furthermore, one part of the brain can take over certain functions for a damaged portion of the brain. Because of these disagreements, we present only those basic brain-function relationships most neurologists agree upon.

Neurologists commonly refer to the brain as being divided into the brain stem, cerebellum, and cerebral cortex, with the latter consisting of four types of lobes: frontal, parietal, occipital, and temporal. The cerebral cortex has a left and a right hemisphere, both of which contain all four kinds of lobes. In other words, there is a left and right frontal lobe, a left and right parietal lobe, and so forth. Figure 2.2A depicts a top view of the brain, showing both hemispheres; Figure 2.2B shows a side view of the left hemisphere, the cerebellum, and the brain stem.

Brain Stem

The two hemispheres of the cerebral cortex rest on the **brain stem,** which serves as a connection to the spinal cord. The brain stem regulates important survival reflexes such as respiration and heart rate.

Cerebellum

The **cerebellum,** located beneath the cerebral cortex and adjoining the brain stem, is more complex than its size suggests. Though comprising only about 10% of the brain's mass, it contains more than half its neurons (Pinel, 1993). The cerebellum regulates several behaviors having to do with movement (e.g., balance, gait, speech, eye movements). Damage to this area of the brain can result in profound difficulties in controlling a variety of movements. Following is an example of a common test neurologists use to assess functioning of the cerebellum, which you can try:

> Have a friend place his or her finger in front of your face, about three-quarters of an arm's length away. While your friend slowly moves his or her finger around to serve as a moving target, alternately touch your nose and your friend's finger as rapidly as you can. If your cerebellum is normal, you can successfully hit your nose and your friend's finger without too much trouble. People with lateral cerebellar damage have great difficulty; they tend to miss the examiner's hand and poke themselves in the eye. (Carlson, 1994, p. 245)

Cerebral Cortex

A layer of tissue covering the cerebral hemispheres, the **cerebral cortex** is divided into four types of lobes: frontal, parietal, occipital, and temporal. The cerebral cortex is deeply furrowed (cortex means "bark"), which greatly increases the surface area of the brain. In fact, about two-thirds of the cortex's surface is contained in the creases (Carlson, 1994). The largest grooves are called *fissures.* The central fissure divides the frontal lobe from the parietal lobe, and the lateral fissure separates the temporal lobe from the frontal and parietal lobes. (See Figure 2.2A and B.)

FIGURE 2.2 (A) A top view of the two cerebral hemispheres; (B) A side view of the left cerebral hemisphere, the brain stem, and the cerebellum

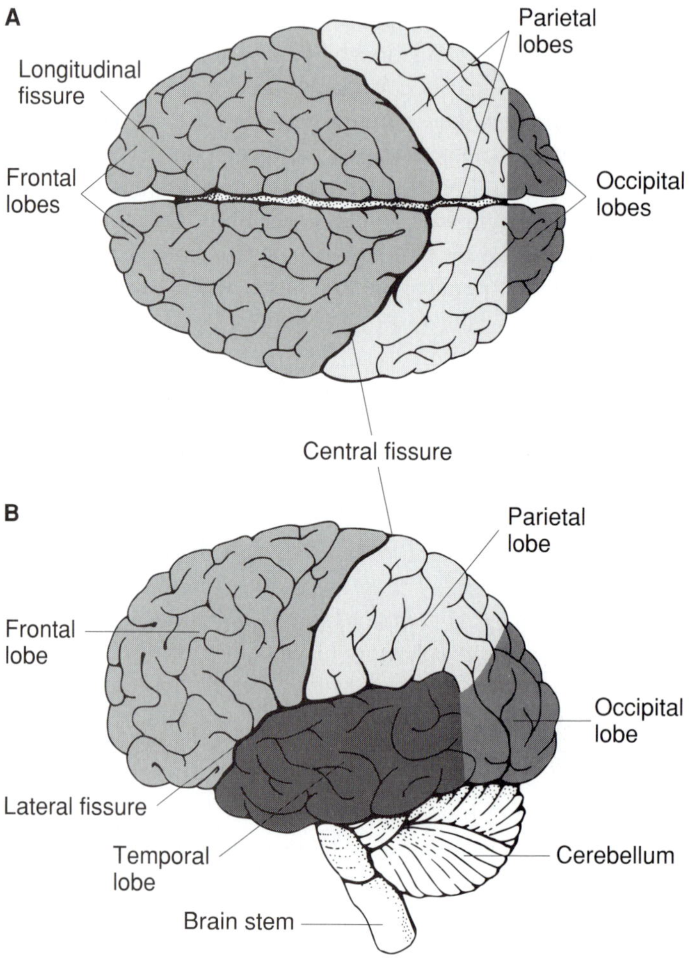

Source: Adapted from *Biopsychology,* 2nd ed. (p. 86, Fig. 3.24) by J. P. J. Pinel, 1993, Boston: Allyn & Bacon. Copyright 1993 by Allyn & Bacon. Reprinted by permission.

The Frontal Lobes of the Cerebral Cortex

The **frontal lobes** have been referred to as the "most mysterious region of the cortex" (Haberlandt, 1994, p. 51). We do know that a relatively thin strip immediately in front of the central fissure is responsible for some motor movements. Researchers have also pointed to the frontal lobes as a site for communication with other areas of the brain. Some have speculated that they "house an 'executive' that schedules cognitive operations like problem solving, speech production, and the execution of daily activities" (Haberlandt, 1994, p. 51).

The first inkling that this brain area plays a crucial role in executive functions came from the celebrated case of Phineas Gage, a dynamite worker in the mid-1800s who had a steel rod accidentally propelled through his cheek and out the top of his head, passing through the front part of the frontal lobes (Figure 2.3). Miraculously, Gage survived; however, he suffered serious alterations in personality. He was no longer the industrious, energetic worker he had been before the accident. He was now "childish, irresponsible, and thoughtless of others. He was unable to make or carry out plans, and his actions appeared to be capricious and whimsical" (Carlson, 1994, p. 341).

The front part of the frontal lobes, the **prefrontal lobes,** have also been implicated in the control of emotions. The outmoded prefrontal lobotomy—severing the connections between the prefrontal lobes and the rest of the brain—was intended as a cure for psychiatric patients who were under severe emotional distress and anguish. Over 40,000 prefrontal lobotomies were performed in the middle part of the 20th

FIGURE 2.3 A bust and skull of Phineas Gage. The steel rod entered his left cheek and exited through his frontal lobes.

Source: From the Warren Anatomical Museum, Harvard Medical School. Reprinted by permission.

century, and its developer was awarded the Nobel Prize in physiology (Pinel, 1993). After several years of careful study, however, researchers concluded that the side effects of prefrontal lobotomies were too devastating, and the surgery was discontinued. They left people almost totally indifferent to the consequences of their actions, childish, and irresponsible. Their pathological emotions were gone, but so were their normal ones (Carlson, 1994).

The Parietal Lobes of the Cerebral Cortex

The **parietal lobes** are involved in the integration of bodily sensations and visual perception. Neurologists think that the parietal lobes are crucial to the ability to perceive objects as integrated entities:

> An object affects different senses, yet we perceive the object as one whole. A cat is furry, purrs, and projects a visual image. Although these sensations travel along different pathways, we perceive only one cat. If there are defects in visuo-spatial centers [of the parietal lobes], the person has difficulty mapping different sensations involved in the same object. She will perceive the cat visually and hear purring but cannot coordinate these two perceptions. (Haberlandt, 1994, p. 51)

The Occipital Lobes of the Cerebral Cortex

Although other parts of the brain are also involved, the **occipital lobes** are primarily dedicated to various aspects of visual perception. Damage to the occipital lobes, for example, can result in a condition known as *visual agnosia,* which is the inability to recognize common objects even though one may have normal visual acuity.

The Temporal Lobes of the Cerebral Cortex

The **temporal lobes** serve a variety of important functions related to learning, being involved in attention, memory, and language production and expression. Because of their significance for learning, there has been much speculation about their role in learning disabilities, as discussed in more detail in the next section.

Left and Right Hemispheres

The **left and right hemispheres** of the brain are relatively distinct with regard to their functions. For the most part, each receives sensory information from and controls movement of the opposite side of the body. For example, objects presented in the left visual field are perceived in the right hemisphere, sounds heard by the right ear are perceived in the left hemisphere, and movement of the left hand is controlled by the right hemisphere.

Another important way in which the two hemispheres differ is with respect to language. In most people, the left hemisphere is more important for language production and comprehension than the right hemisphere. In over 90% of right-handed individuals, the left hemisphere is specialized for language; in about 70% of left-handed individuals, the left hemisphere is specialized for language (Milner, 1974).

Broca's and Wernicke's Areas

Two researchers working in the 19th century were instrumental in drawing attention to the left hemisphere's role in language. Broca performed postmortem examinations of the brains of several persons who had exhibited **aphasia**—severe problems in speaking—and found they all had damage to an area in the left frontal lobe. Several years later, Wernicke identified an area in the left temporal lobe that he hypothesized was largely responsible for speech comprehension. These areas have come to be known, respectively, as **Broca's area** and **Wernicke's area** (Figure 2.4).

Subsequent research has shown that it is not always possible to predict precisely the type of language problem a person will have based on Broca's or Wernicke's area (Pinel, 1993). Documented damage to these areas does not always result in the same kinds of speech problems, and there have been cases of surgical removal of these areas with little disruption of speech production or comprehension. Furthermore, there is evidence that the right hemisphere is also responsible for certain aspects of language and communication. For example, the ability to convey and recognize emotion in one's tone of voice is largely a right-hemisphere activity (Carlson, 1994; Pinel, 1993).

Even though it is dangerous to predict in individual cases the connections between specific brain areas and specific behaviors, the weight of the evidence since the time of Broca and Wernicke indicates that, for most people, the left hemisphere is primarily responsible for many important aspects of language, especially for those who are right-handed. Several methods have been used in pointing to the dominance of the

FIGURE 2.4 The Location of Broca's Area and Wernicke's Area

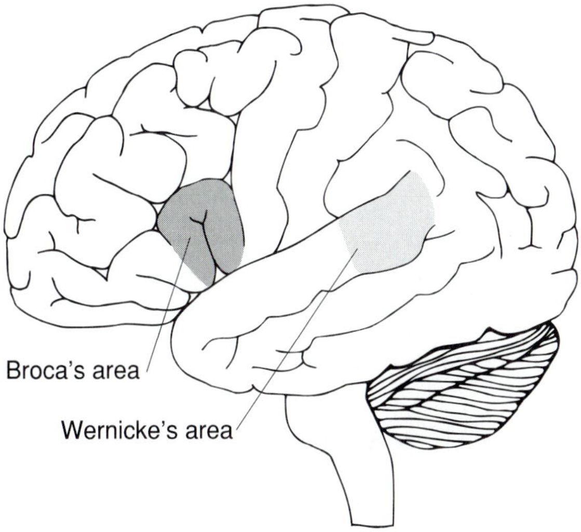

Source: From *Biopsychology,* 2nd ed. (p. 514, Fig. 16.2) by J. P. J. Pinel, 1993, Boston: Allyn & Bacon. Copyright 1993 by Allyn & Bacon. Reprinted by permission.

left hemisphere for language. For example, patients who are about to undergo surgery that might affect speech are often given an anesthetic first in the artery leading to the one hemisphere and then, after the anesthetic has worn off, in the artery leading to the other hemisphere. Researchers have noted that, for the overwhelming majority of right-handed people and for the majority of left-handed people, the anesthetization of the left hemisphere results in an inability to speak.

Split-Brain Studies

Perhaps the most dramatic demonstrations of the differential abilities of the left and right hemispheres have been the much celebrated **split-brain studies** (Gazzaniga & LeDoux, 1978; Sperry, 1964). Split-brain studies came about as the result of a surgical procedure performed on patients with severe cases of epilepsy. In these patients, neurons in one hemisphere stimulate neurons in the other hemisphere, creating seizures so intense that they are not controllable by drugs. Severing the area between the two hemispheres reduces the number of seizures by prohibiting the neurons in one hemisphere from setting off those in the other hemisphere.

Split-brain patients provide testimony to the fact that the two brain hemispheres are primarily responsible for different functions. For example, one of the first things these patients say is that their left hand seems to have "a mind of its own" (Carlson, 1994, p. 12). They may be intently reading a book (a left-hemisphere activity) they are holding in their left hand when suddenly the left hand puts the book down. This occurs because their left hand is controlled by their right hemisphere, and the right hemisphere, not being able to read, gets bored.

Researchers have tested split-brain patients using a variety of laboratory tasks. In one typical procedure, the picture of a common object, such as a ball, is flashed to the right or left visual field of these individuals, and their responses are compared. When it is shown to the right visual field, these patients say they see a ball because it is seen by the left hemisphere, the hemisphere in control of speech. With eyes closed, they can also pick out the ball from among several objects using the right hand. They pick out the ball at a chance level of performance, however, when using the left hand. When objects are shown to the left visual field, the results are the opposite. When the ball is shown to the left visual field and, hence, the right hemisphere, these patients usually say they do not see anything. With eyes closed, however, the left hand, which is controlled by the right hemisphere, is able to pick out the ball from among several objects; but the right hand, which is controlled by the left hemisphere, does no better than chance.

HOW CAN WE INFER NEUROLOGICAL DYSFUNCTION IN CHILDREN?

Historically, much of the rationale for implicating **neurological dysfunction** as a cause of learning disabilities has been inferential. Neurologists and other professionals have noted that many of the behaviors and learning problems of people with obvious and well-documented brain injury are also present, although sometimes to a less pervasive degree, in children with learning disabilities. In other words, the types of learning problems and behavioral deviations that occur in those who have brain tumors or who have had strokes or head wounds are also present in some children with learning disabilities. For example, virtually all the behaviors noted previously as associated with damage to the cerebellum and the cerebral cortex are also evident in some children with learning disabilities. These range from problems of movement associated with damage to the cerebellum to attention, language, and memory difficulties associated with damage to the temporal lobes.

Inferring neurological dysfunction in children with learning disabilities from what we know about the behavior of documented cases of brain injury, however, has its limitations. Without some more direct measure of brain structure or functioning, we cannot be sure whether the behavioral or learning problems of the child with learning disabilities are due to the same causes as those of individuals with documented brain injury. However, research on lateralization suggests a more direct link between the brain and learning disabilities.

Research on Brain Lateralization

Starting in the 1980s, researchers began to uncover more direct evidence of a neurological basis for learning disabilities. Much of this work has focused on the lateralization of brain function in adults with **dyslexia,** or severe reading disabilities. **Lateralization of function** refers to the different roles the two sides of the brain play in controlling behavior. Several researchers have reached similar conclusions: The brains of people with dyslexia are structurally and functionally different from those of people who are nondisabled. Specifically, those with dyslexia do not exhibit the typical left-hemisphere dominance for language that we noted in the discussion of split-brain studies. Researchers have primarily used three methods to arrive at these conclusions: postmortem studies of the brain, MRI and CAT-scan studies, and PET-scan and fMRI studies.

Postmortem Studies

The first evidence suggesting that neurological abnormalities are present in people with dyslexia came from autopsies. Galaburda and Geschwind and their colleagues have conducted more than a dozen autopsies on the brains of individuals who had dyslexia and compared them with results of over a hundred autopsies performed on brains of persons (infancy through adulthood) who were not dyslexic (Galaburda & Kemper, 1979; Galaburda, Menard, & Rosen, 1994; Galaburda, Sherman, Rosen, Aboitiz, & Geschwind, 1985; Geschwind & Levitsky, 1968; Humphreys, Kaufmann, & Galaburda, 1990). Although the number of cases of persons with dyslexia is relatively small, the findings have been consistent. In the majority of nondyslexic brains, a section of the left temporal lobe is larger than the same area in the right hemisphere. This area, which includes a large portion of Wernicke's area (see Figure 2.4), is referred to as the **planum temporale.** The results for those who are dyslexic are dramatically different; in the majority of cases, the planum temporales in the left and right hemispheres are the same size or the planum temporale in the right hemisphere is bigger than that in the left hemisphere.

MRI and CAT-Scan Studies

Studies using neuroimaging techniques have generally confirmed the results of the postmortem studies (Hynd & Semrud-Clikeman, 1989; Kushch et al., 1993; Larsen, Hoien, Lundberg, & Odegaard, 1990). In most cases, MRIs and CAT-scans have revealed asymmetry favoring the left planum temporale for nondyslexic individuals, but symmetry or reversed symmetry (i.e., the right planum temporale is larger than the left) for persons who are dyslexic. In addition, some studies have found similar patterns for the parieto-occipital cortex. The left parieto-occipital cortex tends to be larger than the right in nondyslexic persons, but the two areas tend to be symmetrical or the right is larger than the left in those who are dyslexic.

PET-Scan and fMRI Studies

There have been too few studies to provide definitive results, but researchers using PET-scans and fMRIs (see Box 2.1) have found differences between the brain metabolisms of persons who are dyslexic and those who are nondyslexic. Although not as consistent as the results from MRI studies in pointing to the planum temporale, studies using PET-scans have found that persons with dyslexia have left-hemisphere deficits (Flowers, 1993; Flowers, Wood, & Naylor, 1991; Gross-Glenn et al., 1991; Hagman et al., 1992). Typically, these studies have involved having an individual perform some type of cognitive task while blood flow to various parts of the brain is measured. For example, in one study, researchers required subjects to read words presented once every 5 seconds for 30 minutes (Gross-Glenn et al., 1991). Another presented individuals with consonant-vowel syllables (*da, ga, pa, ta*) once every 2 seconds, requiring them to press a response button whenever the target stimulus, *da,* occurred (Hagman et al., 1992). More recently, researchers using fMRIs have found evidence suggesting that compared to nondisabled adults those with dyslexia show decreased neural activity in the posterior portions of the brain (e.g., Wernicke's area; Shaywitz et al., 1998). (See Figure 2.4.)

Although there is abundant evidence showing, on average, the brains of people with dyslexia do not exhibit the typical left-right asymmetry, the results are not unequivocal. Some people with dyslexia do show the characteristic asymmetry, and some nondisabled individuals exhibit symmetry of the hemispheres. Researchers have yet to agree on exactly what accounts for the tendency for people with dyslexia to lack the left-right asymmetry.

Right-Hemisphere Brain Dysfunction

Most neurological research having a bearing on learning disabilities has focused on the impact of the left hemisphere on brain dysfunction. This is not surprising, given the importance of the left hemisphere for language and the fact that many persons with learning disabilities have language and reading problems. Some researchers, however, have posited that persons who have a dysfunctional right hemisphere exhibit what is referred to as **nonverbal learning disabilities** (Myklebust, 1975; Rourke, 1989; Semrud-Clikeman & Hynd, 1990). This term is somewhat of a misnomer because persons with nonverbal learning disabilities often display subtle problems with using language, especially in social situations (Rourke & Tsatsanis, 1996).

In the perceptual realm, individuals with nonverbal learning disabilities have difficulties with visual-spatial and tactual tasks. In the cognitive arena, they often have difficulty in math and in self-regulation and organization. Terms such as *spacy* and *in a fog* are often used to characterize these children (Denckla, 1993).

But the social area is where persons with nonverbal learning disabilities encounter their most significant problems. They are often socially inept, showing deficits in their ability to interpret the social behavior of others and to understand the impact of their own immature behavior on them. These deficits are especially pronounced in novel situations. Even though some may be academically competent, adults with nonverbal learning disabilities often have trouble holding a job because of their problems in social interaction. Some authorities see these persons as being at risk for depression and suicide (Rourke, Young, & Leenaars, 1989).

WHAT FACTORS CONTRIBUTE TO NEUROLOGICAL DYSFUNCTION?

Given the mounting evidence that persons with learning disabilities may have neurological abnormalities, the question arises as to why these abnormalities occur. One very speculative theory has been advanced concerning the association between language/reading disabilities, immune disorders, left-handedness, and testosterone levels. (See Box 2.2.) In addition to this tentative theory, there is more substantial evidence for the following factors as possible contributors to learning disabilities: hereditary factors, teratogenic factors, medical factors, and environmental factors.

Hereditary Factors

Professionals have long surmised that heredity plays a significant role in many cases of learning disabilities. The authors of some of the first reported cases of reading disability, for example, noted that children with reading disabilities often had relatives who were reading disabled (Hinshelwood, 1907; Stephenson, 1907; Thomas, 1905). Genetics researchers have used two types of studies to look at the issue of whether the condition of learning disabilities is inherited: familiality and heritability.

Familiality

Familiality is said to be operating when a particular condition, such as a reading disability, occurs at a greater than chance rate in a family. In other words, **familiality** is the tendency for something to "run in a family." The turn-of-the-century researchers,

BOX 2.2 ***CURRENT ISSUES***

The Geschwind-Behan-Galaburda Theory of Reading Disabilities

Geschwind, Behan, and Galaburda have put forth some very provocative, but highly speculative, ideas regarding the causes of reading disabilities (Galaburda, 1994; Geschwind & Behan, 1984; Geschwind & Galaburda, 1985). Although far from completely accepted, their model is intriguing because it ties together several strands of findings pertaining to persons who are dyslexic. Specifically, it addresses data suggesting that persons with dyslexia are more likely than nondyslexics to (1) have symmetrical hemispheres or right hemispheres that are larger than left hemispheres, (2) be left-handed, (3) have autoimmune disorders (e.g., asthma, allergies, colitis), and (4) be males.

The G-B-G theory holds that all these findings can be explained by abnormally high testosterone levels or hypersensitivity to testosterone during fetal development. In the normal fetal brain, neurons that will eventually end up in the cortex develop in the neural tube, and as the fetus develops, these neurons migrate to their respective positions in either the left or right hemisphere, with more going to the left than to the right hemisphere. Although there is some overlap, migration to the right hemisphere occurs earlier than that to the left. The fact that the left hemisphere develops more slowly leaves it vulnerable for a longer period to agents that might disrupt its growth. Researchers have demonstrated that testosterone is an agent that slows cell migration, and the G-B-G theory posits that high testosterone levels or hypersensitivity to it in some fetal brains can result in an excessive delay of maturation of the left hemisphere such that the normal asymmetry of the left hemisphere being larger than the right fails to occur.

Geschwind, Behan, and Galaburda hypothesize that the increased size of the right hemisphere relative to the left accounts for the higher prevalence of left-handedness in persons with dyslexia reported by some researchers. (The right hemisphere controls motor movements and receives perceptions from the left side of the body, and vice versa.) They also note that researchers have found that exceptionally high levels of testosterone are linked to malfunctioning of the thymus gland, which affects the immune system. And, finally, they assert that males are more likely to have high levels of testosterone, and this leads to a higher prevalence of dyslexia in males.

The G-B-G theory is highly speculative and not accepted by everyone working in this area. (See Bryden, McManus, and Bulman-Fleming, 1994, for a critical review of the theory.) For example, the evidence for an association between left-handedness and language or reading disabilities is equivocal—some studies have found a relationship; others have not. As we noted in Chapter 1, some have questioned the higher prevalence of dyslexia in males (Shaywitz, Shaywitz, Fletcher, & Escobar, 1990). Little empirical evidence exists to pinpoint testosterone as a causal agent in the associations that do occur. Nevertheless, some researchers think there is enough evidence of an association among these various conditions that the G-B-G theory warrants further investigation (Hugdahl, 1994; Kaplan & Crawford, 1994). An intriguing set of findings is that studies of mice have also suggested an association among autoimmune disorders, learning deficits, and abnormal brain structures.

Questions to Ponder

If the Geschwind-Behan-Galaburda theory were to be proven correct, of what value would this be to teachers or parents?

Can you think of individuals who are left-handed or who have an autoimmune disorder who could be used as evidence to support or to negate the G-B-G theory?

noted previously, who found evidence of familiality were working with small numbers of cases. In more current studies, researchers have used larger samples to document that reading disability is, indeed, a familial condition (Hallgren, 1950; Pennington, 1990). Generally, researchers have found around 35% to 45% of first-degree relatives of children with learning disabilities also have reading disabilities. They have also found evidence for approximately the same degree of familiality for speech and language disorders (Beichtman, Hood, & Inglis, 1992; Lewis, 1992) and spelling disability (Schulte-Korne, Deimel, Muller, Gutenbrunner, & Remschmidt, 1996).

Familiality, however, is not proof of heritability. Learning disabilities may run in families for environmental reasons. For example, one cannot rule out the possibility that parents who have learning disabilities might cause their children to have learning disabilities by the way they raise them. Likewise, siblings may be more likely to have learning disabilities because they share relatively similar environments.

Heritability

The most common way to test for the **heritability** of a condition—the degree to which it is genetically transmitted—is to compare its prevalence in monozygotic (MZ) and dizygotic (DZ) twins. **Monozygotic twins** come from the same egg and share the same genetic characteristics; **dizygotic twins** come from two separate eggs and share the same genetic characteristics as do other siblings. In the case of reading disabilities, for instance, the researcher first finds a group of individuals with reading disabilities who are members of MZ twin pairs and compares them with a group of individuals with reading disabilities who are members of DZ twin pairs. If reading disability is heritable, the proportion of cases in which both twins are reading disabled should be higher in the MZ group than in the DZ group because the MZ twins come from the same egg and share more genetic material than do the DZ twins.

Researchers have consistently found a greater degree of concordance for reading disabilities and speech and language disorders in MZ twins than in DZ twins. For example, in a major study of genetics and learning disabilities, the Colorado Reading Project, 53 of 99 (54%) MZ pairs and 23 of 73 (32%) DZ pairs were concordant for reading disabilities (DeFries, Gillis, & Wadsworth, 1993). In another study, 24 of 32 (75%) MZ pairs and 8 of 25 (32%) DZ pairs were concordant for speech and language disorders (Lewis & Thompson, 1992). In a study of MZ and DZ nondisabled readers, a high degree of heritability was also found on an oral reading measure (Reynolds et al., 1996).

Gene Location

Some of the most recent genetics research on learning disabilities has concentrated on trying to isolate the particular gene or genes involved in these cases. A few researchers have found evidence implicating Chromosomes 6 and 15, especially the former, as being responsible for some cases of learning disabilities (Cardon et al., 1994; DeFries et al., 1993; Grigorenko et al., 1997). Most authorities, however, doubt that there is only one gene responsible for learning disabilities (Pennington, 1995).

Genetic Links with Other Disabling Conditions

The results of research on whether learning disabilities share genetic links with other conditions are mixed. We have long known that learning disabilities and attention deficit hyperactivity disorder (ADHD) tend to occur together (see Chapter 10). This could be due to one causing the other, or they may both be caused by the same neurological condition, which is genetically based. However, evidence for a common genetic influence for ADHD and learning disabilities is tentative at best (Gilger, Pennington, & DeFries, 1992; Stevenson, Pennington, Gilger, DeFries, & Gillis, 1993). One team of researchers found evidence for the notion that the two tend to co-occur because of nonrandom mating patterns (Faraone et al., 1993). In other words, spouses of persons with attention deficit hyperactivity disorder have higher rates of learning disabilities than do spouses of persons without ADHD. The offspring of these couples inherit genes for both conditions and therefore are more likely to have both learning disabilities and ADHD. There has also been speculation concerning the co-occurrence of learning disabilities and Tourette's syndrome, a hereditary condition characterized by tics. Although persons with Tourette's syndrome often have other characteristics, such as ADHD and learning disabilities, studies of a familial link between Tourette's and learning disabilities have been inconclusive (Comings & Comings, 1990; Pauls, Leckman, & Cohen, 1993).

Teratogenic Factors

Teratogens are agents that cause abnormal growth or malformation in the fetus. A variety of chemicals has been implicated as **teratogens.** We briefly discuss three of them: alcohol, cocaine, and lead.

Probably the most common teratogen affecting mental development is alcohol. A pregnant woman who drinks excessively runs the risk of having a baby with **fetal alcohol syndrome.** Although this is most often associated with mental retardation, brain damage, hyperactivity, anomalies of the face, and heart abnormalities, some have speculated that in smaller concentrations alcohol might result in more subtle neurological problems that lead to learning disabilities.

Some researchers have also concluded that crack cocaine use by expectant mothers can cause neurological damage in the developing fetus (Greer, 1990). Although not all authorities agree on whether crack cocaine results in learning problems, at this point, it is reasonable to be on the alert for learning disabilities and other behavioral problems in children born to mothers using crack cocaine.

We have long known that lead ingestion can result in brain damage. When lead-based paint was commonly used, researchers found that infants and young children who ate paint chips suffered brain damage and mental retardation (Byers & Lord, 1943; Smith, Baehner, Carney, & Majors, 1963). Lead-based paint is now banned, but researchers have been studying the effects of lower levels of lead that can result from living near lead smelters or other toxic sites. They have found that children exposed prenatally and postnatally to lead run the risk of exhibiting developmental problems (Feldman & White, 1992; Leviton et al., 1993; Minder, Das-Smaal, Brand, & Orlebeke, 1994).

Medical Factors

There are myriad medical conditions that can contribute to children's problems. The following are sometimes associated with learning disabilities:

- *Premature birth* places children at risk for neurological damage, learning disabilities, and other disabling conditions. One study found that 19% of prematurely born children with very low birthweight had learning disabilities (Ross, Lipper, & Auld, 1991).
- *Diabetes* can lead to neuropsychological problems and learning disabilities. One team of authorities concluded that children with early onset of diabetes (before 5 years of age) are candidates for learning disabilities (Rovet, Ehrlich, Czuchta, & Akler, 1993).
- *Meningitis,* an infection of the brain caused by a variety of viral or bacterial agents, can result in brain damage. There is evidence that this brain damage can lead to learning problems (Taylor & Schatschneider, 1992).
- *Cardiac arrest,* although occurring rarely in children, can lead to loss of oxygen and blood flow to the brain, which results in brain damage. Children who had suffered a cardiac arrest were found to have a variety of deficits on neuropsychological, achievement, and adaptive behavior measures (Morris, Krawiecki, Wright, & Walter, 1993).
- *Pediatric AIDS* is the fastest growing infection that babies can contract from their mothers (Armstrong, Seidel, & Swales, 1993). The effects of pediatric AIDS are not always easy to disentangle from other social and physical causes (e.g., neglect, malnutrition, drug and alcohol addiction), but there is strong evidence that pediatric AIDS can result in neurological damage.

Environmental Factors

The role the environment may play in causing learning disabilities has already been noted. For example, extremely poor parenting or teaching can put children at risk for developing learning difficulties. In addition to having a direct negative influence on learning, the environment can also have an indirect impact on learning by creating situations in which brain dysfunction is more likely. Poor socioeconomic conditions are linked with a host of factors (e.g., malnutrition, poor prenatal and postnatal health care, teenage pregnancy, substance abuse) that can put children at risk for neurological dysfunction. And, unfortunately, there is strong evidence that, since mid to late 1970s, increasing numbers of children and their mothers are living in poverty.

WHAT SHOULD EDUCATORS KEEP IN MIND REGARDING CAUSES?

From an educator's viewpoint, it is important to keep the significance of causal factors in its proper perspective. Knowing the exact cause of a learning disability is of only limited utility to teachers and other educators. For example, knowing that a particular student does or does not have neurological dysfunction is largely irrelevant to how one teaches that student. Furthermore, in considering individual cases, we are rarely able to determine definitively the cause or causes of someone's learning disability because there are no foolproof tests, procedures, or examinations that provide quick and easy answers to the complicated question of causal factors. Nonetheless, as well-rounded professionals able to communicate with professionals from other fields, as well as with parents, teachers have a responsibility to keep abreast of research on causal factors of learning disabilities.

Summary

1. What causes learning disabilities?
   a. The field of learning disabilities grew out of a medical and clinical assumption that *neurological factors* were the basis of learning disabilities. The work of Broca and Wernicke in the 19th century, which identified particular areas of the brain as controlling speaking and understanding of language, laid the groundwork for later work on dyslexia. In the early 20th century, clinicians noted the similarities between children with dyslexia or other learning disabilities and persons with documented brain damage.
   b. The field was slow to accept neurological dysfunction as a viable causal factor because of the *questionable accuracy* of neurological measures and the popularity of behaviorism and environmentalism.
   c. In recent years, professionals have generally taken a more favorable view of neurological explanations of learning disabilities. There has been a decrease in the popularity of behaviorism and environmentalism because intervening to remedy the effects of poverty on child development has been difficult. Furthermore, advances in neurological measures, such as CAT-scans, MRIs, PET-scans, and fMRIs, have probably been the most influential reason for the resurgence of interest in exploring neurological factors in learning disabilities.
2. How does the brain function?
   a. *Neurons* send and receive messages. Neurons consist of a *soma* (cell body), *dendrites* (projections that receive messages), and an *axon* with its *terminal buttons* that secrete chemical *neurotransmitters* into the *synapse* (a small gap between the axon and dendrite).

b. Different parts of the brain have different functions. The brain is commonly divided into the following areas, each of which is generally responsible for different functions:
   (1) *brain stem*—regulates survival reflexes such as heart rate and respiration
   (2) *cerebellum*—regulates several behaviors related to movement, including balance, gait, speech, and eye movements
   (3) *cerebral cortex*—composed of the *frontal lobes* (responsible for some motor movements and executive functions), *prefrontal lobes* (foreparts of the frontal lobes, implicated in control of emotions), *parietal lobes* (involved in the integration of bodily sensations and visual perceptions), *occipital lobes* (primarily dedicated to visual perception, in conjunction with other parts of the brain), and *temporal lobes* (involved in attention, memory, and language production and reception)

c. The left and right hemispheres of the brain are relatively distinct with regard to their functions. For the most part, each receives information and controls movement of the opposite side of the body. In most people, especially those who are right-handed, the left hemisphere is more important for language production and comprehension than the right hemisphere.
   (1) *Broca's area* and *Wernicke's area* are two parts of the left hemisphere associated with language (production and comprehension, respectively). However, damage to these areas does not always result in the same kinds of problems, and there is evidence that the right side of the brain is responsible for some aspects of language and communication.
   (2) *Split-brain studies* involve surgical procedures performed on patients with severe epilepsy in which the number of seizures experienced is reduced by severing the area between the two hemispheres. These studies have resulted in dramatic demonstrations of the differential abilities of the two hemispheres.

3. How can we infer neurological dysfunction in children?
   a. Historically, neurological dysfunction in children with learning disabilities has been largely inferred from what we know about the behavior of people with documented brain injury. This approach has its limitations, however, because it does not involve direct measures of brain function or structure.
   b. More recently, researchers have used postmortem studies and neuroimaging technology (MRI, CAT-scan, PET-scan, and fMRI) to conclude that persons with dyslexia are more likely than those without dyslexia to:
      (1) have symmetrical hemispheres or larger right than left hemispheres (the left cerebral hemisphere tends to be larger than the right in persons without dyslexia)
      (2) have abnormal functioning and structure of the left *planum temporale* (an area that includes a large portion of Wernicke's area in the temporal lobe)
   c. Even though many researchers have pointed to the left hemisphere as involved in learning disabilities, there is also evidence that a dysfunctional right hemisphere may be the cause of *nonverbal learning disabilities.* Nonverbal

learning disabilities may include difficulties with visual-spatial and tactual tasks, math, and self-regulation and organization. The most significant problems for people with nonverbal learning disabilities may be in the social area, in which they may exhibit poor social perception and judgment.

4. What factors contribute to neurological dysfunction?
   a. Hereditary factors may play a role. Researchers have used two types of studies to investigate the genetic basis of learning disabilities:
      (1) *Familiality,* in which a learning disability occurs at a greater than chance rate in a family, has been found in some studies. But familiality is not proof of heritability because learning disabilities may occur in a family for environmental reasons.
      (2) *Heritability* studies often compare the prevalence of a condition in monozygotic versus dizygotic twins. MZ twins share more genetic material than do DZ twins. If learning disabilities are inherited, when one twin has learning disabilities, there should be more cases of the other twin also having learning disabilities in MZ than in DZ twins. Research has consistently found this to be the case.
   b. Teratogenic factors may play a role. *Teratogens* are agents that cause abnormal growth or malformation of the fetus. The following are some examples:
      (1) *Alcohol* is probably the most common teratogen that can affect mental development. Authorities speculate that *fetal alcohol syndrome,* although most often associated with mental retardation, may result in learning disabilities if the alcohol is in smaller concentrations.
      (2) *Crack cocaine* use by expectant mothers may also cause neurological damage to a developing fetus, but opinions vary about long-term exposure as a cause of learning disabilities.
      (3) Ingestion of *lead* can result in brain damage, and we cannot rule out prenatal exposure as a cause of some cases of learning disabilities.
   c. *Medical factors* may play a role. Some examples are *premature birth, diabetes, meningitis, cardiac arrest,* and *pediatric AIDS.*
   d. *Environmental factors* can have an indirect effect on neurological development by creating situations in which brain dysfunction is more likely to occur. For example, poor socioeconomic conditions are linked to many factors that put children at risk for neurological disorders.
5. What should educators keep in mind regarding causes?
   a. In individual cases, we are rarely able to determine definitively the cause of someone's learning disability.
   b. Knowing the exact cause of a student's learning disability does not always translate into knowing what should be done for him or her educationally.
   c. Well-rounded professionals should keep abreast of research on causal factors in learning disabilities.

3

Educational Approaches

People's views about the causes of learning disabilities align closely with their views about how we should assess and treat the problems experienced by those with learning disabilities. For example, if there are fundamental biological differences between people who have learning disabilities and people who do not have them, it would be important to identify the specific biological differences and to provide interventions on that basis; theory about assessment and treatment would naturally follow a biological or medical perspective. In contrast, people who think that learning disabilities are primarily mismatches between the sensory mode of instruction and students' preferred modality of learning will want to identify learners' preferences and recast instruction to fit them. If, however, most learning disabilities are caused by environmental problems, assessment and treatment would probably follow a very different path.

As shown in Chapter 2, the field of learning disabilities is not advanced enough to permit educators to group students based on the causes of their disabilities. Neither biological nor environmental causes are well enough established to permit educators to plan educational programs on the basis of physical diagnosis. Although educators cannot structure the way they address learning disabilities today according to causes of these disorders, they need to have principles—a conceptual model—that organizes their approach to the assessment and treatment of learning disabilities.

WHY UNDERSTAND EDUCATIONAL MODELS OF LEARNING DISABILITIES?

Just as it is difficult to create precise boundaries between the group of students educators say have learning disabilities and those they say have low achievement (see Chapter 1), it is also difficult to delineate the exact boundaries among various conceptual approaches to learning disabilities. Nevertheless, conceptual approaches or models are useful because they help clarify general differences between perspectives on learning disabilities, promote conceptually integrated descriptions of learning disabilities, provide general guidelines from which more specific practices can be deduced, and encourage research that supports or counters the model.

However, conceptual models also have drawbacks. They are problematic because they make more sense conceptually than they do in practice, emphasize differences (and hence mask similarities), encourage advocates to ignore some evidence, and are often based more on ideas than facts.

Despite these problems, educational models offer enough benefits to make them worthy of study. Bear in mind that models are valuable in understanding general approaches to learning disabilities, but there are no sharp boundaries between them. In the regions closer to the boundaries between models, differences become less distinct. Many of the differences are of greater theoretical than practical importance. Indeed, advocates of different models may claim that the same assessment and intervention practices are consistent, at least in part, with very different theoretical models.

WHAT EDUCATIONAL MODELS WERE APPLIED IN THE PAST?

When learning disabilities was first becoming recognized as a separate area of special education, authorities in the field generally discussed three conceptual models as the basis for diagnosis and intervention: medical, diagnostic-remedial, and task-analytic (or behavioral) perspectives (e.g., Bateman, 1967). These models differed on the basis of their theoretical foundations, approaches to assessment of learning problems, and recommendations about interventions.

Medical Approaches

Medical approaches to disorder focus on finding the etiology (cause) of a problem and correcting it. For example, if one knows that a particular learning or behavior problem is caused by an imbalance in blood chemistry, one would prescribe a medication that would correct that imbalance. Learning disabilities were usually presumed to be neurological problems, which could have many different ultimate causes (genetic, biochemical, etc.).

The ultimate causes of problems often would not be subject to direct correction. For example, once established, a person's genetic constitution is not mutable. Ironically, one of the strongest appeals of the medical model is that it often fixes the source of a student's problem as a specific cause that cannot be directly modified. Although the incorrectable nature of such problems might seem demoralizing, the explanations offer advantages. Instead of fretting about the cause, educators and parents must focus on providing students with means of compensating for the problem. A related appeal of etiological theories is that they free the primary caregivers of responsibility for causing the problem; parents, for example, are absolved of guilt and freed to become advocates seeking help for their children.

In the 1960s and 1970s, several individuals in the field emphasized the etiological aspects of learning disabilities. Nowhere is this more obvious than in the work of Samuel Clements, who countered widely held beliefs about faulty parenting causing learning disabilities and other problems (e.g., Clements & Peters, 1962). Clements argued that there were indications of minor problems in children's nervous systems that were at the root of learning problems, which he labeled **minimal brain dysfunction,** or MBD (Clements, 1970).

Etiological approaches usually emphasized many of the factors presented in Chapter 2. Concerns about neurological, genetic, and biochemical factors were paramount. Problems such as anoxia (lack of oxygen at birth), hemispheric asymmetry, and lead exposure were seen as particularly important. Assessment practices emphasized medical and neurological examinations, and interventions often included medications.

Although oversimplified, this description illustrates one of the most powerful early approaches to learning disabilities. The etiological approach to learning disabilities still has advocates, and future research into the causes of learning disabilities will probably be helpful in understanding these difficulties. They offer little direction for the practice of special education today, however. Teachers should strive to be informed about causes of learning disabilities so they can help students and parents understand them, but they should not expect knowing the causes of learning disabilities to help them design effective programs for students with the disabilities.

Diagnostic-Remedial Approaches

The important figures in the history of learning disabilities who promoted diagnostic-remedial approaches were responding, in part, to etiological approaches. This is evident in Kirk's famous speech of 1963; he cautioned against using terminology that focused on "concepts relating to etiology of brain injury or cerebral dysfunction" (Kirk, 1975, p. 8). Instead, he recommended a behavioral label: learning disabilities. This focus would encourage the development of instruments to diagnose children's specific problems and to prescribe appropriate remedial methods.

In diagnostic-remedial approaches, diagnosticians and teachers focused on identifying correlates, rather than causes, of problems. By correlates, they meant associated cognitive and behavioral problems—sometimes called psychological processes. Remediating those difficulties was the next step. For example, when students had difficulty with reading, the diagnostician would assess whether they also had difficulties with auditory memory (remembering things they heard), form constancy (knowing that the identity of an object does not change when it is shown in a different size or orientation), visual closure (recognizing an object after seeing only part of it), or any of many similar areas. If students had difficulty with these, teachers would try to remediate them or design instruction that avoided using the weak areas.

Some of the foremost figures in the history of learning disabilities were closely associated with diagnostic-remedial models (see Chapter 1). Kirk was instrumental in the development of the *Illinois Test of Psycholinguistic Abilities* (ITPA; Kirk, McCarthy, & Kirk, 1968) and provided recommendations about remediating problems that it revealed (Kirk & Kirk, 1971). Kephart coauthored the *Purdue Perceptual-Motor Survey* (Roach & Kephart, 1966) and wrote about remediating perceptual and motor problems that characterized many children with learning disabilities (Kephart, 1971). Frostig coauthored the *Developmental Test of Visual Perception* (Frostig, Lefever, & Whittlesey, 1964) and sets of associated remedial materials (Frostig & Horne, 1964).

The diagnostic-remedial model had two important legacies for the future of learning disabilities. First, it offered hope that, through careful testing, a student's specific learning disabilities could be identified; the emphasis on diagnosis—determining the nature of a condition—is still evident in the extensive use of testing data in learning disabilities. Second, it focused on information processing—the procedures involved in thinking. This focus foreshadowed much of the later emphasis on cognition in learning disabilities.

Behavioral Approaches

Applications of the behavioral views to education drew from the laboratory and applied work of behavioral psychologists, especially B. F. Skinner (1953, 1968). Skinner's work went well beyond stimulus-response psychology (he argued his work was response-stimulus psychology, focusing on how behavior produces certain environmental consequences) and included development of teaching machines. In addition, Skinner advocated a philosophy of education that stressed rewarding appropriate behavior rather than using punishment. Following Skinner, other psychologists and educators such as Bijou (1970), Haring (1968; Haring, Lovitt, Eaton, & Hansen, 1978), and Lovitt (1967) promoted applied behavior analysis in learning disabilities.

The focus of behavioral views is not so much on the learner as on the environment surrounding the learner, particularly the tasks to be learned. Historically, behavioral approaches to learning disabilities disregarded emphasis on biophysical causes of problems and on remediating indirect (psycholinguistic or perceptual-motor) problems. Instead, they stressed explicit remediation of the most obvious problems of students with learning disabilities: academic and social-behavioral deficits.

Many early behavioral efforts in assessing and treating learning disabilities were relatively simple, but they provided powerful evidence of effectiveness. For example, **applied behavior analysis (ABA)** for learning disabilities focused on the systematic analysis of the observable behavior of individual learners (Lovitt, 1975). People used ABA to examine the effects of changes in the environment on how well students acquired academic skills. Some of the important student behaviors included the number of words read correctly, questions answered correctly, arithmetic problems completed correctly, and words written correctly. ABA researchers found that students make many fewer reversal errors (mistakenly writing a *b* for a *d* or Ɛ for 3) when teachers systematically provide rewards for correctly written letters (e.g., Smith & Lovitt, 1973).

Although many of the important teaching procedures behavior analysts examined depend on reinforcement and punishment, behaviorally oriented researchers did not simply reward correct responses with small candies and punish mistakes by yelling "No." They employed far more complex social consequences and self-instructional techniques (see Alberto & Troutman, 1995; Rusch, Rose, & Greenwood, 1988; Wolery, Bailey, & Sugai, 1988).

Applied behavior analyses have revealed many important practices for teachers of students with learning disabilities. Books summarizing these practices are available (Haring et al., 1978; Lovitt, 1995). Although these techniques are important, perhaps the greatest contributions of applied behavior analysis are its tremendous emphasis on empirical verification of outcomes and, in general, its recommendation that teachers collect objective data about pupil performance.

Influences of Historical Models

In contemporary special education, there are many important influences of these early models. The medical models of the 1960s and 1970s still greatly affect research on the causes of learning disabilities, as shown in Chapter 2. Although the diagnostic-remedial model is not widely espoused today, it is still influential; many psychologists concerned with learning disabilities still use extensive batteries of psychological tests to identify learning patterns and make recommendations about what teachers should do to help students. Perhaps the greatest continuing influence of the early models rests with the behavioral approach to assessing and treating learning disabilities.

HOW IS BEHAVIORAL THEORY APPLIED?

Of the historically important models, behavioral theory is the only one that continues to be especially relevant to teaching students with learning disabilities today. The medical model still generates important research about the causes of learning disabilities, but this research has little impact on teaching. The diagnostic-remedial model fell from favor for two main reasons: Researchers found that (1) the tests used in diagnosis had inadequate psychometric properties and (2) the recommendations about remedial practices proved ineffective.

Applied Behavior Analysis

Although applied behavior analysts often focus on students with more severe handicaps (see, for example, the *Journal of Applied Behavior Analysis*), there are many examples of contemporary studies of problems associated with learning disabilities. For example, applied behavior analysts have identified ways to improve students' completion of homework assignments (Olympia, Sheridan, Jenson, & Andrews, 1994) and examined ways that different teaching procedures affect students' spelling skills (Birnie-Selwyn & Guerin, 1997; Gettinger, 1993).

These examples also illustrate that behavior analysts examine more than simple reinforcement procedures. The study by Olympia et al. (1994) assessed the effects of student-managed procedures, and the study by Gettinger (1993) compared the effects of teaching spelling lists with the effects of encouraging children to write without being constrained by having to spell correctly (invented spelling).

Task Analysis

Task analysis refers to specifying the components required to complete an action. "*Task analysis is the process of isolating, describing and sequencing (as necessary) all the necessary sub-tasks which, when the child has mastered them, will enable him to perform the objective*" (Bateman, 1971, p. 33).

Task analysis has obvious applications in motor skills. For example, a task analysis of filling a cup with coffee (given that one has a cup on a flat surface and a pot of coffee) simply describes the steps of (1) gripping the pot by its handle, (2) positioning the pot so its spout is next to and just above the cup, (3) tilting the pot slowly to pour the coffee, (4) stopping pouring when the cup approaches full, and (5) repositioning the pot on a protected flat surface. To be sure, the task can be analyzed in much finer grain; each step can be broken into substeps. The important point is that one can identify the steps and substeps needed to complete the task.

One of the most important aspects of behavioral approaches to learning disabilities is the analysis of cognitive tasks. Cognitive tasks or operations can also be conceptualized as a series of steps. In performing a task analysis, one describes the competencies students must have if they are to use a given strategy to solve a kind of problem. Table 3.1 provides examples of task analyses for two academic strategies.

The purpose of task analyses is to turn the steps in a cognitive process inside out, to make the usually covert parts of a strategy overt. Even though they may not realize it, people perform a complicated series of steps to complete simple tasks such as reading words or adding numbers. Although they may think they are reading a word as a unit, skillful readers are automatically converting the letters into sounds and, aided by their expectations about how those sounds might make sense, are deriving the word's pronunciation. Similarly, people who are skilled at arithmetic computation may think they automatically know the sum of a pair of numbers (e.g., 3 and 4), but they are likely to use counting systems to derive the actual sum. Task analysis specifies the steps through which naive learners go in acquiring facility with reading words, computing sums, writing essays, deducing relative returns on investments, and so forth.

Task analysis forms a foundation not only for behavioral interventions, but also for other interventions that are more closely associated with cognitive theories. Advocates who design cognitive-behavioral treatments, for example, identify the steps that students will learn to use when completing tasks. Task analyses describe cognitive strategies. Promoting students' use of cognitive strategies is a foundational concept in learning disabilities today.

Direct Instruction

Direct Instruction is the foremost example of instruction based on behavioral task analysis. Direct Instruction incorporates teacher actions that have regularly been associated with effective instruction (Brophy & Good, 1986; Rosenshine & Stevens, 1986). Although they share many features, **Direct Instruction (DI)** differs from direct instruction in one very specific way (see Table 3.2).

DI does not refer to a teacher simply lecturing and students sitting passively in rows of desks. Typically, when teachers present a DI lesson, they work with small groups of students, present examples according to a script, and ask questions that have specific answers (often as many as 10 to12 questions per minute). The students answer in unison, and the teacher provides praise or corrective feedback, depending on the accuracy of the students' answers. These aspects of the DI approach represent the teacher behaviors that most observers see when they watch a lesson. When watching any one lesson, however, an observer may not see the sequencing based on the logical analysis that discriminates DI from di.

Direct Instruction's emphasis on logical analysis of concepts and operations is unique (Engelmann, 1997; Engelmann & Carnine, 1982). According to this view, effective teaching requires that teachers show many different examples of a concept or operation and present them in a way that rules out misinterpretation. To ensure that

TABLE 3.1 Illustrative Task Analyses for Academic Strategies

These examples show the rudiments of task analyses. They are not complete analyses; much more detail would be needed to carry them to the level of instruction. But they do provide a level of detail illustrating how tasks can be analyzed logically.

What would the student have to know how to do or have been previously taught to do? These are the questions basic to a task analysis. To answer them, there must be a given task (a group of items that are similar in certain ways) and a system or strategy that students can use to solve the task. This strategy is then analyzed to identify the necessary skills.

■ Task Analysis: Decoding Simple Words

The task: Given written words composed of regularly pronounced consonant-vowel-consonant strings, the student says the words.

The strategy: Start at the left of the word and say the sound for each letter in the order shown, sliding from one letter sound to the next. If needed, say the word at a normal speech rate.

The task analysis: The student will have to know how to:

- *Start here and go that way* 
  This would not necessarily include knowing left and right (gee and haw, port and starboard); more simply, when reading, one begins at the circle and moves in the direction of the arrow.
- *Say sounds for letters*
  This illustrates the sound-symbol, or phoneme-grapheme, relationship (sometimes also called the alphabetic principle) that undergirds the correspondence between spoken and printed English. The student does not need to know the letter names or even how to map all of the 44 sounds of English to letters. He or she simply needs to know, for instance, that when one sees the letter m, one says "mmmm" and that when one sees the letter i one says "iiii."
- *Blend the sounds*
  Blending actually consists of two skills: (1) sliding from one sound to the next without stopping between them and (2) converting the stretched-out pronunciation of words to their normal speech equivalents.

■ Task Analysis: Multiplying Binomials

The task: Given a binomial expression, the student writes the expanded expression.

The strategy: Multiply the first number in the first set of parentheses by the first number in the second set of parentheses; multiply the first number in the first set of parentheses by the last number in the second set of parentheses; multiply the last number in the first set of parentheses by the first number in the second set of parentheses; multiply the last number in the first set of parentheses by the last number in the second set of parentheses. (Note: This is the FOIL strategy: multiply the *f*irst, *o*utside, *i*nside, and *l*ast expressions.)

The task analysis: The student will have to know how to:

- *Identify the first, outside, inside, and last parts of the expressions*
  Because it is useful to use the mnemonic of FOIL here, it is important that the student knows the labels for these parts of the algebraic expressions.
- *Multiply numbers, including combinations of known and unknown variables*
  This competency presupposes that the student knows how to multiply known numbers (e.g., to write 6 when shown $2 * 3$) and unknown numbers (e.g., to write $9x^2$ when shown $3x * 3x$). Furthermore, the student must know how to handle multiplying that involves positive and negative numbers and two unknowns (e.g., that $-2y * 17x = -34yx$).
- *Reduce complex equations to simpler forms*
  Sometimes, applying the strategy results in an expression that has parts that can be combined. The student must know how to determine whether an expression has parts that can be combined and know how to combine them (e,g., to add like parts).

TABLE 3.2 Shared and Distinguishing Features of Approaches Using Direct Instruction

direct instruction	Direct Instruction
Structured, teacher-led lessons	Structured, teacher-led lessons
Small-group instruction	Small-group instruction
Lessons presented in small steps	Lessons presented in small steps
Frequent questions	Frequent questions
Extensive practice	Extensive practice
Feedback, reinforcement, and correction	Feedback, reinforcement, and correction
	Lessons designed according to *Theory of Instruction* (Engelmann & Carnine, 1982)

students are, in fact, acquiring the concepts, teachers must require them to respond in ways that demonstrate they are learning.

DI advocates stress the importance of controlling the details of instruction. The interactions between teachers and students are structured by having lessons presented according to scripts. Authors of DI programs develop these scripts so that they can specify the examples to use and the order in which to present them. As they develop the scripts, the authors test them repeatedly in the field to be sure they do not misteach the students.

A critical goal of the DI approach is to teach students how to solve problems on their own. Teachers or those who write instructional materials cannot identify and teach each and every problem that a student might ever encounter; students will simply see more words than they can be taught, have more ideas than they can write, and come upon more arithmetic problems than they can learn in a few years. So instruction must provide them with generalized skills. DI teachers do this by teaching students strategies for solving problems. Students learn these strategies by practicing using them with carefully selected and sequenced tasks while the teacher provides systematic guidance and feedback.

To teach complex skills, DI follows the task-analytic practice of breaking the skill into component parts, teaching the parts separately, and then teaching students how to use the parts to perform the larger skill. In this sense, DI follows what is often called a bottom-up approach—competent performance is built from smaller parts. The task analyses in Table 3.1 illustrate how component skills in decoding simple words or multiplying binomials can be identified. Figure 3.1 shows three scripts for teaching students the structure and use of analogies.

A DI approach would teach students the component skills in a strategy. In the decoding example from Table 3.1, the strategy would be described verbally in this

FIGURE 3.1 Sample Teaching Scripts for Three Direct Instruction Lessons

THINKING OPERATIONS

■ Exercise 1—Analogies

Task A

The first Thinking Operation today is Analogies.

1. We're going to make up an analogy that tells how animals move. What is the analogy going to tell? (Signal.) *How animals move.* (Repeat until firm.)
2. The animals we're going to use in the analogy are a hawk and a whale. Which animals? (Signal.) *A hawk and a whale.*
3. Name the first animal. (Signal.) *A hawk.* Yes, a hawk. How does that animal move? (Signal.) *It flies.* Yes, it flies.
4. So, here's the first part of the analogy. A hawk is to flying. What's the first part of the analogy? (Signal.) *A hawk is to flying.* Yes, a hawk is to flying. (Repeat until firm.)
5. The first part of the analogy told how an animal moves. So, the next part of the analogy must tell how another animal moves.
6. You told how a hawk moves. Now you're going to tell about a whale. What animal? (Signal.) *A whale.* How does that animal move? (Signal.) *It swims.* Yes, it swims.
7. So, here's the second part of the analogy. A whale is to swimming. What's the second part of the analogy? (Signal.) *A whale is to swimming.* Yes, a whale is to swimming.
8. (Repeat steps 2–7 until firm.)
9. Now we're going to say the whole analogy. First, we're going to tell how a hawk moves and then we're going to tell how a whale moves. Say the analogy with me. (Signal.) (Respond with the students.) A hawk is to flying as a whale is to swimming. (Repeat until the students are responding with you.)
10. All by yourselves. Say that analogy. (Signal.) *A hawk is to flying as a whale is to swimming.* (Repeat until firm.)
11. That analogy tells how those animals move. What does that analogy tell? (Signal.) *How those animals move.*
12. (Repeat steps 10 and 11 until firm.)

Individual Test

(Call on individual students to do step 10 or 11.)

■ Exercise 12—Analogies: Opposites

Now we're going to do some more Analogies.

1. Here's an analogy about words. Old is to young as asleep is to . . . (Pause 2 seconds.) Get ready. (Signal.) *Awake.* Everybody, say the analogy. (Signal.) *Old is to young as asleep is to awake.* (Repeat until firm.)
2. What are old and asleep? (Signal.) *Words.* (To correct students who say "Opposites"):
   a. Old and asleep are words.
   b. (Repeat step 2.)

   Old is to young as asleep is to awake. That analogy tells something about those words. (Pause.) What does that analogy tell about those words? (Signal.) *What opposites those words have.* (Repeat until firm.)

FIGURE 3.1 *continued*

3. Say the analogy. (Signal.) *Old is to young as asleep is to awake.* (Repeat until firm.)
4. And what does that analogy tell about those words? (Signal.) *What opposites those words have.*
5. (Repeat steps 3 and 4 until firm.)

■ Exercise 13—Analogies

(Note: Praise all reasonable responses in this exercise, but have the group repeat the responses specified in the exercise.)

1. Everybody, what class are a towel and a plate in? (Signal.) *Objects.*
2. Finish this analogy. A towel is to rectangular as a plate is to . . . (Pause 2 seconds.) Get ready. (Signal.) *Round.*
3. Everybody, say that analogy. (Signal.) *A towel is to rectangular as a plate is to round.* (Repeat until firm.)
4. The analogy tells something about those objects. (Pause.) What does that analogy tell about those objects? (Signal.) *What shape those objects are.*
5. (Repeat steps 3 and 4 until firm.)
6. A towel is to cloth as a plate is to . . . (Pause 2 seconds.) Get ready (Signal.) *Plastic.*
7. Everybody, say that analogy. (Signal.) *A towel is to cloth as a plate is to plastic.* (Repeat until firm.)
8. The analogy tells something about those objects. (Pause.) What does that analogy tell about those objects? (Signal.) *What material those objects are made of.*
9. (Repeat steps 7 and 8 until firm.)

Note: The scripts come from two different lessons. The second would normally be taught about a month after the first.

Source: From *Thinking Basics: Corrective Reading Comprehension A* (pp. 121, 251) by S. Engelmann. P. Haddox, S. Hanner, and J. Osborn, 1978, Chicago: Science Research Associates. Copyright 1978 by Science Research Associates. Reprinted by permission.

way: "Start at left and move right, say sounds for letters, and blend the sounds into a word." Students would not have to state the strategy orally, however. Instead, they would simply learn to use it by practicing with it repeatedly with different examples (words, in this case). Having built up the ability to read words, students would later apply these simple skills (along with others about, for example, spelling conventions that produce "long" vowel sounds) to read even more complex words. Throughout the development of facility with the decoding strategy, the students would have opportunities to use it in reading brief passages of text.

In teaching students to use strategies according to a DI approach, the teacher teaches students how to

- perform component skills (e.g., letter sounds and blending in reading)
- use the strategies with simple examples

- practice with the strategies on more difficult and diverse examples
- apply the strategies in more realistic situations

Researchers have conducted many studies of DI instructional programming principles involving both nondisabled (e.g., Carnine, 1976, 1980) and atypical learners (e.g., Gersten, White, Falco, & Carnine, 1982; Kameenui, Carnine, & Maggs, 1980). The research has revealed that students learn faster and generalize better when details of instruction such as the choice of examples and the order in which they are introduced are controlled carefully (Engelmann, 1997). Overall, the DI methods have consistently shown substantial benefits in academic learning (Adams & Engelmann, 1996). Texts outline DI programs in general (Kameenui & Simmons, 1990) and for reading (Carnine, Silbert, & Kameenui, 1996) or arithmetic (Stein, Silbert, & Carnine, 1997).

Many of the same factors that can be found in DI methods are present in other methods, too. Teaching strategic behavior, for example, is present in both task-analytic and cognitive approaches. Cognitive approaches are having substantial influence on learning disabilities today.

HOW IS COGNITIVE THEORY APPLIED?

In learning disabilities, approaches based on cognitive theory are related to the psychoeducational, process, or diagnostic-remedial approaches of the 1960s and 1970s. Like those models, contemporary cognitive theory emphasizes the processes involved in human thinking; thus, they are sometimes called **information-processing models.** The earlier process models stressed the reception, organization, and expression of information. Contemporary cognitive models have gone much further. Today they emphasize more specific functions, particularly those related to memory (e.g., rehearsal), thinking (e.g., metacognition), and specific skills (e.g., the role of phonological awareness in reading competence).

Proponents of cognitive models base their ideas on cognitive psychology. They draw heavily on the work of Piaget and his interpreters (e.g., Inhelder, Sinclair, & Bovet, 1974; Piaget & Inhelder, 1969a, 1969b), Flavell (1977a, 1977b), and Bruner (e.g., Bruner, Goodnow, & Austin, 1956). Contemporary scholars who contribute to our understanding of cognition and learning disabilities include John Borkowski (e.g., Borkowski, Johnston, & Reid, 1986), Keith Stanovich (1986), Lee Swanson (1990), Joe Torgesen (1977), and Bernice Wong (1986).

A basic premise underlying cognitive theory is that learners actively manipulate mental processes such as memory and attention to integrate prior experiences with current information. Attention and memory, then, are ways of processing information during learning. Combining previously acquired information with observations about a current learning situation leads to understanding of the new information. In processing information, students probably use *executive* or *metacognitive* processes—reflective consideration of their own approaches to solving problems.

Information Processing

Studies of how students with learning disabilities process information have advanced greatly since the 1960s and 1970s, when pioneers in learning disabilities first studied this matter. Early work in learning disabilities focused on understanding relationships among sensory systems. As shown in Figure 3.2, information received by the visual, auditory, and tactile senses would be integrated by the various cognitive processes. Emphasis on sensory systems led to instructional recommendations about adapting instruction to the student's modality preferences or learning style, an idea that has found little support in research (Kavale & Forness, 1987; Snider, 1992)

More recent work has stressed the role of attention, memory, and executive function (Borkowski & Burke, 1996; Swanson, 1994; Torgesen, 1996). Today researchers

FIGURE 3.2 Early Model of Information Processing Illustrating Emphasis on Sensory Pathways

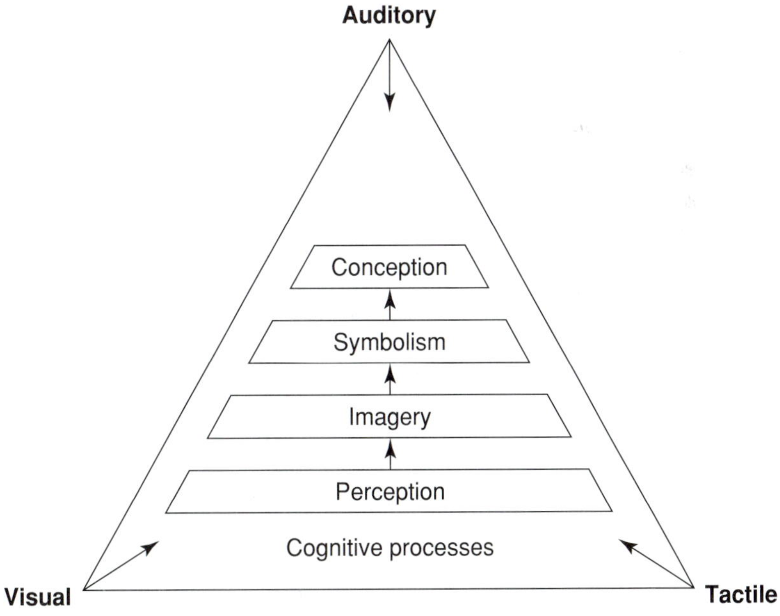

Source: From "Learning Disabilities and Cognitive Processes" by H. R. Myklebust, M. N. Bannochie, and J. R. Killen in H. R. Myklebust (Ed.), *Progress in Learning Disabilities* (vol. 2) (p. 215), 1971, New York: Grune & Stratton. Copyright 1971 by Grune & Stratton. Reprinted by permission.

represent information processing as a group of functions or processes. In learning disabilities, there is particular concern about memory and executive function. There are usually three broad types of memory:

- *sensory storage:* very temporary memory that resides mostly in the nervous system, where information is sensed (e.g., the visual system)
- *working memory:* more active memory that is used in operating on information, changing it in some way
- *long-term memory:* complex storage of information for extended times, probably with similar types of memories stored in similar ways

Figure 3.3 illustrates a contemporary view of memory. One critical concern for professionals in learning disabilities is the section of the model referring to working memory.

> Working memory contains a controlling system referred to as the central executive, which is a limited capacity work space that can be devoted to a variety of processing activities, including executive routines and decision making. . . . The central executive coordinates a number of slave systems. The two that have been studied most

FIGURE 3.3 Model of the Human Memory System Showing the Various Types of Memory in the Left Column and the Functions in the Diagram

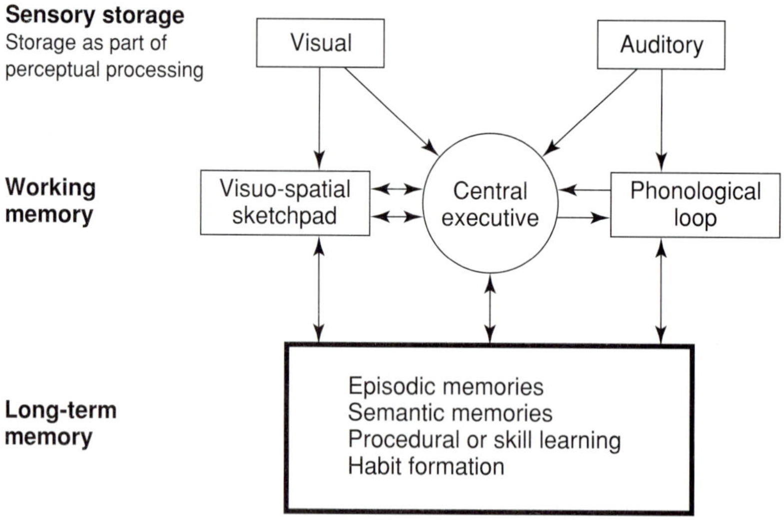

Source: From "A Model of Memory from an Information Processing Perspective: The Special Case of Phonological Memory" by J. K. Torgesen in G. R. Lyon and N.A. Krasnegor (Eds.), *Attention, Memory, and Executive Function* (p. 158), 1996, Baltimore: Paul H. Brookes. Copyright 1996 by Paul H. Brookes. Reprinted by permission.

extensively are the visuospatial sketchpad and the phonological loop. The sketchpad is responsible for generating and storing visual images, and the phonological loop is responsible for the manipulation and storage of speech-based information. (Torgesen, 1996, pp. 159–160)

One can conceptualize information coming into the memory system along the sensory memory paths, being manipulated by the executive in working memory, and then being stored in long-term memory. For example, a student might hear a description of a kind of animal ("a large brown bear"). For a few moments, the sounds of that statement would persist in sensory memory. Then working memory would take over and hold the words verbatim briefly in the phonological loop; if the student *rehears* (i.e., rehearses) the phrase, it would persist for a little longer. Then the central executive may work with long-term memory, perhaps to locate related information (e.g., the word "grizzly," images of grizzlies) or to store new information the student is hearing with related information in long-term memory.

Contemporary studies indicate that many students with learning disabilities have problems with memory, particularly in using strategies regularly used by their nondisabled peers. These strategies include **rehearsal** (repeating things to be remembered, as one would do to remember a phone number), **organization** (sorting things to be remembered according to similar features, such as remembering what one needs from the grocery by remembering that one needs things to make a dinner of salad, French bread, and chili beans), and **mnemonics** (remembering that the order for multiplying binomials is FOIL—multiply the *f*irst terms, the *o*utside terms, the *i*nside terms, and then the *l*ast terms).

Metacognition

In educational models influenced by cognitive theory, metacognition assumes a crucial role in learning disabilities. Deficits in metacognition even come close to assuming the status of a cause for learning disabilities in some accounts (e.g., Larson & Gerber, 1992).

Metacognition is closely related to cognition: In simple terms, cognition refers to thinking, and metacognition refers to thinking about thinking. Cognitive strategies are used to accomplish mental tasks such as remembering, but metacognitive strategies are used to monitor whether such tasks are being accomplished. People's understandings of their own thinking processes affect how they seek new information, perceive it, relate it to stored information, store it, select parts of it for further consideration, and recall it.

The concept of metacognition arose from Flavell's study of memory processes (Flavell, 1977a; Flavell & Wellman, 1977). Flavell noted that although young children can learn to use memory strategies such as rehearsal, they revert to developmentally younger strategies unless experimenters regularly prompt them to use the higher-order strategies. Flavell argued that such findings compel researchers to consider other factors when explaining the development of cognitive skills, particularly people's understandings of how to influence their own thinking. Thus, when children revert to developmentally younger strategies, one might suspect that they have metacognitive deficits, that they are failing to monitor, check, or maintain the use of effective strategies. On laboratory tasks, many students with learning disabilities appear to use strategies of younger students (see Hallahan, Kneedler, & Lloyd, 1983).

Metacognitive strategies are self-regulatory processes. That is, people use them to regulate their own cognition. According to Borkowski (1992), these strategies are presumed to include several elements:

- awareness of viable strategies
- selection of appropriate strategies
- monitoring of the use of these strategies
- adjusting or revising of the strategies

Much of cognitive theory's emphasis on self-regulation has affected learning disabilities. It is apparent in work on reading (Borkowski, Wehring, & Carr, 1988; Palincsar & Brown, 1984), writing (e.g., Harris, Graham, & Pressley, 1992), mathematics (Seabaugh & Schumaker, 1993), and attention (Hallahan et al., 1983).

Cognitive-Behavior Modification

The cognitive-behavioral approach adds features of cognitive theory to behavioral theory. It is an outgrowth of a larger movement in psychology that retains the empirical base of behavioral approaches in clinical work on such problems as hyperactivity, social isolation, schizophrenia, and other areas. But advocates of cognitive-behavioral approaches also accept certain features of behaviorism's nemesis—mentalism, the idea that thoughts and feelings affect people's behaviors. Advocates of an integrated cognitive and behavioral approach, often called **cognitive-behavior modification (CBM),** also stress the role of metacognition (e.g., Meichenbaum, 1977).

CBM supporters take a somewhat eclectic approach to theory, adopting whatever aspects of cognitive or behavioral literature suit. Leading advocates such as Meichenbaum (1977)—his book was the first comprehensive presentation of the idea—draw from sources as diverse as the works of B. F. Skinner and L. S. Vygotsky. The resulting synthesis includes strong emphasis on the influence of self-talk or inner language as a means of guiding overt behavior. Combined with a concern about metacognition, these components should provide not only changes in actual behavior, but also increased awareness of one's own behavior and the thinking associated with it.

Mnemonic Instruction

One of the foremost contemporary examples of the application of cognitive psychology to education employs *mnemonics* (a helper for one's memory; *Mnemosyne* was the

Greek goddess of memory). Most people are familiar with little tricks used to help one remember common information. For example, people use the mnemonics such as "Every Good Boy Does Fine" to remember the notes on a musical scale (e, g, b, d, f) or "*I* before *E* except after *C*" to remember spelling patterns (though this pattern does not always apply). However, as used in learning disabilities, mnemonics is a much more sophisticated strategy.

Mnemonics has been used to help students with learning disabilities learn content knowledge. Scruggs and Mastropieri (1992) developed extensive sets of materials for teaching social studies, science, and other content using mnemonics. In a mnemonic approach, students learn systems for remembering facts and relationships among them. In learning mnemonics, students learn to associate *key words* with terms to be remembered and *peg words* for features that occur in an order; the information is presented in a visual image to help foster memory for the facts and relationships. For example, Mastropieri and Scruggs (1987) taught students to use

- the key word "wolf" to remember the name of a mineral, "wolframite"
- the "black" feature of the wolf to remember that wolframite is black in color
- the peg word "floor" to remember the hardness ("four") of wolframite
- the image of a wolf turning on a lightbulb to remember that wolframite is used in making lightbulbs (see Figure 3.4)

Thus, students learned the related facts about this mineral. In other similar lessons, they learned about other minerals using different key words, peg words, and images. Studies of these methods reveal that students learn and retain more information when taught with mnemonics than when taught by most other methods (Brigham, Scruggs, & Mastropieri, 1995; Mastropieri & Fulk, 1990; Mastropieri & Scruggs, 1989).

Cognitive theory emphasizes people's thinking and their thinking about their own thinking. As a result of cognitive theory, the field of learning disabilities has been influenced by such techniques as cognitive-behavior modification and mnemonics. However, learning disabilities do not occur only in an individual's head. They are social phenomena and occur in a sociopolitical context.

HOW IS CONSTRUCTIVIST THEORY APPLIED?

Some theorists concerned with learning disabilities place special emphasis not only on cognition, but also on subjective and contextual influences on learning. They argue that individuals with or without disabilities create or construct their own perspectives of the world. Constructivism is based on two meanings of the word *construct(ive)*:

1. building by assembling parts ("constructing one's own reality")
2. serving to improve or help ("She made a constructive comment.")

FIGURE 3.4 Key Word–Peg Word Mnemonic Text Passage

Wolframite is number *4* on the hardness scale and is *black* in color. Wolframite is used for making *lightbulbs*.

WOLFRAMITE (wolf)

Hardness level 4 (floor)
BLACK Color
Used for LIGHTBULBS

In the picture above, notice that a *wolf* (wolframite) that is *black* in color (black color) is standing on a *floor* (hardness level 4) and is turning on the *light* (used for lightbulbs).

When you are later asked to remember the facts about wolframite, you should think of the *wolf*, which will bring this picture to mind with wolframite's three facts.

Remember this picture of a *black wolf* (black in color) standing on a *floor* (hardness level 4) turning on a *light* (used for lightbulbs).

Source: From *Effective Instruction for Special Education* (p. 290) by M. A. Mastropieri and T. E. Scruggs, 1987, Austin, TX: PRO-ED. Copyright 1987 by PRO-ED, Inc. Reprinted by permission.

Students base these constructions on their own experiences and their interpretations of them. This is the constructivist perspective, the model of learning disabilities based on the most subjective and least formal view of the world.

Constructivism—also known as **holism** or **structuralism**—is less a theory about learning disabilities than it is a philosophy, a group of beliefs about how people learn. Advocates of constructivism stress relationships or the interplay between stages of development and the developmental mechanisms of change. They emphasize a "holistic" presentation of material, arguing that material analyzed into its constituent parts is meaningless. Among the advocates of constructivism in special education are Heshusius (1989, 1994), Iano (1986), Poplin (1988a, 1988b), and Reid (Reid, Hresko, & Swanson, 1996).

Disciplines outside education and psychology—particularly anthropology and philosophy—provide much of the theoretical foundation for constructivism. It aligns with these views by drawing ideas from philosophy and social sciences, including feminist theoreticians, human science researchers, and structuralists (Poplin, 1988a). One of the most important, if not the animating, concepts underlying the constructivist view is a rejection of behaviorism and the task-analytic perspective. Constructivism represents a fundamental change in thinking that reaches far beyond special education:

> Structuralist philosophy, constructivist theory, and holistic beliefs define the learning enterprise in opposition to reductionistic behavioral learning theory and suggest that the task of schools is to help students develop new meanings in response to new experiences rather than to learn the meanings others have created. This change in the very definition of learning reveals principles of learning that beg consideration in designing classroom instruction. (Poplin, 1988a, p. 401)

In favor of more subjective means of knowing, some advocates of constructivism reject empirical research. Some, however, see empirical research and constructivism as mutually beneficial sources of knowledge (Kronick, 1990). Despite reservations about empiricism, most constructivists embrace research by Piaget (Piaget & Inhelder, 1969b) and Vygotsky (1962). The work he pursued later in his career "convinced Piaget that children's understanding of *interrelationships* (e.g., correspondences, mappings, and morphisms) were essential to developmental progress," causing Piaget to shift his focus from describing stages of development "to a *process approach concerned with the interplay between macrostructure* [stages] *and the mechanisms of change*" (Reid, 1991, p. 249). Constructivists emphasize similar aspects of Vygotsky's work, particularly his ideas about meaning and structure. Vygotsky, for example, stresses structural rather than associative relationships between words and thoughts and contends that these evolve as a natural consequence of experience: "Word meanings are dynamic rather than static formations. They change as the child develops" (1962, p. 124).

Such a view leads to a different perspective on teaching, but it is a difficult one to specify.

> [U]nlike the well-articulated intervention systems generated by empirical thinking, educational interpretations of constructivism are difficult to label because they are dependent on learners' behavior. The whole language movement is one example of a constructivist intervention that is difficult to define. (Meltzer & Reid, 1994, p. 339)

Part of the reason for this difficulty is that the principles of constructivist teaching can be made operational in many different ways (Harris & Graham, 1994).

One of the central tenets of constructivism is to consider the student as something more than a mere repository for information, to "portray the student as a thinker, a creator, and a constructor" (Brooks & Brooks, 1993, p. 126). In doing so, teachers should adhere to fundamental guidelines (Brooks & Brooks, 1993) for creating constructivist classrooms:

1. Pose problems of emerging relevance to students—an idea that emphasizes the relationship to teaching at the zone of proximal development.
2. Structure learning around primary concepts—focusing not on lesser or insignificant points, but instead stressing instruction on the big ideas that underlie later learning.
3. Seek and value students' points of view—promoting the worthiness of each student's experiences.
4. Adapt curricula to address students' suppositions—taking into account what they bring to the learning situation rather than simply imposing the views of teachers and curriculum planners.
5. Assess student learning in the context of teaching—using authentic, not artificial, means of evaluation.

These and other features are common to recommendations about learning disabilities, too. Table 3.3 lists several recommendations from perspectives on constructivist teaching in learning disabilities (Meltzer & Reid, 1994; Poplin, 1988a). Several of the features in Table 3.3 deserve amplification. They represent important contributions to the field of learning disabilities.

Authentic Tasks and Experiences

One of the strongest emphases of constructivism is providing learning situations that have intrinsic goals for learners. This aspect of constructivism is closely akin to the project method of teaching popular among educators since the early 1900s. The project method, sometimes called the unit method, requires teachers to develop integrated sets of activities.

According to constructivists, a primary goal of teachers is to create learning situations that require students to solve real-world problems and, at the same time, lead to understanding of fundamental principles (primary concepts). For example, a constructivist science lesson might challenge small groups of students to determine what materials were used to build otherwise identical miniature boats. The teacher would encourage the students to explain (perhaps in writing and illustration) why boats constructed of one material float and those constructed of another material sink. One of the crucial tasks for the teacher would be to lead the students to measuring the level of water in a container before and after the objects were placed into it. When students offered an explanation incompatible with hydrostatics (Archimedes' principle about density), the teacher would encourage the students to test the explanation. Such a sci-

TABLE 3.3 Basic Tenets of the Constructivist Approach

Tenets of constructivist/holistic theory include, but are not limited to:

1. New experiences are integrated into the whole (spiral of knowledge) such that the new pieces of knowledge, the new meanings, are much larger than the sum of their parts.
2. Two or more learning experiences transform one another and transform the structure of present knowledge. Thus, learning is not merely additive, it is transformative.
3. The learner is *always* learning, and the process of self-regulation, not reinforcement theory, determines best when, what, and how things are learned.
4. Instruction is best derived from student interest and talent and not from deficits or curriculum materials.
5. The assessment of student development, interests, and involvement is more important to teachers than student performance on reductionistic subskills and subprocesses.
6. Good teaching is interactive rather than unidirectional.
7. Real-life activities form better educational experiences than synthetically contrived ones.
8. Errors are necessary and should not be penalized.
9. Goals of instruction should be more life related (such as literacy, and cooperative learning) than school related (such as reading basals, worksheets, and textbooks).
10. Reflection, creation of questions, and construction of personal interpretations are more critical than "correct," "accurate," "right" answers to prepared questions.
11. Problems in learning are the result of interactions of personalities, interests, development, expectations, and previous experiences.
12. Learning involves a process of going from whole to part to whole with accurate forms (parts) being secondary to the whole.
13. Form follows purpose (function) and meaning, and premature instruction in accurate forms will inhibit fluency.
14. Passion, trust, and interest are paramount—subjectivity surrounds learning, and cognitive processes are only one part of the picture.

Source: From "Holistic/Constructivist Principles of the Teaching/Learning Process: Implications for the Field of Learning Disabilities" by M. S. Poplin, 1988. *Journal of Learning Disabilities, 21,* P. 414. Copyright 1988 by PRO-ED, Inc. Reprinted by permission.

ence lesson should be both entertaining and informative. With careful guidance, students should discover the principle of density. Of course, if students deduced Archimedes' principle, they should run about the classroom and shout "Eureka!"

Socially Mediated Learning

Learning situations should be based on social interactions. Cognitive learning is tightly bound to the social situations in which it occurs. Part of the rationale for this emphasis is that most students will wind up living and working in social situations. Special educators should be preparing their students—even those destined for college and graduate school after K–12 education—for the world of work. Job situations usually require people to work collaboratively with coworkers and clients. Therefore, schools should provide opportunities to solve problems in social situations, as will be demanded in the world of work.

Students should learn by participating in social situations, particularly situations in which they are required to communicate clearly with their peers. Students should learn the natural consequences of their behavior. If they miscommunicate, they should learn from their peers that they need to restate or clarify their messages. Given the difficulty with communication of many students with learning disabilities, the idea of communicating clearly is of obvious importance.

The emphasis on social aspects of constructivism makes it an appealing means of promoting inclusion. Many goals associated with inclusion have to do with promoting social relationships between students with disabilities and their nondisabled peers. Students should participate in classrooms that are communities of learners where social interactions serve as catalysts for learning and where students must learn to deal with the diverse range of human differences.

WHAT DOES RESEARCH TELL ABOUT EFFECTIVE PRACTICES?

Many of the people working in the field of learning disabilities emphasize empirical research. They say that practices should be validated by systematic testing, and this information should be made available so that teachers and parents can choose those practices that benefit students. Many of the practices recommended for learning disabilities have been evaluated.

An evaluation of a practice often compares the experimental practice and some other practice. Students are usually divided into two groups; one receives the experimental practice, and the other receives another one (i.e., a control condition). Researchers compare the outcomes for the two groups and, using statistical techniques, determine whether one group on average had better outcomes than the other group.

Because any one study may yield inaccurate results, researchers usually combine the results of many studies. One important way to combine studies is to conduct a meta-analysis (Cooper & Hedges, 1994). They combine the results of the studies by determining the extent to which the experimental practice produced better outcomes than the control practice. Technically, they take the difference between the average scores of the experimental and control groups, then divide this difference by the standard deviation of the control group. This produces what is called an "effect size." The formula is

$$\frac{\text{(Mean Experimental)} - \text{(Mean Control)}}{\text{Standard Deviation}} = \text{Effect Size}$$

If experimental practices consistently produce better outcomes than the control practices to which they are compared, the mean of the experimental group will consistently be higher than that of the control group. This produces positive average effect sizes. If the differences favoring the experimental practice are substantial, the average effect sizes will be large. There are no exact rules about how large an effect size must be to be considered important, but there are some general guidelines (Forness & Kavale, 1994; Forness, Kavale, Blum, & Lloyd, 1997). If an effect size is

- less than 0.30, it indicates that the experimental practice is not very powerful
- greater than 0.30 but less than 0.70, it indicates that the experimental practice makes a modest difference in outcomes
- greater than 0.70, it indicates that the experimental practice is consistently producing substantial benefits

Researchers have determined effect sizes for many of the practices that have been recommended in learning disabilities. Figure 3.5 shows the average effect sizes for several practices that have been studied extensively in the field. The figure summarizes hundreds of studies. Most of these practices are discussed in subsequent chapters, so we only describe them briefly here. The lowest four practices shown in the chart produced effects of little or no clear benefit.

- *Perceptual-motor training.* Training designed to remedy weak perceptual-motor skills produced an effect size of only 0.08 (180 studies; Kavale & Matson, 1983).
- *Feingold dietary therapy.* The Feingold diet, which restricts children's intake of foods containing certain acids, such as those found in synthetic colorings and flavorings, in order to reduce hyperactivity, produced an average effect size of 0.12 (23 studies; Kavale & Forness, 1983).
- *Modality-styles instruction.* Teaching reading on the basis of students' modality learning styles produced an average effect size of 0.15 (39 studies; Kavale & Forness, 1987).
- *Social skills training.* Teaching social skills to students with learning disabilities produced an average effect of only 0.21 (52 studies; Forness & Kavale, 1996).

The next two practices, going up from the bottom of the chart, produced more substantial benefits. However, these benefits are not so large that they should merit a stampede of support.

- *Psycholinguistic training.* In training based on the ITPA (see earlier discussion), students received substantial teaching in understanding and using language. This practice produced an average effect size of 0.39 (34 studies; Kavale, 1981a). The effect is large enough to move the average student in the experimental group to a level higher than nearly two-thirds of the students in the control group.

FIGURE 3.5 Effects of Various Practices in Learning Disabilities

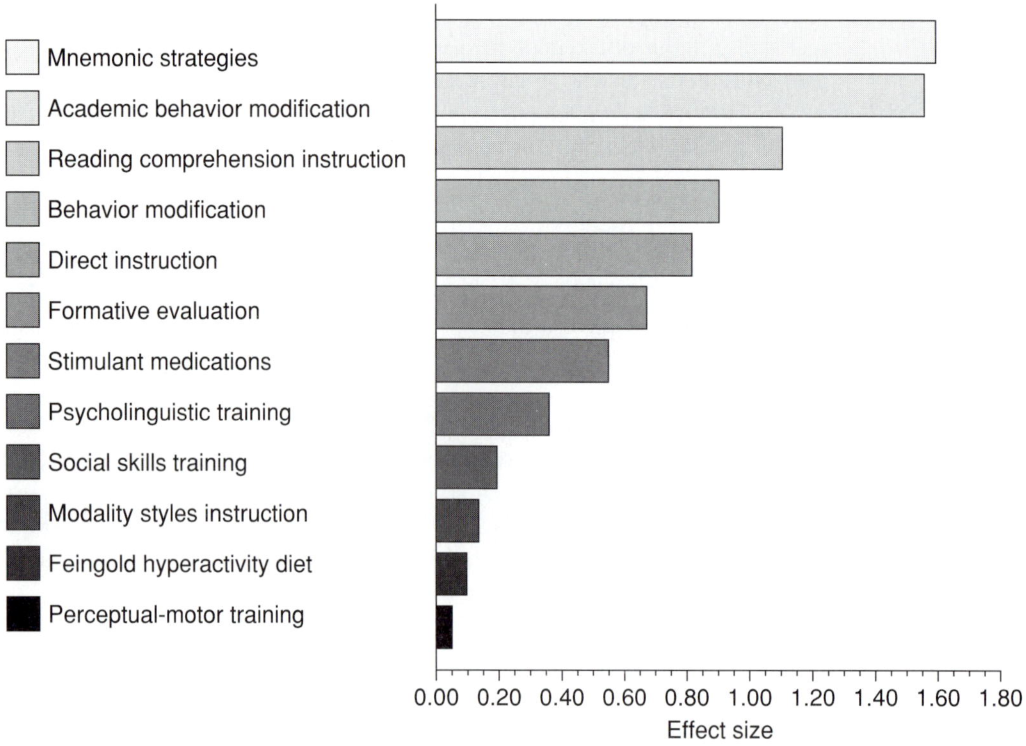

- *Stimulant medication.* Providing prescription stimulant drugs such as methylphenidate (Ritalin) or dextroamphetamine (Dexedrine) produced an effect size of 0.58 (135 studies; Kavale, 1982). The medications had greater benefits for behavioral outcomes (effect size of 0.80) than for academic or cognitive outcomes (effect size of 0.38).

The benefits of the remaining practices shown in Figure 3.5 are quite substantial. Teachers should incorporate these into instruction for students with learning disabilities.

- *Formative evaluation.* Systematic ongoing assessment of the effectiveness of instruction, which is discussed extensively in Chapter 4, produces an effect size of 0.70 (21 studies; Fuchs & Fuchs, 1986a). That is, when teachers use curriculum-based assessment to help guide their instruction, the children in their classes will have better outcomes than two-thirds of the students in classrooms where curriculum-based instruction is not used.

- *Direct Instruction.* The DI programs discussed previously produced an average effect size of 0.82 (25 studies; White, 1988). Of the practices described here, these are the most comprehensive; whereas other effective practices are specific and targeted, DI methods include entire programs of instruction.
- *Behavior modification.* Using behavior modification techniques such as modeling and reinforcement produces an effect size of 0.93 (41 studies; Skiba & Casey, 1985).
- *Reading comprehension instruction.* Systematically teaching reading comprehension strategies using strategy training, Direct Instruction, or cognitive-behavior techniques produces substantial benefits for students with learning disabilities. The average effect size is 1.13 (48 studies; Talbott, Lloyd, & Tankersley, 1994).
- *Academic behavior modification.* When teachers focus behavior modification techniques on academic responding, the effect size grows to 1.57 (Skiba & Casey, 1985).
- *Mnemonic strategies.* Using mnemonics (e.g., key words, peg words, etc.) to promote acquisition and retention of content produced an average effect size of 1.62 (24 studies; Mastropieri & Scruggs, 1989).

Many other practices in special education and related services have also been evaluated (see Forness et al., 1997). Some practices have not. Thus, the meta-analyses discussed here do not provide a comprehensive comparison of all methods. For example, few practices associated with the constructivist approach are specific enough to be testable. Also, many advocates of constructivism downplay the importance of empirically testing practices, saying that students—especially those with learning disabilities—are too different from each other for average scores to have any meaning.

There are also other reasons teachers should regard the results of meta-analyses with caution. Features of the original studies that a meta-analysis summarizes influence the effect size. One concern has to do with the control practices used for comparison. For example, if many studies compared a relatively weak practice to some other very bad practice, the weak practice would produce much better outcomes and therefore have a larger average effect size. Another concern has to do with the measures used in comparisons. For example, one practice may be consistently compared to controls on broad measures that are reliable and valid, but another may be compared on measures that have lower reliability and validity. The overall effect sizes will not show which used the broad, reliable measures.

Despite these caveats, the meta-analyses described here provide help. They tell teachers and parents which practices appear to have the best chances of benefiting students with learning disabilities. In that way, they should help guide contemporary practice in learning disabilities.

HOW DO EDUCATIONAL MODELS RELATE TO CONTEMPORARY PRACTICE?

Arguments about the appropriateness of contemporary approaches to learning disabilities abound. Two of the journals that publish scholarly work on learning disabilities—*Journal of Special Education* (volume 28 [2], 1994) and *Remedial and Special Education* (volume 14 [3], 1993)—provided extensive discussions of models. Because no one model has a corner on explanatory power, it is helpful to compare them on important matters. However, it is not only worthwhile to analyze the ways in which these models differ, but also to examine the features that they share.

Points of Difference

Tarver (1986) contrasted models that correspond to those here labeled cognitive, behavioral, and constructivist. Although she omitted some aspects of the cognitive model, her comparison of these models is helpful. She focused on how the models differ along four dimensions: specific versus general emphases, bottom-up versus top-down programming, more structured versus less structured teaching, and effectiveness versus ineffectiveness.

Specific versus General Emphases

Whereas some models emphasize broader and more general strategies, others emphasize task-specific strategies (Tarver, 1986). Broader strategies emphasize solving real-life problems, but specific strategies focus on acquiring narrower skills, such as decoding or computing.

Advocates of both cognitive-behavioral and DI approaches seek to help students learn broad strategies by teaching more specific strategies. Following these approaches, teachers would teach students the more fundamental skills, such as planning an essay, and then have them use the skills to solve the higher-order problems encountered in content area studies. Similarly, to help students with attention problems, advocates of these models would alter the environment by changing the features of instruction or teaching the students a self-management strategy for maintaining attention.

Advocates of a constructivist approach to teaching make clear that they reject explicit teaching of learning strategies. They contend that students will acquire the needed strategies when they require them. For example, when teachers ask students to write up the findings of an experiment, they will need to produce a well-constructed essay. From a combination of this need and social interactions with people who read their essays, they will gradually acquire facility in communicating.

Bottom-Up versus Top-Down Programming

Models also differ in whether teaching should proceed from the general to the specific or from the specific to the general. Working from the general to the specific is often called "top-down" programming because it emphasizes deducing the parts from the whole. Working from the specific to the general is called "bottom-up" programming because it stresses acquiring the parts and from them inferring the whole.

Tarver (1986) used the example of reading instruction to contrast the two approaches. The constructivist model emphasizes top-down programming: Get the meaning first and do not worry about the details of decoding. The DI approach is expressly built on bottom-up programming: Teach decoding skills early and systematically integrate them with comprehension (meaning-getting) strategies. As Tarver (1986) put it:

> The [constructivists] express a primary concern for the whole of reading; they do not attempt to specify the parts that constitute the whole. In contrast, DI curriculum developers begin with an analysis of the whole knowledge system known as reading; this analysis produces many parts which are then sequenced and recombined to reconstitute the whole. (p. 371)

Although Tarver (1986) did not describe the position of the cognitive model on the question of top-down versus bottom-up programming, advocates of cognitive approaches emphasize some combination of the two. Given the evidence from cognitive psychology that reading competence requires mastery of decoding (Juel, 1991), cognitive theorists are obliged to promote teaching of the components of reading, a bottom-up emphasis. However, there is also likely to be an emphasis on top-down features: When reading text, students should be prompted to think about their prior knowledge of the topic.

More Structured versus Less Structured Teaching

When used in the context of teaching, structure usually refers to the consistency or predictability of classroom routines. Tarver (1986) argued that advocates of constructivism support less structured, more child-centered instruction, and advocates of DI approaches favor highly organized, teacher-directed instruction.

One way to conceptualize this difference is to imagine people standing outside a classroom door and being told, "This is the 27th day of remedial instruction in fractions." How well could those people predict what would be happening in the classroom?

- If the observers knew the teacher was using *Mastering Fractions* (Systems Impact, 1986) and were familiar with the program, they would probably be able to say not only how the room would be structured, but what kinds of tasks the teacher was presenting.
- If the observers knew that the teacher was following a constructivist approach, they might guess that the teacher would be engaged in any of a variety of activities (measuring for baking, listening to a passage about dividing food among people, manipulating objects of various physical proportions, etc.).

Cognitive approaches emphasize student-directed learning more than DI approaches. However, their stress on drawing strategies from research-based practices separates cognitive approaches from constructivist approaches; using research-based practices is inconsistent with the constructivist notion that student-developed strategies are preferable outcomes.

Effectiveness versus Ineffectiveness

Presumably, advocates for students with learning disabilities would recommend practices that have produced evidence of effectiveness. But what research demonstrates effectiveness? Differing perspectives about research methods cloud this comparison of the major models.

Constructivist approaches differ from cognitive and behavioral (DI) approaches in whether effectiveness can be demonstrated by research. From a constructivist perspective, learning is too idiosyncratic for any general findings to be useful. Students—especially those with learning disabilities—differ too much for any results from traditional research methods to apply to them; teachers must find their own personally satisfying approaches for each individual student.

In evaluating the research evidence, Tarver (1986) gave greater credence to findings based on traditional research methods. She based her judgments of the effectiveness of practices on research using quantitative methods, that is, methods in which the outcomes of different practices are compared statistically on explicit measures (e.g., achievement tests). "Research to date provides strong support for DI, equivocal support for some CBM programs and little or no support for the [constructivist] approach" (p. 373). Since Tarver prepared her analysis, other evidence supporting the cognitive model has emerged. Tarver (1994) acknowledged the evidence supporting these other models; however, she argued that the good outcomes reported in those studies cannot be a result of the cognitive model's inherent strength, but from its newfound emphasis on features of instruction that have been the focus of DI for many years. For example, she illustrated by noting that Engelmann (1967b) had emphasized phonological segmentation and blending long before these skills became popular in contemporary cognitive models of reading.

Tarver's (1986) analysis points to important ways to understand the differences among models. These differences are also stressed by people with quite different views (e.g., Heshusius, 1989; Poplin, 1988b). Despite the clear emphasis on differences among the models that is evident in many discussions of them, there are important similarities that can guide people concerned with learning disabilities.

Shared Emphases

During the 1960s, authorities in learning disabilities emphasized assessment and remediation of psychological processes that were correlated only with academic competence. Teachers often required students to practice completing tasks that looked a lot like those on tests developed by advocates of the diagnostic-remedial approaches. Advocates hoped that building competence in related processes (e.g., visual perception) would indirectly remedy the underlying problems of learning disabilities.

In contrast, contemporary models approach learning disabilities much more directly. Even though they differ in many ways, current models focus more squarely on actual academic skills and recommend instructional practices designed to facilitate students' development of competence. Cognitive and instructional research fits together to reveal the importance of presenting new material in small steps, helping students use strategies and organize the material sensibly, and providing copious practice opportunities (Rosenshine, 1997).

Many of the differences among the models are in word choice. For example, in referring to remarkably similar ideas, advocates of one model might use the label "cognitive strategies" to refer to what advocates of another model might call "covert operations" (see deBettencourt, 1987). Furthermore, among the activities and practices used under the auspices of the various models, there are substantial similarities (Dixon & Carnine, 1994).

The factors the various approaches share are noteworthy because they indicate some growing consensus about how to approach learning disabilities. Although there are other bases for integration (see Harris & Graham, 1994), contemporary models agree on at least the following purposes of instruction:

- to incorporate *direct assessment* of performance
- to promote acquisition of useful cognitive *strategies*
- to provide extensive opportunities for students to *practice* using those strategies in useful situations

Direct Assessment

The models discussed in this chapter emphasize different assessment methods. Whereas the cognitive approaches stress students' verbal descriptions obtained from interviews, the task-analytic approaches stress students' actual academic performances. Whereas the constructivist approaches argue for focusing on students' capabilities, the cognitive and task-analytic approaches add assessments of students' mistakes.

These differences, however, are not hard and fast. For example, in their paper advocating constructivist approaches to assessment, Meltzer and Reid (1994) comment favorably on using curriculum-based assessment, a behaviorally based method. Across all three types of approaches, then, there are shared emphases on assessment. All the models stress the following:

- evaluating students' performance frequently, while they are learning, rather than waiting until they are supposed to have finished learning
- assessing students' performance on the actual tasks of concern, not on psychological instruments of related areas

- examining students' performance under differing conditions rather than examining only under testlike conditions
- linking the results of assessment directly to the provision of instruction

Strategies

Another commonality among contemporary models is that each is concerned with the strategies students use in solving problems. They differ in the ways described by Tarver (1986), but none of these models expects students simply to learn isolated facts. Not only do advocates of the various approaches use a similar word—*strategies*—in referring to this idea, but the idea is remarkably similar. From the cognitive model's interest in memory and attention strategies to the task-analytic model's emphasis on cognitive operations, each model stresses the importance of students learning systems of actions that lead to solutions of problems.

Although it was not a highlighted feature of early work in learning disabilities, the centrality of strategies appeared earlier in the history of learning disabilities. In reviewing the work of the five research institutes on learning disabilities funded in the late 1970s and early 1980s, McKinney (1983) wrote:

> The central concept that emerges from this research is that many LD students have not acquired efficient strategies for processing task information and therefore cannot use their abilities and experience to profit from conventional instruction. Most of this research, however, also demonstrates that they are capable of acquiring the strategies that account for competent performance and that they can improve their academic skills and adaptive functioning when they are taught task-appropriate strategies. (pp. 130–131).

The treatment of learning disabilities in this book is consistent with the idea that strategy deficits and strategy instruction play a major role in learning disabilities. Chapter 1 stresses the importance of students with learning disabilities acquiring systematic approaches to tasks (viz., strategies), and this idea is reemphasized in subsequent chapters on problems in cognitive, social, and academic domains. Indeed, the concern with strategies will probably be one of the most enduring and substantial contributions of the field of learning disabilities to the field of education in general.

Practice

Although each emphasizes strategies at some level, the major contemporary models recommend different procedures and techniques for teaching them. For example, advocates of constructivism stress the importance of providing social context for the use of strategies, having students practice them in situations where they would need them. Advocates of cognitive approaches recommend creating opportunities for students to reflect on alternative strategies (metacognition). DI proponents follow initial instruction in the use of strategies by having students practice them in ever more complex situations. Each model promotes students' repeated use of strategies.

The models share more than a simple concern with practice, however. They all stress that students benefit from applying strategies to real problems. Stripped of their specific terminology, these approaches recommend that students practice strategies under conditions in which they are likely to be valuable. The practice is embedded in realistic situations.

Summary

1. Why understand educational models of learning disabilities?
   a. Educational models help people understand the similarities and differences in approaches to learning disabilities.
   b. Educational models help guide research and practice.
2. What educational models were applied to learning disabilities in the past?
   a. Early educational models were often identified as medical, diagnostic-remedial (or process), and task-analytic (or behavioral) approaches.
   b. The medical and behavioral models have evolved, but they are still influential in learning disabilities today.
3. How is behavioral theory applied to learning disabilities today?
   a. Applied behavior analysis has less influence than it had during the 1960s and 1970s, but it continues to offer ways to evaluate innovations in learning disabilities.
   b. Direct Instruction is the major contemporary representative of behavioral theory in learning disabilities today. Direct Instruction methods for teaching concepts and strategies have a strong research basis.
4. How is cognitive theory applied to learning disabilities today?
   a. Cognitive theory offers a conceptually integrated way of understanding the problems in thinking and remembering that are experienced by many students with learning disabilities.
   b. Cognitive approaches include a diverse range of practices. Chief among these are such methods as cognitive-behavior modification and mnemonic strategy training.
   c. Many interventions associated with cognitive theory have strong empirical support.
5. How is constructivist theory applied to learning disabilities today?
   a. Constructivist approaches place special emphasis on the role of philosophy in understanding learning disabilities. Some constructivists even dismiss much empirical evidence.
   b. From a constructivist viewpoint, learning is more a process of discovery than of direct teaching, and it is most appropriately mediated by authentic and social situations.

   c. Constructivist practices emphasize teaching at the zone of proximal development, focusing on central concepts, and valuing students' views and starting from those views when teaching new information and skills.
6. What does research tell us about effective practices?
   a. Research reveals that many practices that were popular earlier (e.g., perceptual training) or are still popular today (e.g., instruction based on modality styles) are ineffective.
   b. Other practices, such as psycholinguistic training and having physicians prescribe stimulant medications, have modest but clear benefits.
   c. Five educational practices have consistently been found to be very likely to help students with learning disabilities:
      (1) Assessing instruction on a systematic, ongoing basis
      (2) Teaching using Direct Instruction
      (3) Applying principles of behavior modification to both social and academic behaviors
      (4) Teaching systematic reading comprehension strategies
      (5) Teaching content using mnemonic strategies
7. How do educational models relate to contemporary practice?
   a. Educational models differ in their emphasis on several points:
      (1) The behavioral approaches place greater emphasis on *specific rather than general strategies,* in contrast to the cognitive and constructivist models.
      (2) The cognitive and constructivist approaches stress *bottom-up programming* less than they do *top-down programming;* this contrasts with the behavioral views.
      (3) The behavioral and cognitive models are generally more *structured,* whereas the constructivist approaches are less structured.
      (4) The behavioral and cognitive approaches emphasize use of practices with *documented effectiveness.*
   b. Despite these differences, contemporary models share emphasis on
      (1) Direct assessment—evaluating students' performances frequently, on actual tasks, under varying conditions, and linking assessment directly to instruction
      (2) Strategies—understanding how students solve problems and teaching them to approach tasks systematically
      (3) Practice—promoting frequent use of knowledge and strategies in realistic situations

4

Assessment

Persons should be said to have learning disabilities only if assessments of their learning problems show that they meet the criteria spelled out in the definition of learning disabilities. Ideally, students are provided special education because assessments of their learning indicate that instruction of a specific nature is most likely to be effective in addressing a learning disability in a particular area of performance. Thus, assessment has specific purposes and must address particular domains of learning. The process of assessment is complex, and in some respects, assessment is controversial.

WHAT ARE THE PURPOSES OF ASSESSMENT?

The assessment of learning disabilities has five major purposes, which are to:

- *screen* individuals who may have learning disabilities for more detailed study
- *identify* whether the individual has a learning disability
- *classify* the type of learning disability the individual has
- *guide remediation* of the learning disability
- *evaluate progress* in remediation of the learning disability

Each step is critical for effective education of students with learning disabilities (NJCLD, 1997) (see Box 4.1). However, the most important purposes of assessment are guiding instruction and evaluating progress. Assessment procedures should help the teacher know what skills to focus on, how to deliver instruction, and how to correct instructional errors (Lloyd & Blandford, 1991). If assessment is to do this, it must yield information that is useful in selecting students for special instruction, guiding instructional practices, and evaluating outcomes. Some of the questions teachers might ask themselves in thinking about assessment include:

- How do I determine that a student is at risk for school failure or might have a disability? What information confirms that a student has a learning disability?
- How do I decide what to teach this student and at what level to begin teaching it?
- On what basis do I select an instructional method for this student?
- How do I write reasonable goals and objectives for this student in a specific area of performance?
- How do I determine whether this student is making adequate or inadequate progress?

Answering any of these questions may be complicated because every assessment strategy has its limitations. Some are better suited than others to specific objectives. Standardized testing is particularly valuable for comparing a student's performance to

BOX 4.1 ***EXAMPLE***

Four Steps in Operationalizing Assessment

In 1997, the National Joint Committee on Learning Disabilities released a report suggesting four steps for operationalizing the definition of learning disabilities through ongoing assessment. The report also provides the purposes of each step and lists processes for achieving them.

Step 1. Describe learning problems prior to referral for formal assessment. The key questions are:

1. What are the student's learning strengths and problems?
2. How do the strengths and problems vary within the educational environment, both academic and nonacademic?
3. What interventions and accommodations, as well as the modifications of typical teaching strategies, might help the student learn?

Step 2. Identify individuals as having learning disabilities. The key questions are:

1. What is the nature of the learning problems and how pervasive and severe are they?
2. Is performance in the problem areas unexpectedly low compared with the student's performance in other areas?
3. Are the learning problems the result of learning disabilities (as opposed to some other explanation)?

Step 3. Determine eligibility for special education and related services. The key question is: Given the student's learning disabilities and current performance in important academic and social contexts, does the student require special education and related services at this time?

Step 4. Bridge assessment to specialized instruction and accommodations. The key questions are:

1. What special education and related services and accommodations should be provided?
2. Based on the entire assessment process, what goals should be targeted on the student's IEP?
3. Is this a time to prepare for special transition (such as preschool to elementary school, elementary school to middle school, middle school to high school, high school to postsecondary education or employment) (NJCLD, 1997)?

Questions to Ponder

Which of these four steps is most critical to achieving effective education for students with learning disabilities?

How are cultural standards and expectations involved in each of the key questions?

What are the legal requirements for each step in assessment?

What theory should guide someone in seeking to answer the key questions?

Source: From *Operationalizing the NJCLD Definition of Learning Disabilities for Ongoing Assessment in Schools: A Report from the National Joint Committee on Learning Disabilities,* by NJCLD, February 1997.

that of a large normative group. Such tests can be helpful in identifying students at risk and in identifying disabilities. But standardized tests are not very useful in guiding instruction. Teacher-made tests, curriculum-based assessment, behavioral assessment, and other alternatives to standardized testing may be better tools for guiding instruction, but have limited usefulness in judging how a student is performing compared to a large representative sample of other students. Thus, assessment strategies must be selected to fit the question we are asking about a student.

Assessing something means measuring it. What we choose to measure and the assessment tools we use will depend to some extent on what we believe learning disabilities are and what causes them. That is, our choice of assessment tools and procedures will be guided by a conceptual model (a theory).

WHAT ARE TWO GENERAL APPROACHES TO ASSESSMENT?

There are two major conceptual models of assessment or general approaches. Both are built on assumptions about what should be measured. Some people assume that the most important things to measure are the traits, abilities, cognitive processes, or developmental stages underlying learning disabilities. This approach is called the **trait assessment/classification theory** of assessment. Other people assume that it is more important to measure the student's actual performance on tasks involving academic and social skills. This approach is called the **direct measurement/instruction theory** of assessment. From each perspective, the expectation is that assessment involves a cycle of measuring, teaching, and measuring again—a **test-teach-test cycle** in which the teacher measures to identify a problem, uses this information to guide teaching, and then checks progress by remeasuring. Here we compare several features of these two theories of assessment, including differences in the nature of the test-teach-test cycle suggested by each conceptual model.

Trait Assessment Approach

The trait assessment/classification theory focuses on measurement to determine eligibility for special education. It is based on the belief that learning disabilities are caused by deficits in underlying processes, such as memory or the ability to process information. This approach may lead directly to a student's classification as having learning disabilities. It identifies patterns of strengths and weaknesses in basic abilities or processes underlying academic performance and social acceptance.

The instruments used in this approach to assessment are usually standardized or informal tests that are assumed to be reliable and valid. Strengths and weaknesses in certain characteristic traits such as intelligence, auditory processing, impulsiveness, visual-motor abilities, and academic knowledge are assessed. The pattern of strengths and weaknesses provides the basis for selecting instructional methods to address the underlying ability or process that produced the learning difficulty. To assess the remediation of learning disabilities, students may be tested again to determine whether the underlying characteristic has been changed and whether there has been any improvement in academic or social skills. The major features of this approach to assessment are depicted in the top part of Figure 4.1.

The trait assessment/classification approach is associated with what has been called **diagnostic-prescriptive teaching.** In this approach, testing is assumed to

FIGURE 4.1 Two Theories of Assessment and the Test-Teach-Test Cycle

Trait Assessment/Classification Theory

Measure →	to Identify →	to Teach →	and Measure
trait, ability, process, or stage	eligibility, classification, strength, or weakness	to strength or weakness in trait, ability, process, or stage	test performance revealing trait, ability, or process

Primary tools of assessment: standardized and informal tests

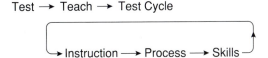

Test → Teach → Test Cycle

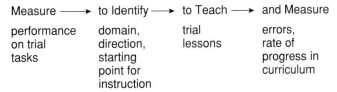

→ Instruction → Process → Skills ↺

Direct Measurement/Instruction Theory

Measure →	to Identify →	to Teach →	and Measure
performance on trial tasks	domain, direction, starting point for instruction	trial lessons	errors, rate of progress in curriculum

Primary tools of assessment: samples of performance taken directly from curriculum

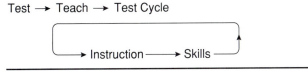

Test → Teach → Test Cycle

→ Instruction → Skills ↺

lead to a "diagnosis" of the underlying difficulty. For example, testing might reveal a weakness in auditory discrimination that is the basis for difficulties in listening and reading skills, or we might interpret test results as indicating an impulsive cognitive style that has led to social rejection. Once the diagnosis is made, an instructional "prescription" can be written. For example, the prescription might be to teach the student to tell the difference between a variety of sounds or to work on getting the student to slow down and consider alternatives before reacting in social situations. The prescribed instruction addresses the underlying weakness in a psychological process and, one hopes, results in improved academic performance. For example, auditory discrimination training might be provided on the assumption that learning to discriminate sounds will lead to improved skills in listening and reading.

Direct Measurement Approach

The direct measurement/instruction theory of assessment focuses on the academic or social performance problem itself, not on traits, abilities, processes, or stages assumed to underlie learning disabilities. Measurement begins with trial lessons on the actual academic or social tasks the student is expected to perform. The intention is to identify precisely the domain, direction, and starting point for instruction. Initial measurement should lead directly to subsequent trial lessons designed to improve performance. For example, if the student is having difficulty in beginning reading, assessment may start with measuring the extent of the student's knowledge of letter-sound correspondence and identification of those correspondences the student does not know. This information is then used to construct lessons to teach the student the skills needed to say the correct word sounds when the student is shown letter combinations. The outcome of interest is not test performance, but performance in the academic curriculum itself—in this example, errors and rate of progress in oral reading. The major features of this approach to assessment are shown in the bottom part of Figure 4.1.

The direct measurement/instruction approach to assessment is associated with **curriculum-based assessment (CBA)** or **curriculum-based measurement (CBM),** behavioral assessment, and direct instruction. The key assumption about assessment from this perspective is that learning problems and progress in learning are best measured directly as performance in the curriculum rather than indirectly as test performance related to underlying processes. The contrasts between trait assessment/classification and direct measurement/instruction theories are depicted further in Figure 4.1.

Our discussion of contrasting theories of assessment and their relationship to instruction is greatly simplified. The problems of measurement involved in identifying and classifying learning disabilities are numerous, technical, and complex (see Kavale & Forness, 1985; Kavale & Mundschenk, 1991; Lyon & Flynn, 1991; Taylor, 1997). Likewise, direct measurement using curriculum-based or behavioral methods requires attention to numerous details of method and understanding how to construct trial lessons and use knowledge of student errors to guide subsequent instruction (see Choate, Enright, Miller, Poteet, & Rakes, 1995; Engelmann & Carnine, 1982; Howell & Morehead, 1987; Lovitt, 1991). Some of these complexities will become apparent in our discussion of assessment strategies in this and subsequent chapters.

In practice, assessment need not be guided exclusively by either of the theories we have outlined. Assessment procedures guided by both theories have legitimate roles in identifying students who should receive special services and the specific problems these students have and in guiding the selection of instructional procedures.

WHAT ARE THE DOMAINS OF ASSESSMENT?

Regardless of the theoretical frame of reference for approaching assessment, specific domains of performance, including aptitude, intelligence, attitude, and a variety of abilities related to sensory and social perception, must be assessed. These domains may also involve the basic processes or curriculum areas in which learning disabilities may be suspected or confirmed. Each domain presents unique challenges in conceptualizing the problem of poor performance as well as unique difficulties in measuring the characteristics and abilities deemed most important. However, as will become apparent in this discussion, these domains are interrelated. That is, problems in one may be intimately connected to problems in others. For example, we cannot assess language without attention to cognition, socialization, and the learning environment. Assessment of mathematical abilities requires attention to cognitive and language skills as well.

Here we provide a brief overview of the domains of assessment that we discuss in more detail in other chapters. Although we do not address every possible area of the typical school curriculum (which includes science, health and physical education, and other areas of instruction), the domains covered here provide the basis for identifying learning disabilities and for designing interventions with implications for all aspects of the curriculum.

Language Abilities

Language, more than any other area of performance, is critical to human interaction. Communication—the ability to **decode** (receive and understand) and **encode** (express and send) messages—is at the heart of language. Language is the communication of ideas by an arbitrary code or system of symbols. These symbols may be sounds, as is the case in oral language, or visual forms, as in reading, writing, and sign language. Without the ability to use language effectively and efficiently, an individual in contemporary society is seriously handicapped in everyday life. Despite its importance, language, perhaps the most complex human ability, remains poorly understood. Much about how it develops and about how brain injury affects language and how impaired language can be restored remains to be learned (see Bernstein & Tiegerman-Farber, 1997; Nelson, 1998).

Because language difficulties are increasingly seen as the basis of most learning disabilities, classroom teachers are expected to master the basic concepts underlying language development, language disorders, and instruction designed for students with language disabilities. Thus, teachers must learn the concepts underlying spoken language, reading, and written language and be conversant with basic assessment procedures in these areas. In order to assess students' language competencies and particular problems, teachers must understand how language develops and how spoken and written languages interrelate. They must also understand how language learning communities vary and how to distinguish cultural differences in language from language disabilities (van Keulen, Weddington, & DeBose, 1998).

The language problems related to learning disabilities may involve oral language or written language. Written language includes reading and writing. Some students with learning disabilities have pervasive language problems involving all aspects of language usage. Others have difficulties primarily in one aspect of language, such as reading or writing.

Mathematics Abilities

Disabilities in mathematics were given relatively slight attention, compared to language-related disabilities, in the early development of the field. However, in contemporary American education, the various branches of mathematics are seen as increasingly important to students' success upon leaving school. Teachers today are expected to offer instruction in a variety of math skills and to be able to help their students learn not only basic computational skills, but also the quantitative reasoning that allows for solving advanced problems, often with the aid of ever more sophisticated computational devices.

The domain of mathematics learning is very broad and includes basic concepts related to numeracy, computational skills, and problem solving requiring reasoning about quantities. Computational and reasoning skills may be applied to whole numbers or fractions, money, a variety of types of measurement, algebraic equations, geometry, and more advanced areas of mathematics. As with language, the teacher assessing difficulties in mathematics must be able to identify precisely what the student knows and does not know and to understand what concepts and skills are prerequisites for learning more complex ideas and competencies (Smith & Rivera, 1991). The most fundamental concepts and skills in the mathematics domain are often those with which students with learning disabilities have problems (see Taylor, 1997, for further discussion).

Cognitive Abilities

We generally refer to pervasive disabilities in cognition as *mental retardation*. Individuals with learning disabilities have adequate cognitive skills in most areas, but difficulty with specific cognitive tasks, such as deploying their attention or processing specific types of information. Cognition includes a wide variety of information-processing skills, including perception, attention, memory, comprehension, and guidance of one's own thinking (see Conte, 1991; Swanson & Cooney, 1991; Taylor, 1997; Wong, 1991). One or more of these processes (e.g., attention) may be impaired across all types of academic tasks, leaving the individual with inadequate task-approach skills even though the other cognitive processes are intact. Alternatively, an individual may have difficulty processing information only in a particular area, such as a poor ability to remember words or word sounds even though memory for other information is unimpaired.

The assessment of cognitive processes should be designed to help teachers understand how students think about academic tasks and social interactions, how they approach problems and evaluate solutions, and where their cognitive processes go awry. Understanding how students think about the tasks we ask them to perform may provide important clues for devising the systematic strategies they need for learning.

Social Skills

Learning disabilities have always been seen primarily as problems of academic performance. However, problems in social relationships have always been associated with academic inadequacy. Some individuals with learning disabilities have excellent social skills, but many have very poor social skills and consequently experience serious social problems (Bryan, 1991; Taylor, 1997). Although social and academic learning are intertwined in most cases (Kauffman, 1997), social skills are a distinctive area of learning and curriculum development. Teachers are expected to be able to help children learn to perceive social circumstances accurately and to form desirable patterns of interpersonal interaction. Furthermore, as we pointed out in Chapter 1, individuals with learning disabilities are a very diverse group, and learning disabilities may coexist with other disabilities. Many students with learning disabilities have emotional or behavioral problems, and a substantial percentage of these can be said to have a coexisting emotional or behavioral disorder. Thus, assessment of social perceptions and interactions is a critical aspect of the assessment of learning disabilities.

Environmental Factors

Learning problems do not exist without a context or environment. An important aspect of the assessment of learning disabilities is finding out whether an inadequate environment could be the primary cause of the student's difficulty or a factor contributing significantly to inadequate performance (see Lloyd & Blandford, 1991; Taylor, 1997; Ysseldyke & Christenson, 1987). Teachers need to be aware of how the learning environment they provide and the way they control or modify it may affect the outcomes of their instruction.

The learning environment includes the physical space (classroom arrangement, work areas) and the things (desks, tables, instructional materials, equipment) and people (pupils, teachers, other adults) in it. It also includes the home, community, and culture in which the student lives. All of these may play important roles in how a student responds to instruction, but a teacher's first attention must be given to the classroom environment and how it may be contributing to learning problems (Hallahan & Kauffman, 1997).

As already discussed, the social environment is also important to learning. The social aspect of a learning environment is defined by the emotional tone or climate of the classroom and the interactions among pupils and adults. The instructional environment must also be assessed, including such variables as the amount of time allocated to instruction, the difficulty and interest level of tasks, the sequence in which tasks are presented, the pace of instruction, the frequency of opportunities to respond, and the structure of expectations and rewards.

WHAT ARE SOME ASSESSMENT STRATEGIES?

Assessing learning disabilities requires that we assess an individual student's academic and social learning. However, besides finding out what a student knows or can do, we also must have a basis for comparing the student's performance to what we assume is "normal" or typical for students similar in age, gender, cultural group, intelligence, and opportunities to learn. The same strategies are used to assess learning disabilities and all students' learning, but particular attention is paid in the former to how performance in specific areas differs from what the student's other characteristics lead us to expect.

Regardless of the assessment strategy being considered, basic concepts of measurement must be applied to its evaluation. We must ask whether the measurement we obtain is **valid:** Did I measure what I intended? We must also ask whether the measurement is **reliable:** Could I or someone else obtain the same result again? **Validity** and **reliability** are psychometric concepts that raise complex issues beyond the scope of our discussion here (see Taylor, 1997; Wallace, Larsen, & Elksnin, 1992, for further discussion). The important point is that the accuracy (validity) and dependability (reliability) of measurement are critical issues in the selection and use of any assessment strategy.

Neuropsychological Assessment

Historically, learning disabilities have been linked to neurological factors. Assessment that attempts to link neurological problems to psychological characteristics is called **neuropsychological assessment.** This assessment strategy usually involves giving a battery of tests assumed to measure a variety of processes known to be affected by brain dysfunction. For example, the tests might measure muscle tone, posture and gait, motor skills and coordination, auditory and visual perception, memory, attention, receptive and expressive language, cognition, and academic achievement. However, these tests do not measure neurological functioning directly. Furthermore, many neuropsychological test batteries are of questionable reliability and validity for measuring learning disabilities (Obrzut & Bolick, 1991). Many neuropsychological test batteries were designed for use with adults with known brain damage, and the downward extension of these tests to children makes their appropriateness all the more questionable because of the developmental differences between children and adults in neurological and psychological functioning.

The popularization of neurological explanations for learning disabilities, combined with advances in neuroscience and its technologies, has led many people to accept tentative findings as facts and to overestimate the extent to which psychological tests can reveal neurological phenomena and provide guidance for instruction (Lyon, Newby, Recht, & Caldwell, 1991). Another way of putting this is to say that the sophistication, glamour, and mystery of the neurosciences and psychological testing lead many people to exaggerate the reliability and validity of neuropsychological assessment and overvalue its usefulness for teachers.

A complete neurological assessment can be done only by a physician, usually one with special training in neurology. A neuropsychological (or psychoneurological) assessment, however, might be done by a psychologist specializing in brain-behavior relationships. Very few teachers can do neuropsychological testing competently, but teachers should know about the kinds of tests given and their implications for selecting educational methods.

Because some of the same standardized tests included in neuropsychological batteries are commonly administered by school psychologists or teachers, it is tempting to look for patterns of test results that might be said to indicate neurological problems. It has become popular to use psychological or educational testing to ascribe learning problems to neurological dysfunction or to cognitive processing peculiar to the right or left hemisphere of the brain. However, the instructional implications of neuropsychological assessment are actually very limited (Lyon et al., 1991). Teachers can obtain far more enlightening and helpful information from other assessment strategies.

Contextual Assessment

Comprehensive and competent assessment of students with learning disabilities involves more than testing or measuring specific performance outcomes of instruction. It also requires attention to context, to the student as a person living in various environments. The student's perceptions and thoughts about the environment of the school and classroom, the objective characteristics of the learning environment itself, and other aspects of the student's life outside of school must be assessed. Assessing these contexts usually involves interviewing the student and others and directly observing the student in various contexts.

A thorough contextual assessment may also require researching school records to determine the history of the student's problems. Such a search can often be highly informative about the social and academic contexts that the student has experienced. Some teachers may avoid looking at a student's records because they do not want to be biased by what others have said. However, a systematic search of archival records may turn up information that will help the teacher anticipate problems, avoid mistakes that others have made, and choose strategies with a higher probability of success (see Walker, Block-Pedego, Todis, & Severson, 1991). Fear of bias must not prevent teachers from using the information available to them.

Interviews

One means of obtaining important information about students and their environments is interviewing them and significant others in their lives (Lopez-Reyna & Bay, 1997). Getting students who have academic or social trouble in school to speak candidly is no minor feat (Hughes & Baker, 1990; Kauffman, 1997). Extracting accurate and relevant information from interviews requires keen judgment and excellent communication skills (Morgan & Jenson, 1988), as does interviewing parents and school personnel. But skillful interviews can reveal much that is useful in planning for teaching, such as the student's most and least preferred activities, the student's thoughts about his or her capabilities, and the parent's ability and willingness to supervise homework activities.

Observations

Observations can add significantly to the information obtained through interviews. Sometimes there are important discrepancies between what individuals say in interviews and what we find through observation. Moreover, direct observation of the student's behavior in the classroom and other settings (hallways, cafeteria, playground) can provide more precise measurement of academic and social problems. Classroom observations can also be the basis for assessment of the learning environment, helping to pinpoint ways in which the environment might be altered to address the student's learning problems. To be most helpful, observations of the student and the environment must be carefully planned and systematic so that behavior and environmental conditions are defined precisely, appropriate samples of activity are obtained, and results are presented understandably (see Alberto & Troutman, 1995; Kerr & Nelson, 1998).

Error Analysis

Skillful teachers take note of errors that students repeat. The pattern of mistakes a student makes, whether on an academic task or in a social situation, often provides the key to successful instruction (Colvin, Sugai, & Patching, 1993; Lopez-Reyna & Bay, 1997; Taylor, 1997). When the teacher can anticipate a student's error, she or he can devise a plan to help the student learn to avoid it (see Box 4.2).

Standardized Testing

All tests are designed to measure something in comparison to a standard, expected, or desired value for the purpose of evaluation or prediction. The tests educators are interested in are most often measures of skill, knowledge, or aptitude related to school success. These are considered **standardized tests** if there are set procedures for administration, objective scoring criteria, and a specific frame of reference for interpreting scores. Standardized tests may be designed for administration to individuals or groups.

Set procedures for administration means that the test instructions (including any time limits that are set) and materials (as well as examiner responses to questions) are fixed. Standardized tests usually have detailed manuals that state exactly how they are to be given, including exactly what the examiner is to say. The purpose of having set procedures is to make the testing conditions as consistent as possible so that fair comparisons can be made among the scores of the people taking the test. Set procedures for administration are important for all types of standardized tests, including those with multiple-choice answers, and other forms of standardized assessment, such as rating scales or direct observation.

Objective scoring criteria are obvious when there is only one correct answer to a test item. For items having more than one possible right answer and those for which some responses might be better than others, specific criteria are needed for making judgments. Adequately standardized tests have manuals with explicit scoring criteria to use in judging answers; these criteria make the scoring process more objective and reliable.

A specific frame of reference for interpreting the scores means there is a comparison group, standard, or expectation for use in judging what the test scores mean. The frame of reference may be a specific normative group (in norm-referenced tests),

BOX 4.2 ***EXAMPLE***

Miscue or Error Analysis

Are particular students consistently making the same kinds of errors in their work? When you carefully scrutinize a student's work—oral reading, a written assignment, or a math quiz—you may find patterns of errors or misinformation. For example, you may note that a student consistently substitutes one vowel sound for another or repeatedly ignores punctuation in oral reading, thereby distorting the meaning of a passage. Through careful analysis of the errors, a remediation plan can be tailored to the student's instructional needs.

Source: From "Enriching Assessment Using Varied Assessments for Diverse Learners" by N. A. Lopez-Reyna and M. Bay, 1997, *Teaching Exceptional Children, 29*(4), pp. 33–34. Copyright 1997 by Council for Exceptional Children. Reprinted by permission.

Questions to Ponder

Why is it important for a teacher to note both what a student performs correctly and the errors the student makes?

If you find that a student's error is highly predictable, what instructional strategies could you use to help the student avoid making it?

How do coaches and music teachers use modeling, practice of isolated skills, practice in context (rehearsal), imagery, prompts, and reinforcement to help students avoid errors and perform correctly?

a specific performance criterion (in criterion-referenced tests), or a specific way of evaluating answers (in nonreferenced tests). In interpreting standardized test scores, we must always keep in mind the way the standardization sample—the group to whom the student is being compared on the test—was selected. If the comparison group is substantially different in demographic characteristics (e.g., region of the country, age, sex, socioeconomic level, ethnicity), then the norms or performance criteria used for comparison may be misleading.

Standardized testing can provide an indispensable picture of how a student's performance under standard testing conditions compares to that of others or to a specified criterion. Knowing how a student compares to others is valuable in determining whether his or her performance is adequate to meet social expectations. Standardized tests can also provide useful information about how students approach problems under specified conditions. The information from standardized tests can thus help teachers aim initial instruction at the right academic targets (see Hammill & Bryant, 1991; Taylor, 1997). Furthermore, teachers appear to rely most heavily on standardized tests in assessing learning disabilities (Lopez-Reyna, Bay, & Patrikakou, 1996). However, standardized testing has limitations. It is not very useful in guiding instruction. It has been criticized as offering misleading information regarding students' capabilities, being biased or unfair to certain groups, distracting attention from instruction, and being an exorbitantly expensive approach that yields trivial information, particularly for exceptional children (see Choate et al., 1995; Choate & Evans, 1992; Poteet, Choate, & Stewart, 1993). Thus, although standardized testing is extremely valuable in assessing learning disabilities, other assessment strategies must be considered as well.

Norm-Referenced Tests

Norm-referenced tests allow us to measure how a student performed on a test compared to other students. The normative group used for comparison may be any specified collection of students (e.g., other students in the school or district, the state, or the nation). The normative group's scores have a **range** (highest and lowest score), **mode** (the most frequent score), **median** (the score in the middle of the range, with half the scores higher and half lower), and **mean** (the average score, calculated by adding all the scores and dividing by the number of scores).

These basic statistical components can be used to describe how a student's test score compares to that of others in any defined comparison group for which scores are available. **Percentile** rank—what percentage of the normative group scored the same or lower on the test—is another useful and easily understood comparison. For example, if a student's score is at the 77th percentile, we know that 77% of the individuals in the normative sample scored the same as or lower than this student (and, of course, 23% scored higher); if the student's percentile is 48, then 48% scored the same or lower and 52% scored higher. **Standard scores** are additional statistics depicting how a student performed in comparison to the **normative group.** The normative group is the group that is assumed to be a representative sample and is used to establish a typical or normal distribution of scores, including a normal range, mean, and percentiles. Table 4.1 contains comparisons of percentile ranks to a variety of standard scores. Teachers frequently encounter test scores of the types shown in Table 4.1 to indicate how a student's test scores compare to a normative group.

Criterion-Referenced Tests

Criterion-referenced tests are designed to measure the extent to which students have mastered specific skills. The test items are administered under standard conditions, and there are objective criteria for scoring, but students' scores are compared to a standard expectation (e.g., at least 90% correct) rather than to a comparison group's performance. The standard expectations or criteria were undoubtedly derived from an analysis of what most students of comparable age were able to learn, but the idea of criterion-referenced testing is to compare the student's performance only to the criterion itself, not to the performances of others.

Nonreferenced Tests

Some tests with standardized administration and objective scoring do not use a normative group or criterion for comparison, but instead focus on the problem-solving strategies used by students in approaching problems. The assumption behind these **nonreferenced tests** is that it is important to find out how the student formulates answers to problems, not to compare the student to a group or expected level of performance. For example, if a student is asked to solve the problem $x - 27 = 53$, then we may assess how the student attacks the problem and thereby obtain a better understanding of what he or she needs to learn, if anything, in order to solve similar problems efficiently.

TABLE 4.1 Relation of Various Standard Scores to Percentile Rank and to Each Other

Percentile Rank	Standard Scores: Quotients	NCE scores	T-scores	Z-scores	Stanines	Deficit
99	150	99	83	+3.33	9	none
99	145	99	80	+3.00	9	
99	140	99	77	+2.67	9	
99	135	99	73	+2.33	9	
98	130	92	70	+2.00	9	
95	125	85	67	+1.67	8	
91	120	78	63	+1.34	8	
84	115	71	60	+1.00	7	
75	110	64	57	+0.67	6	
63	105	57	53	+0.33	6	
50	100	50	50	+0.00	5	
37	95	43	47	–0.33	4	
25	90	36	43	–0.67	4	
16	85	29	40	–1.00	3	mild
9	80	22	37	–1.34	2	
5	75	15	33	–1.67	2	moderate
2	70	8	30	–2.00	1	
1	65	1	27	–2.33	1	severe
1	60	1	23	–2.67	1	
1	55	1	20	–3.00	1	

Source: From "The Role of Standardized Tests in Planning Academic Instruction" (p. 377) by D. D. Hammill and B. R. Brvant, 1991, in H. L Swanson (Ed.). *Handbook on the Assessment of Learning Disabilities* (pp. 373–406). Austin, TX: PRO-ED. Copyright 1991 by PRO-ED, Inc. Reprinted by permission.

Teacher-Made Tests

Teacher-made tests may include a variety of procedures devised by a classroom teacher or other professional to assess specific skills. Such testing has the advantages of flexibility and low cost and offers the possibility of deriving data with direct relevance to classroom instruction in that the tests measure small increments of knowledge or skill and thus indicate how close the student has come to mastering the material being taught. The disadvantages of teacher-made tests are that there are no norms, aside from comparisons to the student's classmates, and the tests can be so poorly constructed or administered that they are misleading (Taylor, 1997).

All teachers prepare periodic tests to determine what their students know about what is being taught. These tests may range from exams at the end of grading periods to shorter tests at the end of instructional units to immediate quizzes to determine whether the student has acquired a new concept. Skill in constructing and using informal tests is likely to be highly correlated with the teacher's instructional skill. That is, the informal tests teachers use to assess students' progress in the curriculum are likely to reflect their level of understanding of the concepts being taught and their knowledge of how and when to test. Informal testing is an intrinsic and implicit part of effective instruction. The skillful teacher knows when and how to probe students' understanding and how to use these informal measurements in planning the next step in instruction.

Informal teacher-made testing is indispensable in assessing students with learning disabilities. These students' progress in the curriculum must be monitored more frequently and more accurately than that of typical learners.

Curriculum-Based Assessment

Curriculum-based assessment or curriculum-based measurement is a way of addressing the mismatch between what is taught and what is tested by sampling the student's performance very frequently. Performance is sampled at least twice weekly, usually more often, in the curriculum materials that are being used for daily instruction in reading, math, or other curriculum areas (Choate et al., 1995; Deno & Fuchs, 1987; Howell & Morehead, 1987; Lovitt, 1991). For example, three days per week a student might be asked to read orally for 2 minutes from a story being used in reading instruction, and the teacher might record the number of words read correctly per minute and the number and types of errors made. As samples of the student's performance are collected on subsequent days, the information is entered systematically in a table and also plotted on a graph to reveal the student's progress (in this example, progress in oral reading fluency). The student's performance in the curriculum is tracked, and decisions about changing instructional materials or procedures are based on the extent to which the student reaches the performance goals.

The core methods of CBA—frequent systematic performance sampling, results recorded systematically and plotted on a graph, and both quantitative and qualitative results used to guide teaching procedures—can be applied to a wide variety of curricular areas and performances. For example, CBA is not limited to oral reading fluency, but can also be applied to reading comprehension, as indicated by reactions to what is read, perhaps in the form of story retelling (Tindal & Marston, 1990). In fact, a wide variety of language, math, and social skills has been assessed using CBA.

Some proponents of CBA have suggested that this form of assessment depends on drawing testing material from the students' actual instructional materials or tasks. However, Fuchs and Deno (1994) have shown that sampling from the actual curriculum materials or tasks is not essential to obtaining instructionally useful measurement. They concluded that, in constructing instructionally useful performance tests, teachers "may sample testing material from their instructional material; from other, more controlled material that deliberately is structured to mirror curricular materials; or from material representing the generalized outcomes or goals of the curriculum" (p. 23). That is, the procedures used in CBA can be instructionally useful as long as the test materials are much like those used in instruction and as long as three other critical conditions are met:

1. There is repeated testing over time on material of comparable difficulty.
2. Critical behavioral outcomes of instruction are measured directly, not indirectly, through assessment of traits or processes.
3. The data obtained are both qualitative and quantitative, so that teachers know not only when to change their instructional approach, but also how they might adapt and enhance their instruction most effectively.

CBA is typically focused on the core curriculum areas of reading and math. However, it is possible to use it in any curriculum area. An often overlooked area is teaching social skills—the classroom conduct that the teacher would like the student to demonstrate (Colvin et al., 1993; Walker, Colvin, & Ramsey, 1995).

Behavioral Assessment

The essential features of CBA—repeated measurement under controlled conditions, direct measurement of desired outcomes, and decisions based on quantitative and qualitative data—are also the essential features of **behavioral assessment** (see Alberto & Troutman, 1995; Kerr & Nelson, 1998; Lovitt, 1991). Behavioral assessment is often thought to apply primarily to emotional or behavioral problems, but this method encompasses much more (Colvin et al., 1993; Walker et al., 1995). The specific behaviors measured may be academic or social. However, in both CBA and behavioral assessment, precise specification of the desired outcome is important, direct and frequent measurement of the desired performance is continued across time, and decisions about teaching the student academic or social skills are made on the basis of the data.

Behavioral assessment is particularly important because students' individualized education plans (IEPs) must now by law include plans for managing behavior problems if the student exhibits serious inappropriate behavior (Yell & Shriner, 1997). The IEP must include positive behavioral interventions, strategies, and supports to address such difficulties. Teachers must have a proactive behavior intervention plan based on a functional behavioral assessment, and such assessment should delineate the inappropriate behavior, the expected behavior, and the positive and negative consequences that will be applied to help the student learn to behave appropriately. (See Alberto & Troutman, 1995; Kauffman, Mostert, Trent, & Hallahan, 1998; Kerr & Nelson, 1998; Walker, 1995; Walker et al., 1995, for further discussion of behavior management.)

Interactive Assessment

Standardized tests administered according to the instructions in the test manual provide a static measure of the student's ability. This measure is fixed by what the student has learned up to the time of testing. A relatively new way of testing, one that bridges standardized and teacher-made tests, is **interactive assessment.** Feuerstein (1979) introduced this way of testing, which he called **dynamic assessment.** Feuerstein's methods have been modified and elaborated by others (e.g., Budoff, 1987; Campione & Brown, 1987; Carlson & Wiedl, 1992).

Interactive assessment is a way of assessing how the student uses cues, prompts, and instruction to learn during testing (Haywood, 1992; Palinscar, Brown, & Campione, 1991). This method attempts to assess the potential of the student to learn with specific instruction; the intention is to use the information gained through this assessment for prescribing more effective instruction (Palinscar, et al., 1991).

Feuerstein (1979) suggests that learning has two aspects: **Incidental learning** is acquired simply by exposure to the environment; **mediated learning** is acquired through the training of someone who helps the learner frame a question and focus attention on critical features and who provides feedback and support. A child gradually internalizes the guidance received through mediated learning, and it is this ability to learn through mediation that is important to assess.

To measure low-performing children's ability to profit from instruction, Feuerstein (1980) developed the Learning Potential Assessment Device (LPAD). This instrument assesses children's responsiveness to mediated learning and helps remediate their cognitive deficits. Others also have developed a variety of procedures to assess the extent to which children can learn to perform better on tests if they are given appropriate assistance. In the following vignettes, Palinscar and colleagues (1991) illustrate the difference between static and interactive, or dynamic, assessment. First, they describe how an examiner might respond in a static assessment.

> The child is seated with an examiner and presented a page that has five rows of letters, with eight letters in each row. At the end of each row of letters are four blank lines. The examiner tells the child that she is to look at the letters in each row and then figure out what letters belong in the blank spaces. The task is structured in such a way that, with each problem, the relationship among the letters is increasingly more complicated. The child, with furrowed brow, examines the first row of letters (GWHWIWJW__ __ __ __) pointing to each letter. After a few moments, she smiles, and proceeds to fill in the blank spaces (KWLW). She moves on to the second problem (PZUFQZFV__ __ __ __). She puzzles over it, looks to the examiner who shrugs her shoulders and gently urges "just try your best." (p. 75)

Because this is a typical "by-the-book" static examination, the examiner gives no assistance. The child writes four seemingly random letters in the blanks for each of the remaining problems, spending less time pondering her answers as she proceeds.

Now consider what might have happened after the child had completed the first problem successfully and was studying the second problem, but this time with an examiner using an interactive assessment procedure.

> After a few unsuccessful minutes, the examiner asks the child, "Is this problem like any other that you have seen before?" The child responds, "I thought it was like this one but it doesn't work." The examiner urges the child to "read the letters in the problem out loud. . . . Did you hear a pattern in the letters?" The prompt failing, the examiner continues with "Are there any letters written more than once in the problem? Which ones? Does this give you any ideas about how to continue?" With this prompt, there is a smile of recognition and the child successfully completes the problem. When she is presented with the third problem, a problem identical in nature to the second, she is heard to say, "Oh, I know how to do this one. . . . Which letters are here more than one time?" The session continues with the examiner presenting problems either similar to the one presented previously, or differing in degree of difficulty. With each problem, the examiner provides, as needed, a series of prompts facilitating the child's successful completion of the problem. (pp. 75–76)

The interactive assessment of intelligence or learning potential has been criticized as lacking reliability and validity as well as implications for remedial methods (see Frisby & Braden, 1992; Laughon, 1990). One of the reasons reliability of measurement is difficult to achieve with interactive assessment is that the prompting procedures cannot be standardized. The approach requires that the prompts be tailored to each child, so it is difficult to obtain results that can be duplicated at another time or by another examiner. Validity is particularly difficult to achieve when the tasks given in the assessment are substantially different from those the student is given in the curriculum. That is, it is difficult to show that what is being measured is a cognitive skill that applies to other tasks. Although the idea of interactive assessment is quite appealing, it has proven to be extremely complex to implement in ways that are useful to teachers or psychologists, who are expected to assess students with tools that are reliable and valid (Taylor, 1997).

Authentic Assessment

Traditional testing, whether standardized or teacher-made, has been severely criticized since the late 1980s, and reformers have called for assessment techniques that better reflect education's emphasis on critical thinking and problem solving (Wiggins, 1993). Although the idea of authenticity of assessment is inherently appealing, the meaning of "authentic" in assessment procedures is anything but clear (Terwilliger, 1997).

To some educators, typical test scores lack authenticity, failing to represent the real abilities of the student and not accurately representing what the student can do or, more important, is expected to do in real life. Interactive assessment procedures may be somewhat more authentic in that they demonstrate what the student can do in a situation more closely approximating real life, in which the individual is likely to get appropriate help from a teacher, peer, parent, or supervisor in learning new tasks. Teacher-made tests can be more authentic if they consist of samples of tasks the student has been taught, are administered under typical instructional conditions, or address real-life problems. However, alternative assessment practices are considered necessary if measurement of student abilities is to be most meaningful.

Alternatives to typical assessment procedures may take a wide range of forms and are described by a variety of labels, including **authentic assessment** (Poteet et al., 1993; Taylor, 1997; Wiggins, 1993; Worthen, 1993). They are thought to give a more "real" or authentic, useful picture of what the student can and cannot do. The emphasis is on examination of what the student has produced as a completed piece of work, not on fragments of performance (as in CBA) or test items taken out of context.

Performance Assessment

Performance assessment includes a wide variety of samples of student work. The teacher offers or examines as evidence of the student's abilities what the student has done in response to assignments or independent study (Taylor, 1997). For example, the following might be used:

- constructed-response items, in which the student must offer a response rather than choose from alternatives
- essays or other writing samples, such as letters, instructions, or stories
- oral discourse, such as recitations, speeches, or oral responses to questions
- exhibitions, including recitals or other performances
- experiments and their results or reports

Portfolio Assessment

Portfolios are collections of a student's work over a period of time (Feuer & Fulton, 1993; Taylor, 1997). Collecting samples of the student's best work into portfolios is thought to provide authentic assessment and offer advantages for assessing students with learning disabilities or behavioral disorders (Swicegood, 1994). Constructing and evaluating these portfolios, however, present numerous challenges. Some performance measures are relatively easy to identify if the performance always results in a permanent product (written story, visual art project). Other performances exist for only a short time (storytelling, oral reading, dance, oral description of an experiment). Unless they are preserved on audio- or videotape, measuring performance is difficult. Some of the items included in a portfolio may involve secondary measures of the student's behavior. That is, an observer's anecdotal record, checklist, summary, or evaluation, rather than the student's performance or the product itself, may be included in the portfolio. Table 4.2 shows a suggested list of the types of information that might be considered for inclusion in a student's portfolio.

TABLE 4.2 Possible Pieces of Information to Include in Student Portfolios

■ Measures of Behavior and Adaptive Functioning

Anecdotal records or critical incident logs

Observations of behavior across settings and conditions

Behavior checklists

Interviews about interests, motivation, and attributions

Videotapes of student behaviors

Social skills ratings and checklists

Peer ratings and sociometric measures

■ Measures of Academic and Literacy Growth

Criterion-referenced tests

Curriculum-based assessments

Teacher-made tests in selected literacy or content area domains

Analysis of oral reading such as informal reading inventories

Writing samples collected over time

Photographs of student projects

Running records in reading, writing, or math, such as "stories read and completed"

Classroom tests in spelling, math, and so forth

■ Measures of Strategic Learning and Self-Regulation

Ratings and checklists of skills or strategies a student is using

Student self-evaluations of task performance

Miscue analysis procedure in oral reading

Interviews and questions about how a student performs in literacy and classroom tasks

Student think alouds—verbal descriptions of strategies and operations used in different academic situations

Excerpts from teacher-student dialogue journals

Observations and ratings of study skills

■ Measures of Language and Cultural Aspects

Cultural interviews with student and parents

Primary language sample

Observations of student responses to changing social and classroom situations

Simulations and role-plays

Source: From "Portfolio-Based Assessment Practices" by P. Swicegood. 1994, *Intervention, 30*(l), p. 9. Copyright 1994 by PRO-ED. Inc. Reprinted by permission.

The idea of portfolio assessment may initially seem simple. On closer examination, such assessment becomes much more complex. How does the teacher decide just what to include, how and to whom to present it, and how to evaluate it? Table 4.3 includes some of the initial questions a teacher might ask about portfolio assessment and indicates that the process is much more demanding than merely keeping a folder of a student's work. Table 4.4 provides guidelines for implementing portfolio assessment and suggests how time-consuming the task might be.

Evaluating the products of a portfolio requires developing a scoring system for various aspects of the products in it. Examine the production of Mike, a seventh-grader with learning disabilities, in Box 4.3. If the evaluation of such portfolio items is to be reliable and valid, the teacher must not only be able to specify the criteria for scoring, but also communicate those criteria effectively to students, parents, and other teachers.

Cautions about Authentic Assessment

Appealing as the notion of authentic assessment may be, it is important to remember that "authenticity" is difficult to define because knowledge and expertise in compo-

TABLE 4.3 Reflective Questions for Evaluating and Monitoring Student Portfolios

What does this excerpt say about the student's current literacy or biliteracy levels, social/behavioral progress, and acculturation?

How can I use this unique sample of information to assist this student to grow and develop academically, behaviorally, and socially?

How can I use information about the child's language and home culture to plan for future instruction?

How do pieces collected from diverse sources and measurement techniques interrelate?

What patterns of behavioral and social functioning are shown through an analysis of various portfolio pieces collected over time?

Does information about the student's attitudes and attributions relate both to social behavior and academic functioning?

Does the portfolio create a profile of strengths and instructional needs across different domains?

What levels, types, and topics in reading materials are appropriate for this student?

What do writing samples reveal about the student's use of prewriting drafting, editing, and peer evaluation competencies?

Is collaboration with other professionals and practitioners as well as increased student ownership being fostered over time?

Source: From "Portfolio-Based Assessment Practices" by P. Swicegood, 1994, *Intervention, 30*(l), p. 10. Copyright 1994 by PRO-ED, Inc. Reprinted by permission.

TABLE 4.4 Guidelines for Implementing Portfolio Assessment

1. Initially, the teacher of students with behavioral or learning disabilities will assume responsibility for organizing and compiling pieces for the portfolio. Contact individuals and select sources of information that will contribute to each of the portfolio domains. Over time. it is hoped, other professionals and the student will come to contribute more and more information. Remember the concept of scaffolding.
2. Stay on a quest to locate and identify innovative informal assessment techniques that might yield pieces for the portfolio.
3. Construct a set of goals to be accomplished through portfolio assessment and periodically review the portfolio to see if these goals are taking shape. Such goals might take the form of statements such as "The portfolio will contain a sampling of the student's work, projects, interpersonal relationships, and social-emotional functioning."
4. Consider various ways that the portfolio might be used for decision-making purposes. Does the student's emotional, behavioral, or learning problem occur with such frequency, or beyond standards of adaptive functioning, as to merit special education programming? Have prereferral interventions been documented prior to making a placement decision? Are pieces being included in the portfolio that directly translate into instructional interventions?
5. Label each piece included in the portfolio with a caption—a brief statement or paragraph describing the piece and its significance for the portfolio. What does the piece show about the student?
6. Read primary sources describing the theory and practices associated with portfolio assessment and development.
7 Document your experiences with student portfolios. Describe advantages and disadvantages. What have been the specific positive and negative outcomes for teacher-practitioners and other educators, as well as measures of student growth and learning?
8. Consider the type of packaging that will contain the portfolio. Loose-leaf notebooks with additional pockets and subsections have sometimes been used.

Source: From "Portfolio-Based Assessment Practices" by P. Swicegood. 1994, *Intervention, 30*(l), p. 14. Copyright 1994 by PRO-ED, Inc. Reprinted by permission.

nent skills are essential to competent performance in everyday life. As Terwilliger (1997) pointed out, "authentic" inappropriately implies that some approaches to assessment are inherently more "genuine" or "real" than others. "Authentic assessment" also suggests that knowledge and skills are of little importance in competent performance in real-life settings and that assessment of the components of performance in any domain is misguided. It is inappropriate to ignore the importance of assessing a student's ability to perform tasks in everyday settings. It is also inappropriate to ignore assessment of the knowledge and skill components of performance.

BOX 4.3 ***EXAMPLE***

Portfolio Entry from History Class

My favorite historical person
is John F. Kennedy. He is my
favorite because his assassination
might be a conspiracy. Same people
say there might have been two
assassins. In my opinion Jack Ruby
shot Oswald so no one would know
the truth.

J F K ran for congress in 1946.
Kennedy served three terms in the
House of Representatives in 1947–1953
Kennedy ran for the U.S. Senate
and beat Henry Cabot Lodge Jr. with
Seventy thousand votes. He enhanced
his electorial appeal in 1953 when he
married Jacqueline Bouvier.

Source: From *Assessment of Exceptional Students: Educational and Psychological Procedures,* 4th ed. (p. 158) by R. L. Taylor, 1997, Boston: Allyn & Bacon. Copyright 1997 by Allyn & Bacon. Reprinted by permission.

Questions to Ponder

If you were evaluating this written performance of Mike, a seventh-grade student with learning disabilities, what scale would you use for various aspects of this item (e.g., 1 = poor, 2 = fair, 3 = good, 4 = excellent)?

What features of Mike's writing would you score? How would you evaluate the accuracy and coherence of his ideas? Would you judge his handwriting, and, if so, how? Would you evaluate his spelling? How would you judge his word usage and the mechanics of his written product, such as capitalization and punctuation?

How specifically and in what form would you convey information about this portfolio item to Mike, to his parents, and to other teachers?

WHAT ARE SOME ISSUES IN ASSESSMENT?

Assessment is controversial because it is the process through which students are labeled and selected for special education programs. Throughout the history of the field, the critical issues have involved questions about *who* should have the authority to identify learning disabilities and *how* they should do so. Because assessment involves many issues of authority and procedure, it is now governed by federal law (Yell, 1998). Thus, teachers, school administrators, psychologists, and parents cannot avoid the legal issues surrounding assessment. However, besides strictly legal issues, other questions of professional conduct in assessment must be considered. These ethical issues, such as nondiscriminatory assessment, may be addressed in part by the law. Although it specifies important guidelines for practice, the law does not address all of the ethical issues teachers face in assessment (Howe & Miramontes, 1992).

Legal Issues

Assessment for special education is constrained by laws and regulations. The single most important law governing special education assessment is the federal law known as the Individuals with Disabilities Education Act (IDEA). The law now known as IDEA was initially passed by Congress in 1975 as Public Law 94–142 (the Education of All Handicapped Children Act), but it was amended in 1990 and 1997 to include new requirements (see Yell, 1998; Yell & Shriner, 1997). IDEA is important because it regulates assessment for determining students' eligibility for special education and students' periodic reevaluation. Assessment is also necessary for writing the individualized education plans (IEPs) required by the law. The IEP is the heart of IDEA's intent to provide each student with a disability an appropriate, individualized education (Bateman, 1996).

Under IDEA, every student thought to have a disability that affects his or her education is entitled to an individualized assessment of educational needs. Such assessment has several distinct phases, beginning with referral for evaluation by a multidisciplinary team to determine eligibility for special education. The evaluation can be initiated only with parental consent, and after parental consent is given, it must be completed within a specific time limit (usually about 60 days). If a student is found eligible, then an IEP must be written based on evaluation of the student's educational needs before he or she can be placed in a special education program. Subsequently, the student's progress in the program must be assessed at least yearly. A full multidisciplinary reevaluation (a triennial evaluation) must be completed at least every three years to determine whether the student's placement is still appropriate.

Assessment for Special Education

The classroom teacher is the most critical member of the team that completes a student's educational evaluation. This evaluation cannot be handled solely by a psychologist or other person designated to do testing and observations. Although formal testing and structured observations may be necessary to assess a student's eligibility, the teacher needs to provide data on the student's performance and behavior in the classroom. The teacher should be able to answer such questions as the following:

1. Is the student lagging behind his or her peers academically? If so, by how much is he or she delayed? What evidence is there of this delay (e.g., work samples, test scores, curriculum-based assessment)? What are the student's instructional levels in the subjects you teach?

2. Does the student perform much better in some curriculum areas than in others? How even or uneven is his or her performance across the curriculum and across time (i.e., day to day and week to week)? How does classroom performance compare to what you would expect from standardized test results?
3. What is the student's record of completing in-class and homework assignments correctly and on time?
4. Does the student exhibit problem behavior in school? If so, how often, in what circumstances, and with what consequences does it occur?
5. To what extent does the student exhibit discrepancies in his or her ability to learn through listening and speaking compared to reading and writing? That is, what evidence do you see that the student has particular problems related to language in its oral and written forms?
6. What support services has the student received (e.g., speech-language therapy)? What evidence do you see that these have been beneficial?
7. What instructional or behavior management strategies have you tried with the student, for how long, and with what results? What support and guidance in using these strategies have you received from other professional personnel (e.g., principal, special education teacher, school psychologist)?

Clearly, assessment for special education entails amassing a lot of information about the student. Questions then arise about who should have access to the information and how differences of opinion about it should be resolved. Test results and other records about the student must be kept confidential. No one but teachers and other professionals who work with the student can be allowed access to this information without parental permission. It is illegal and unethical to share information from the assessment with others who are not directly involved with the student's education. However, parents must, by law, be informed of the results of the assessment in language they can understand and must be allowed to see their child's records if they so request. If the parents and school personnel do not agree that the assessment has been adequate, the parents have a right to have their child evaluated somewhere else and present the results to the school. Then, if the parents and school cannot reach an agreement about the assessment, they may ask for mediation by a third party. By law, either the parents or the school system may request a due process hearing, which is much like a court proceeding. If the hearing fails, either party may file a formal legal suit to resolve the issue.

Referral for Evaluation

Referral of students for evaluation for special education is a topic about which many complaints have been lodged. The most frequent are that teachers are too quick to refer students for evaluation and that the reasons for referral are more often misperceptions of the student's behavior, perhaps created by cultural or gender bias, than the student's actual learning difficulties (Patton, 1998; see also Ysseldyke, Algozzine, &

Thurlow, 1992, pp. 187–188, 371). However, referrals might be interpreted to mean that the teacher genuinely needs assistance (Gerber & Semmel, 1984), and some studies of referral have found that students' academic problems, not misbehavior, are the primary reasons for referral (e.g., Lloyd, Kauffman, Landrum, & Roe, 1991). Other research has indicated that teachers' concern about students' performance leading to referrals does not appear to be racially or gender biased (e.g., MacMillan, Gresham, Lopez, & Bocian, 1996).

The referral process has been criticized not only because too many students are referred, but also because most referrals do eventually result in the student's being found eligible for special education services. In a survey of directors of special education, Algozzine, Christenson, and Ysseldyke (1982) found that 73% of students who were referred were found eligible for special education. These and similar findings have led some to criticize referral and placement practices, particularly for learning disabilities, and to suggest that referral and placement rates are unjustifiably high (Ysseldyke et al., 1983; Ysseldyke et al., 1992). However, no one has suggested an ideal rate of referral (e.g., that 1% of students should be referred each year) or an ideal ratio of referred to eligible students (e.g., 2 to 1, meaning that one student would be found eligible for each two referred).

IDEA requires that schools make efforts to identify all students with disabilities, and teachers have a legal responsibility to refer any student they suspect of having a disability. Thus, schools and teachers cannot legally simply limit the number of referrals. Nevertheless, procedures designed to prevent unnecessary and inappropriate referrals are both legal and professionally desirable. Nearly all schools have instituted **prereferral strategies** of some type. Typically, these approaches involve groups of teachers and other professional personnel (e.g., school psychologist, social worker) called child study teams, student assistance teams, teacher assistance teams, and so on. A teacher having problems teaching or managing the behavior of a student asks for the assistance of the team, which then helps the teacher implement and monitor the effects of alternative instructional or behavior management methods. Only after these alternative approaches have been implemented and have failed to resolve the problems is the student referred to a multidisciplinary team (MDT) consisting of representatives from the medical, psychological, social, and educational arenas for evaluation for eligibility for special education. A referral to an MDT for evaluation for special education (an expensive, time-consuming procedure) must be made if the teacher believes the student has a learning disability.

However, before concluding that a referral is appropriate, the teacher must take certain actions. First, the teacher must discuss the problems with the student's parent or guardian. Referral should never come as a surprise to the student's parent. Next, the teacher must obtain written permission from the parent before initiating an evaluation for special education. Finally, the teacher must document the student's academic or behavioral difficulties and the effects of reasonable attempts to resolve them before referral. This means that the teacher must keep careful, systematic records not only of the student's achievement and behavior, but also of what interventions were tried and how the student responded.

After concluding that a referral for special education evaluation is appropriate but before the referral, the teacher must again take certain actions. The teacher must first make a careful search of the student's academic records and speak with other teachers about specific concerns regarding the student. Then the teacher must hold at least one conference with the student's parent or guardian to discuss the problems. Finally, the teacher must document the efforts made to resolve the problems.

Hasty referrals and those for problems that can be resolved without special education are not justifiable. However, undue delay in referral in the face of clear indications that the student may have a disability and need special education is unprofessional and illegal, even if prereferral interventions are being implemented. Referral does not, of course, guarantee that the student will be found eligible for special education.

Eligibility Determination

A student in today's schools cannot legally be said to have a disability or be given special education services without a thorough evaluation in each area of the suspected disability and after consideration of the data so obtained by a multidisciplinary team. Ideally, each member of the MDT contributes significantly to the eligibility determination, although some researchers have found that one individual, often the school psychologist, usually seems to determine the outcome (Ysseldyke et al., 1983; Ysseldyke et al., 1992). The MDT must weigh all evaluation data and determine the student's eligibility in the light of the federal and state definitions of disability. Because many issues about the definition of learning disabilities remain unresolved, eligibility decisions are often difficult.

A multidisciplinary eligibility evaluation typically includes medical, social, psychological, and educational components necessary to determine the student's eligibility for special education. It must be completed by a multidisciplinary group of professionals qualified to evaluate the student's problems, and at least one of these professionals must be a teacher or specialist qualified to teach students with disabilities like the one the student is known or suspected to have. The student must be evaluated in each area of known or suspected disability. The evaluation must be done using methods or tests that are not racially or culturally discriminatory, and it must be done in the student's native language or usual mode of communication. The tests must be reliable and valid for the purposes for which they are used. Furthermore, no single test or evaluation strategy can be used as the sole criterion for determining the student's eligibility for special education. The evaluation should yield assessment information that is helpful in planning the special instruction that is needed if the student is found eligible.

Individualized Education Plan

An IEP is a written agreement between the student's parents and the school about what the student needs and what will be done to address those needs. It is, in effect, a contract about services to be provided for the student, and it is to be written by the MDT in collaboration with the parents, if possible, and the student, if appropriate.

The IEP must have the parents' approval, whether they were involved in writing it or not. It must be written within 30 calendar days after the student has been found eligible for special education services, and a new IEP must be written each year. The IEP cannot be changed without parental approval. By law, IEPs must be written to address or include statements about each of the key points shown in Table 4.5. The law specifies that regular education teachers must participate in writing the IEP and that considerable emphasis be placed on how the student will be involved in the general education curriculum.

The IEP must contain measurable annual goals, including benchmarks or short-term objectives that allow teachers and parents to monitor the student's progress. It must also state how and to what extent the student will be involved in the general education curriculum, participate in state- or districtwide assessments, and be included in assessment procedures through special accommodations or alternative procedures. If the student has behavior problems, regardless of his or her special education category, the IEP must also include strategies for managing behavior (a matter we consider in more detail in Chapter 9).

The IEP must be written before the decision is made about the least restrictive environment for the student (see Bateman, 1996; Yell, 1998). As is perhaps clear from the components of the IEP, a good plan cannot be written on the basis of standardized test information alone. Performance data from teacher-made tests related to the curriculum as well as observations, interviews, and other nonstandardized assessment strategies are indispensable for writing adequate instructional goals and objectives and specifying the instructional services to be provided.

The most important steps leading from recognition that a student is having difficulty through prereferral strategies to preparation of an IEP, if the student is found eligible for special education, are shown in Table 4.6. The table also contains a checklist of procedures teachers should follow before making a referral and information they should be ready to provide at the time of referral.

Nonbiased Assessment

IDEA requires that students with disabilities be evaluated in ways that are nondiscriminatory (i.e., not biased because of the student's native language, culture or ethnicity, gender, and so on). A major concern prompting the legal requirement of nonbiased assessment is the disproportionate representation of ethnic minority students in some categories of special education (cf. MacMillan & Reschley, 1998; Ortiz, 1997; Patton, 1998; van Keulen, Weddington, & DeBose, 1998). IDEA demands that schools select and administer tests that are not racially or culturally discriminatory. Assessment must be done in the student's native language, the tests must be appropriate for the abilities they are purported to measure, and decisions regarding the student's education may not be made on the basis of a single test or source of information. Nevertheless, the law does not provide specific guidance on how assessment is to be accomplished or the criteria for judging that assessment has been nondiscriminatory (Yell, 1998).

TABLE 4.5 IDEA Requirements: Individualized Educational Programs and Placement

Key Points	Explanation
Required Participants Sec. 614 (d)(1)(B)	Parent Regular education teacher Special education teacher LEA [local education agency] representative knowledgeable about general curriculum Person who can interpret the instructional implications of evaluation results (may be one of the above members)
Development Considerations Sec. 614 (d)(3)	The team should consider: child's strengths, parents' concerns, most recent evaluation, language needs of LEP [limited English proficient] children, child's communication needs, and assistive technology; braille instuction when appropriate When behavior is an issue, strategies and supports to address that behavior Regular educators will participate in all above decisions
Placement Decisions	The IEP team will make most decisions, but when they don't, LEAs must "ensure" parent participation
Content Sec. 614 (d)(1)(A)	Present levels of performance (including how disability affects involvement and progress in general curriculum) Measurable annual goals including benchmarks or short-term objectives (related to meeting the child's needs to enable him or her to be involved in the general curriculum and other needs resulting from the disability) Special education and other services, supplementary aids, any program modifications or support for school personnel necessary for student to meet annual goals Explanation of the extent to which child will not participate in general education Individual modifications in administration of achievement tests, or explanation of why this is not appropriate and how child will be assessed Projected date for beginning services, anticipated service frequency, location, and duration Measures of progress toward annual goals and how parents will be kept informed of progress
Transition Services Sec. 614 (d)(1)(A)(vii)	Beginning at age 14 and updated annually, statement of transition service needs that focus on student's existing program or courses Beginning at age 16, specific transition services including interagency responsibilities Beginning at least 1 year before the student reaches the age of majority, student informed of his or her rights
Review Schedules Sec. 614 (d)(4)	At least once a year by IEP team, using the following criteria: any lack of progress toward annual goals and in the general curriculum, results of any reevaluation, information about child provided by parents, new informaton about child's anticipated needs

Source: From "The IDEA Amendments of 1997: Implications for Special and General Education Teachers, Administrators, and Teacher Trainers" by M. L. Yell and J. G. Shriner, 1997, *Focus on Exceptional Children, 30*(1), pp. 4–5. Copyright 1997 by Love Publishing, Co. Reprinted by permission.

TABLE 4.6 Steps from Prereferral to IEP and Checklists of the Teacher's Responsibilities

■ Steps to the IEP

1. A teacher notices a student having serious academic or behavioral difficulty.
2. The teacher consults the student's parents and tries the instructional or behavior management strategies she or he believes will resolve the problem.
3. If the problem is not resolved, the teacher asks for the help of the child study (or teacher assistance) team.
4. With the help of the team, the teacher implements and documents the results of strategies designed to resolve the problem.
5. If the problem is not resolved after reasonable implementation of the team's suggestions, the teacher makes a referral for evaluation by a multidisciplinary team (MDT).
6. The MDT evaluates the student in all areas of known or suspected disability, including medical, psychological, social, and educational evaluations.
7. With the results of the evaluation components in hand, the MDT determines whether the student is eligible for special education.
8. If the student is found eligible, then an IEP must be written.

■ What Should I Do Before Making a Referral?

Hold at least one conference to discuss your concerns with the parents (or make extensive and documented efforts to communicate with the parents).

Check all available school records and interview other professionals involved with the student to make sure you understand the student's history and what has been tried.

Ask the child study (or teacher assistance) team—or the principal, the school psychologist, and at least one other teacher who knows the student—to help you devise strategies to solve the problem.

Implement and document the results of the academic and behavior management strategies you have tried.

■ What Information Should I Be Able to Provide at the Time of Referral?

A statement of exactly what you are concerned about

An explanation of why you are concerned

Detailed records from your observations of the problem, including samples of academic work

Records documenting the strategies you have used to try to resolve the problem and the outcomes of those strategies

Note: Referrals for evaluation may also be initiated by parents or administrators who believe the student may have a disability.

From referral to placement to judgment of progress and reevaluation, the assessment process in special education is subject to careful scrutiny for possible bias. Failure to identify and provide services for minority students who need special education is as serious a problem as is overidentification of minority students for special education (Ortiz, 1997). However, the primary emphasis in assessment is on recognizing ethnic and cultural differences in language and behavior that are different from the white, middle-class norm but not indicative of disability (van Keulen et al., 1998).

Participation in State- and Districtwide Assessments

Another issue is the extent to which students with disabilities should be included in minimum competency testing and systemwide evaluations designed to ensure accountability. As the press for higher educational standards has increased emphasis on standardized testing and other statewide or systemwide evaluations, concern for including students with disabilities has grown (McDonnell, McLaughlin, & Morison, 1997). The concern is that students with disabilities be included in assessments that will allow them to demonstrate their competence and give them access to later education and employment (Yell & Shriner, 1997).

IDEA now requires that states make public information regarding the participation of students with disabilities in typical and alternative assessment procedures and report on their performance. Whenever possible, they must be included in the general or typical testing or other assessment procedures used by the school district or state to monitor all students' performance. For some students, special accommodations may be necessary. Table 4.7 shows examples of accommodations involving time, setting, and changes in the format of presentation or response.

The inclusion of students with disabilities in state- and districtwide assessments is relatively recent, having been added as a requirement under IDEA only since the 1997 amendments to the law. Just what accommodations are required for most students with learning disabilities and how these students fare in the assessments are matters of considerable concern.

Manifestation Determination

A thorny issue involving student misconduct, especially if suspension or expulsion is possible, is whether the behavior is a manifestation of the student's disability (Yell, 1998; Yell & Shriner, 1997). That is, if a student engages in serious misbehavior (e.g., bringing a weapon to school, fighting, destroying property, threatening others), is it a manifestation of his or her disability, or is it unrelated to it? If the latter is the case, the typical disciplinary consequences can usually be applied. But if the misbehavior is a manifestation of disability, educators may not apply a long-term suspension or expulsion as a consequence. Understandably, assessing the reasons for misconduct is fraught with difficulty, especially the case with students who have learning disabilities, because they are typically thought to have the cognitive and social understanding required to be held accountable for their actions. We return to discussion of this topic in Chapter 9.

TABLE 4.7 Examples of Accommodations for Assessments

Flexible Time	Flexible Setting	Alternative Presentation Format	Alternative Response Format
Extended time	Test alone in test carrel or separate room	Braille or large-print edition	Pointing to response
Alternating lengths of test sections (e.g., shorter and longer)	Test in small-group setting	Signing of directions	Using template for responding
More frequent breaks	Test at home (with accountability)	Interpretation of directions	Giving response in sign language
Extended testing sessions over several days	Test in special education classroom	Taped directions	Using a computer
	Test in room with special lighting	Highlighted keywords	Allow answers in test book

Source: From "The IDEA Amendments of 1997: Implications for Special and General Education Teachers, Administrators, and Teacher Trainers" by M. L. Yell and J. G. Shriner, 1997, *Focus on Exceptional Children, 30*(l), pp. 8. Copyright 1997 by Love Publishing Co. Reprinted by permission.

Ethical Issues

All aspects of special education present ethical problems for teachers and administrators (Howe & Miramontes, 1992). Many of these are connected to assessment. Ethical assessment requires, first, that the tests or other procedures be valid measures of the knowledge or skill in question. Assessment procedures must be administered properly by adequately trained personnel, be interpreted appropriately, and not be biased or discriminatory on the basis of gender, ethnicity, or other characteristic unrelated to the knowledge or skill being measured. The findings of assessment must be restricted to those having a compelling need to know them. These requirements for ethical assessment are well known, but in actual practice, knowing what course of action to follow is often difficult.

Many of the ethical problems teachers face involve the testing they are expected to do. Given what they are told to do, teachers may struggle with questions like these: Am I qualified to administer and interpret this test? If I am not, then what are the implications of my refusal to give it? What should take precedence, given the finite amount of time and energy I have—teaching or testing? The quandaries teachers may face in trying to live up to the expectations of their school systems to do both testing and teaching have long been recognized (Katzen, 1980). As one resource teacher put it: "We have been warned that disciplinary letters may be placed in our files if we don't complete evaluation and placement of newly referred kids within 30 days of obtaining their parents' signature. Nobody can tell me how to teach 40 kids and still have time to do testing" (Kauffman, 1992, p. xii).

Other ethical dilemmas may arise from issues of confidentiality or the selection or findings of assessment procedures (Taylor, 1997; Wiggins, 1993; Yell, 1998). Parents have a right to know how their children are doing in school. But what if the teacher knows that informing parents of their child's poor performance will result in child abuse? And what is a teacher's professional duty when he or she hears gossip in the teachers' lounge about things that are supposed to be held in confidence? Under what conditions should we send information to another school? Under what conditions should student teachers or researchers be allowed to see student records? Eligibility criteria must be stated, and they must be taken seriously. But what if a student does not quite meet the eligibility criteria as stated, yet desperately needs special services that are available only if he or she is found eligible? Is denying the services or is "fudging" the eligibility rules the lesser evil? Teachers have an obligation to respect other professionals and work collaboratively with them. But how should we handle a situation in which another professional's assessment is in error? Aside from the testing that the school system may prescribe, how do we select assessment procedures that evaluate the student's learning most meaningfully and provide maximum benefit to the student?

The ethical dilemmas that arise around issues of assessment have no easy solutions, nor can any prescription for resolving them be written. They can be addressed adequately only by the painstaking and often painful consideration of the details of the individual case. (See Howe & Miramontes, 1992; Salvia & Ysseldyke, 1991; Yell, 1998, for further discussion.)

Summary

1. What are the purposes of assessment?
   Primary purposes of assessment include:
   a. screening and selecting individuals who may have learning disabilities for more detailed study
   b. identifying whether the individual has a learning disability
   c. classifying the type of learning disability the individual has
   d. guiding remediation of the learning disability
   e. evaluating progress in remediation
2. What are two general approaches to assessment?
   a. One approach is trait assessment, which assumes that the most important things to measure are the traits, abilities, cognitive processes, or developmental stages underlying learning disabilities.

   b. An alternative approach is direct measurement, which assumes that the most important things to measure are students' actual performance on tasks involving academic and social skills
3. What are the domains of assessment of learning disabilities?
   Five major domains are:
   a. language abilities—oral language, reading, and writing
   b. mathematics abilities—mathematics concepts and operations, reasoning, and problem solving
   c. cognitive abilities—control of attention and control of mental processes
   d. social skills—social perceptions and social interactions
   e. environmental factors in school, home, and the community
4. What are some strategies for assessing learning disabilities?
   Various assessment strategies include:
   a. neuropsychological assessment—focuses on how brain function affects learning
   b. contextual assessment, which includes:
      (1) interviews with the student and important others
      (2) observations of the student in the classroom and other places in school
      (3) error analysis to discover predictable mistakes
   c. standardized testing, which includes:
      (1) norm-referenced tests of cognitive ability and achievement: compare the student to a large normative group
      (2) criterion-referenced tests—reveal what specific standards of performance the student has reached
      (3) nonreferenced tests—may reveal how the student approaches problems
   d. teacher-made tests—cover material presented in class
   e. curriculum-based assessment—systematic and frequent sampling of the student's performance on the instructional tasks in the daily curriculum
   f. behavioral assessment—direct observation and recording of specific target behaviors
   g. interactive assessment—observation of the student's response to instruction during testing
   h. authentic assessment, which includes:
      (1) performance assessment—samples of what the student can do
      (2) portfolio assessment—a compilation of the student's completed work
5. What are some issues in the assessment of students with learning disabilities?
   a. Many legal issues emanate from IDEA, including:
      (1) assessment for special education—general requirements of fair and accurate assessment leading to special services
      (2) referral for evaluation—the initial actions required before a full evaluation for eligibility may be initiated
      (3) eligibility determination—judging whether the student is entitled to special education and related services under IDEA

(4) individualized education plan (IEP), including persons involved in writing the IEP and the components included in it
(5) nonbiased assessment—testing should be nondiscriminatory on the basis of ethnicity, culture, language, gender, and so on
(6) participation in state- and districtwide assessment, including necessary accommodations for the student's disability or alternative assessment procedures
(7) manifestation determination—judging whether misconduct is a result of or unrelated to the student's disabilities

b. Ethical issues accompany the law or arise in addition to the law and may involve confidentiality, professional qualifications, and difficult judgments based on evaluation data.

5

Service Delivery Models

Service delivery models have been among the most controversial topics in special education throughout the history of the field. The controversy surrounds how to answer several questions about special education:

- Which students shall be served?
- What services shall be provided to them?
- Who shall provide these services?
- How shall these services be provided?
- Where shall these services be offered?

These are perpetual questions about special education for children with all types of exceptionalities, including those with learning disabilities (Bateman, 1994).

WHAT LAWS GOVERN THE DELIVERY OF SPECIAL EDUCATION?

The primary law governing special education services is the Individuals with Disabilities Education Act (IDEA). This federal law, initially passed in 1975, was amended in 1990 and 1997. State laws also govern special education, but they must conform to the requirements of IDEA.

When we refer to IDEA requirements, we include not only what is written in the actual law (the statute), but also what is written in the federal regulations related to the law. These federal regulations have the same force as the law, and courts require that schools implement the regulations as if they were written into the law itself (cf. Bateman, 1996; Yell, 1998).

The Influence of IDEA on Service Delivery

IDEA does not require, nor does it prohibit, a specific service delivery model for students with disabilities of any kind. However, it does require educators to give careful attention to how and where special education will be offered. Much of the controversy about special education has to do with interpretations of certain aspects of IDEA. The requirements of the law are ambiguous on many points, and they are often misunderstood or misinterpreted. So far, federal district courts have offered a variety of interpretations of many of the service delivery requirements of the law; the United States Supreme Court has not ruled on how special education service delivery is to be designed (Yell, 1998).

One influence of the 1997 amendments to IDEA was to bring general educators more clearly into the process of providing special education. As we discussed in Chapter 4, the assessment of students for special education must be done by **a multidisciplinary team (MDT).** This team includes the student's general education teacher, who will be expected to bring critical information to light about the student's performance in his or her regular classroom. Box 5.1 provides an example of the kind of information general education teachers may provide.

BOX 5.1 ***EXAMPLE***

Information Shared by Classroom Teacher Jackie Darnell at a Multidisciplinary Conference

Name: Cassandra

Age: 10-10

Grade: 5th

Literacy:

4th to 5th grade level

Enjoys reading as a leisure-time activity, and uses the library on a regular basis.

Enjoys writing fantasy and drama, and uses both character and plot development; patterns many of her stories after the popular girl-oriented series.

Participates in literature discussion groups and can answer a variety of questions about the literature, including underlying theme and application questions.

Can write a report with introduction and two supporting paragraphs.

Spells at fourth-grade level, using phonic and structural analysis for unknown words.

Can use a word processor to write and revise written work.

Math:

Second-grade achievement level.

Adds and subtracts with regrouping, but makes computation errors in the process and basic facts.

Understands basic concept of multiplication but does not know basic facts or how to use for computations.

Has difficulty understanding simple, one- and two-step word problems.

Has not yet memorized 50% of the basic addition and subtraction facts.

Knows multiplication facts 0, 1, 5, and 10.

Understands concept of multiplication as repeated addition. Does not compute multiplication problems.

Does not demonstrate concept of division and does not know division facts.

Demonstrates concept of simple fractions 1/2, 1/3, 1/4.

Solves word problems. Errors are generally in computation and basic facts rather than problem representation.

Describes math as least favorite subject.

Struggles to learn basic math facts, despite incentive program, coordination with parents, and use of computer programs at school.

Social/Emotional:

Well liked by peers, both boys and girls.

Quiet, does not ask for help when needed.

Works well in cooperative groups but usually does not take leadership roles.

Good sense of humor.

Source: From *Teaching Maintstreamed, Diverse, and At-Risk Students in the General Education Classroom* (p. 138) by S. Vaughn, C. Bos, and J. S. Schumm, 1997, Boston: Allyn & Bacon. Copyright 1997 by Allyn & Bacon. Reprinted by permission.

Questions to Ponder

If you were in the MDT conference at which Jackie presented this information, what questions would you have for her regarding Cassandra?

On the basis of the information provided by Jackie, do you think Cassandra is likely to be found to have a learning disability?

Given Cassandra's characteristics as described by Jackie, what service delivery model do you think would be most appropriate if Cassandra is to be given special education?

Individualized Education Plan

The primary intent of IDEA is to ensure that students with disabilities receive an appropriate, individualized education. The major vehicle for doing this is the **individualized education plan (IEP).** The IEP must detail the student's needs and state what special services will be provided. It also must include short-term goals for the student that allow progress to be monitored. The general education teacher must be included in preparing the IEP (see Table 4.5 and accompanying discussion of IEPs in Chapter 4).

Free Appropriate Public Education

IDEA and accompanying federal regulations require first and foremost that every student with a disability be provided a **free and appropriate public education (FAPE).** FAPE is the central issue of the federal law; without it, the other requirements of the law are irrelevant. That is, none of the other requirements of the law can be interpreted for an individual case until the FAPE requirement has been satisfied. Moreover, FAPE and other requirements of IDEA must be determined on an individual basis. A state or school system cannot make generalizations about FAPE and other requirements of the law that apply across the board to all students.

The "free" aspect of the law means that the parent or guardian cannot be charged for the special services that the student requires; the education must be provided at public expense. However, public funds may be used to send the student to a private school if that is required to ensure that the student receives an appropriate education.

The special education provided under IDEA must be "appropriate," which is a difficult term to interpret in some circumstances. The law refers to education designed to meet the individual ("unique") needs of the student with disabilities. Whatever instructional methods, materials, equipment, or type of educational environment is required for the student to learn must be provided. Educators may not, under IDEA, assume that all students with a particular category of disability (e.g., learning disability) will have the same educational needs or that education will be appropriate because it is designated for a particular category. The requirement is clearly that appropriateness be judged on a case-by-case basis (Bateman, 1996; Yell, 1998).

Least Restrictive Environment

IDEA requires that a student's FAPE be delivered in the **least restrictive environment (LRE).** LRE is the least restrictive or most "normal" place in which appropriate education can be offered. The LRE also is the environment in which the student has the maximum feasible opportunities to have contact with peers who do not have disabilities. Students are to be removed from regular classes and schools only when their needs cannot be met satisfactorily in those environments with supplementary aids and services.

Since the reauthorization of IDEA in 1997, LRE also refers to the extent to which the student is involved in the **general education curriculum** (Yell & Shriner, 1997). The student's educational program and placement must be designed to provide meaningful access to the typical curriculum for nondisabled students to the extent possible. A variety of factors must be taken into account in determining what is the LRE for a given student. Table 5.1 includes the five major considerations that educators must make in determining what environment will be least restrictive in a particular case.

The ambiguities inherent in these provisions of the law have resulted in uncertainty and conflict in some cases. Again, IDEA requires that LRE be judged in the individual case; it does not allow educators to assume that the LRE will be the same type of place for all students or for all students with a particular category of disability (Bateman, 1996; Huefner, 1994; Osborne, 1997; Yell, 1998).

IDEA has clearly moved many educators toward including more students with disabilities in general education. When implemented appropriately, placing some students with learning disabilities in regular classrooms can work well. Successful inclusion in general education requires a competent teacher who will make appropriate adaptations and accommodations for the student with a disability, as well as support of the teacher by specialized personnel (Bassett et al., 1996). The interview featuring Tammy Gregory in Box 5.2 provides an example of how inclusion can work when the match between teacher, class, and student is good.

TABLE 5.1. Determination of the Least Restrictive Environment

School district decisions should be based on formative data collected throughout the LRE process.

1. Has the school taken steps to maintain the child in the general education classroom?
   - What supplementary aids and services were used?
   - What interventions were attempted?
   - How many interventions were attempted?
2. Benefits of placement in general education with supplementary aids and services versus special education.
   - Academic benefits
   - Nonacademic benefits (e.g., social, communication)
3. Effects on the education of other students.
   - If the student is disruptive, is the education of other students adversely affected?
   - Does the student require an inordinate amount of attention from the teacher, thereby adversely affecting the education of others?
4. If a student is being educated in a setting other than the general education classroom, are there integrated experiences with nondisabled peers to the maximum extent appropriate?
   - In what academic settings is the student integrated with nondisabled peers?
   - In what nonacademic settings is the child integrated with nondisabled peers?
5. Is the entire continuum of alternative services available from which to choose an appropriate placement?

Source: From "Least Restrictive Environment, Inclusion, and Students with Disabilities: A Legal Analysis." by M. L. Yell, 1995, *Journal of Special Education,* 28 (4). Copyright 1995 by PRO-ED, Inc. Reprinted by permission.

BOX 5.2 ***EXAMPLE***

Interview with Tammy Gregory

Tammy Gregory is one of four second grade teachers at Canyon Verde Elementary School in Tucson, Arizona. This is Tammy's third year teaching. In her class of 31 students, Tammy has one student with learning disabilities, Adrian, and one student with attention deficit disorder, Lenny.

When you talk with Tammy and watch her teach, it is clear that she believes all students can be successful learners, and that her job is to modify the content and the curriculum for the different learners in her classroom. This is certainly the case with Adrian, whose learning disabilities relate most to the speed at which he processes information. It takes him longer to understand what is being said during classroom discussions and presentations. He reads slowly whether he is reading aloud or to himself. His responses to questions are often slow and labored, and the ideas are not clearly stated. He also writes slowly. He is almost always the last or next-to-last student to finish a written assignment, and often does not complete work in the time allowed.

Tammy regularly makes accommodations for Adrian so that he is a successful learner in her classroom. Because his writing is slow, she sometimes reduces the length of the assignment so that he can complete it in the time allowed. Tammy says, "The key is that Adrian understands and has mastered the skill. If he can demonstrate mastery answering five problems instead of ten problems in math, then he has learned and reached his goal."

Tammy has also set up an informal buddy system in her room. Students regularly help each other with assignments. Tammy has Adrian sitting next to one student who is an able helper and high achiever and another student who is an average achiever and who likes to problem solve and work with Adrian on assignments. This arrangement gives Adrian the opportunity to work with two very different students who like to work with other students and provide support for him. Although speed of processing can make Adrian appear slow and not very adept at many skills, his teacher has taken the time to learn about his interests and his strengths and to share those with the other students. It is not unusual to hear Tammy say to the class, "Check with Adrian on that, he's a real expert."

Tammy has also made accommodations for Lenny, a student with attention deficit disorders including hyperactivity and impulsivity. At the beginning of the year, Tammy thought that Lenny would be "the child that led her into early retirement." He moved constantly (even when sitting), and was out of his seat, sharpening his pencil, talking to and bothering the other students. During class discussion he would answer before Tammy had a chance even to ask the students to raise their hands. He rarely completed assignments. Tammy felt that Lenny could do much of the work, but that his attention problems got in the way of his being a successful learner. To help Lenny, Tammy thought about and modified the structure of her classroom and schedule. Tammy comments,

> Lenny attends best when he knows what is "on tap" for the day. Each day I review the schedule for the day and put a copy of it on the board, on the corner of Lenny's desk, and on my desk. As each activity is completed, Lenny checks it off and rates himself for that activity on three criteria: paying attention, effort, and work completed. At first I also rated Lenny, but now I am comfortable with his self-monitoring. At lunch and during the end of the day wrap-up, I take several minutes to review with Lenny his self-monitoring. Based on his performance, Lenny receives good work day certificates to take home for his parents to sign, and on Friday afternoon he can receive a "Job Well Done" pass to watch a video or participate in other activities with the other good workers in the school. For me, taking this extra time with Lenny is well worth the progress Lenny has made and the sanity that has been restored to my classroom.

Tammy also makes other modifications for Lenny, such as reducing the number of math problems as-

BOX 5.2 *continued*

signed by having him complete only the odd or even numbered problems. She also helps Lenny, Adrian, and other students in her class break multiple-step or complex tasks and projects into smaller tasks. Tammy comments, "Even reading a book and writing a book report can be divided into five or six steps the students can complete one-by-one. This substantially increases the likelihood of students getting these projects done in a timely manner."

Adrian and Lenny have made good progress this year in school, both in terms of their learning and their positive self-concepts as learners. Tammy is concerned, however, about their transition into third grade, where more emphasis will be placed on written work and complex assignments and less time will be spent on teaching basic skills and individualizing for different students' needs. She is wondering what to communicate to Adrian and Lenny's teachers next year, so that they can continue as successful learners.

Source: From *Teaching Maintstreamed, Diverse, and At-Risk Students in the General Education Classroom* (p. 130) by S. Vaughn, C. Bos, and J. S. Schumm, 1977, Boston: Allyn & Bacon. Copyright 1997 by Allyn & Bacon. Reprinted by permission.

Questions to Ponder

Why do you think Tammy is concerned about Adrian's and Lenny's transition to third grade? What should she do about it?

How do Adrian and Lenny fit the definition and characteristics of students with learning disabilities that we have provided so far?

What questions would you have for Tammy about how she makes accommodations for Adrian and Lenny?

The LRE for students with learning disabilities is rarely thought to be a separate class or school. In the mid-1990s, only about 20% of students with learning disabilities were educated primarily in special classes or schools, about 40% were taught primarily in regular classrooms, and about 40% were in resource rooms from 20% to 60% of the school day. The trend since 1990 has clearly been toward placement of a greater percentage of students with learning disabilities in regular classrooms for a greater part of their school day and less reliance on placement in separate settings (U.S. Department of Education, 1996).

Continuum of Alternative Placements

Because a basic assumption of IDEA is that the LRE will differ from student to student, it also requires that a full **continuum of alternative placements (CAP)** be available. The CAP ranges from full-time placement in regular classes, with supplementary aids and services, through resource room programs, special self-contained classes, special day and residential schools, and programs provided in hospitals or through home-based instruction.

Again, the law requires educators to choose from the CAP a service delivery option for each student. That is, the law prescribes case-by-case decisions and proscribes uniform decisions that apply to all students with learning disabilities or to all students in any other category. There is no ambiguity in this provision of the law. Thus, the suggestion that a single educational plan—including any single service delivery model—

will be the only option is clearly at odds with the law (Bateman, 1996; Bateman & Chard, 1995; Dupre, 1997).

The controversies regarding the law typically involve attempts to answer two central questions in this order: (1) What is appropriate education? (2) What is the least restrictive environment? Neither of these is easy to answer by itself, but answering either one is complicated by the order in which they are addressed. Legally and logically, the first question must be answered before the second; we cannot determine the LRE for delivering services until we have described what we are going to deliver (i.e., what will be appropriate for the individual student). Much of the controversy about service delivery is precipitated by misunderstandings of the law. IDEA does not require that all students with learning disabilities be served in neighborhood schools or regular classrooms; the CAP provision of the law applies to learning disabilities as well as all other categories of disability. IDEA does not allow making a placement decision first, then deciding what can be provided in that place. Defining the needed educational program must come first, then defining the LRE in which the program can be provided (Bateman, 1996; Yell, 1998).

The inclusive schools movement, which emphasizes delivering all services to students with disabilities in neighborhood schools and regular classes, should prompt careful reflection on the history of special education as well as on the provisions of the law (cf. Dupre, 1997). One legal scholar summed up the implications of court cases for choosing service delivery models as follows:

> It would be premature for school districts to provide all special services in mainstream classes, just as it would be intransigent to refuse to provide individualized support services there. Although separate services have done an injustice to many students, forcing all students into mainstream regular education classrooms will also be an injustice. Students with disabilities need options based on their individualized needs—not just a shift from a separation paradigm to an inclusion paradigm. Of course, that is part of the great challenge for both regular and special educators: how to see a diversified student body with a variety of needs that do not respond to one administratively imposed model. The individualized and flexible legal standard of least restrictive environment serves students with disabilities well. We need to pay it more than lip service. (Huefner, 1994, p. 52)

HOW IS *SPECIAL EDUCATION* DEFINED?

By definition, *special education* involves special instruction designed to address special problems in teaching and learning. The special problems may have to do with a wide variety of disabilities, including physical, sensory, cognitive, speech and language, emotional/behavioral, or academic problems or combinations of all of these.

Students with learning disabilities require special education primarily, but often not exclusively, because of atypical problems in our teaching (and in their learning) of academic tasks for reasons that are often obscure but may involve neurological anomalies.

These students need special instruction—something different from what can be provided by general education. They also need related services that will help them obtain and benefit from special education. In fact, they are assured of both special education and related services under federal law (the Individuals with Disabilities Education Act).

Definition and Practice of Special Education

Education reformers have sometimes suggested that special education is little or nothing more than good general education. The contention is that if general education were transformed in certain ways, it could address the individual needs of every child and so be special for all (Thomas, 1994). However, as others have pointed out, education cannot be truly special for all any more than other services provided to the public at large can be specially designed for everyone, except in the most superficial sense (Dupre, 1997; Kauffman & Hallahan, 1993). Moreover, when special education is practiced as it should be, it is different from general education along several critical dimensions of instruction (Fuchs & Fuchs, 1995b). At a minimum, these instructional differences involve the training and support teachers receive, class or group size and composition, degree of individualization and teacher direction, accuracy and scope of pupil assessment, precision of implementation of instructional strategies, closeness of monitoring of instructional progress, and empirical validation of teaching practices.

Teacher Training and Support

Special education teachers receive additional training that informs them of the nature and characteristics of the disabilities of their students and the instructional and behavior management practices that will be most effective with them. Appropriate special education teacher training offers skills in addition to those taught in general education teacher preparation and helps special educators understand how their role is different from and complements the role of general education teachers (Kauffman, 1994). Teacher training alone is not enough to produce viable special education. A professional infrastructure of support services, including consultation, supervision, curriculum, instructional materials, and paraprofessional assistance, is required to enhance teaching practice (Vaughn, Bos, & Schumm, 1997; Worrall & Carnine, 1994).

Class or Group Size and Composition

The pupil-teacher ratio is lower in special than in general education instructional settings. This is achieved by congregating students with special instructional needs in special schools, classes, or resource rooms or by adding a consulting teacher or co-teacher to work with a general education teacher in a regular class. The class or group size in which instruction is offered is necessarily smaller in special education to allow for the degree of individualization required to meet extraordinary instructional problems. Moreover, although heterogeneous grouping is popular in general education and has advantages for some school activities, effective instruction of students with special learning problems may require teaching small groups of students with similar skills in the curriculum being taught. Thus, special education may involve not just lower pupil-teacher ratios, but also homogeneous grouping of students for instruction in specific skill areas (Grossen, 1993b).

Individualization and Teacher Direction

All good general education teachers individualize instruction to the extent possible, given the limits of their time and efforts in teaching a relatively large group of students. In special education, the degree of individualization is necessarily higher, as reflected in the individualized education plan that must be written for each child. The required individualization extends to assessing, planning, instructing, and monitoring progress. In addition, instructional materials that are adequate for most students but unusable for students with particular problems may need to be specially adapted. Besides individual attention, special education may require a higher level of teacher direction. Although many or most students in general education may be successful in directing much of their own learning, effective special education often requires that the teacher be more directive and offer more explicit instruction (Grossen, 1993a).

Assessment

Students in general education are routinely assessed, but those in special education require closer scrutiny than can be afforded for all students. The assessment required in special education is broader in scope and more detailed than that required for the successful practice of general education. In special education, teachers must assess all areas of known or suspected disability. They must also give more careful attention to the analysis of students' errors, the patterns of relative strength and weakness, and the effects of particular instructional and behavior management practices than is necessary in general education.

Instructional Precision

Instruction in general education is, of necessity, designed for typical learners—the vast majority of students. As such, it need not be controlled as precisely as in special education. Questioning, sequencing, pacing, opportunity to respond, wait time, positive and negative examples, repetition, feedback, reinforcement of desired behavior and academic performance, and other instructional elements must be used with greater precision by special than by general educators. Many of the same basic instructional procedures used in general education apply to special education and vice versa, but in special education, there is less room for error in instruction, because these students will not learn given the typical instructional procedures and level of precision that are successful with most students.

Progress Monitoring

In general education, student progress need not be monitored as closely as in special education. Special educators must be aware daily, if not moment to moment, of the progress individual students are making. Close monitoring is essential to avoid small instructional errors that can lead to later catastrophes in learning for students with special problems. Competent general education teachers may assess their students' progress once a week and run relatively little risk of losing touch with their students' learning. This is not the case with special education teachers, who must be more finely attuned to their students' headway.

Empirical Validation

General education instructional practices have often been based on fads, not derived from careful field tests and scientific confirmation of their effectiveness (Carnine, 1993). The best practices in special education are derived from research and development and have been empirically validated through careful field tests. Progress in special education depends on the accumulation of scientific evidence that its methods are effective (Kauffman, 1993b). Empirical validation has been one of the hallmarks of the competent practice of special education (Fuchs & Fuchs, 1995a).

The seven features just described have not always characterized the practice of special education, which has too often been poorly implemented (Kauffman, 1994). However, when special education does have these features, it can and does work because it is truly special (Fuchs & Fuchs, 1995a, 1995b).

General education teachers can also tailor some of these features to accommodate students who have special needs (Schumm & Vaughn, 1992). Although general education practices can and should be substantially improved, special instruction will nonetheless be required to address the problems of students and teachers for whom general education has been a failure. Moreover, at present, there appear to be large gaps between general education teachers' beliefs and their practices and skills in accommodating the needs of students with learning disabilities. Special education in the context of general education—or general education that actually meets the needs of students with learning disabilities—is likely quite rare (Schumm, Vaughn, Gordon, & Rothlein, 1994).

Related Services

Related services are those services necessary to allow a student to benefit from special education. These must be provided as needed for all students who receive special education. For example, transportation to and from the location at which special education is offered is a related service that cannot be withheld. Physical and occupational therapies, recreation, speech and language therapy, psychological services, counseling, and medical diagnostic services may also be related services. Special education must be delivered in such a way that related services are made available at no cost to the student's parents.

Continuum of Alternative Placements

IDEA envisions an array of plans and variations of service delivery arrangements suited to students' particular needs. The law does not allow schools to employ only one or two service delivery options, but instead requires a continuum of alternatives ranging from placement in regular classes to placement in residential schools.

Most school systems are constantly seeking to improve how they group and instruct students to deliver the special services that those with disabilities need to be successful in school. Special educators are also looking for ways to combine a variety of instructional approaches with all the service delivery options. Strategies such as peer tutoring and cooperative learning, for example, are often suggested as approaches that can help to make teaching more successful. Direct instruction may be a particularly effective approach for most students with learning disabilities, but it is seldom feasible to provide it in the context of a regular classroom in which student-directed learning is the norm.

Clearly, some instructional approaches are more feasible than others in some service delivery models. Some are more workable than others for different grade levels. The problems of finding the right combinations of instructional methods and service delivery systems for students of different ages and disabilities—not to mention the demands of individualization—contribute to the controversy surrounding service delivery issues.

WHAT ARE SOME SERVICE DELIVERY MODELS?

Given that special instruction and related services are to be provided, we must construct a model for how they are to be delivered to students. A **service delivery model** is a plan for bringing students, teachers, and instructional methods and materials together—a model of the physical and interpersonal environment required to foster effective teaching and learning. Many of these models of service delivery have been constructed. Each has certain advantages and disadvantages. None is without merit for some students, and none is without fault if applied universally. Six such models are briefly described, along with a summary of possible advantages and disadvantages of each.

We can speak of possible advantages and disadvantages of each service delivery model only in the abstract because different individuals perceive and respond to any given environment in very different ways (Gallagher, 1993; Kauffman, 1995). Furthermore, a service delivery model offers only potential advantages and disadvantages; poor implementation can undermine the benefits of any model, and adroit implementation can minimize drawbacks. All six of these models have existed in some form for decades, and it is possible to find many variations and combinations of them in practice.

The order in which these models are presented might be considered a ranking from less to more restrictive. Because the LRE provision of IDEA emphasizes removing students with disabilities from the ordinary school environment only as necessary to meet their needs for special education, we begin with the model that involves pulling students out of their regular classrooms as little as possible. Many people associate pullout with restrictiveness—the longer or more obvious the pullout, the more restrictive the environment. However, what makes an environment more or less restrictive is open to debate (Kauffman, 1995). Least restrictive must be interpreted in the light of what the student learns in the classroom and school environment (Bateman, 1996).

Collaborative Consultation in the General Education Classroom

In an effort to avoid the difficulties inherent in pullout models, special educators of the 1980s devised **collaborative consultation.** In this model, special education teachers do not have classrooms of their own and do not pull students out of their regular classes for special instruction. Rather, special educators serve as consultants to general education teachers, collaborating with them in planning and implementing instructional accommodations in regular classrooms. Students with learning disabilities are not clustered in particular classes, but rather dispersed throughout the classes they would attend if they had no disabilities. One special educator might work with ten or more general educators, rotating among classrooms to help teachers assess and instruct a variety of students. The special educator's role may be defined as consulting not only about students identified as having learning disabilities, but about any student who is having difficulties. This service delivery plan became quite popular in the special education reform movement of the early 1990s. It was further encouraged by the 1997 amendments to IDEA, which allow special educators to provide services to students without disabilities as long as students with disabilities are receiving appropriate education.

Possible advantages of collaborative consultation include blurring of the distinctions between general and special education among students and teachers and the opportunity for preventive work with students not identified as having disabilities. This plan may minimize the stigma of being identified as receiving special education and help general education teachers learn how to approach instructional and management problems and make successful accommodations for learners with special needs.

The primary disadvantage of collaborative consultation as a service delivery system is that the special educator's work is spread over a number of classrooms, which prevents intensive, sustained work with individual students. A special educator can be in only one classroom at a time, so the primary responsibility for implementing special services often falls to the general education teacher (Jenkins, Jewell, Leicester, Jenkins, & Troutner, 1991). Another possible disadvantage of collaborative consultation, therefore, is that both general and special education teachers can feel that the services they provide are insufficient to meet their students' needs (Schulte, Osborne, & Kauffman, 1993b).

Co-teaching in the General Education Classroom

Another way around both the scheduling problems and the stigma inherent in pullout models is to use a **co-teaching** approach in which the general and special educator team up to teach a class together. Typically, a group of students with disabilities and a group of students without disabilities are combined in one class; thus, it is not apparent that the class is "special." The two teachers, perhaps assisted by one or more paraprofessionals, share responsibility for teaching all the students. In effect, there is a special class within a general class—a melding of 20 to 30 students, a quarter to a half of whom may have disabilities, and two teachers with complementary skills. Co-teaching is a service delivery plan of growing popularity.

Co-teaching has the potential advantage of fully integrating special and general education, both students and teachers. Students with disabilities are not labeled so obviously as in pullout models, and teachers need not be identified by the students as "special" or "regular." Co-teaching may offer the advantages of a special self-contained class without the separation of those with and without disabilities. Thus, co-teaching can avoid the problems of stigma and of uncoordinated general education and special education curricula (Bear & Proctor, 1990; Johnston, Proctor, & Corey, 1994).

A potential disadvantage of co-teaching is that both teachers can fall into stereotyped roles with students and with each other so that they are actually on very different tracks that are parallel only in the sense that the teachers share physical space. Coordinating the work of two teachers and a diverse group of learners is not simple, and not all teachers are successful in working out a true partnership. Furthermore, it is possible for students with learning disabilities to play highly predictable roles in the class and to be stigmatized by their differences in academic performance or behavior. Some of the potential problems are discussed in Box 5.3.

Special Education Resource Room

The **resource room** was popularized in the 1970s as a way of keeping students with learning disabilities in greater contact with their nondisabled peers in regular classes and of improving the collaboration of general and special educators. The special education teacher takes students into the special class for instruction only in specific areas in which they have difficulties, perhaps for as little as 30 minutes several times a week, perhaps as much as half of each school day. The resource teacher is expected to serve a larger number of students than the teacher of a self-contained class, sometimes with the assistance of a paraprofessional. Caseloads for resource teachers may include 30 students or more. Furthermore, resource teachers are frequently expected to consult with the general education teachers of resource room students and to offer help in adapting instruction and materials, advising on behavior management, and coordinating the instruction in the resource and regular classes. The resource room is a very common service delivery plan for students with learning disabilities.

The obvious potential advantage of the resource room is that students can spend the majority of their time in the regular classroom with nondisabled peers. The resource room model can be a way of providing special, intensive instruction in one or more specifically targeted areas of the curriculum with minimum disruption of the students' school experience. It can also be a way of improving the articulation between general and special education so that the integration of the two is heightened and the separation is minimized. Thus, well-designed resource room programs appear capable of producing good outcomes for many students with learning disabilities (Carlberg & Kavale, 1980; Marston, 1987–1988; Sindelar & Deno, 1979).

Possible disadvantages of the resource room plan include the difficulty of coordinating students' and teachers' schedules to avoid disrupting students' general education and of coordinating general and special teachers' schedules so that there is time for consultation. With a heavy caseload, the resource teacher can find it virtually impossible to offer adequately intensive and sustained instruction to students in the resource room as well as sufficient consultation with students' regular classroom teachers. Also, students who receive services in resource rooms may be stigmatized by leaving their regular classes and attending a special class, even if for only a relatively brief time.

Self-Contained Special Education Classroom

A **special self-contained class** is generally thought to be appropriate for students who need a more highly structured and intensive instructional and behavior management program than can be afforded in a regular classroom. A well-designed and well-functioning special class usually has a dozen or fewer students enrolled, with a special education teacher and a paraprofessional staffing the classroom. The purpose of such a class is to provide an environment in which intensive instruction can be offered to individuals and small groups. Few students with learning disabilities are placed in these classrooms, and even fewer spend the entire school day there. Virtually all students in self-contained classes are included with their nondisabled peers in regular classes for part of the day. They are generally mainstreamed for those subjects in which their disabilities do not put them at great disadvantage (e.g., art, music, or physical education) or for nonacademic activities (e.g., home room, recess, lunch, and extracurricular activities). However, the self-contained class is their primary placement, the home base from which they operate.

The possible advantages of a self-contained class include the opportunity for intensive, individualized, and small group instruction. Certainly, it is advantageous to have a curriculum designed for one's special needs rather than one appropriate for the typical student. Especially at the middle-school and secondary-school levels, students placed in a special self-contained class may need to make fewer transitions from one class and teacher to another than they would were they placed in regular classes.

Potential disadvantages of a self-contained class include the stigma attached to attending a different class, the added difficulty in making friends with students in regular classes, and the difficulty of making the transition back to regular classes. Another potential disadvantage is a curriculum that is not aligned with that of the regular class, making a student's integration into the mainstream of the school more difficult.

Special Day School

A **special day school** is designed to serve a special student clientele during the entire school day, but not before or after school hours. Typically, a special day school is a regional program, and most of the students who attend are from other districts or

BOX 5.3 ***EXAMPLE***

Common Co-teaching Issues

Based on extended observations and interviews with more than 70 general education/special education teacher teams, we have identified several issues that co-teachers must address if they are to be successful.

Whose Students Are These?

Address this issue before co-teaching begins: Who is responsible for the students in the classroom? The general education teacher is responsible for all of the students in the class, but how do these responsibilities change when the special education teacher is in the room? Who is responsible for the students with special needs? Under what conditions do these responsibilities change?

Perhaps the issue that warrants the most discussion *prior* to co-teaching is grading. Special education teachers are accustomed to grading based on the effort, motivation, and abilities of the students. General education teachers are accustomed to grading based on a uniform set of expectations that is only slightly adjusted to reflect issues of effort, motivation, and student abilities. Making joint decisions about how grades will be handled for in-class assignments, tests, and homework will reduce the frictions frequently associated with grading special education students in general education classrooms. Working together, teachers can develop guidelines for grading to use with both students and parents.

Whose Classroom Management Rules Do We Use?

Most general and special education teachers know the types of academic and social behaviors they find acceptable and unacceptable. Over the years, they have established consequences for inappropriate behaviors. Rarely is there disagreement between teachers about the more extreme behaviors. The subtle classroom management difficulties that are part of the ongoing routines of running a classroom, however, can cause concerns for teachers. Often, the special education teacher is unsure about when he or she should step in and assist with classroom management. Teachers should discuss their classroom management styles and the roles they expect of each other in maintaining a smoothly running classroom.

What Space Do I Get?

When special education teachers spend part of their day instructing in general education classrooms, it is extremely useful to have a designated area for them to keep their materials. A desk and chair that are used only by special education teachers provide them with a "base" from which to work and contribute to their position of authority.

What Do We Tell the Students?

An issue repeatedly brought up by teachers is how much information should be given. Should students be informed that they will have two teachers? Should students know that one of the teachers is a special education teacher and that she will be assisting some children more than others? The students should be informed that they have two teachers and that both teachers have the same authority. We think it is a good idea to introduce the special education teacher as a "learning abilities" specialist who will be working with all of the students from time to time. It is our experience that students willingly accept the idea of having two teachers and like it very much. In interviews we have conducted, many students who have participated in co-teaching classrooms tell us that having two teachers is better because everyone gets more help.

What Do We Tell the Parents?

Teachers are often unsure of how much they should tell parents about their new teaching arrangement. One of the concerns that teachers have is how parents might react to having a special education teacher in the classroom for part of the day. It is our experience that these programs are most successful when parents are brought in early and are part of the planning process. Thus, parents are part of the process from the beginning and are able to influence

BOX 5.3 *continued*

the development of the program. Parents of average- to high-achieving children may express concerns that their children's education may be hampered because students with special needs are placed in the classroom. Teachers report that these students fare as well or better, academically and socially, when students with special needs are in the general education classroom; and all students benefit from the support provided by the special education teacher (Arguelles, Schumm, & Vaughn, 1996).

How Can We Get Time to Co-Plan?

The most pervasive concern of both general and special education teachers in co-teaching situations is obtaining sufficient time during the school day to plan and discuss instruction and student progress. This is of particular concern for special education teachers who are working with more than one general education teacher. Teachers report that planning often comes on their own time. Even when a designated period is established for co-planning, teachers report that this time gets taken away to be used for meetings and other school management activities. Teachers need a *minimum* of 45 minutes of uninterrupted planning time each week if they are likely to have a successful co-teaching experience. One suggestion made by several of the teacher teams with whom we have worked is to designate a day or a half-day every 6–8 weeks when teachers can meet extensively to plan and discuss the progress of students, as well as changes in their instructional practices.

Source: From "The ABCDEs of Co-Teaching" by S. Vaughn, J. S. Schrumm, and M. E. Arguelles, 1997, *Teaching Exceptional Children, 30* (2), p. 8. Copyright 1997 by Council for Exceptional Children. Reprinted by permission.

Questions to Ponder

What additional questions might arise about co-teaching?

Can you think of any additional possible solutions to the issues discussed here?

In what service delivery models besides co-teaching might the same or similar issues arise?

attendance areas. Like residential schools, special day schools are relatively costly on a per pupil basis, and only a very small percentage of students with learning disabilities ever attend one.

Major potential advantages of special day schools include those described for residential schools in the next section, except that the day school does not have any direct control over the student's environment during nonschool hours. Major potential disadvantages are also those of the residential school, except that contact with the home and transition back to the regular neighborhood school may be easier.

Residential School

In a **residential school,** students live in dormitories or other residential units, at least during the school week if not seven days a week, and attend a special school on the campus. Residential schools are most often the placement of choice if the student's learning disabilities are severe or pervasive (i.e., affect multiple areas of the school curriculum, including social relations) and of long standing. Many students placed in residential schools have experienced repeated failure, even with special assistance in more normal environments. Residential schools are quite expensive, and only a tiny percentage of students with learning disabilities are ever placed in one. In fact, residential schools are often available only to students whose parents are of considerable financial means and are willing and able to pay the cost or to students who have for years frustrated the efforts of public school personnel to provide effective but less expensive programs.

The major potential advantages of residential schools are that they can provide a highly structured environment 24 hours a day. For some students, this is important in bringing order and predictability as well as intensive instruction into their lives. A residential program may allow work on a student's self-control, work habits, and social relationships that is hard to duplicate when educators have little or no control over what happens outside the school building and before or after the school day. In a good residential school, special education and related services are highly concentrated and continuously available. A residential program may also offer the advantage of a mutually supportive staff, all of whom are in constant close communication about the student's needs and progress. Camaraderie is an important element for teachers and other professionals working with students who have special difficulties, and the interpersonal support found in the best residential schools is difficult to duplicate in a less structured, less intensive environment. Finally, a significant advantage for some students is being in a community in which all the other students share many of the same problems. In such a community, some students gain self-confidence, learn from peer role models who are overcoming similar difficulties, and develop a renewed sense of self with which to face the outside world.

An obvious disadvantage of a residential school is its high per pupil cost. Typically, the school is a long distance from the student's home, which may be a disadvantage for keeping the student's family involved and for helping the student make a transition back to his or her original school. Also, residential schools are "artificial" environments in that they are quite different from the typical home and neighborhood school. Some students may feel stigmatized by attending a special residential school, and some may gravitate toward the worst peer models in the school. Another drawback is the limited opportunity to spend time with students who do not have learning disabilities. Finally, many residential schools are small, and academic and extracurricular options may be limited, especially in the upper grades.

WHAT ARE SOME ISSUES IN SERVICE DELIVERY?

The variety of plans or models for delivering special education and related services has led to much controversy about legal, philosophical, and research issues. These issues are interdependent and overlapping. One set of legal and philosophical issues centers on teaching students in inclusive settings, usually interpreted to mean in regular classrooms with little or no pullout. Another set of issues has to do with maintaining the full continuum of alternative placements so that there are service delivery options. Research can inform decision makers about these issues, but research has not answered all the important questions about service delivery and policy decisions.

Teaching Students in Inclusive Settings

Teaching in inclusive settings is often different from what is portrayed in the literature by proponents of the full inclusion of all students with disabilities (e.g., see the cases "Yours, Mine or Ours" [pp. 170–174] and "What's Inclusion Got to Do with It?" [pp. 164–169] in Kauffman, Mostert, Trent, & Hallahan, 1998). Much of the literature on teaching in inclusive settings describes working with students who have severe physical disabilities and/or mental retardation, and these descriptions do not fit the typical situation confronting a teacher of a student with learning disabilities (cf. Bassett et al., 1996; Deno, Foegen, Robinson, & Espin, 1996; Manset & Semmel, 1997). Zigmond and Baker (1996) describe some of the frustrations felt by general education and special education teachers alike in attempting to include students with learning disabilities in regular classrooms. The first quote is from a second-grade general education teacher; the second, from a special education teacher.

> The thing that is so amazing about these special ed kids is you always have to teach them: "Look at me, I'm talking; look at me; here I am, where's your eyes supposed to be?" Every day. Usually second grade, by the second week of school, you just say, "These are rules; here's the signal; I do this, you look." But, you just have to keep [going over it again and again]. (p. 30)
>
> We're not teaching them *how* to read. I think we're just doing total accommodation. Nobody has time to teach these kids [fifth graders] how to read back at their second grade level. In about two periods a week, I'm not going to teach kids how to read. (p. 31)

Teachers in inclusive settings often find that they do not have enough time for planning. Special education teachers often find that they are expected to work with too many teachers and that their time in any one class or with a particular child is too short. Sometimes special education teachers are relegated to the role of teacher's aide or find that the instruction they believe the student with learning disabilities should have is not what the general education teacher wants them to give. Pulling students aside for special instruction in the regular classroom can be more stigmatizing than pulling them out to a separate classroom. Resources of time, personnel, training, and materials are often inadequate, and in the absence of the needed supports, teachers often are ineffective. In short, there are many potential problems in teaching in inclusive settings, and research strongly suggests that poorly implemented or inappropriate inclusion frustrates teachers and shortchanges students (Deno et al., 1996; Zigmond & Baker, 1996).

Nevertheless, when inclusion is properly implemented for students for whom it is appropriate, teaching in inclusive settings can be highly rewarding for teachers and beneficial to students. The key is planning carefully, allocating adequate resources to support inclusion, and understanding that inclusion in general education is neither best for all students nor necessarily best done for the entire school day. Vaughn, Schumm, and Arguelles (1997) describe how two fifth-grade teachers—Tiffany, a general educator, and Joyce, a special educator—were successful in co-teaching to include students with disabilities.

> [Tiffany] We learn so much from each other. Really, Joyce has taught me how to implement strategies that are good for other students in the class, not just the students with special needs. It is wonderful to have a partner to bounce ideas off who really understands kids.
>
> [Joyce] I think I'm a better teacher now, and I definitely have a much better understanding of what goes on in the general education classroom and what kinds of expectations I need to have for my students . . . . I am able to provide some support for all of the students in the class. Mind you, I never lose sight of why I'm in here, to assist the students with identified special needs, but there are benefits for other students as well. (p. 4)

Working out the specifics of co-teaching and other inclusionary models requires careful attention to the details of what is going to be taught, what specific roles each teacher will play, what materials will be used, and how teaching and learning will be evaluated. For example, Vaughn et al. (1997) describe five different plans for working out co-teaching:

1. one group: one lead teacher, one teacher "teaching on purpose" (i.e., giving specific instruction to individuals or groups, not merely playing the part of a paraprofessional)
2. two groups: two teachers teaching the same content, usually to heterogeneous groups, the primary advantage being simply that instructional groups are smaller
3. two groups: one teacher reteaching, one teacher teaching alternative information (This usually means the general education teacher provides basic instruction for the whole class and the special education teacher works with students who need additional teaching, reteaching, or adaptations.)
4. multiple groups: two teachers monitoring/teaching (The content may vary. The two teachers work with specific groups by monitoring student progress or teaching minilessons to individuals or small groups.)
5. one group: two teachers teaching the same content, working cooperatively in providing instruction for the whole class at the same time

Teaching in inclusive settings can be successful and highly rewarding. However, success will not occur automatically, and many educators argue for alternatives to inclusion.

Maintaining a Continuum of Alternative Placements

The idea of a full array of placement options in special education has been under serious attack since the mid-1980s. The alternative—full inclusion—has been proposed as a way of serving all students effectively. However, the presumption that a single model of service delivery can effectively meet the needs of *all* students inevitably dilutes the focus on individuals that is the hallmark of special education. "Because of its wholesale nature, the concept of inclusion contradicts the individualization that is central to a 'special' education" (Manset & Semmel, 1997, p. 176). Overenthusiasm for inclusion may bring what Zigmond and Baker (1996) call "too much of a good thing."

> Based on our research, we cannot support elimination of a continuum of services for students with LD. Inclusion is good; full inclusion may be too much of a good thing . . . .
>
> Scheduling and excessive case loads have prevented special education teachers from accomplishing their intended purposes. Nevertheless, for students with LD, there are skills and strategies that need to be acquired if instruction in the mainstream is to be meaningful and productive, and these skills and strategies must be taught explicitly and intensively. Providing a venue and the resources for delivering this instruction is not only our moral obligation to students with LD, it is also our obligation under the law. (p. 33)

Zigmond and Baker (1996) and Marston (1996) note that proponents of full inclusion recommend the drastic reduction, if not the complete elimination, of all models but those keeping students with disabilities in regular classrooms on a full-time basis. However, research does not support such drastic measures, and many leaders now note the necessity of maintaining the full continuum of placement options that has characterized special education and that is required by IDEA. Marston (1996) concludes:

> The movement toward full inclusion of special education students in general education settings has brought special education to a crossroads and stirred considerable debate on its future direction. Proponents of full inclusion argue that the needs of students with disabilities are best met in the general education setting. For these supporters, the direction to take is to reduce, if not eliminate, special education as a service delivery model. Some critics of full inclusion argue for a different direction, one that returns the special education focus to unique instructional settings such as the resource room. (p. 129)
>
> What is needed in special education is not a retreat from the basic principles that support a continuum of services for students with disabilities, but rather a renewed commitment to the thoughtful deployment of these ideas. Serious attention to the least restrictive environment, including a shared philosophy and commitment by general and special educators, will insure that a variety of learning opportunities across educational settings will exist for all students. (p. 131)

WHAT IS THE EFFECTIVENESS OF SERVICE DELIVERY MODELS?

For those who want to make decisions about service delivery issues based on reliable evidence about outcomes for students, research is critical. Consequently, there has been great interest in finding out which service delivery model produces the best outcomes. Research to date does not provide evidence that any one service delivery model meets the needs of all students, particularly all students with learning disabilities (Deno et al., 1996; Manset & Semmel, 1997; Marston, 1996; Zigmond & Baker, 1996). The research most often cited as evidence that inclusive models are successful was done with students having severe physical and/or cognitive disabilities, not students with learning disabilities.

Research Issues

Much of the research intended to shed light on the effectiveness of various placement options (e.g., special self-contained classes, resource rooms) has actually done little but demonstrate the difficulty of doing such research. Three major problems have frustrated researchers: (1) disagreement about the choice and adequacy of the outcome measures (i.e., about the criteria for stating that one plan "works better" than another), (2) inability to assign students randomly to the different placements that are to be compared, and (3) difficulty in separating the effects of a type of placement from the quality of education that is offered in that place. Besides these difficulties in doing research, misunderstanding and misinterpretation of research findings also contribute to the controversy.

Definition of "Works Better"

When someone says that one service delivery plan works or is better than another, it is often difficult to know exactly what he or she means. By "works better," some might mean that students, teachers, administrators, or parents report positive impressions of the plan, regardless of any objective evidence of improved student achievement. To others, the phrase might mean that the student's academic achievement is significantly higher; that achievement is about the same, but the cost is lower; that the cost is the same, but achievement is lower; or that both cost and achievement are lower, but the student is spending more time in contact with nondisabled peers. In short, the criteria for "works better" can involve preferences, academic achievement, cost, contact or friendships with nondisabled students, or some other criterion or combination of criteria. Furthermore, researchers may agree about what should be measured, but not agree about how to measure it. For example, some researchers may feel that the specific tests, questionnaires, interviews, observation techniques, or other instruments used in a given study are poorly designed. Thus, there are many possible points of controversy among people who do the research. In addition, those who read the research sometimes misinterpret findings by failing to note what the outcome measures were in a given study, not examining the particulars of the research, or making overgeneralized statements about the findings (Gerber, 1995).

Random Assignment of Students to Classes

One of the most serious flaws in most studies of the effectiveness of special self-contained classes, resource rooms, and all other service delivery plans is the failure to assign students randomly to the types of placements being compared (Hallahan &

Kauffman, 1994). For research purposes, random assignment is critically important, for it is the best way to ensure that students are not being selected on the basis of the nature or severity of their problems. For example, if a researcher shows that students placed in regular classes achieve more than those placed in special classes but has failed to assign students randomly, we cannot rule out the possibility that the students placed in regular classes had less severe problems or higher ability than those placed in special classes (Osborne, Schulte, & McKinney, 1991). As necessary as random assignment is for research purposes, it is difficult to achieve, for understandable reasons. Few parents or educators want to see children used as research "guinea pigs." Besides, IDEA requires that students be placed in the least restrictive environment in which the appropriate education specified in their IEPs can be ensured. The need for sound research to tell us what produces better outcomes is sometimes in direct conflict with the need to do what we assume or believe but do not know (based on research) is best for students.

Separation of Effects of Place from Effects of Instruction

Even if we have research in which students are randomly assigned to different service delivery plans and adequate measures of the outcomes are used, we must be cautious in interpreting the findings. The instruction and social experiences offered may be considerably more important than the type of class in which they occur. There is no "magic," in regular or special classes, and placement may actually be a minor factor, compared to instruction, in determining outcomes (Kauffman, 1993b, 1994). *What* happens to students is perhaps more important than *where* it happens. Thus, if studies comparing special and regular classes do not make sure that the same instructional methods are used—and that they are used consistently and skillfully in both types of placement—then the results may tell us more about instruction than about placement. A fair comparison of different service delivery models must invest equal resources in each model and provide equal attention to ensuring the quality of instruction in each (Zigmond et al., 1995).

Misunderstanding and Misinterpreting Research Findings

Numerous studies of the effects of service delivery models have been done, but most have been so seriously flawed that the results are not reliable (Hallahan & Kauffman, 1994; MacMillan, Semmel, & Gerber, 1994). Reviews of these studies and commentaries on the findings of both individual studies and research syntheses have sometimes compounded the problem by presenting a distorted picture of what research has actually shown. For example, critics of special education have frequently cited Carlberg and Kavale's (1980) statistical synthesis of previous research to buttress the argument that education in separate settings (i.e., special self-contained classes and resource rooms) is ineffective and that inclusive education (i.e., placement in regular classes) produces better outcomes for students with disabilities (e.g., Baker, Wang, & Walberg, 1994; Lipsky & Gartner, 1987, 1991). Gartner and Lipsky (1989) suggested that Carlberg and Kavale's work leads to the conclusion that there is "little or no benefit for students of all levels of severity placed in special education settings" (p. 13).

Carlberg and Kavale's analysis did show that regular classroom placement produced slightly better results than special class placement when all types of students were considered together and when students with below-average IQ were considered alone. However, special class placement produced substantially better outcomes than regular class placement for students classified as having learning disabilities (LD) and emotional or behavioral disorders (EBD or ED/BD).

> For LD and BD/ED children in special classes . . . an improvement of 11 percentile ranks resulted from their placement. Thus, the average BD/ED or LD student in special class placement was better off than 61% of his/her counterparts in regular class . . . . When exceptional children were placed in special classes on the basis of low IQ, they did not respond as well as their regular class counterparts. The situation was reversed with respect to LD and BD/ED children, who were found to show greater improvement in the special class. A 99% confidence interval around the ES [effect size] for the LD and BD/ED categories ranged from 0.7 to .75; there is a high probability that these children demonstrate a better response in special classes than their counterparts in regular classes. (Carlberg & Kavale, 1980, pp. 301–302)

The common misunderstanding or misinterpretation of Carlberg and Kavale (1980) is but one example of the ways research findings can be distorted to support a particular point of view regarding service delivery. A dispassionate review of all the available research indicates that the evidence for the effectiveness of all service delivery models is mixed. Some studies have found evidence to support the model; others have not (Manset & Semmel, 1997; Zigmond & Baker, 1996). Claims that a given service delivery plan has been successful for all students with learning disabilities should therefore be viewed with considerable skepticism. Although there has been much enthusiasm for programs of full inclusion, the results of three major research projects in which the effects of inclusion on students with learning disabilities were carefully evaluated were disappointing: "Taken together, the findings from these three studies suggest that general education settings produce achievement outcomes for students with LD that are neither desirable nor acceptable" (Zigmond et al., 1995, p. 539). Zigmond et al. (1995) found that although some students in inclusionary programs made adequate academic progress, about half of them did not. The achievement outcomes were disappointing even though "these three projects invested tremendous amounts of resources—both financial and professional—into the enhancement of services for students with LD in the mainstream setting" (p. 539). Given the mixed findings of research, it is perhaps understandable that many advocates for students with learning disabilities call for the full range of placement options to be maintained.

Final Note on Service Delivery

The legal, philosophical, and research issues discussed here suggest that we should be cautious about promoting a particular service delivery model or saying that research has provided much guidance for selecting service delivery models. Therefore, our first concern should be improving instruction wherever it is offered; we should be more concerned about the integrity of the services delivered than about the location in which they occur (Crockett & Kauffman, in press; Kauffman, 1994). Our second concern should be finding out where instruction of a given type can be delivered most effectively (Kauffman & Lloyd, 1995; Kauffman, Lloyd, Astuto, & Hallahan, 1995). Our third concern should be helping students understand that no shame or stigma is attached to receiving the special instruction one needs, being taught by a specialist, or going to a special place to receive that instruction (Bateman, 1994; Hallahan & Kauffman, 1994).

Educating students with learning disabilities in the least restrictive environment is an important facet of service delivery. But what is the least restrictive environment for a student? Cruickshank (1977) noted that we must ask whether we are talking about physical or psychological restriction. Students can be in a regular class, which is assumed to be least physically restrictive, but be severely restricted in their learning and social relationships. The degree of psychological restrictiveness is very much a matter of individual differences in perception and behavior (Kauffman & Hallahan, 1997). As Gallagher (1993) stated, "An everyday setting that inclines one individual to feel and function well can push another in the opposite direction" (p. 18). Because the restrictiveness of an environment has multiple dimensions and highly individual meanings, a diversity of service delivery models must be constructed to meet the intent of the LRE provision of IDEA—"ensuring that [each individual] student has basic needs met and is travelling a well thought-out road to a career and a satisfying life style" (Gallagher, 1994, p. 528).

Summary

1. What laws govern the delivery of special education?
   a. The principle law governing special education is the federal law known as IDEA (Individuals with Disabilities Education Act). Its provisions include:
      (1) an individualized education plan (IEP) detailing the student's needs and the services to be provided
      (2) an appropriate education at no expense to parents or guardians (i.e., at public expense)
      (3) placement in the least restrictive environment compatible with the student's needs and allowing as much access to the general education curriculum as possible
      (4) a continuum of alternative placements ranging from regular classrooms in neighborhood schools to special classes and schools designed for students with disabilities
2. How is special education defined?
   a. Special education is instruction designed to meet the unusual or unique needs of the individual student with disabilities. It includes:
      (1) special training and support for teachers
      (2) reduced class or group size and controlled class composition

(3) individualization and a high degree of teacher direction
(4) frequent and accurate pupil assessment
(5) precision in implementation of instructional strategies
(6) close monitoring of instructional progress
(7) empirical validation of teaching practices

(b) Special education includes related services that are necessary for the student to benefit from special instruction, such as physical and occupational therapies, recreation, speech and language therapy, psychological services, counseling, and, in some cases, medical diagnostic services.

(c) A continuum of alternative placements is necessary to realize the goals of IDEA, because it is impossible to offer all types of instruction simultaneously in the same place.

3. What are six service delivery models for educating exceptional students?
Six alternative models are:
(a) collaborative consultation, in which general and special educators work together in regular classrooms without pulling students out for special instruction
(b) co-teaching, in which the general and special educator team up to teach a class together, usually serving a group of students with disabilities and a group of students without disabilities who are combined in one class (Thus, it is not apparent that the class is "special.")
c. resource room, in which the special education teacher pulls students into a special class for instruction only in specific areas in which the students have difficulties, perhaps for as little as 30 minutes several times a week, perhaps as much as half of each school day
d. special self-contained class, which is generally thought to be appropriate for students who need a more highly structured and intensive instructional and behavior management program than can be afforded in a regular classroom, usually serving a dozen or fewer students with a special education teacher and a paraprofessional
e. special day school, designed to serve a special student clientele during the entire school day but not before or after school hours
f. residential school, in which students live in dormitories or other residential units, at least during the school week, if not seven days a week, and attend a special school on the campus

4. What are some issues in service delivery models for special education?
a. Teaching students in inclusive settings can be a rewarding and successful experience, but it often is not, due to poor planning and inadequate resources to support it.
b. Maintaining a continuum of alternative placements is not only necessary to provide appropriate education for all students, but a requirement of IDEA.

5. What does research suggest about the effectiveness of service delivery models for students with learning disabilities?

a. Definition of what "works better" is problematic, and controversy is often a result of failure to agree about what outcomes indicate what "works."
b. Random assignment of students to classes is often not accomplished, meaning that the results of studies are not definitive.
c. Separation of effects of place from effects of instruction is often impossible, meaning that studies are inconclusive regarding placement options.
d. Misunderstanding and misinterpretation of research findings are frequent.
e. Greater attention should be given to the quality of instruction that students are given, regardless of the place they are taught.

6

Parents and Families

Historically, parents of children with learning disabilities have played a critical role in advocating for services for their children. In fact, the area of learning disabilities has probably been influenced by parents more than any other area of special education. It was largely through the efforts of a parent group known as the Association for Children with Learning Disabilities (now known as the Learning Disabilities Association [LDA] of America) in the 1960s that the category of learning disabilities was created. Although teachers and administrators tended to view the academic difficulties of some students as due to laziness or obstinacy, parents argued long and vociferously that their children had bona fide learning problems that needed special attention. Their efforts have paid off in funding and legislation for learning disabilities programs.

HOW HAVE PROFESSIONALS' VIEWS OF PARENTS CHANGED?

Professionals' views of the role of parents of children with disabilities have changed dramatically. At one time, it was common for professionals to discount or ignore the concerns of parents regarding their children's development or, worse, automatically blame parents for their children's learning and social problems. The neurological organization theory of the late 1950s and 1960s is an example of how parents were sometimes blamed for the learning problems of their children. This theory held that external manipulation of the limbs of children with learning disabilities would remediate supposedly damaged pathways of the brain and hence improve these children's reading ability (Delacato, 1959). Not only did research fail to demonstrate the effectiveness of this treatment approach, but the program was soundly criticized for placing undue stress on parents to carry out the treatment regimen strictly (Robbins & Glass, 1969). In 1968, several professional and parent organizations adopted an official statement listing concerns about this approach, including the following:

> 1. Promotional methods . . . appear to put parents in a position where they cannot refuse such treatment without calling into question their adequacy and motivation as parents;
> 2. The regimens prescribed are so demanding and inflexible . . . that they may lead to neglect of other family members' needs;
> 3. It is asserted that if therapy is not carried out as rigidly prescribed, the child's potential will be damaged, and that anything less than 100% effort is useless. (quoted in Hallahan & Cruickshank, 1973, p. 94)

Because of its popularity, this treatment program was much publicized for its allegedly questionable treatment of parents; however, one could make the case that its view of parents was not that atypical for the time. Many professionals, including teachers, viewed parents with little respect, focusing on the negative rather than the positive contributions they could make toward their children's development.

Today, however, the knowledgeable professional understands that parents can play a critical part in helping meet the needs of children with disabilities. Although there are still far too many instances in which teachers ignore or blame parents and although there are undoubtedly some parents who are detrimental to their children's progress, teachers and parents are increasingly working together for the benefit of students with learning disabilities. There have been at least two reasons for this shift toward a more positive working relationship: the recognition of reciprocal effects and the use of individualized family service plans.

Reciprocal Effects

Evidence has accumulated that not only can parents influence the development of their children, but also the reverse can occur—children can exert effects on their parents. This concept is referred to as **reciprocal effects,** the notion that causation between child and adult behavior can go in either direction (Bell & Harper, 1977). Researchers, for example, have shown that some babies, especially those with disabilities, are born with difficult temperaments, which can influence how their parents respond to them (Brooks-Gunn & Lewis, 1984; Mahoney & Robenalt, 1986). This body of research has made professionals more aware that parents are not necessarily to blame for their children's behavioral and learning problems. These findings have also helped teachers gain a better understanding of why some parents of children with learning disabilities sometimes act differently than other parents. That is, it is not difficult to imagine how living with a child with learning disabilities might put parents under stress.

Individualized Family Service Plans

A second reason professionals are now working more closely with parents is that Congress has passed laws stipulating that they be given the opportunity for more involvement. The reauthorization of IDEA, the Individuals with Disabilities Education Act of 1997 (first passed as P.L. 94-142 in 1975), stipulates that schools make a good faith effort to include parents of children with disabilities in the development of their individualized education program (IEP). Federal law (P.L. 99-457) also dictates that parents of children under three years of age be involved in the design of an individualized family service plan (IFSP), which specifies services for the child as well as the family.

Research and legislation have thus created a greater appreciation of the importance of being able to work constructively with families of students with disabilities. Most children, after all, spend a much greater percentage of their time with their parents and families than they do with individual teachers. To ignore parents is to miss out on a potentially powerful source of support for teachers.

WHAT TREATMENT MODELS ARE USED WITH FAMILIES?

Recognizing the potentially positive influence parents of children with disabilities can have in the treatment of their children, professionals are more likely than they once were to involve parents as much as possible in the treatment process. It is no longer as common as it once was for professionals to view themselves as the sole source of expertise and parents as the recipients of that expertise. Gaining in popularity are **family-centered models** of treatment, which adopt the consumer-driven philosophy that professionals work *for* families in seeking ways to increase their decision-making power (Dunst, Johanson, Trivette, & Hamby, 1991).

Today's approaches to working with families are also characterized by attention to social systems. Bronfenbrenner (1979), a renowned child development and family theorist, was one of the first to promote a **social systems approach** to understanding behavior. It posits that an individual's behavior can be best understood by considering the context in which it occurs, a significant part of which is the family. Bronfenbrenner stressed that the family, in turn, is influenced by other social systems, such as the extended family (e.g., grandparents), friends, and professionals. The philosophy that there is a reciprocal relationship between a person's behavior and that of family members and that there is a reciprocal relationship between the family and society has had an impact on how the field views the role of the family in the educational process.

Several practitioners and researchers have developed models that take into account the fact that persons fit within families and families fit within a broader social context. Two such models are the family systems approach of the Turnbulls (Turnbull & Turnbull, 1996) and the social support systems approach of Dunst and colleagues (Dunst, Trivette, & Deal, 1988). These frameworks are helpful in understanding the role of families in the educational process.

Family Systems Approach

The **family systems model** consists of four interrelated components: family characteristics, family interaction, family functions, and family life cycle.

Family Characteristics

Descriptive information on the family is referred to as **family characteristics.** These include characteristics of the disability (e.g., type and severity), characteristics of the family (e.g., size and cultural background), personal characteristics of each family member (e.g., health), and special conditions (e.g., child abuse or poverty).

These family characteristics are important considerations for teachers when working with students with learning disabilities. Although it is not always the case, such things as poverty, abuse, or ill health of family members can make it difficult for the family to offer support for the child with learning disabilities. Parents are living under more stress than ever, and even financially stable families whose members are in the best of health can operate under considerable stress in just meeting the demands of living in a complex society (Hallahan, 1992). As a result, parents may be distracted and seem uninterested or otherwise nonsupportive of their children's education when, in fact, they are doing the best they can to cope.

Family Interaction

Interaction among family members can range from facilitative to dysfunctional. Cohesion and adaptability determine the quality of family interaction. **Cohesion** refers to the degree to which individual family members are free to act independently. Parents of children with learning disabilities often struggle with how much freedom to give their children. Research has shown that parents of children with learning disabilities have a tendency to be overprotective (Green, 1992). Although parents may want to encourage independence in their children, they are also aware that these children require more than the usual amount of supervision. For example, the parents of a young child who has difficulties with directions (a relatively common characteristic of children with learning disabilities) may wrestle with whether they should allow him or her to go alone to visit friends in the neighborhood. Similarly, the parents of a teenager who is highly distractible, impulsive, and has poor coordination may debate whether to let him or her obtain a driver's license.

Adaptability refers to the amount of flexibility family members display in their interactions with one another. Some family members can be very rigid, which makes it difficult for them to adjust to the variable behavior often displayed by children with learning disabilities. Some family members may be so unpredictable or chaotic in their responses that it increases their children's problem behavior. Maintaining the proper amount of adaptability can be very difficult when dealing with children with learning disabilities. It is important that parents be able to "roll with the punches" while maintaining a degree of firmness that communicates appropriate expectations for behavior.

Family Functions

The many activities in which families engage to meet their everyday needs are considered **family functions.** Families must do a wide variety of things to meet their economic, medical, social, and educational needs. All of these competing demands on the family can make it difficult for parents to be as involved in the education of their children as some teachers would like. Parents of children with learning disabilities tend to be relatively passive participants in IEP meetings (Vaughn, Bos, Harrell, & Lasky, 1988). Teachers need to keep in mind, however, that, although parental involvement is ideal, there may be good reasons for some parents being less than totally engaged in their child's education. Minimal parental involvement may indicate apathy, or it may signify that the family is overwhelmed in meeting its other living demands. A single parent with three children, one with learning disability and another with serious medical problems, for example, may decide to leave educational matters up to the schools because he or she has neither the time nor the energy to meet with school personnel.

Family Life Cycle

The impact that a child with a disability has on the family varies according to the stage of the **family life cycle.** In the early childhood years, for example, there may be little impact on parents of children with learning disabilities because these children are usually not identified as having problems until they enter school. The early elementary years, however, are typically a time of much unrest. Usually at this time, parents and siblings are learning to adjust to the child's disability, and parents are faced with myriad decisions pertaining to diagnosis and treatment. Adolescence is a period of turmoil for many families as teenagers strive to find their own identities. For families of children with learning disabilities, adolescence can be even more rocky. Issues pertaining to such things as dating, planning for postsecondary education or work, and interactions with peers are all likely to be more problematic for teenagers with learning disabilities. As we discuss in Chapter 8, most adults with learning disabilities will struggle to some degree with their problems throughout their lives.

Social Support Systems Approach

The **social support systems model** stresses the importance of informal rather than formal sources of support for families. Instead of immediately assuming that families need to rely solely on professionals for help, this model proposes that families turn to friends, neighbors, social clubs, and extended family members for support. Although Dunst and colleagues probably had in mind families who have children with relatively severe disabilities, one can also make the case that this model would apply for families of children with learning disabilities. These parents might not be as likely to need respite care, but they might benefit from at least having someone with whom they can share their concerns and worries. And if their child has been recently diagnosed, they can also learn from others whose children with learning disabilities are older.

Some authorities have lamented the decline in the number of informal sources of support available in our society (Zigler & Black, 1989). Families are more geographically and psychologically isolated from one another than was once the case. Poverty has taken a toll on families, sapping their resolve to become involved with neighborhood resources, and even those who are not in poverty live hectic lives that interfere with developing and drawing on informal sources of support.

When families do not have their own sources of informal support, a social systems approach attempts to help establish them. Putting families in contact with the local chapter of the LDA, for example, can help them get in touch with other parents for support as well as valuable information on child-rearing approaches and educational options.

WHAT ARE SOME CURRENT TRENDS IN AMERICAN FAMILY LIFE?

Students and their families can belong to a number of different cultural groups. They are part of a **macroculture,** a national or shared culture, as well as several **microcultures,** smaller groups sharing values, styles of living, frames of reference, and identities (Banks, 1994). Figure 6.1 portrays how the individual and his or her family can belong to several microcultures. These microcultural groups can have a profound influence on families and how they respond to having a child with a learning disability.

With each passing year, the number and diversity of microcultures in America continue to grow. This growth is due to a number of factors, especially the influx of immigrants. Three important, interrelated areas of diversity that teachers need to be aware of are the family unit; race, ethnicity, and language; and socioeconomic status.

The Family Unit

Whereas 30 years ago it was possible to describe the typical family in the United States as consisting of a father and mother with only the father working outside the home, today it is difficult to portray a typical family because of the wide assortment of family configurations in existence. There has been a rapid expansion of the number of families in which both parents work outside the home as well as of single-parent families. Although not great in number, there have also been increases in other nontraditional families (e.g., gay and lesbian couples who have adopted or given birth using surrogate fathers or mothers).

Race, Ethnicity, and Language

Demographers have projected that by the beginning of the next century, over one-third of the school population will be students of color. In California and Texas and in the 25 largest cities, children of color already constitute over half the student population (Gollnick & Chinn, 1994). In schools in and around large cities, it is not unusual to find over a dozen different languages representing students' primary language.

Although it is dangerous to generalize about individuals based on their cultural backgrounds (see Box 6.1), it behooves teachers to be aware of some of the most common cultural differences they will likely encounter. There are at least three areas in which teachers should be alert for cultural differences: family structure, discipline, and communication style.

Family Structure

Teachers may be used to dealing with the student's mother and/or father in the typical white family. In some ethnic groups, however, the extended family plays an important role in the student's life, and the teacher needs to be prepared to consider these "extra" adults when communicating with the family. In some African American and Mexican American families, for example, decisions pertaining to children are made in consultation with extended family members and sometimes with local community organizations such as churches (Salend & Taylor, 1993). Likewise, in Native American families, the clan and tribe can play a critical role in matters related to children's education.

Within the family unit, too, there can be definite role differentiations for different cultural groups. For example, in some Mexican American families, the father is the

FIGURE 6.1 The Individual's and Family's Relationship to Different Microcultural Groups

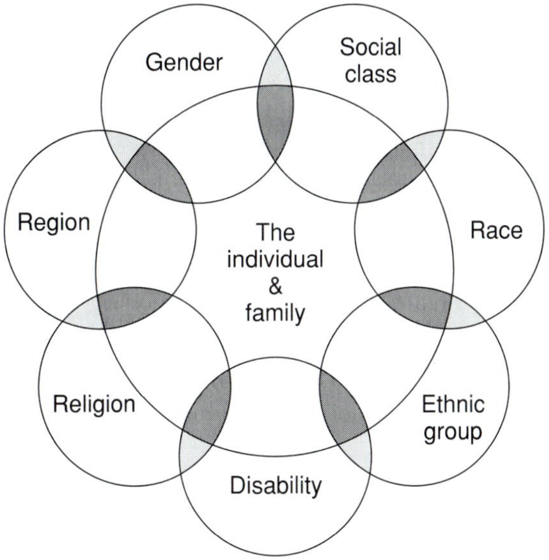

Source: Adapted from *Multiethnic Education: Theory and Practice,* 3rd ed. (p. 89) by J. A. Banks, 1994, Boston: Allyn & Bacon. Copyright 1994 by Allyn & Bacon. Reprinted by permission.

chief decision maker in financial matters, and the mother is in charge of child care. Knowing who wields the power in particular matters can help teachers in their interactions with families.

Discipline

How parents reward and punish their children is also culturally determined to a degree. For example, some have stated that physical punishment is more prevalent among poor urban African American families and that shame is sometimes used by Asian American parents as a way of showing displeasure with their children. At times, such cultural differences may raise for teachers the question of whether the disciplinary practices are abusive (McIntyre & Silva, 1992). Many teachers who come from the dominant white middle-class culture may find themselves in a quandary over how to handle parental discipline practices with which they are unfamiliar. At the least, they may be faced with trying not to overreact to what they consider inappropriate; at the most, they may struggle with whether they should report suspected child abuse. In any case, knowing the cultural norms for discipline in families is of utmost utility.

BOX 6.1 *MULTICULTURAL PERSPECTIVES*

Are There Distinct Cultures in the United States?

Although there is merit in the U.S. school system's attempts to recognize cultural differences among the families it serves, the idea of unique, clearly differentiated "cultures" is confounded by the tremendous cultural variation *within* identified minority groups. By emphasizing cultural differences and ignoring the diversity within ethnic groups, we may actually be supporting ethnic stereotypes. The following excerpt from a report of a study based on in-depth interviews with second-wave Southeast Asian immigrants (Smith & Tarallo, 1993) suggests that educators should be wary of assuming that individuals who come from this ethnic group are likely to experience exceptional success in school:

The Unsettling Resettlement of Vietnamese Boat People

> The practice of similar customs and traditions by both first- and second-wave immigrants from Vietnam to Sacramento conceals real differences between their patterns of adaptation to American life. The diversity often is masked by the promotion by the popular media of the Vietnamese as the contemporary model minority through images of strong family unity, children as valedictorians, and successful businessmen. . . . In fact, discussing the Vietnamese by extrapolating from the backgrounds and experiences of the most well-equipped first-wave settlers tends to ignore the splits both within and between them and the second-wave refugees. . . .
>
> The adjustment of the first wave is attributable in part to their social backgrounds in Vietnam—many refugees were from urban areas, educated, with professional and military experience. . . . Their relatively high educational and occupational backgrounds, plus their familiarity with urban living and exposure to Western culture, helped to contribute to their relatively successful adaptation.
>
> The situation of the second-wave refugees has been quite different. Arriving from 1979 onward, they generally are less educated, not as well off financially, and often from rural areas with limited exposure to Western culture. . . .
>
> What some have called the "politics of difference" exists as much within as between new immigrant groups in their relations with each other and their new society. The shapers of public expectations of receptivity or opposition to the new minorities often fail to give due recognition to the complexity of these internal differences, thus contributing to the development of new ethnic and racial stereotypes. (Smith & Tarallo, 1993, pp. 27–29)

In a study of parenting attitudes, behaviors, and parental involvement in children's education, researchers compared survey responses from a total of 3,511 male and female African American, Hispanic, Caucasian, and Asian American parents (Julian, McHenry, & McKelvey, 1994). The analysis of responses to 21 questions about parenting children 5 to 18 years old revealed a variety of significant differences on 10 of the questions. Despite the array of differences, the authors stated:

> There were far more cultural similarities than differences found when socioeconomic status was controlled. It should also be noted that the percentage of variance accounted for by culture did not exceed 4% on any of the dependent measures. These data suggest that although there are some cultural differences in parenting, these differences are not as extensive as would be predicted by cultural variant models and related literature. . . . Within-group diversity makes it extremely difficult to develop monolithic schemes for examining the structures and functions of racial and ethnic minority families. (p. 35)

According to these researchers, the general lack of cultural differences suggests that parents from different cultural groups are more alike than differ-

BOX 6.1 *continued*

ent. However, practitioners should be aware that cultural groups may vary widely, depending on factors such as level of acculturation, specific ethnic group, and economic background. The authors did note that "the cultural variations that were detected in this study indicated that the ethnic parents in this study were perhaps stricter—placing greater demands and expectations on their children because of the difficulty they perceive their children to face" and that "instead of being the model minority, many Asian-Americans are disadvantaged and require special services" (p. 36). They also pointed out that there were as many differences between the perceptions of fathers and mothers as there were variations by cultural group.

The importance of this study and others like it is that they illustrate the diversity within and among cultural groups and the range of issues that need to be addressed. More research regarding practices specifically related to parenting children with disabilities is needed before educators and other practitioners can be said to understand cultural differences and their implications for instruction of children and collaboration with parents.

Communication Styles

How parents approach meetings with school personnel may differ according to their cultural background (Salend & Taylor, 1993). For example, some Asian American and Mexican American parents are much more deferential toward authority figures such as teachers, psychologists, and principals. Their reluctance to question authority can make it more difficult to find out exactly what they are thinking about their child's education. For example, they might be less likely than a white parent to offer suggestions regarding their child's education at an IEP meeting. Another challenge for teachers concerns how much to respect a parent's desire not to be involved in the child's education versus how much to encourage parental involvement.

Socioeconomic Status

Teachers are also involved with increasing numbers of families in poverty. Whereas the number of 3- and 4-year-olds increased by 16% in the 1980s, the number of these same children in poverty grew by 28% (U.S. Senate Committee on Labor and Human Relations, 1993). The U.S. Census Bureau reports that 38.1 million Americans, about 15% of the population, live below the poverty level (U.S. Census Bureau, 1996). The rate of poverty is even higher for children, with about one in five children living in poverty—that is, in an environment of substandard housing, malnutrition, and inadequate health care (Baumeister, Kupstas, & Klindworth, 1990). The factor of poverty is related to the factors of family unit and ethnic diversity in that poverty is disproportionately represented in single-parent families and ethnic minority groups. For example, 46% of African American children and 41% of Hispanic children live in poverty, compared to 14% of white children (Children's Defense Fund, 1995).

Because of its relationship with poor health care, inadequate nutrition, and so forth, poverty not only places children at greater risk of having a disability, but also affects how families are able to cope with the child once he or she has a disability. Severely strained financial and psychological resources may seriously impede a family's ability to work with school personnel.

WHAT IS THE FAMILY'S ROLE?

Families are amazingly complicated phenomena to study. So-called normal families are fertile ground for a variety of intricate interactions, both positive and negative. Most of us have strong reactions to and memories about our families. We can recall vividly the good and bad times we experienced. And it is not uncommon to receive very different interpretations of family dynamics from different members of the same family. Families that contain a member with learning disabilities are even more complicated. Just the extra time required to parent a child with learning disabilities can alter how parents and siblings interact with the child who has learning disabilities as well as with nondisabled family members.

Family Adjustment

For many years, the customary way of viewing parental reactions was to consider them in terms of stage theory—the notion that parents, on learning that their child has a disability, go through a set sequence of emotional reactions over a period of time. Much of the impetus for a stage theory approach comes from work done on reactions people have to the death of a loved one. A typical sequence of reactions, based on interviews of parents of infants with serious physical disabilities, is shock and disruption, denial, sadness, anxiety and fear, anger, and adaptation (Drotar, Baskiewicz, Irvin, Kennell, & Klaus, 1975). Although such a theoretical framework has been more popular when considering children with more serious disabilities, some professionals have used it in working with parents of children with learning disabilities.

More recently, many researchers have rejected the idea of a fixed sequence of stages through which all parents of students with disabilities pass (Turnbull & Turnbull, 1996). Some parents do not experience some of these stages; of those who do, not all experience them in the same order. One particularly controversial stage in the area of learning disabilities is that of denial. In fact, professionals have had a tendency to accuse parents of "doctor shopping"—going from one physician, psychologist, or educator to another in search of someone who will come up with a diagnosis of learning disabilities or attention deficit hyperactivity disorder. Although there are undoubtedly parents who deny that there is anything wrong with their child when in fact the child has a learning disability, parents probably more commonly complain that schools do not recognize that their child has a bona fide learning disability. Many parents say they have known there was something wrong with their child but were told by teachers, psychologists, or physicians that the child would outgrow it or was simply being lazy.

Parental Guilt

Of the many emotions parents may feel when they first learn that their child has a disability, perhaps the most common is guilt. This reaction may occur because the causes of most disabilities are unknown (see Chapter 2). Some parents respond to this uncertainty about cause by blaming themselves for their child's disability.

A factor that has begun to receive a great deal of attention as a causal agent is that of heredity. There are, however, no quick and easy tests to determine that a child has inherited a learning disability from one or both parents. This leads many parents to speculate that their child may have inherited a learning disability from them. For some, this can arouse feelings of guilt; for others, a biological explanation may help alleviate guilt and even help explain some of their own problems.

Parental Stress

Raising any child can be stressful. Although helping children to negotiate the many pitfalls of childhood and adolescence can be very rewarding, the responsibility for the well-being of a child in a society that is undergoing as many changes as ours can be overwhelming. Influences on children of the media, violence, and drugs, to mention a few, make being a parent complex and difficult.

There is abundant evidence that being the parent of a child with learning disabilities increases the chances of experiencing stress (Dyson, 1996; Green, 1992; Konstantareas & Homatidis, 1989; Margalit & Almougy, 1991; Margalit, Raviv, & Ankonina, 1992). Although the deficits of learning disabilities are often not as conspicuous as those of children with physical or psychological disabilities, the very fact that students with learning disabilities do function within or close to the mainstream may ironically create some very difficult decisions for parents and students, especially during adolescence. In particular, parents of adolescents with learning disabilities are likely to have difficulty deciding how much freedom and independence to allow (Morrison & Zetlin, 1992). For example, deciding when the child is ready to assume the responsibility of driving a car is often more difficult for parents of children with learning disabilities.

Another complicating factor is that many parents of children with learning disabilities exhibit external attributions; that is, they view themselves as being powerless to help their children cope with their problems (Green, 1992). How much their attributions are caused by their children's problems, or vice versa, is open to speculation, but the end result is that some of these parents either become despondent and give up trying to direct their children's lives or become overly rigid and controlling (Margalit & Almougy, 1991; Margalit et al., 1992; Michaels & Lewandowski, 1990).

Adding to the plight of some of these children with learning disabilities and their families is a higher prevalence of family instability and disruption today. Researchers have found that children with learning disabilities are more likely than those without such disabilities to experience parental divorce, change of schools, or parental or sibling death or illness (Lorsbach & Frymier, 1992). There is speculation about whether such factors are causal. That is, does a child with a learning disability make the family more susceptible to some of these disruptions, or do some of these traumas contribute to the child's learning disability? Regardless of whether there is a causal connection and in which direction it is manifest, family instability makes it difficult for some families to cope with a child who has a learning disability.

Sibling Reactions

Research on whether siblings of children with learning disabilities experience more problems in adjustment is mixed. Some siblings have trouble adjusting, some adjust well, and some report that they actually benefit from the experience (Dyson, 1996; Seligman & Darling, 1989; Senapati & Hayes, 1988). There is little doubt, however, that sisters and brothers of children with disabilities are at a greater risk of having problems in their relationships with their siblings than are siblings of children without disabilities. Resentment can build, for example, because the child with a learning disability receives more attention from parents. It is often difficult for parents to provide an equal amount of care and attention to the child with a learning disability and to his or her siblings. Furthermore, some of the same social problems children with learning disabilities have with their peers (see Chapter 9) are likely to play a role in interactions with siblings. Poor impulse control, difficulties in reading social cues, and so forth can make for volatile sibling relationships.

Family Adjustment

Although a number of problems can confront families of children with learning disabilities, the majority of families adapt very well. Some parents experience having a child with a disability as actually having some positive benefits. They say they have become more concerned about social issues and more tolerant of differences in other people; some believe that their families and marriages have been brought closer together because of their child's disability. They think that the common purpose of rallying behind their child has resulted in greater family cohesiveness.

Professionals working with children with learning disabilities and their families must keep in mind that there is no universal set of reactions experienced by these families. Most adjust well, some experience minor difficulties, and some few experience enough turmoil and stress to be considered dysfunctional.

Family Values and Attitudes toward Learning

Parents and families often play a significant role in determining the social, intellectual, and physical well-being of all children, not just those with learning disabilities. Parents can exert influence on their children through interactions with them as well as through attitudes. For example, parents can challenge their children intellectually and expose them to a variety of learning experiences, or they can subtly discourage their intellectual development through their attitudes toward school and learning.

Perhaps there is no better example of how important families can be to the academic achievement of their children than that of Southeast Asian boat children who have immigrated to the United States. Despite severe economic disadvantages, many of these children do exceedingly well in school. In particular, Indochinese families that maintain their traditional values, which emphasize strong support from the family for achievement and learning, outperform their American peers of the same economic status. However, if Indochinese families allow their children to become acculturated to certain American values (e.g., pursuing material possessions and entertainment), the achievement of these children is lower, being closer to that of their American peers (Caplan, Choy, & Whitmore, 1992).

Regardless of which cultural group one belongs to, children whose parents value education are at an advantage. And for the child with learning disabilities, it is even more important that the family instill a positive attitude toward learning and school.

Parents and Homework

Ask parents of children with learning disabilities what their greatest areas of concern regarding schooling for their children are, and they are very likely to put homework at the top of the list. Ask teachers whether this concern is valid, and they are very likely to concur. Several researchers have documented that parents and teachers view homework as a major stumbling block for students with learning disabilities (Bryan & Donahue, 1994; Bryan, Nelson, & Mathur, 1995; Epstein, Polloway, Foley, & Patton, 1993; Polloway, Foley, & Epstein, 1992; Salend & Schliff, 1989). Homework can cause a great deal of stress in families of these students, as is revealed in this parent's statement: "Homework has dominated and ruined our lives for the past eight years" (Baumgartner, Bryan, Donahue, & Nelson, 1993, p. 182). Unfortunately, this negative perception of homework starts in the early primary grades (Bryan et al., 1995).

Given that students with learning disabilities have academic problems, it makes sense that they will have difficulties with homework. Not only the academic work, but also their cognitive and metacognitive difficulties cause them problems with homework (see Chapter 10). Many of their homework troubles are due to such things as poor memory and organizational skills. For example, these students are more likely than students without learning disabilities to forget to bring their homework home, to forget to take their completed homework to school, to lose their homework, not to complete their homework, and to make careless mistakes on homework. In sum, there are few aspects of homework that do not pose major problems for students with learning disabilities.

What Teachers Can Do

There are at least four ways that teachers can increase the chances of making homework a successful experience for students with learning disabilities. First, teachers, especially in elementary school, should not assign homework that emphasizes the acquisition of new information (Cooper, 1989). In the case of students with learning disabilities, it is probably even more important that the homework not require students to perform skills they have not already been taught in school. Instead, the homework should focus on proficiency and maintenance of skills already within the student's repertoire (Polloway et al., 1992).

Second, teachers need to be careful that students with learning disabilities understand their assignments. Because these students have problems listening and copying directions accurately, they often misunderstand assignments or forget them. Teachers should therefore be explicit in their assignments. Some suggestions for making sure students understand their assignments are (1) encourage students to ask questions, (2) specify resources and how much help they can get, (3) choose students to review the directions for the class, and (4) allow students to begin homework in class under the teacher's guidance (Salend & Schliff, 1989; Sawyer, Nelson, Jayanthi, Bursuck, & Epstein, 1996).

Third, teachers should set up a system whereby they can efficiently monitor students' homework. One popular method is for each student to have an assignment book wherein (1) the teacher initials the assignment before the student leaves school to make sure he or she has written it down correctly, (2) the parent signs the assignment after the student has completed it, and (3) the teacher checks it the next day at the start of class (Epstein et al., 1993).

Finally, some research suggests that involving parents in the homework process can be beneficial (Rosenberg, 1989). How much involvement is helpful will vary with the particular parents. It is a good idea, however, that teachers at least make parents aware of homework policies and seek their feedback regarding their views on homework. Communicating with parents about homework is important because, as the following quote suggests, parents are often frustrated by what they perceive to be a lack of sympathy for their plight: "Sure, I'd like to get involved, but when? There's just not enough time. I can't come home to conferences during school hours! And then the teacher makes me feel like a bad parent" (Baumgartner et al., 1993, p. 182).

What Parents Can Do

By definition, homework is done primarily at home; therefore, it is logical that parents can be influential in reducing homework problems. In addition to contingencies that most parents use with their children regarding homework (e.g., allowing the child a privilege or special reward—TV, visits with friends, etc.—if homework is finished), parents of students with learning disabilities also need to be particularly attentive to organizational factors. As already noted, it is not just academic work that may be difficult for many students with learning disabilities. These students also need help in planning and organizing their work time. First, parents can help them decide on the best time and place for their homework, assisting them in choosing a quiet, distraction-free area for studying.

Because children engage in a variety of activities in addition to homework, parents can help them by setting up a schedule of activities for the week. One team of researchers found that the systematic use of a such a schedule resulted in improvement in homework submission, grades, and school and home behavior (Sah & Borland, 1989). This home plan was instituted on a contractual basis, that is, the parents and children signed off on each day's activities. Table 6.1 shows the home plan for one of the students in the study.

TABLE 6.1 The Home Plan Form Completed for One of the Subjects

		Home Plan for ______________			
	Monday	Tuesday	Wednesday	Thursday	Friday
4:15–4:45	Home, snack	Home, snack	Home, snack	Home, snack	Home, snack
4:45–5:50	Homework: reading, math, language arts, social studies, science, Spanish	Homework: reading, math, language arts, social studies, science, Spanish	Homework: reading, math, language arts, social studies, science, Spanish	Homework: reading, math, language arts, social studies, science, Spanish	Homework: reading, math, language arts, social studies, science, Spanish
5:50–6:00	Set table	Set table	Set table	Set table	Set table
6:00–6:45	Dinner	Dinner	Dinner	Dinner	Dinner
6:45–7:20	Finish homework or Free time	Finish homework or Free time	Finish homework or Free time	Finish homework or Free time	Finish homework or Free time
7:20–8:00	Study for tests or Work on projects	Study for tests or Work on projects	Study for tests or Work on projects	Study for tests or Work on projects	Study for tests or Work on projects
8:00–8:55	Shower; reading or television	Shower; reading or television	Shower; reading or television	Shower; reading or television	Shower; reading or television
9:00	Lights out	Lights out	Lights out	Lights out	Lights out

Source: From "The Effects of a Structured Home plan on the Home and School Behaviors of Gifted Learning-Disabled Students with Deficits in Organizational Skills" by A. Sah and J. H. Borland, 1989, *Roeper Review, 12*(1), p. 55. Copyright 1989 by Roeper Review. Reprinted by permission.

What Students Can Do

Students need to take an active role in managing their own homework routine. No amount of teacher or parent involvement will be enough if the student does not have the desire to do well on homework assignments. Unfortunately, students with learning disabilities are renowned for their poor study habits. For example, when researchers interviewed students about their homework practices, those with learning disabilities differed on several questions pertaining to attention, motivation, and study skills (Gajria & Salend, 1995). Table 6.2 lists those questions on which the students with learning disabilities differed from their nondisabled peers.

One of the most difficult things students must learn is to allocate their time efficiently for homework. For many students with learning disabilities, it is not enough to

TABLE 6.2 Items Regarding Homework on Which Students with Learning Disabilities Differ from Nondisabled Peers

- After working for 30 minutes on my homework, I lose interest and quit or take a long break.
- I get easily distracted when I am doing my homework.
- It takes me a long time to begin my homework.
- I feel unsure about which homework assignment to do first.
- It takes me a very long time to do my homework, so I get tired and cannot finish my work.
- I must be reminded to start my homework.
- I need someone to do my homework with me.
- I feel teachers are unfair and give too much homework.
- I go to school without completing my homework.
- I complain about homework.
- I forget to bring my homework assignments back to class.
- I have problems completing extralong assignments such as projects and lab reports because I do not divide the work into smaller parts and work on it a little at a time.
- When I do not understand an assignment or find it too hard, I stop working on it.
- I start my homework with subjects I like and then find no time or feel too tired to complete the assignment in other subjects.
- I have difficulty estimating the time needed to complete my homework, so my homework is incomplete.
- After I finish my homework, I do not check to see that I have completed all my assignments.

Source: Adapted from *Homework Practices of Students with and without Learning Disabilities: A Comparison* by M. Gajria, & S. J. Salend, 1995. *Journal of Learning Disabilities, 28*(5), p. 294. Copyright 1995 by PRO-ED, Inc. Reprinted by permission.

set aside a block of time for homework. They need to specify when and how much time to spend on each subject. One strategy for scheduling homework uses wheels, or ovals, as visual organizers (Rooney, 1988). Figure 6.2 is an example of a time management plan for one week's homework. (Students can also use this technique to schedule each night's homework.)

Finally, parents should give careful thought to who, if anyone, will give the child direct help with homework. Depending on the particular family, a sibling, parent, or family friend might be designated as the helper. But for many students, learning disabled or not, family members and close friends are not good choices as helpers. Disagreements, arguments, and so forth that are likely to arise over other matters can interfere with the homework session. For parents who can afford it, tutors are often an excellent alternative.

FIGURE 6.2 Time Management of Weekly Homework

The following assignments are due within a week:

1. Read chapter 10 for history test on Thursday (150 pages).
2. Do math problems 14–21 on p. 28 (Tuesday).
3. Read first chapter in novel (50 pages) due on Friday.
4. Review notes for science quiz on Wednesday.
5. Complete worksheet on commas by Wednesday.

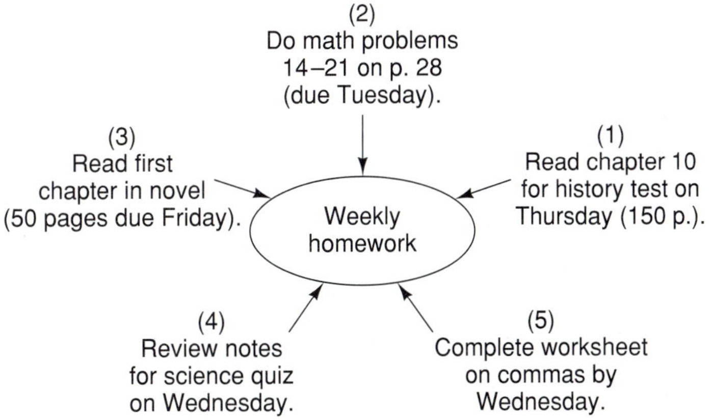

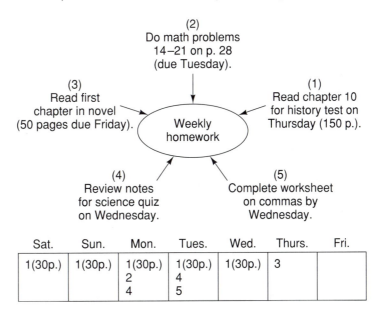

Sat.	Sun.	Mon.	Tues.	Wed.	Thurs.	Fri.
1(30p.)	1(30p.)	1(30p.) 2 4	1(30p.) 4 5	1(30p.)	3	

Source: From *Independent Strategies for Efficient Study* (p. 6) by K. Rooney, 1990. Richmond, VA: Educational Enterprises. Copyright 1990 by Educational Enterprises, Inc. Reprinted by permission.

Parents as Advocates

Even though IDEA protects the rights of students with disabilities to receive a free, appropriate education, there are times when the schools or other community agencies are not completely responsive to their needs. Even the best of schools are not perfect, and given the myriad learning and social problems presented by most students with learning disabilities, it is only natural that there are times when the student can benefit from having someone speak on his or her behalf. At some point, most parents of students with learning disabilities find it necessary to advocate for their children to ensure that they receive the best education possible.

Some parents may not be able to assume the role of advocate because of the time commitment it entails. As one manual for parents of children with learning disabilities states:

> If you do decide to undertake the role of advocate for your child, it should be with the realization that this is not a skill you will learn and then use for a year or two. Parents of LD children need to acknowledge that they will be the person (actually the only person) who has the overall picture of their child's disability, not only at a single point in time but throughout the years. You will find yourself playing the role of facilitator, coordinator, and overseer—no matter how good your child's school program and no matter how competent the professionals working with your child. That sounds like a time-consuming and perhaps exhausting prospect? It's much better to undertake the job realizing that it's a long-term commitment that will demand the best of your skills and energy than to approach the situation with the idea that your responsibilities will be to find the right school and the right teacher, and, that done, you will be able to relax while others take over. (Learning Disabilities Council, 1989, p. 12)

The Learning Disabilities Council (1989) manual for parents also recommends that parents or guardians keep a file containing information pertaining to the student's academic, health, and work experiences (see Box 6.2). This information can be used by the parent, and later by the child, to advocate for services and provisions.

As children with learning disabilities mature, they must become more and more comfortable with being their own advocates, especially after they finish secondary school. For example, it is helpful for students who attend college to know how to talk about their disability and the accommodations they need with their advisor, the staff from the office providing assistance to students with disabilities, and individual instructors.

HOW CAN COMMUNICATION BE ENHANCED BETWEEN THE FAMILY AND PROFESSIONALS?

Implicit in much of what has been said thus far is the maxim that good communication between professionals and parents is the key to successful programming for students with learning disabilities. Unfortunately, communication between parents and professionals does not always go well. This is understandable, given that parents of students with learning disabilities are often under stress and that teachers are often frustrated by the enigma of a child with complex learning and behavioral problems. Furthermore, except for parent-teacher days or nights that occur once or twice per year and annual IEP meetings, which are attended by several people and are quite formal, schools do not usually have established mechanisms for parents and teachers to meet. Unless the parent or teacher initiates contact, there is little opportunity for the two to discuss the student's progress.

The ability to work with parents can often be one of the last skills that teachers develop. Because many beginning teachers are not yet parents themselves, they may not readily empathize with the parental point of view. The sooner both teachers and parents recognize that they need each other, however, the better off the student with learning disabilities will be. Each has something to offer the other that will ultimately benefit the student. Because parents spend considerably more time with the child, they are a source of information for the teacher on the child's behavior and interests. By keeping them informed about what the student is doing in the class, the teacher can keep the parents apprised of his or her progress.

In time, most teachers are able to work with parents reasonably well. Some become truly adept at communicating with parents, having learned that being able to understand and communicate with parents enhances their own teaching. These teachers often devise creative ways to communicate with parents. Some, for example, have installed messages on their home telephone answering machines that inform parents about class assignments. Others send home periodic newsletters. And many are now communicating with parents via e-mail. We discuss two of the most common modes of communication: parent-teacher conferences and school-home note programs.

Parent-Teacher Conferences

Teachers can use parent-teacher conferences to serve at least four general purposes: (1) impart information to the parents about the student's academic and social behavior; (2) gather information from parents regarding such things as the student's interests, hobbies, and homework; (3) plan for the student's educational program; and (4) solve problems the student may be having in school (Schulz, 1987).

Some have recommended that the conference be combined with a letter and a telephone call, if possible (Kauffman, Mostert, Trent, & Hallahan, 1998). The teacher uses the phone call to indicate that a conference would be a good idea and follows up with a letter reminding the parents of the time and place of the meeting.

Planning is crucial in conducting a successful conference. Planning involves not only gathering pertinent information prior to the meeting, but also preparing for the meeting itself as well as for postconference activities. Teachers should attend to as many details as possible before the meeting. Advance preparation includes reviewing the student's cumulative records, consulting with other involved professionals, noting down problem behaviors as well as positive behaviors, and mentally rehearsing what they will say in the meeting (Turnbull & Turnbull, 1996).

BOX 6.2 ***TIPS FOR PRACTICE***

Keeping a File on Your Child

Parents of children with learning disabilities never know when they will need to find information already collected on the child. It may be that an English paper from a prior year would be helpful to pinpoint for the new teacher the child's strengths and weaknesses. It may be that the new physician wants to know what the child's dosage of Ritalin was two years ago. Because most parents, but especially those of children with learning disabilities, have busy, almost chaotic, schedules, the Learning Disabilities Council, a group of parents and professionals, recommends that parents keep a systematic file on their child. Although the keeping of such a file can be time-consuming, it may actually save time in the long run. Having these kinds of data readily accessible can save parents from searching for information that might not be readily available. Following is an excerpt from the Learning Disabilities Council manual for parents:

> The suggestions that follow have come from parents, educators, and legal experts.
>
> - Date each item in the lower right-hand corner in pencil. Do this even if the date appears elsewhere on the document. This date will be used to keep and to locate documents in chronological order. In case of documents which span a period of time, such as report cards and telephone logs, use date of the last entry.
> - Maintain records in a standard 8½" × 11" 3-hole looseleaf notebook, whenever possible. (The one you purchase in which to keep this guide would serve the purpose well.) Arrange records in chronological order, oldest document first, most recent last. Use this notebook to keep **all** records pertaining to your child's learning disability and educational progress. You will want to include the following:
>
> Report cards: Official school and interim report cards, as well as written comments from all teachers, camp counselors, Sunday School teachers, tutors, etc.
>
> Correspondence: All correspondence received as well as copies of letters which you have written about your LD child.
>
> Medical test reports: Significant birth and developmental history, visual exams, auditory, evaluations, etc.
>
> Psychological and educational test reports: Also include any notes you made during interpretive conferences following these evaluations.
>
> Telephone log: This would include a record of significant telephone conversations with teachers and other professionals. Be sure to include the date, time, name of the person you talked with, the subject and substance of the conversation, and any follow-up steps to be taken.
>
> Special education documentation: Referral, child study, eligibility, IEP, and all other official documents pertaining to your child's special education process and program.
>
> - Never highlight or write on the documents (excepting date in lower right corner). If you wish to call attention to particular passages, affix "post-it" notes with your comments.
> - Do keep a log of your telephone communications (see above).
> - Do keep a written summary of each meeting you have with teachers and other professionals.
> - Secure a complete and entire copy of your child's cumulative and confidential file from the school system and from all agencies that have ever evaluated or worked with your child. Familiarize yourself with these records and place them in the notebook in chronological order.
> - Maintain a table of contents or chronological list of documents. Each document is entered according to date, author, description of type of document, and brief summary or explana-

BOX 6.2 *continued*

tion. If author is unknown or not available, use name of the agency or school system. It is helpful to store this chronological list of documents on a word processor, if one is available, for ease in making insertions and changes.

- Keep dated samples of your child's school papers in a separate notebook.
- Never leave your notebook with a professional or school system for more than a day or two. Have extra copies of your chronological list of documents available for them so they can indicate which reports they want you to copy and provide to them.

Source: From *Understanding Learning Disabilities: A Parent Guide and Workbook* (p. 56) by Learning Disabilities Council, 1989, Richmond, VA: Learning Disabilities Council. Copyright 1989 by Learning Disabilities Council, Inc. Reprinted by permission.

The meeting itself often requires a great deal of sensitivity and tact on the teacher's part. This is particularly true if the reason for it is the child's misbehavior or poor academic progress. How the teacher starts the meeting, for example, can set the tone for the entire session. Thanking the parents for coming, allowing time for informal conversation before the meeting starts, and using language free of jargon can help put the parents at ease (Turnbull & Turnbull, 1996). Following are some questions teachers can use to ensure tact in their meetings with parents:

- Am I able to avoid blaming parents? One of the least helpful things a teacher can do is lay the blame on parents for the misbehavior of their children. Parents will already be on the defensive because you have called them to have this meeting. Weigh your words carefully so as not to give the impression that you think they are the culprits. Even if you are convinced that they are the cause of their children's problems, you should avoid accusations. If they are at fault, it is better to let them arrive at that judgment on their own.
- Am I willing to admit it when I'm wrong? Some teachers, especially those who are relatively inexperienced, feel that it is a sign of weakness to acknowledge to parents that they have made mistakes. We don't think you need to see the meeting as an opportunity to reveal all of your shortcomings, but if you have doubts about how you have handled the student it is a good idea to concede this point.
- Am I willing to admit it when I don't know the answer to parents' questions? Again, be careful not to fall into the trap of feeling that you need to have answers to every question posed by the parents. Confident teachers are more than willing to say that they are not all-knowing. In fact, teachers should view the parent-teacher conference as an opportunity to learn more about the child from the parents.
- Can I accept the family as it is? Some teachers view parent-teacher conferences as quasi-therapy sessions in which they should try to influence family dynamics. Your focus should be on what the student is doing in your classroom. To be sure, you will want to talk about how the child behaves at home, and you

may want to suggest that parents carry out certain procedures in the home to back up what you are doing at school, but you should not see yourself as a family therapist.

- Am I attuned to cultural differences between myself and the parents? It is important that you respect the cultural backgrounds of parents and not misinterpret their behavior or offend them because their customs vary from yours.
- Can I find something positive to say about the child and something positive about the parent that I can support? It is very important that you try to find something positive and supportive to say about the child and the parent in every parent contact. Sometimes this may be difficult. Nevertheless, if all the parent receives is negative information, you are not likely to get very far in resolving the problem. (Kauffman et al., 1998, pp. 137, 139)

School-Home Note Programs

If parents are willing, a **school-home note program** can be an excellent way for teachers to involve parents in the child's educational program. This can also benefit teachers because it gives them another means of reinforcing appropriate social and academic behavior. Sometimes referred to as home contingency programs, school-home note programs involve the teacher in evaluating the student's behavior and the parents in providing the reinforcement at home. Based on a brief report filled out and signed by the teacher, the parents deliver a reinforcement that has already been negotiated with the child. Program particulars are usually decided by the teacher in consultation with the parents and sometimes with the student.

Considerable research has been conducted on the use of school-home note programs (e.g., Kelley & McCain, 1995; McCain & Kelley, 1994). Most researchers suggest that the school-home note program be implemented in the beginning on a daily basis and later adjusted to a once-per-week accounting. The use of punishment is discouraged because some parents can become too punitive. In addition, the target behaviors must be clearly defined; the student, teacher, and parent must all be committed to the program and understand their respective roles; and the note should be minimally intrusive (Kelley, 1990). Figure 6.3 is an example of a school-home note.

Future school-home note programs undoubtedly will include the use of the Internet, specifically e-mail. Although no formal studies have yet been conducted, adapting the school-home note paradigm so it could be implemented via e-mail would be easy and efficient.

HOW CAN PARENTS USE THE INTERNET AND WORLD WIDE WEB AS RESOURCES?

The Internet and the World Wide Web have become useful resources for many parents. The "information highway" has opened up new ways for families to gain access to support and information. There are several news groups and lists available through

FIGURE 6.3 A School-Home Note

Teacher Completes

Today, in math I rated Kim's behaviors as follows (using a 1 to 5 pt. scale [1 = lowest, 5 = highest]):

	Rating	Points Earned
1. work completed	5	15
2. accuracy	3	6
3. neatness	4	4
	TOTAL POINTS =	25

Teacher Comments:

This is Kim's best day this week. Accuracy should improve—a lot of today's material was new.

Signature and date: Maria Lopez 3/10/98

Parent Completes

I gave the following reward(s): one hour of T.V.

Parent Comments:

It was really great to see the "5" in work completed, and the neatness is much improved.

Signature and date: Ray Mort

Teacher Completes

Signature and date: Maria Lopez 3/11/98

Source: From *Home-School Collaboration: Evaluating Effectiveness of a School-Home Note Program for Children with Attention Deficit Hyperactivity Disorder* by E. Cotton, 1998, unpublished doctoral dissertation, University of Virginia. Reprinted by permission.

the Internet for people with learning disabilities and their families. Some of these groups function very much like support groups except that subscribers communicate with one another over computers rather than in face-to-face meetings. Participants exchange information and opinions on a variety of topics pertaining to disabilities. For example, they may discuss issues concerning educational techniques, provide advice on how to work with school officials, or offer support to someone whose child has just been diagnosed. Figure 6.4 contains an example, with names and addresses changed, of one such communication between two parents belonging to a listserve devoted to attention deficit hyperactivity disorder.

The World Wide Web also contains many potential resources for parents. Table 6.3 lists some examples of sites that might be of interest to parents of children with learning disabilities or to learning disabled children or adults themselves. Like the newsgroups and listserves, some of these resources are devoted more specifically to practitioners than parents, and some are focused on parents of children with any kind of disability. But each of them holds some interest for parents of children with learning disabilities.

FIGURE 6.4 Parents' Use of Listserves for Information and/or Support

Miranda,

My name is Emily and I am a new member. I have a 6½ year old conclusively diagnosed with ADHD in Feb. I'm still trying to figure out if the medication (Ritalin) is doing what it is supposed to. Does it take months to figure out? Do neurologists just base effectiveness on focusing and staying on task? What about behavioral issues? Everyone seems to think Ritalin creates great positive changes—in some of the parent info I read—not for us exactly. The rebound is worse than any ADHD behavior before medication. HELP! Thanks,

Emily

Emily,

Welcome to the list, Emily. First of all, Ritalin has pretty much immediate effects "when it works." Ritalin is not the right medication for all people. I don't even know if it's the right medication for most people. It is the right medication for my children, and I am profoundly grateful that we don't have to do the medication tango.

When Ritalin (or other medication which covers a short period of time) works, some people find there is a rebound effect. Some people don't (not counting the contrast between the on-time and off-time behaviors). If you and your child's teachers are not noticing any effect after a few days (at most), the dosage may need to be increased or it may not be effective with your child. My children's dosages have been modified either over time or because the initial prescription was obviously too low a dosage.

Effectiveness can be judged both from focusing and behavioral issues. If you are only seeing improvement in one area, that's still better than no improvement, isn't it? You can continue to experiment with Ritalin and/or try other medications. Good luck,

Miranda
(Miranda O'Brien; e-mail: mira@dallas.com)

TABLE 6.3 World Wide Web Resources for Parents

Ability OnLine Support Network
http://www.ablelink.org/

C.H.A.D.D. (Children and Adults with Attention Deficit Disorders) Online
http://www.chadd.org/

Council for Learning Disabilities
http://www1.winthrop.edu/cld/

Division for Learning Disabilities
http://edhd.bgsu.edu/faculty/seanj/DLD/

Family Education Network
http://www.familyeducation.com/

Family Village
http://familyvillage.wisc.edu/

International Dyslexia Association
http://www.interdys.org

Learning Disabilities Association of America
http://www.ldanatl.org/

LD Online
http://www.ldonline.org/

Internet Resources for Special Children (IRSC)
http://www.irsc.org/

The National Adult Literacy and Learning Disabilities Center
http://novel.nifl.gov/nalldtop.htm

National Center for Learning Disabilities, Inc.
http://www.ncld.org/

ParentsPlace.com
http://www.parentsplace.com

Note: Web addresses are known to change. The addresses listed here were current when this book went to press.

There is, of course, a potential downside to using the Internet for support and especially as a source of information. Not everything on the Internet is accurate. Therefore, parents, just like everyone else, need to be cautious in taking at face value everything they read on the Internet.

Summary

1. How have professionals' views of parents changed?
   a. At one time, professionals viewed parents of children with disabilities negatively. They often blamed them for the problems their children had.
   b. Professionals now view parents more positively. This is owing to two factors:
      (1) Research has demonstrated the principle of reciprocal effects—that not only do parents influence children's development, but also that children have effects on parents.
      (2) Congress has passed laws stipulating that parents be given more opportunities for involvement.
2. What treatment models do professionals use with parents?
   Today's methods of working with parents often are characterized as family-centered and stressing social systems. Two such approaches are:
   a. the Turnbulls' family systems model, which includes the following components:
      (1) family characteristics
      (2) family interaction

        (3) family functions
        (4) family life cycle
    b. Dunst's social support systems model, which stresses informal sources of support
3. What are some patterns and trends in American life today?
   Students and their families belong to a macroculture and several microcultures. Microcultures are becoming more and more diverse with respect to:
    a. the family unit
    b. race, ethnicity, and language; teachers should be aware of cultural differences of families with respect to:
        (1) family structure
        (2) discipline
        (3) communication styles
    c. socioeconomic status
3. What is the family's role in helping students with disabilities?
    a. At one time, a stage theory, similar to that used with people who experience the death of a loved one, was used to explain family reactions to having a child with a disability. The typical stages were shock and disruption, denial, sadness, anxiety and fear, anger, and adaptation.
    b. Two reactions that parents often have are:
        (1) guilt
        (2) stress
    c. Siblings often experience stress, too.
    d. Most families adjust well, some experience minor difficulties, and a few experience enough stress to be considered dysfunctional.
    e. Homework is a major problem area for many students with learning disabilities and their families.
        (1) Teachers can help by:
            i. assigning homework that does not require acquisition of new skills
            ii. making sure that the students understand their assignments
            iii. setting up a system so that they can monitor the students' homework
            iv. attempting to involve parents
        (2) Parents can help by:
            i. providing contingencies to get their children to finish homework
            ii. helping students plan and organize their work time
            iii. setting up a schedule of activities in addition to homework for a comprehensive plan
            iv. organizing homework time specifically
            v. carefully considering who will give direct help to the student
        (3) Students can help by attempting to allocate their time efficiently. One such method involves the use of visual organizers in the form of wheels or ovals.
    f. Parents can be effective as advocates for their child.

5. How can communication among students, parents, and professionals be enhanced?
   Two of the most common methods of parent-teacher communication are:
   a. parent-teacher conferences—meetings for imparting information about students' academic and social behaviors; gathering information about students' interests, hobbies, and homework; planning for students' educational programs; and solving problems students are having in school. Conferences should be carefully planned.
   b. school-home note programs—a system of communication between teacher and parent in which the teacher evaluates the child's behavior at school on a simple form that goes home to the parent, and the parent then reinforces the child.
6. How can parents use the Internet and the World Wide Web as resources?
   a. Parents and their children can gain information and support from the Internet through newsgroups and listserves.
   b. Parents and their children can also explore the Web for sites devoted to parenting issues and other aspects of learning disabilities.

7

Prevention and Intervention in Early Childhood

How Can Learning Disabilities Be Prevented?

Addressing Risk Factors in Infancy and Early Childhood

Distinguishing Disabilities from Cultural Differences

How Are Learning Disabilities Identified in Infancy and Early Childhood?

Two Approaches to Early Identification

Promises and Pitfalls of Early Identification

How Is Early Childhood Intervention Provided?

Popular Early Intervention Programs

Legal Requirements of Early Intervention

Evaluating Early Childhood Program Quality

What Are Some Trends and Controversies in Early Childhood Education?

Inclusive Education

Developmentally Appropriate Practices

Alternative Assessment

Education for Transition

Family-Based Education

Summary

If we could prevent most disabilities, we could avoid most of the personal disadvantages and social costs that go with having them. Most people agree that if a child's disability cannot be prevented, then intervention should be started as soon as it is detected. In fact, if we detect a disability in its earliest stages and begin effective intervention at once, we may be able to avoid a variety of complications, and the ultimate outcome for the child may be much better. Thus, prevention and early intervention are closely linked in concept and in practice (Hightower & Braden, 1991).

HOW CAN LEARNING DISABILITIES BE PREVENTED?

Prevention is usually described as primary, secondary, or tertiary, depending on when and why preventive action is taken. The prevention of learning disabilities may involve all three types.

Primary prevention means keeping the disability from occurring in the first place. That is, strategies designed to reduce the risk of acquiring a disability or disease are called primary prevention. For example, immunizing babies against polio and other infectious diseases is primary prevention; it reduces or eliminates the risk that children will get the disease. Fluoridating water is an example of primary prevention of tooth decay because it reduces the risk of tooth decay, although it does not eliminate cavities altogether. Primary prevention in learning disabilities might involve reducing the chances of brain injury, improving teachers' skills in instruction and behavior management, or teaching parents child-rearing skills. For primary prevention to work, the strategy must be aimed at reducing or eliminating the cause(s) of learning disabilities or protecting against causal factors. Box 7.1 suggests that if we were able to decrease the number of babies having very low birthweight, we might prevent some learning disabilities altogether. Intervening to prevent low birthweight is, in fact, an example of primary prevention of learning disabilities and a variety of other disabilities as well.

Secondary prevention means correcting the disability after it occurs, or at least keeping it from getting worse. The purpose of secondary prevention is to nip the disability in the bud or minimize its effect. If we already see signs that the individual has acquired or is acquiring a problem or disability, it is too late for primary prevention, but secondary prevention may be possible. In dentistry, filling a tooth cavity once it occurs prevents further decay and the loss of the tooth. In medicine, using an antibiotic to cure an infection is secondary prevention because it avoids complications or the spread of the infection to other organs. In education, remedial instruction is a secondary preventive strategy. In fact, most of the interventions for learning disabilities involve secondary prevention because the child's learning problems have been noticed and the aim is to correct the problems or prevent them from getting worse. If a special education teacher works not only with students already identified as having learning disabilities but also others who are struggling academically but have not yet been identified, she or he may be practicing secondary prevention with both labeled and nonlabeled students.

BOX 7.1 ***EXAMPLE***

Low Birthweight and Learning Problems

Extremely low-birthweight infants whose lives have been saved by the aggressive use of expensive new technologies are likely to suffer from serious and often irreversible physical and intellectual disabilities, researchers reported last week.

The first wave of "miracle" babies, born nearly a decade ago, are alive today because advances in neonatology made it possible to save infants born three months premature who weigh less than 2 pounds—small enough to fit in the palm of a hand. A study published last week in the *New England Journal of Medicine* of 68 babies born weighing less than 750 grams—1 pound, 10 ounces—conducted by researchers from Rainbow Babies and Children's Hospital and Case Western Reserve University, both in Cleveland, is one of the first to track these infants' progress in childhood and school.

"These children are at serious disadvantage in every skill required for adequate performance in school," concluded the authors, led by physician Maureen Hack. Early school performance, the researchers note, is closely linked with "how these children will ultimately function in society."

The study's sobering conclusions are likely to fuel the continuing debate over the moral and economic implications of saving infants who surely would have died as recently as 15 years ago.

Among their findings:

- 50% of extremely low-birthweight children have IQs that are borderline normal or lower; 21% are mentally retarded.
- 45% are in special education classes.
- 9% suffer from cerebral palsy.
- 25% have a significant vision problem.
- 25% have a measurable hearing loss.
- 25% have serious growth problems, and 35% have abnormally small heads, a measure of brain development.

Extremely low-birthweight children, who were born on average at 26 weeks gestation—14 weeks early—also scored lower on behavioral assessments and evaluations of school performance conducted by the child's parent, usually the mother, and by a teacher.

Hack's study involved infants born between 1982 and 1986 in a six-county region of Ohio that included Cleveland. Her team compared three groups of infants: extremely low-birthweight babies who weighed less than 1 pound, 10 ounces and were admitted to specialized neonatal intensive care units; another group of very low-birthweight babies who were larger than the first and weighed less than 3 pounds, 5 ounces; and a group of full-term, normal-sized babies who weighed more than 5.5 pounds.

By every measure, full-term babies outperformed their low-birthweight counterparts; the smallest babies fared the worst. Rates of mental retardation, for example, varied from 21% in the extremely low-birthweight group to 8% among the very low-birthweight to 2% among the normal-sized children. The variation in retardation rates may be due to prolonged dependence on oxygen, Hack hypothesized. There were no demographic differences among the three groups. Two-thirds were female, Hack said, "because of the greater survival of girls."

Researchers noted that the babies were born in the vanguard of the movement to save very tiny premature newborns "before many recent innovations in care," such as surfactants to treat lung problems. It is doubtful, they added, that these advances would reduce lung problems or other chronic disabilities.

The problem of extreme prematurity and low birthweight is not likely to improve any time soon, noted pediatrician Marie C. McCormick in a companion editorial. McCormick, a professor at Harvard Medical School, notes that the rate of low-birthweight babies is rising, in part due to fertility treatments, which have resulted in multiple births. Twins and triplets are likely to be born early and much smaller than full-term babies.

McCormick said that poverty also continues to be a critical factor in the rising rate of extremely premature low-birthweight infants.

BOX 7.1 *continued*

In another small study of very premature newborns published last week in the *Journal of the American Medical Association,* a group of Harvard researchers studied the medical effects of individualized treatment provided to some babies in the neonatal intensive care unit of Boston's Brigham and Women's Hospital.

The team led by psychologist Heidelise Als found that low-birthweight babies who are treated by nurses trained to pick up and react to their individual cues gain weight faster and leave the hospital sooner than do those who are treated according to the standard hospital regimen where care is delivered on schedule rather than on demand.

Two groups of babies were studied: 16 were randomly assigned to an experimental unit that responded to the baby's sleep and wake schedules, emphasized holding the babies, and instituted dark and quiet periods. An equal number was assigned to the regular neonatal ICU, which is brightly lit at all times and tends to be noisy.

Babies in both groups were born between 24 and 30 weeks gestation, none was drug or alcohol affected, and all were placed on respirators shortly after birth.

The group in the experimental unit had fewer brain hemorrhages and lung problems and left the hospital on average two months earlier than infants in the regular ICU. They also gained weight faster and began bottle feeding sooner than their counterparts. At nine months of age, they scored significantly higher on a developmental assessment.

"This is not a glamorous, high-technology form of neonatal intensive care," said Gerald B. Merenstein, a perinatologist at the University of Colorado School of Health Sciences Center, in an editorial. While Merenstein noted that the study was small and the results need to be replicated, "the clear differences in medical morbidity and neurodevelopmental outcome cannot be ignored."

Source: From "Low Birthweight Babies: Problems Persist as Infants Grow and Learn" by S. G. Boodman, September 27, 1994, *Washington Post Health,* p. 11. Copyright 1994 by *The Washington Post.* Reprinted by permission.

Questions to Ponder

What are some of the most effective ways of preventing low birthweight?

What preventive steps can be taken to minimize the effects of low birthweight on later development?

Tertiary prevention means keeping the effects of the problem or disability from spreading to other areas of functioning. To continue the dentistry example, root canal surgery might not only prevent the loss of an infected tooth, but also avoid complications involving other teeth or other tissues. It would thus be tertiary prevention. The objective of tertiary prevention in special education is to limit or contain the disability to a particular area of the individual's life or abilities. When remedial interventions are initiated long after a learning disability has developed, the primary goal may be tertiary prevention. For example, if a student has had learning disabilities in reading that have been known since the early grades and these have not been corrected, tertiary prevention at the high school level may involve teaching the student skills that will prevent failure in finding and holding a job.

The main purpose in this chapter is to discuss prevention strategies that might be employed to reduce the risk of learning disabilities or be initiated after at least the early signs of disability are already evident. The first step is to identify risk factors associated with learning disabilities so that we know how to reduce the chances that children will have such problems. The next step is to identify learning disabilities as early as possible so that interventions have the maximum potential to correct them.

Addressing Risk Factors in Infancy and Early Childhood

Children said to be at risk of developing learning disabilities are those who are likely to be identified later, given their present behavior, learning characteristics, or life circumstances. What should we look for in preschool children's characteristics or life circumstances that puts them at risk for learning disabilities? Precisely what behavioral, emotional, or learning characteristics are reliable precursors of learning disabilities? Is the child actually at risk for developmental problems, or does the child merely exhibit behavior different from that expected in school owing to the circumstances or culture in which he or she has been reared? These questions are not easy to answer, as we will see.

Learning disabilities have a wide variety of possible and suspected causes and are a very heterogeneous group of disorders. Moreover, they may coexist with a wide range of other disabilities. The risk of learning disabilities varies along multiple dimensions. That is, the factors giving rise to risk of learning disabilities are those that increase risk for a wide variety of other disabilities as well. For example, risk for disabilities of any type is heightened if the child is reared in poverty, experiences abuse or neglect, is malnourished, has a very low birthweight, inherits genetic markers for the disability, is exposed to substances that cause birth defects, or is not nurtured and taught specific skills necessary for normal cognitive, social, and physical development. Box 7.1 describes the link between low birthweight and a variety of problems, including learning disabilities.

Other adverse conditions besides low birthweight that may put children at high risk for learning disabilities include:

- children and mothers living in poverty, having poor nutrition, and being exposed to environmental conditions likely to cause disease and disability
- babies being born to teenage mothers
- babies being born to mothers who receive inadequate prenatal care and poor nutrition during pregnancy and who use substances that can harm the fetus
- environmental hazards, including both chemical and social dangers
- children being subjected to abuse, neglect, and an environment in which violence and substance abuse are pervasive
- cuts in social programs that widen the gap between the needs of children and families and the availability of social services

Unfortunately, more children than ever are being born and reared under adverse conditions. Such conditions will result in more children being identified as having disabilities of all types, including learning disabilities (Baumeister, Kupstas, & Klindworth, 1990).

Learning disabilities also vary tremendously in severity and pervasiveness. Their hallmark is intraindividual differences, and individuals with specific learning disabilities have extraordinary differences between their abilities in some areas (e.g., skill in sports or mechanical abilities) and in others (e.g., reading or math). These individuals vary not only in the type and severity of disabilities, but also in their vulnerability to specific causal factors and their resilience or ability to resist potential causes. This means that although children at extremely high risk may be easily identified, those at relatively low to moderate risk may be difficult or impossible to pick out reliably.

Moreover, learning disabilities are developmental disorders persisting over the life span. The implication is that changes in risk may occur over time. Children and youths may go through periods during which they are especially vulnerable and others during which they are relatively immune to the development of learning disabilities (Keogh & Sears, 1991).

Thus, the factors that increase risk for learning disabilities are particularly difficult to assess because (1) the possible causes of learning disabilities are multiple and complex and overlap with the causes of other disabilities, (2) learning disabilities vary enormously in severity and may affect a wide range of areas of abilities, and (3) vulnerability to various causal factors may change with age. However, if learning disabilities are to be prevented, risk factors must be evaluated carefully and action must be taken to reduce the risk.

Distinguishing Disabilities from Cultural Differences

Cultural difference may be mistaken for developmental delay. Different cultures prepare children to accomplish developmental tasks in different ways. Children from low-income homes may not be prepared to meet the expectations that most middle-class schools have for students, yet these children may not be at risk for developmental failure. It is important to distinguish between developmental and cultural differences so that the assessment, prevention, and remediation of disabilities are not misguided and children are not inappropriately placed in special education (Bowman, 1994; Hallahan & Kauffman, 1997).

Educators must be particularly careful in assessing the abilities of children who are culturally and linguistically diverse (CLD), because language differences and their implications for learning can be mistaken for learning disabilities. Language differences are particularly important to understand; language is the basis for reading and other forms of communication in schools (Battle, 1997; van Keulen, Weddington, & DeBose, 1998). Some children are not provided with many opportunities for language learning because their parents do not read to them and they seldom observe reading and writing in their homes. These children may have normal cognitive skills, and their primary need may be simply a heightened level of exposure to literacy. Other children come from homes in which there is a high degree of literacy, but not in English; so the teacher who does not speak their language may underestimate their language competence. Still others may have learned a variation of English that they seldom or never have seen in print and that is not typically used by teachers. Teachers not aware of such differences and their meanings may mistakenly believe that such a child has a learning disability. Box 7.2 provides an example of how such linguistic differences may affect children learning to read.

Failure of teachers and others to differentiate between difference and disability may account for the misidentification of students for special education and the overrepresentation of minority students in special programs. Thus, teachers must be familiar with multicultural issues in special education (Hallahan & Kauffman, 1997). Familiarity with multicultural issues and understanding that many differences are not disabilities should not, however, lead teachers to neglect the referral of CLD students for evaluation when difference signifies a disability. Ortiz (1997) cautions that the neglect of CLD students with disabilities is just as serious as mistaking cultural differences for disabilities.

> Patterns of underrepresentation pose problems as serious as those associated with overrepresentation but are more difficult to explain, as underrepresented students are an invisible population. A possible explanation is that teachers do not refer CLD students to special education because they inaccurately attribute their academic difficulties to differences of language and culture. In some cases, school districts discourage referrals because (a) they do not have personnel with the expertise to assess CLD students; (b) they fear they will not be able to defend assessment procedures; and/or (c) if students qualify for services, schools lack personnel who can address disability-related needs in linguistically and culturally appropriate ways. It is not uncommon, for example, for districts to prohibit referrals of LEP [limited English proficiency] students until these students have been in school for at least 2 years. Presumably, such policies are intended to give students time to adjust to the school culture and acquire English, thus increasing the likelihood of accurate diagnoses if they are eventually referred. . . . Such policies, though well-intentioned, not only violate the right of CLD students to an appropriate education, but also can have long-term negative effects because the lack of access to early intervention and specialized services can prevent students from realizing their social and academic potential. (Ortiz, 1997, p. 322)

One implication of the discussion here is that teachers must be keenly aware of both cultural and linguistic differences that are not disabilities and the distinguishing features of disabilities. Another implication is that teachers must be more understanding and accepting of the cultural diversity of the families of young children and work more closely with families (Linan-Thompson & Jean, 1997; Saint-Laurent, Glasson, & Couture, 1997; Thorp, 1997).

HOW ARE LEARNING DISABILITIES IDENTIFIED IN INFANCY AND EARLY CHILDHOOD?

The more severe the child's disability, the easier and earlier it can be identified (Kenny & Chekaluk, 1993). Few learning disabilities are severely disabling to children younger than 5 years old, and therefore their detection before the child enters school is quite difficult (Satz & Fletcher, 1988; Vaughn, Bos, & Schumm, 1997).

BOX 7.2 ***EXAMPLE***

Culture, Language, and Reading

Black children who come from print-rich environments where the parents model and reinforce emerging literacy skills will likely enter first grade equal to their White counterparts having had the same or similar experiences. The primary differences will most likely be in the language spoken by Black children and the written language in print. This means that Black children may bring different assumptions about the world to the printed page, so teachers must be aware that Black children's interactions with text may be different from White mainstream American English speaking children. These differences are often caused by not having written word–spoken word correspondence, and these differences are what most teachers do not understand. Typically, Black children's spoken home language is not represented in conventional storybooks or textbooks. Therefore, learning to read for some Black children involves making meaning of the letters, words, and sentence structure, as well as the identification of words. On the other hand, White children typically have congruence in the language they speak at home with the written words found in conventional print. This lack of congruence for African American children is where culture and language variation makes a difference in language, speech, and learning. These are also areas where teachers need knowledge and understanding of cultural differences to prevent the promotion of misconceptions about Black children as individuals and false perceptions about their abilities to learn.

Questions to Ponder

What are some of the different assumptions about the world that black children and white children may bring to the printed page?

How might the lack of congruence between African American children's oral language and the print they read be addressed most effectively?

How might issues similar to those described here for African American children arise for children who speak Spanish or another language other than standard American English at home?

Source: From *Speech, Language, Learning, and the African American Child* (pp. 231–232) by J. E. van Keulen, G. T. Weddington, & C. E. DeBose, 1998, Boston: Allyn & Bacon. Copyright 1988 by Allyn & Bacon. Reprinted by permission.

Some of the children who will be identified in school as having learning disabilities are slower than average in reaching early developmental milestones in motor, language, and social skills, but not so limited in cognitive skills as to be considered clearly mentally retarded. For example, they may be slower than most children in learning to walk, dress themselves, and use the toilet. They may begin saying words and using sentences at a later age than most children or have particular difficulty making themselves understood. Or by the age of 3 or 4 years, they may have begun exhibiting an unusually persistent pattern of aggressive behavior, tantrums, hyperactivity, and refusal to follow adults' directions (Loeber, Green, Lahey, Christ, & Frick, 1992). These children may be identified early if their parents seek help from a clinic or other community social service because they are concerned about their child's slow development or difficult behavior. If the parents are not concerned about the child's development, the problem may be detected by a preschool teacher. Preschool programs that provide prekindergarten education for 3- to 5-year-olds may identify disabilities, including incipient learning disabilities (Sinclair, 1993).

The identification procedures used in clinics and preschools may involve a variety of standardized tests or developmental scales that compare a child's skills to a norm. However, many standardized instruments, particularly intelligence tests, have substantial limitations in assessing preschoolers (Neisworth & Bagnato, 1992; Shepard, 1994). Careful observation of the child in a variety of contexts by experienced teachers and assessment of preacademic skills are more appropriate procedures for identifying the early stages of learning disabilities. An important caution in reliance on teacher observation is that the teacher must be sensitive to the ways in which the child's home and community have shaped her or his behavior (Harry, 1995; Midgette, 1995; Ortiz, 1997).

Most of the young children later identified as having learning disabilities may appear to be developing quite similarly to their age-peers unless we look closely at the specific skills that are the most immediate precursors of reading problems. Research is increasingly indicating that key aspects of reading problems involve phonology, syntax, and semantics—difficulties in understanding how sounds and words are put together to make sense. Children who have trouble in understanding and using language when they are in kindergarten and first grade, for example, typically have problems learning to read and are likely to be clearly identified as poor readers by the third grade (cf. Seidenberg, 1997).

Two Approaches to Early Identification

The discussion to this point suggests that recognizing children who later will be identified as having specific learning disabilities in school before they enter school is extraordinarily difficult. Given this, it is not surprising that there is some debate as to how to approach early identification. Educators attempting to do this may take a generic or a specific approach.

Generic Approach

Many early childhood educators propose a generic approach to early identification, that is, recognizing children as being at risk based on developmental lags, which might indicate any of a variety of disabilities, including mental retardation, learning disabilities, or emotional or behavioral disorders. Many early childhood educators suggest that we identify preschoolers whose characteristics suggest disability in the general case (Haring et al., 1992). The general case includes slow development in motor skills, language, and learning the skills associated with reading and other areas of the school curriculum. These skills might include, for example, developmentally and culturally relevant skills in manipulating objects precisely, describing objects, carrying on a conversation, naming shapes and colors, associating sounds with letters, being able to reproduce sounds, counting, paying attention to a given task for an appropriate amount of time, following adults' commands, and making appropriate social approaches and responses to others.

The generic approach to early identification is not concerned with differentiating learning disabilities from other disabilities. Therefore, it directs attention to a wide variety of developmental milestones, to lags in the acquisition of skills required for successful academic and social learning in school, regardless of the disability category into which the child might eventually be placed. Some schools choose not to use specific labels such as "learning disability" during the primary grades. Instead, they may use a more generic designation such as "developmentally delayed" to cover all types of identified disabilities for children below fourth grade.

A major advantage of a generic approach is that if relatively small lags in these skills result in early identification, then most children with learning disabilities will be included. A major disadvantage is that it can result in a high number of false identifications. For example, if relatively small lags result in early identification, the percentage of false identification will be high; if only large lags in development result in early identification, the percentage of children with true disabilities who are not identified will be high.

Specific Approach

The younger the child, the greater the benefit of a generic approach because there is no real measure for learning disabilities prior to school. However, as children approach school age, enter kindergarten, and proceed through the grades, a more specific approach to identifying learning disabilities becomes more desirable. A specific disability label (e.g., "learning disability" or "reading disability") might be used. Moreover, specific skills, such as language or reading, may be identified as the basis for identifying the child as having a disability and as targets for remediation.

From kindergarten on, it is possible to begin focusing more specifically on reading-related skills, which are most often the central problem in learning disabilities. At the kindergarten level, these skills—often referred to as **phonological awareness**—involve the ability to blend sounds, segment the sounds of words, rhyme, and in other ways manipulate the sounds of spoken words. By the time a child is in the third grade, a reading disability is usually painfully obvious to the teacher, the child, and the parents in test scores, the child's everyday classroom performance, and the experienced teacher's observations. The key question regarding early identification is this: Can we identify in kindergarten the children who will, without intervention, have reading disabilities by third grade? The findings of reading research suggest that we may be able to do this and offer effective instruction (cf. Jerger, 1996; O'Connor, Jenkins, & Slocum, 1995; O'Connor, Notari-Syverson, & Vadasy, 1996; Vaughn et al., 1997).

Promises and Pitfalls of Early Identification

Early identification of learning disabilities intuitively seems a promising practice. The common wisdom is that it will be followed by early intervention, which will lead to effective secondary and tertiary prevention. The pitfalls of early identification are not so obvious, and only after careful reflection have many people seen the possible downside of efforts to catch learning disabilities in their very earliest stages.

The earliest stages of learning disabilities are not so easy to recognize as one might think. Furthermore, the early identification procedures available today are far from perfect. Ideally, identification of a child as having a learning disability will not only be accurate (i.e., there will be no misdiagnoses), but will also lead to effective programming to address the disability. If the identification is accurate and appropriate intervention is promptly provided, we might expect overwhelmingly positive consequences. The only possible negative consequences of accurate early identification followed immediately by effective intervention are the stigma and anxiety created by the identification of any disability, and these are clearly outweighed by the advantages of early and effective help in coping with learning problems. Given that we can accurately identify children who have learning disabilities and provide effective intervention, we should do so as early as possible.

Over two decades ago, Keogh and Becker (1973) warned of the dangers of early misidentification and of early identification that is not followed promptly by effective intervention. Misidentification carries with it not only the stigma and anxiety of disability, but also the costs of any intervention provided. Accurate early identification without prompt and effective intervention is likely to make the problems worse for both child and family. Major issues in early identification thus involve accuracy (avoiding errors) and the availability of early intervention.

More recently, Haring et al. (1992) questioned the identification of preschoolers as having learning disabilities. They suggested that a learning disability is defined specifically by lack of academic progress in school; therefore, one cannot define learning disabilities in preschool children. Furthermore, they noted that special services to preschool children with disabilities do not require categorical labels and can be channeled through more generic labels such as "developmentally disabled" or "at risk." Labels associated with specific disabilities, Haring et al. (1992) maintain, create lowered expectations for children that may follow them throughout their school careers. Whether more generic labels are more or less problematic than more specific ones we do not know. How to provide special services to children with special needs without any label at all—except primary prevention that is given equally to all children, regardless of identified problems—is a puzzle not likely to be solved (Kauffman & Hallahan, 1993).

HOW IS EARLY CHILDHOOD INTERVENTION PROVIDED?

Special education and early childhood education are separate entities, yet they are intertwined. We cannot fully understand one without considering the other.

> Special and general early educators are engaged in the same function: designing early educational experiences for young children—children who often are similar in many ways, although on occasion stark differences are apparent. The two disciplines share many assumptions about young children, a joint commitment to high quality in early education, and some common disciplinary (e.g., child development) and theoretical (e.g., constructivism) origins. Many good reasons exist for understanding and acting on the similarities in the two fields; for example, we might learn to use

> our meager resources more efficiently, avoid some negative effects of segregation, promote more positive attitudes toward difference, and expose ourselves to various thoughts and traditions that in turn may produce improvements in practice. (Wolery, 1993, p. viii)

The best known early intervention programs straddle the line between general and special education. Most of the students for whom they are designed have not been identified as having disabilities, although they are at risk for later identification if they do not receive effective instruction. Thus, these programs are focused on primary and secondary prevention. That is, they are intended to prevent learning disabilities from emerging and to correct learning problems that have been perceived.

Popular Early Intervention Programs

Three early intervention programs are particularly well known nationally. All are designed to provide prevention and early intervention for young children who are at high risk for school failure (Vaughn et al., 1997).

Project Head Start

Perhaps the most visible historical link between general and special early childhood education is Project Head Start. In the 1960s, the federal government launched Head Start with the intention of addressing the needs of preschool children from low-income families for educational experiences prior to their entry into kindergarten. Head Start remains one of the most popular government social programs, and its basic premise—that early educational intervention can prevent school failure and related developmental problems—remains the foundation for other early childhood education programs serving children at risk.

Although Head Start was not focused on children with disabilities, they may be identified and served in the context of Head Start classrooms (Sinclair, 1993). However, federal legislation separate from Head Start now requires early intervention programs for preschoolers with disabilities, and these children may be served in a variety of environments. Most often today they are served in the context of integrated preschools attended by both normally developing and developmentally delayed children.

Reading Recovery

Reading Recovery is a program imported from New Zealand (Clay, 1985; Pinnel, 1990). It requires special teacher training in how to provide individual tutoring for low-achieving first-graders. The tutoring sessions last for 30 minutes, and a typical session involves the following:

1. child rereading a familiar book
2. teacher analyzing the reading by keeping a running record
3. letter identification activities, if necessary
4. child writing a story, with emphasis on hearing the sounds of words

5. putting together a cut-up story
6. child becoming acquainted with and reading a new book (Vaughn et al., 1997, p. 320)

The success of Reading Recovery depends not only on having a well-trained teacher who knows how to assess reading skills and teach those the child needs, but also on having enough such teachers to provide individual sessions with all the students who need them.

Success for All

Success for All (SFA) is a program designed at the Center for Research on Effective Schooling for Disadvantaged Students at Johns Hopkins University in Baltimore (Madden, Slavin, Karweit, Dolan, & Wasik, 1991; Slavin, Madden, Dolan, & Wasik, 1994). It focuses on children in kindergarten through third grade who are at risk of school failure. SFA combines emphasis on reading in the regular class curriculum with tutoring, small group instruction, and work with families to try to ensure that every child learns to read. During reading instruction, which is scheduled for 90 minutes, the pupils are pulled out of their regular grade-level class for instruction in smaller, more homogeneous groups. These groups are comprised of 10 to 20 children who are all reading at about the same level, although their regular classrooms might range from grades 1 to 3. The primary components of the program are:

1. a family support team (including a social worker and a parent liaison)
2. reading tutoring for students with particular problems for as long as necessary
3. an innovative curriculum that integrates reading and writing instruction in meaningful contexts
4. regrouping of students across grades for reading instruction (Vaughn et al., 1997, p. 321)

All popular early intervention programs focus on teaching young children in small groups or individual tutoring. There appears to be no substitute for intensive, focused, and skillful teacher attention. The fact that a program is popular and widely used across the nation does not necessarily mean it is highly effective. Further research on the effects of early intervention programs on children's learning and school success will tell which approach is most effective and efficient.

Legal Requirements of Early Intervention

Federal laws require that all preschool children, including infants and toddlers, receive free and appropriate services if they have disabilities (Yell, 1998; Yell & Shriner, 1997). These laws are the Individuals with Disabilities Education Act (IDEA) and other laws enacted primarily to address severe disabilities of preschool-age children. The 1997 amendments of IDEA extended the law to cover infants and toddlers (Yell & Shriner, 1997). As we have already noted, however, most children with learning disabilities are not identified until they are in school; the pitfalls of earlier identification of learning disabilities are great.

The 1997 amendments to IDEA allow special education teachers to work with general education students who do not have identified disabilities as long as the needs of those with identified disabilities are being met. This opens additional possibilities for prevention in the form of early intervention—additional help before a learning problem becomes a learning disability.

If children are identified as needing special services due to a disability during their preschool years, federal laws require a plan for working with the child's family. Specifically, the families of infants and toddlers must be involved in developing an **individualized family service plan (IFSP),** which is similar to the individualized education plan (IEP) required for school-age children under IDEA. An IFSP must include:

- present levels of the child's cognitive, physical, language and speech, psychosocial, and self-help development
- family resources, priorities, and concerns relating to the child's development
- major expected outcomes for the child and family, including criteria, procedures, and time lines for assessing progress
- specific early intervention services necessary to meet the child's and the family's needs, including frequency, intensity, location, and method of delivery
- projected dates for initiating and ending the services
- name of the case manager
- steps needed to ensure a smooth transition from the early intervention program into a preschool program

IFSPs, like IEPs, are not easy to implement well (Bateman, 1992, 1996; Brown, 1991; Campbell, Strickland, & LaForme, 1992; Minke & Scott, 1993). However, they do provide a structure for ensuring that families are involved and that the child's needs are being addressed.

Federal mandates to provide early intervention programs for children with disabilities are perceived as among the least burdensome or wasteful and most cost-effective social programs of government. Research data will likely provide increasing support for this perception.

Evaluating Early Childhood Program Quality

An early intervention program is not necessarily of high quality just because it meets the legal requirements. A high-quality program goes beyond the law to provide a nurturing and effective learning environment for the child. Box 7.3 describes six ways teachers and others can promote the learning and attitudes of young children that are the goals of early education, both general and special.

BOX 7.3 ***TIPS FOR PRACTICE***

Ways to Promote Cognitive Development and Good Attitudes toward Learning

Encouragement of Exploration
Children need to be encouraged by caring adults to explore and to gather information about their environments.

Mentoring in Basic Skills
Children need to be mentored by trusted adults in basic cognitive skills, such as labeling, sorting, sequencing, comparing, and noting relationships between means and ends.

Celebration of Developmental Advances
Children need to have their developmental accomplishments celebrated and reinforced by others—especially adults with whom they spend a lot of time.

Guided Rehearsal and Extension of New Skills
Children need to have responsible adults help them rehearse and then elaborate on (extend) their newly acquired skills.

Protection from Inappropriate Disapproval and Teasing or Punishment
Children need to be spared the negative experiences associated with adults' disapproval, teasing, or punishment for behaviors that are necessary in children's trial-and-error learning about their environments (e.g., mistakes in trying out a new skill or unintended consequences of exploration or information seeking). This does not mean that constructive criticism and negative consequences cannot be used for behaviors that children have the ability to understand are socially unacceptable.

A Rich and Responsive Language Environment
Children need to have adults provide a predictable and comprehensible communication environment, in which language is used to convey information, provide social rewards, and encourage learning of new materials and skills.

Source: From "The Transition to School: Why the First Few Years Matter for a Lifetime" by S. L. Ramey and C. T Ramey, 1994, *Phi Delta Kappan, 76,* p. 197. Copyright 1994 by Phi Delta Kappan. Reprinted by permission.

Questions to Ponder
Exactly what can teachers do with young children to implement these tips?
How would a teacher take into consideration children's cultural and linguistic diversities in implementing these procedures?

Katz (1994) provides an overview on program quality from the perspectives of the preschool children served, parents, staff, and community and suggests some of the questions each participant in early childhood programs might ask in evaluating program quality. For example, the following are questions we might expect children to ask—if they could—about their program. (Affirmative answers would indicate high program quality.)

- Do I usually feel that I belong to the group and am not just part of the crowd?
- Do I usually feel accepted, understood, and protected by the adults rather than scolded or neglected by them?
- Am I usually accepted by some of my peers rather than ignored or rejected by them?

- Am I usually addressed seriously and respectfully rather than being treated as someone who is "precious" or "cute"?
- Am I usually glad to be here rather than reluctant to come and eager to leave?
- Do I find most of the activities engaging, absorbing, and challenging rather than just amusing, fun, entertaining, or exciting?
- Do I find most of the experiences interesting rather than frivolous or boring?
- Do I find most of the activities meaningful rather than mindless or trivial?
- Do I find most of my experiences satisfying rather than frustrating or confusing? (Katz, 1994, p. 201)

Certainly, these questions are relevant to both general and special education programs, in both the higher grades and preschool. One final question posed by Katz (1994) seems essential in judging program quality, particularly for students with disabilities: Am I acquiring the specific skills necessary for my satisfactory progress through school?

WHAT ARE SOME TRENDS AND CONTROVERSIES IN EARLY CHILDHOOD EDUCATION?

There may be overwhelming public support for early intervention programs, but there is also controversy among early childhood educators regarding the most effective practices. These controversies encompass both general and special early education and concern contemporary trends in educating young children. Trends in the 1990s in both general and special early childhood education center on:

- greater reference to and involvement of children's families and communities
- assessment based less on testing and more on the child's performance
- an emphasis on satisfying the consumers (i.e., children and their parents)
- coordination of services across the various agencies serving children
- instructional practices that are considered developmentally appropriate
- concern for transition from family to preschool and then to elementary school
- a broader definition of education than that offered by traditional academic or preacademic instruction (See Kleinhammer-Tramill, Rosenkoetter, & Tramill, 1994.)

Five current trends with particular relevance to special education are:

1. greater inclusion of young children with disabilities in preschools serving normally developing youngsters
2. widespread acceptance of practices described as developmentally appropriate
3. new approaches to the assessment of young children

4. emphasis on transition of children from home to preschool and preschool to kindergarten
5. emphasis on family involvement in the education of young children and family-based education

The controversies surrounding these trends will probably continue well into the 21st century.

Inclusive Education

In early childhood special education, considerable controversy has been generated by the inclusive schools movement, which promotes the full inclusion of children with severe disabilities in classes with nondisabled pupils (e.g., Buysse & Bailey, 1993; Demchak & Drinkwater, 1992). However, relatively little of this controversy involves children likely to be categorized as having learning disabilities (Manset & Semmel, 1997; Wolery et al., 1993).

Virtually all early childhood educators suggest that children with mild disabilities and those considered at risk for school failure should be included in programs designed to serve a diverse group of learners (Bowman, 1994; Katz, 1994; Ramey & Ramey, 1994; Sainato & Strain, 1993). The controversy surrounding integration of children likely to be identified as having learning disabilities tends to be centered on the relationship between general and special early childhood education. The extent to which practices in one are appropriate for children served by the other and the extent to which children at risk of school failure need special services that are not an integral part of general early childhood education programs are matters of controversy (McLean & Odom, 1993).

Developmentally Appropriate Practices (DAP)

Among the similarities and differences between general and special early childhood education, perhaps the most hotly debated issue is what has become known as developmentally appropriate practice (DAP). The features of DAP were introduced in the late 1980s in a publication of the National Association for the Education of Young Children (Bredekamp, 1987). DAP involves providing an educational program that is appropriate for the child's age and individual needs, given knowledge of child development. This program takes into consideration the child's progression through developmental stages and emphasizes avoidance of pushing children's achievement beyond their current developmental levels. Another way of describing DAP is that it is based on the assumption that learning must be child centered and child directed, that teachers should do relatively little to direct children or teach specific skills.

DAP is controversial in early childhood special education because the mission of special educators has been to speed up the rate at which children with disabilities develop important skills. Moreover, special educators typically have emphasized the need for teachers to direct learning by explicitly teaching the skills important to overcoming or compensating for learning disabilities. One group of early childhood special educators noted, "While DAP has focused primarily on preventing attempts to artificially accelerate the progress of children who are developing normally, the explicit mission of [early childhood special education] is to produce outcomes that would not occur in the absence of intervention or teaching" (Carta, Schwartz, Atwater, & McConnell, 1991, p. 4). Thus, the differences between early education programs designed for normally developing children based on a DAP philosophy and the basic premises of special education programs for preschool children with disabilities make integrating general and special early education difficult (Carta et al., 1991; Johnson & Johnson, 1992; Mallory, 1992). Wolery (1991) raised several questions that are important in weighing the value of DAP versus the more teacher-directed approach of special educators:

- For what types of outcomes are child- and teacher-directed instruction best suited?
- What balance, if any, should exist between the two types?
- Which children, if any, learn best from either type or given combinations of the two types?
- What phases of performance (acquisition, fluency, maintenance, generalization) are promoted by the two types? (p. 130)

Further research will be necessary to reveal how DAP and early childhood special education are compatible.

Alternative Assessment

Educational assessment, including that of special education, is undergoing substantial changes. Standardized testing, the traditional approach, is being deemphasized in favor of alternative procedures. The alternatives to standardized testing include those we discussed in Chapter 4, such as performance testing, portfolio assessment, and curriculum-based assessment. In early childhood special education, too, a similar shift in thinking about assessment is occurring (Barnett, Macmann, & Carey, 1992; Neisworth & Bagnato, 1992). Following are five key principles that undergird assessment, including that of young children with disabilities:

- No testing of young children should occur unless it can be shown to lead to beneficial results.
- Methods of assessment, especially the language used, must be appropriate to the development and experiences of young children.
- Features of assessment—content, form, evidence of validity, and standards for interpretation—must be tailored to the specific purpose of an assessment.
- Identifying children for special education is a legitimate purpose for assessment and still requires the use of curriculum-free, aptitude-like measures and

normative comparisons. However, [disabilities of young children] are rare; the diagnostic model used by special education should not be generalized to a larger population of below-average learners.

- For both classroom instructional purposes and purposes of public policy making, the content of assessments should embody the important dimensions of early learning and development. The tasks and skills children are asked to perform should reflect and model progress toward important learning goals. (Shepard, 1994, p. 212)

The trends in assessment are clearly away from testing and toward performance criteria directly related to the preschool curriculum. However, controversy continues about the role specific types of tests (e.g., IQ tests, developmental scales) should play in diagnosis and evaluation and about the relative value of various alternative procedures such as portfolios and teacher observation (Taylor, 1997).

Education for Transition

A major trend in early childhood education, both general and special, is to plan for the transition of young children from home to school and from preschool to kindergarten (Chandler, 1993; Fowler, Schwartz, & Atwater, 1991; Hadden & Fowler, 1997; Rous, Hemmeter, & Schuster, 1994). Much of the thinking about transition is based on child development literature indicating the importance of transitions in cognitive and social characteristics that occur at certain ages (Kleinhammer-Tramill et al., 1994; Sameroff & McDonough, 1994). Furthermore, as children move from families to preschools and from preschools to kindergarten and on to first grade, they must become more self-directed and less dependent on adults. Table 7.1 contains a list of social, communication, task-related, and self-help behaviors that preschoolers must learn for successful transition to kindergarten. The child who does not exhibit these expected behaviors in kindergarten is likely to be at risk of failure in later grades.

Table 7.2 provides a list of important signs that an educational program is meeting these needs and that children are making successful transitions. Notice that the items listed in Table 7.2 include not only child behavior, but family and community involvement as well.

Family-Based Education

As we discussed in Chapter 6, parent and family involvement in special education is usually highly desirable. Particularly strong emphasis is placed on families in early childhood education for children with disabilities. So much of early education is grounded in the home that family participation is required for effective early intervention. The language experiences—being talked to and read to and observing others using written and oral language—provided by the family environment are critical to children's early learning (Hart & Risley, 1995). Two aspects of families are points of critical concern and controversy: cultural diversity and diversity of family structure.

TABLE 7.1 Transition Skills Related to Successful Transition from Preschool to Kindergarten

■ Social Behaviors and Classroom Conduct

Understands role as part of group
Respects others and their property
Interacts and defends self without aggression
Plays cooperatively, shares toys and materials
Expresses emotions and affections appropriately
Takes turn, participates appropriately in games
Is willing to try something new
Follows class rules and routines
Lines up and waits appropriately
Imitates peer actions
Sits appropriately
Plays independently

■ Communication Behaviors

Follows two- to three-part directions
Initiates and maintains peer interactions
Modifies behavior when given verbal feedback
Asks peers or teachers for information or assistance
Recalls and follows directions for tasks previously described
Follows group instructions
Relates ideas and experiences
Answers questions
Communicates own needs and wants

■ Task-Related Behaviors

Finds materials needed for tasks
Does not disrupt peers during activities
Complies quickly with teacher instructions
Generalizes skills across tasks and situations
Follows task directions in small or large group
Replaces materials and cleans up work space
Monitors own behavior, knows when a task is done
Begins and completes work at appropriate times without extra teacher attention
Makes choices
Stays in own space
Follows routine in transition
Uses a variety of materials
Seeks attention appropriately
Attends to teacher in a large group

■ Self-Help Behaviors

Recognizes when a problem exists
Locates and cares for personal belongings
Avoids dangers and responds to warning words
Takes outer clothing off and puts it on in a reasonable amount of time
Tries strategies to solve problems
Feeds self independently
Cares for own toileting needs

Source: Adapted from "Steps in Preparing for Transition: Preschool to Kindergarten" by L. K. Chandler, 1993, *Teaching Exceptional Children,* 25(4), p. 54. Copyright 1993 by Council for Exceptional Children. Reprinted by permission.

TABLE 7.2 Indications That Successful Transition Is Occurring

1. Children like school and look forward to going to school regularly.
2. Children show steady growth in academic skills.
3. Parents become actively involved in their children's education at home, in school, and in the community.
4. Classroom environments are emotionally positive ones for both teachers and children.
5. Teachers and families value each other.
6. Schools celebrate the cultural diversity in their communities and in the nation as a whole.
7. Developmentally appropriate practices are visible in the classrooms.
8. The community shows consistent investment in the education of children and strives to increase the learning opportunities available.

Source: Adapted from "The Transition to School: Why the First Few Years Matter for a Lifetime" by S. L. Ramey and C. T. Ramey, 1994, *Phi Delta Kappan, 76,* pp. 196–197. Copyright 1994 by Phi Delta Kappan. Reprinted by permission.

Cultural diversity is important because of the variety found in families' language and literacy traditions, views of disability, assumptions about learning, and ways of relating to school personnel. Inviting and encouraging parent participation in special education will be effective only if teachers accept and understand the reality of cultural differences (Harry, 1995; Linan-Thompson & Jean, 1997; van Keulen et al., 1998). Effective communication with families is the key to their involvement. Box 7.4 provides information about resources to help teachers and families develop better communication links.

The structure and composition of families vary tremendously, and traditional assumptions about the strengths and weaknesses of diverse families may need to be revised (Hanson & Carta, 1996; Hanson & Lynch, 1992). The very definition of family has become controversial due to the frequent dissolution of family units by divorce and the changing, multicultural groupings that constitute families. One definition is that in a family, "the members of the unit see themselves as a family, are affiliated with one another, and are committed to caring for one another" (Hanson & Lynch, 1992, p. 285). Teachers must learn to set aside stereotypes of family constitution and strength or weakness and work with families regardless of their structure. Hanson and Carta (1996) suggest that teachers must work with other professionals to:

1. provide critical and positive interactions with students and demonstrate these for parents
2. find and support the strengths of individual families
3. help families find and use informal sources of support from friends, neighbors, coworkers, or others in the community

BOX 7.4 ***EXAMPLE***

Training and Information for Diverse Families of Children with Disabilities

A national network of organizations for parents of children with disabilities can be an important resource for culturally and linguistically diverse families of children in your classroom. Each state has a parent training and information center funded by the U.S. Department of Education's Office of Special Education Programs. The centers are guided by the view that parents are full partners in the educational process and a significant source of support and assistance to each other. Often centers have materials available for families from varied cultural and linguistic communities. In addition, some may have staff members who can translate information for families with limited English. The centers provide training and information to help parents and family members

- Better understand the nature and needs of the disability of their child
- Provide home follow-up to support their child's school program
- Communicate with school personnel
- Participate in educational decision making
- Obtain information about available programs, resources, and services

For the address or phone number of the center nearest you, contact

Technical Assistance for Parent Programs Project (TAPP)
Federation for Children with Special Needs
95 Berkeley St., Suite 104
Boston, MA 02116
617/482–2915 or their Web site at http://www.fcns.org

Source: From "Increasing Opportunities for Partnership with Culturally and Linguistically Diverse Families" by E. K. Thorp, 1997, *Intervention in School and Clinic, 32,* p. 263. Copyright 1997 by PRO-ED, Inc. Reprinted by permission.

Questions to Ponder

How can families and parents be supportive of each other in the education of their children?

What should be the first steps of a teacher in establishing communication with the parents of a child with disabilities?

4. become competent in understanding and valuing cultural differences in families
5. provide a broad spectrum of coordinated services so that families receive comprehensive, flexible, and usable services that address their needs

Summary

1. How can learning disabilities be prevented?
   a. Prevention of learning disabilities may be:
      (1) primary—keeping the disability from occurring at all
      (2) secondary—correcting a problem or keeping it from getting worse
      (3) tertiary—keeping the problem from spreading to other areas of functioning
   b. Addressing risk factors for learning disabilities in infancy and early childhood requires identifying and removing the conditions that increase the

chances that a child will develop a disability. These factors are multiple and complex and vary greatly from individual to individual and with the age of the child.

   c. Distinguishing disabilities from cultural differences of young children requires knowledge of the cultural and linguistic diversity of families. Sensitivity to cultural differences should reduce both the overrepresentation of minority children in special education and the underidentification of children with disabilities from culturally and linguistically diverse groups.

2. How are learning disabilities identified in infancy and early childhood?
   a. Two approaches to early identification are:
      (1) a generic approach—specific disability labels are not assigned to children's difficulties, but instead a very general designation (e.g., "developmentally delayed") is used to indicate problems that may indicate a variety of disabilities
      (2) a specific approach, meaning that specific labels (e.g., "learning disability," "reading disability") are used and specific skill areas are targets for remediation
   b. Promises and pitfalls of early identification include the promise of prevention and the pitfall of misidentification.
3. How is early childhood intervention provided?
   a. Popular early intervention programs include:
      (1) Project Head Start, a preschool program for disadvantaged youngsters begun in the 1960s and now frequently including preschoolers with disabilities
      (2) Reading Recovery, a reading tutorial program imported from New Zealand
      (3) Success for All, a program designed for disadvantaged primary-grade children involving special reading instruction in small, homogeneous groups plus tutoring for individual children
   b. The legal requirements of early intervention include the Individuals with Disabilities Education Act and other federal laws. Preschoolers with disabilities must have an individualized family service plan detailing what services they will be provided and how their families will be involved.
   c. Guidelines for evaluating early childhood program quality include questions relevant to both general and special education, including the type and intensity of instruction offered, the way the child feels about the program, and family and community involvement.
4. What are some trends and controversies in early childhood education? Contemporary issues and trends include:
   a. greater inclusion of young children with disabilities in preschools serving normally developing youngsters
   b. the widespread acceptance of practices described as developmentally appropriate, although there is controversy about the extent to which such prac-

tices, which do not focus on accelerating the child's acquisition of specific skills, are appropriate for children with disabilities

c. new approaches to the assessment of young children, including alternate assessment that relies less on standardized testing and accommodates cultural and linguistic diversity
d. emphasis on transition of children from home to preschool and preschool to kindergarten so that the child is more likely to experience success in the primary grades
e. emphasis on family involvement in the education of young children and family-based education, with recognition of the need to adapt to cultural and linguistic diversity and diversity of family structure

8

Transition Programming in Adolescence and Adulthood

What Are Learning Disability Outcomes across the Life Span?
- Higher Dropout Rates
- Higher Underemployment
- Greater Dependency on Others

What Transition Programs and Services Are Available?
- Federal Initiatives
- Interagency Collaboration and Service Delivery
- Social Skills and Self-Advocacy Training
- Parental Involvement
- Vocational Training and College Preparation

How Are Students with Learning Disabilities Prepared for College?
- Programming Goals for College Preparation

How Can Students with Learning Disabilities Succeed in College?
- Guidelines for Choosing a College
- Predictors of Success in College
- Instructional Accommodations

How Can Students with Learning Disabilities Prepare for the Work World?
- Programming Goals for Vocational Training
- School-Business Partnerships

A once-ignored population, adults with learning disabilities are coming into their own. More and more researchers are turning their attention to issues pertaining to this group. Whereas professionals used to believe that children with learning disabilities outgrew their problems during adolescence, we now recognize that many adults are in need of special programming. And more and more adults are taking an active role in the recognition and treatment of their problems.

This interest in adults with learning disabilities has spawned a variety of programs designed to enhance the transition of adolescents into adulthood. **Transition** has been defined as:

> a change in status from behaving primarily as a student to assuming emergent adult roles in the community. These roles include employment, participating in post-secondary education, maintaining a home, becoming appropriately involved in the community, and experiencing satisfactory personal and social relationships. The process of enhancing transition involves the participation and coordination of school programs, adult agency services, and natural supports within the community. The foundations for transition should be laid during the elementary and middle school years, guided by the broad concept of career development. Transition planning should begin no later than age 14, and students should be encouraged, to the full extent of their capabilities, to assume a minimum amount of responsibility for such planning. (Halpern, 1994, p. 117)

This definition stresses the need for a comprehensive array of services and does not focus solely on employment. This broad conceptualization is in keeping with the attitude of many in the field who consider transition from a quality of life perspective, which includes such things as independence, happiness, and contentment (Halpern, 1993; Szymanski, 1994).

WHAT ARE LEARNING DISABILITY OUTCOMES ACROSS THE LIFE SPAN?

Two general types of evidence lead us to the conclusion that learning disabilities usually persist into adulthood: research on characteristics and research on outcomes. A body of research, largely conducted in the 1970s and 1980s, focused on the characteristics of secondary students and adults. It shows that the same academic and social problems manifested in childhood are likely to continue into adulthood (Kavale, 1988). Even intensive programming at the elementary and secondary levels will not "cure" most learning disabilities, especially those that are relatively severe. The disabilities may change their form slightly as older persons with learning disabilities learn to cope with their problems, but for the most part, to have a learning disability is to have a lifelong condition.

The second type of evidence suggesting the intractability of learning disabilities focused on outcomes related to major phases in life. Researchers have found that learning disabilities are associated with higher rates of dropping out of secondary school, underemployment, and greater dependency on others.

Higher Dropout Rates

Obtaining national data on outcomes pertaining to secondary-school attendance (e.g., graduation rates, dropout rates) should be fairly straightforward. But researchers have pointed out that it is difficult to compare students with disabilities to those without disabilities using national statistics related to secondary-school outcomes because the two federal agencies responsible for collecting the information on each population use different methodologies (MacMillan et al., 1992).

However, smaller-scale studies of secondary-school outcomes have used comparable data collection measures for students with and without learning disabilities. Although their relatively small size and geographical scope limit the conclusions we can draw from them, these studies suggest that students with learning disabilities are far more likely than their nondisabled peers to drop out of school. One survey found that 54% of students with learning disabilities who attended secondary school ended up dropping out, compared to 33% of students without disabilities (Zigmond & Thornton, 1985). Another survey found a dropout rate of 36% for students with learning disabilities and 13% for students without disabilities (deBettencourt, Zigmond, & Thornton, 1989).

Another revealing statistic is that 48% of students with learning disabilities leave secondary school without a diploma (U.S. Department of Education, 1994). In other words, almost half of students with learning disabilities either drop out or receive a certificate of completion rather than a diploma.

Higher Underemployment

Several large-scale studies have been relatively consistent in finding that the employment rates of persons with learning disabilities are similar to those of the general population. For example, data from the National Longitudinal Transition Study (NLTS) on students out of high school three to five years showed that 71% of those with learning disabilities were employed, compared to 69% of those in the general population (Blackorby & Wagner, 1996). And looking over a ten-year span at high school graduates from three large school districts, researchers found that the employment rates for graduates with learning disabilities did not differ most years from those without learning disabilities (Murray, Goldstein, & Edgar, 1997). There are some indications that the employment status for women with learning disabilities may be lower, but that may be because some of them have chosen to stay at home with their children (Murray et al., 1997).

Whereas the best available data suggest that, except for the possible exception of females, unemployment rates for adults with learning disabilities are generally not critically high, there is abundant evidence that underemployment is a major problem. For example, data from the NLTS survey of students with learning disabilities out of school three to five years indicated that only 45% earned more than $6 per hour. The types of jobs held by young adults with learning disabilities tend to require low-level skills; many are part-time service, fast-food, or laborer positions (Gajar, 1992; White, 1992).

Greater Dependency on Others

Although few data exist on the residential status of adults with learning disabilities, those available suggest that a disproportionate number live with their parents or relatives. For example, one research team found that, in a sample of 21-year-olds with learning disabilities, 79% were living with their parents or relatives (Haring, Lovett, & Smith, 1990). And researchers using the NLTS data found that only 44% of persons with learning disabilities were living independently three to five years after high school, compared to 60% of the general population (Blackorby & Wagner, 1996).

WHAT TRANSITION PROGRAMS AND SERVICES ARE AVAILABLE?

Results from outcome studies of adults with learning disabilities as well as adults with other types of disabilities (e.g., mental retardation, emotional or behavioral disorders) have done much to convince policy makers that major initiatives need to be directed toward transition programming. There has been a series of federal government initiatives to strengthen educational programming for secondary-school students with disabilities to enable them to make a more successful transition to adulthood.

Federal Initiatives

Prior to the passage of P.L. 94-142 in 1975, public school programming for students with disabilities beyond elementary-school age was minimal. This law mandated that students with disabilities receive an appropriate education until graduation from high school or until 21 years of age. In the mid-1980s, the federal government announced the "transition initiative" (Will, 1984). Based on this call for action, Congress passed several pieces of legislation, the most important of which was IDEA (P.L. 101-476, passed in 1990 and amended in 1997 as P.L. 105-17), which mandates that schools provide transition services for all students with disabilities.

In order to ensure proper and timely planning for the implementation of transition services, the law requires that a transition plan be integrated into each student's individualized education program (IEP). The 1997 reauthorization of IDEA requires the IEP to contain the following:

> 1. beginning at age 14 and updated annually, a statement of the transition service needs of the child under the applicable components of the child's IEP that focuses on the child's courses of study (such as participation in advanced-placement courses or a vocational education program)
> 2. beginning at age 16 (or younger, if determined appropriate by the IEP Team), a statement of needed transition services for the child, including, when appropriate, a statement of the interagency responsibilities or any needed linkages. (IDEA Amendments of 1997, Sec. 614(d) (I) (A) vii, p. 55)

By mandating that the transition plan be part of a student's IEP, Congress has underscored the importance of each student's need for a unique transition experience. With the wide variety of employment and postsecondary experiences, as well as the many living options available, individualization becomes increasingly important as the student with learning disabilities progresses through secondary school. Very few students with learning disabilities will have exactly the same transition training needs. The needs of many will change as they progress through secondary school. Adolescence is a time of rapid physical and emotional alterations. Students at this age frequently modify their vocational and educational aspirations.

Interagency Collaboration and Service Delivery

Implicit in current conceptualizations of transition services is the idea of a coordinated set of services. This coordination

> helps ensure that transition outcomes, service needs, and expectations for how they will be provided are communicated among and agreed to by key participants. . . . It also guards against duplication of services and, therefore, the more unfortunate occurrence of students who "fall through the cracks" and fail to access needed services. (DeStefano & Wermuth, 1992, p. 540)

For example, vocational rehabilitation personnel might be involved for those headed toward employment, as might college representatives for those headed toward college. Although it may not always be practical for college personnel to participate in IEP meetings, some have noted that if a student plans to attend a college nearby, it can be beneficial for the college learning disabilities specialist to become involved as early as possible in the transition process (Aune & Johnson, 1992). This gives the specialist an opportunity to inform the student and the family of the college's services and expectations while learning more about the student's interests.

Social Skills and Self-Advocacy Training

One of the most persistent problem areas for students with learning disabilities is that of social skills. Because social skills deficits can have profound effects on adults' functioning at work and in college, many authorities point to the need for social skills training as a part of transition programming. Unfortunately, social skills are not easily trained, and many adults with learning disabilities continue to face problems interacting with friends and colleagues. One of the problems in training social skills for transition is that, although identifying the social skills necessary to function in school is difficult, doing so may be even more difficult in the workplace. Among other things, there is a wider variety of work settings, rules of the workplace may be less well defined, and feedback for poor performance may be more subtle (Mellard & Hazel, 1992).

Social skills are also extremely important for successful transition to college. Students, with or without disabilities, who are able to interact with other students and faculty are in a better position to be successful in college. It may be even more necessary that students with learning disabilities display good social skills. For example, being able to act as their own advocate serves college students with learning disabilities well, and being able to talk with professors about their learning disabilities in order to receive accommodations requires a great deal of social poise and tact. Because learning disabilities are "invisible" and poorly understood by so many, an articulate spokesperson is often needed to explain their ramifications. Students who are either too aggressive or too timid may have great difficulty talking with professors about their learning disabilities.

Many authorities have pointed out that secondary-school students need to take the initiative in developing their transition programming (see Box 8.1). Being actively involved in their own transition planning does not come easily for some students. Some authorities think it is important that **self-advocacy** be a part of transition training in high school, and there is some evidence that self-advocacy can be taught (Durlak, Rose, & Bursuck, 1994; Phillips, 1990). For example, one team of researchers taught students with learning disabilities to state the nature of their disability and its impact on academic and social functioning and to identify accommodations and strategies for implementing them with their general education teachers (Durlak et al., 1994). Another team of researchers successfully implemented a self-awareness and self-advocacy program for persons with learning disabilities who had graduated from high school and were enrolled in college in a nondegree program focused on achieving independence (Roffman, Herzog, & Wershba-Gershon, 1994).

Parental Involvement

The role of parents can be crucial to many aspects of educational programming for students with learning disabilities. As the student enters transition programming, parents begin to grapple with issues pertaining to their child's emerging sexuality, vocational choices, and dependency. It is at this time that many parents begin to face the prospect that their child's learning disability is a lifelong condition that will require

BOX 8.1 ***EXAMPLE***

Preparing for Transition: Things the Student Should Do

Many authorities have pointed out that secondary students should play an active role in their own transition programming. The National Joint Committee on Learning Disabilities, consisting of several major professional and parent organizations concerned with learning disabilities, has identified the following responsibilities of secondary students with learning disabilities:

To contribute to successful transition planning, the student should

- understand his or her specific LD, including its effect on learning and work;
- establish realistic goals;
- present a positive self-image by stressing strengths, while understanding the influence of the LD;
- know how, when, and where to discuss and request needed accommodations;
- develop personal qualities, such as realistic self-assessment, willingness to take risks, and ability to sustain efforts;
- develop and use social skills;
- develop and apply effective studying, test-preparation, test-taking, time-management, and note-taking strategies;
- seek instructors and learning environments that are supportive;
- maintain an ongoing personal file that includes school and medical records, individualized education program (IEP), résumé, and samples of academic work;
- know rights and responsibilities necessary to prepare for and access postsecondary education;
- identify and access resources that will provide needed support;
- explore postsecondary education options and entrance requirements;
- select courses that meet postsecondary requirements; and
- prepare for and participate actively in the postsecondary application process.

Source: From "Secondary to Postsecondary Education Transition Planning for Students with Learning Disabilities" by National Joint Committee on Learning Disabilities, 1996, *Learning Disability Quarterly, 19,* pp. 62–63. Copyright 1996 by Council for Learning Disabilities. Reprinted by permission.

Questions to Ponder

Which do you think are the three or four most important responsibilities?

Which responsibilities would generally be the most difficult for most students with learning disabilities to assume? Can you think of some strategies to help them learn these responsibilities?

Can you think of any other responsibilities?

relatively constant emotional and financial support. Many young adults with learning disabilities live at home with their parents (Haring et al., 1990).

Some strategies that professionals have recommended for increasing parental participation in transition programming are to encourage parents to (1) begin precareer development activities with their children by assigning them chores and paying them a small allowance, (2) honor their children's choices in order to increase their independence, and (3) develop informal sources of support such as friends, relatives, and community organizations (Brotherson, Berdine, & Sartini, 1993). In addition, students with learning disabilities who achieve successfully are often supported by their parents. One thing that parents can do is help them find areas in which they can excel in order to compensate for the areas in school in which they perform poorly. By finding an area in which they can develop talent and succeed, children with learning disabilities may begin to think that they could do better in school if they worked harder (Reis, Neu, & McGuire, 1997).

Vocational Training and College Preparation

Although transition plans are individualized, by the time students near graduation, they should be pointed toward either employment or postsecondary schooling. The need to decide how much a particular student's transition program should be oriented toward one or the other is one of the biggest challenges facing students, parents, and teachers.

Some think that many students with learning disabilities do not live up to their academic potential because they are routed into a non-college-bound track from which they are unable to escape. These authorities assert that there are diminished expectations for students with learning disabilities that result in an unchallenging curriculum. One team of researchers, for example, found that secondary-school learning disabilities classrooms exhibited an "environmental press against academic content" (Zigmond & Miller, 1992, p. 25).

But some think that an overemphasis on academics can leave some students with learning disabilities ill prepared for the workplace. They maintain that many students with learning disabilities have such severe problems that it is unrealistic to expect them to succeed in college. Investigators have found that vocational training has a certain degree of "holding power" by helping to keep students in school rather than dropping out. Furthermore, students who do not attend college but participate in vocational training end up with higher paying jobs than those who do not receive vocational training (Evers, 1996).

In some cases, students, parents, and teachers agree from the start about the direction the student is headed—college or work. The advantage to determining direction early is that it allows for a longer period of appropriately focused instruction; however, one needs to be cautious about starting the student off on a sequence of courses that are a waste of time.

HOW ARE STUDENTS WITH LEARNING DISABILITIES PREPARED FOR COLLEGE?

As described by Zigmond (1990), the college-bound model of programming for secondary-school students with learning disabilities should include five features:

1. LD students are assigned to mainstream classes for math, content subjects required for graduation, and elective courses. . . .
2. One special education teacher is assigned as a support or consulting teacher to work with mainstream teachers in whose classes LD students are placed. . . .

3. Additional special education teachers are responsible for yearly English/reading courses, one survival skills class, and a supervised study hall, which LD students are scheduled to take each year of high school. . . .
4. From the start of ninth grade, LD students interact regularly with a counselor for transition planning. . . .
5. Courses required for graduation are spaced evenly throughout the four years to reduce academic pressures, particularly in ninth grade. (pp. 16–17)

An advantage of this model is that it stresses the strengths of special education teachers by not requiring them to teach in all content areas. Many secondary special education teachers are not prepared to teach a variety of subjects, such as social studies, science, and math. Instead, this model requires them to teach only English/reading courses and survival skills (e.g., behavior control and study and organizational skills) and to consult with general education teachers on how to modify their instruction to accommodate students with learning disabilities. Table 8.1 presents a sample four-year schedule for students in the college-bound model. (Note that this schedule meets Pennsylvania graduation requirements but might not meet those in other states.)

Programming Goals for College Preparation

An important aspect of preparing for college is taking courses that meet the entrance requirements. In Zigmond's model, for instance, there are several electives that need to be chosen carefully. It is usually better for students to take college prep classes, even

TABLE 8.1 Sample Four-Year Schedule for College-Bound Students

Year 1	Year 2	Year 3	Year 4
English/Reading[a]	English/Reading[a]	English/Reading[a]	English/Reading[a]
Math	Math	Math	Social Studies
Social Studies	Science	Social Studies	Science
Survival Skills[a]	Study Hall[a]	Science	Study Hall[a]
Study Hall[a]	PE	Study Hall[a]	PE
PE/Health	Elective[b]	PE/Health	Elective[b]
Elective[b]	Elective[b]	Elective[b]	Elective[b]

[a]Course taught by special education teacher.

[b]Electives selected with advice from counselor to meet distribution requirements for graduation, college entrance requirements for students considering postsecondary education, and/or student's vocational interests. (This schedule meets Pennsylvania requirements for graduation.)

Source: From "Rethinking Secondary School Programs for Students with Learning Disabilities" by N. Zigmond, 1990, *Focus on Exceptional Children,* 23(1), p. 17. Copyright 1990 by Love Publishing Co. Reprinted by permission.

though they will probably obtain a lower grade, than to take mostly general education classes (Brinckerhoff, 1996).

Another key aspect of transition programming for students with learning disabilities who are headed for college is to provide them with organizational, time management, and study skills. These students are notorious for their deficiencies in these skills that most college-bound students have in their repertoires. Zigmond's model also emphasizes classes devoted to these important skills.

HOW CAN STUDENTS WITH LEARNING DISABILITIES SUCCEED IN COLLEGE?

Although it is difficult to obtain accurate statistics on how many students with learning disabilities go on to college, our best estimates indicate that, five years after leaving secondary school, about 12% and 4% of students with learning disabilities go to two-year and four-year colleges, respectively (Wagner, Blackorby, Cameto, Hebbeler, & Newman, 1993). Although this is not a large percentage, most authorities agree that there has been a dramatic increase in the number of students with all kinds of disabilities, including learning disabilities, attending college.

Some of the increase in students with learning disabilities attending college is undoubtedly due to legislation prohibiting discrimination against persons with disabilities. At one time, college was out of the question for many students with learning disabilities. Beginning in the mid-1970s, however, federal law prohibited institutions of higher education from discriminating against students with disabilities. Section 504 of the Rehabilitation Act of 1973 mandates that "no otherwise qualified handicapped individual . . . shall, solely by reason of his/her handicap, be excluded from participation in, be denied the benefits of, or be subject to discrimination under any program or activity receiving financial assistance."

Applying the phrase "otherwise qualified" in individual cases is not always easy. It is clear, however, that the courts have interpreted it not to mean the lowering of admissions standards. The Supreme Court, in *Southeastern Community College v. Davis* (1979), ruled that a nursing program could deny admission to a student who was hearing impaired and unable to understand speech because, being unable to hear patients, she might put them in danger. What the law did mean was that decisions should be based on actual abilities rather than prejudicial assumptions (Brinckerhoff, Shaw, & McGuire, 1992). In addition, colleges are to make adjustments in requirements for courses, but these accommodations are not expected to alter the essential aspects of the curriculum.

Immediately following the passage of Section 504, colleges and universities did not suddenly throw open their doors to students with disabilities. Over time, as the courts have helped to define the parameters of the law and public opinion about persons with disabilities has improved, many colleges and universities have become more comfortable with the idea of admitting and accommodating students with disabilities, including learning disabilities. Some now have a full-time faculty or staff person who specializes in learning disabilities. This coordinator may have a variety of support staff, such as a full-time assistant and graduate-level interns who provide a number of services, including tutoring, acting as a liaison to the faculty, and developing individualized semester plans similar to IEPs (Shaw, McGuire, & Brinckerhoff, 1994). In fact, some institutions of higher education have gained reputations as good places for students with learning disabilities to attend because of the level of support offered.

Guidelines for Choosing a College

Choosing a college is difficult for any student. Reputation, academic rigor, location, types of majors offered, extracurricular activities, and cost are just some of the many variables that parents and students consider. In the case of students with learning disabilities, the choice can be even more difficult. They and their parents will also want to consider the level of support offered for those with learning disabilities. See Box 8.2 for a list of questions that students and their parents can use in assessing colleges.

Secondary-school teachers and counselors now recommend that students with learning disabilities who are likely to be college bound begin to seek information on different colleges early in their secondary schooling. In fact, some advocate that one of the transition goals on the IEP be that students be able to research various colleges' entrance requirements, curricula, and learning disabilities services (Blalock & Patton, 1996).

One issue students need to address when considering colleges is whether they should attend a two-year or a four-year institution. This decision depends on several factors. Many students value two-year colleges because they more often "have open admissions policies; smaller class ratios; comparatively low tuition fees; academic and personal counseling; and a wide range of vocational, remedial, and developmental courses" (Brinckerhoff, 1996, p. 127). Some students, especially those whose disabilities are less severe, are able to handle the less structured setting of a four-year college.

Predictors of Success in College

Most college admissions officers will tell you that predicting how well a particular student will do in college is nearly impossible. Some who have excelled in high school have not been able to do the same in college. Some who barely scraped by in high school suddenly find their niche in college. College and university officials have developed a relatively uniform set of criteria based on predictive studies involving large numbers of applicants. These criteria, such as high school grade-point average (GPA) and SAT scores, are often used because they are the best predictors available, but they are far from perfect.

Selecting which students with learning disabilities are likely to succeed in college is even riskier. We do not yet have a well-established research base on which to make these kinds of predictions with much accuracy, and using traditional criteria is prob-

BOX 8.2 ***EXAMPLE***

Questions to Ask Before Selecting a College

The following set of questions, proposed by Michaels (1987, pp. 486–487), are designed to serve as guidelines for choosing a college.

Does the college provide the following:

- a full-time coordinator of services for learning-disabled students
- preliminary diagnostic services in order to determine student ability to work at the college level
- preadmission advisement
- short-term and long-term student counseling
- study skills course work
- remedial and basic classes
- feedback systems from professors to coordinators of services for learning disabled students
- termination services (counseling, testing, etc.) for those learning disabled students who leave college

Does the college furnish the following:

- access to required course syllabi
- access to tutors, readers, and note-takers
- computers for student use
- taped textbooks and recorded lectures

Does the college allow the following:

- modified college admission procedures
- visits to college classrooms in advance of enrolling in the college
- untimed exams
- varied testing options
- advance acquisition of required reading assignments

Does the college supply the following:

- full-time or part-time educators to assist with the needs of the learning disabled population
- guidance in structuring the student workday
- student groups that facilitate making friends
- access to early registration procedures

Does the college give the following:

- assistance with class scheduling
- listings of outside services and support groups in the college community for use by learning disabled students

Questions to Ponder

Which do you think are the three or four most important questions to ask?

Which questions would generally be the most difficult for colleges to answer satisfactorily?

Can you think of any other questions that should be asked?

lematic. Students with learning disabilities may not "test well" on standardized tests such as the SAT, even though they are entitled to accommodations, and their GPAs may be difficult to interpret because the courses and accommodations they received may vary considerably, depending on the high schools they attended.

The little research that has been done on predicting college success for students with learning disabilities suggests that admissions officers should look at factors pertaining to performance in high school rather than at admissions tests such as the SAT or the ACT. One team of researchers found that, although far from perfect, such things as high school GPA and number of mainstream English courses completed with a grade of C or better were better predictors than standardized test scores (Vogel & Adelman, 1992). Demands placed on students differ from high school to college, but college requires a great deal more student independence than secondary school. For example, there is considerably less classroom instruction in college, the implication being that students will spend more time outside of class reading and studying on their own. Many students have problems adjusting to the decreased structure of college. Students with learning disabilities may have an even more difficult time because they are prone to have problems in independence and their high school programs may have been even more structured than those of most students (Brinckerhoff et al., 1992). These observations have led many college admissions officers to point to motivation and the ability to work independently as important attributes to consider in selecting students with learning disabilities (Spillane, McGuire, & Norlander, 1992).

Instructional Accommodations

As noted, Section 504 of the Rehabilitation Act requires that colleges make reasonable adjustments for students with disabilities in order that they not be discriminated against on the basis of their disabilities. These adjustments can take three general forms: "adaptations in the manner in which specific courses are conducted, the use of auxiliary equipment, and modifications in academic requirements" (Brinckerhoff et al., 1992, p. 421). The following are some examples of relatively common accommodations for students with learning disabilities:

- adjustments in course requirements and evaluation
  - giving extra time on exams
  - allowing students to take exams in a distraction-free room
  - allowing students to take exams in a different format (e.g., substituting an oral exam for a written one)
- modifications in program requirements
  - waiving or substituting certain requirements (e.g., a foreign language)
  - allowing students to take a lighter academic load
- auxiliary aids
  - providing tape recordings of textbooks
  - providing access to a Kurzweil Reading Machine (a computer that scans text and converts it into auditory output)
  - recruiting and assigning volunteer note-takers for lectures

Although the intent of the law and subsequent litigation is fairly clear relative to modification of course requirements, program requirements, and evaluation of students, it is less obvious with regard to individual instructor's approaches to instruction.

One can make a strong case that, especially with regard to lectures and discussion courses, some of the same pedagogical strategies that make for good instruction for many students without learning disabilities are of particular benefit to those with them. Starting lectures with a review of past material, providing advance organizers, and using an overhead projector or computerized graphic displays to emphasize main points are just a few of the techniques that help most students, especially those with learning disabilities, attend to and retain information presented in lectures. As yet, however, the law has not been used to dictate that instructors use such techniques.

Institutions of higher education vary widely in how they handle implementation of accommodations for students with disabilities. Although Section 504 has been in effect since the 1970s, the process of interpreting the law through litigation continues. Many universities have adopted policy advisory committees to help university administrators educate faculty about accommodations and resolve disputes when they arise. The notion of academic freedom is ingrained deeply into the consciousness of many faculty, and some are immediately suspicious of anything they think will impinge on it. Policy advisory boards, some of whose members are faculty, can do much to alleviate tension concerning appropriate accommodations.

Some have also pointed out that providing accommodations can help faculty better understand their own programs. Determining what are appropriate accommodations and what are essential components of a program takes more than a cursory review of program requirements:

> Defining the essential requirements of academic programs and courses is, in some respects, a Herculean task. Faculty and academic departments are being asked to define and come to consensus on the core of their disciplines. Often, faculty are faced with this task in response to an immediate request for accommodation by a student currently enrolled in a course. On a short-term basis, faculty must apply their best professional judgment in defining the essential elements of a course or program. However, determining essential requirements should ultimately be viewed as an ongoing dialogue for professional examination, perhaps extending beyond individual faculty members and departments to a topic to be addressed within fields or disciplines. (Scott, 1994, p. 408)

HOW CAN STUDENTS WITH LEARNING DISABILITIES PREPARE FOR THE WORK WORLD?

As described by Zigmond (1990), the programming model for non-college-bound secondary-school students should include five features:

1. All basic skills are taught by a special educator and instruction in basic skills is linked to transition planning. . . .
2. Required "content" subjects are taught by special educators. . . .

3. Vocational education is provided in the mainstream and coordinated with transition planning provided within special education. . . .
4. All ninth grade students with learning disabilities will take a required course on survival skills taught by a special educator. . . .
5. Students' schedules would reflect a light academic load in ninth grade to ensure successful completion of the first year of high school. (pp. 18–19)

One problem with this model, conceded by Zigmond, is that it requires special education teachers to teach in content areas in which they might not be completely proficient, although the level of the content would be less than that typically taught in these subjects.

An important advantage of this model is that it provides two classes of vocational education for each of four years. Table 8.2 presents a sample four-year schedule for students in this model. (Note that this schedule meets Pennsylvania graduation requirements but might not meet those in other states.)

Programming Goals for Vocational Training

More and more authorities are moving toward a developmental approach to vocational programming. This assumes that an individual's career development occurs well into adulthood. Most developmental models of career development include three stages: career awareness, career exploration, and career experiences (Morningstar, 1997).

TABLE 8.2 Sample Four-Year Schedule for Non-College-Bound Students

Year 1	Year 2	Year 3	Year 4
English/Reading[a]	English/Reading[a]	English/Reading[a]	English/Reading[a]
Math[a]	Math[a]	Math[a]	Social Studies[a]
Social Studies[a]	Social Studies[a]	Science[a]	Science[a]
Survival Skills[a]	Science[a]	PE/Health[a]	PE
PE/Health[a]	PE	Voc Ed	Voc Ed
Voc Ed	Voc Ed	Voc Ed	Voc Ed
Voc Ed	Voc Ed	Elective[b]	Elective[b]

[a]Course taught by special education teacher.

[b]These courses would have to meet graduation requirements of two credits in Art and/or Humanities. (This schedule meets Pennsylvania requirements for graduation.)

Source: From "Rethinking Secondary School Programs for Students with Learning Disabilities" by N. Zigmond, 1990, *Focus on Exceptional Children,* 23(1), p. 19. Copyright 1990 by Love Publishing Co. Reprinted by permission.

Researchers have suggested several student-centered objectives for vocational preparation:

- Develop and implement assessment procedures which identify functional skills and interests related to current and future employment and training opportunities in the community. . . .
- Provide necessary support services to ensure access to mainstream vocational classes. . . .
- Provide at least four work experiences, six to eight weeks each, in identified areas of interest and skill for students between the ages of 15 and 18. . . .
- Assist the student in locating and securing employment prior to graduation. . . .
- Provide supervision and follow-up services to students in full-time or part-time employment until graduation (or the student's twenty-second birthday). . . .
- Develop individual transition plans with appropriate adult services agencies (i.e., vocational rehabilitation, community college, state employment service, or mental health) for students who need continued services following graduation. (Brody-Hasazi, Salembier, & Finck, 1983, pp. 207–208).

School-Business Partnerships

Most vocational specialists promote the idea that non-college-bound students with disabilities have a great deal to gain from on-the-job experiences with employers in the community. It is often difficult to arrange consistent work experiences for students, however. That is one of the reasons some have advocated formal school-business partnerships that facilitate the placement of students in real jobs while they are still in school (Tilson, Luecking, & Donovan, 1994). In addition to providing useful job training for students, such arrangements can help businesses prepare well-trained personnel for their workforce (Goldberger & Kazis, 1996).

Apprenticeship experiences for secondary-school students in general education are commonplace in some European countries, such as Germany. They have not been widely adopted in the United States because of the reluctance to identify students too early for non-college-bound "tracks." In the case of students with disabilities, the issue of tracking students too early into a vocational orientation is no less real. But many see this potential problem outweighed by the advantages of building relationships with businesses so that students can have ready access to training in meaningful job settings.

HOW CAN EMPLOYERS ENCOURAGE SUCCESS FOR ADULTS WITH LEARNING DISABILITIES?

Recent changes in the workplace are making the employment picture look less optimistic for adults with learning disabilities. Although generally seen as improvements necessary to make American business more competitive worldwide, many of these changes have worked to the disadvantage of adults with learning disabilities.

Brown and Gerber (1994) have identified four trends in the workplace that have created more problems for adults with learning disabilities. First, teamwork is replacing a more bureaucratic, hierarchical structure. Unfortunately, because they often have difficulties in social interactions (e.g., reading social cues), workers with learning disabilities may be perceived as unfriendly and uncooperative.

Second, although some technology (e.g., computer software such as spell-checkers) has made the workplace more accessible to adults with learning disabilities, technology has also placed more cognitive demands on the worker. And technological innovations are introduced at such a rapid pace that workers with learning disabilities have difficulties keeping up with these advances, thus putting them at a disadvantage to their nondisabled peers.

Third, there is an increased emphasis on credentials and passing standardized tests for certain jobs. Many jobs that used to require only a high school diploma now require a college degree. The President's Committee on Employment of People with Disabilities has estimated that, by the year 2000, more than half the jobs in the United States will require some education beyond high school and one-third will be filled by college graduates (Brown, Gerber, & Dowdy, 1990). Furthermore, some jobs (e.g., truck driver and plumber) now require passage of a licensing exam.

Fourth, in order to compete in the global economy, American businesses have placed a greater emphasis on productivity. Corporations are restructuring and reducing their work force, which means that greater demands are being placed on workers. Those employees who require less supervision and are more efficient in carrying out their assignments are more likely to be kept in the work force and to advance in their careers.

> In keeping with all of these changes in the workplace, it is important to keep in mind that the proverbial bottom line for businesses is profit: While they acknowledge that good corporate citizens hire persons with all kinds of disabilities, they also take the position that they are not running a social service agency. . . . [T]hey are looking for those who have mastered basic skills as well as other skills that will make them successful employees (i.e., social skills). (Gerber, 1992, p. 331)

Workplace Accommodations

Although employers are generally not interested in "running a social service agency," federal law requires that they make accommodations for workers with disabilities in the job application process and the job itself (so that the employee can perform the job's essential functions) and also make adjustments that allow the worker to enjoy privileges enjoyed by other workers. Specifically, the Americans with Disabilities Act (ADA) of 1990 defines accommodations in the following way:

> Reasonable accommodation means (i) modifications or adjustments to a job application process that enable a qualified applicant with a disability to be considered for the position such qualified applicant desires; or (ii) modifications or adjustments to work environment, or to the manner or circumstances under which the position held or desired is customarily performed, that enable a qualified individual with a

disability to perform the essential functions of that position; or (iii) modifications or adjustments that enable a covered entity's employee with a disability to enjoy benefits and privileges of employment as are enjoyed by its other similarly situated employees without disabilities. (*Federal Register,* July 26, 1991, pp. 35735–35736)

There are two keys to making accommodations: Employers need to know the functional limitations associated with a particular disability, and they need to understand the job's requirements (Jacobs & Hendricks, 1992). Employers often, but not always, have a grasp of the latter, but they usually need help in comprehending the former. Transition specialists can help explain the characteristics of the disability and specify the job requirements, if need be. Employers need to gain a fuller understanding of all disabilities, including learning disabilities. The Committee on Employment of People with Disabilities (Brown et al., 1990) identified widespread ignorance about learning disabilities as the major impediment to furthering the employment success of adults with learning disabilities.

As more and more employers comply with federal laws and hire and accommodate workers with learning disabilities, attitudes toward these employees may improve. A better strategy, however, is for professionals involved in transition programming to take active roles in promoting a realistic portrayal of what adults with learning disabilities can do on the job, given appropriate support and accommodations. In addition, investigators need to continue developing and testing transition models and accommodation strategies.

Ironically, in some cases, employers may need to take a more active role in making accommodations for employees with learning disabilities than they would for employees who have more severe disabilities, such as mental retardation. This is because workers with mental retardation are often provided more support under a **supported employment model,** which uses job coaches to integrate retarded workers into competitive employment situations. This has become very popular, but it is rarely used with workers who have learning disabilities because the prevailing professional opinion is that the latter group is not disabled enough to need that much support. Some professionals disagree. See Box 8.3 for a discussion of this emerging issue.

Most accommodations that have been recommended by transition specialists have addressed the first two types of accommodations—those having to do with applying for a job and those dealing with enabling the worker to perform essential job functions. Here are some examples of accommodations for the latter:

- reading problems

  Consider verbal rather than written instructions.

  Assign a coworker who is responsible for letting them know about important information contained in memos.

- listening and distractibility problems

  Assign them to quiet work space.

  Use short, simple sentences; enunciate clearly; and repeat instructions when necessary.

BOX 8.3 ***CURRENT ISSUES***

Should Supported Employment Be Used with Employees Who Are Learning Disabled?

In 1990, when Congress enacted legislation (IDEA, P.L. 101–476) mandating that schools provide transition services for all students with disabilities, it specifically mentioned supported employment as an example of a service that should be used to encourage integrated employment. Although there are different supported employment models, they all have one thing in common: They all use a job coach who, among other things, provides on-the-job training and support as needed. Supported employment is thus designed for employees who cannot work completely independently, at least initially.

Supported employment has become one of the most, if not the most, popular types of service delivery models for workers who are mentally retarded. It is virtually nonexistent as a model for employees who have learning disabilities, however. Apparently, the prevailing attitude of most special educators is that workers with learning disabilities are not disabled enough to need supported employment. This raises the question of whether these persons are being discriminated against because their disabilities are not as severe as those with mental retardation.

A few authorities have questioned why supported employment is not being used with adults with learning disabilities (e.g., Inge & Tilson, 1994; Siegel, Greener, Prieur, Robert, & Gaylord-Ross, 1989). Given the difficulties that many adults with learning disabilities have with independence, this type of model would seem ideally suited to their needs. College graduates might not need the degree of support that supported employment offers, but it might be appropriate for those with more severe learning disabilities.

There are several types of supported employment models, many of which place workers with disabilities in small groups of no more than eight and integrate these groups into competitive employment alongside nondisabled workers (Rusch & Hughes, 1990). For workers with learning disabilities, an individual placement model would probably be more appropriate (Inge & Tilson, 1994). Under this model, a job coach provides onsite training that is gradually reduced as the worker is able to function on the job more independently.

Supported employment also offers some advantages for employers. The job coach assumes many of the responsibilities that would otherwise fall to the employer. The job coach can "shadow" the worker and ensure that he or she is performing the job correctly. If something goes wrong, the job coach can be there to help the employee correct mistakes. Thus, the employer does not have to be as vigilant in watching out for the worker with learning disabilities.

Over the next several years, as more and more research and attention are given to supported employment with employees who are retarded, it will be interesting to see if supported employment will be used more often with workers with learning disabilities.

Questions to Ponder

What kinds of jobs would be most applicable to a supported employment model?

What kinds of criteria would you use to determine whether a job coach would be helpful for a particular job?

What might be some disadvantages to using a supported employment model?

Provide them with a written copy of important instructions.

Demonstrate exactly what needs to be done, rather than merely describing the task.

- organizational problems

Encourage them to use a daily checklist to keep track of their duties/ assignments.

Encourage them to use an appointment calendar.

Provide them with a three-ring binder to keep track of important written materials.

- social problems

Be patient if they misinterpret social interactions.

Make all communications direct, without sarcasm, hints, or hidden messages they might misinterpret. (Luecking, Tilson, & Wilner, 1991)

The following excerpt provides a case example of an accommodation that was made for the job application process:

> An employer in the transportation business contacted the JAN [Job Accommodation Network] office to request accommodation information for a prospective employee. He had just interviewed a person who mentioned that she had an SLD [specific learning disability] in spelling and writing. Although the applicant presented herself well during the interview, and her résumé was well done and neatly typed, she had mentioned difficulties in writing cohesive papers in school and taking notes when teachers lectured. For the job of radio dispatcher, she was required to complete a timed, multiple-choice and essay pre-employment test.
>
> The JAN consultant asked the employer to describe what the test was designed to measure. The employer responded that it was a test of verbal abilities, basic math skills, and logic. Next, the employer was asked to describe the "essential functions" of a radio dispatcher. The employer indicated that at this company, dispatchers received typewritten instructions, which they relayed to drivers.
>
> Since the test measured some skills that might not be "essential" to the job, possible suggestions discussed with the employer to handle the situation included (a) providing the test on audio-cassette tape or having someone else read the test aloud to the individual, (b) allowing the use of a tape recorder to record the individual's responses to test items, and (c) allowing extended time to complete the test (usually either time and a half or double time). (Jacobs & Hendricks, 1992, pp. 281–282)

HOW CAN EMPLOYEES WITH LEARNING DISABILITIES SUCCEED IN THE WORKPLACE?

Transition specialists have identified a number of ways that adults with learning disabilities can enhance their chances of successfully obtaining and holding jobs (Adelman & Vogel, 1993; Gerber, 1992; Gerber, Ginsberg, & Reiff, 1992; Siegel & Gaylord-Ross, 1991). One way of looking at these strategies is that the more one is able to use them, the less one will need to rely on employer accommodations. Some of the most frequently cited methods are:

- Choose a job that is a good match.
- Use personal contacts to find a job.
- Become a self-advocate.
- Develop compensatory strategies.
- Take advantage of technology.
- Gain control over one's life.

Choose a Job That Is a Good Match

Adults with learning disabilities must be realistic about what jobs they are suited for. They need to realize that some jobs will be more difficult because of their particular disabilities. An individual who has severe problems with math, for example, should not expect to pursue engineering as a profession. Adults with learning disabilities need to consider jobs that utilize their strengths. A person with excellent social skills, for example, might consider a job that requires meeting the public, such as sales.

The ability to choose an appropriate job or profession requires a thorough understanding of one's disability and its impact on cognitive and social functioning. Special education teachers, transition specialists, and career counselors can work together to offer assistance in identifying jobs that bring out a person's strengths and minimize weaknesses.

Use Personal Contacts to Find a Job

Several researchers have found that adults with learning disabilities often obtain employment by relying on personal contacts (Adelman & Vogel, 1993). Although job skills will ultimately determine whether the worker with learning disabilities is able to perform the job, being able to prove that one has the ability to do the job is often difficult, especially in a tight job market. Getting one's foot in the door can make all the difference in securing a job. Thus, networks developed through family or friends can be helpful to adults with learning disabilities, and they should be encouraged to cultivate such contacts.

Become a Self-Advocate

Although having others who can serve as advocates is helpful, this should not be done at the expense of being a self-advocate. Adults with learning disabilities who are able to speak for themselves are at a distinct advantage in obtaining and holding jobs. Given the fact that many employers do not have a good understanding of learning disabilities, sometimes confusing them with mental retardation or other disabilities, they often must rely on these workers themselves to explain their disabilities (Gerber, 1992). Box 8.4 lists questions the employee with learning disability should be able to answer if asked.

BOX 8.4 ***EXAMPLE***

Questions the Employee with Learning Disability Should Be Prepared to Answer

The decision of whether to self-disclose one's learning disability to an employer is often a difficult one. When individuals do decide to inform an employer or potential employer, they should be prepared to answer several questions, such as these proposed by Gerber, Reiff, and Ginsberg (1996, p. 101):

1. What exactly is your disability?
2. What does learning disability or dyslexia mean?
3. What kinds of modifications do you need in your work environment?
4. What reasonable accommodations do you need? Why/how do you see them as reasonable?
5. How can you best be efficient?
6. Will your learning disability interfere with your productivity?
7. If we need to train you, how do you learn best?
8. Can you work well on a team?
9. Can you be given a lead role in a work group?
10. Why should I hire you when I can hire another person who is not disabled? Aren't I taking a risk?

Questions to Ponder

How would you answer questions 2 and 10?

Which would be the two or three most important questions to be able to answer?

What other questions might an employer be likely to ask?

Even though adults with learning disabilities are potentially in the best position to explain their strengths and weaknesses, they are not always skilled in doing so. Not only does self-advocacy mean being aware of how one's learning disability affects one specifically, it also requires social skills in order to communicate effectively with the employer.

Evidence indicates that many persons with learning disabilities are reluctant to disclose them during the application process or after they are hired for fear of discrimination (Greenbaum, Graham, & Scales, 1996). Even the most skilled communicator should be extremely cautious when approaching the issue of self-disclosure. Although workers with learning diabilities are protected by the Americans with Disabilities Act,

> in the downsizing and restructuring efforts of business and industry in the early 1990s, persons with learning disabilities who are already employed should be aware of the risks of self-disclosure. . . .
>
> While ADA provides for reasonable accommodation and other protections in the workplace, individuals with learning disabilities should carefully plan how they wish to self-disclose and think through the implications of their action. (Gerber, 1992, p. 331)

Develop Compensatory Strategies

Adults with learning disabilities who are successful in work often employ strategies to compensate for their disabilities. Two of the most common involve taking extra time to complete work and rechecking work several times for possible errors (Adelman &

Vogel, 1990). **Compensatory strategies** may also involve relying on others for certain aspects of work as well as putting out extraordinary effort oneself, as shown by the following case of a highly successful lawyer with learning disabilities:

> The severe reading difficulties posed problems early on in his law practice. He found trial law to be particularly stressful. He related, "I would be anxious that I'd have to read a document with people around, and I knew I couldn't do it. So I was *always* overprepared." As his law practice and businesses have become more established, he has learned to compensate for his weaknesses in reading by hiring a highly competent staff. Associates and assistants do most of his law and business reading. He explained, "To this day, now that I'm out of trial practice, I have a lady in particular who has been with me for seventeen years and who in effect is my reading eye. If I have to read under pressure, I go off to my office and deal with it."
>
> During the developing years of his practice and business, [he] used to read everything in order to keep up. . . . "When things got better financially and I didn't have to depend on law, I threw my reading material away." Now he has a CPA who tells him what he needs to know. However, when he needs to do his own reading and research, he knows how to outline and pull out important information (a skill he used in law school). He has self-tailored organizational skills that he developed for himself, and they work well for him. (Gerber & Reiff, 1991, pp. 49–50)

Take Advantage of Technology

There is a variety of technological products that can assist employees who have learning disabilities. Much of this **assistive technology** has been in the form of computer software, including that for problems in written language, reading, and organization and memory. Some examples of software to help with written language are spell-checkers, outlining programs, proofreading programs, and voice recognition systems. Spell-checkers scan documents, flag words that are likely misspellings, and present several possible correct alternatives. Outlining programs allow the user to type phrases or sentences; the software then automatically assigns numbers or letters, depending on the position of the cursor. Proofreading programs search documents, stopping at places where there is a probable error in punctuation, grammar, capitalization, word usage, and so forth. With voice recognition systems, the user speaks into the computer, which then types out what the user said.

Another software aid is personal data managers. These can help persons with organizational and memory problems by permitting them to set up daily schedules, address books, telephone directories with automatic dialers, check registers, and monthly calendars.

The Kurzweil Reading Machine, although relatively expensive, can be helpful to those with reading problems. Originally developed for use by people who are blind, this machine converts print into sound. The portable version allows the user to scan text with a handheld scanner, which sends the information to a computer, which converts it to auditory output (i.e., it "reads" the text aloud).

There is a downside to the infusion of so much technology into the marketplace: Consumers often have a difficult time sorting out the various products. The following are some guidelines for selecting assistive devices:

1. Products should be selected that are directly tied to the functions that need to be performed. . . .
2. Whenever possible, assistive technologies need to be identified that are appropriate across contexts . . . home, workplace, school, and social settings.
3. An effort should be made to identify technologies that are compatible with one another. . . .
4. In consideration of the various contexts in which adults with LD function, products should be identified that can be easily transported.
5. Assistive technology products should be intuitive and straightforward to learn and operate. . . .
6. Technologies should be reliable. . . .
7. Products should be selected that provide clearly written and easy-to-understand documentation. . . .
8. If possible, products should be supported with hot lines (1-800 numbers) linked to readily available company representatives and support service centers.
9. Products should be selected that are easy to install and set up.
10. An attempt should be made to identify technologies with a high "benefit/cost ratio," that is, a high potential for compensation relative to cost. . . .
11. Standard technologies should be chosen whenever possible. "Standard technology" refers to technology that is commercially available from a number of sources, is widely used in a variety of settings, and is designed for the general population. (Raskind, 1993, p. 193)

Gain Control over One's Life

Perhaps the single most important thing that adults with learning disabilities can do to ensure employment success is to gain control of their lives—not only of the physical environment, but also psychological and emotional control of their lives. Extensive interviews with highly successful adults with learning disabilities have revealed that "control was the fuel that fired their success" (Gerber et al., 1992, p. 479).

Researchers have found that a major way for adults with learning disabilities to achieve success is through reframing (Reiff, Gerber, & Ginsberg, 1997). **Reframing** is the recognition that the disability itself is not the biggest problem; one must accept the weaknesses caused by the disability while finding ways to shore them up and exploit one's strengths. Reframing consists of four stages. First, one needs to recognize the disability. Knowing that one is different from others is important. Second, one needs to accept the disability in the sense of recognizing that one can still be a worthwhile person with something to offer. Third, one needs to understand the disability and the limitations it imposes. Fourth, one needs to take action to achieve realistic goals of achievement. The following excerpt from a highly successful practicing dentist with learning disabilities who is also a clinical professor in New York University's College of Dentistry provides a good description of some of the components of reframing:

> Needless energy is wasted on what I call the "Why me?" syndrome. Why do I have this problem? Why must I face so many difficulties presented by this problem? In my position, as director of the Learning Disability Program for students in a professional school, I have found that those students who have the "Why me?" syndrome usually fare the worst because they waste so much energy. Those who say "OK, this is what I have, now I understand some of my problems, how do I deal with it in the future" fare the best. They accept their status, and this creates understanding and hope. Desire and motivation alone are not always enough to create success. The research corroborates that reframing or acceptance of the problem is a necessary ingredient. (Reiff et al., 1997, p. 129)

Summary

1. What are learning disability outcomes across the lifespan?
   Outcomes for those with learning disabilities include:
   a. higher dropout rates
   b. higher underemployment
   c. greater dependency on others
2. What transition programs and services are available for students with learning disabilities?
   a. In the mid-1980s, the federal government announced a "transition initiative."
   b. Legislation (IDEA of 1990 and amended in 1997) mandates that schools provide transition services and that a transition plan be included in the IEP.
   c. Interagency collaboration is essential to ensure that service needs are communicated between high school program representatives and representatives at receiving agencies, including vocational rehabilitation facilities and colleges.
   d. Many young adults with learning disabilities have problems with social skills, and these are important. Training to overcome these problems is not easy, for one reason, because of the difficulty identifying the social demands of various workplace or postsecondary education settings. One social skill that is particularly important and that appears to be teachable is self-advocacy—that is, the ability to describe specific needs resulting from the disability.
   e. It is also crucial that transition programs include parent involvement because parents often play an important role in the lifelong treatment of learning disabilities.

f. Transition programming needs to take into account how much the student should be prepared for work through vocational training versus how much he or she should be prepared for college.

3. How are students with learning disabilities prepared for college?
   a. In a college-bound model of secondary instruction, the special educator is responsible for most of the instruction, and students are mainstreamed in vocational education classes and take a light academic load. An advantage to this model is that special education teachers, who may not be proficient in every subject, are not required to teach all content areas.
   b. Key aspects of programming for college-bound students are:
      (1) to have students take as many courses as possible in mainstreamed settings
      (2) to teach students organizational, time management, and study skills
4. How can students with learning disabilities succeed in college?
   a. There has been a dramatic increase in the number of students with learning disabilities attending college. Five years after leaving secondary school, about 12% attend a two-year college and about 4% attend a four-year college.
   b. One reason for this increase can be attributed to Section 504 of the Rehabilitation Act of 1973, which prohibits institutions of higher learning from discriminating against disabled students.
   c. There are a number of factors to consider in choosing an appropriate college, including the amount of support provided for students with learning disabilities.
   d. Students need to seek information on possible colleges as early as possible in their secondary schooling.
   e. Many students opt to attend a two-year college because of their open admissions policies, smaller class sizes, lower tuition fees, and a variety of counseling services and vocational, remedial, and developmental courses.
   f. In predicting college success, college and university officials tend to rely on a relatively uniform set of criteria, such as high school GPA and SAT scores, based on predictive studies involving large numbers of applicants. However, students with learning disabilities may have difficulty with standardized tests such as the SAT, and their GPAs may be difficult to interpret because courses and accommodations vary widely, depending on high schools attended. Admissions officers should consider the following as predictors of college success for students with learning disabilities:
      (1) high school GPA
      (2) the number of mainstream English courses completed with a grade of C or better
      (3) motivation
      (4) ability to work independently

   g. Accommodations often used for college students with learning disabilities are:
      (1) adjustments in course requirements and evaluation
      (2) modifications in program requirements
      (3) auxiliary aids
5. How are students with learning disabilities prepared for the world of work?
   a. In a non-college-bound model of secondary instruction, the special educator is responsible for most of the instruction, and students are mainstreamed in vocational education classes and take a light academic load.
   b. Key aspects of vocational programming are that there are:
      (1) assessment procedures focused on functional skills related to future employment
      (2) support services to ensure access to mainstream vocational classes
      (3) at least four work experiences, six to eight weeks each
      (4) assistance in locating and securing employment
      (5) individual transition plans with appropriate adult service agencies
   c. Many professionals advocate school-business partnerships to help vocational programming for students with learning disabilities.
6. What can employers do to help adults with learning disabilities succeed in the workplace?
   a. Four trends in the workplace have created problems for those with learning disabilities:
      (1) emphasis on teamwork
      (2) technology is sometimes placing excessive cognitive demands on the worker
      (3) increased emphasis on credentials and the passing of standardized tests
      (4) emphasis on productivity
   b. The Americans with Disabilities Act requires employers to make accommodations for workers with disabilities. To do this, employers need to know:
      (1) the functional limitations associated with particular disabilities
      (2) the job task requirements
   c. Supported employment, often used with workers who are mentally retarded, has been suggested as a possible model for those who have learning disabilities.
7. What can employees with learning disabilities do to succeed in the workplace?
   a. choose a job that is a good match
   b. use personal contacts to find a job
   c. become a self-advocate
   d. develop compensatory strategies
   e. take advantage of technology
   f. gain control over one's life
      (1) use the technique of reframing—recognizing that the disability itself is not the biggest problem
      (2) accept one's weaknesses and exploit one's strengths

9

Social, Emotional, and Behavioral Problems

The problems of inattention and hyperactivity, which many students with learning disabilities exhibit, are disconcerting to teachers, parents, and many students. These problems are incompatible with the skills teachers consider critical for classroom success, such as following classroom rules, listening to teachers' instructions, following written instructions and directions, complying with teachers' commands, and exhibiting good work habits (Kauffman, 1997; Kauffman, Mostert, Trent, & Hallahan, 1998; Walker, 1995; Walker, Colvin, & Ramsey, 1995). Consequently, these behavioral characteristics often put a strain on interpersonal relationships and may result in a student's negative self-evaluation. In fact, many students who have learning disabilities have social and emotional problems that are part of their learning disabilities (Haager & Vaughn, 1997; Pearl & Bay, in press).

Learning disabilities may coexist with or predispose children and youths to a wide variety of emotional or behavioral problems. In the contemporary language of special education, there is no attempt to distinguish between "emotional" and "behavioral" problems because both are indicated by the individual's inappropriate behavior (cf. Forness & Kavale, 1997; Kauffman, 1997). When distinctions among types of problems are made, they are more often between **internalizing** and **externalizing behavior** (Achenbach, 1985; Achenbach & Edelbrock, 1989). Internalizing behavior is characterized by anxiety and social withdrawal, which are often taken as indications of emotional (affective) problems. For example, internalizing behavior often indicates depression. Externalizing behavior is characterized by acting out or antisocial behavior. For example, fighting, tantrums, property destruction, and hyperactivity are externalizing behavior. A given individual may exhibit either or both types of maladaptive behavior.

Inattention and hyperactivity may be part of the condition known in federal law as "emotional disturbance" and commonly referred to as "emotional or behavioral disorders" (Kauffman, 1997). Some students with learning disabilities have such severe problems in focusing and controlling attention and activity or other inappropriate behavior that they are labeled as having emotional or behavioral disorders instead of—or in addition to—learning disabilities. The dividing line between emotional or behavioral *problems* and emotional or behavioral *disorders* is not precise. The difference between problem and disorder is primarily a matter of judgment of severity. Disorder indicates a problem so severe that it becomes a critical concern and interferes significantly with the individual's everyday functioning (cf. Forness & Kavale, 1997; Kauffman, 1997). Put another way, all disorders are problems, but not all problems are disorders. Our discussion of problems includes those serious enough to be considered disorders.

There is considerable overlap among the groups of students having learning disabilities (LD), emotional or behavioral disorders (EBD), and attention deficit hyperactivity disorder (ADHD), as shown in Figure 9.1. Some have speculated that problems in focusing and sustaining attention are associated primarily with learning disabilities, whereas impulsive behavior and hyperactivity are associated primarily with behavioral disorders (Shaywitz, Fletcher, & Shaywitz, 1995). Our discussion is limited to those who have learning disabilities, although many of these students have emotional or behavioral problems, some have ADHD, and some have emotional or behavioral disorders in addition to learning disabilities. Thus, it is not surprising that many

FIGURE 9.1 Hypothetical Relationships among Learning Disabilities (LD), Emotional or Behavioral Disorders (EBD), and Attention Deficit Hyperactivity Disorder (ADHD)

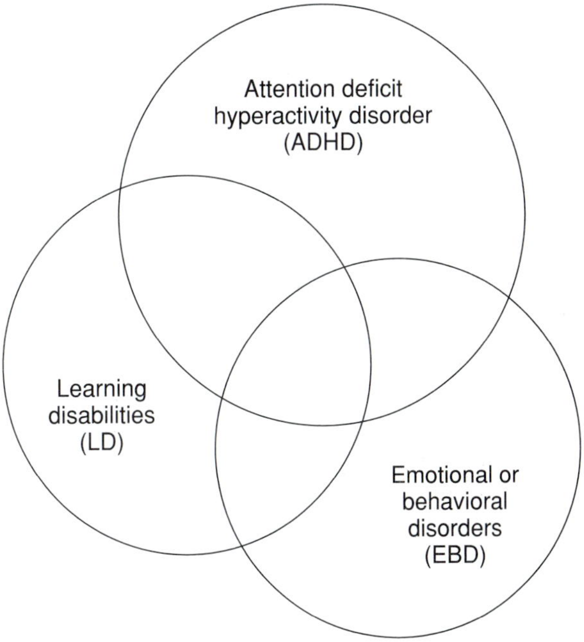

school systems have combined classes for students with learning disabilities and emotional or behavioral disorders (i.e., have classes designated as "LD/ED" or similarly combined labels).

WHAT SOCIAL, EMOTIONAL, AND BEHAVIORAL PROBLEMS SOMETIMES COEXIST WITH LEARNING DISABILITIES?

An informed guess is that the majority of students with learning disabilities exhibit serious problem behavior in school and that perhaps 30% of students with learning disabilities could have a dual diagnosis—that is, they have ADHD or another emotional or behavioral disorder as well as a learning disability. This speculation is based in part on decades of child development research showing that most normal children exhibit behavior problems at home or at school—or in both environments—at some time during their development (Kauffman, 1997). More important are two additional facts: (1) Emotional and behavioral disorders are frequently accompanied by serious academic difficulties (Forness & Kavale, 1997; Kauffman, 1997). (2) Numerous studies of students with learning disabilities have found them to exhibit behavior problems in school or to have emotional or behavioral disorders in addition to their learning disabilities (Forness & Kavale, 1997; Haager & Vaughn, 1997; Kavale & Forness, 1995b, 1997; Pearl & Bay, in press).

In short, the typical student with learning disabilities is likely to present behavior management problems more demanding that those presented by typical students. Teachers of students with learning disabilities should be equipped with skills for managing the emotional and behavioral problems or disorders that a significant percentage of their students will exhibit.

However, *not all individuals with learning disabilities have emotional or behavioral problems.* Many children and adults with learning disabilities are well adjusted, pleasant, well liked, and self-fulfilled. In fact, for some students with LD, the social domain is their area of strength, as evidenced by the testimony of an adult with severe reading disabilities: "I could talk my way out of anything. I couldn't read in high school but I always managed to do 'OK' because I could get the teachers to believe anything I told them." (Haager & Vaughn, 1997, p. 130). Our discussion focuses on those who have social and emotional problems—a majority of people with learning disabilities, but not all of them.

Problems of Social Competence

Social competence may be thought of as having several components, all of which are important to being liked, accepted, and self-confident. Haager and Vaughn (1997) suggest that social competence has four elements or dimensions: (1) effective use of social skills, (2) absence of maladaptive behavior, (3) positive relations with others, and (4) accurate/age appropriate social cognition. Thus, being socially competent does not mean just having good social skills, nor does it mean merely exhibiting no maladaptive behavior. Social competence is a complex concept, consisting of the combination of all these elements.

Many students with learning disabilities are not high in social competence. They may have lower social status and fewer friends than students without learning disabilities. They may be ignored or socially rejected by their peers. Their difficulty in social relationships may be due to deficits in social skills. They may not be able to "read" social situations as skillfully as most youngsters and, as a consequence, not understand how others are trying to influence them, what they want them to do, or how they are perceiving them. They may lack social tact in approaching others, making evaluative social comments, or offering or receiving criticism or praise (Pearl, 1987; Pearl & Bay, in press; Pearl, Donahue, & Bryan, 1985). They may not have skills in resisting negative peer pressure and choose the wrong peer models to imitate. They may exhibit behavior that others find highly irritating or unacceptable (i.e., maladaptive behavior), yet be unaware that others are upset with them. Sometimes they know that what they are doing is socially inappropriate, but either do not know what is appropriate or are unable to behave as expected. They may have few friends and be unable to figure out why or how to make and keep them. Consider how the behavior of John, described in Box 9.1, reflects problems like those we have been discussing.

BOX 9.1 ***EXAMPLE***

"If He Touches Me or My Stuff One More Time . . . !" The Case of John

When other kids start telling you, "If he touches me or my stuff one more time I'm going to kill him!" you know you have a problem. John is a 7th grader who bugs his peers until they scream. He makes me want to scream too. He's been screamed at a lot, but that hasn't changed his behavior.

John reminds me of a fast-moving mink, poking his nose in and out of hollow logs hunting for mice. He's always on the hunt. But he's doing more than hunting. He's looking for the next moment of excitement, aggravation, or distraction. John is always in motion, squirming, tapping, twitching, and darting. He is unable to keep his hands to himself. If he is not bopping someone on the head as he passes by, then he forces attention from the other 7th grade students in his class by knocking their books and lunch bags to the floor, where they become great soccer toys as he kicks them down the hall. There is a permanent red ring around his mouth where he habitually sucks on his lips and licks his perpetually chapped skin.

John knows that at the age of 13 he should be able to quiet down for his teacher. Many days, he tries to sit still at his desk and "behave himself." But the moment he sees the small printed words page after page in his textbook, or numbers, symbols, and letters all jumbled up together on the math review, he blows up, scattering his papers as they fly off the desk. Often, as he escapes the room, he is the target of jokes as he trips over himself in his haste. For although he moves with lightning speed, it is not with grace or agility.

In private moments, John sadly tells me how hard it is to feel so jittery all the time, how hard it is to concentrate. He hates the way little kids in elementary school tower over him, and especially how his younger brother is stronger, taller, better looking, and more athletic than he thinks he will ever be. The other day he said to me, "I'm always the bad one. Why can't I be the good one sometimes? Mrs. Armand, why am I this way?" I wanted to tell him, "You *know* how to behave better. *Just DO it!*"

Source: From *Characteristics of Emotional and Behavioral Disorders of Children and Youth,* 6th ed. (p. 325) by J. M. Kauffman, 1997, Upper Saddle River, NJ: Prentice-Hall. Copyright 1997 by Prentice-Hall, Inc. Reprinted by permission.

Questions to Ponder:

How is John's behavior typical or atypical of students with learning disabilities or ADHD?

How is John's behavior reflective of problems in social competence?

What do you think Mrs. Armand should have said in response to John's questions?

What strategies would you recommend for improving John's relationships with his peers?

If you had to choose, what behavior(s) would you focus on as targets for intervention?

The self-perceptions or self-concepts of students with learning disabilities are often a matter of concern. They tend to have lower opinions of themselves or their abilities, because they typically have both academic and social problems. However, it is important to distinguish self-concept in various areas: academic, social, and general self-esteem.

When it comes to their academic self-concepts, students with learning disabilities tend to perceive themselves in more negative terms than do students without learning disabilities and to attribute their academic failure to things they cannot change. Socially, too, students with learning disabilities tend to see themselves as less competent and less accepted than their normally achieving peers. However, two points are important: (1) Not all students with learning disabilities have lowered academic and social self-concepts. (2) Some students maintain a normal degree of general self-esteem although their academic and social self-perceptions are lower than normal. The self-concepts of students with learning disabilities are more varied and a more complex issue than is often realized. The peers to whom they primarily compare themselves and the specific comparisons they make may shape their self-perceptions. If they have high athletic ability, for example, and focus on comparisons in this area, they my have high self-concepts in spite of their academic limitations.

A common concern is the presumed negative effect that receiving special education in a pullout setting (i.e., being taught in a resource room or self-contained class) has on students' self-esteem. Contrary to popular belief, research suggests that receiving such pullout services has a positive effect, if any, on self-esteem (Pearl & Bay, in press). Students with learning disabilities may be encouraged to see themselves more positively when they compare themselves to others who are academically more like them than when they compare themselves to normally achieving students in the regular classroom (cf. Coleman, McHam, & Minnett, 1992; Coleman & Minnett, 1992).

Exactly why most students with learning disabilities experience more problems of social adjustment than typical students is not known for certain. Perhaps their low social status and problems of social adjustment are shaped by their low academic achievement, lack of social understanding, inappropriate behavior, deficient social motivation, inability to resist peer pressure, undesirable social environments (e.g., negative peer or teacher bias, parent or teacher rejection, social gravitation toward poorly adjusted peers), or some combination of these (Pearl & Bay, in press).

Conduct Problems

Particularly troublesome are conduct problems—overt antisocial behavior such as aggression, tantrums, and disruption and covert antisocial behavior such as lying and stealing. All conduct problems involve noncompliance—not obeying adults or meeting normal social demands. Such problems are highly related to ADHD; many children with conduct problems have ADHD as well. Children with serious conduct problems are at high risk for developing lifelong patterns of social maladjustment, particularly when they experience low academic achievement as well (Kauffman, 1997). Thus, students with learning disabilities who show conduct problems need particularly effective intervention for academic and behavioral difficulties.

Conduct problems are not necessarily indications of delinquency. However, many children and youths who have conduct problems become involved with the juvenile justice system—they become juvenile delinquents. Youths with learning disabilities constitute a high percentage of the population of correctional institutions (Murphy, 1986).

The conduct problems of students with learning disabilities may be due in part to deficient social skills in understanding expectations, social roles, and consequences. Whatever the causes, conduct problems make children and youths more likely to fail academically and socially and to become involved with the law. Conduct problems carry the most severe social consequences of any type of maladaptive behavior that students may exhibit, and they are among the most difficult to change (Kazdin, 1995).

Other Emotional or Behavioral Problems

Students with learning disabilities may have any of the other emotional or behavioral problems or disorders cataloged in the American Psychiatric Association's diagnostic and statistical manual (DSM-IV) (American Psychiatric Association, 1994). These may include disorders that are primarily affective (i.e., involving emotional states), such as anxiety disorders and depression. Most often, as we have noted, these disorders are considered internalizing, as opposed to the externalizing disorders of conduct in which the individual strikes out against others.

Anxiety and depression are frequently seen in children with learning disabilities (Cullinan & Epstein, 1985; Forness & Kavale, 1997; Kavale & Forness, 1997). They may be particularly sad, discouraged, and hopeless. These problems may be in part a result of academic and social failure, but they may also contribute to them. As is the case for most emotional and behavioral problems, there is a reciprocal relationship among them and achievement. Academic and social failures contribute to the emotional or behavioral problem, which in turn makes academic and social failure more likely.

WHAT CAUSES EMOTIONAL AND BEHAVIORAL PROBLEMS?

When someone behaves badly or oddly, our tendency is to ask such questions as "What makes him behave that way?" and "What on earth could she have been thinking that would lead her to do that?" Popular notions about the causes of problem behavior usually contain elements of truth, but are simplistic, ascribing nearly all the fault to a single factor. In explaining behavior problems or disorders, most people are prone to oversimplifications like the following:

"It's the parents' fault because of the way they raised her."

"The school and those teachers are really to blame for the way they handled him."

"It's a neurological thing that she just can't control."

"In today's culture, with all the bad models and nobody setting limits, how could you expect him to behave?"

We know that a variety of factors can contribute to the growth and development of problem behavior, and in the typical case, we have good reason to believe that several of these are involved. A youngster's misbehavior may be partly biological in origin, partly attributable to the family's child-rearing practices, partly due to mismanagement at school, and partly a function of cultural influences (see Kauffman, 1997). All possible causes of learning disabilities are potential causes of emotional and behavioral problems. Moreover, some of the characteristics of learning disabilities—problems of memory and communication, for example—may contribute to problems of social competence.

Among the possible causes, those most pertinent to teachers are the ones involving schooling. In fact, most of what we know about the social problems of students with learning disabilities is related to the school context (Haager & Vaughn, 1997). Teachers cannot do very much directly about biological, family, or cultural factors, but they can do a lot to ensure that the student's experience at school does not contribute to misbehavior (see Kauffman, 1997; Kauffman et al., 1998; Walker, 1995; Walker et al., 1995). Teachers can ask several questions about their own behavior, their classroom, and the school to assess whether the educational environment might be contributing to a student's misbehavior.

1. *Is my instructional program sound?* A sound instructional program is the first defense against emotional or behavioral problems in school. Effective instruction offered at the student's level is critically important as a way of preventing the student's feelings of threat, failure, resentment, and defeat. We should not expect students to behave well if they are not being taught well. Often students do not see the relevance of the skills they are being taught in school. If they see what they are being asked to do as a waste of their time, they are likely to behave inappropriately in protest or out of boredom or frustration. One of the teacher's tasks is to teach skills that are important to students' lives and to find ways of making "uninteresting" skills worth students' time to learn, sometimes by modifying teaching methods or learning activities, sometimes by offering meaningful rewards for learning. Moreover, if students have deficits in social skills or social cognition, then the instructional program must include effective instruction in these areas.

2. *Are my expectations of the student appropriate?* Expectations that are too high for a student's ability lead to constant feelings of failure; expectations that are too low lead to boredom and lack of progress. A good teacher adjusts expectations to fit the student's level of ability so that improvement is always both possible and challenging. Unless an appropriate level of expectations is set for the individual, the teacher will set the student up for failure. Getting the expectations just right is no small task, but this fundamental task, if not accomplished, is virtually certain to induce misbehavior.

3. *Am I sufficiently sensitive to the student as an individual?* A school environment that is conducive to appropriate behavior must allow students sufficient freedom to demonstrate their individuality. Teachers who demand strict uniformity and regimentation and who are unable to tolerate and encourage appropriate differences among their students are likely to increase the tendency of some to exhibit troublesome behavior. Finding the balance between conformity to necessary rules and tolerance for difference is a key to building a school and classroom environment conducive to appropriate behavior. Particularly important is knowing the difference between cultur-

ally based and appropriate though different behavior and behavior that is inappropriate regardless of the student's culture.

4. *Do I offer positive reinforcement expertly?* In many classes, students with emotional or behavioral problems are ignored when they are behaving well and given lots of attention (usually in the form of criticism and reminders or threats) when they misbehave. This arrangement is certain to perpetuate the student's emotional or behavioral difficulties. Expert **positive reinforcement** (reward) is typically given frequently, immediately, interestingly, and contingent on desired behavior. To be used expertly, reinforcement must be combined with other behavior management strategies for maximum effect (Rhode, Jenson, & Reavis, 1992). These other strategies include careful instructional programming, knowing when and how to ignore misbehavior, using nonviolent **punishment,** and talking with students in ways that enhance their self-confidence and self-control.

5. *Am I consistent in managing behavior?* One of the most significant features of a good school experience for any student, but especially one who exhibits emotional or behavioral problems, is a high degree of structure. Structure means that instructions are clear to the student, the teacher holds firm expectations that the student will follow instructions, and the consequences for behavior are consistent. When the student is being managed consistently, the classroom routine and the consequences for behavior are highly predictable. Inconsistent management is one factor that is almost certain to increase any student's tendency to misbehave.

6. *Are desirable models being demonstrated and used?* Children and adolescents, not to mention adults, are great imitators. If the teacher's behavior is a desirable model for students, then appropriate conduct may be encouraged. Students also imitate their classmates, but just having classmates whose behavior is desirable is not sufficient to ensure that they will be imitated. If it were, then how do we account for some students' misbehavior in classes in which most of their peers are well behaved? Appropriate peer models are found not only in regular classes, but also in special classes. The best models often are not those who are perfect, but those who share many of the characteristics of and are only somewhat better than the student who is experiencing problems. The teacher must choose models carefully, call attention to the behavior to be imitated, and reward imitation of these models if they are to be effective (Hallenbeck & Kauffman, 1995).

HOW ARE EMOTIONAL AND BEHAVIORAL PROBLEMS ASSESSED?

The assessment of students' emotional or behavioral problems, like that of problems in various academic areas, should identify those students who need special help, guide the planning of programs to address their problems, and provide the basis for monitoring progress toward specific goals. An adequate assessment does not focus exclusively on the student's behavior. Rather, it includes consideration of the student's social and physical environments and the student's thoughts and feelings about these circumstances. Assessment should be solution centered—that is, it should not merely be descriptive of what is, but also should be a process that leads to interventions. It should be based on the most accessible and reliable sources of information, not on speculation that cannot be confirmed, and should yield a picture not only of the student, but also of the context in which his or her behavior is causing concern (Haager & Vaughn, 1997).

An important principle of the assessment of social competence and emotional or behavioral problems is that information must be obtained from multiple sources. That is, all aspects of assessment should include multiple perspectives, never rely entirely on one person's judgment. The multiple sources of information should include the student, parent(s), and peers, in addition to the teacher. Moreover, a complete assessment will include social skills, maladaptive behavior, interpersonal relationships, and social cognition (see Forness & Kavale, 1997; Haager & Vaughn, 1997).

The full range of assessment strategies includes screening for possible problems, prereferral strategies, and evaluation; these guide the writing of the individualized education plan (IEP). Since enactment of the 1997 amendments to the Individuals with Disabilities Education Act (IDEA), the IEP must include plans for dealing with problem behavior if behavior problems become evident in the student's assessment. In addition, IDEA makes special provisions for disciplining students with disabilities.

Systematic Screening

Systematic screening for emotional or behavioral problems is relatively uncommon in American public schools, primarily because it would likely turn up many more problems than school personnel could address effectively. However, a variety of screening instruments and strategies is available. Most of these are behavior rating scales that have been normed on a comparison population (see Kauffman, 1997, for a description of several of these instruments). Some are appropriate for screening entire school populations, and many would be useful for screening students already identified as having academic learning disabilities to determine whether they may have emotional or behavioral problems as well.

Screening is a process of eliminating or confirming the suspicion that a student *may* have a problem. Ideally, it requires a series of steps in which the criteria for selecting students are successively narrowed so that in the end only those students who actually have problems have been identified. The instrument conforming most closely to the ideal screening process in the elementary grades is the *Systematic Screening for Behavior Disorders,* or SSBD (Walker & Severson, 1990). It assesses both adaptive and maladaptive behavior.

The SSBD is a "multiple-gating" process designed to ensure not only that just those students who actually have problems are identified, but also that equal attention is given to internalizing and externalizing problems (Walker et al., 1988). The first step

(Gate 1) through which students pass is a teacher nomination procedure. The teacher lists in rank order the students in the class who best fit descriptions of externalizing and internalizing problems. Only six students—the three ranked as most similar to the externalizing description and the three ranked as most similar to the internalizing description—pass through Gate 1. Gate 2 is a rating procedure. The teacher rates the six students who passed through Gate 1 on two checklists. One asks whether the student exhibited specific maladaptive behaviors during the past month (e.g., "steals," "has tantrums," "uses obscene language or swears"); the other asks how often ("never," "sometimes," "frequently") each student shows certain desirable characteristics (e.g., "follows established classroom rules," "cooperates with peers in group activities or situations"). Students pass through Gate 2 if their ratings exceed established norms. Gate 3 involves direct observations in the classroom and on the playground by a school professional other than the teacher (usually a school psychologist, counselor, or resource teacher). If the observations and teacher ratings place the student outside accepted norms, the student passes through Gate 3 and is referred for evaluation for special education. Students passing through Gate 3 but not yet identified as needing special education could eventually be classified as having either learning disabilities or emotional or behavioral disorders. Those passing through Gates 2 or 3 but already identified as having learning disabilities might be identified as having emotional or behavioral problems or disorders in addition to their academic disabilities.

Screening should not depend entirely on one individual's opinions, one measure of behavior, or student behavior in one setting. It should represent the convergence of data from a variety of sources and situations indicating that the student needs further study.

A major concern is that cultural difference or nondeviant personal idiosyncrasies might be mistaken for emotional or behavioral problems (cf. Kauffman, Hallahan, & Ford-Harris, 1998). In fact, bias in screening and identification could result in the overidentification of students based on ethnic, gender, or individual differences. In 1989, the Council for Children with Behavioral Disorders (CCBD) issued a white paper calling for particular care in assessment to guard against such bias. Among the council's recommendations were the following:

- Focus attention on assessment of classroom and school learning environments that may foster behavioral problems.
- Attend to predisposing factors (e.g., cultural expectations, prior learning, family conditions) that may play a role in students' behavior.
- Focus on observable student and teacher behavior in the classroom and the conditions under which these occur.
- Establish specific, measurable, and instructionally relevant standards for acceptable academic performance and social behavior.
- Develop and implement careful prereferral interventions.
- Implement effective and efficient instructional approaches.

The CCBD recommendations on avoiding bias suggest the importance of assessing the school and classroom environment as well as the student's behavior (Council for Children with Behavioral Disorders, 1989). These recommendations are entirely consistent with the foregoing discussion of the school as a possible causal factor in emotional or behavioral disorders.

A variety of rating scales for social skills, peer relationships, and self-perceptions is available. These may be useful, but perhaps more important is the careful observation of teachers. Much of the information on which effective assessment is based, including screening, comes from the teacher's informal observations regarding the quality of the student's friendships, responses to adults, and behavioral adaptation (cf. Gerber & Semmel, 1984).

Prereferral, Referral, Observations, and Record Keeping

Referral for evaluation for special education launches a time-consuming, expensive, and often anxiety-provoking experience for teachers or parents. Therefore, using prereferral strategies is critically important because they are designed to avoid unnecessary referrals (see also Chapter 4).

Many problems in the referral process could be eliminated by prereferral strategies. Before making a referral, the teacher should document the strategies he or she has used to meet the student's educational needs. Regardless of whether the student is later found to have a disability, documentation of these strategies will be useful. Prereferral strategies have the following advantages:

1. The teacher will have evidence helpful to or required by the committee of professionals that will evaluate the student and determine his or her eligibility.
2. The teacher will be better able to help the student's parents understand that methods used for other students in the class are not adequate for their child.
3. The teacher will have records of successful and/or unsuccessful methods of working with the student, and these will be useful to any other teacher who works with the student in the future.

Documentation of prereferral strategies may appear to require a lot of paperwork, but careful record keeping will pay off. If the student is causing serious concern, the teacher will be wise to keep written records of the following:

- exactly what behavior the teacher is concerned about (i.e., a behavioral definition of the problem)
- why the teacher is concerned about it (its developmental or academic significance)
- dates, places, times of day, and frequency with which the problem behavior has been observed
- precisely what the teacher has done to try to resolve the problem

- who, if anyone, helped the teacher devise the plans or strategies
- evidence that the strategies have been successful or unsuccessful

Although critics of special education have sometimes charged that teachers refer students quickly and typically for minor behavioral rather than for serious behavioral or academic reasons, research has not shown this to be the case (Lloyd, Kauffman, Landrum, & Roe, 1991). When a teacher refers a student, in the vast majority of cases, it appears to be out of concern for the student's lack of academic progress or academic problems combined with inattentive or disruptive classroom behavior. Teachers do not see the problems for which they refer students as minor (Gerber & Semmel, 1984; Lloyd et al., 1991).

Confirmation of Eligibility

Confirmation of a student's eligibility for special education due to a learning disability is, by law, to be the decision of a **multidisciplinary team (MDT).** Confirmation that a student with learning disabilities has emotional or behavioral problems needing intervention is part of the assessment process for determining eligibility. If the student has behavior problems, the IEP must include behavioral objectives, and the parents and other team members need to be involved in and approve of the plan, just as they would for academic objectives (Yell, 1998; Yell & Shriner, 1997).

Confirmation of emotional or behavioral problems requires obtaining information from multiple sources (e.g., classroom teacher, other teachers, parents, and peers) and assessing the student's behavior in multiple settings (e.g., classroom, playground, and lunchroom). Information from tests, behavior ratings, interviews, and direct observations should be used to obtain as complete and detailed a picture as possible of what the student does in a variety of settings and how others perceive and respond to the student. Ultimately, confirmation hinges on the combined judgment of a team of individuals that the student's behavior is problematic and is not a reasonable response to an inadequate school environment. Confirmation that the student has such a problem depends on eliminating school factors that may be the cause of unacceptable behavior.

Including Behavior Problems in the IEP

Given confirmation that a student has an emotional or behavioral problem in addition to a learning disability, teachers must plan a program designed to change the student's behavior. The plan must be based on information from multiple sources and be included in the IEP.

Obtaining and Using Information from Multiple Sources

As is true of all assessments for eligibility and IEP development, the information that is the basis for the services to be offered and the goals of intervention are to be obtained from multiple sources. This means that no teacher, school psychologist, or administrator alone can provide the information necessary for writing the IEP and that the information cannot be obtained from a single assessment strategy or instrument. The purpose of requiring multiple sources of information is not only to help eliminate bias in assessment, but also to make sure that the problem is as fully understood as possible and that all important aspects of the problem are addressed.

Planning the program requires careful consideration of questions that might be addressed through interviews or direct observations or both. Kanfer and Grimm (1977) suggest seeking answers to questions such as the following, particularly through interviews. Notice that adequate answers to these questions will involve multiple sources and address the many dimensions of social competence described by Haager and Vaughn (1997)—social skills, maladaptive behavior, relationships with others, and social cognition.

1. *What behavioral deficits does the student exhibit?* What skills does the student lack that, if acquired, would foster more desirable behavior? What appropriate behaviors does the student need to learn to be perceived as socially skilled?
2. *What behavioral excesses does the student exhibit?* What specific things does the student do too often or too intensely?
3. *What does the student do that is "out of place"?* What does the student do that is considered deviant because of its social context or that demonstrates inefficient organization or personal skills?
4. *What does the student do that reflects inappropriate responses to self?* How does the student's behavior reflect misperceptions of his or her abilities, unrealistic evaluations of self, or inaccurate descriptions of his or her internal feelings?
5. *To what extent does the student's behavior seem to be a function of inappropriate reinforcement or punishment?* Under what circumstances and for what specific behaviors is the student rewarded or punished?
6. *What does the student's behavior communicate to others?* How do others, including adults and peers, interpret the student's behavior? What does the student appear to be saying or asking for by his or her behavior?

In addition to interviews or rating scales, adequate assessment requires direct observation of the student's behavior. Direct observation and recording of behavior allow teachers to pinpoint the problem, analyze the environmental factors that contribute to it, and plan an intervention designed to produce specific behavioral improvement. The first step in planning a program of behavioral change often is doing an ABC analysis. This involves observing and recording the antecedents (A, events occurring immediately before the behavior and setting the stage for it) and consequences (C, events occurring immediately after the behavior and changing its future probability) of behavior as well as the behavior itself (B) (Alberto & Troutman, 1995; Kauffman, Mostert,

Trent, & Hallahan, 1998; Kerr & Nelson, 1998). In performing an ABC analysis, the teacher might be able to answer some of the following questions:

1. In what settings (e.g., home, school, math class, playground) is the problem behavior or behavioral deficit exhibited?
2. With what frequency, duration, and amplitude does the behavior appear in various settings?
3. What happens immediately before the behavior occurs that seems to set the occasion for it? Is there a pattern of the behavior occurring under particular circumstances?
4. What happens immediately after the behavior occurs that may be reinforcing or punishing it? Is there a consistent response to the behavior?
5. What other appropriate or inappropriate behavior does the student exhibit besides the particular behavior being observed? Does the definition of the problem need to be revised or extended?
6. What specific skills could be taught or strengthened as replacements for the student's inadequate or inappropriate behavior?

Behavior Intervention Plan

The 1997 amendments to IDEA require that if a student with disabilities has behavior problems, regardless of the student's disability category, the IEP must include specific strategies and supports designed to manage them. The plan must be proactive—designed to avert problems, not merely react to behavior once it has occurred. "The behavior intervention plan for each student should delineate expected behaviors, inappropriate behaviors, and positive and negative consequences. The disciplinary process that will be followed, including intervention techniques, should be outlined in the plan. The plan also should include procedures for dealing with behavioral crises" (Yell & Shriner, 1997, p. 12).

Figure 9.2 shows a behavior intervention plan that might be included in an IEP, using a format suggested by Yell (1998). Box 9.2 shows an excerpt from an IEP that includes a behavior intervention plan.

The requirement that behavior intervention plans be included in IEPs is relatively new (i.e., enacted into law in 1997 and specified in regulations in 1998), and writing such plans to federal specifications is uncharted territory. As yet, there are no models for specifying certain required components, such as the disciplinary process to be followed, procedures for dealing with behavioral crises, or basing the plan on a "functional analysis" of behavior (Nelson, Roberts, Mather, & Rutherford, in press). Moreover, when students exhibit multiple behavior problems, there is no clear guidance for selecting the particular behavior(s) that should be the target(s) of an intervention plan. However, behavior intervention plans developed during the 1990s, especially proactive **precorrection** plans, include many components that fit IEP requirements.

FIGURE 9.2 Sample Behavior Intervention Plan for IEP

Student: Patrick Milton Wills **Date:** March 17, 1998

Teacher(s): Patricia Pullen

Parent(s): Judith & John Wills

Administrator(s): Rebecca Dailey, principal

Other(s): Ron Reeve, school psychologist

Problem behaviors: Patrick violates other students' personal space and property by touching, grabbing, or using others' possessions without their permission. He also annoys other students by aggressively touching them. Inappropriate touching of others or their possessions occurs on average about 5 times per day.

Antecedents of problem behaviors: These problems occur throughout the day in a variety of settings, but are particularly likely when students are making a transition from one activity to another and when Patrick is excluded from an activity in which he wants to participate.

Positive procedures to redirect behaviors: Ms. Pullen will explain to Patrick that he sometimes touches others and their possessions inappropriately and needs to learn alternative ways of relating to his peers. She will also explain and demonstrate alternative, expected behaviors (e.g., keeping hands to self, touching your own possessions, requesting permission, avoiding touching by using self-talk). She will make a plan with Patrick about how she will remind him prior to transitions and other times to exhibit the expected behavior.

Intervention plan (reinforcers and consequences): Ms. Pullen will offer frequent praise and encouragement for Patrick's appropriate behavior. Patrick will chart his behavior daily, based on a log kept by Ms. Pullen, and take his parents a daily report of his behavior. Mr. & Mrs. Wills will offer praise for improvement and a small tangible reward for each week in which there is improvement over the previous week or fewer than 3 incidents per week reported by Ms. Pullen. Mr. & Mrs. Wills agree not to provide criticism or other negative consequences for poor reports.

Procedures to teach positive replacement behaviors: Mr. Reeve will give Patrick instruction in how to obtain permission to touch others' belongings, how to refrain from inappropriate touching, and how to obtain peer attention in appropriate ways. The instruction in these social skills will involve modeling, role playing, and rehearsal. Mr. Reeve will keep Ms. Pullen informed of the instruction Patrick has been given, and Ms. Pullen will encourage Patrick to use these strategies by giving him prompts and praise for demonstrating them.

Method of evaluation: Ms. Pullen will keep a log of Patrick's inappropriate touching, recording the date, time, and activity during which each incident occurs. At the end of each school day, Patrick will be given a copy of the day's log to take home to his parents. He will also plot the number of inappropriate touching incidents for the day on a graph to be kept by Ms. Pullen.

Goal and criteria for success: Patrick will touch other students and their property only with their permission and in an appropriate manner as judged by the teacher's observation of students' reactions. Successful intervention will reduce recorded incidents of inappropriate touching to 2 or fewer per week for 6 weeks.

BOX 9.2 ***EXAMPLE***

Individualized Education Program

Student: Curt **Age:** 15 **Grade:** 9 **Date:** 10/12/94

Unique Characteristics/ Needs	Special Education, Related Services, Modifications	(begin duration)	Present Levels, Objectives, Annual Goals (Objectives to include procedure, criteria, schedule)
Social Needs: ■ To learn anger management skills, especially regarding swearing ■ To learn to comply with requests Present Level: Lashes out violently when not able to complete work, uses profane language, and refuses to follow further directions from adults	1. Teacher and/or counselor consult with behavior specialists regarding techniques and programs for teaching social skills, especially anger management.	30 min., 3 × week	Goal: During the last quarter of the academic year, Curt will have 2 or fewer detentions for any reason. Objective 1: At the end of the 1st quarter, Curt will have had 10 or fewer detentions.
	2. Provide anger management training for Curt.	30 min., 2 × week	Objective 2: At the end of 2nd quarter, Curt will have had 7 or fewer detentions.
	3. Establish a peer group which involves role playing, etc. so Curt can see positive role models and practice newly learned anger management skills.		Objective 3: At the end of 3rd quarter, Curt will have had 4 or fewer detentions.
	4. Develop a behavior plan for Curt which gives him responsibility for charting his own behavior.		Goal: Curt will manage his behavior and language in a reasonably acceptable manner as reported by faculty/peers.
	5. Provide a teacher or some other adult mentor to spend time with Curt (could be talking, game play, physical activity).	30 min., 2 × week	Objective 1: At 2 weeks, asked at end of class if Curt's behavior language was acceptable or not, 3 out of 5 teachers will say "acceptable."
	6. Provide training for the mentor regarding Curt's needs/goals.		Objective 2: At 6 weeks, asked same question, 4 out of 6 teachers will say "acceptable." Objective 3: At 12 weeks. 6 out of 6 will say "acceptable."

Adaptations to regular program:

- In all classes, Curt should be near front of class
- Curt should be called on often to keep him involved and on task
- All teachers should help Curt with study skills as trained by spelling/language specialist and resource room teacher
- Teachers should monitor Curt's work closely in the beginning weeks/months of his program

Source: From *Better IEPs,* 2nd ed. (p. 89) by B. D. Bateman, 1996, Longmont, CO: Sopris West. Copyright 1996 by Barbara D. Bateman. Reprinted by permission.

Questions to Ponder

Does this IEP excerpt specify all the components required by IDEA for a behavior intervention plan? If not, what needs to be added?

In Curt's case, what do you think would be an acceptable discipline plan?

Special Discipline Considerations

Disciplining students with disabilities is a controversial topic that leaves many teachers and school administrators confused about what is legal. Special rules apply to managing some of the behavior problems of students who are identified as having disabilities. In some cases, the typical school rules apply, but in others, they do not (see Yell, 1998; Yell & Shriner, 1997).

The disciplinary action about which there is uncertainty or controversy usually involves a change in the student's placement or suspension or expulsion due to a very serious matter such as bringing a weapon or illegal drugs to school. IDEA discipline provisions for students with disabilities are designed to maintain a safe school environment without violating the rights of students with disabilities to fair discipline, taking the effects of their disability into consideration.

> School officials may discipline a student with disabilities in the same manner as they discipline students without disabilities—with a few notable exceptions. If necessary, school officials may unilaterally [without parental approval] change the placement of a student for disciplinary purposes to an appropriate **interim alternative educational setting (IAES),** another setting, or by suspending the student to the extent that these disciplinary methods are used with students without disabilities. The primary difference is that with students who have a disability, the suspension or placement change may not exceed 10 school days. (Yell & Shriner, 1997, pp. 11–12)

However, if a student with disabilities brings a weapon or illegal drugs to school or to a school function, school officials may unilaterally place him or her in an IAES for up to 45 days.

If a student with disabilities presents substantial risk to the safety of others, school authorities may ask for a special hearing about the student's placement. A hearing officer may be asked to consider the evidence that "(a) maintaining the current placement is substantially likely to result in injury to the student or others, (b) the IEP and placement are appropriate, (c) the school has made reasonable efforts to minimize the risk of harm, and (d) the IAES meets the criteria set forth in the IDEA amendments" (Yell & Shriner, 1997, p. 12). If the evidence that all four are true meets the legal definition of "substantial," then the hearing officer may order a change of placement to an IAES for up to 45 days.

Manifestation Determination

If a serious disciplinary situation arises and school officials want to change the student's placement or suspend the student for more than 10 days, or expel the student, then a special review of the relationship between the student's disability and the misbehavior must be made.

> A student's IEP team and other qualified personnel must conduct this review, called a manifestation determination. If a determination is made that no relationship exists between the misconduct and disability, the same disciplinary procedures as would

> be used with students who are not disabled may be imposed on a student with disabilities (i.e., long-term suspension or expulsion). Educational services, however, must be continued. If the team finds a relationship between a student's disability and misconduct, school officials still may seek a change of placement but cannot use long-term suspension or expulsion. (Yell & Shriner, 1997, p. 12)

A student's parents may, of course, challenge the school officials' decision. Those conducting the **manifestation determination** must consider all relevant information related to the student's misbehavior, including evaluation results, direct observation of the student, and information provided by parents. An IEP team may conclude that misconduct was *not* a manifestation of disability only when all three of the following criteria are met:

> 1. The student's IEP and placement were appropriate (including the behavior intervention plan) and the IEP was implemented as written;
> 2. The student's disability did not impair the ability of the student to understand the impact and consequences of the behavior subject to the disciplinary sanction;
> 3. The student's disability did not impair the student's ability to control the behavior at issue. (Yell & Shriner, 1997, p. 13)

Interim Alternative Educational Setting

An IAES is an alternative setting chosen by the IEP team that will allow the student to continue participating in the general education curriculum and continue to receive the services described in the IEP. Students must be able to continue working toward their IEP goals and objectives, including those related to the behavior that resulted in placement in the IAES. IAES may include alternative schools, instruction at home ("homebound instruction"), and other special settings. A key requirement of the law is that the student's special education must be continued.

WHAT INTERVENTIONS CAN HELP WITH EMOTIONAL OR BEHAVIORAL PROBLEMS?

The focus of behavior management in special education has changed from reacting effectively to misbehavior to planning proactive programs intended to avoid problems. Proactive plans are consistent with the 1997 IDEA amendments and can be much more effective and efficient than reactive techniques. The idea of precorrection—a strategy for anticipating misbehavior and avoiding it by teaching desired behavior—is extremely useful to classroom teachers (Colvin, Sugai, & Patching, 1993; Walker et al., 1995).

Nevertheless, not all behavior problems can be predicted or avoided, and teachers still must have strategies for dealing reactively when problems occur. Teachers must be prepared to deal with ordinary misbehavior and the kind of rule infraction that invokes the special discipline considerations we discussed earlier. A crucial point in planning programs of behavioral change, whether proactive or reactive, is that *focusing on eliminating inappropriate behavior without teaching desirable behavior is unacceptable.* The teacher's first line of attack on emotional or behavioral problems should be to ensure competent academic instruction. The second should be to teach the social skills needed to function well in society and to reinforce (reward) appropriate behavior exhibited by the student. The third should be to decrease or eliminate the student's socially inappropriate behavior.

Our focus in this chapter on managing behavior should not be taken as an indication of unconcern for students' self-esteem or emotional lives. How students feel about themselves and about school is very important. However, the surest way to help them feel better about school and themselves is to help them achieve academic success and behave in a socially acceptable, if not socially skillful, manner. The teacher who focuses on effective instruction and is sensitive to students' feelings will surely be the most effective in improving students' self-perceptions.

Modifying the Learning Environment for Proactive Management

Proactive management means avoiding behavior problems. Increasingly, research suggests that the best single proactive strategy for avoiding behavior problems in school is effective academic instruction—in which students give frequent correct responses and have a low error rate (cf. Gunter & Coutinho, in press; Gunter, Hummel, & Conroy, in press; Kameenui & Darch, 1995). Students who experience frequent success in the tasks they are given have fewer reasons to resist instruction and avoid academic work through misbehavior.

Assuming that academic instruction is effective, teachers still need to have proactive plans for dealing with behavior problems that can be anticipated. Many students with learning disabilities, even with effective academic instruction, exhibit predictable misbehavior in particular contexts. Their misbehavior is not predictable in the sense that any student is likely to misbehave, but it is predictable in that the teacher has learned through observation that a particular context is a rough spot in which the student is likely to make a mistake. The teacher might be compared to an athletic coach who can anticipate that a player is likely to make a particular mistake (Colvin, 1992). The teacher needs to adopt a good coaching model—to anticipate behavioral mistakes in various classroom contexts and offer effective coaching in how to avoid them. This is also the approach used by teachers who are skillful in all types of instruction—knowing where a student is likely to have trouble understanding or performing and teaching the student how to avoid the predictable errors.

The most effective approach to managing emotional or behavioral problems is to assume that the expected, desirable behavior needs to be taught. Social competence is acquired through learning particular behavioral skills and knowing when and how to demonstrate them. Teaching these skills can be approached using the same basic principles expert teachers use for helping students learn any other type of performance—not only in athletics, but in music, drama, or reading, for example.

The precorrection checklist and plan devised by Colvin et al. (1993) provides a convenient format for organizing one's thinking about proactive behavior management (see also Kauffman, Mostert, Trent, & Hallahan, 1998; Walker et al., 1995). It is a way of thinking through how to anticipate and prevent behavioral mistakes. Precorrection focuses on teaching students to do what is expected.

The precorrection strategy begins with the context—the setting, circumstances, or situation in which a predictable misbehavior occurs. Through observation, the teacher learns that, in a given context (e.g., the class is making a transition from one activity to another), a behavioral mistake (e.g., failure to follow instructions) is highly likely on the part of a student. Identifying the context of predictable misbehavior is critically important. The basic idea is to see recurrent patterns in misbehavior so that the context can be modified to avert them.

The second step in precorrection is stating the expected behavior—what the teacher wants the student to do instead of making the behavioral mistake. This step is essential because precorrection involves teaching students what to do, not simply what to avoid.

Third, the teacher must devise a plan for modifying the context in a way that will reduce the likelihood that the student will make a behavioral mistake. The modification can be very simple and straightforward, but small changes can often be critical in helping students learn to behave as desired. The context modification might be a change in location of the student or the teacher, a change in the teacher's behavior, a change in the way the assignment is presented, and so on. Whatever the change, it must be calculated to lower the probability that the student will exhibit the predictable misbehavior and increase the chances that the student will do what is expected.

The fourth step involves the student in rehearsal—either practice runs through the expected behavior or cognitive rehearsal in which the student describes the expected behavior. Rehearsal, or trying the behavior out before the expected performance, is basic to learning all skills, including those required for behaving as expected in school. The rehearsal should occur just before the performance is expected so that it is fresh in the student's mind.

Fifth, the teacher must arrange strong reinforcement for correct performance of the expected behavior. Reinforcement refers to a rewarding consequence, which may be social or tangible. To ensure high motivation to perform the expected behavior, the teacher must ensure that doing what is expected results in some highly satisfying consequence—a privilege or perk beyond the ordinary. However simple or ordinary the task or expectation may seem to someone else, strong reinforcement typically results in faster and more permanent learning whenever a person is learning to do something new or not customary *for him or her.*

Sixth, the teacher must arrange prompts or signals that the student understands to mean "remember" or "do it now." Like strong reinforcement, prompts are typically necessary to help students acquire a new skill. At first, if students do not have a special prompt, they may miss the typical cue and forget to apply what students know. As they become accustomed to performing as expected, they begin reading more subtle cues or prompting themselves.

Finally, precorrection requires a monitoring plan to help the teacher judge whether the student is acquiring the expected behavior. Effective monitoring involves systematic, direct observation and recording so that progress, or lack of it, is not a matter of guesswork. It is a reliable check on the effectiveness of the plan.

Figure 9.3 is a completed precorrection checklist and plan. Notice that although the plan is for a particular student (Dominic), the entire class is included in most parts of it. The precorrection strategy may be applied to single students only, small groups, individuals within groups, or entire classes.

Notice also how the precorrection plan fits with the requirements of IDEA for a behavior intervention plan. It is proactive, states what is expected, details the positive behavioral interventions, strategies, and supports that will be used, and includes an evaluation component (the monitoring plan). The precorrection plan could also be written to specify procedures for disciplinary action or management of behavioral crises.

FIGURE 9.3 Precorrection Checklist and Plan

Teacher: *Sarah Endow*
Student: *Dominic Smith*
Date: 11/15/94

❑ 1. Context	Students enter classroom immediately after recess. Students shouting, laughing, and pushing before complying with teacher directions.
❑ 2. Expected Behavior	Enter the room quietly, go to desks, begin task, keep hands to self.
❑ 3. Context Modification	Teacher meets students at door, has them wait, and then go to desks to begin entry tasks.
❑ 4. Behavioral Rehearsal	Teacher reminds students just before recess of expected behaviors. Teacher asks Dominic to tell what expected behaviors are.
❑ 5. Strong Reinforcement	Students are told that if they cooperate with teacher requests, they will have additional breaks and 5 extra minutes for recess.
❑ 6. Prompts	Teacher gives signals at the door to be quiet and points to activity on chalkboard. Teacher says "hush" to noisy students and praises students who are beginning work.
❑ 7. Monitoring Plan	Teacher uses a watch to measure how long it takes for all students to get on-task and counts how many students begin their tasks immediately (within 10 seconds).

Source: From *Antisocial Behavior in School: Strategies and Best Practices* by Hill M. Walker, Geoffrey Colvin, and Elizabeth Ramsey. Copyright © 1995 by Wadsworth. Reprinted by permission.

Teaching Desired Behavior

Precorrection is a general, proactive plan for teaching expected behavior. However, the effective implementation of such plans depends on careful attention to details of a variety of teaching tactics, many of which have long been used by master teachers. Moreover, many are seemingly simple. As is true in any area of art or science, the difference between the master and less skilled performers is often found in the details of execution—doing the seemingly simple things with extraordinary finesse.

Intervening Early

Research of the past several decades has led to increasing emphasis on early intervention (Colvin, 1992; Walker et al., 1995; Walker et al., in press). Early intervention does not mean merely intervention beginning when the child is young. It also means intervening before misconduct has progressed to more serious levels (Cyprus Group, 1996).

Teachers tend to wait until misbehavior goes through its earliest stages and has become intolerable before attempting to stop it. However, it is much more effective to step in at the earliest indications of problem behavior to prevent misconduct from developing further. Misbehavior tends to proceed through a predictable cycle from a state of calm to a crisis or state of being out of control (Colvin, 1992; Walker et al., 1995). The earlier the teacher intervenes effectively, the greater the chance of avoiding more serious problems. When using the early intervention strategy, teachers are making special efforts to give students attention when they are calm—compliant and on task.

Giving Effective Instructions

In approaching emotional or behavioral problems, it is easy to overlook the most obvious and simplest of intervention strategies: telling students what you want them to do. Research suggests that teachers and parents often make serious errors in the way they give instructions to children and youths, mishandling in the most mundane ways the simplest instructional interactions (Haring & Phillips, 1962; Lovitt & Smith, 1972; see also Kauffman, 1975; Kauffman, Mosert, Trent, & Hallahan, 1998).

Giving good instructions and following them with appropriate monitoring and consequences are not as simple as they might seem. Teachers must give their directions simply and clearly, in a firm but polite and nonangry voice, and when the student is paying attention. Too many instructions at a time will confuse students. Finally, to be effective, the teacher must monitor the student's compliance, give the student a reasonable amount of time to obey, and follow through with consequences. Students need recognition and social praise for following instructions and mild negative consequences for failing to comply.

Effectively Modeling

Showing students how to behave—providing observable examples or models—is often a highly effective instructional strategy. Teachers should set good examples by their own behavior, but in addition, they should use peer models. However, a careful review of the research on modeling and regular classroom environments suggests that if peer models are to be effective, the teacher must make sure that students see and understand exactly what they are to imitate and that they receive reinforcement for imitation (Hallenbeck & Kauffman, 1995). Moreover, the modeled performance must be something the student can do. Students are more likely to imitate models they see as like themselves. Modeling alone is likely to be effective only for students who are already highly motivated. Strong positive reinforcement for imitating desirable models will be required for most students with emotional or behavioral problems.

Structuring Choices

A simple but frequently overlooked technique of managing emotional or behavioral problems is giving students choices. All of us are likely to be more compliant with authority when we have the power to make choices that are important to us. Conversely, we often behave badly when we feel "boxed in," perceiving that we have no alternatives. The alert teacher finds ways to give students meaningful choices about classroom tasks. Master teachers understand that options must be structured for students to prevent catastrophic consequences, but also must foster interest and personal responsibility.

Constructing alternatives is a simple strategy that can be used very creatively and often successfully to manage problem behavior. These options may seem trivial to some teachers, but to students, they may be significant. The choices may be as simple as which assignment or problem to do first, which assignment from an array of acceptable alternatives to choose, or even what color paper or pen to use or where to sit for a particular activity. Also, students might be allowed to choose one of two or more tangible rewards or special activities when they have earned it or to pick a friend with whom to work. Box 9.3 illustrates how one teacher used choice of academic assignments to deal with the undesirable behavior of a student with ADHD in a regular classroom. Research shows that, for some students with emotional or behavioral problems, choices increase achievement and desirable behavior (Dunlap, et al., 1994; Powell & Nelson, 1997).

Using Positive Reinforcement

The staple of effective behavior management is positive reinforcement—supplying effective reinforcing consequences for the behavior one wishes to encourage (Alberto & Troutman, 1995; Kauffman, Mostert, Trent, & Hallahan, 1998; Kerr & Nelson, 1998; Rhode et al., 1992; Walker, 1995). Positive reinforcement is elegantly simple in concept (i.e., reward the behavior you want), but teachers must make astute choices about what and how to reinforce and must practice the procedure so they can use it with finesse and maximum effect. Finding words, activities, or tangible things that are effective reinforcers for individual students who are "tough kids" may present a real challenge (Rhode et al., 1992; Walker, 1995). Giving the right amount or magnitude of reinforcers and making them accessible only for desired behavior are critical.

Positive reinforcement is likely to be most effective when it includes variety and choice of reinforcers. Other variables that determine how effective reinforcement will be include immediacy, frequency, enthusiasm of the teacher, description of the

BOX 9.3 ***EXAMPLE***

Using Choices to Reduce Undesirable Behavior

Evan was a 7-year-old boy who had been diagnosed with ADHD. . . . Prior to this study, his teacher described the majority of his behaviors as undesirable. . . . Evan had poor peer relations and did not understand second-grade work.

This study was conducted in Evan's classroom. Observations were taken during language arts instruction between 1:30 and 2:00 p.m., when Evan's undesirable behaviors were reported to be the most severe. . . . For Evan, undesirable behavior included noncompliance, being away from his desk, disturbing others, staring off, and not doing work. . . .

For both the choice and no-choice conditions, Evan's classroom assignments were given by the teacher. During data collection in the baseline no-choice phases, Evan was directed to work on the same assignment as the rest of the class. During the choice phases, the teacher presented Evan with three different language arts assignments taken from the class curriculum, and he chose one to complete. The assignment choices were identical in length and difficulty. They varied in content (e.g., spelling lists, silent reading assignments, grammar and punctuation exercises, etc.) because they were taken from the language arts assignments the class was completing. In addition, the assignment choices varied, and Evan was not given the same choice of assignments twice. . . .

Compared to no-choice conditions, Evan's levels of undesirable behaviors decreased during choice conditions. . . . [See Figure A.]

These results suggest that choice procedures may be helpful to educators in managing the behaviors of students in general education classrooms.

Source: From "Effects of Choosing Academic Assignments on a Student with Attention Deficit Hyperactivity Disorder" by S. Powell & B. Nelson (1997), *Journal of Applied Behavior Analysis, 30,* pp. 181–183. Copyright 1997 by *Journal of Applied Behavior Analysis.* Reprinted by permission.

Questions to Ponder

What do you think were the most serious of Evan's behavior problems?

What additional interventions, besides choices, might Evan's teacher have considered?

What might Evan's teacher have done to increase the chances that Evan would imitate the appropriate peer models in his class?

FIGURE A Percentage of Intervals Rated as Containing Undesirable Behaviors across Conditions

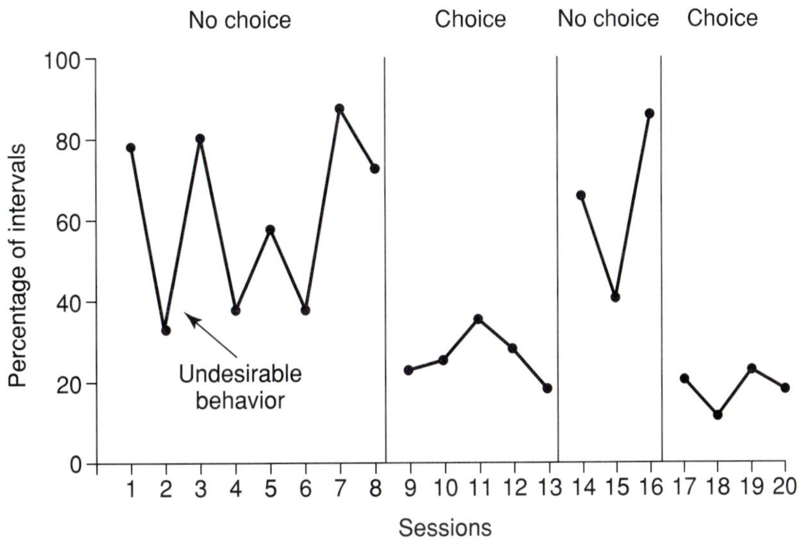

behavior being reinforced, anticipation of receiving reinforcement, and eye contact with the teacher (Rhode et al., 1992). Furthermore, the effort required to obtain the reinforcer, the quality of the reinforcer, and the availability of other competing reinforcers will likely alter the effectiveness of positive reinforcement (Neef, Shade, & Miller, 1994).

Teaching Social Skills

A notion popularized in the 1980s is that social skills can be readily assessed and taught through explicit training (e.g., Goldstein, 1988; Walker & McConnell, 1988; Walker et al., 1983). Although social skills and social competence are notoriously difficult to define, programs to teach such skills have involved instruction intended to improve students' perceptions and understanding of social interactions, modeling the skill to be learned, shaping approximations of the skill through verbal cues and reinforcement, and rehearsal or guided practice. In other words, effective social skills training requires the masterful use of all the teaching procedures discussed to this point.

Intuitively, social skills training seems to offer great promise because the majority of students with learning disabilities have serious problems of social competence. However, analyses of research on social skills training offer only scant evidence that it has typically been an effective strategy (Kavale & Forness, 1995). The results may be frequently disappointing because the social skills training has been too brief, been given to students who are already socially skilled, or did not follow a well-designed and field-tested curriculum. The training may too often have focused on social skill deficits themselves, rather than on correction of the low achievement that may have given rise to poor self-esteem and peer rejection. If social skills training is to be effective, it must be systematic, prolonged, based on a field-tested curriculum, and combined with effective instruction to address the academic failure that may contribute to low self-esteem, peer rejection, and inadequate social skills (Mastropieri & Scruggs, 1994).

Discouraging Undesired Behavior

This point cannot be overemphasized: *Correcting behavior problems requires that procedures for teaching desired behavior be already in place.* Traditional discipline has tended to emphasize punitive procedures for misbehavior rather than positive procedures for teaching and correction. Yet positive procedures designed to instruct and strengthen desired behavior are more effective in the long run and create a classroom climate in which students are more likely to learn. Hence, teachers should use the most positive procedures possible and be very cautious in the use of procedures designed to discourage unwanted behavior—particularly, the procedures that constitute punishment.

Punishment has a technical definition in behavioral psychology that is often misunderstood by the general public, and it can easily be misused or abused (see Kauffman, 1997; Rhode et al., 1992; Walker, 1995). It means any consequence that reduces the future probability of a particular behavior. As such, it is a legitimate if not indispensable tool of teachers (cf. Pfiffner & O'Leary, 1987; Pfiffner, Rosen, & O'Leary, 1985). Not all misbehavior can be anticipated, and proactive behavior intervention plans do not prevent all misconduct. Therefore, teachers must have additional humane and effective procedures for discouraging students' misbehavior.

The consequences that educators intend to be punishing (e.g., yelling, criticizing, lecturing, or sending a student out of the classroom) often are not perceived as such by students. Effective punishment need not cause pain or embarrassment. In fact, corporal punishment and strategies that rely on embarrassment or humiliation place educators at risk of legal sanctions and cannot be justified on ethical grounds. Used properly and as a secondary strategy to supplement positive strategies for teaching expected behavior, some forms of nonviolent punishment are appropriate and legally and morally defensible. However, strategies other than punishment (some of which we have already discussed) may discourage misbehavior, and these are always preferable when punishment is not required to resolve a problem.

Response Cost

The most effective and defensible type of punishment involves withdrawing a privilege or reward contingent on a particular unacceptable behavior. This type of punishment is known as **response cost** because the unacceptable response "costs" a privilege or reward. It is, in effect, a "fine" levied for inappropriate behavior. For example, suppose that a student who frequently disturbs others in the class finds it highly reinforcing to sit with his friends rather than next to the teacher at lunch. This student might be given five points (perhaps represented as symbols on an index card) at the beginning of the day, with the understanding that if he still has two or more points at lunchtime, he will be allowed to sit with his friends at lunch. The teacher will mark off one point each time he disturbs another student. An unacceptable behavior (disturbing others) costs him a point; if he loses more than three of his five points, he loses a special privilege.

Response cost, like positive reinforcement, is a simple idea that requires careful attention to implementation if it is to work well. If managed well, the withdrawal of rewards and privileges is less likely than other punishment procedures to produce aggression and lead to legal liabilities. The wise teacher consults and follows detailed guides for using such procedures (e.g., Alberto & Troutman, 1995; Kerr & Nelson, 1998; Rhode et al., 1992; Sprick & Howard, 1995; Walker, 1995).

Positive Reinforcement of Alternative Behavior

The preferred tactic for discouraging undesirable behavior is reinforcing competing or incompatible behavior—replacing undesirable behavior with expected behavior by using positive reinforcement rather than punishment (Deitz & Repp, 1983; Kauffman, Mostert, Trent, & Hallahan, 1998; Walker et al., 1995). Choosing the particular behaviors to reinforce is a key issue. Competing behaviors are those that are difficult to do simultaneously. Incompatible behaviors are those that are impossible to do at the same time. Misbehavior can sometimes be successfully discouraged simply by offering reinforcement for expected behavior that makes misbehavior more difficult or impossible. For example, reinforcing attention to and completion of seat work makes out-of-seat behavior less likely; doing seat work and being out of the seat are competing behaviors. Reinforcing in-seat behavior tends to decrease out-of-seat behavior because in-seat and out-of-seat behaviors are incompatible; they cannot be done at the same time. The suggestion is simply this: Focus first on using positive reinforcement for appropriate behavior as a means of correcting behavior problems, and then give thought to reinforcing specific behaviors that make concurrent misbehavior more difficult or impossible.

Another way to use positive reinforcement to decrease behavior problems is to make reinforcement contingent on the problem behavior not occurring at all or occurring less than a stated number of times for a specific period. For example, earning a rewarding consequence might depend on a student's not talking out or talking out less than three times during a 20-minute lesson. Rewarding the omission or reduced level of undesirable behavior is a strategy that can be used very effectively with many types of classroom behaviors. As with other strategies, however, reinforcement requires careful attention to detail and understanding of the behavior principles on which it is based (Kerr & Nelson, 1998; Rhode et al., 1992; Walker et al., 1995).

Summary

1. What social, emotional, and behavioral problems sometimes coexist with learning disabilities?
   Attention-deficit hyperactivity disorder and the full range of other emotional and behavioral problems may accompany learning disabilities. Some problems are internalizing (social withdrawal); others are externalizing (acting out, antisocial behavior). Not all students with learning disabilities have emotional or behavioral problems. However, a majority of students with learning disabilities present behavior management problems for teachers.
   a. Problems of social competence include difficulties in using social skills effectively, avoiding maladaptive behavior, developing positive relations with others, and acquiring age-appropriate social cognition. Such problems may have a negative influence on the self-concepts of students with learning disabilities. However, the issue of self-concept is complex, and low achievement may be the primary factor responsible for lowered self-concepts of students with learning disabilities.
   b. Conduct problems include overt antisocial behavior such as aggression, tantrums, noncompliance, disruption, and covert antisocial behavior such as lying and stealing. These problems are common among students with learning disabilities, who are overrepresented among youths detained by the juvenile justice system.
   c. Other emotional or behavioral problems, such as anxiety and depression, may accompany learning disabilities.

2. What causes students' emotional and behavioral problems?
   All potential causes of learning disabilities are potential causes of emotional or behavioral problems, including biological, family, cultural, and school factors. Teachers should be particularly concerned about causes related to schooling, including inadequate instructional programs, inappropriate expectations, insensitivity to students' individuality, reinforcement of undesirable behavior, inconsistency in behavior management, and inappropriate models.
3. How are students' emotional and behavioral problems assessed?
   Like academic assessment, the assessment of emotional or behavioral problems should guide intervention. IDEA now requires that the behavior problems of students with disabilities be assessed in ways that will help in writing IEPs.
   a. Systematic screening is often not done because of the number of problems that would likely be detected. However, a useful multiple-gating procedure (the SSBD) is available for screening students for internalizing and externalizing problems. A major concern in screening, and in all other aspects of assessment, is cultural sensitivity.
   b. Prereferral strategies provide useful information regardless of whether the student is later found to be eligible for special education services.
   c. Confirmation of eligibility must be based on the combined judgments of a multidisciplinary team, including teachers.
   d. IDEA requires that all students with disabilities who have behavior problems have a behavioral assessment and a behavior intervention plan included in their IEP.
      (1) Obtaining and using information from multiple sources is required in writing a behavior intervention plan
      (2) The behavior intervention plan must delineate expected behaviors, inappropriate behaviors, positive and negative consequences, disciplinary procedures, and procedures for handling behavioral crises.
   e. Special discipline considerations may be necessary if the student's placement is changed or the student is suspended for more than 10 school days. However, in most cases, the same discipline that applies to nondisabled students applies to those with disabilities. The major exceptions usually arise when a student brings a weapon or illegal drugs to school. In any case, the special education of a student with disabilities may not be discontinued. It may be continued in the student's current placement or an interim alternative setting.
      (1) Manifestation determination means that the IEP team and other qualified personnel must assess the student to determine whether the misbehavior was a result of the disability. Usual disciplinary action may not be allowed if the student's misconduct was related to the disability, but in all cases, the student's special education must be continued.
      (2) Interim alternative educational settings include alternative schools, special classes, special schools, the student's home, and other settings in which education can be provided.

4. What interventions can help students with emotional or behavioral problems? The focus should be on proactive plans for teaching appropriate behavior, not reaction to misconduct. IDEA requires proactive behavior intervention plans as well as plans for dealing with discipline and behavioral crises.
   a. Modifying the learning environment for proactive management is a key concept. Precorrection is a proactive teaching plan that appears to be consistent with IDEA requirements. It is a way of anticipating predictable misbehavior in particular contexts and devising a strategy for teaching expected behavior. Precorrection involves describing the context of misbehavior, stating the expected behavior, modifying the context, planning rehearsal of the expected behavior, arranging strong reinforcement for exhibiting the expected behavior, arranging prompts or cues to perform the expected behavior, and devising a monitoring plan.
   b. Effective tactics for teaching desired behavior include those that are simple and well known. The key is implementing these procedures with finesse.
      (1) Intervening early means not only intervening when the child is young, but also intervening early in the misbehavior so that it does not become more serious.
      (2) Giving effective instructions may seem simple, but it depends on attention to a variety of factors, such as getting the student's attention, giving clear directions, and rewarding compliance.
      (3) Effective use of models requires both that models be present and that the teacher call attention to what is to be imitated and reward imitation. The student must be able to perform the modeled behavior.
      (4) Structuring choices can be a powerful tool for defusing student resistance to tasks; the key is providing choices that the student sees as meaningful.
      (5) Positive reinforcement is the staple of good behavior management, and effective teachers learn how to reward desired behavior frequently and effectively.
      (6) Teaching social skills is intuitively appealing, but may be effective only if it is systematic, prolonged, based on a field-tested curriculum, and combined with effective instruction to address the academic failure.
   c. Effective strategies for discouraging undesired behavior are important because not all misbehavior can be anticipated and proactive behavior intervention does not prevent all misconduct. Punishment has a technical definition—a consequence that reduces the likelihood of a particular behavior. Though punishment can be abused and some forms (e.g., corporal punishment) cannot be defended, certain forms of nonviolent punishment are defensible. Positive means of discouraging undesired behavior are, when sufficient, preferable to punishment.
      (1) Response cost punishment means withdrawing rewards or privileges contingent on particular misbehaviors.
      (2) Positive reinforcement of alternative behavior is preferred to punishment, and this may involve rewarding specific competing or incompatible behaviors or giving rewards for omitting particular misbehaviors.

10

Cognitive, Metacognitive, Motivational, and Attention Problems

What Cognitive and Metacognitive Problems Sometimes Occur with Learning Disabilities?

Early Research—Cognitive Styles

Recent Cognitive Research—Memory Abilities

Metacognitive Problems

How Can Cognitive and Metacognitive Needs Be Addressed?

Self-Instruction

Self-Monitoring of Academic Performance

Mnemonic Strategies

Metamemory Training

Metacomprehensive Training

Scaffolded Instruction

What Motivational Problems Occur and What Can Be Done about Them?

External Locus of Control

Negative Attributions

Learned Helplessness

Strategies for Improving Motivation

What Attention Problems Sometimes Occur with Learning Disabilities?

Early Work—Strauss Syndrome

Selective Attention and Maintaining Attention

More Recent Work—Attention Deficit Hyperactivity Disorder

Cognition refers to our ability to think, metacognition refers to our ability to think about thinking, attention refers to our ability to concentrate, and motivation refers to our desire to engage in all three. In many ways, all four are interconnected: A person who has a problem with one is likely to have problems with one or more of the others. In addition, educational methods developed for each of these areas are frequently similar.

WHAT COGNITIVE AND METACOGNITIVE PROBLEMS SOMETIMES OCCUR WITH LEARNING DISABILITIES?

For many years, the special education profession was not very interested in cognition, largely because of the popularity of behaviorism. Strict behaviorists are interested solely in observable behavior—that is, behavior that can be measured. **Cognition,** or the ability to think and solve problems, is primarily unobservable, so strict behaviorists dismiss it as a legitimate area of scientific inquiry.

Beginning in the mid-1970s, however, many psychologists, including some behaviorists, began to criticize behavioral theory as too simplistic. They seriously questioned whether complex human behavior could be explained solely by stimulus-response connections, as behaviorists maintained. As Mahoney (1974) put it:

> There is now an overwhelming body of evidence indicating that a "passive organism" input-output model is sorely inadequate. Not only are there complex causal interactions among environmental and internally-based stimulations, but we know that much of what is "external" is actually mediated. Humans do not passively register the world as it really is; they filter, transform, and construct the experiences which constitute their "reality." (p. 29)

This growing dissatisfaction with behaviorism prompted the growth of cognitive psychology. Whereas behaviorists are concerned with the association of stimulus (S) and response (R), cognitive psychologists concentrate on what occurs between the S and the R. They want to know what goes on "inside our heads."

Early Research—Cognitive Styles

In the 1960s, there was a rapid growth in an area of study that came to be called **cognitive styles**—ways of approaching problem-solving tasks. The two cognitive styles that have received the most attention, first in populations without learning disabilities and then in children with them, were the dimensions of field independence–field dependence and reflectivity-impulsivity.

Field Independence versus Field Dependence

The concept of **field independence–field dependence** refers to how much individuals are influenced by their physical surroundings when asked to make decisions on perceptual tasks. Persons who are heavily influenced by their environment are considered field dependent. Their perceptions are less accurate because they can be "thrown off" by misleading information in their environment. Individuals who are able to focus on the most essential perceptual data without being influenced by inessential details are referred to as field independent. Their perceptions tend to be more accurate than those of persons who are field dependent.

Researchers have used several methods to assess field independence. In the most elaborate one, the person is seated on a chair within a small room. Both the chair and the room can be tilted by the experimenter and the person in the chair. After both the chair and room are tilted so that neither is in a vertical position, the individual is requested to "right" his or her chair to the true vertical. Those who are able to ignore cues from the room and place the chair in a position close to true vertical are categorized as field independent. Those who cannot are classified as field dependent. Children become more field independent with age (Witkin, Goodenough, & Karp, 1967). Children who have learning disabilities are generally more field dependent than their nondisabled peers (Blackman & Goldstein, 1982).

Reflectivity versus Impulsivity

The idea of **reflectivity–impulsivity** refers to whether a person takes time to reflect on various alternatives before making a choice on difficult but solvable tasks. Most studies of reflectivity-impulsivity have used a visual-perceptual matching task. The child is presented with the line drawings of familiar figures (e.g., car, teddy bear, etc.) one at a time and is asked to find one exactly like it from several figures (Kagan, Rosman, Day, Albert, & Phillips, 1964). Two things are recorded: response time, or how long it takes the child to make his or her first choice, and errors, or how many incorrect choices the child makes before he or she gets the correct answer. Reflective children respond more slowly and make fewer errors, whereas impulsive children respond quickly but make many errors.

Researchers have generally found the reflectivity-impulsivity dimension to be developmentally sensitive, with children becoming more reflective with age. Students with learning disabilities are more apt to be impulsive than are their nondisabled peers (Blackman & Goldstein, 1982).

Cognitive style research was immediately appealing to special education practitioners. Teachers and school psychologists could easily associate laboratory researchers' findings with their own experiences with students with learning disabilities. Teachers are the first to acknowledge that many of these students do not seem to think before they respond, but instead blurt out the first thing that comes into their heads. More educationally oriented researchers made several efforts to train students with learning disabilities to be more reflective. Generally, they found that they could make students more reflective on the perceptual matching task, but that this did not carry over to classroom behavior (Epstein, Hallahan, & Kauffman, 1975).

Even though training did not lead to educational benefits, this early research on cognitive styles has had a substantial impact on how we now view persons with learning disabilities and also on educational programming for them. These studies also laid the groundwork for later work on cognitive and metacognitive training (discussed later in this chapter) by showing that students with learning disabilities do approach problem-solving tasks in a different manner than nondisabled students and that attempting to train them to think in a more "normal" manner is not likely to be successful if the training is based on laboratory tasks rather than on classroom behavior.

Recent Cognitive Research—Memory Abilities

Much recent research on cognition in students with learning disabilities has focused on memory abilities. Like the work on cognitive styles, the study of memory processes of students with learning disabilities has gained impetus from the fact that teachers see it as relevant to the everyday functioning of these students. Teachers are quick to agree that many students with learning disabilities display significant difficulties with memory. "In one ear and out the other" is a commonly heard phrase when teachers discuss these students.

There are numerous research studies demonstrating that persons with learning disabilities have problems with various types of memory tasks (Beale & Tippett, 1992; Hulme & Snowling, 1992). We briefly explore two types of memory: short-term memory and working memory.

Short-Term Memory

The ability to remember information over a relatively short period of time—a few seconds or a minute or so at most—is referred to as **short-term memory.** (This is in contrast to long-term memory, which requires the retention of information over several hours, days, or longer.) Short-term memory tasks can vary in several ways. For example, they can require the retention of auditory or visual information. In a typical auditory short-term memory task, the individual hears several trials of five to seven digits. After each trial, the individual is to repeat back the sequence in the correct order. In a typical visual short-term memory task, the person is shown several trials of five to seven pictures. After each trial, he or she is to say the names of the pictures in the correct order. Although researchers have found that students with learning disabilities have problems with visual short-term memory (e.g., Hallahan, Kauffman, & Ball, 1973; Tarver, Hallahan, Kauffman, & Ball, 1976), most learning disabilities research has focused on auditory short-term memory. The evidence that students with learning disabilities perform more poorly than their nondisabled peers on auditory short-term memory tasks is overwhelming (Hulme & Snowling, 1992).

Working Memory

There is evidence that working memory problems are even more important than short-term memory problems in the reading difficulties of students with learning disabilities (Swanson, 1994). **Working memory** refers to a person's ability to keep a small amount of information in mind while simultaneously carrying out further cognitive operations. Swanson (1994) has described the difference between short-term memory and working memory in the following way:

> Everyday examples of WM [working memory] would thus include holding a person's address in mind while listening to instructions about how to get there, or perhaps listening to the sequence of events in a story while trying to understand what the story means. Described in this way, WM differs from the concept of short-term memory that is typically used to describe situations in which small amounts of material are held passively (e.g., digit- or word-span tasks) and then reproduced in an untransformed fashion. (p. 48)

In this same study, children and adults with learning disabilities and normally achieving children and adults were compared on several types of working memory and short-term memory tasks (Swanson, 1994). In one of the working memory tasks, for example, the subject was presented with a string of words (e.g., lip, slip, clip), asked whether ship or lip was in the list, and then required to recall the previously presented words (lip, slip, clip) in the correct order. There were several strings presented, each containing from 2 to 14 words. Results of this study indicate that, for individuals with learning disabilities, working memory is even more important than short-term memory for predicting reading and mathematics performance. And results from another study (Ashbaker & Swanson, 1996) suggest that both reading comprehension and word recognition ability depend more on working memory than short-term memory in adolescents with learning disabilities.

Metacognitive Problems

As noted in Chapter 3, metacognition refers to the ability to think about thinking. Metacognition has two components: (1) an awareness of what is needed in the way of strategies, skills, or resources to perform a task and (2) an ability to regulate one's performance by monitoring it and making adjustments if one starts to make errors in performance (Baker, 1982). Students with learning disabilities can be deficient in a variety of metacognitive areas such as metamemory, metalistening, and metacomprehension in reading.

One of the first studies of the metacognitive abilities of students with learning disabilities (Torgesen, 1979) compared these students' abilities with those of nondisabled students to answer such questions as "If you wanted to phone a friend and someone told you the phone number, would it make any difference if you called right away after you heard the number or if you got a drink of water first? Why? What would you do if you wanted to try to remember a phone number?" These questions assess metamemory skills—the ability to think about memory strategies. Students with learning disabilities had more difficulty than their nondisabled peers in answering these metamemory questions. For example, in answer to the last one, most students in both groups said they would write it down. When asked what they would do if they did not have a pencil and paper, nondisabled students were almost twice as likely to reply that they would use verbal rehearsal as a strategy.

Teachers often describe students with learning disabilities as looking as though they understand what you are telling them, although their subsequent behavior reveals that they have not understood a word you've said. This anecdotal observation was corroborated by a study that involved metalistening—the ability to conceptualize the listening process (Kotsonis & Patterson, 1980). In this study, children were told they were going to play a game that involved several rules. An adult presented one rule at a time, asking the children after each rule presentation if they thought they now had enough information to play the game. Students with learning disabilities were much more likely than their nondisabled peers to voice a readiness to play even though by objective standards they had not yet heard enough information to play the game appropriately.

The concept of metacomprehension—the ability to think about how one understands—has helped special educators better understand the reading comprehension problems of students with learning disabilities (e.g., Anderson, 1980; Baker & Anderson, 1982; Bos & Filip, 1982; Forrest & Waller, 1981; Paris & Myers, 1981; Wong, 1982). This research has shown that many students with learning disabilities lack the following metacomprehension strategies:

1. *Clarifying the purposes of reading.* Before efficient readers even begin to read, they have a mind-set about the general purpose of their reading. For instance, their approach to reading to obtain the gist of a news article is different from their approach to reading to gain information from a textbook on which they will be tested. Students with learning disabilities are not adept at adjusting their reading styles to fit the difficulty level of the material and tend to approach all reading passages with the same degree of concentration and effort.

2. *Focusing attention on important parts of passages.* Students with learning disabilities have difficulties in picking out the main idea of a paragraph. Good readers spend more time and effort focusing on the major ideas contained in the paragraphs they read.

3. *Monitoring one's level of comprehension.* Efficient readers know when they are not understanding what they are reading. Knowing when you are and are not understanding something is an important metacomprehension skill.

4. *Rereading and scanning ahead.* When good readers do note that they are having problems comprehending, they often use a couple of basic metacomprehension strategies that students with learning disabilities do not readily use. They stop and reread portions of the passage and/or scan ahead for information that will help them understand what they are reading.

5. *Consulting external sources.* When good readers encounter a word they do not know, they are more likely than poor readers to turn to external sources such as a dictionary or an encyclopedia for help.

HOW CAN COGNITIVE AND METACOGNITIVE NEEDS BE ADDRESSED?

A number of educational techniques have been developed to combat the constellation of cognitive and metacognitive problems of students with learning disabilities. Several different names have been used to refer to these techniques, including cognitive training, cognitive-behavior modification training, and metacognitive training. The differences among the use of these terms is often relatively subtle, and sometimes they are used virtually interchangeably. Depending on which theorist you read, the methods are referred to in slightly different terms. In other words, one person's cognitive training techniques might be another's cognitive-behavior modification techniques, which might be another person's metacognitive training techniques. For purposes of simplicity, in this book, the classification **cognitive training** refers to techniques and methods that address the combination of cognitive and metacognitive problems of students with learning disabilities. Cognitive training involves:

1. changing the thought processes of students
2. providing students with strategies for learning
3. teaching students self-initiative

Several specific techniques fall under the rubric of cognitive training, and we discuss some briefly: self-instruction, self-monitoring of academic performance, mnemonic strategies, metamemory training, metacomprehension training, and scaffolded instruction. Box 10.1 lists principles characteristic of cognitive training methods.

Self-Instruction

One of the first cognitive training methods to be used with students with learning disabilities was **self-instruction,** which involves verbalizing the steps in a task. Meichenbaum was the pioneer in this area, relying heavily on the earlier work of well-known Russian language theorists (Luria 1961; Vygotsky, 1962). The following

BOX 10.1 ***TIPS FOR PRACTICE***

Eight Principles of Effective Cognitive Training Programs

Many specific techniques fall under the rubric of cognitive training. Because of this diversity, it is sometimes difficult for teachers to know which strategies are most likely to be successful. After examining several effective cognitive training programs, Pressley and colleagues arrived at a list of eight common features (Pressley, Symons, Snyder, & Cariglia-Bull, 1989; Symons, Snyder, Cariglia-Bult, & Pressley, 1989). Teachers can use them as a guide when choosing among cognitive training options.

1. *Teach a few strategies at a time.* Rather than bombarding children with a number of strategies all at once, teach them just a few. In this way, there is a better chance that the students can learn the strategies in a comprehensive and not a superficial fashion.
2. *Teach self-monitoring.* It is helpful if students keep track of their own progress. When checking their own work, if they find an error, they should be encouraged to try to correct it on their own.
3. *Teach them when and where to use the strategies.* Many students with learning disabilities have problems with the metacognitive ability of knowing when and where they can use strategies that teachers have taught. Teachers must give them this information as well as extensive experience in using the strategies in a variety of settings.
4. *Maintain the students' motivation.* Students need to know that the strategies work. Teachers can help motivation by consistently pointing out the benefits of the strategies, explaining how they work, and charting students' progress.
5. *Teach in context.* Students should learn cognitive techniques as an integrated part of the curriculum. Rather than using cognitive training in an isolated manner, teachers should teach students to employ cognitive strategies during academic lessons.
6. *Don't neglect a nonstrategic knowledge base.* Sometimes those who use cognitive training become such avid proponents of it that they forget the importance of factual knowledge. The more facts children know about history, science, math, English, and so forth, the less they will need to rely on strategies.
7. *Engage in direct teaching.* Because the emphasis in cognitive training is on encouraging students to take more initiative in their own learning, teachers may feel that they are less necessary than is actually the case. Cognitive training does not give license to back off from directly teaching students. Students' reliance on teachers should gradually fade. In the early stages, teachers need to be directly in control of supervising the students' use of the cognitive strategies.
8. *Regard cognitive training as long term.* Because cognitive training often results in immediate improvement, there may be a temptation to view it as a panacea or a quick fix. To maintain improvements and have them generalize to other settings, however, students need extensive practice in applying the strategies they have learned.

---

training sequence, based on that developed by Meichenbaum and Goodman (1971), has served as the prototype for many subsequent self-instruction efforts:

1. The teacher performs the task while verbalizing the following aloud:
   a. questions about the task
   b. self-guiding instructions on how to perform the task
   c. self-evaluation of performance

2. The child performs the task while the teacher instructs aloud.
3. The child performs the task while verbalizing aloud.
4. The child performs the task while verbalizing in a whisper.
5. The child performs the task while verbalizing covertly.

An example of using self-instruction with students with learning disabilities involved a five-step strategy for solving math word problems (Case, Harris, & Graham, 1992): (1) saying the problem out loud, (2) looking for important words and circling them, (3) drawing pictures to help explain what was happening, (4) writing the math sentence, and (5) writing the answer. The students were also prompted to employ the following self-instructions: (1) "What do I have to do?" (2) "How can I solve this problem?" (3) "The five-step strategy will help me look for important words." (4) "How am I doing?" (5) "Good job. I got it right."

An example of the use of self-instruction with handwriting problems involved students using the following instructions: (1) saying the word to be copied, (2) saying the first syllable of the word, (3) saying the name of each letter in the syllable three times, (4) naming each letter in the syllable as it is being written, and (5) repeating the first four steps for each syllable remaining in the word (Kosiewicz, Hallahan, Lloyd, & Graves, 1982).

After a decade of research on his own and with others, Meichenbaum (1981) set forth ten guidelines for the development of self-instruction programs. These are listed in Box 10.2.

Self-Monitoring of Academic Performance

Students employ **self-monitoring** of their academic performance by keeping track of their own work and making some type of recording of it. Although self-monitoring was originally used with students with learning disabilities as a means of monitoring attention, some have also applied it specifically to academic performance. Students have improved their spelling, for example, by being taught to count the number of words they have correctly spelled on spelling lists and recording this number on a graph (Harris, Graham, Reid, McElroy, & Hamby, 1994). This method led to more words being spelled correctly. Self-monitoring has also resulted in an increase in the length and quality of written stories (Harris et al., 1994). The procedure involved having the students count the number of words in their stories and record this number on a graph.

Although self-monitoring of performance can be highly effective, its effectiveness is limited to skills that the student already possesses. In other words, "self-monitoring does not create new behaviors . . . rather, it affects behaviors that are already in the child's repertoire" (Reid, 1996, p. 322). The fact that students with learning disabilities often have problems fluidly executing skills they possess, however, makes self-monitoring a very useful teaching technique.

BOX 10.2 ***TIPS FOR PRACTICE***

Ten Guidelines for Developing Self-Instruction Programs

1. Carefully analyze the target behaviors that you want to change.
2. Listen for the strategies that the student is presently using, paying special attention to whether they are inappropriate.
3. Use training tasks that are as close as possible to those you want to change.
4. Collaborate with the student in devising the self-instruction routine, rather than imposing the regimen on him or her.
5. Be sure that the student has all the skills that are necessary to use the self-instructions.
6. Give the student feedback about the utility of the self-instructions for performance.
7. Explicitly point out other tasks and settings in which the student can use the self-instructions.
8. Use a variety of trainers, settings, and tasks to increase the chances that the student will learn to use the self-instructions successfully outside the training setting.
9. Anticipate failures and include failure management in the training activities.
10. Train until a reasonable criterion of performance has been reached. Then follow up with "booster" sessions in order to provide a better chance that the trained skills will be maintained.

Source: Adapted from "Teaching Thinking: A Cognitive Behavioral Approach" by D. Meichenbaum, April 1981, paper presented at the meeting of the Society for Learning Disabilities and Remedial Education, New York. Reprinted by permission.

Mnemonic Strategies

Teachers can use **mnemonic strategies** to enhance the memory performance of students with learning disabilities. Several such strategies have been used successfully with students at a variety of age levels. The rationale behind mnemonics is that students with learning disabilities will remember information better if they can use concrete cues and draw on prior knowledge. For example, to teach young children letter-sound correspondence, teachers can present each letter as an integrated part of a familiar figure (Fulk, Lohman, & Belfiore, 1997). (See Figure 10.1.)

Another mnemonic technique that has been used successfully with middle-school students with learning disabilities involves helping them remember the order of the presidents of the United States (Mastropieri, Scruggs, & Whedon, 1997). Each president was represented by a picture with two elements—one for his name and one for his ranking. For example, for Washington, the picture showed someone *washing* (a cue for Washington) *buns* (a cue for 1). For Franklin Pierce, the picture showed a *purse* (a cue for Pierce) being stabbed by a *fork* (a cue for 14).

Teachers can also use mnemonics to help teach abstract concepts. For example:

> To teach that "radial symmetry" refers to structurally similar body parts that extend out from the center of organisms, such as starfish, an acoustically similar keyword ("radio cemetery") was constructed from the unfamiliar term, *radial symmetry.* In the picture, radio cemetery was shown in the shape of a star, with radios as headstones, and skeletons dancing to the music from the radios. Each arm of the star is shown

FIGURE 10.1 Mnemonic Illustration for the Letter K

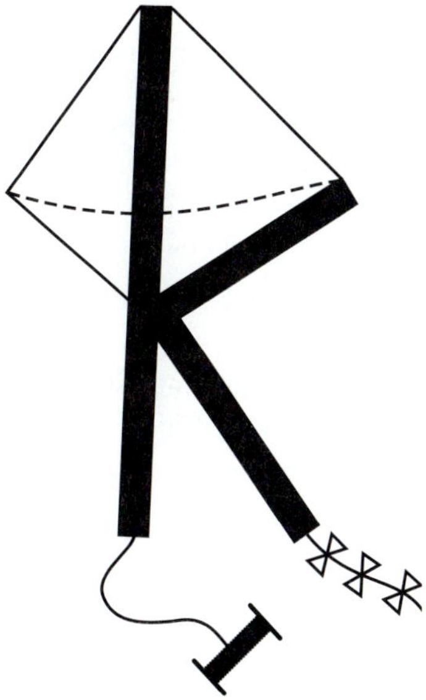

Source: From "Effects of Integrated Picture Mnemonics on the Letter Recognition and Letter-Sound Acquisition of Transitional First-Grade Students with Special Needs" by B. M. Fulk, D. Lohman, & P. J. Belfiore, 1997, *Learning Disability Quarterly, 20,* p. 36. Copyright 1997 by Council for Learning Disabilities. Reprinted by permission.

to be similar in appearance to each other arm, to enforce the concept. (Scruggs & Mastropieri, 1992, p. 222)

Metamemory Training

In addition to mnemonics, teachers can also use techniques that encourage students to use metacognitive strategies to help them remember important information. One team of researchers found that they were able to help students with learning disabilities by teaching them such things as being aware that they can forget things but that they can do things to help them remember, that there are individual differences in memory, and the importance of repetition (Lucangeli, Galderisi, & Cornoldi, 1995). For example, to stress the importance of being aware that forgetting is normal but that one can do things to help prevent it, they engaged in the following dialogue with students:

Do you sometimes forget?

Do you think that other people can forget things, too?

For any answer you may have given, try, together with a classmate of yours, the following activity. You will discover if you are right or wrong.

Look at the objects represented and pronounce their names. [Teacher shows student picture containing 12 common objects.] Turn your head while your schoolmate covers one of them. You have to remember the object . . . hidden. Repeat and answer again. Have you remembered . . . every figure? . . .

Now you have to remember the 12 figures you have seen in the previous picture. How many do you think you can remember? Write the names of the objects you have seen . . . here. Count how many of them you have remembered and compare . . . with your prediction. How close was your prediction? . . . Now try to answer these . . . questions:

1. Do you remember what things you did in school yesterday?
2. What things did you do in school a week ago?
3. Do you remember exactly the names and faces of your classmates when you were in kindergarten?
4. Do you remember any poetry you learned last Christmas?
5. Could you recite it completely?

Have you forgotten anything we asked you? Write it in the first column. Could you do something to try to remember? Report in the second column the solutions you have thought of. (Lucangeli et al., 1995, p. 20)

Metacomprehension Training

In **metacomprehension training,** teachers provide students with strategies for thinking about and remembering the major points of material they are reading. In one study (Wong & Jones, 1982), for example, students with learning disabilities were taught to use the following set of metacomprehension strategies: (1) Ask yourself, "What am I studying the passage for?" (2) Find the main ideas and underline them. (3) Think of a question about each main idea and write it down. (4) Look back at your questions and answers to see how they provide you with more information.

In another study, students were given practice in adjusting their reading speed to match the type of material they were reading (e.g., quickly, very slowly, skimming some but not all the material) (Lucangeli et al., 1995). For example, students were asked which strategy they should use in trying to find a particular word on a dictionary page. This type of training led to better reading comprehension.

Scaffolded Instruction

The technique of **scaffolded instruction** requires the teacher to provide assistance when a student is first learning a task but then gradually to remove the help so that the student is able to do the task independently. This method is based on Vygotsky's (1978) theory of a **zone of proximal development**—the gap between a child's level of performance when working independently and when helped by an adult. According to Vygotsky, children learn from their elders in ways that are similar to apprentices who learn their crafts from masters. Scaffolded instruction is designed to bridge this gap between independent and dependent performance. One way to think about scaffolded instruction is to consider the teacher a "cognitive coach" (Englert, 1990; Tharp & Gallimore, 1988).

One type of scaffold that teachers can provide is referred to as **reciprocal teaching,** which involves the teacher and students taking turns reading passages. In this way, students can see reading strategies modeled by the teacher and try them out while being monitored by the teacher (Brown & Campione, 1984).

Although scaffolded instruction looks relatively easy, it is extremely demanding (Pressley, Hogan, Wharton-McDonald, Mistretta, & Ettenberger, 1996). It requires that the teacher have in-depth knowledge of the students and the curriculum.

WHAT MOTIVATIONAL PROBLEMS OCCUR AND WHAT CAN BE DONE ABOUT THEM?

Many authorities have noted the close link between metacognitive problems and motivation problems. As one researcher put it:

> *Every important cognitive act has motivational consequences, and, furthermore, these consequences potentiate future self-regulatory actions* (Borkowski et al., 1989). For instance, as strategic and executive processes become more refined, the young student comes to recognize the importance of being strategic. As a result, feelings of self-efficacy emerge. Simultaneously, children learn to attribute successful academic outcomes to effort (and sometimes ability) rather than to luck or ease of the to-be-learned task. (Borkowski, 1992, p. 253)

Given the metacognitive problems of many students with learning disabilities, it is not surprising that so many of them also have motivational problems. These students appear to let events occur without attempting to take control. Their motivational problems stem from three interrelated areas: external locus of control, negative attributions, and learned helplessness.

External Locus of Control

Locus of control refers to whether you view yourself as being controlled by internal or external forces. Persons with learning disabilities are more likely than those without disabilities to have an external rather than an internal locus of control (Hallahan, Gajar, Cohen, & Tarver, 1978; Short & Weissberg-Benchell, 1989). For example, when asked a question such as "Suppose you did a better than usual job in reading at school. Would it probably happen (1) because you tried harder or (2) because someone helped you?" these students are more likely to choose the second response.

Negative Attributions

What you think are the causes of your successes and failures are known as **attributions.** Researchers have consistently found that, unlike their nondisabled peers, students with learning disabilities do not take pride in their successes, are prone to minimize those they do have, and tend to accept more readily responsibility for their failures. These negative attributions can lead to damaging effects on self-esteem:

> LD children do not seem to employ the self-serving attributional bias that is associated with normal self-esteem. . . . This bias is the tendency to attribute success to internal causes and failure to external factors: that is, to take more personal responsibility for one's triumphs than for one's defeats. (Groteluschen, Borkowski, & Hale, 1991, pp. 89–90)

Learned Helplessness

Closely related to locus of control and attributions is the concept of **learned helplessness**—the belief that your efforts will not result in the desired outcomes (Seligman, 1992). Persons with learned helplessness have come to expect failure no matter how hard they try; therefore, they tend to lose motivation. It is easy to see why students with learning disabilities are frequently referred to as exhibiting learned helplessness, given their propensity for academic failure and their external locus of control and negative attributions.

Strategies for Improving Motivation

Whether these motivational problems cause academic problems, or vice versa, is not known. It is logical, however, to assume that a vicious cycle is operating. For example, because of difficulties in learning, the student with learning disabilities learns to expect failure; therefore, he or she tends to give up when faced with new learning tasks that are the least bit difficult, which results in more failure.

This cycle of failure has led some to refer to students with learning disabilities as inactive learners (Hallahan, Kneedler, & Lloyd, 1983; Torgesen, 1977). Many students with learning disabilities do not actively involve themselves in the learning situation. Their cognitive, metacognitive, and motivational problems combine to make them passive in the face of situations that require active task involvement. They are likely to have difficulties working independently and are not likely to be "self-starters."

Authorities have suggested several strategies for working with students who have motivational problems. Box 10.3 lists several suggestions for teachers to consider. Many of these techniques fall under the rubric of attribution training (Borkowski, Weyhing, & Carr, 1988). **Attribution training** involves attempting to recognize the relationship between hard work and success. Most of it takes the form of pointing out to students that when they do well, it is due to having tried hard and not giving up. For example, in one study (Fulk, 1996), every time the student got an answer correct on a spelling task, the experimenter said, "Why do you think you spelled that word correctly? Right, you tried hard, used the study strategy, and spelled the word correctly." And after an incorrect spelling, the experimenter reminded the student to try hard and to use the study strategy.

As compelling as the arguments for the use of attribution training appear, research on its effectiveness has been mixed (Fulk, 1996). There is enough positive evidence

BOX 10.3 ***TIPS FOR PRACTICE***

Motivating Students with Learning Disabilities

Teachers can use the following strategies to try to motivate students with learning disabilities and keep them actively involved:

1. Reduce the amount of external reinforcement and focus on reinforcing student performance. Rather than saying, "Good work" or "Excellent job," focus on the behaviors, such as, "You really concentrated and finished this biology assignment. You needed to ask for help, but you got it done. How do you feel about it?"
2. Link students' behaviors to outcomes. "You spent ten minutes working hard on this worksheet and you finished it."
3. Provide encouragement. Because they experience continued failure, many students are discouraged from attempting tasks they are capable of performing.
4. Discuss academic tasks and social activities in which the student experiences success.
5. Discuss your own failures or difficulties and express what you do to cope with these. Be sure to provide examples of when you persist and examples of when you give up.
6. Encourage students to take responsibility for their successes. "You received a 'B' on your biology test. How do you think you got such a good grade?" Encourage students to describe what they did (e.g., how they studied). Discourage students from saying, "I was lucky," or "It was an easy test."
7. Encourage students to take responsibility for their failures. For example, in response to the question, "Why do you think you are staying after school?" encourage students to take responsibility for what got them there. "Yes, I am sure Billy's behavior was hard to ignore. I am aware that you did some wrong things to get you here. What did you do?"
8. Structure learning and social activities to reduce failure.
9. Teach students how to learn information and how to demonstrate their control of their learning task.
10. Teach students to use procedures and techniques to monitor their own gains in academic areas.

Source: Adapted from *Strategies for Teaching Students with Learning and Behavior Problems* (3rd ed.) by C. S. Bos and S. Vaughn, 1994, Boston: Allyn & Bacon. Copyright 1994 by Allyn & Bacon. Reprinted by permission.

to indicate that teachers should definitely consider using it with students who have motivational problems. But an external locus of control, learned helplessness, and negative attributions can become deeply entrenched in students with learning disabilities and are highly resistant to change in some cases.

WHAT ATTENTION PROBLEMS SOMETIMES OCCUR WITH LEARNING DISABILITIES?

Just as cognition and metacognition are closely linked, so too is attention—the ability to concentrate—intimately related to both cognition and metacognition. Teachers and parents frequently describe students with learning disabilities as inattentive and hyperactive. Parents of these children can often relate numerous incidents from the early years that depict them as always "getting into things they shouldn't." These same children, when confronted with the demands of school, can quickly become a nightmare for even the best of teachers, and it often takes only one in a classroom to create chaos.

Early Work—Strauss Syndrome

Much of the early interest in attention problems and hyperactivity in students with learning disabilities was triggered by the work of Werner and Strauss in the 1930s and 1940s with students who were mentally retarded (Strauss & Werner, 1942; Werner & Strauss, 1939, 1940, 1941). Werner and Strauss focused on documenting distractibility in children who were mentally retarded and considered brain-damaged. They conducted a series of experiments in which they compared the performance of supposedly brain-injured children with mental retardation to that of non-brain-injured children with mental retardation on a variety of figure-background tasks. For example, each child was shown slides of familiar objects (e.g., sailboat, hat, iron, cup) embedded in backgrounds (e.g., wavy lines) at very fast exposure times, such as half a second. When asked what they had seen, the children in the brain-injured group were more likely to refer to the background and less likely to recall the figure correctly.

Werner and Strauss's work has been aptly criticized on the grounds that the diagnostic classification of their children as brain-injured was faulty (see Chapter 2); however, they did find a subgroup of students with mental retardation, brain-injured or not, who were highly distractible. They brought attention to the particularly devastating consequences that distractibility and hyperactivity could have on children's functioning. Children with high levels of distractibility and hyperactivity soon came to be referred to as exhibiting the Strauss syndrome.

More than a decade later, Cruickshank replicated the work of Werner and Strauss. Instead of working with students who were mentally retarded, he tested the figure-background abilities of students with cerebral palsy who were of near-normal, normal, or above-normal intelligence (Cruickshank, Bice, & Wallen, 1957). This work served as a conceptual bridge between persons who were retarded and those of average intelligence. In other words, it showed that a person did not need to be retarded in order to display inattention and hyperactivity.

Bolstered by the results of his study of students with cerebral palsy, Cruickshank went on to set up educational programs for children who today would be referred to as having learning disabilities and/or attention deficit hyperactivity disorder. These were students whose intelligence levels were above those of persons with mental retardation, but who exhibited academic achievement problems and high levels of inattention and hyperactivity. (Cruickshank's approach is discussed later in this chapter, as is the concept of attention deficit hyperactivity disorder.)

Selective Attention and Maintaining Attention

Once the category of learning disabilities became formally recognized, researchers began to investigate whether the conclusions of Werner and Strauss and Cruickshank would apply to these students. Much of this work, conducted in the 1970s and 1980s, comes under the rubrics of selective attention and maintaining attention.

Selective Attention

Selective attention is the ability to focus on the relevant features of a task without being distracted by its irrelevant aspects. A number of researchers, using a variety of experimental tasks, have concluded that students with learning disabilities have selective attention problems with both auditory and visual material (see Hallahan & Reeve, 1980, for a review of these studies). Teachers have also noted how much difficulty students with learning disabilities tend to have with focusing their attention. These are the students who, although they have not completed the assigned work, are able to tell the teacher how many stray pencil marks there are on the page. When faced with a new assignment, such students have difficulty determining the relevant cues to which they should be attending, Some researchers have speculated that some of this seemingly inattentive behavior may in fact be these students' ways of seeking to gain information (Hallahan, 1975; Keogh & Margolis, 1976). Instead of concentrating on the task before them, they may be looking for cues from extraneous sources in their environment on how to perform the task.

Maintaining Attention

Students with learning disabilities also have difficulty sticking to a task once they begin it. This finding has been noted both in research conducted in laboratory settings and in observations of classroom behavior. In laboratory studies, for example, students with learning disabilities have been found deficient on vigilance tests (Pelham, 1981). On a typical vigilance test, the person views for several minutes the continuous presentation of letters on a computer screen. The person is instructed to press a response key every time a particular letter (e.g., an *x*) or sequence of letters (e.g., an *x* preceded by an *a*) appears.

Because virtually all teachers attest to the fact that students with learning disabilities have problems staying on task, classroom observation of the attention of students with learning disabilities was among the first areas of study in the field of learning disabilities. These studies typically involved observing students while they were engaged in normal classroom activities. The research consistently showed that, compared to their nondisabled peers, students with learning disabilities are less on task (Hallahan, 1975).

More Recent Work—Attention Deficit Hyperactivity Disorder

When someone's attention problems are very severe, this person is often diagnosed by a psychiatrist as having **attention deficit hyperactivity disorder (ADHD).** There are three types of attention deficit hyperactivity disorder: inattention, hyperactivity, or a combination of the two. Psychiatrists use the criteria listed in Table 10.1 to determine whether a person has ADHD.

TABLE 10.1 Diagnostic Criteria for Attention Deficit Hyperactivity Disorder

A. Either (1) or (2):

(1) six (or more) of the following symptoms of *inattention* have persisted for at least 6 months to a degree that is maladaptive and inconsistent with developmental level:

Inattention

(a) often fails to give close attention to details or makes careless mistakes in schoolwork, work, or other activities

(b) often has difficulty sustaining attention in tasks or play activities

(c) often does not seem to listen when spoken to directly

(d) often does not follow through on instructions and fails to finish schoolwork, chores, or duties in the workplace (not due to oppositional behavior or failure to understand instructions)

(e) often has difficulty organizing tasks and activities

(f) often avoids, dislikes, or is reluctant to engage in tasks that require sustained mental effort (such as schoolwork or homework)

(g) often loses things necessary for tasks or activities (e.g., toys, school assignments, pencils, books, or tools)

(h) is often easily distracted by extraneous stimuli

(i) is often forgetful in daily activities

(2) six (or more) of the following symptoms of *hyperactivity-impulsivity* have persisted for at least 6 months to a degree that is maladaptive and inconsistent with developmental level:

Hyperactivity

(a) often fidgets with hands or feet or squirms in seat

(b) often leaves seat in classroom or in other situations in which remaining seated is expected

(c) often runs about or climbs excessively in situations in which it is inappropriate (in adolescents or adults, may be limited to subjective feelings of restlessness)

(d) often has difficulty playing or engaging in leisure activities quietly

(e) is often "on the go" or often acts as if "driven by a motor"

(f) often talks excessively

Impulsivity

(g) often blurts out answers before questions have been completed

(h) often has difficulty awaiting turn

(i) often interrupts or intrudes on others (e.g., butts into conversations or games)

B. Some hyperactive-impulsive or inattentive symptoms that caused impairment were present before age 7 years.

C. Some impairment from the symptoms is present in two or more settings (e.g., at school [or work] and at home).

TABLE 10.1 *continued*

D. There must be clear evidence of clinically significant impairment in social, academic, or occupational functioning.

E. The symptoms do not occur exclusively during the course of a Pervasive Developmental Disorder, Schizophrenia, or other Psychotic Disorder and are not better accounted for by another mental disorder (e.g., Mood Disorder, Anxiety Disorder, Dissociative Disorder, or a Personality Disorder).

■ **Code Based on Type:**

314.01 Attention-Deficit/Hyperactivity Disorder, Combined Type: if both Criteria A1 and A2 are met for the past 6 months

314.00 Attention-Deficit/Hyperactivity Disorder, Predominantly Inattentive Type: if Criterion A1 is met but Criterion A2 is not met for the past 6 months

314.01 Attention-Deficit/Hyperactivity Disorder, Predominantly Hyperactive–Impulsive Type: if Criterion A2 is met but Criterion A1 is not met for the past 6 months

Coding note: For individuals (especially adolescents and adults) who currently have symptoms that no longer meet full criteria, "In Partial Remission" should be specified.

Source: From *Diagnostic and Statistical Manual of Mental Disorders: DSM-IV* (4th ed.) (pp. 83–85) by American Psychiatric Association, 1994, Washington, DC: Author. Copyright 1994 by American Psychiatric Association. Reprinted by permission.

There is considerable overlap between persons identified as having learning disabilities and those identified as having attention deficit hyperactivity disorder. Estimates vary, but a conservative estimate would be that about 20% of children identified as learning disabled could also be diagnosed as having ADHD (Riccio, Gonzalez, & Hynd, 1994).

There are at least three possible reasons for so much overlap between learning disabilities and attention deficit hyperactivity disorder:

1. The learning disability may precede the attention problems. The child may develop inattentive behaviors because of being frustrated by repeated failures.
2. The attention problems may precede the learning disability. Because of problems in attending to relevant academic information, the child may develop learning disabilities.
3. The attention problems and learning disabilities may be separate conditions that co-occur.

It is likely that each of the three scenarios is in operation for some of the cases of overlap, although it is very difficult to tell which of the three applies in individual cases.

The overlap between learning disabilities and attention deficit hyperactivity disorder has created considerable controversy in the field. This has occurred because the

Individuals with Disabilities Education Act (IDEA) does not recognize ADHD as a separate category of special education. For a period of time, the only way a child with attention deficit hyperactivity disorder could qualify for special education services was if he or she also exhibited a learning disability. In 1991, in response to the lobbying of parents and professionals, the U.S. Department of Education issued a memo to state departments of education stating that students with ADHD may be eligible for special education under the category "other health impaired"—that is, "in instances where the ADD is a chronic or acute health problem that results in limited alertness, which adversely affects educational performance." Some parents are still disappointed that ADHD is not recognized as a separate category because they believe that the "other health impaired" category is too indirect a means of identification.

Causes of ADHD

The causal factors discussed in Chapter 2 pertaining to learning disabilities are the same ones authorities point to with regard to attention deficit hyperactivity disorder. Heredity and neurological factors, in particular, are suspected in many cases of ADHD (Faraone et al., 1993; Faraone et al., 1995).

For many years, the frontal lobes have been thought to play a role in attention deficit hyperactivity disorder. This is because research on patients with bona fide frontal lobe damage (e.g., from accidents or strokes) has demonstrated that this area of the brain is responsible for response inhibition and attention. (As discussed in Chapter 2, the frontal lobes play a role in executive functioning, or problem solving.)

Recently, advances in neuroimaging techniques (see Chapter 2) have begun to corroborate the early speculation about involvement of the frontal lobes in attention deficit hyperactivity disorder. The **basal ganglia,** located beneath the cortex (the outer layer of the brain) and behind the frontal lobes, have also been implicated. Neurologists have known for some time that the basal ganglia are responsible for controlling movement and are damaged in patients with Parkinson's disease. Recent research indicates that the connections between the frontal lobes and the basal ganglia are dysfunctional in persons with attention deficit hyperactivity disorder (Castellanos, 1997).

Assessment

Reliable and valid measurement of attention deficit hyperactivity disorder is not easily accomplished. Although some have recommended the use of various paper-and-pencil and computerized tests, most authorities think that detailed histories, or interviews, and rating scales are the best way to determine if a person has ADHD (Hallowell & Ratey, 1994). In the case of children, the interview might take place with the child's parents.

Rating scales are usually filled out by the student's parents and/or teachers. One of the most common rating scales (Conners, 1969; Goyette, Conners, & Ulrich, 1978) requires the person to rate such behaviors as "restless (overactive)," "excitable, impulsive," or "inattentive, distractible," using the four categories of "not at all," "just a little," "pretty much," or "very much."

Outcomes

For many years, persons with attention deficit hyperactivity disorder were thought to outgrow their attention problems as they grew up. Most authorities now agree, however, that this is not always the case. Estimates vary, but available data suggest that at least half the children with ADHD will continue to have some of the symptoms in adulthood. Researchers have found that adults with the condition are at risk for impaired social skills and lower levels of educational and occupational achievement (Greene, Biederman, Faraone, Sienna, & Garcia-Jetton, 1997; Mannuzza, Klein, Bessler, Malloy, & Hynes, 1997; Mannuzza et al., 1991; Weiss & Hechtman, 1993).

Medical Treatment of ADHD

Persons whose attention problems are severe enough to be diagnosed as having attention deficit hyperactivity disorder are often helped by medication. The medication of choice is usually some type of psychostimulant, and methylphenidate (Ritalin) is the most frequently prescribed. For a number of years, some professionals and laypeople were very skeptical about the use of medication with children with ADHD. In fact, some claimed that the use of such drugs was a disguised attempt to keep children docile and that it encourages teachers to shirk their teaching responsibilities (Schrag & Divoky, 1975). Today most professionals see a place for medication in a total treatment package. Also, with the increasing recognition of attention deficit hyperactivity disorder in adults has come an increase in the prescribing of psychostimulants for these adults (Hallowell & Ratey, 1994).

Research has demonstrated that medication can be very effective in helping children and adults attend better. (See Hallahan & Cottone, 1997; Henker & Whalen, 1989; Shaywitz & Shaywitz, 1987; Weiss & Hechtman, 1993, for reviews.) In addition, the major organization for parents of children with ADHD, Children with Attention Deficit Disorders (CHADD), has endorsed the use of medication as a viable treatment approach (Children with Attention Deficit Disorders, 1992). Even though medication may be the single most effective method of treating ADHD, there are some cautions to keep in mind:

- Although medication works for most persons, there are a few for whom it is not effective.
- There are some relatively common side effects of psychostimulants, such as difficulty falling asleep and diminished appetite.
- Parents and teachers need to monitor dosage levels closely in order to arrive at the proper dosage that is effective but not too strong.
- Every effort should be made by parents and teachers not to send the message that the medication serves as a complete substitute for self-responsibility and self-initiative.
- Parents and teachers should not view the medication as absolving them of their responsibilities in dealing with the very difficult challenges presented by children with ADHD.

- These medications are controlled substances; the decision to prescribe them should not be taken lightly.
- Communication among parents, physicians, and teachers is the key to the effective use of the medication.

Given these cautions, medication is often an indispensable part of the treatment package for ADHD.

HOW CAN PROBLEMS OF ATTENTION BE ADDRESSED IN THE CLASSROOM?

There are several educational approaches to attention problems. Classroom interventions can be categorized under three general headings: stimulus reduction and structure, functional assessment, and cognitive training. These approaches should not be viewed as competing; professionals often recommend a combination of them, as well as medication.

Stimulus Reduction and Structure

As noted earlier in the chapter, Cruickshank, expanding on the prior work of Werner and Strauss, made educational recommendations for hyperactive and inattentive students. Believing that their major problem was their distraction by extraneous stimulation, Cruickshank developed a program that emphasizes the reduction of inessential stimuli and the enhancement of stimuli essential for learning. In addition, his program is highly structured, that is, highly teacher directed (Cruickshank, Bentzen, Ratzeburg, & Tannhauser, 1961).

Stimulus Reduction

Cruickshank recommended that students who are distractible be placed in a classroom that is as devoid as possible of extraneous environmental stimuli. Recommended classroom modifications include soundproofed walls and ceilings, carpeting, enclosed bookcases and cupboards, limited use of colorful bulletin boards, and cubicles and three-sided work areas. To contrast with the blandness of those aspects of the environment not involved in the teaching activity itself, the material directly necessary for instruction should be designed to draw the student's attention to it. For example, in the early stages of reading, the teacher would present the child with only a few words per page, and these would be in bold colors. This modification differs from the more common reading text, in which a page of print usually contains many words plus miscellaneous pictures.

Structure

Cruickshank reasoned that because students who are distractible are so much at the mercy of their impulses, their educational program should be heavily structured. He proposed that these students, being unable to provide their own structure, may become disoriented in a classroom that promotes the idea of having students make their own decisions. Thus, Cruickshank and colleagues (1961) advocated that the teacher maintain a tightly prescribed schedule of educational activities for the students so that they would have very little opportunity to engage in nonproductive behaviors.

Teachers today rarely use all the components of Cruickshank's program. Most authorities agree that not all students with attention problems are distracted by things in their environment. For those who are, many advocate the use of cubicles and other such arrangements. It is also thought that structure and teacher direction may be critical in the early stages of learning for students with attention problems, but that these students gradually need to assume more responsibility for their learning.

Functional Assessment

Many authorities advocate the use of functional assessment with many kinds of behavioral and learning problems, including those associated with attention deficit hyperactivity disorder (DuPaul, Eckert, & McGoey, 1997). **Functional assessment** centers on the functions that behaviors serve for individuals. Using it, the teacher tries to determine which events trigger target behaviors (e.g., inattention) and which factors maintain them (Horner, 1994; Kratochwill & McGivern, 1996). For example, some students may exhibit inattention in order to avoid work or to gain the attention of adults or peers.

Once the teacher conducts the functional assessment, he or she can develop an intervention that changes the factors triggering and/or maintaining the undesirable behavior. Several studies have found functional assessment effective in reducing inattentive behavior in students with attention deficit hyperactivity disorder. For example, in one study,

> the intervention for one student involved altering the nature of the task (i.e., requiring assignments to be completed on a computer rather than in writing) because this student's off-task behavior appeared to be motivated by escape from written tasks. Alternatively, the intervention for a second student involved providing peer attention contingent on the display of on-task behavior given that this student's off-task activities appeared to be an attempt to gain peer attention. In both cases, the interventions were effective. (DuPaul et al., 1997, p. 376)

Cognitive Training

Some have pointed out that cognitive training techniques may be particularly appropriate for students with attention problems because these approaches stress teaching students self-initiative (Hallahan et al., 1983; Kneedler & Hallahan, 1984). These researchers point out that all the other major approaches to dealing with attention problems—stimulus reduction and structure, functional assessment, and medication—emphasize external controls. That is, these approaches all involve doing something to students—shielding them from distractors, manipulating environmental events, giving them pills. Some are concerned that those using these techniques might unwittingly be reinforcing the very passivity they hope to address.

One cognitive training technique that has been used with considerable success for attention problems is self-monitoring. Self-monitoring of academic performance was discussed in an earlier section. Teachers can also teach students to self-monitor their attention. The technique involves students asking themselves the question "Was I paying attention?" and recording a "yes" or "no" on a score sheet every time they hear a tone on a tape recorder. (The time between tones varies randomly.) The following is a set of sample instructions:

> "Johnny, you know how paying attention to your work has been a problem for you. You've heard teachers tell you, 'Pay attention,' 'Get to work,' 'What are you supposed to be doing?' and things like that. Well, today we're going to start something that will help you help yourself pay attention better. First, we need to make sure that you know what paying attention means. This is what I mean by paying attention." (Teacher models immediate and sustained attention to task.) "And this is what I mean by not paying attention." (Teacher models inattentive behaviors such as glancing around and playing with objects.)
>
> "Now you tell me if I was paying attention." (Teacher models attentive and inattentive behaviors and requires the student to categorize them.) "Okay, now let me show you what we're going to do. While you're working, this tape recorder will be turned on. Every once in a while, you'll hear a little sound like this:" (Teacher plays tone on tape.) "And when you hear that tone quietly ask yourself, 'Was I paying attention?' If you answer 'yes,' put a check in this box. If you answer 'no,' put a check in this box. Then go right back to work. When you hear the sound again, ask the question, answer it, mark your answer, and go back to work. Now, let me show you how it works." (Teacher models the entire procedure.) "Now, Johnny, I bet you can do this. Tell me what you're going to do every time you hear a tone. Let's try it. I'll start the tape and you work on these papers." (Teacher observes student's implementation of the entire procedure, praises its correct use, and gradually withdraws his or her presence.) (Hallahan, Lloyd, & Stoller, 1982, p. 12)

Research has demonstrated the effectiveness of self-monitoring of attention in increasing on-task behavior and academic productivity. This technique has been used with students ranging from elementary (Hallahan, Lloyd, Kosiewicz, Kauffman, & Graves, 1979; Harris et al., 1994) to the secondary grades (Prater, Joy, Chilman, Temple, & Miller, 1991). The technique has been successful with students whose attention problems are severe enough to have the diagnosis of attention deficit hyperactivity disorder (Mathes & Bender, 1997). Researchers have also found that adding the component of having students graph the results of their assessments is beneficial (DiGangi, Maag, & Rutherford, 1991). Some have speculated that self-monitoring of attention is successful because it helps students become more aware of and in control of their attention.

Summary

1. What cognitive and cognitive problems sometimes occur with learning disabilities?
   a. Cognition refers to the ability to think and solve problems. In the past, cognition was not considered a legitimate area of scientific inquiry in the special education field because of the popularity of behaviorism. Over the past two decades, behavioral theory has been criticized as too simplistic; there is now more focus on mental processes.
   b. Some early cognitive psychologists suggested that people have different cognitive styles of approaching tasks, such as:
      (1) field independence–field dependence—how much people are influenced by their environment when asked to make decisions on perceptual tasks
      (2) reflectivity-impulsivity—whether a person takes time to reflect on alternatives before making a choice
   c. Students with learning disabilities tend to be more field dependent and more impulsive than their peers without disabilities.
   d. Much of the more recent cognitive research in learning disabilities has focused on memory, specifically:
      (1) short-term memory—the ability to remember information over a few seconds or a minute or so at most
      (2) working memory—the ability to keep a small amount of information in mind while carrying out other operations
   e. Short-term memory appears to be affected in people with learning disabilities. Working memory is even more important than short-term memory in the reading and mathematics performance of those with learning disabilities.
   f. Metacognition refers to the ability to think about thinking. Students with learning disabilities are deficient in a variety of metacognitive areas, including metamemory, metalistening, and metacomprehension. These problems are generally due to students' lack of awareness of strategies they can use in different situations. For example, in reading, it is necessary to:
      (1) clarify the purposes of reading
      (2) focus attention on important parts of a passage
      (3) monitor one's level of comprehension
      (4) reread and scan ahead
      (5) consult other sources when unsure of something
2. How can students' cognitive and metacognitive needs be addressed?
   a. Cognitive training involves three elements:
      (1) changing the thought processes of students
      (2) providing students with strategies for learning
      (3) teaching students self-initiative

   b. There are several different cognitive training techniques:
      (1) self-instruction—verbalizing the steps in a task
      (2) self-monitoring—keeping track of one's academic performance
      (3) mnemonic strategies—using concrete cues to enhance memory
      (4) metamemory training—being aware of memory strategies
      (5) metacomprehension training—understanding the purposes of reading and strategies for enhancing comprehension
      (6) scaffolded instruction—having the teacher provide help in the early stages of learning a task but then gradually removing that help (This technique is based on the concept of the zone of proximal development.)

3. What motivational problems affect students with learning disabilities and what can be done about them?
   a. There is a close link between metacognitive and motivation problems.
   b. Motivation problems come from three interrelated areas:
      (1) external locus of control—viewing oneself as controlled by external forces
      (2) negative attributions—discounting successes as due to luck
      (3) learned helplessness—believing that one will fail no matter how hard one tries
   c. Strategies for improving motivation often involve attribution training—emphasizing that effort can have a positive payoff

4. What attention problems occur with learning disabilities?
   a. Early work in this area was conducted by Werner and Strauss with children who were mentally retarded. They used a task that focused on the ability to differentiate figure from background.
   b. Cruickshank extended the work of Werner and Strauss to children of normal intelligence.
   c. Researchers have also found students with learning disabilities to have problems in selective attention and maintaining attention.
   d. More recently, researchers and practitioners have focused on attention deficit hyperactivity disorder (ADHD), a condition of severe attention problems. Many students with learning disabilities have ADHD. A person with ADHD may have problems primarily in inattention, hyperactivity, or a combination of the two.
      (1) Causes of ADHD have focused on heredity and neurology, with the frontal lobes and the basal ganglia being possible sites of neurological dysfunction.
      (2) Assessment of ADHD usually involves taking a detailed history.
      (3) Adult outcomes for children with ADHD are often negative.
      (4) Many individuals with ADHD take psychostimulant medication, such as methylphenidate (Ritalin). Although there are side-effects (e.g., reduction of appetite and difficulty in sleeping), medical treatment is often successful in reducing inattention and/or hyperactivity.

5. How can problems of attention be addressed in the classroom?
   a. stimulus reduction—reducing saliency of irrelevant information and increasing value of to-be-attended material
   b. structure—scheduling students' activities rigorously
   c. functional assessment—determining which events trigger and maintain inattention and then changing these events
   d. cognitive training (in particular self-monitoring)—having students keep track of when they are on- and off-task

11

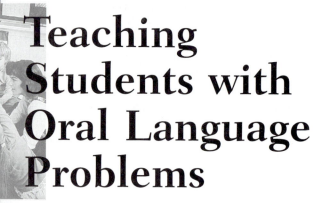

Teaching Students with Oral Language Problems

What Are the Major Dimensions of Language?
- Reception
- Expression
- Phonology
- Syntax
- Morphology
- Semantics
- Pragmatics

How Does Language Develop Normally?

What Are the Characteristics of Students with Oral Language Problems?
- Problems with Reception and Expression
- Problems with Language Systems

How Are Oral Language Abilities Assessed?
- Comprehensive Assessments
- Specific Assessments
- Methods of Monitoring Progress

How Can Oral Language Problems Be Addressed?
- Theoretical Approaches
- Psycholinguistic Interventions
- Task-Analytic Interventions
- Effective Practices

Summary

Oral language—often considered a capability unique to humans—is the primary way that most of us communicate most of the time. We listen to what others say. We tell others what we have to say. We write to tell others what we have to say. We read what others have to say. Without language skills, we could not enjoy a stand-up comic's routine, listen to a play, explain an answer, or write lyrics for a song. Much of what happens in schools either is transmitted in oral language or, as in the case of reading and writing, requires an understanding of it.

The obvious relationships among listening, speaking, reading, and writing make clear that much of academic learning is based on language. Thus, it is important to remember that these different areas of language are part of a larger whole. Although there is "little consistency . . . in those attributes thought to be the focus of whole language" (Bergeron, 1990, p. 312), part of the reason many people emphasize whole language is that speaking, listening, writing, and reading are all language arts.

Clearly, when students have problems using oral language, they are likely to struggle in school. Moreover, when not remedied, problems with oral language can have debilitating effects on a person's life. Language deficits not only affect one's fundamental ability to communicate on a day-to-day basis, but also impede the acquisition of language skills such as reading and writing. They even influence—often negatively—other areas such as social interaction.

Language problems are common in learning disabilities. That difficulties in learning language skills are common in learning disabilities has been known throughout the history of the field. Influential figures such as Orton (1937), Kirk (1976), Strauss and Kephart (1955), and Johnson and Myklebust (1967) emphasized the importance of language in their work (see Chapter 1). Early in the history of learning disabilities, emphasis on perceptual processes probably overshadowed these pioneers' concern about language. It took many in the field of learning disabilities a long time to realize the importance of language problems (Hallahan & Cruickshank, 1973).

The neglect of language skills in the early development of learning disabilities was unfortunate for many reasons. First, because of the basic importance of language in everyday life, students' language difficulties should be a foremost target for remediation. Second, the need for language skills in virtually all areas of academic achievement means that these skills are crucial to success in school. Third, estimates of the prevalence of disorders of spoken language among students with learning disabilities reveal that they are among the most common problems experienced by these students.

Language deficits were specifically emphasized in most definitions of learning disabilities (see Chapter 2). When discussing learning disabilities, authorities often note the special emphasis on language in these definitions:

> The rapid expansion of research on oral language development with LD students . . . provides much support to the fact that the 1969 definition's emphasis on oral language disorders was not misplaced. A sizable body of research now indicates that, as a group, LD children are less skilled than normal achievers on a wide variety of phonological, semantic, syntactic, and communicative tasks. . . . Furthermore, efforts to delineate subgroups of LD children have found that the largest single

subgroup can be characterized as language-impaired and usually constitutes over half of the LD sample. (Bryan, Bay, Lopez-Reyna, & Donahue, 1991, p. 119)

Today in learning disabilities, there is renewed concern with language problems, particularly young children's skill with the phonological aspects of language. Many children who have difficulty developing certain early language skills later experience substantial difficulty in acquiring reading and writing skills (Lyon, 1995). To understand these problems, one must understand some aspects of how language develops normally. To understand development, one needs to know about the major aspects of language.

WHAT ARE THE MAJOR DIMENSIONS OF LANGUAGE?

Linguists (people who study language) divide language into several major aspects. One division has to do with *receptive* or *expressive* language; this division refers to whether the language is being received or expressed. Another important division identifies language systems, and they include *phonology, syntax, morphology, semantics,* and *pragmatics.* Students who have problems with language may have difficulties in any of these language systems. Figure 11.1 represents the relationships among the dimension of reception and expression and the language systems of phonology, syntax, morphology, semantics, and pragmatics.

Reception

Receptive language refers to the listener's behavior. Except for those who communicate using sign language, people receive most language by hearing it. However, when one is reading, one is also receiving language. So receptive language is similar to but not synonymous with hearing.

When receiving language, people not only hear it, but also must comprehend it. Comprehension of language is based on many complex and related skills. For example, listeners both perceive the difference between very similar words (e.g., "mist" and "must") and have those words in their *receptive vocabulary* (the store of known words).

Expression

Expressive language refers to the production of language. Usually, people express language by speaking, but they also express themselves in writing.

Expressing ideas in language requires using many language abilities. When people express themselves, they not only use their ability to make sounds (or write letters), but also make certain sounds in a specific order so that they create words, order the words to make phrases and sentences, and so forth. Just as was true with recep-

FIGURE 11.1 Important Components of Language

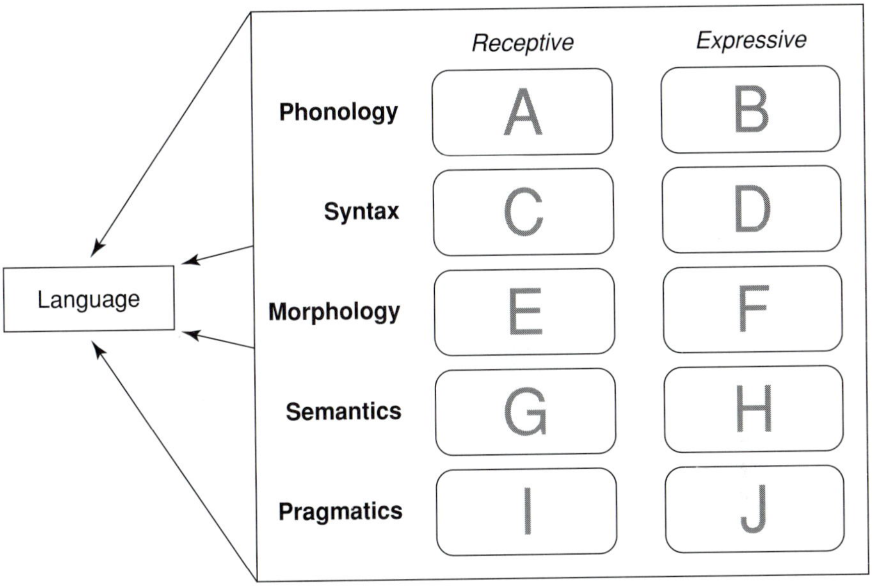

Note: A—hearing, discrimination of sounds in language; B—speaking, production of sounds of language; C—comprehending how structure of language or order of words affect meaning; D—producing language with structure that communicates meanings; E—comprehending meaning units; F—producing meaning units; G—comprehending word meanings (vocabulary); H—producing language using word's meaning (vocabulary); I—comprehending language in light of its social context; J—producing language suitable to the social situation.

tive language, expressive language can be broken into many parts, but the parts are actually closely connected.

Understanding the difference between reception and expression is helpful in describing language. However, language theorists emphasize another very important distinction called the competence-performance dichotomy. **Competence** refers to the hidden knowledge of language that nearly all people are presumed to have. **Performance** refers to language behavior, both listening and speaking. The competence-performance issue is sometimes confused with the reception-expression dichotomy. The competence-performance dichotomy is more general. It applies to both comprehension and production.

The competence-performance dichotomy is important for two reasons. First, it alerts us to the possibility that someone may have fundamental language competence but problems in performance. Second, it helps describe how language develops:

> Almost all children can detect fine shades of differences before they can themselves produce them. A child may persist in his "kicky" for kitty, but reject this pronunciation from an adult; he may still produce "wawipop" at age five but resent such an

offering from an older person. What the child is demonstrating by this apparently inconsistent language behavior is that at age four or five he has better phonemic discrimination, and so better expectations in regard to listening, than he has motor control over his own production. (Eisenson, 1972, p. 17)

Phonology

Phonology refers to the study of the sound system of language. Although we communicate with gestures or body language, most of our communication is based on the sounds we make when using expressive language (e.g., speaking) or hear via receptive language. People can make many different sounds, but only some of them are used in each language. For example, in English, we do not use clicks as a part of our talk, but some African languages do. Infants learn the unique sounds of their language from their environment; although they can make all the sounds used in all languages when they are very young, they gradually stop making those sounds that are not used in the language they hear regularly in their environment.

A **phoneme** is the smallest unit of sound. As people talk, they exhale slightly and move the muscles in their mouths and throats to shape the escaping air and form phonemes. In English, there are 44 phonemes. Table 11.1 shows how some of the basic sounds of English are written in the International Phonetic Alphabet. Some of the sounds are not obvious, and, unfortunately, too few teachers are taught how the sound system of English works (Moats, 1995). For example, the word "sin" has three phonemes—/*s*/, /*i*/, and /*n*/. But the words "sing," "thin," and "thing" also have three—/*s*/, /*i*/, and /*ng*/, /*th*/, /*i*/, and /*n*/, and /*th*/, /*i*/, and /*ng*/.

Phonological skills play an important role in acquisition of higher-order skills, too. For instance, facility with phonology influences children's acquisition of two-word utterances (Donahue, 1986) and reading (e.g., Muter, 1998).

Syntax

Syntax refers to the patterns or rules people use to put words together into sentences. It is roughly equivalent to "grammar," but not grammar in the sense that it is taught in schools. These rules are not the kinds that someone creates and others memorize; instead, they are understood implicitly by the people who speak the language. In this sense, syntax refers to the way in which words can be arranged to create meaningful sentences.

Studies of syntax have been greatly influenced by N. Chomsky's (1965) view of language as an innate ability of humankind. According to this view, people have an underlying understanding of language that gives them the ability to use different sentence structures to say the same things and very similar structures to say things with different meanings. For example, compare these two sentences:

Kids are faster than kittens.

Kids are not faster than kittens.

TABLE 11.1 Some Sounds of English

Common Spelling[a]	Pronunciations	IPA Symbol
a	as in at or can	æ
a	as in ate or cane	eɪ
au	as in autumn	ɔ
b	as in bat or cab	b
c	as in cat or fact	c
d	as in dog or cad	d
e	as in edge or bed	e
ee, ea	as in each or seed	i
f	as in fin or shaft	f
g	as in go or lag	g
h	as in hat	h
i	as in itch or list	ɪ
i	as in I or twine	aɪ
j	as in jelly or Jack	dʒ
k	as in king or lake	k
m	as in man or ham	m
n	as in nimble or can	n
o	as in odd or cot	o
o	as in ode or code	ɔ
p	as in pat or cap	p
q	as in queen	q
q	as in antique	k
r	as in run	ɹ
s (unvoiced)	as in sip or mist	s
s (voiced)	as in has	z
sh	as in ship or mash	ʃ
t	as in time or late	t
th	as in thin or path	θ
th	as in these or smooth	ð
u	as in ugly or cup	u
v	as in vast or cave	v
w	as in we	w
y	as in yellow or lanyard	j
z	as in zoo or lizard	z
z	as in azure	ʒ
ng	as in sing	ŋ
ou	as in ouch or mouse	au
a, e, i, o, u (unstressed)	as in spoken	ə

[a]Not all spellings for the sounds are shown here.

The syntax of these sentences differs in only one word, "not." That difference, however, completely reverses the meaning of the sentence.

The syntactic structure of our language allows us to understand some parts of a message even when we do not know the words in it. For example, most adult speakers of English could answer the questions in Table 11.2 because they know enough about the syntax (and other aspects) of English that the exact word meanings are not required to deduce many of the ideas expressed by a speaker.

Morphology

Children learn not only the phonology and syntax of their language, but also how to change parts of words in ways that change meaning. For example, they learn that, by adding an ending to most nouns, they can indicate more than one of that thing (e.g., girl + s = more than one girl). These special rules of grammar are called morphological rules, and the aspect of language is called **morphology.** Morphology is particularly important for learning disabilities.

A *morpheme* is the smallest unit of meaning in a language. In the example of "girls" just considered, there are two morphemes, one for the concept of "juvenile female" and one for the concept of "more than one" or "plural." Morphology is important not only in its own right; it also provides important cues in reading and spelling. Some students with learning disabilities experience problems with the morphology of our language.

Semantics

Semantics is the system of language having to do with meaning. Morphology is closely related to semantics. Because understanding and conveying meaning are the

TABLE 11.2 How General Knowledge of Language Helps People Understand Messages

Given this passage:

> Before the flangbong, the smarmly gribbles were very murggy. So, they went to the libenstar and libensed their smarmly zwibucks. Then the gribbles went to their yibode counsiber's nebber and libensed themselves. Once they were all flarkly and foebush, the gribbles borrowed their counsiber's marbork and went happily to the flangbong.

See if you can answer these questions.

1. Who was very murggy?
2. What did the gribbles do to their zwibucks? When did they do it?
3. What did the gribbles do to themselves? Where did they do it?
4. Whose marbork did the gribbles borrow?
5. Why do you think the gribbles wanted to be flarkly and foebush?

main activities of language, semantics is very important. Semantics involves the study of the meanings of words and words in groups, particularly sentences.

There are many competing theories of semantics. Most of them seek to explain where the meaning of language is located (Hedge, 1991). Experts differ about whether the meaning of language is its

- *content* (A listener who knows the words of a language will know the meaning of statements.)
- *referents* (The words of a language refer to objects or events.)
- *concepts* (The words of a language refer to abstract concepts evoked by the speaker.)
- *responses* (The words of a speaker evoke particular responses, even covert responses, from the listener.)

Semantics plays a central role in language. People often talk about semantics in a less formal sense. For example, they may say "It's just a matter of semantics" as a way to dismiss the importance of what someone has said. However, because using language to convey meaning is very important, semantics is very important. For example, if one's life depended on libensing zwibucks (see Table 11.2), semantics would be quite important.

Pragmatics

Pragmatics refers to the way in which language is used in social situations (Thompson, 1997). People alter how they speak, depending on whom they are speaking to, why they are speaking, and other factors. For example, most of us talk differently when conversing with our friends than we do when speaking in a class or visiting with our parents at a restaurant.

Most children use shorter and simpler sentences when talking to someone clearly younger than themselves than when talking to someone nearly the same age or older (Shatz & Gelman, 1973). Speaking in short, simple sentences might be insulting to some listeners, however. Thus, speakers must take into account the social situation when they speak, changing their language to fit it. When people fail to adapt their language to fit social situations, they increase the chances that they will have social problems. As discussed in Chapter 10, this is a problem for many students with learning disabilities.

HOW DOES LANGUAGE DEVELOP NORMALLY?

The major milestones in the normal development of language have been documented (Bloom, 1993; Carrow-Woolfolk, 1988; Menyuk, 1972). Although we may see language capabilities as greatly affected by environments, many language competencies have biological bases, too (Bloom, 1993).

At birth, the infant cries. Starting with the birth cry, believed to be a reflex response to the pain of breathing on his or her own, the infant for several weeks engages in crying as a response to discomfort. Crying of this sort is called "undifferentiated crying" because it does not seem to change on the basis of various states of discomfort (Eisenson, 1972).

At about 2 months of age, the infant begins to use two new responses. Cooing sounds emerge, and the infant's crying seems to differ according the situations in which it occurs. These differences in crying can be thought of as based on whether the child is physically uncomfortable or socially isolated.

From about 3 to 6 months of age, the infant engages in babbling. This stage is often considered crucial for the later development of speech because it causes changes in the infant's environment (Eisenson, 1972; Owens, 1988; Sachs, 1989). It is important for the child to learn that he or she can operate on the environment by making noises. Infants learn this when adults, particularly parents, attend to and reinforce babbling. Shortly after birth, infants are capable of discriminating between sounds on the basis of frequency, intensity, and duration; a few months later, they can discriminate between speech and nonspeech sounds and friendly and unfriendly voices (Menyuk, 1972).

Children learn to discriminate sounds on the basis of their distinctive features (Jacobson, 1968), much as they use distinctive features to discriminate visual patterns. Some of the aspects that children use to hear differences are the consonantal, nasal, strident, and voiced features of speech sounds. These and other distinctive features of speech can be used to predict which sounds will be more or less difficult to learn. The first actual speech sounds children use are those that are highly discriminable on the basis of distinctive features. That children's first words often are "mama" and "papa" is predicted by a distinctive features analysis because these words are composed of easily discriminable speech sounds (Menyuk, 1972) and are most likely to be reinforced and shaped by attention and other social interactions with parents, siblings, and others.

At about 8 or 9 months of age, most children enter a stage of echolalia (Eisenson, 1972). *Echolalia* refers to parrotlike repetition of what the child hears; in children with autism, echolalia is a problem, but it is only temporary in normally developing children. The infant begins to imitate speech sounds. If an adult says something, the child will attempt to say the same thing. This is probably the precursor to children learning to use language as a tool, a means of changing what happens in their own environments.

At about 1 year of age, the child utters his or her first words. They form primitive sentences at about 18 months. Most children learn that their expressions affect others and cause changes in their environments. This is part of the reason that Skinner talked about how language is operant behavior, that children use it to operate on the environment (Skinner, 1957). Because adults in their world share a language, children learn to use language as a tool to influence others and make things happen (Bloom, 1993).

From about the end of the first year on, language acquisition occurs exceedingly rapidly. Children master the complexities of language very quickly. For one thing, most of them experience the *vocabulary spurt,* a period during early language development when the number of different words they say suddenly increases rapidly. Whereas they may use a few words repetitively at one time during their first year or two, when they are about 18–24 months old, children suddenly begin to use lots of words (Bloom, 1993; Owens, 1988; Sachs, 1989). Children who hear more words and more different sentences during the early years are likely to have higher scores on cognitive and academic measures given many years later (Hart & Risley, 1995).

Before the age of 3 or 4 years, children often use one-word utterances to stand for entire sentences. Later they begin to string words together in rudimentary sentences that omit nonessential words such as articles. For example, a child may say "All gone shoe" in place of the sentence "The shoe is not here." Usually, these beginning forms of syntax give way to more sophisticated forms long before children enter preschool. As they grow toward adulthood, children and adolescents learn to use sentences that are longer, include more clauses, and so forth (McNeill, 1970).

Children develop morphological rules at a young age. One rule refers to the addition of a letter to the end of a word to indicate that it is plural, as illustrated previously. Of course, some words do not follow the usual rules of inflection. The word "fish" may be both the singular and the plural form; the plural of the word "man" does not require the addition of a phoneme, but the change of one (the *ah* becomes an *eh* to make men). Initially, children often mistakenly apply general rules to all examples and only later learn the exceptions. For example, in making plurals, a young child might say "three mans" but later learn to say "three men."

By 3 or 4 years, children are able to use most of the basic types of sentences of the language. However, subtle and complex ones must still be learned during later years (Chomsky, 1969). Children of 5 or 6 years will have mastered the fundamental vocabulary and structures of their language (Hedge, 1991). Although they may still make mistakes (e.g., saying "cars's" for "cars"), they will sometimes surprise adults with their vocabularies and expressions of concepts. One 2-year-old child answered a question about picking her nose by saying, "A butterfly pooped in my nose."

Teachers of students with learning disabilities often work with speech pathologists on diagnostic and remedial procedures for those who have disabilities in spoken language. The field of speech pathology has produced a great deal of work on language problems. One area of study of speech problems that is related to learning disabilities but considered more in the realm of speech pathology is aphasia—difficulty in acquiring a system of language (Carrow-Woolfolk, 1988; Eisenson, 1972; Hedge, 1991).

WHAT ARE THE CHARACTERISTICS OF STUDENTS WITH ORAL LANGUAGE PROBLEMS?

Language performance can be divided into components in several different ways. One is to consider receptive and expressive language; as previously noted, receptive language refers to people understanding what they hear (or read), and expressive language refers to what they say (or write). As also shown previously, language may be divided into the language systems (e.g., phonology). Students with learning disabilities may experience difficulties in any of these areas.

Problems with Reception and Expression

In the 1970s and early 1980s, researchers studied whether students with learning disabilities differed from normally achieving students on both expressive and receptive language skills. Although some studies showed that they had great difficulty with both, most found that they had greater difficulty using spoken language to express themselves than understanding the spoken language of others (Hessler & Kitchen, 1980; Noel, 1980; Semel & Wiig, 1975; Wong & Roadhouse, 1978).

When people concerned with learning disabilities encounter a student who is having difficulty with language, one of the first questions they can ask is, "Does this student have problems primarily with receptive or expressive language?"

Reception

Some children have difficulty understanding what they hear (Bishop, 1997). When a student's facility with receptive language is particularly low, that student is more likely to have mental retardation than learning disabilities (see Chapter 2). For example, problems understanding individual words—an inadequate *receptive vocabulary*—are often reflected in low scores on measures of vocabulary. Inadequate receptive vocabulary is usually associated with lower intelligence. Some children have low scores on the vocabulary subtest of the *Weschler Intelligence Scale for Children—III* or on the *Slosson Intelligence Test—Revised.*

When students have less pervasive and more specific problems in receptive language, these may be considered learning disabilities. Such problems may manifest themselves in any of the language systems.

Expression

Children who have difficulty expressing themselves may have several different problems. One is called *dysnomia.* Children who have dysnomia, which is also known as a "word-finding problem," often seem to talk in fits and starts; they may stumble over words, rephrase what they are saying, or substitute the word "thing" for words they cannot remember at the moment (Kail & Leonard, 1986). Of course, most people do this sometimes; it is a problem when it occurs especially frequently. A student with dysnomia might say, "Well, we had to take the, the . . . big car . . . door in the back . . . uhm . . . the van. So, anyway, we went to . . . to, you know, groceries . . . that place where you get food and, you know, and we were, uhm, you know, looking for . . . shopping! . . . shopping for things, you know, food and stuff and my mom wanted to, uhm, get, uhm, some . . . you put 'em on your legs. . . ."

Dysarthia and *apraxia* are other expressive language problems. Both are difficulties with articulation, that is, the production of speech sounds. Students with *dysarthia* slur their speech and sound hoarse. Students with *apraxia* seem to be trying very hard to speak, talk slowly, and have greatest difficulty with starting to say words (Caplan, 1992).

Students may have trouble expressing themselves quickly. Studies reveal that some students with learning disabilities speak slowly (Ackerman, Dykman, & Gardner, 1990). The problems usually are not severe enough to be called dysarthia, however. It is not clear whether slow speech is caused by slow processing of the information or disorganized control of the muscles used in speaking (similar to apraxia). Regardless of the cause, the result can be described as a problem in expressive language.

Certain aspects of expressive language problems appear to be controlled more by genetic factors, but others are influenced by environmental factors. Variation in production of the sound *r* is affected relatively equally for monozygotic twins. However, variation in production of the sounds *l, j,* and *w* show greater sensitivity to environmental factors (Dixon, Matheny, & Mohr, 1995).

Problems with Language Systems

Students with learning disabilities may have difficulties with any of the various language systems. Because learning disabilities are a heterogeneous group of disorders, some students will have problems with one area of language but not with another. However, some students may have trouble with multiple areas.

Problems with Phonology

Some problems with phonology involve production of speech and are referred to as articulation problems. Mastery of articulation requires the development of control over the muscles used in speaking but does not necessarily imply difficulties with understanding spoken language. Dysarthia and apraxia are examples of problems with the production of phonemes.

Students with articulatory problems may or may not have trouble understanding speech or learning other skills. That is, their competence may exceed their performance. In other words, only some students who have articulatory problems have learning disabilities, and only some who have learning disabilities have articulatory problems. The two are not synonymous.

Problems with auditory discrimination have often been discussed in the field of learning disabilities. Auditory discrimination refers to an individual's skill in telling the difference between sounds. One test of auditory discrimination would be to show a child pictures of a rake and a lake and then tell him or her to touch the picture of a lake; in this way, one could tell whether the child hears the sounds correctly. Many studies of the relationship between phonological skills and reading reveal that auditory discrimination correlates with reading achievement (Kavale, 1981b). However, the correlation is small, and to what extent this relationship indicates a need for training is unclear (Gersten & Carnine, 1984; Hammill & Larsen, 1974b; Rozin & Gleitman, 1977; Sabatino, 1973).

Problems with phonological awareness are said to exist when children cannot separate words into their parts (sounds). *Rhyming,* for example, requires that the last sounds of a word be held constant while the first sounds are changed.

In another form of phonological awareness, **phoneme segmentation,** students hear an entire word and say only part of it; for example, a teacher might direct students to say "sand" but to omit the *sss* (leaving "and"). Skill in segmenting words into their constituent sounds is important in early reading achievement, and difficulties with phonological awareness probably are fundamental to the difficulties students with learning disabilities have in mastering simple reading tasks (Adams, 1990; Juel, Griffith, & Gough, 1986; Liberman, 1970; Liberman & Shankweiler, 1991; Rozin & Gleitman, 1977; Tarver & Ellsworth, 1981). Furthermore, these difficulties are almost certainly related to problems in other areas, such as written expression (Lyon, 1995).

Problems with sound blending may also reflect children's difficulties with phonology. **Sound blending**—essentially the opposite of phonemic segmentation—is used to collapse separated phonemes into a whole. For example, the sounds *m, i, s,* and *t* can be blended into the word "mist." Poor readers have weaker sound-blending skills (Adams, 1990; Kass, 1966; Kavale, 1981b; Richardson, DiBenedetto, & Bradley, 1977; Richardson, DiBenedetto, Christ, & Press, 1980). However, the relationship between sound blending and reading is thought to be less obvious when scores are controlled for IQ (Hammill & Larsen, 1974b; Harber, 1980; Larsen, Rogers, & Sowell, 1976), although some evidence contradicts this (e.g., Richardson et al., 1980).

Problems with segmenting, rhyming, and blending may all reflect deficits in working memory (see Chapter 10). To complete a segmenting, rhyming, or blending task, students perform a complex series of cognitive operations. As illustrated in Table 11.3, they operate on a stream of sounds several times, swapping information in and out of working memory and then generating the result.

Problems with Syntax

Some students with learning disabilities experience problems with syntax. For example, they may have difficulties repeating sentences in the declarative form and other sentences with special kinds of clauses (Hresko, 1979). Students who have learning disabilities also have greater trouble than their nondisabled peers selecting a picture to which a sentence refers and choosing a sentence that describes a picture (Semel & Wiig, 1975). Furthermore, when the syntax of a sentence makes it ambiguous (e.g., "He laughed at the church"), those with learning disabilities are less likely to realize that it can be interpreted in more than one way (Wiig, Semel, & Abele, 1981).

Some problems with syntax remain even after many years of schooling. For example, adolescents with learning disabilities may not understand to what a pronoun refers as well as their nondisabled peers (Fayne, 1981) and are more likely to produce grammatically incorrect sentences (Wiig & Semel, 1975). In addition, although their sentences become longer and more complex as they grow older, children and adolescents with learning disabilities still seem to use sentences that are simpler than those others use (Simms & Crump, 1983).

Problems with Morphology

Students with reading disabilities do not use morphological rules as well as their peers (Kass, 1966; Vogel, 1974; Wiig, Semel, & Crouse, 1973), regardless of whether they

TABLE 11.3 A Simple Illustration of How Memory Might Be Used in Creating a Rhyme

Step	Overt Action	Covert Action	Requires Working Memory?	Example
1	Hear word		yes	"Think"
2		Parse word into parts	yes	"th" + "ing" + "k"
3		Chunk parts for rhyming	yes	"th" + "ink"
4		Hold rhyming chunk in memory	yes	"ink"
5		Consider alternative sounds to prepend to "ink"	yes	Hmmmm . . . does "f" work? How about "k?" How about "p?"
5a		Combine new sound with "ink" and compare result to dictionary of known words	yes	Sheesh, "fink?" How about "kink?" Uhm, how about "pink?"
5b		Select new word	yes	Hey, *pink* . . . That's it!
6	Say word		yes	"Pink! Teacher. I know. I know! It's pink!

are being tested on real or nonsense words (Vogel, 1974). Many students with language problems have difficulty with certain morphemes that indicate tense. Although their peers may have advanced to the level of adults, young children with difficulties continue to make mistakes with these tasks (Rice & Wexler, 1996).

As illustrated in Figure 11.2, the difficulties of students with learning disabilities often are particularly striking (Vogel, 1977; Wiig et al., 1973). They have great difficulty

- when the plural of a word requires adding a complex ending, such as box, boxes
- when they must give the third person singular possessive
- when they must create the adjective form of a word

Problems with Semantics

Studies of the semantic problems of students with learning disabilities have produced conflicting findings. For example, two studies showed that these students have relatively impoverished vocabularies (Ackerman, Peters, & Dykman, 1971; Myklebust, Bannochie, & Killen, 1971), but a third study did not show this (Wiig & Semel, 1975). Similarly, students with learning disabilities have been reported to have more difficulty

FIGURE 11.2 Examples of Morphological Tasks with which Children with Learning Disabilities Have Trouble

This dog has spots. He is spotty. But this dog has even more spots. He is________.

This boy can shake things. Here he is shaking. He does it every day. Every day he________.

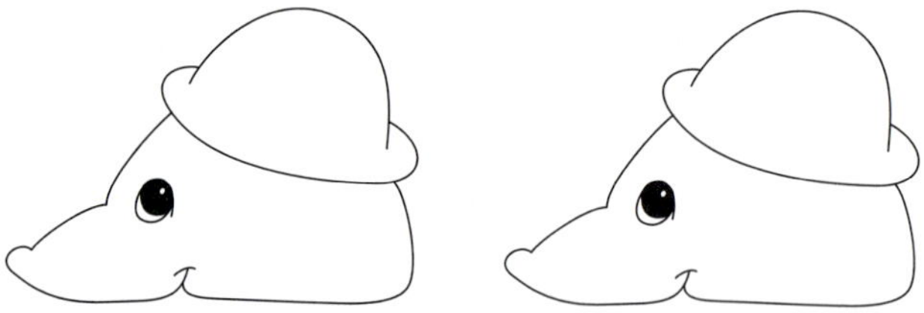

These are lags. They have hats. Whose hats are they? They are the________.

Source: From *Introduction to Learning Disabilities,* 2nd ed. (p. 182) by D. P. Hallahan, J. M. Kauffman, and J. W. Lloyd, 1985, Upper Saddle River, NJ: Prentice-Hall. Copyright 1985. Reprinted by permission of Allyn & Bacon.

than their normally achieving peers in using words to label pictures in one study (Wiig & Semel, 1975), but not in another (German, 1979). These disagreements among studies may be attributed to differences in how the researchers defined learning disabilities when selecting their samples (see discussions of definition in Chapter 1), how the students' performances were measured, or the ages of students tested. The inconsistencies in these studies support one of the important ideas developed in Chapter 1: Individuals with learning disabilities form a diverse group.

Many students with language disabilities have at least some problems with semantics. Some have difficulty completing an orally presented sentence that has a common word missing, and some struggle to name an object that has been described by its features (parts and function). Their problems are more apparent when the missing words and the words for the objects described are "low-frequency" words (do not occur often in children's reading materials) (German, 1979). Students with learning disabilities may have difficulties understanding sentences in which an ambiguous word is used; for example, they may not realize that the sentence "He was drawing a gun" can have two different meanings (Wiig et al., 1981). Adolescents who have learning disabilities take longer and make more errors than their normally achieving peers when asked to name antonyms (e.g., told "brother," they were to say "sister") and make more errors when trying to define common words such as "robin" "bridge," and "opinion" (Wiig & Semel, 1975).

Problems with Pragmatics

Problems with pragmatics represent one of the most important difficulties for students with learning disabilities. Boys (but not girls) who have learning disabilities use more complicated and longer communication patterns when explaining to younger children how to play a game than when explaining to their age-mates how to play the same game (Bryan & Pflaum, 1978). These students are also less effective than their nondisabled peers in providing descriptive information about objects. That is, when they are required to describe something so that another person can select it from an array of choices, they will not do as well. Normally learning students use labels more frequently, but students with learning disabilities use terms referring to the shape of objects more frequently (Noel, 1980).

Mistakes in how they use language may lead to social problems for these students, as discussed in Chapter 9 (see Donahue, 1987). For example, students who have learning disabilities use more competitive statements in their conversations with peers, but normally achieving students make more comments showing consideration (Bryan, Wheeler, Felcan, & Henek, 1976). Speaking competitively may cause hard feelings and even lead to arguments and fights. Thus, poor spoken language skills may be related to the social problems that students with learning disabilities experience (Camarata, Hughes, & Ruhl, 1988).

HOW ARE ORAL LANGUAGE ABILITIES ASSESSED?

Skills and deficits in oral language are most often assessed by administering tests. Reliance on tests to the exclusion of careful observation is a mistake (see Chapter 4). However, knowledgeable teachers and other clinicians should know about the tests that are frequently used.

Many tests have been developed to assess different aspects of language skills. The decision about how to assess language performance depends largely on the purposes of the assessment (see Chapter 4).

Comprehensive Assessments

Children's general language competence and performance are usually assessed by measuring their IQ. Because intelligence tests rely heavily on language abilities, IQ can be a good indicator of verbal ability. This was thought to be particularly true with such IQ tests as the *Wechsler Intelligence Scale for Children,* now the WISC-III (Wechsler, 1974), which have subtests designed to assess language performance (e.g., vocabulary). During the 1960s and 1970s, leaders in learning disabilities developed tests specifically designed to measure language abilities (Kirk & McCarthy, 1962; Kirk, McCarthy, & Kirk, 1968). Occasionally, these instruments were used as screening devices (i.e., they were administered to determine whether individual students were so different from their peers that they needed further testing). More often, however, they were used as diagnostic devices (i.e., they were administered to determine what deficits should be remedied or at what point in an instructional program a student should begin work).

More recently, psychologists and other clinicians have used newer tests of general language ability. Some of these tests are shown in Table 11.4. Many of these comprehensive tests, such as the *Test of Language Development* or TOLD (Hammill & Newcomer, 1988, Newcomer & Hammill, 1988), have become popular. The TOLD and special versions of it for students of different ages focus on assessing the major aspects of spoken language, including phonology, syntax, and semantics. Like the TOLD, many of the tests shown in Table 11.4 provide not only an overall language ability score, but also scores in specialized areas.

The language test that had the greatest influence on the field of learning disabilities is the *Illinois Test of Psycholinguistic Abilities,* or ITPA (Kirk, McCarthy, & Kirk, 1968; see also Kirk, 1976). The ITPA was designed to allow clinicians to assess specific processes presumed to be associated with school success. The history of the instrument (Kirk, 1969, 1976) reveals that its purpose was to enable identification of a student's deficit areas and then adjust instruction to meet that student's individual needs. The presumption underlying this approach is that individuals have unique strengths and weaknesses that can be identified by examining performance on tasks that tap specific skills.

To permit assessment of specific strengths and weaknesses, the ITPA assesses skill in 12 areas (see Table 11.5) that correspond to a model of communication (Osgood, 1957a, 1957b). The model classifies these skills according to two *channels* of communication (auditory-vocal and visual-motor modalities), two *levels* of communication (representational or thought-based and automatic or unconscious), and three *processes* of communication (reception, organizational, or expression). Because not all processes occur at the automatic level, there is not a subtest for each of the 12 cells (2 channels · 2 levels · 3 processes = 12) in the model. Each subtest is designed so that responding to the items for it requires that the child use only one ability. Table 11.5 describes the subtests.

TABLE 11.4 Selected Comprehensive Tests of Language

Test	Age Range[a]	Some Areas Assessed (Scores)
Detroit Tests of Learning Aptitudes—Adult (Hammill & Bryant, 1991a)	16-0 to 17-11 years, adults	Word Opposites Sentence Imitation Basic Information Word Sequences Story Sequences
Detroit Tests of Learning Aptitudes—Primary (Hammill & Bryant, 1991b)	3-0 to 9-0 years	Word Opposites Sentence Imitation Basic Information Word Sequences Story Sequences
Test of Adolescent Language, 3 (Hammill, Brown, Larsen, & Wiederholt, 1994)	12 to 25	Listening Speaking Reading Spoken Language Written Language Vocabulary Grammar Receptive Language Expressive Language General Language
Test of Auditory Comprehension of Language—Revised (Carrow-Woolfolk, 1985)	3-0 to 17-11, adults	Word Classes and Relations Grammatical Morphemes Elaborated Sentence Constructions
Test of Language Development 2—Intermediate (Hammill & Newcomer, 1988)	8-6 to 12-11	Syntax Semantics Speaking Listening Spoken Language
Test of Language Development 2—Primary (Hammill & Newcomer, 1988)	4-0 to 8-11	Phonology Syntax Semantics Speaking Listening Spoken Language

[a]Age in years-months format.

TABLE 11.5 Subtests of the *Illinois Test of Psycholinguistic Abilities*

Subtest	Content and Example	Channel	Level	Process
Visual Reception	Child is shown picture of an object and then shown pictures of four other objects; she or he must select the one from the same category.	V-M	Rep	Rec
Auditory Reception	Child is asked to answer "yes" or "no" to questions such as "Do dogs eat?" "Do dogs fly?" "Do mute musicians vocalize?"	A-V	Rep	Rec
Visual-Motor Association	Child chooses a picture of an object that goes with a stimulus (e.g., shown a bone, child chooses dog rather than pipe, rattle, or pencil).	V-M	Rep	Org
Auditory-Vocal Association	Child completes verbal analogies (e.g., "Bread is to eat; milk is to______).	A-V	Rep	Org
Motor Expression	Child demonstrates what to do with a pictured object (e.g., strums and fingers the frets of a guitar).	V-M	Rep	Exp
Verbal Expression	Child describes common objects (e.g., nail), earning a higher score by giving more complex and thorough descriptions.	A-V	Rep	Exp
Visual Sequential Memory	Child is shown a card depicting a series of shapes and then must arrange tiles with those shapes on them into the same order from memory.	V-M	Auto	N/A
Auditory Sequential Memory	Child repeats sequences of numbers said by examiner.	A-V	Auto	N/A
Visual Closure	Child is shown a line drawing and directed to find objects in it, many of which may be shown only in part.	V-M	Auto	N/A
Auditory Closure	Child is asked to say what examiner said, although examiner omits some sounds when saying item (e.g., given "re____ig____ator," child should say "refrigerator").	A-V	Auto	N/A
Grammatic Closure	Child gives correct grammatical form to complete statements shown in pictures (e.g., given "This man is painting. He is a____ ," child should say "painter").	A-V	Auto	N/A
Sound Blending	Child is given words separated into sounds and asked to say them (e.g., given "z-ee-f," child should say "zeef").	A-V	Auto	N/A

A child might have difficulty with one or more skills assessed by the ITPA. The testing data would allow a teacher to diagnose the child's problem in a way similar to the way a physician would diagnose illness by examining a patient. Based on this diagnosis, teachers could prescribe interventions. Hence, approaches based on the ITPA were sometimes called "diagnostic-prescriptive teaching."

Although there were many variations in prescriptions, there tended to be two basic types: (1) Provide remedial exercises to patch up the weak areas. (2) Avoid teaching through the weaknesses and capitalize on the child's strengths. For example, to patch up deficits in motor expression, a teacher might develop a series of lessons that required the child to act out events and that gradually increased in difficulty and then have students practice those lessons over a period of months. In contrast, a teacher might decide to avoid the weaknesses (in this case, select instructional practices that did not require motor expression), making sure that the lessons always permitted children with motor expression deficits to respond orally.

Performance on just one subtest rarely formed the basis for diagnoses and prescriptions. Most students showed general patterns of strengths and weaknesses. For example, some generally scored better on subtests assessing the visual-motor channel; others scored better on subtests assessing the auditory-vocal channel. The former might be called "visual learners" and the latter, "auditory learners."

Today people readily recognize these terms; they are called learning styles. But in the 1960s and 1970s, the ITPA offered the first carefully developed means of determining learning styles. According to the learning styles model, different learners should get different kinds of instruction. If learners score better on the visual-motor subtests, they should receive instruction that taps their strengths and does not require them to use their weaknesses—a sight or visual approach to reading in which they do not have to use phonics. If learners score better on the auditory-vocal subtests, they should receive instruction that taps their strengths and does not require them to use their weaknesses—a sound-based or phonics approach to reading in which they do not have to depend on the visual modality.

The ITPA and diagnostic-prescriptive teaching received substantial criticism (Engelmann, 1967a; Hallahan & Cruickshank, 1973; Mann, 1971; Mann & Phillips, 1967; Sedlak & Weiner, 1973; Waugh, 1975; Ysseldyke & Salvia, 1974). People questioned the psychometric adequacy of the instrument (e.g., whether the subtests actually measure what they are purported to measure). They also questioned the effectiveness of providing remedial exercises for deficits in specific areas (patch-up teaching) and basing instruction on learning styles.

One of the important contributions that resulted from experience with the ITPA was an emphasis on intraindividual differences. As noted in Chapter 1, intraindividual differences are a hallmark of learning disabilities. Another important contribution was an emphasis on fostering a close connection between assessment and instruction. These are recurring themes in learning disabilities. As a result, people in the field continue to search for tests that will permit them to identify deficits in specific areas of language.

Specific Assessments

As the previous discussion indicates, language includes the areas of phonology, syntax, morphology, semantics, and pragmatics. People who work with students who have learning disabilities may sometimes need to assess students' performance in one or more of these specific aspects of language. The comprehensive tests of language performance may help satisfy this need, but teachers may want to conduct more extensive assessments.

Table 11.6 lists some common tests of specific areas of language learning. The table does not list tests for each of the aspects of language learning included in the

TABLE 11.6 Tests of Specific Language Areas

Test	Age Range[a]
■ **Auditory Discrimination**	
Goldman-Fristoe-Woodcock Test of Auditory Discrimination (Goldman, Fristoe, & Woodcock, 1974)	3-0 to 17-11, adults
Wepman Test of Auditory Discrimination (Wepman, 1973)	3-0 to 7-11
■ **Phonological Awareness**	
Lindamood Auditory Conceptualization Test (Lindamood & Lindamood, 1979)	2-0 to 17-0, adults
Test of Phonological Awareness (Torgesen & Bryant, 1994)	4-0 to 7-11
■ **Syntax**	
Carrow Elicited Language Inventory (Carrow-Woolfolk, 1974)	3-0 to 7-11
Northwestern Syntax Screening Test (Lee, 1971)	
■ **Vocabulary**	
Comprehensive Receptive and Expressive Vocabulary Test (Wallace & Hammill, 1994)	4-0 to 17-11
Expressive One–Word Picture Vocabulary Test, Revised[b] (Gardner, 1991)	2-0 to 11-11
Peabody Picture Vocabulary Test—III[b] (Dunn & Dunn, 1997)	2-0 to 18-0
Receptive One–Word Picture Vocabulary Test, Revised (Gardner, 1985)	2-0 to 15-11

[a]Age in years-months format.

[b]There is also a Spanish version of this test.

earlier discussion of language features. For additional information on tests of language skills, see works on assessment of learning disabilities (Overton, 1996; Salvia & Ysseldyke, 1998; Swanson, 1991; Swanson & Watson, 1989).

Because phonological awareness is a critical skill in the development of literacy (Juel et al., 1986; Smith, Simmons, & Kameenui, 1998), it is the phonological skill of foremost importance in language learning. Young students' phonological awareness should be assessed routinely as part of literacy screening. Some states have established programs to screen for problems in phonological awareness among kindergarten and first-grade students (e.g., Invernizzi, Meier, Juel, & Swank, 1997; Swank, Meier, Invernizzi, & Juel, 1997).

In addition to rhyming and phoneme segmentation, phonological awareness includes other skills. Table 11.7 shows examples of different tasks that can be used in informal assessments of phonological awareness. Research indicates that tasks 4, 5, and 6 assess isolation of phonemes and tasks 8 and 9 assess phoneme deletion (Yopp, 1988). Evaluations of phonological awareness should include both types of tasks.

Auditory discrimination tasks differ from phonological awareness tasks. In them, students may or may not have to use phonological awareness. For example, some auditory discrimination activities do not involve words, although phonological awareness is explicitly about the sounds in words.

Interest in auditory discrimination arose because of the theory that students with learning disabilities might perceive sounds differently than their normally achieving

TABLE 11.7 Tasks Used to Assess Phonemic Awareness

Task	Example
1. Sound-to-word matching	Is there a /f/ in *calf?*
2. Word-to-word matching	Do *pen* and *pipe* begin the same?
3. Recognition or production of rhyme	Does *sun* rhyme with *run?*
4. Isolation of a sound	What is the first sound in *rose?*
5. Phoneme counting	How many sounds do you hear in the word *hot?*
6. Phoneme counting	How many sounds do you hear in the word *cake?*
7. Phoneme blending	Combine these sounds: /c/-/a/-/t/.
8. Phoneme deletion	What word would be left if /t/ were taken away from the middle of *stand?*
9. Specifying deleted phoneme	What sound do you hear in *meat* that is missing in *eat?*
10. Phoneme reversal	Say *os* with the first sound last and the last sound first.
11. Invented spellings	Write the word *monster.*

Source: From "The Validity and Reliability of Phonemic Awareness Tests" (p. 161) by H. K. Yopp, 1988, *Reading Research Quarterly,* 23. Copyright 1988 by International Reading Association. Reprinted by permission.

peers (Goldman, Fristoe, & Woodcock, 1970; Wepman, 1958, 1973). To test auditory discrimination, an examiner might say a pair of words (e.g., "mop," pause, "pop"), and the student is to say whether the words are the same or different. In a variation, a tape-recorded voice pronounces a word, and the student selects one of several pictures that vary from the stimulus word only in one particular sound. Figure 11.3 illustrates such items. Tasks such as these are not particularly useful in predicting students' acquisition of rudimentary reading skills (Yopp, 1988).

There may be, however, two separate aspects of phonological awareness, and these have important implications for intervention (Yopp, 1988). One area has to do with separating words into their constituent parts; the other has to do with combining parts to form words. To the extent that there are two (or more) component skills in phonological awareness, assessment and instruction may have to address each separately. Although additional studies are needed, sound blending may be the easier task (Slocum, O'Connor, & Jenkins, 1993; Yopp, 1988). However, teaching students either blending or segmenting alone does not necessarily lead to improvement in the other skill, thus supporting the idea that these may be separate skills (Slocum et al., 1993).

Methods of Monitoring Progress

Plans for monitoring progress should be developed according to individual needs. For example, monitoring a student's progress on phonological awareness makes little sense

FIGURE 11.3 An Auditory Discrimination Task

Directions: Examiner says stimulus word. Child points to correct picture at right.

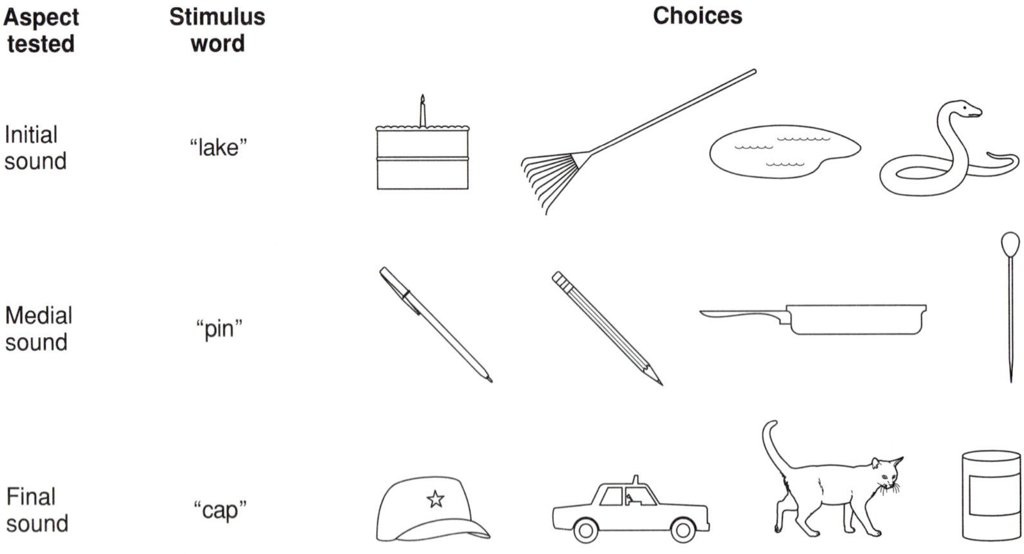
Aspect tested
Stimulus word
Choices
Initial sound
"lake"
Medial sound
"pin"
Final sound
"cap"

when her primary language problems are in word knowledge. Decisions about which problem areas to monitor should be based on students' IEPs.

Progress in some specific areas can be measured by means similar to those used in curriculum-based assessment. The assessment strategies described in Chapter 4—frequently repeated measurement of specific skills—can be applied to areas such as phonological awareness and receptive vocabulary. For example, teachers might construct lists of simple words and test how many of them students can segment correctly within 2 minutes. Similarly, to assess pragmatic use of language, teachers might simply observe students during particular activities and count the proportion of socially appropriate statements they make.

Expressive language can profitably be assessed by collecting and analyzing samples of spoken language. Using language samples to assess language is a time-honored method (Lee, 1971). Teachers who can collect samples repeatedly can use them to evaluate whether certain aspects of students' language abilities are improving.

To collect language samples, teachers should create a situation in which students can produce their best language performance because one wants to know how well the student can do. With younger children, the teacher may want to use toys or activities to promote language, but with adolescents, social situations are probably sufficient. Rather than asking many specific questions, teachers gathering language samples should use strategies that encourage the student to talk a lot. The idea is to obtain a sample of student language that includes about 50 to 100 utterances. Teachers may want to record the sample on video- or audiotape.

The most daunting part of using language samples is scoring them. The first step is to transcribe the sample (transferring it to paper or computer disk) and segment it (mark off individual utterances or units of language). Then the individual utterances must be analyzed. Some important measures for analysis are mean length of utterance, type-token ratio, and T-units. Table 11.8 describes these measures. In addition, the sample can be analyzed for appropriate use of various language features, such as use of particular morphemes. Other sources provide additional and more detailed information about language samples and learning disabilities (Johnson, 1994; Nelson, 1993).

HOW CAN ORAL LANGUAGE PROBLEMS BE ADDRESSED?

Intervention in the language problems of students with learning disabilities is influenced by several factors. Among these are the theoretical conceptions of language and learning disabilities that teachers adopt (see Chapter 3) and the programs and materials available for teaching.

Theoretical Approaches

Although there are many theoretical explanations of how best to teach language, there are two primary perspectives. A behavioral position explains language behavior in terms of learning; a psycholinguistic position considers language to be a native ability.

TABLE 11.8 Some Common Measures of Expressive Language for Analyzing Language Samples

Measure	Description
Mean length of utterance (MLU)	Calculating MLUs requires counting the number of words in the sample and dividing by the number of utterances. How the sample is segmented into utterances will affect the MLU.
Type-token ratio	Type refers to the number of different words, and token refers to the total number of words in a writing sample. For example, the sentence "The girl gave the other girl a smile" has eight tokens and six types. In general, as students get older, the type-token ratio increases, indicating that they are using proportionally more different words.
T-unit	A T-unit is a single main clause and the subordinate clauses that accompany it. For example, "The movie we saw" is not a T-unit and neither is "we saw about Moby Dick, the white whale." The following are T-units: "I like the movie we saw" and "I like the movie we saw about Moby Dick, the white whale." T-units may be very brief (e.g., "Birds fly") or longer (e.g., "Flying continuously for many months, the swallows eat and mate in midair while circumnavigating the globe").

The former is closest to the task-analytic model, and the latter is closest to the constructivist models described in Chapter 3.

Task-Analytic Model

Many people think that learning principles can be used to explain language acquisition. Skinner (1957) popularized the position that operant conditioning is the primary means of learning language. Others expanded on these ideas (Jenkins & Palmero, 1964; Staats, 1968, 1974). In the 1990s, they gained strength from longitudinal research showing the lasting influences of early language experiences on children's subsequent achievement (Hart & Risley, 1995).

According to the behavioral approach, an individual's speaking behavior is, at least in part, learned. Children's language skills are "taught" by the environment. Processes such as modeling (children hear others saying words and observe the effects of speaking) and reinforcement (using language affects the child's environment) influence performance. Production of words is shaped: Environmental contingencies may reward a toddler for saying "cah-cah" but will reward an older child only for saying "car." Word meanings are learned by differential reinforcement: People around a child will react one way if he or she says "blue" when pointing to a blue object and another way if he or she says "blue" when pointing to a red object. Syntactic skills are developed by learning response classes: Children can say "I see" and then nearly anything else (e.g., "you," "dogs," "a girl who is running," "the point you are trying to make"), depending on the circumstances.

Behavioral interventions are direct and systematic. Specific language skills are identified, and activities are designed to get students to use them. Table 11.9 shows an analysis of the components of language that a task-analytic (or behavioral) approach might assess and teach. As the student uses them, the teacher reinforces accurate usage and corrects mistakes. For example, if a student does not know the usual plural form of man (e.g., the student says "mens" rather than "men"), the teacher might model the correct form ("Listen to me say it: *men*"), provide the student with an opportunity to repeat it correctly ("How do you say it?"), and praise common usage ("That's it! Men. You said it correctly!"). The teacher might then provide other opportunities for practice under different conditions to help the student remember the pronunciation. For example, while showing a picture of adult males, the teacher might say, "Tell me about these people. Are they boys? That's correct; they're not boys. What are they? Yes! They are men." Related morphological forms (e.g., women) would be assessed and taught as necessary.

More contemporary applications of behavioral principles have expanded the view of language behavior to include an emphasis on the context in which language is used (e.g., Warren & Yoder, 1994). This emphasis corresponds to the concern about pragmatic competence in learning disabilities. Thus, though it may be tempting to dismiss behavioral views of language acquisition and instruction as mechanistic, to do so would misrepresent contemporary behavioral research and practice.

Psycholinguistic Approach

In contrast to the task-analytic perspective, which stresses the importance of the environment and its influence on the speaker's behavior, the psycholinguistic approach emphasizes the importance of innate abilities and the listener's interpretations. The psycholinguistic orientation was originally based largely on N. Chomsky's (1957) work on syntax, then received a big boost from his review of Skinner's (1957) work (N. Chomsky, 1959). Leading advocates of the psycholinguistic position emphasize the idea that language abilities are genetically transmitted, that there is an understanding of language "wired" into the brain at birth (McNeill, 1966, 1970; Wexler, 1990). Studies of identical and fraternal twins indicate there is even a genetic component to important language skills, including such fundamental skills as articulation, phonological awareness, and correct grammar (Dixon et al., 1995; Olson, Wise, Conners, Rack, & Fulker, 1989; Tallal, Townsend, Curtiss, & Wulfeck, 1991; van der Lely & Stollwerck, 1996; see also Chapter 2). That there is a genetic contribution to these skills does not mean they are completely determined by genes. There is still room for environmental influence and, hence, teaching.

One of the main arguments advanced by proponents of a psycholinguistic view is the idea that language performance is incredibly diverse. Any page of a newly written book, for example, is very unlikely to have on it lines of print that have appeared in the exact same form anywhere else (except quotations). Similarly, children speak sentences

TABLE 11.9 Content Analysis of Language Domains

1 Syntax/Morphology	2 Semantics/Vocabulary	3 Pragmatics
A. Syntax/Morphology	**A. Basic**	**A. One-Way Communication**
1. Noun phrase/verb phrase	1. Body parts	1. Expresses wants
2. Regular plurals	2. Clothing	2. Expresses opinions
3. Subject pronouns	3. Classroom objectives	3. Expresses feelings
4. Prepositional phrases	4. Action verbs	4. Expresses values
5. Adjectives	5. Verb tasks	5. Follows directions
6. Interrogative reversals	6. Animals and insects	6. Asks questions
7. Object pronouns	7. Outdoor words	7. Narrates event
8. Negatives	8. Family members	8. States main idea
9. Verb *be* auxiliary	9. Home objects	9. Sequences events
10. Verb *be* copula	10. Meals	10. Subordinates details
11. Infinitives	11. Food and drink	11. Summarizes
12. Determiners	12. Colors	12. Describes
13. Conjunction *and*	13. Adverbs	13. Compares and contrasts
14. Possessives	14. Occupations	14. Gives instructions
15. Noun-verb agreement	15. Community	15. Explains
16. Comparatives	16. Grooming objects	**B. Two-Way Communication**
17. *Wh* questions	17. Vehicles	1. Considers the listener
18. Past tense	18. Money	2. Formulates messages
19. Future aspect	19. Gender	3. Participates in discussions
20. Irregular plurals	20. School	4. Uses persuasion
21. Forms of *do*	21. Playthings	5. Resolves differences
22. Auxiliaries	22. Containers	6. Identifies speaker's biases
23. Derivational endings	23. Days of the week	7. Identifies speaker's assumptions
24. Reflexive pronouns	24. Months	8. Formulates conclusions
25. Qualifiers	25. Emotions	
26. Conjunctions *and, but, or*	26. Numbers	
27. Conjunctions	27. Celebrations and holidays	
28. Indirect and direct objects	28. Spatial concepts	
29. Adverbs	29. Quantitative concepts	
30. Infinitives with subject	30. Temporal concepts	
31. Participles	31. Shapes	
32. Gerunds	32. Greetings and polite terms	

TABLE 11.9 *continued*

1 Syntax/Morphology	2 Semantics/Vocabulary	3 Pragmatics
33. Passive voice	33. Opposites	
34. Complex verb forms	34. Materials	
35. Relative adverb clauses	35. Music	
36. Relative pronoun clauses	36. Tools	
37. Complex conjunctions	37. Categories	
	38. Verbs of the senses	
	B. Advanced	
	1. Reading material vocabulary	
	2. Content area vocabulary	
	3. Idioms/figurative language	
	4. Multiple meaning of words	
	5. Influence of context on meaning	

Source: From *Curriculum-Based Evaluation: Teaching and Decision Making,* 2nd ed. (p. 256) by K. W. Howell, S. L. Fox, and M. K. Morehead, 1993, Pacific Grove, CA: Brooks/Cole. Copyright 1993 by Brooks/Cole Publishing Company, a division of Thompson Publishing, Inc. Reprinted by permission.

they have never previously heard. According to nativists, such diversity negates any possible behavioral explanation of language. Furthermore, according to the psycholinguistic position, the fact that different sentences can convey the same meaning indicates there is an innate, underlying structure to language. For example, the idea in the sentence "Jane played the song" can be stated in another form without changing the idea: "The song was played by Jane." Not only do these two sentences have the same "deep structure"—the same abstract basis—but children possess the innate ability to understand that these two sentences have the same meaning.

Psycholinguistic interventions deemphasize the importance of direct teaching and stress the value of discovery learning. Although nativists consider environment important, their approach is based less on having teachers initiate instruction and more on having them respond to children's use of language. According to McNeill (1970):

> A language is thus acquired through [a child's] discovering the relations that exist between the surface structure of its sentences and the universal aspects of the deep structure, the latter being a manifestation of children's own capacities. The interaction between children's innate capacities and their linguistic experience occurs at this point, in the acquisition of transformations—and it is here that parental speech must make its contributions. (p. 1088)

One of the primary means advocates of psycholinguistic views use to encourage acquisition of language is **expansion.** Expansion refers to an adult responding in an interpretive way to children's utterances: The adult expands on what a child says. For example, if the child says "Doggie gone," the adult might say "Yes, the doggie is gone." In this way, it is hoped that the child will learn the more grammatically complete form for the idea he or she expressed when saying "Doggie gone."

An Effective Approach

Most of the actual interventions used with children and adolescents who have learning disabilities have not been aligned exclusively with one or the other of the basic approaches to language. In fact, the interventions have been based more on clinical and classroom experience than on any theory.

Deemphasis on theoretical orientation does not mean advocacy for mindless eclecticism. Teachers should not simply adopt practices because they appear entertaining or new. Instead, they should base their decisions about language instruction and other areas on the benefits the instruction provides for students.

Today in learning disabilities, concern about effectiveness of interventions should overshadow theoretical orientations. Regardless of the theoretical basis of an intervention, if it can be clearly shown that the intervention benefits students, it should be used. This perspective places increased emphasis on teachers collecting data to monitor progress and basing instructional decisions on them. Using these data, teachers can make informed decisions about the benefits of the psycholinguistic and task-analytic interventions described in the next sections.

Psycholinguistic Interventions

Psycholinguistic interventions have a long history in learning disabilities. Some of the earliest work using these methods focused on addressing isolated language subskills. These subskills were identified by testing using the ITPA (Kirk et al., 1968). Others have been more general and less modular. They have also sought to incorporate concepts from cognitive psychology.

ITPA-Based Programs

Psycholinguistic interventions were particularly popular during the 1960s and 1970s. Among the interventions in this group were many that were based on the ITPA (Kirk et al., 1968) and others that, although not expressly related to the test, were based on many of the same assumptions. For the most part, early psycholinguistic interventions focused on students' strengths or weaknesses. Some held that teachers should provide activities that would strengthen weak abilities, and others argued that instruction should be based on a pupil's strengths or learning style.

Remedial programs assumed that specific language abilities or processes could be isolated and that each skill could be trained using educational techniques. For example, inability to remember sequences as measured by the Auditory Sequential Memory subtest of the ITPA might be remedied by providing extensive practice in following multistep directions (e.g., "Go to the door, open it, close it, walk backward to the bookshelf, touch a big red book, come back to your seat, and sit down in front of your chair") and other activities.

There were many programs and recommendations about psycholinguistic training. For example, Kirk and Kirk (1971) provided specific remedial recommendations, and a book by Bush and Giles (1977) had chapters that corresponded exactly with the subtests of the ITPA. Similarly, there were kits that included many activities for work on various processes. For example, the MWM Program for Developing Language Abilities (Minskoff, Wiseman, & Minskoff, 1972) and the GOAL program (Karnes, 1972) both contain teaching manuals that describe activities and materials for carrying them out (e.g., picture cards) that are designed to teach the processes measured by the ITPA.

Probably the most widely known program related to psycholinguistic training is the Peabody Language Development program (Dunn, Smith, Dunn, Horton, & Smith, 1981). This program, the revised version of an immensely popular earlier one, is composed of four kits and is designed to be used with children of preschool, primary-school, and elementary-school age. Unlike many other programs with ties to psycholinguistics, the Peabody program does not recommend activities for specific processes; instead, it is aimed at general language development. The kits include teachers' manuals and other materials (e.g., picture cards, puppets) for use in daily lessons. The Peabody program also emphasizes the use of behavior modification techniques.

Many studies of remedial training based on the ITPA have reported that these activities are ineffective. For example, Hammill and Larsen (1974a) reviewed the results of 39 studies and found that fewer than half of the comparisons made in the studies favored students given psycholinguistic training. Advocates of psycholinguistic training disagreed with these analyses (Lund, Foster, & McCall-Perez, 1978). Careful and comprehensive analysis of the literature on psycholinguistic training reveals that there is modest evidence of effectiveness but that other interventions have more substantial effects (Forness, Kavale, Blum, & Lloyd, 1997; Kavale, 1981a).

Cognitive-Psycholinguistic Interventions

In the early development of the field of learning disabilities, the term *psycholinguistic* was almost invariably associated with the ITPA. Today, however, it is used to refer to approaches affected by the study of the mixture of psychology and linguistics—an area strongly influenced by advocates of constructivist (and antibehavioristic) theory. Today, cognitive-psycholinguistic authorities generally do not align themselves with the ITPA and related training programs.

Cognitive-psycholinguistic interventions are closely associated with psycholinguistic theory. Cognitive-psycholinguistic views embrace nativism, emphasize strategies, and reflect a top-down approach. The emphasis on strategic competence is consistent with the emphasis on strategies developed in Chapter 1 and reiterated in Chapter 3. Strategic competence presupposes competence with such lower-order skills as phonemic and morphemic awareness emphasized by proponents of cognitive-psycholinguistic interventions (Wiig, 1990; Semel & Wiig, 1981; Wiig & Semel, 1984).

The following are some crucial factors in classrooms based on a cognitive-psycholinguistic approach (Carrow-Woolfolk, 1988; Galda, Cullinan, & Stickland, 1997; Nelson, 1993).

- creating language-rich environments, places where students are free to express themselves and where language is used to accomplish diverse tasks
- providing explicit instruction in situations where students need to learn clear and consistent steps for accomplishing tasks (strategies)
- capitalizing on spontaneous opportunities to help students acquire language skills (incidental teaching)
- using techniques to evoke and facilitate spontaneous communication by students
- encouraging students to converse with peers

Some techniques used in cognitive-psycholinguistic interventions are rooted in conversation with children and are very similar to the process of expansion discussed previously (Lee, Koenigsknecht, & Mulhern, 1975). In this approach, the teacher presents stories (arranged according to level of linguistic difficulty) and asks questions so that students must use various forms of sentences. Using the sentence that a student utters as a base, the teacher employs one of several techniques to encourage a more grammatically acceptable sentence. For example, when a student uses the wrong inflection of a verb in a sentence (e.g., "He eated bananas"), the teacher might do one of the following.

1. Ask the student to repeat the sentence ("What did you say?") in the hope that he or she will then say it correctly.
2. Repeat the mistaken statement ("He eated bananas?") to encourage the student to make the correction.
3. Ask the student whether the statement was correct ("Is 'He eated bananas' correct?") to encourage self-correction.

Based on their experience, advocates of cognitive-psycholinguistic interventions believe that these techniques are effective, and some experimental data confirm their belief (Lee et al., 1975).

Two commercial programs are good illustrations of a combination of cognitive-psycholinguistic interventions. One is the Sound-Order-Sense program, or SOS (Semel, 1970), and the other is the Semel Auditory Processing Program, or SAPP (Semel, 1976). The SOS program is designed to help children develop listening skills they can use in comprehending spoken language. As its name implies, SOS program activities stress sound (perception of sounds), order (remembering the order of things that have been said), and sense (semantics). There are special features of the program, such as books printed in a way that allows students to know immediately whether they have answered correctly. SOS includes two years of daily lessons designed to be used with children of primary-school age.

The SAPP is designed to help children develop skills in processing and interpreting language. Activities were selected to provide work on auditory memory, morphology, syntax, semantics, and other types of language skills. The activities (e.g., morphemic segmentation, sentence completion) used to encourage learning of language skills are deliberately varied to induce more general learning. The entire program is composed of three levels and can be used with students ranging from 3 years old to the teen years. A study undertaken to evaluate the results of the SAPP showed that elementary-school-age students with learning disabilities made substantial gains on several measures of language development during the time their teachers were following the program (Semel & Wiig, 1981).

Task-Analytic Interventions

Task-analytic interventions are most closely associated with a behavioral perspective on language. They are based much less than cognitive or constructivist interventions on students gaining insight about language. Instead, they are based on systematic teaching of language structures and skills. In task-analytic interventions, activities are designed to teach specific subskills of language and to help students integrate these into more general language competence. DISTAR (Direct Instruction System for Teaching Arithmetic and Reading) Language (Engelmann & Osborn, 1977) and the comprehension strand of the Corrective Reading program (Engelmann, Becker, Hanner, & Johnson, 1978, 1988) are the foremost examples of task-analytic approaches to language instruction.

Many language abilities are based on knowing concepts. That is, concepts are semantic tasks. Because concepts are the building blocks not just of thinking, but also of communicating to others, Direct Instruction programs seek to teach them effectively and efficiently. Concepts can be thought of as existing along a continuum from simple labels for objects (e.g., "chair" as a type of furniture) to subtle descriptions of relationships among other concepts (e.g., "inverse"). Because there can be many different examples of a concept—a lot of different chairs—teachers cannot hope to show students each and every example of a concept. Instead, they must show carefully selected examples of the concept to teach the general idea.

> To learn a concept such as *on, chair,* or *orange,* a student need not observe or experience every example of the concept *on,* sit on every chair to learn the concept of *chair,* or rub, peel and eat every orange to identify a novel instance of the concept *orange.* Because the teacher cannot show the learner every possible example and nonexample of a concept, the general notion of teaching concepts is that by the teaching of a sufficient range of examples, the learner should be able to identify new examples of a concept. (Kameenui & Simmons, 1990, pp. 152–153)

Table 11.10 describes many different classes of concepts. An important feature of DI teaching is that one can use similar techniques to teach similar concepts. "If we are able to design a teaching sequence for a positional concept such as between, then we should be able to design teaching sequences for all positional concepts" (Kameenui & Simmons, 1990).

The DISTAR Language program (Engelmann & Osborn, 1977) includes three levels and was designed to be used with children in the primary grades. Kinder and Carnine (1991) provided an overview of the principles of DISTAR as well as some of the research documenting the benefits of using Direct Instruction. Unlike the psycholinguistic and cognitive-psycholinguistic programs, which are concerned with global language ability, DISTAR's purpose is to teach the language used in the classroom. In doing so, it fosters general language development. Daily lessons with scripts for the teacher to follow include activities for work on basic skills (e.g., descriptions, pronouns, asking questions) and lead up to work on traditional language activities (e.g., identification of subjects and predicates). Teaching techniques include group instruction, modeling, frequent responding, correction, and reinforcement. DISTAR Language programs were a part of the Direct Instruction model tested in Project Follow-Through.

TABLE 11.10 Concept Classes and Examples

Positional Concepts	Color Concepts
on, between, up, under, above, in, to the side, left, right, over, in front of, first, last, middle	red, blue, green, orange, yellow, chartreuse, puce, magenta, pink, red, lavender, black
Polar Concepts	Action Concepts
hot/cold, open/close, high/low, clean/dirty, big/little, full/empty, smooth/rough, up/down	run, push, lift, bounce, cut, fight, evade, play, jump, hit
Comparative Concepts	Superlative Concepts
wider, faster, brighter, bigger, deeper, heavier, harder, smoother, steeper	widest, fastest, brightest, biggest, deepest, heaviest, hardest, smoothest, steepest

Noun Concepts

General	Specific	Proper
food, fruit, plants, tools, vehicles, toys, people, pets, furniture, clothes, geometric shapes	meat, oranges, pliers, car, boy, chair, table, shirt, pants, circle, square	German shepherd, Albert, Chevrolet, *Newsweek,* Oshkosh B'Gosh, Polo

Source: From *Designing Instructional Strategies: The Prevention of Academic Learning Problems,* by E. J. Kameenui, and D. C. Simmons, 1990, Columbus, OH: Merrill. Copyright 1990, by Merrill Publishing Company, an imprint of Prentice-Hall, Inc. Reprinted by permission.

According to evaluations of Project Follow-Through, the DI model was the most effective of nine major approaches (Abt Associates, 1976, 1977) and was the only model that had positive effects on children's language performance (House, Glass, McLean, & Walker, 1978). Other studies have revealed similar evidence of effectiveness (Gersten & Maggs, 1982; Maggs & Morath, 1976; Weller, 1979).

The comprehension strand of the Corrective Reading Program (Engelmann et al., 1978, 1988) is very similar to DISTAR Language. It includes two levels, Thinking Basics and Comprehension Skills, with scripted daily lessons for the teacher to follow. Unlike DISTAR Language, which is designed for young children, the remedial comprehension programs are written for older students who

> do not have well-developed recitation skills. They cannot repeat sentences they hear, so they have trouble retaining and answering questions about information that is presented. These students are often prevented from comprehending what they read because they don't even understand the material when it is presented orally. (Engelmann et al., 1978, p. 8)

The program teaches language and thinking skills such as description, classification, definition, analogies, deductions, and vocabulary. After the skills have been taught, they are systematically integrated into the students' reading and writing tasks. The program has significant effects on oral vocabulary and reading comprehension (Lloyd, Cullinan, Heins, & Epstein, 1980; see also Adams & Engelmann, 1996; White, 1988).

Effective Practices

A factor of particular importance in language assessment and intervention today is sensitivity to language differences (see Box 11.1). There are practices that promote specific aspects of language performance but do not align with only one of the programs described in the foregoing sections. For example, there is widespread agreement about the importance of teaching phonological awareness (Simmons & Kameenui, 1998). Methods for teaching phonological awareness appear in both task-analytic and cognitive-psycholinguistic approaches.

Phonological Awareness

Recommendations about teaching phonological awareness abound (Adams, Foorman, Beeler, & Lundberg, 1997; Baker, Kameenui, Simmons, & Stahl, 1994; Ball & Blachman, 1991; Smith et al., in press; Snider, 1995). In the simplest form, training activities closely resemble those described previously in tests of phonology (see Table 11.7). For example:

Teacher: Listen to this word: fan. Say that word.
Students: Fan.
Teacher: Now I want you to say that word without saying the *f* sound.
Students: An!
Teacher: That's it! An . . . you've got it.

BOX 11.1 ***MULTICULTURAL PERSPECTIVES***

Teaching Students Whose Primary Language Is Not English

Teaching students whose primary language is not English requires that teachers consider special techniques. Gersten, Brengelman, and Jiménez (1994) provide recommendations about adapting instruction to meet the needs of those students. The following outline articulates the key components of effective, comprehensible instruction for language-minority students.

1. Scaffolding and strategies
   a. Provide story maps and visual organizers.
   b. Encourage transfer of native language skills.
   c. Elicit or provide relevant background knowledge.
   d. Stress and reiterate underlying big idea with range of examples.
2. Challenge
3. Involvement
   a. Provide extended discourse.
   b. Use complex linguistic structures.
   c. Foster active engagement of all.
4. Success
5. Mediation and feedback
   a. Make it frequent and comprehensible.
   b. Focus on meaning.
   c. Use recall strategies.
   d. Ask for supporting evidence.
6. Responsiveness to cultural and individual diversity
   a. Link content to experience.
   b. Use personal experience. (p. 9)

In a popular variation, teachers give students tiles representing individual sounds and direct them to move one tile for each sound as they say the sounds in a word.

Regardless of the type of activity used, phonological awareness training tasks can vary in difficulty (Smith et al., in press). Teachers can adjust the difficulty of phonological awareness tasks by varying the following.

- Word length. Words with fewer phonemes are easier than longer words to manipulate.
- Size of phonological unit. Segmenting compound words is easier than segmenting syllables, which is easier than segmenting individual phonemes.
- Position in the word of the phonemes to be manipulated. Segmenting the first sounds is easier than segmenting the last sounds in words.
- Characteristics of the phonemes. Continuous sounds such as *s* and *m* are easier to segment than consonant clusters such as the first sounds in "school."

Teaching phonological awareness is very important today. There are at least two cautions teachers should know. First,

> How good do you have to be at phonological awareness activities . . . to get the maximum advantage out of these important insights about the phonological structure of words? . . . When does additional teaching of phoneme awareness per se stop becoming productive? (Blachman, 1997, p. 416)

Second, although there is considerable evidence that promoting phonological awareness has beneficial effects on reading and spelling for young students, there is much less evidence about its benefits for students in later elementary or secondary grades. Educators must be careful not to overgeneralize the evidence.

Statement Repetition

Another prominent problem for many children with learning disabilities is the repetition of sentences. We have known for a long time that students with learning disabilities do poorly on statement repetition tasks (Hessler & Kitchen, 1980; Hresko, 1979; McNutt & Li, 1980; Vogel, 1974; Wiig & Roach, 1975; Wong & Roadhouse, 1978). Statement repetition forms the basis for many other skills. Some of these skills are quite rudimentary; others are more complicated. The ability to repeat a statement itself is relatively simple; one must say only what one heard.

However, statement repetition is fundamental, for without this skill, students cannot hold a statement in memory long enough to think about it, change it, or do much of anything else with it. Performance on statement repetition tasks may be affected by many of the spoken-language skills described elsewhere. For example, pupils with weaker phonemic skills may have to work so hard at pronouncing words they have heard that when they try to say a complicated word, they forget the remainder of a sentence they are repeating. When this happens, it is easy to see why a student might simply shrug, sigh, and stop in mid-sentence. Statement repetition is clearly one of the skills required for successful learning and one in which many students with learning disabilities are deficient.

The following example illustrates how statement repetition might be used while practicing changing sentences to active voice.

Teacher: Say this sentence: The overdue books were lost by the teachers.
Students: The overdue books were lost by the teachers.
Teacher: Now, I want you to say that sentence in the active voice.
Students: The teachers lost the overdue books.
Teacher: That's it! Whoa! Now, wait a minute . . . who are you saying lost those books?

Summary

1. What are the major dimensions of language?
   a. Language can be divided on the basis of a person's behavior as either receptive or expressive.
   b. Another important division identifies the language systems, including phonology, syntax, morphology, semantics, and pragmatics.

2. How does language develop normally?
   a. Children acquire language skills gradually over time.
   b. Early development centers around the phonology of language. Later development centers around the subtler aspects or nuances of development, such as pragmatics.
   c. Although most language development occurs before the school years, later development occurs during the primary grades.
3. What are some oral language characteristics of students with learning disabilities?
   a. Students with learning disabilities may have problems in either receptive or expressive language or in both.
   b. Students with learning disabilities may have difficulties with any of the various language systems, including phonology, syntax, morphology, semantics, and pragmatics.
   c. Problems in these various areas affect not only language facility itself, but also other areas, such as reading, spelling, and even social relations.
4. How are oral language abilities assessed?
   a. Skills and deficits in oral language are best assessed by using both tests and less formal, direct measurement methods, such as observation.
   b. Comprehensive tests of language ability may be used to assess general language ability (verbal intelligence).
   c. Teachers often use specific tests for language areas such as phonological awareness, vocabulary, understanding of sentences, and so forth.
   d. Teachers need to be able to assess progress in oral language skills and usually do so by devising informal measures of skills such as phonological awareness.
5. How can oral language problems be addressed?
   a. Intervention in language problems is often guided by pyscholinguistic or task-analytic theory. However, concern about effectiveness of interventions should overshadow theoretical orientations. Regardless of the theoretical basis of an intervention, if it can be clearly shown that the intervention benefits students, it should be used.
   b. Effective practices include explicitly teaching students such skills as phonological awareness, statement repetition, and transformation of sentences.

12

Teaching Students with Reading Problems

What Are the Characteristics of Students with Reading Problems?

Problems with Reading Performance

Problems with Aspects of Language

What Is the Prevalence of Students with Reading Difficulties?

How Is Reading Performance Assessed?

Comprehensive Measures

Diagnosing Problems and Planning Programs

Monitoring Student Progress

How Should Beginning Literacy Be Taught?

Code-Emphasis Approach

Whole-Language Approach

Effectiveness of Beginning Reading Approaches

Emerging Synthesis in Beginning Reading Instruction

Promoting Phonological Awareness

How Should Reading Problems Be Corrected?

Traditional Approaches

Current Remedial Reading Instruction

Instructional Strategies

Summary

People use reading as a means of accomplishing other things. They read novels about romances, balloons about what cartoon characters say, signs about products, manuals about how to use computers, and cookbooks about how to make bread. By reading, they can learn the order of the planets in our solar system or entertain themselves with a novel or poem. Students who read well have great advantages in studying not only literature, but also social studies, science, and even mathematics. Reading has become nearly essential for adult employment and is almost a necessity for obtaining adult privileges such as getting a driver's license.

Reading disabilities negatively affect students' schooling. Children who are behind in kindergarten and first grade are likely to be behind in second and third grade (Juel, 1988). By the second grade, teachers often have recognized children's difficulties and have referred them for special education evaluation (Lloyd, Kauffman, Landrum, & Roe, 1991). By the third grade, students with reading problems begin to fall behind their peers in other school subjects. One consequence of falling behind in other areas is that students with reading problems have less access than their peers to sources of information; thus, as capable readers gain new information from reading, those with disabilities continue to fall behind in other areas, losing ground to their peers in the knowledge and information that provides the working material for intelligence (Stanovich, 1986b). As adults, people who had severe reading problems in childhood may be successful in life and work, but they continue to have substantial reading problems (Bruck, 1998).

Not only do reading disabilities put children at risk for referral to special education and for difficulty in other school subjects, but these deficits are related to other problems as well. Children who have difficulty learning to read often develop negative views of their own competence (e.g., Bryan, 1986) and lose interest in academics. By the middle of elementary school, reading is so aversive for poor readers that they would rather clean their rooms than read (Juel, 1988).

Becoming a capable adult reader requires that students acquire five generalized competencies (Anderson, Hiebert, Scott, & Wilkenson, 1985):

1. *Fluency.* Capable readers recognize words readily. They appear to read effortlessly. They can do this because they have practiced *decoding* (turning print into oral language) enough that it is *automatic* (requires no conscious work) (Laberge & Samuels, 1974). When readers do not have to focus on decoding—when they are fluent readers—they are free to devote their attention to learning from and enjoying what they read.

2. *World knowledge.* Capable readers use their knowledge of the world to construct the meaning of what they read. They do more than simply extract the meaning from the text; they try to make what they are reading correspond with what they have experienced. Young readers (especially those with disabilities) sometimes construct mistaken representations of what they read; their personal experience may intrude to such a great extent that they read what they think should be on the page, not what is actually there. As readers become more sophisticated, they can suspend their own be-

liefs and ideas, follow an author's argument, and acquire new world knowledge from the text.

3. *Flexible strategy use.* Capable readers adapt their reading to fit the material they are reading and their understanding of it. When they encounter unfamiliar or difficult words, they slow down and read more carefully. When they realize that they have not been understanding what they have been reading, they employ strategies such as rereading. To help themselves remember what they have read, they use strategies such as paraphrasing and others discussed in Chapter 10.

4. *Motivation.* Capable readers read because of what it gives them. They may gain new knowledge, learn the resolution of a story, or avoid doing some less pleasant task, such as housework. Early in the acquisition of reading skill, there is little intrinsic reinforcement in reading for children; they may pursue it because they have been told it is fun, but they have not had enough practice with it to find reading easy and inherently interesting. Later, if people read well, reading new information becomes very rewarding.

5. *Continued reading.* Capable readers not only learn fundamental reading skills, but also continue to read. As they do so, they become more and more skillful. Reading becomes a lifelong pursuit.

Many students with learning disabilities have difficulty with many of these competencies. To understand the relationships between reading and learning disabilities, it is important to examine the characteristics of students with reading disabilities, how to assess reading performance, and how to teach reading effectively.

WHAT ARE THE CHARACTERISTICS OF STUDENTS WITH READING PROBLEMS?

Many students with learning disabilities have severe problems with reading. Reading deficits are the most common academic deficit among students considered to have learning disabilities (Norman & Zigmond, 1980), and teachers in learning disabilities programs report that they emphasize reading instruction more than any other area (Kirk & Elkins, 1975). The overlap of reading disabilities and learning disabilities explains why some people might equate remedial reading with learning disabilities. This overlap has caused debate among professionals working in these two areas (Council for Exceptional Children, 1997a; Lerner, 1975). Regardless of their differences, educators affiliated primarily with remedial reading and those affiliated primarily with special education agree that many students have severe reading problems. Usually, those students with the most severe reading problems are identified as having learning disabilities.

Severe reading problems are often referred to as dyslexia. The term *dyslexia* comes from Greek and means "an impairment in the ability to read." The label *dyslexic* is sometimes used to distinguish a person with quite severe reading problems from other remedial readers who may not have the presumed neurological problems. These terms have medical connotations and are more often used by physicians and by those who believe that reading problems are the result of biological (particularly neurological) problems. Part of the reason for the medical connotations is that students who have quite serious deficits are more likely to be taken to medical clinics than are students with less severe problems.

Problems with Reading Performance

Understanding exactly why students have trouble with reading should guide development of interventions that would overcome those fundamental stumbling blocks. After all, if there are some fundamental skills that students lack—some keys to learning to read that children with learning disabilities do not have—then we could focus on those skills and create interventions that would prevent reading problems.

Simply listening to a student read gives rise to many hypotheses about those key problems. As shown in Box 12.1, students make many different mistakes. Some of them seem to be based on the student diligently trying to make sense of the passage. For example, this boy substituted "a better idea" for "another idea," using a phrase that was common in television advertising at the time. Similarly, he worked hard to make the passage fit with the picture, as illustrated by his comment about the absence of an obvious rope. Also, he used some letters—usually the first letter of a word—to cue his reading.

Whereas much of the early emphasis in learning disabilities was on the apparent visual confusion of students with learning disabilities, we have since come to understand that these difficulties are not as fundamental in reading as we originally thought. Indeed, some mistakes that children make may appear to be visual but in fact could be the result of their difficulty with using language to label objects (see Hulme, 1988; Liberman & Shankweiler, 1979; Vellutino, 1977). For example, consider the familiar task in which a student is shown a row of designs that differ in only minor ways; the tester directs the student to choose a design that matches the left-most item in an array (see Figure 12.1). Children may perform poorly on this sort of task not only because they confuse the shapes, but also because they do not use for the objects verbal labels that help them remember the target object as they scan the choices. For example, for the first item, a student may use words to describe the sample ("Oh. A face under an ironing board.") and then repeat the description while scanning the choices. How might a student use language to help with the second example in the figure?

Vision problems have little to do with reading problems (American Academy of Ophthalmology, 1987, 1997). The deemphasis on visual aspects of reading should not be extended to the point of excluding all visual factors. On some visual tasks assessed in laboratories, there are differences between students with and without reading problems (Lovegrove, 1991). These disparities do not lead directly to remedial practices,

BOX 12.1 ***TIPS FOR PRACTICE***

How It Sounds to Hear a Student with Learning Disabilities Read

The following example shows what the reading of a student with learning disabilities sounds like. This passage was drawn from an elementary-level social studies textbook (Fiedler & Feeney, 1972, p. 211). Next to the passage were pictures of factory workers and automobiles with prominent white tires.

Here is what the student said:

> Then Ford had uh other i . . . a better idea. Take the worrrk to the men. He deee . . . A long rope was hooked onto the car . . . wheels . . . There's no rope on there. The rope pulled the car . . . auto . . . the white wheels along . . . pulled the car all along the way. Men stood still. Putting on car parts. Everybody man . . . put on, on, a few parts. Down the assembly line went the car. The assembly line saved . . . time. Cars costed still less to buh . . . bull . . . d . . . build. Ford cuts their prices on the Model T again.

Here is the actual passage the student was to read:

> Then Ford had another idea. Take the work to the men, he decided. A long rope was hooked onto a car axle and wheels. The rope pulled the axle and wheels along. All along the way, men stood still putting on car parts. Down the assembly line went the car. The assembly line saved more time. Cars cost still less to build. Ford cut the price of the Model T again.

Source: From *Introduction to Learning Disabilities,* 2nd ed. (p. 203) by D. P. Hallahan, J. M. Kauffman, and J. W. Lloyd, 1985, Upper Saddle River, NJ: Prentice-Hall. Copyright 1985. Reprinted by permission of Allyn & Bacon.

but even if they did, they would probably differ from those regularly advocated in the field of learning disabilities in the 1960s and 1970s (Blachman, 1997).

In contrast to the concern about the visual aspects of reading, a mounting body of evidence indicates that phonological aspects of language should be a greater concern. Evidence about phonology (Chapter 11) and working memory (Chapter 9) show that these aspects of language are important in reading. Although it is clear that capable readers must use other skills, phonological skills are especially important in the acquisition of reading.

FIGURE 12.1 Match-to-Sample Tasks Showing How Language Competence Might Help Students Even on What Appear to Be Visual Tasks

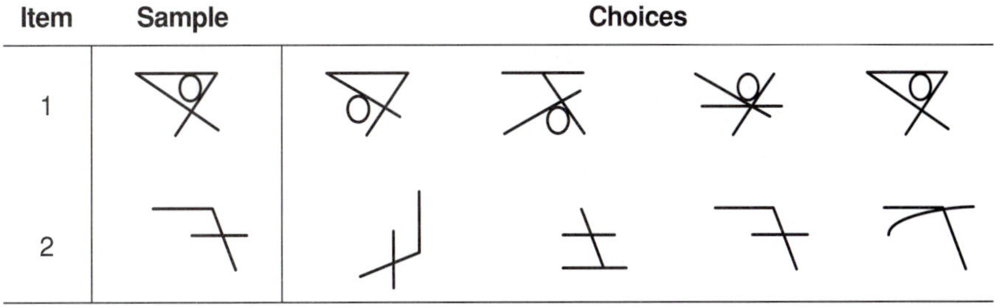

Plodding versus Problem Solving

The history of efforts to understand reading performance goes back even farther than Huey's (1908) classic book, *The Psychology and Pedagogy of Reading.* Throughout that history and into the present, there has been a tension between two opposing perspectives on what happens when a person reads. The conflicting theories about the psychology of reading have an interesting parallel with perspectives on reading instruction.

> At one pole stand those who claim that the reader is a plodder. He literally ploughs through text a letter at a time, building the words and sentences out of the individually identified phone-sized squiggles on the page; he converts the letters to sounds which are then formed into phonological representations, which in turn contact the previously learned meanings. This plodder view is essentially a speeded-up, smoothed-out version of what the stumbling first grader seems to do in "sounding out" the words of his primer. It is probably the common-sense view of any Phoenician on the Street. Because, on this account, meaning is derived through the systematic combination of minimal elements, the plodder view can be described as a "bottom up" approach. At the opposite extreme stand those romantics who view the reader as an explorer of the printed page. They suppose the fluent reader . . . looks at the printed page as he does at other aspects of the visual world, sampling selectively from among many available cues, developing expectations for words or meanings, seeking confirmation of these guesses and, in general, bringing to bear at all levels his considerable linguistic, intellectual, and perceptual skills. On this view, then, reading is more problem solving than plodding through phonology. Because the reader is here conceived as arriving at the details of the printed message after deriving its meaning, the explorer view can be characterized as a "top down" approach. (Rozin & Gleitman, 1977, p. 59)

These opposing views of reading stress different skills in explaining reading competence. The plodder view clearly depends more on phonology, whereas the explorer view depends more on syntax. As discussed in Chapter 11, students with learning disabilities have difficulties in both of these areas.

False Starts: Reversals and Modalities

The history of learning disabilities is full of attempts to identify factors that are key in reading problems. Many of these efforts have created "contention, false starts, fads, dead ends, [and] pseudoscience" (Stanovich, 1989, p. 487). Some attempts appear suspect from the start. For example, parents and teachers have been told that reading disabilities result from imperfect balance and atypical closure of the parts of the skull (see Worrall, 1990, for a critique). Such theories make many teachers roll their eyes. Other questionable ideas, however, have received enthusiastic support.

Some ideas from learning disabilities have penetrated deeply into our society, going beyond the field itself. Perhaps one of the most widely accepted ideas is that certain kinds of mistakes—particularly reversals—in reading and writing indicate that a student has learning disabilities. Most people have heard someone say "Oh, it's just my LD coming out" as an explanation for transposing letters or numbers. In the case of reversals, this is probably not true. If one considers the percentage of total errors that are reversal errors, students with reading problems make no more of these than their peers who read relatively well. Students with reading problems make more errors of all types, and thus they make more reversal errors (e.g., Fischer, Liberman, & Shankweiler, 1978; Holmes & Peper, 1977).

Beliefs that reversals indicate learning disabilities is only one of several myths that have permeated the treatment of reading problems. Another false start has been the pervasive notion that learning styles based on modalities should guide instruction. Multimodality instruction has been a topic of discussion in learning disabilities since the pioneering work of such luminaries as Orton (1937), Hegge, Kirk, and Kirk (1970), and Fernald (1943). According to this theory, if students who have different learning styles are given instruction that matches their styles, learning should be easier for them (Lloyd, 1984). Thus, students who are considered to have strengths in the visual aspects of information processing—those who might score higher on tasks that require visual skills than they would on those that require auditory skills—would be considered visual learners; they should get visual instruction. Those whose patterns of scores were the opposite—auditory higher than visual—would be considered auditory learners; they should get auditory instruction. Visual instruction would emphasize the shapes of words; auditory instruction would emphasize the phonology.

According to advocates of learning styles (e.g., Barbe & Milone, 1980; Carbo, 1990; Wepman, 1964), matching instruction to individuals' learning styles should result in greater reading achievement—"different strokes for different folks." In the 1970s, many teachers were taught to believe that consideration of modalities was important and that research supported it (Arter & Jenkins, 1977). As appealing as the learning styles approach may be, though, it has little if any empirical support (Arter & Jenkins, 1977; Bateman, 1979; Kavale & Forness, 1987b; Snider, 1992; Tarver & Dawson, 1978; Ysseldyke, 1973). Of course, advocates of learning styles (e.g., Carbo, 1990; Dunn, 1990; Dunn, Griggs, Olson, Beasley, & Gorman, 1995) disputed these conclusions.

Problems with Aspects of Language

Not only do students who have problems with reading have poor prospects for later learning, but they often have other related problems as well. Although a few do not, most students with reading problems also have difficulties with aspects of written expression. They often have barely legible handwriting, spell poorly, and compose simplistic and disorganized written products.

Students who have reading problems also are likely to have difficulties with some aspects of language. It makes sense that students with reading problems will have difficulties with written expression: Both written expression and reading depend on some of the same aspects of language. One aspect of written expression, spelling, requires many skills that are similar to those used in the decoding aspects of reading. Among these are phonological awareness, blending, and letter-sound correspondences. However, these skills are used somewhat differently for spelling. For example, the letter-sound skill used in reading requires pupils to see a letter and say a sound; in spelling, it requires them to hear a sound and write a letter. Nevertheless, spelling and reading are intimately connected, and students who have difficulty with reading are likely to have problems with spelling. Students with learning disabilities have significantly poorer spelling skills and produce more unrecognizable spellings than their nondisabled peers (Carpenter, 1983; Carpenter & Miller, 1982). Although in one study the former appeared to be using the same cognitive processes as their more capable peers, their spellings usually resembled those of younger children (Bruck, 1988).

Reading and writing are both language-based tools. Hence, teachers can expect that some of the problems that students experience in acquiring skill with them will be related to problems with the fundamental aspects of language. Indeed, the phonologic, syntactic, and semantic aspects of language are very important in understanding reading problems.

Problems with Phonological Awareness

Since the 1970s, when psychologists began in earnest to study the cognitive aspects of reading, more and more emphasis has been placed on children's competence in manipulating the phonemes of our language. One of the most consistent findings in the recent research on reading problems has been that phonological skills are intimately linked to reading skill (Muter, 1998; Perfetti, 1991; Snider, 1995; Wagner & Torgesen, 1987; see also Chapter 11).

Many authorities in reading and learning disabilities (e.g., Chall, 1967; Chall, Roswell, & Blumenthal, 1963; Engelmann, 1967a; Myklebust, Bannochie, & Killen, 1971) recognized the importance of phonological awareness before the 1970s. The work of the cognitive psychologists strengthened the argument that children must gain skill in manipulating the phonemes of our language if they are to become capable readers. More recent developments make it clear that deficits in phonological awareness play a central role in the problems of students who have difficulty learning to read (Liberman & Shankweiler, 1991).

Cognitive psychologists stressed the importance of phonological awareness in the development of early reading skills. Ball and Blachman (1991) described the importance of phonological awareness in this way:

> The student must come to realize that words can be broken into syllables and phonemes, and that the phoneme is the unit in the speech stream represented by the symbols in an alphabetic script. To a person with a well-developed phoneme awareness, our alphabetic system appears to be a reasonable way to represent our language. To those with little or no phoneme awareness, the system probably appears arbitrary. (p. 51)

Despite its importance, the role of phonological awareness should be kept in perspective. Words are not identified simply by applying phonological rules. Children apparently use analogies between words to derive the pronunciation of some words (Goswami, 1991, 1998). In theory, students read by analogy when they use what they know about some words to determine the pronunciation of others; in practical terms, use of analogies is particularly evident when children read rhyming words. Although phonological awareness does not necessarily predict later skill in reading words by analogy (Muter, Snowling, & Taylor, 1993), some fundamental decoding skills are required to be able to read words in this way (Ehri & Robbins, 1992). Competent readers probably use multiple sources of information—letter features, letters themselves, phonemes, groups of letters, and even words—almost simultaneously when identifying words. Sensible models of word identification (Perfetti, 1991; Stanovich, 1980) stress that readers probably use enough of the phonological representation to derive the word's pronunciation and make a connection to its meaning; the context confirms the meaning of the word.

Fluent decoding requires great skill with the phonological aspects of language. Without it, reading problems abound. Many difficulties with reading comprehension can be attributed to poor decoding skills. If one does not read accurately, then one will have trouble getting meaning from what one reads. If one does not read fluently and smoothly—that is, if one . . . reads . . . haltingly with . . . lots . . . of . . . pauses—then the meaning of a passage may be obscured. Imagine how hard it would be for the child described in Box 12.1 to understand what he read.

Problems with Syntax

Syntax refers to the grammatical structure of language, whether spoken or written (see Chapter 11). Although there are many other aspects of syntax that make differences in our language, one—word order—helps illustrate the importance of syntax. The sentence "Jane kissed John" means something different from "John kissed Jane" or from "John was kissed by Jane." The slight differences in the relationships among the words modify the meaning in subtle but important ways. Clearly, even if one can read one of these sentences without hesitation but still has difficulty understanding the subtleties of syntax, one might get the wrong idea from the sentences.

Psychological perspectives on reading vary in their emphases on the influences of syntax and phonology. There is a tension between phonology and syntax in understanding what transpires when someone reads—what happens between the brief time the eye sees the printed page and the reader speaks words corresponding to that print (Gough, 1972). In part, this is the tension described in the quotation on plodding and exploring earlier in this chapter.

Some students who have decoding problems have difficulty with certain aspects of syntax, particularly morphology. Students who read neither accurately nor fluently apparently also have difficulty with the kinds of tasks illustrated in Figure 11.1, especially those tasks that use nonsense words (Lovett, 1987). These findings are essentially consistent with early research showing similar difficulties (e.g., Kass, 1966). It is interesting to speculate that the automatic skills required in giving morphological variations of words may also be required in fluent, accurate decoding.

Problems with understanding the syntax of written sentences probably are involved in students' problems with reading comprehension. When reading, older students make greater use of syntax than do younger readers (Resnick, 1970). Students with reading problems do not use the clusters of words that occur in English to guide their phrasing of what they read (Clay & Imlach, 1971) and make other mistakes that indicate they are not using syntax to help make sense of passages (Pflaum & Bryan, 1981). However, when students with reading problems are compared with younger peers who have the same level of decoding skills, they are just as adept at using semantic and syntactic cues (Stanovich, Cunningham, & Freeman, 1984). In fact, they may depend upon these aspects of language too much. Thus, their understanding of what they read apparently is not inhibited as much by their problems with syntax as it is by their problems with decoding.

Problems with Semantics

Semantic cues, which refer to the meaning of language, are bits of ideas that help one understand the ideas of a passage and also help one decode. For example, consider the following sentence: "The student turned in her ______." The meaning of the first part of the sentence helps reduce the number of possible words that could complete the sentence. The missing word probably will not be "pajamas" or "ear" because those have little to do with students and school. It is not likely to be "grades" or "classroom" because teachers, not students, turn in grades, and almost no one turns in classrooms. A reader would find words such as "paper," "books," "homework," and "test" sensible.

That reading comprehension is greatly influenced by decoding skills seems obvious, and research supports the logical connection between the two. This connection between phonological skills and word meaning is quite high and appears causal (Lomax, 1983). Many students with comprehension deficits have inferior performance on tasks requiring simple reading of words (Perfetti & Hogoboam, 1975). Students with poor comprehension do not differ from their nondisabled peers in reading familiar words, but they are much slower in reading unfamiliar words (Golinkoff & Rosinski, 1976) and more likely to make mistakes that change the meaning of the passage (Pflaum & Bryan, 1981). When asked to reason aloud while deducing answers to comprehension questions, competent readers use efficient strategies and reach accurate conclusions; students with learning disabilities use inefficient strategies and produce incorrect answers. Furthermore, students with learning disabilities are hampered in reasoning out answers by their inaccurate decoding and impoverished vocabularies (Kavale, 1980).

One of the important assertions of advocates of the explorer approach (Rozin & Gleitman, 1977) is that children can use context (a combination of syntax and semantics) to guide their reading. According to an often-cited study (Goodman, 1965), children read words in context much better than they do in lists. People interpret these results as indicating that the context in the passages must have facilitated the decoding of words. More recent research (e.g., Nicholson, 1991) reveals that the facilitative improvement probably resulted from the research methods. In the original study, children always read the lists first. After they saw the words in the lists, reading them in the passages was easier, so they made fewer mistakes on words in passages. Actually, poor readers probably rely on context to compensate for their deficits in decoding (e.g., Stanovich, 1980, 1986b).

Difficulties in reading comprehension may also have to do with deficits in vocabulary and general world knowledge. Even if one can decode words accurately and rapidly, a limited vocabulary can prevent making connections between words and their meanings. Many students with learning disabilities also have minor vocabulary deficits that contribute to their lower scores on comprehension tests (Ackerman, Peters, & Dykman, 1971; see also Chapter 11).

Unfortunately, the orthography of words (their spelling), which guides their pronunciation, does not help much in deriving their meaning. "One can learn to pronounce most written words, familiar or not, by learning the rules that relate spelling and sound . . . [but] word meaning must be learned on a case-by-case basis" (Rueckl & Dror, 1994, p. 571). Effective programs can teach students to decode print, but it takes a powerful, sustained effort to overcome the deficits in vocabulary that some students also bring with them to school (Becker, 1977). The implication is plain: Teachers must not only teach decoding competence; they must also teach vocabulary (and other aspects of reading comprehension).

In addition to vocabulary, other factors also influence students' understanding of what they can decode. General knowledge about the world—what is often called *world knowledge*—affects reading comprehension. Students may use their previous experiences of events or situations to guide comprehension (Williams, 1991). For example, a student who has taken train trips would likely have an easier time understanding a reading assignment about a surly conductor than would a student who has traveled only by car or bus.

The reading problems of students with learning disabilities cannot be attributed solely to phonemic difficulties; they can also stem from problems with comprehension. Students with learning disabilities may have difficulty associating printed words with their meanings, a factor that is clearly important in understanding text (Perfetti, 1991). Students with learning disabilities also use language comprehension strategies less well than their more skilled peers and have trouble determining the underlying themes of materials they read. These difficulties are related to students' abilities to monitor their own understanding of what they read (Garner, 1980).

One possible reason that students with learning disabilities have greater difficulty with **gist comprehension**—understanding the theme of a narrative—is that their background knowledge intrudes too much into their interpretation of what they read. For example, whereas students without learning disabilities might base their interpretations on the information in the passage they have read, some students with learning disabilities might focus on a thematically less important part of the passage because of its similarity to something in their own experiences. Students may read a passage about a child who wears a blue sweater and is supposed to remember to buy cat food on the way home. The child in the story forgets to buy the food and then feels miserable when it is time to feed the family kitten. Although most students would focus on the theme of responsibility for pets, some students with reading problems may focus on less relevant parts of the passage. For example, asked to discuss the meaning of the passage, a student with learning disabilities might reply, "Oh, yeah. I had a blue sweater. One day I wore it and it got dirty at school. My mama was mad at me." Students who often make idiosyncratic responses make more mistakes in identifying the themes of passages they read. Students with learning disabilities have specific difficulty getting the main points of the passages and are somewhat more likely to give answers that reflect idiosyncratic information (Williams, 1991).

These findings indicate that instruction for students with learning disabilities should be comprehensive and thorough. As developed in Chapter 1, there are no magic solutions in learning disabilities. Despite the great importance of such factors as phonological awareness in understanding reading problems, learning disabilities will not be overcome by identifying and remediating one simple key factor. Teachers must not only teach rudimentary reading skills, but also probably will have to teach students higher-order thinking skills. (See Carnine & Kameenui, 1992, for valuable discussions on teaching higher-order thinking.)

WHAT IS THE PREVALENCE OF STUDENTS WITH READING DIFFICULTIES?

Some authorities suggest that reading disabilities are quite common, affecting from 15% to 20% or more of children and adolescents (Lyon, 1997). Determining exactly how many students have reading disabilities depends on the same variables that influence estimates of the prevalence of learning disabilities, including (1) how the problem is defined, (2) how it is measured, and (3) how samples are selected to study prevalence.

By definition, learning disabilities are based on a discrepancy between ability and achievement, so their prevalence will be influenced by how one measures ability. Should IQ be used as the marker of ability in identifying dyslexia (Joshi, Williams, & Wood, 1998; Stanovich, 1991; see also Chapter 1)? If dyslexia is defined using a different marker of ability (say, oral comprehension instead of IQ), different prevalence estimates would emerge from the same sample of pupils. Nevertheless, discrepancies between IQ and achievement are used to estimate the prevalence of disabilities.

Studies of the prevalence of reading disabilities indicate that between 6.2% and 7.5% of children have reading achievement scores that are substantially lower than their IQs (Lewis, Hitch, & Walker, 1994; Shaywitz, Shaywitz, Fletcher, & Escobar, 1990). Although not all students whose aptitude-achievement discrepancies are this great will be identified as having learning disabilities, many of them will. There are also likely to be other students (e.g., those with arithmetic problems) who would qualify for learning disability services but who do not have highly discrepant scores between ability and reading measures.

Differences in the prevalence of reading disabilities by gender is another matter of concern. In some studies, strict formulas for classifying students as having reading disabilities reveal about equal numbers of boys and girls. However, when one counts the number of children receiving services instead of using the strict research formula, more boys than girls are classified (Shaywitz et al., 1990). The difference between school- and research-identified cases appears to be a consequence of differential referral of boys and girls for services, probably prompted by the boys' behavior (Shaywitz et al., 1990). In other studies, however, research-based formulas reveal that boys outnumber girls about two to one (Lewis et al., 1994). Because we know that teachers base referral on more than just reading problems (Speece & Cooper, 1990), we can suspect that other factors such as behavior contribute to the differences between prevalence numbers based on teacher referrals and tests.

Another factor affecting prevalence is the interplay of reading disabilities with learning disabilities. There almost surely are some students who would meet the standards for having a reading disability but who might not be identified as having learning disabilities and some who would meet the standards for learning disabilities but not for reading disabilities. Students in the former group might have difficulties that are not severe enough to warrant special education services, and those in the latter group might have disabilities in other areas. That most, but not all, students with learning disabilities have problems with reading reinforces the theme that individuals with learning disabilities form a diverse group (see Chapter 1).

HOW IS READING PERFORMANCE ASSESSED?

Assessment of reading performance may take many different forms, depending largely on the purpose of the assessment. Thus, different measures are employed according to whether the purpose of assessment is to identify students who may need additional services, to plan an instructional program, or to assess whether instructional practices are promoting better student performance. Comprehensive reading tests are often used to screen students. More detailed tests—sometimes called diagnostic instruments—are usually used to gather data to plan programs. Curriculum-based assessment is the most useful means of monitoring progress.

Despite the seeming straightforwardness of these assessment goals, no simple set of rules or practices guides the assessment of reading skills. Assessment is complicated by such factors as the level of the student being assessed, the theoretical model of assessment used, and the nature of reading.

Comprehensive Measures

Schools identify students as having learning disabilities so that the identified students can receive additional services. To identify these students, schools must screen large numbers of students and then evaluate these individuals more closely to determine eligibility (see Chapter 4).

Some school systems develop explicit practices for assessing students' reading competence and then examining more closely those whose reading skills fall below a certain level (say, the 20th percentile). To identify students in this way, schools use screening tests, particularly general achievement batteries such as the *Iowa Tests of Basic Skills* (Hieronymus, Hoover, & Lindquist, 1986) and the *Metropolitan Achievement Tests—7th Edition* (Balow, Farr, & Hogan, 1992). However, individually administered achievement batteries such as the *Peabody Individual Achievement Test—Revised*, or PIAT (Markwardt, 1989), and the *Woodcock-Johnson Psychoeducational Battery—Revised* (Woodcock & Johnson, 1989/1990), as well as some devoted specifically to diagnosing reading problems, probably are the instruments most commonly used to identify students.

Although tests may help identify students who need to be assessed more carefully, teachers are often key in screening for referral and initiate nearly 75% of referrals for special education (Lloyd et al., 1991). Teachers' judgments may be imperfect, but they more than anyone else have experience with a wide range of students and usually with the student in question (Gerber & Semmel, 1984). Furthermore, they are sensitive to subtle variations in student characteristics that may not be evident from standardized testing.

Teachers probably do not base their evaluations on reading performance alone (Cooper & Speece, 1988; Speece & Cooper, 1990), but many of the important clues in identifying reading problems have to do with reading performance. Although some clues are false leads (e.g., reversals of letters' orientation or letter order do not indicate learning disabilities), others are particularly important. Students' oral reading proficiency provides probably the most valuable indication of reading competence.

Given that reading rate is important as an index of fluency and as an indicator of comprehension, teachers need guidelines for assessing it. Table 12.1 provides guidelines for reading speeds at different age levels that permit adequate comprehension of text (Carnine, Silbert, & Kameenui, 1996; Lovett, 1987). Teachers can use these to ascertain whether a student's reading fluency is weak enough to merit further evaluation and remediation.

Diagnosing Problems and Planning Programs

Planning reading programs requires that one assess performance. Planning based on trait theory is usually not as valuable as planning based on direct measurement. Diagnostic reading assessment may be directed at identifying causes of problems, but it is probably more profitably focused on identifying precisely what reading skills students lack.

Knowing the causes of students' disabilities rarely provides instructional guidance (see Chapter 2). Instead, teachers need to identify those factors they can manipulate—instructional factors—and plan reading programs accordingly. Assessment for

TABLE 12.1 General Guidelines for Evaluating Independent-Level Fluency of Reading

Student's Grade[a]	Rate (words per minute)	Errors (words per minute)	Notes
1	50–60	1–2	In the earlier months of first grade, rate may be lower.
2	75–100	1–2	Generally, during second grade, students' fluency should increase rapidly. They should move from the lower end of this range toward the higher end as the year progresses.
3	130–140	1–3	At this rate, the students are reading quite fluently. If a student is in the second half of the third grade and reads below 100 wpm on third-grade material, she or he probably needs instruction in decoding.
4–12	150–175	1–3	At the higher grade levels, students will not read much faster, but they should be able to maintain fluent reading even as the text becomes more complex.

[a]Student fluency is evaluated based on the student reading a passage of text at his or her grade level.

program planning often requires using diagnostic tests, informal reading inventories, and clinical teaching.

Diagnostic Testing

When diagnosing and planning programs, many teachers of students with learning disabilities use tests in hopes of identifying more specific deficits. Table 12.2 describes some instruments used by teachers to help diagnose reading problems. As the table shows, diagnostic tests in reading are usually composed of several subtests that are designed to measure specific parts of general reading skill. For example, a diagnostic test may include subtests of letter recognition, word recognition, reading rate, and comprehension. If a student has lower scores on some subtests than on others, he or she is judged to be weaker in those areas, and the teacher might prescribe specific remedial activities accordingly.

Diagnosing specific reading problems requires teachers to go beyond simply administering tests. They must interpret the results carefully. Unfortunately, sometimes those charged with administering diagnostic tests and recommending or planning programs for students with disabilities may not follow the most desirable practices. For example, psychologists' recommendations sometimes are unrelated to data about

TABLE 12.2 Examples of Tests of Specific Reading Areas

Test	Areas Assessed	Age Range[a]
■ Phonological Awareness		
Test of Awareness of Language Segments (Sawyer, 1987)	Segmenting sentences into words, words into syllables, and words into sounds	5–17 years
Test of Phonological Awareness (Torgesen & Bryant, 1994)	Segmenting	Grades K–2
■ Oral Reading		
Gilmore Oral Reading Test (Gilmore & Gilmore, 1968)	Oral reading accuracy, words per minute, and comprehension	Grades 1–8
Gray Oral Reading Test—3rd Ed. (Wiederholt & Bryant, 1992)	Rate, accuracy, and comprehension	7-0 to 18-11 years
■ Diagnostic Batteries		
Gates-McKillop-Horowitz Reading Diagnostic Tests (Gates, McKillop, & Horowitz, 1981)	Oral reading, word reading (flash and untimed), word attack, blending, auditory discrimination, written expression	Grades 1–6
Stanford Diagnostic Reading Tests—4th Ed. (Karlsen & Gardner, 1995)	Phonetic analysis, vocabulary, comprehension, and scanning	Grades 1.5–12.9
Woodcock Reading Mastery Tests—Rev. Ed. (Woodcock, 1987)	Visual-auditory learning, letter identification, word identification, word attack, word comprehension, passage comprehension	Grades K–16 plus adults
Woodcock Diagnostic Reading Battery (Woodcock, 1997)	Letter-word identification, word attack, reading vocabulary, passage comprehension, incomplete words, sound blending, oral vocabulary, listening comprehension, memory for sentences, and visual matching	5-0 through 9-0 years
■ Reading Comprehension		
Test of Reading Comprehension—3rd Ed. (Brown, Hammill, & Wiederholt, 1995)	General vocabulary, syntactic similarities, paragraph reading, sentence sequencing, mathematics vocabulary, social studies vocabulary, science vocabulary, and reading directions	7-0 to 17-11 years

[a]Age in years–months format

children's performance; rather, their prescriptions reflect their personal experiences with students who have learning disabilities (Bus & Kruizenga, 1989).

Individual diagnostic testing probably yields more useful information than group tests (Lloyd, Cameron, & Lloyd, 1984). Some of the same instruments that may be used for screening also provide diagnostic information. Individually administered achievement batteries, such as the PIAT (Markwardt, 1989), give scores on separate aspects of reading—decoding and comprehending. The *Woodcock-Johnson Psychoeducational Battery—Revised* (Woodcock & Johnson, 1989/1990) provides scores on some of the component skills in reading, including prereading skills, word recognition, and passage comprehension.

Other useful tests for individually assessing students' reading competence are expressly designed as diagnostic instruments. For example, the *Roswell-Chall Diagnostic Test of Word Analysis Skills* (Roswell & Chall, 1978) is designed for use with young children and gives information about skill in reading words and letters as well as assessing decoding and encoding skills. Similarly, the *Woodcock Diagnostic Reading Battery* (Woodcock, 1997), which follows from the widely used *Woodcock Reading Mastery Tests* (Woodcock, 1973), provides many useful scores. By judiciously employing tests such as these, as well as informal methods, teachers can identify appropriate areas for instruction.

Students at the upper elementary and higher grades already know a lot about reading; they simply make many mistakes, reading some words correctly sometimes and misreading them at other times. These mistakes probably reflect a greater deficit in computational knowledge than in phonological awareness (Perfetti, 1991). In such cases, formal diagnostic testing may be of less value. Such mistakes in decoding will be quite obvious if a teacher administers an informal reading inventory.

Informal Reading Inventories

An informal reading inventory (IRI) is a series of reading passages or word lists graded in order of difficulty. A student reads from the series of lists or passages, beginning with one the teacher thinks is likely to be easy. If the student reads well at a given level, the teacher gives the next most difficult level; the student continues to progress through increasingly more difficult lists or passages until she or he is making many mistakes.

As the student reads, the teacher monitors performance and the kinds of errors being made (e.g., omitted word, mispronunciation, hesitation). If the IRI is composed of passages, the teacher may ask questions to probe the student's understanding of the material. The teacher records the errors and answers for later scrutiny.

The mistakes students make in reading during IRIs can be classified. Figure 12.2 shows a classification system. Such a system not only provides an informal perspective about a student's strengths and weaknesses, but also can suggest the reasons for some errors. Such information aids in designing instructional interventions to address deficits. For example, if a student makes many mistakes on words involving vowel conversions (e.g., con → cone, rid → ride), the teacher might plan specific instructional

FIGURE 12.2 System for Classifying IRI Mistakes

Error Pattern Checklist: Specific-Level Procedure 4

Compare each error in the passage to the checklist (ignore errors on proper names). Make a mark next to the category in which the error seems to fit. Identify the strategic categories in which most errors occur and begin additional testing in those areas. Continue to monitor changes in error patterns.

Error Categories	No. Errors
Mispronunciations	
Errors are substitutions of real words	
Errors are not real words	
Errors are phonetically similar to stimulus word	
Insertions	
Insertions are contextually appropriate	
Insertions are contextually inappropriate	
Omissions	
Omission affects passage meaning	
Omission does not affect meaning	
Hesitation	
Repetition	
Repeats a portion of a target word	
Repeats preceding word	
Repeats preceding words or phrases	
Does not attend to punctuation	
Does not pause at punctuation	
Pauses at end of line	
Self-corrects	

Directions for Using the Error Pattern Checklist

Use the Error Pattern Checklist to categorize all decoding errors made on the passage. Ask yourself what the most probable reading strategy explanation is for each error. Check it off by marking the appropriate category. If more than two errors were made on a word, categorize only the first two.

Question	Recommendation
1. Are there clear patterns of errors?	If yes, correct the erroneous pattern by targeting it as an instructional objective.

Content Error Checklist: Specific-Level Procedure 5

Compare the words in the passage to the student's errors and categorize errors by content area and content subskill. Make a mark next to the subskill indicated by each error. Do not record more than two errors per word. Identify the content areas in which the most errors occurred and begin additional testing in those areas. Continue to monitor changes in error patterns.

Content Categories	No. Errors
Words: Errors involving whole words	
Polysyllabic Words	
Contractions	
Compound Words	
Sight Words	
Silent Letters	
Units: Errors involving combined letter units	
Endings (Suffixes)	
Clusters	
R-controlled Vowels	
Vowel Teams	
Consonant Digraphs	
Consonant Teams	
CVC Words	
Conversions: Errors involving sound modification	
Double Consonant Words	
Vowel + e Conversions	
Sounds: Errors involving individual letters and sounds	
Vowels	
Consonants	
Sequence	
Sounds	
Symbols	

Directions for Using the Content Error Checklist

Use the Content Error Checklist to categorize all errors made on the passage. Ask yourself what the most probable content explanation is for each error. Decide what content category the error is from and check it off by marking the appropriate category. If more than two errors were made on a word, categorize only the first two.

Question	Recommendation
1. Are there identifiable problems of content?	If yes, conduct specific-level testing of decoding skills reflected in the errors.

Source: From *Curriculum-Based Evaluation for Special and Remedial Education: A Handbook for Deciding What to Teach* (p. 216) by K. W. Howell and M. K. Morehead, 1987, Columbus, OH: Merrill. Copyright 1987 by Merrill Publishing Co. Reprinted by permission.

lessons to help the student read words of this spelling pattern correctly (Deno, 1997; Howell & Davidson, 1997; Howell, Fox, & Morehead, 1993; Howell & Morehead, 1987; Howell, Zucker, & Morehead, 1985).

One result of administering an IRI is that the teacher can estimate the appropriate grade or difficulty level of material to assign a student for reading practice. Table 12.1 gives reading rates teachers can use to help determine grade level. Instructional methods textbooks in reading also suggest ways to classify reading materials on the basis of reading rate, accuracy, and comprehension as being at a student's independent, instructional, or frustration levels. In combination with curriculum-based measures of performance (Howell et al., 1993), teachers can use IRI data to assign appropriate reading materials for students (often referred to as "placing" the student in the curriculum).

When teachers determine students' reading materials based on their performance on IRIs, their decisions are consistent with assignments made on the basis of traditional test scores (Eaton & Lovitt, 1972; Lovitt & Fantasia, 1980). Lovitt and Hansen (1976a) demonstrated how IRI techniques can be used to make careful and useful decisions about placing students in reading materials. They selected passages from books in a reading series and wrote comprehension questions for each passage. Students then read passages at each level for several days. Lovitt and Hansen placed learners in the books from which they correctly read an average of 45 to 60 words per minute with 4 to 8 errors per minute and for which they could answer 50% to 75% of the comprehension questions. These researchers found that it was possible to assign students to readers in a way that allowed them not only to read with little frustration, but also to work through challenging materials (Lovitt & Hansen, 1976b).

Clinical Teaching

The methods used by Lovitt and his colleagues are sometimes called clinical (or trial) teaching because they are based on specific experiences with individual students. Sometimes clinical teaching is used in a pejorative way to refer to flying by the seat of one's pants. In the seminal work by Lovitt and his colleagues (Haring, Lovitt, Eaton, & Hansen, 1976), however, the methods are carefully shaped by applied behavior analysis.

Clinical teaching is surely the most informal method of assessment. In it, one tests students' performances by presenting lessons and observing whether they succeed (Lloyd & Blandford, 1991). Clinical teaching requires a teacher to sequence lessons carefully so each successive lesson is more difficult than the last and easier than the next. If students perform well on one lesson but have trouble with subsequent ones, the teacher knows to begin instruction at the point where they began having difficulty. Because it is integral to instruction, clinical teaching should be a fundamental part of assessment for instructional planning (Howell & Davidson, 1997; Zigmond & Miller, 1986).

Clinical teaching as an assessment strategy should focus first on a student's most likely problem areas. As concerns decoding, these areas would include phonological awareness, letter–sound knowledge, single-word decoding (perhaps of both real and nonsense words), and passage reading. Regarding comprehension, clinical teaching should focus on the extent to which students remember information from what they have read; comprehension can be assessed most extensively by having students retell orally the content of a passage they have read.

Monitoring Student Progress

As with clinical teaching and informal reading inventories, progress-monitoring systems for assessing students' progress can be constructed using classroom reading materials. They can be program specific (designed to monitor specific areas) or can employ curriculum-based assessment methods.

Monitoring progress is an important part of reading instruction because it allows teachers to make changes in reading programs according to individual student needs. If students are behind their peers—and students with learning disabilities are—they are unlikely to begin catching up by working on skills and knowledge they already have acquired. If they are working on new material and making little progress, it is probably wise to change the instruction they are receiving rather than continue with ineffective teaching practices (Deno, 1997).

Sadly, progress is monitored too infrequently and too haphazardly. Monitoring should consist of more than a teacher's opinion about a student's improvement or lack of it. It should be systematic and consistent. The students of teachers who use curriculum-based assessment (CBA) to monitor progress have higher scores than about two-thirds of the students whose teachers do not use it (Fuchs & Fuchs, 1986b).

Although touted by some as a way to monitor progress, portfolio assessment is useful in only some ways with reading. Portfolios work well when students do something that can be captured and maintained—that is, when they create a product, such as an essay. But much of reading performance is ephemeral; teachers may listen to their students read aloud or retell the contents of a passage, but they have no product of these performances unless they make audio- or videotape recordings of them.

We can and should preserve the products related to some reading performances. For example, when students write book reports, we have a permanent product from which we can glimpse their reading skills, but such products as book reports primarily reflect writing skills. So we must look to the progress-monitoring systems that are built into some programs or to curriculum-based assessments developed by teachers for means of keeping tabs on how students are progressing.

Reading Program Assessments

In keeping with the popularity of portfolio assessment, some reading instruction programs have incorporated systems for monitoring progress within the reading program. For example, Heath Literacy (Alvermann et al., 1995) provides assessment guides to accompany each of the levels of its reading programs; in one section of the manuals, under the heading Ongoing Assessment, there are directions for portfolio assessments, evaluations of writing, and tests of dictation and writing as well as recommendations for conducting observations, preparing anecdotal records, holding conferences, and administering self-assessments. Other traditional reading programs, such as Connections (Macmillan Publishing Company, 1987), provide unit tests to be administered at specific times during the school year (e.g., at midyear, end of the year, etc.). Teachers are advised to set aside entire class periods for testing; test items resemble the familiar multiple-choice items.

In contrast, the mastery tests that accompany the Corrective Reading Program, or CRP (Engelmann, Becker, Hanner, & Johnson, 1988), are scheduled to occur much more frequently (about every five days) and are brief and explicitly connected to what students have been learning. Figure 12.3 gives an example of a mastery test from CRP. This test would be given as part of a regular lesson, and students would read the words independently. Based on their performance, the teacher would continue to the next lesson or repeat the lesson to address any difficulties. Depending on their performance as a group, students may complete one level of the program in as few as 30 days by skipping unneeded lessons or as many as 70 days by adding extra practice for those who need it. The mastery tests also allow teachers to restructure groups. For example,

FIGURE 12.3 Example of Mastery Test from the Corrective Reading Program

Mastery test 5

Note: Test each student individually. Administer the test so that the other students do not overhear the student being tested.

me

Task A Vowel variations: ē

1. **First tell me the sound the letter makes in the word and then tell me the word.**
2. Point to **e** in **me**. **What sound?** Touch. *ēēē*.
3. (Test item.) Touch the ball of the arrow. **What word?** Slash right. *Me.*
4. Repeat steps 2 and 3 for **the, she.**

the

she

met

Task B Vowel variations: ĕ

1. Point to **e** in **met**. **This letter does not say ēēē in the words you're going to read now.**
2. Point to **e** in **met**. **This letter says ĕĕĕ. What sound?** Touch. *ĕĕĕ*.
3. (Test item.) Touch the ball of the arrow. **What word?** Slash right. *Met.*
4. Repeat steps 2 and 3 for **them, shed.**

them

shed

Evaluating results

If more than 25 percent of the students missed any words, repeat lessons 24 and 25. Then retest.

Source: From *Corrective Reading* (p. 119–120) by S. Englemann, W. C. Becker, S. Hanner, and G. Johnson, 1988, Chicago: Science Research Associates. Copyright 1988 by Science Research Associates. Reprinted by permission.

if one student in a group is performing at a high level, the teacher can move him or her to a higher group to facilitate progress.

Curriculum-Based Assessments

Curriculum-based assessment has been part of the learning disabilities field since the 1960s. Much of the early impetus for this approach came from work by Lovitt (1967) and Deno (Deno & Mirkin, 1977), which was continued and amplified by others as well as by Lovitt and Deno themselves (e.g., Fuchs & Deno, 1991; Haring et al., 1976; Lovitt & Fantasia, 1980; Starlin, 1971). Although distinctions can be made among different variants of what might be called direct assessment (Fuchs & Deno, 1991), CBA and its cousins, applied behavior analysis (Lovitt, 1975) and precision teaching (Starlin, 1971), share the same basic tenets. (See Chapter 4 for an in-depth discussion of CBA.)

To use CBA in reading, teachers have students read aloud several times a week for perhaps 2 minutes at a time. Although it is not mandatory (Fuchs & Deno, 1994), the reading passages for CBA assessments usually are taken directly from the school's reading materials.

Assessment procedures such as CBA compare favorably with traditional achievement tests in reading. Not only do CBA reading measures correlate highly with achievement test scores, but they also permit teachers to gather other useful information. As stressed by Howell et al. (1993), such measures permit teachers to make their instruction more efficient, thus helping students progress at an optimal pace.

HOW SHOULD BEGINNING LITERACY BE TAUGHT?

Preventing reading failure among young children should be one of the foremost goals in education. This relates to the idea that it is the educator's responsibility to minimize poor teaching practices. Although there is not a consensus on what methods permit us to prevent or remediate reading problems, specialists in learning disabilities have provided some evidence about important features of effective practices in reading instruction.

Beginning reading instruction has been beset by many disputes and much controversy. Some of the public outcry about reading instruction that accompanied the publication of *Why Johnny Can't Read and What You Can Do About It* (Flesch, 1955, 1981) probably contributed to the founding of the field of learning disabilities. In her classic book on reading instruction, Chall (1967) described the fundamental issues:

> What is the best way to teach a young child to read? No two people, it seems, agree on the answer.
>
> For over a decade almost every basic issue in beginning reading instruction—how to begin, when to begin, what instructional materials to use, how to organize classes for instruction—has been debated with intense heat and considerable rancor. . . . Each side has claimed that it knows how to give our children "the best"

in reading instruction. And in the United States, where dedication to the best is tantamount to belief in democracy, the debate has often taken on political proportions. (p. 1)

Of the various approaches stressed from the 1950s through the 1970s, the whole-word approach was originally the most popular, but it was challenged by the linguistic, language experience, and code-emphasis approaches:

- Whole-word approach. Advocates of this approach did not want to divert students from getting meaning from the text. Teaching decoding was considered a dull, mechanical approach to reading that would turn students away from reading for meaning. The whole-word approach was also called the "sight" or "look-say" method and was a meaning-emphasis approach.
- Linguistic approach. Advocates of the linguistic view argued that children need to get meaning, but acknowledged that they also have to learn to decode. However, materials consistent with the linguistic approach (e.g., Fries, 1963) did not break words into letters and sounds. Instead, to help students learn the code, these materials presented words with rhyming patterns in story form (e.g., "Nat the fat cat sat on a mat").
- Language experience approach (LEA). Advocates of this view contended that learning to read is a natural part of language development. Instruction in reading should begin with material that is meaningful to students, particularly stories that they dictate. This was the main forerunner of today's whole-language approach.
- Code-emphasis approach. Advocates of a code-emphasis, or phonics, view argued that students should be explicitly taught the component skills of decoding (sounds for letters, blending, etc.) at the very beginning of reading instruction. They contended that students can learn these aspects of reading and quickly progress to reading meaningful text.

Research on alternative approaches to beginning reading makes it clear that the reading method used to teach children will affect how they read. The mistakes students make when reading will almost certainly differ, depending on how they were taught to read (Adams, 1990). For example, the mistakes made by children who have had phonics-based (code-emphasis) instruction are likely to involve letters and letter sounds. The mistakes made by children who have had meaning-based (whole-word) instruction are likely to involve aspects of the context (e.g., syntax).

Over the last few decades, the linguistic and whole-word approaches have mostly disappeared as separate perspectives on reading. Many of the features of the linguistic approach merged with the code-emphasis approach, though some were subsumed under the whole-language approach. Most of the whole-word and language experience approaches merged with the whole-language approach. The resultant two primary approaches to reading instruction today—the code-emphasis approach and the whole-language approach—are explored in the following sections.

Although most authorities now agree that children must receive at least some phonics instruction (see Adams, 1990), disagreements over reading instruction persist. Two of the most important areas of debate concern phonological awareness instruction and the character of initial instruction. Because phonological awareness training can be incorporated into either approach, we include a section on teaching phonological awareness.

Code-Emphasis Approach

Although a few writers would disagree (e.g., Carbo, 1990), most reading authorities concur that to become competent readers, children must master the fundamental building blocks of our written language. These include the following ideas:

- Written language represents spoken language ("talk written down").
- Words in our language can be segmented into sounds, and sounds can be blended into words.
- Letters represent sounds.

The last two of these fundamental building blocks of reading have to do with how our spoken language corresponds to our written language. Although there is some continuing controversy about which instructional practices are fundamental, which are frivolous, and which are more advanced, the general recommendations for effective teaching are clear (see Stahl, 1992). For beginning readers, the fundamental components of instruction include those revealed in a task analysis for **decoding** simple words (see Table 12.3).

Children who learn to use decoding strategies fluently and accurately (i.e., to convert printed language into oral language) will have less trouble understanding what they read. Accordingly, students with good word-reading skills should have high reading comprehension. This is consistent with evidence about the relationship between decoding and comprehension (e.g., Dykstra, 1968b; Perfetti & Hogoboam, 1975). Also, when students have learned code-cracking skills, they should be able to read most words they have not previously seen. Because students must read many words they never have seen previously, skill in figuring them out is very important to their reading progress. Those who cannot decode unknown words must depend on teachers, peers, parents, and others for help or must disregard the unknown words at the risk of not understanding what they are reading.

Virtually all publishers and authors of commercial reading series claim that decoding skills are taught as a part of their programs. However, those that emphasize teaching phonics can be discriminated from others by what they teach and how they teach it. An approach emphasizes decoding skills if it provides "intensive teaching of all the main sound-symbol relationships, both vowel and consonant, from the start of formal reading instruction" (Gurren & Hughes, 1965, p. 340). But some code-emphasis programs go beyond teaching the main sound-symbol relationships. For example, Glass (1971) rec-

TABLE 12.3 Task Analysis of Subskills for Word-Attack Strategy

■ **Objective** Given a page of regularly pronounced real CVC words, the student will say each word aloud at a rate of 40 words per minute with no more than 2 errors per minute

Examples: mat, fin, lop, dip, bet, can, rap

■ **Strategy** Start at beginning of the word and, moving to the right, say the sound for each letter; slide from one sound to the next without stopping between sounds and then say the word.

Steps	*Examples*
1. Start saying sounds at the beginning:	*mmm*
2. Move toward the right and slide into the next sound:	*mmmaaa*
3. Slide into the next sound:	*mmmaaannn*
4. Say the word:	*man*

■ **Objectives for Subskills Required for This Strategy**

Given a list of words, the student will point to the beginning of each word and move his or her finger in the direction of reading (toward the right) with 100% accuracy.

Given a page with individual letters arranged in no particular order, the student will say the most common sound for each letter at a rate of 40 letters per minute with no more than 2 errors per minute.

Given printed words, the student will say the sounds for each letter in each word, sliding from sound to sound without pausing between them with 100% accuracy.

Given a stretched-out pronunciation of a word (e.g., *sssiiit*), the student will say the word at a normal rate of speech for 10 out of 10 trials correctly.

Source: From *Introduction to Learning Disabilities,* 2nd ed. (p. 218) by D. P. Hallahan, J. M. Kauffman, and J. W. Lloyd, 1985, Upper Saddle River, NJ: Prentice-Hall. Copyright 1985. Reprinted by permission of Allyn & Bacon.

ommends teaching frequently occurring letter clusters such as *ate.* From this, students can deduce (perhaps by analogy—see earlier discussion) d*ate,* sk*ate,* l*ate*r, and so forth.

Whole-Language Approach

One of the difficulties in describing whole-language approaches is that they are defined differently, even by their advocates (Bergeron, 1990; Gunderson, 1997). An analysis of 64 articles about the meaning of the term *whole language* showed that:

> The term whole language, common now to most educators, has become a unique enigma. . . . [It] has been described as being an approach . . . , a belief . . . , a method . . . , a philosophy . . . , an orientation . . . , a theory . . . , a theoretical

> orientation . . . , a program . . . , a curriculum . . . , a perspective on education . . . , and an attitude of mind. (Bergeron, 1990, pp. 301–302)

Overall, whole language is most often used to describe a philosophy of instruction, not a specific method or set of techniques (Gunderson, 1997). The diversity of opinion about this philosophy emphasizes two common themes about whole language (Bergeron, 1990): It involves *constructing meaning* and promotes use of *functional language*.

Constructing meaning and using functional language are important guides for the practice of whole-language teaching. Advocates of whole language hold that learning to read is a natural part of normal language development and that children should do it like they learn to listen and talk. That is, they should actively engage in inquiring about the meaning of print and gradually come to use print just as they do spoken language (Goodman, 1986). The connections with the constructivist approach (see Chapter 3) are clear. This emphasis on meaning and the deemphasis on decoding are also consistent with older meaning-emphasis approaches such as the whole-word approach.

Children must realize that print is meaningful as a prerequisite to learning to read. This idea is consistent with an emphasis on understanding the relationship between spoken and written language. Just as children develop spoken-language skills by learning that different sequences of sounds and words have different meanings,

> a similar insight—that differences on a printed page have a function, that they are meaningful—must also be the basis for learning written language. As long as children see print as purposeless or nonsensical, they will find attention to print aversive and will be bored. Children will not learn by trying to relate letters to sounds, partly because the task does not make sense to them and partly because written language does not work that way. In my view reading is not a matter of decoding letters to sound but of bringing meaning to print. (Smith, 1977, p. 387)

Whole-language methods of teaching reading usually incorporate what was previously called the language experience approach (LEA). In LEA, the material to be read is based on students' experiences and the language they use to express them. Beginning reading students in an LEA program will often have a group activity and then dictate a story about it to their teacher. Each child may contribute one sentence, which the teacher writes on a chalkboard or other large display. Later the students read and illustrate their story. Gradually, the students will make more extensive contributions to their group stories and introduce more complex vocabulary and syntax. Eventually, they will write and illustrate their own stories and read from textbooks. Texts about using whole language provide more detail about this approach (Edelsky, 1991; Goodman, 1986; Hall, 1981; Stauffer, 1980).

Effectiveness of Beginning Reading Approaches

Comparisons of code-emphasis and meaning-emphasis approaches to beginning reading programs are clear: Early reading instruction should explicitly show students how to crack the alphabetic code of English (Chall, 1967, 1983). In one of the most important books on reading published during the 20th century, Adams (1990) put it this way:

> The findings reviewed [here] are suggestive of the conclusion that something about the large and general class of programs that purport to teach phonics is of genuine and lasting value. In particular, each of [three] categories of evidence suggests that students must appreciate the alphabetic principle to become proficient readers. They must acquire a sense of the correspondences between letters and sounds upon which it is based. (p. 29)

Some studies favoring the code-emphasis approach have been conducted in highly controlled settings by teaching one group of kindergartners phoneme-grapheme relationships and another group whole words composed of those graphemes. The instruction received by the first group is similar to a code-emphasis approach, and that received by the second group is similar to a whole-word or meaning-emphasis approach. When the children later have to learn a list of new words (a test of generalization), those who had received phoneme-grapheme training read more of the new words correctly on the first try and took fewer trials to learn all the words in the new list than did the students who had learned by the word method (Jeffrey & Samuels, 1967). Similar studies have shown that the same findings occur even when the words on the new list do not have regular pronunciations (Carnine, 1977) and when the students have disabilities (Vandever & Neville, 1976).

Additional supportive evidence has been reported in reviews of the research. Researchers examined 18 early studies and found 22 comparisons between code-emphasis and other approaches. Three were favorable to neither the code-emphasis approach nor the other approaches, none was favorable to the other approaches, and 19 were favorable to the code-emphasis approach. On measures of reading comprehension, they found that 22 of 24 comparisons were favorable to the code-emphasis programs (Gurren & Hughes, 1965). In *Learning to Read: The Great Debate,* Chall (1967, 1983) concluded

> Under a code emphasis, the child shows, from the very beginning, greater accuracy in word recognition and oral reading; this may or may not give him an immediate advantage on reading-for-meaning tests. . . . However, by the end of the first or some time during the second grade the early advantage in word recognition produces better vocabulary and comprehension scores on silent reading tests. These advantages persist through about the third grade. . . . Under a meaning emphasis, the child has an early advantage . . . on reading-for-meaning tests. . . . However, he has an early disadvantage in accuracy on oral word recognition (pronunciation) and connected oral reading tests . . . which ultimately dissipates the early advantage on the standardized silent reading tests. At about the end of the first grade (or the beginning of the second grade), and continuing through about the third grade, meaning-emphasis programs tend to affect comprehension and vocabulary test scores adversely, mainly because the child does less well in word recognition. (1967, p. 137)

Research reported after the publication of these reviews provides additional support for the superiority of code-emphasis programs (Bliesmer & Yarborough, 1965; Dykstra, 1968a, 1968b; Pflaum, Walberg, Karegianes, & Rasher, 1980; Potts & Savino, 1968; Stahl & Miller, 1989). Research conducted on the effectiveness of code-emphasis approaches with students having learning disabilities has shown much the same results (Stein & Goldman, 1980; Wallach & Wallach, 1976; Williams, 1980). Texts on reading instruction present the code-emphasis approach in detail (e.g., Carnine, Silbert, & Kameenui, 1996).

In contrast, some sources cite evidence that supports the effectiveness of LEA. For example, Hall (1981) wrote, "research confirms this method's effectiveness in teaching beginning reading. In a review of thirteen research studies on the language experience approach from 1926 to 1965, Hildreth reports positive results for this approach in eleven instances" (p. 14). However, what Hildreth (1965) actually wrote was,

> The following are references to comparison studies of teaching initial reading through experience-related material in contrast to the use of standard traditional textbook methods. . . . In only two cases were the results negative for the [LEA] group. (pp. 283–284)

Thus, there were not 11 favorable studies, as Hall implied, but rather 11 studies that did not favor either LEA or the approach to which it was compared, 2 that favored an approach other than LEA, and none that favored LEA.

Evidence about the effectiveness of whole-language instruction is generally discouraging. In several studies where scores favored the LEA over traditional basal reader approaches, differences were also present in pretest measures: Students in the LEA programs had significantly higher scores before teaching began (Bond & Dykstra, 1967). When the pretest scores were taken into account, the differences favoring LEA programs disappeared. Results at the end of the second grade also revealed no significant differences favoring the LEA approaches (Dykstra, 1968b). Thus, LEA was not found to be any better than traditional meaning-emphasis basal programs. Similarly, the Tucson Early Education Model in Project Follow Through, which emphasized an experience-based approach to language and reading (Maccoby & Zellner, 1970), failed to produce favorable effects; it actually resulted in worse achievement scores than the comparison programs (Abt Associates, 1976, 1977).

Systematic reviews of the research disclose other discouraging evidence about the effectiveness of whole-language or LEA approaches. Fifty-one studies of whole-language instruction revealed it was no more effective than the basal programs to which it was compared (Stahl & Miller, 1989). Given that code-emphasis programs were consistently more effective than basal programs (see Chall, 1967; Dykstra, 1968a), we can deduce the relationship among approaches: Code-emphasis programs are more effective than basal programs, which, in turn, are about as effective as whole-language programs.

Many advocates in the field of learning disabilities have expressed concerns about whether whole-language instruction is appropriate for students with reading problems. Based on the evidence described in the foregoing paragraphs and other evidence, they conclude that the whole-language approach is not best for everybody. The practices of whole-language instruction may permit some students with disabilities to learn to read, but teachers will need to provide more explicit and more intensive instruction for many others (Lerner, Cousin, & Richeck, 1992; Mather, 1992; Pressley & Rankin, 1994).

Despite these reservations, there are some good things about whole language (Pressley & Rankin, 1994):

- The emphasis on whole language has encouraged teachers to have students write frequently. Writing has too often been neglected in many classrooms. Students with learning disabilities are unlikely to develop competence without opportunities to practice whatever it is they are learning. Thus, they probably will not learn to write coherent sentences, paragraphs, and passages simply by reading.
- Whole language has stressed the connectedness of reading, writing, and spelling. Artificial separation of these closely related areas is likely to hinder the progress of students with learning disabilities. Indeed, part of the success of programs that have emphasized using multisensory teaching (e.g., the Orton-Gillingham and Fernald approaches) may be attributable to the integration of reading and writing inherent in them.
- Because of concern for reading authentic literature, students in whole-language classrooms are reading works written by acclaimed authors. In place of the easily parodied prose of the basal readers used in the 1950s and 1960s (e.g., "Look! Look! See Bowser! See Bowser run! Run, Bowser, run."), students now read from books that represent better quality children's literature.

Emerging Synthesis in Beginning Reading Instruction

There are benefits to teaching children both fundamental decoding skills (phonics and more) and promoting motivation to read and helping them understand the connections among reading, writing, and speaking (whole language). Integrating the two makes sense. However, teachers should avoid mindless eclecticism. Methods for early reading instruction should adhere to the idea that a primary duty of teachers of students with learning disabilities should be to minimize the contribution of instruction to learning problems. Teachers can integrate features of whole language into a sensible early reading program. Because code-emphasis approaches are more effective than other methods of beginning reading instruction, early reading instruction for students with learning disabilities should focus on teaching them the skills required to master the code of written English.

When teachers teach students phonological awareness skills, they are likely to do so within the context of reading and writing. Such lessons present instruction in cracking the code within the context of reading rather than in the abstract. For students with learning disabilities, instruction in such skills as phonological awareness should show the use of those phonological skills in useful tasks.

Given the broad range of interpretations of whole language (Bergeron, 1990), aspects of it are clearly compatible with teaching children to decode, and instruction in phonemic segmentation can be incorporated into whole-language approaches (e.g., Wethy, 1993). Teachers need not eschew teaching students phonics just so they can use children's literature in their classes or have students write about what they read and read what they write. As the National Research Council (1998) noted, there is, indeed, a need to move the debate about whole language onto another level so that teachers can incorporate the benefits of both whole-language and direct instruction practices (see Gersten & Dimino, 1993; Palincsar & Klenk, 1993; Reid, 1993; Stein & Osborne, 1993).

Promoting Phonological Awareness

Since nearly the inception of the field, authorities in learning disabilities have recommended teaching what we now call phonological awareness. Although recent emphasis on them makes the skills of analysis and blending seem new, they were fundamental parts of the instructional practices incorporated into programs for students who have difficulty learning to read (Engelmann, 1967b; Williams, 1977, 1980).

As evidence linking poor phonological awareness to reading disabilities accumulated during the 1970s and 1980s, more and more people began to examine the utility of teaching phonological skills to students. By the early 1990s, it was plain that young children who learned to manipulate the sounds of their spoken language had much lower chances of developing reading disabilities than did their peers who did not learn phonological skills. Although some studies have not found evidence that explicit instruction on phonological awareness tasks causes improvements in reading (Kennedy & Bachman, 1993), there is likewise little evidence that doing something else is better than teaching students phonological awareness. The control groups in these studies do not do any better than the group receiving phonological instruction.

There is a wealth of evidence on the benefits of teaching phonological skills to beginning readers. Most studies show the benefits of teaching students segmenting, rhyming, and similar skills (Ball & Blachman, 1988; Bradley & Bryant, 1983; Byrne & Fielding-Barnsley, 1991, 1993; Content, Kolinsky, Morais, & Bertelson, 1986; Cunningham, 1990; Hurford et al., 1994; Lundberg, Frost, & Peterson, 1988; Torgesen, Morgan, & Davis, 1992; Vellutino & Scanlon, 1987; Williams, 1980). But phonemic segmentation training alone is not sufficient. Indeed, improving phonemic segmentation may not improve blending (Slocum, O'Connor, & Jenkins, 1993), so children should be taught both segmentation and blending skills (Torgesen et al., 1992), how to apply the phonological skills they learn (Cunningham, 1990), and how to connect letters with letter sounds (Foorman, Francis, Novy, & Liberman, 1991). Children's facility with phonological tasks also appears to be promoted in part by learning about letters themselves (Wagner, Torgesen, & Rashotte, 1994). Beginning reading programs should be evaluated on the basis of how well they incorporate these features. See Chapter 11 for examples of procedures for teaching phonological awareness.

But there are limits on teaching phonological awareness. It is not a magic bullet. Evidence for the benefits of teaching phonological awareness is based, for the most part, on work with primary-grade children. Although there is evidence about the relationships between phonological skills and the decoding competence of older students (e.g., Lenchner, Gerber, & Routh, 1990), there have been no studies on whether explicit training in analysis and blending alone facilitates the remediation of reading deficits. Because corrective readers already know a lot about reading but apply it inconsistently and inaccurately, they are unlikely to require different instruction than developmental readers.

HOW SHOULD READING PROBLEMS BE CORRECTED?

Too often, developmental reading instruction fails. Too often, when young children are not learning to read, teachers and parents decide to wait in hopes that the passage of time will make them riper for instruction. The children are passed along while people wait for them to mature. And, too often, these young children who have been passed along become older children who cannot read, are losing ground in content areas to their peers (Stanovich, 1986b), and would rather do just about anything but read (Juel, 1988).

When students have not learned to read, teachers face the more difficult task of correcting reading problems. It is more difficult to correct problems because those students who need corrective reading probably (1) differ from their peers in some other important ways (see earlier discussion), (2) suffer from declining self-confidence, perhaps promoted by their reading failure (Bryan, 1986), (3) continue some mistaken strategies for reading from their prior instruction, and (4) must learn faster than normal if they are to catch up to their peers (Engelmann, 1997).

Traditional Approaches

As indicated by the evidence we examined in our description of the characteristics of students with reading problems, to prevent or remedy reading problems requires more than simply teaching phonics. As Adams (1990, p. 29) noted, "However critical letter-to-sound correspondences may be, they are not enough. To become skillful readers, children need much more." Although Adams made this comment about reading instruction for all students, her point is particularly relevant for those with disabilities. As has been stressed throughout this text, adequate instruction for students with disabilities cannot be based on some simple curative, and this applies to phonics instruction as well as other approaches. We must teach these students fundamental reading skills, but we also must teach them more advanced skills.

One of the strongest currents in the history of learning disabilities has been an emphasis on sensory modalities—visual (seeing), auditory (hearing), kinesthetic (body or muscle feeling), and tactile (touch feeling). This concern with modalities forms the basis for two historically important approaches to remedial instruction: the Fernald and the Orton-Gillingham approaches. It is also evident in a third, the Hegge-Kirk-Kirk approach. These are associated with some of the most important pioneers in the field: Fernald, Orton, Gillingham, and Kirk (see Chapter 1).

VAKT Approach

Fernald (1943) is probably the figure most readily associated with the visual-auditory-kinesthetic-tactile (VAKT) approach. The rationale for the Fernald approach (also known as the Fernald Word Learning Approach) is that, by being taught to use as many senses as possible, the child comes to use additional experiences or cues in learning to read. If the child is weak in any one modality, the other modalities will help convey the information. In practice, the VAKT approach is not confined to reading; it is also used in spelling and writing instruction. It is essentially a language-experience and whole-word approach. Fernald believed that overcoming the emotional problems failing students have with reading would be easier if their reading material was of interest to them. Therefore, stories are written down as suggested by the students, with as much help from the teacher as needed, and then read. Students also select words they wish to learn and work on them, repeatedly tracing and saying a word until they can write them from memory. Mastered words are kept in a file so students may refer back to it as needed. Fernald was opposed to having students "sound out" words; she emphasized the reading and writing of words as wholes. Although there are strong advocates of the Fernald approach who can provide case studies of its successful use, research evidence does not show it has been particularly successful (Myers, 1978).

Hegge-Kirk-Kirk Approach

Although not usually considered a multisensory approach, the Remedial Reading Drills of Hegge, S. Kirk, and W. Kirk (1970) emphasize use of multiple modalities during reading instruction. S. Kirk (1976) became interested in reading during his work with Monroe (1932). At the Wayne County Training School (see Chapter 1), he studied psychological research related to learning and applied it to these instructional programs. The Remedial Reading Drills of the Hegge-Kirk-Kirk approach are designed to help students remember phoneme-grapheme relationships by providing extensive practice and by simplifying the relationships between letters and their sounds (e.g., using only one sound for a letter until it has been thoroughly mastered; see Carnine, 1976). In the program, students are taught to (1) say sounds for individual letters, (2) blend combinations of sounds, (3) write letters for sounds from memory, and (4) practice reading words aloud from prescribed word lists. Practice in reading from connected prose has to be provided by the teacher because the program is limited to reading letters and words in isolation. Revised versions of the materials are available in *Phonic Remedial Reading Lessons* (Kirk, Kirk, & Minskoff, 1985).

Orton-Gillingham Approach

Another multisensory approach to reading has been advocated by Gillingham and Stillman (1965). Based on work the authors did with Orton in the 1930s, it is often known as the Orton-Gillingham approach. Orton, a neurologist, theorized that the brain stores information in both hemispheres and that the information stored in one is a mirror image of what is stored in the other. Thus, in one hemisphere, the printed word "was" would be represented in its usual form, but in the other hemisphere, it would be represented as "saw." Children who had not completely developed lateral dominance (meaning one side of their brains had not grown dominant over the other, as usually happens) would be confused about which image was correct when reading. This theory accounted for reversals in reading and writing that Orton (1937) had observed. Orton suggested that the "whole-word" or "sight" approach to instruction only makes these children's problems worse and that they should be taught reading and spelling according to a phonics approach.

Gillingham and Stillman (1965) made Orton's recommendations into a practical procedure. They created a program designed to remediate not only problems in reading, but also related problems in spelling and handwriting. They recommended that students learn associations between letters and their sounds in all of the modalities required by the reading, spelling, and handwriting tasks. Thus, students are taught to see a letter (visual) and say its sound (auditory), hear a sound (auditory) and write it (kinesthetic), and so forth. Initially, instruction is based on five letters. When they have been practiced until they are mastered, five more letters are introduced and practiced until all ten have been mastered. More letters are then introduced one at a time. After mastering the first ten letter associations, the student begins work on blending letters into words. Spelling and story reading are gradually introduced as the student develops facility with the vocabulary that can be built from the mastered grapheme-phoneme associations.

Beyond the case study reports of Orton (1937), there is little careful research about the effectiveness of this approach to instruction. Those studies that are available reveal improved reading and spelling for elementary-school children (Kline & Kline, 1975; Vickery, Reynolds, & Cochran, 1987) and improved spelling for college students (Guyer, Banks, & Guyer, 1993) given Orton-Gillingham remedial instruction. Some of the method's features are consistent with other effective approaches. For example, the Orton-Gillingham approach is a code-emphasis approach, and in beginning reading, a code-emphasis approach is well supported. But other aspects of the Orton-Gillingham approach do not receive the same strong support (e.g., returning to rudimentary grapheme-phoneme work with remedial readers).

Current Remedial Reading Instruction

Contemporary remedial instruction must emphasize some of the same features present in developmental instruction. In particular, students' reading performances must come under control of the print on the page. Despite the allure of teaching students alternative routes to decoding (e.g., "Look at the picture" and "What do you think that word should be?"), students have to learn to read the text (to decode). To different degrees, contemporary remedial approaches stress acquisition of skillful decoding.

Some programs and kits—such as the Peabody Rebus Reading Program (Woodcock, Clark, & Davies, 1979), the Sullivan Reading Program (Sullivan, 1966), the Specific Skills Series (Boning, 1990), or the Reading Labs from Science Research Associates—may still be found in classrooms. However, today the major contenders in remedial reading are other materials and methods. These include Reading Recovery, Corrective Reading Program, behavior analysis, and computer-assisted instruction.

Reading Recovery

Recently, Reading Recovery (Clay, 1985; Pinnell, 1989) has been among the most popular methods advocated in learning disabilities. This intensive, tutorial approach is designed to help developmental readers who are likely to have difficulty acquiring reading skills. Although the basic program has been extended for use with older students, it was originally focused on young children who had not benefited from developmental instruction.

Reading Recovery is based on several valuable practices: (1) Screen first-graders early in the school year. (2) Select the lowest rank (usually the lowest 20%). (3) Deliver intensive instruction to the selected students. Reading Recovery also emphasizes reading of familiar texts and promotes writing of words in ways that encourage discovery of phonological relationships. Although flawed, preliminary research showed encouraging gains for students taught with Reading Recovery. In part because of these encouraging results and in part because the techniques correspond with some tenets of whole language, Reading Recovery caught on strongly and quickly when it was introduced in the United States.

After early studies, more rigorous evaluations of the Reading Recovery program soon became available. For example, in one study, researchers compared the growth of three groups of students. One group received a standard remedial program, one group received regular Reading Recovery, and a third group received a modified version of Reading Recovery. The modified version of the Reading Recovery program was much more explicit than the usual version; it provided practice in phonological awareness and showed the students symbol-sound relationships. Students in both the regular and the modified Reading Recovery programs improved more than their peers in the control group. However, the students in the Reading Recovery group that also received instruction in phonological skills progressed more rapidly (Iversen & Tunmer, 1993).

Researchers have aggregated numerous studies about Reading Recovery so they can assess whether it is effective in many studies or just one or two. Generally, they found that Reading Recovery has short-lived and very special benefits, but it provides nowhere near the acceleration required for students who need to gain ground against their peers (Grossen, Coulter, & Ruggles, 1996; Heibert, 1994; Iversen & Tunmer, 1993). According to its own standards (whether students can read a specific book),

Reading Recovery looks pretty good. When teachers assess its benefits on generalization tasks (reading other books) or sustained benefits (improvements several years later), the results are less encouraging.

Corrective Reading Program

The DI materials for remedial reading are called the Corrective Reading Program or CRP (Engelmann et al., 1988). CRP is designed to teach students general-case strategies for attacking and solving types of reading tasks. A sound-it-out strategy is a general-case procedure for decoding; this is based on a task analysis similar to the one provided in Table 12.3. Because corrective readers already know some things about the alphabetic code, in CRP, there is relatively less emphasis on teaching the basics of the strategy (e.g., individual sounds for letters) and more emphasis on teaching use of those skills to increase oral reading accuracy.

CRP includes scripted daily lessons designed to teach the component skills needed for fluent, accurate decoding. Students read from carefully structured word lists and then participate in group and individual reading of stories. Research shows the Corrective Reading Program improves the reading of pupils with learning disabilities (Lloyd, Epstein, & Cullinan, 1981; Maggs & Maggs, 1979; Polloway, Epstein, Polloway, Patton, & Ball, 1986; see also White, 1988) and may be particularly valuable for students who have relatively greater deficits in reading (Pflaum & Pascarella, 1980).

Behavior Analysis

Although some research using applied behavior analysis (ABA) has examined comprehensive classroom programs for improving reading performance (e.g., Haring & Hauck, 1969), most studies of reading problems using ABA procedures have provided information about specific intervention techniques. For example, there have been many demonstrations that a student's reading accuracy can be improved by providing reinforcement for reading more words correctly and for reading with fewer errors (e.g., Jenkins, Barksdale, & Clinton, 1978; Roberts & Smith, 1980; Swanson, 1981).

Simply reinforcing more accurate oral reading, however, may not be a sufficient intervention. Even though oral reading and reading comprehension are intimately related, improvement in oral reading accuracy often does not lead to improvement in answering comprehension questions correctly (Jenkins et al., 1978; Roberts & Smith, 1980; Swanson, 1981). When the desired outcome of a reading intervention is greater accuracy in answering comprehension questions, interventions that are directly focused on that behavior are more desirable, perhaps with something as simple as pennies for correct answers (Lahey, McNees, & Brown, 1973). Teachers also can prompt students to raise their hands and ask questions when they do not understand what to do or how to do it. This simple procedure causes substantially better accuracy on reading comprehension tasks (Knapczyk & Livingston, 1974).

A more complete intervention focusing on both reading accuracy and comprehension could use a reinforcement-based technique for improving the oral reading and comprehension of students with learning disabilities (Lovitt & Hansen, 1976b).

After identifying reading books at appropriate levels for each student (Lovitt & Hanson, 1976a; see also Diagnosing Problems and Planning Programs earlier in this chapter), a special procedure called "contingent skipping and drilling" can be used. When students read from their readers and answer comprehension questions quickly and accurately, they are allowed to skip parts of the text they would usually be assigned for the next few lessons. However, when they do not meet the criteria for speed and accuracy, they are required to practice skills until they can do so. Over the course of a school year, the contingent skipping and drilling procedure results in great improvement in student reading performance.

Computer-Assisted Instruction

Despite the potential value of computer-assisted practice in learning, technology has little value in teaching the decoding aspects of reading because students themselves must turn the written letters into sounds. Given rules, computers can convert print to sound, but when computers do this, students do not get the practice they need to gain proficiency. Also, students will likely rely on the computer's decoding of the words rather than learning how to do it themselves.

Computer technology has not advanced far enough to make sophisticated comparisons between a student's reading of a word and its correct pronunciation. Despite progress in vocal recognition technology, computers cannot decipher subtle differences in pronunciation. Thus, clinical experience and experimental evidence (e.g., Farmer, Klien, & Bryson, 1992) show that computers can have only limited value listening to students read. Computers can, however, be used to improve students' reading of individual words (Cohen, Torgesen, & Torgesen, 1988; Rashotte & Torgesen, 1985; Torgesen, Waters, Cohen, & Torgesen, 1988).

Although they are not good listeners, computers can produce speech. This feature allows teachers to use them in innovative ways. For example, computers can provide feedback for difficult words; students can select an unknown word in a passage and have the computer pronounce it. In fact, the computer can segment a word, much like the stretching activities used in phonological awareness training. When students with reading problems practice reading passages on a computer that permits them to have words pronounced for them, their reading improves (Wise & Olson, 1998).

Instructional Strategies

There are many specific techniques teachers can use to help students acquire reading skills. We describe some that have been effective with students with reading problems.

Fluency Enhancement

Fluency in reading is important. When students do not read fluently, their rendition of a passage is choppy, halting, and stumbling. But problems of disfluent reading also affect other areas. For example, students with reading problems may read material about science at only half the speed of their nondisabled peers (Parmer, Deluca, & Janczak, 1994).

Students should have opportunities to practice reading fluently (Sindelar & Stoddard, 1991), and there are many ways to provide it. For example, high school students can learn to read vocabulary words appropriate for different subject areas by practicing reading them in unison with a tape recording. This technique helps students read the texts for the subject areas (Freeman & McLaughlin, 1984). They can also practice reading and rereading passages until their rate and accuracy approximate fluency. Students who have a reasonably good idea about how to convert print into sound but do not do so fluently may be helped by practice.

One popular method for providing practice is called repeated readings (e.g., Samuels, 1979, 1981). Samuels (1981) noted that many special education students do not have enough opportunity to practice reading:

> This is not done in training athletes and musicians. Basketball players practice jump shots over and over again; musicians practice short musical selections repeatedly. Their goal is to develop skills to a level of fluid accuracy. With enough practice, they do not have to devote much attention to the mechanics of their skills. With enough practice, readers will not have to devote much attention to the mechanics of decoding. (pp. 23–24)

Research with students who have learning disabilities shows that repeated practice aids both fluency and comprehension, not only for those with severe difficulties, but also for those who experience moderate problems with reading (Bos, 1982; Sindelar, Monda, & O'Shea, 1990). However, the benefits of repeated reading occur mostly when the same passage is reread; otherwise, repeated reading helps only to the extent that there are common words in the practiced passage and the material read later (Rashotte & Torgesen, 1985). It is probably the repeated practice included in techniques such as the neurological impress method (Heckelman, 1969) that makes them effective despite their otherwise shaky theoretical bases (see Hollingsworth, 1970; Lorenz & Vockell, 1979).

Previewing Text

Another way to provide additional practice is to give a preview of the reading materials (e.g., the teacher may lead students in a discussion of the story in a passage they are about to read). Although previews may take different forms, the most widely studied method with students who have reading problems is for someone else to read the passage aloud before the students read it themselves. The previewer is usually an adult, but a peer may read the passage (Salend & Nowack, 1988), or it can be tape recorded (Rose & Beattie, 1986). Multiple studies show that previewing improves the rate and accuracy of students' reading of passages (Rose, 1984a, 1984b, 1984c; Rose & Sherry, 1984).

Context Training

Some evidence about how students with learning disabilities read indicates that they may benefit from using context clues to help them decode (Pflaum & Bryan, 1981). Pflaum and Pascarella have investigated training procedures for helping these students develop this skill. In one study, they found that children with more severe reading deficits benefited from Direct Instruction, but that children with less severe problems benefited from context training, which showed them how to monitor their own reading performance for errors and correct only those that seemed to change the meaning of what they were reading (Pflaum & Pascarella, 1980). In a second study, Pascarella and Pflaum (1981) found that children with a more external locus of control benefited from a more teacher-directed instructional program for learning context usage, but that children with a more internal locus of control benefited from a more student-directed program for learning the same skills.

Reciprocal Teaching

Reciprocal teaching integrates features of several models, particularly the cognitive and constructivist views of learning disabilities (see Chapter 3). It emphasizes scaffolded instruction, an important feature of instruction for students with learning disabilities (Kameenui & Carnine, 1998). Although it can be conducted in a tutorial format, reciprocal teaching often

> [r]efers to an instructional procedure that takes place in a collaborative learning group and features guided practice in the flexible application of four concrete strategies to the task of text comprehension: questioning, summarizing, clarifying, and predicting. The teacher and group of students take turns leading discussions regarding the content of the text they are jointly attempting to understand. (Palincsar & Klenk, 1992, p. 213)

Advocates of reciprocal teaching stress the importance of having instruction occur within a social context, of initially providing supports (prompts or "scaffolds") to help students perform activities, and of having students demonstrate their increasing competence by explaining to others how to do things. In teaching reading comprehension, the instructors model how to derive ideas from a text, help students do so by asking questions, and have students explain to teachers and peers what they have learned from reading a passage. Reciprocal teaching is also readily applied to composition instruction.

Comprehension Strategies

Although it is crucial for students to be able to decode the printed word fluently, competent decoding does not ensure adequate comprehension of the material. Thus, teachers must also teach students how to use strategies to comprehend what they read. But strategy training by itself may not be sufficient. Furthermore, students rarely know how to extract themes from what they read. Research on reading comprehension in learning disabilities has led to methods that address these needs, including procedural facilitation, enhanced strategy training, and gist comprehension training.

Procedural Facilitation One method for improving comprehension that has gained substantial currency in the last few decades is the use of procedural facilitation, in which students are taught a strategy or set of procedures for accomplishing a task. A valuable application of procedural facilitation to reading comprehension is called story grammar, which is a general or fairly standard system for organizing the content of what one reads or writes (See the discussion in Chapter 13). A story grammar might include important features one would expect to find in a passage of prose, such as who was involved, where the action took place, and what happened.

This strategy and others like it have been used successfully with students with learning disabilities (e.g., Carnine & Kinder, 1985; Gurney, Gersten, Dimino, & Carnine, 1990; Idol & Croll, 1987). Moreover, the connection between using story grammar for reading comprehension and for written expression makes it a good candidate for inclusion in an integrated language arts program for students with learning disabilities.

Strategy Training Teachers can also teach students general-case strategies for comprehension skills. For example, there are strategies to help students answer questions about the sequence of events in stories they read. Sequence questions require readers to indicate which event happened first, next, and last in the story. Many students have difficulty with this type of task. Teachers can show them how to locate each part of the possible answer in the story and mark it. Then the students can determine the order of those parts and use that order to answer the question (Carnine, Prill, & Armstrong, 1978). Another type of comprehension task has students answer questions that require understanding sentences with clauses. Passive voice clauses often cause confusion; a sentence of this type is "Henry, who was kissed by Joan, ran home crying" (Kameenui, Carnine, & Maggs, 1980). Students can be taught to restate the original sentence as two separate sentences so they can answer questions about it (e.g., "Who did the kissing? Who was crying?").

Borkowski and his colleagues (e.g., Grotelushchen, Borkowski, & Hale, 1991) maintain that strategy training in itself is insufficient. They agree that teaching students to use strategies is very important, but add that students also must learn to persist in using strategies and to attribute their success to their own efforts (see also Chapter 11). In one study, Borkowski, Wehring, and Carr (1988) had teachers demonstrate the use of strategies with memory tasks so that students learned that using those strategies improved their performance on the memory tasks. Then the teachers taught the students a strategy for summarizing the main ideas and other aspects of what they read. Later, the teachers modeled how to use the strategies even under difficult conditions. When the teachers made mistakes, they reverted to using the strategies, thus illustrating the value of persistence in using the original plan. Throughout the demonstrations and practice sessions, the teachers emphasized positive attributions for success. Students who received the entire package of training had better scores on comprehension measures than those who were taught only the reading comprehension strategy.

Gist Comprehension Training One of the most challenging things to teach students with learning disabilities is gist comprehension. As discussed earlier in this chapter, Williams (1991) found students with learning disabilities particularly deficient in getting the theme or message from what they read. In subsequent research (Williams, Brown, Silverstein, & deCani, 1994), Williams evaluated an instructional program for helping students identify and interpret themes. She and her colleagues taught upper-elementary-school-aged students a general strategy for extracting themes from what they read. This strategy encouraged the students to use a series of organizing questions, some of which are similar to those a teacher would use as part of teaching story grammar (e.g., "Who is the main character?") and some of which guided students to evaluate the story situation (e.g., "Was this good or bad?"). Teachers modeled how these organizing questions could lead to the development of statements about what the main character should do and then helped the students generalize these themes to real-life situations. The program Williams and her colleagues provided helped both students with and without learning disabilities gain greater facility in identifying themes, regardless of whether they were compared to noninstructed peers or to peers who received an alternative form of instruction.

Because teachers hope they can teach students to learn things on their own, preparing students to extract themes from what they read is an important skill. Students with learning disabilities apparently have trouble with this aspect of higher-level comprehension, so procedures for teaching this are still sorely needed. The work of Williams and her colleagues represents important progress in teaching these complex, subtle skills and points the way toward future developments in high-quality instruction.

Summary

1. What are the characteristics of students with reading problems?
   a. Students with reading problems first and foremost have difficulty with the primary aspects of reading: decoding and comprehending.
   b. These students also have difficulty with other aspects of language, particularly with phonological awareness, syntax, and semantics.
   c. They also are likely to have difficulty with other academic skills—particularly spelling and written expression—and, later, in academic content areas where much of what is to be learned is presented in print.
2. What is the prevalence of the students with reading difficulties?
   a. Prevalence estimates range from a low of 2%–3% to a high of 15%–20% of the school-age population.
   b. Studies of the prevalence of reading disabilities indicate that between 6% and 8% of children have severe reading problems.
   c. Although the percentage of boys with reading problems is often greater than the percentage of girls, this may be the result of bias in referrals because of boys' greater activity levels.

3. How is reading performance assessed?
   a. Skills and deficits in reading are best assessed by using both tests and less formal, direct measurement methods, such as performance samples.
   b. Comprehensive tests of reading ability may be used to assess general ability (reading grade level).
   c. Teachers often use specific tests for more specific reading skills areas, such as decoding and comprehension.
   d. Teachers need to be able to assess progress in reading skills and usually do so by devising informal measures (e.g., probes) of such skills as oral reading fluency.
4. How should beginning literacy be taught?
   a. Although advocates differ about how heavily to emphasize learning of the alphabetic code of English, evidence indicates that doing so is essential to reading success.
   b. There are benefits to both teaching children fundamental decoding skills (phonics and more) and promoting motivation to read and helping students understand the connections among reading, writing, and speaking (whole language).
   c. Regardless of philosophical orientation, there is a wealth of evidence on the benefits of teaching phonological skills to beginning readers.
5. How should reading problems be corrected?
   a. Choices of remedial reading methods should be based on whether the methods are effective.
   b. Contemporary remedial instruction must emphasize both decoding and comprehension.
   c. Specialized methods, such as those emphasizing sensory modalities (visual, auditory, kinesthetic, and tactile), have a long history in learning disabilities. These include Fernald's VAKT, the remedial reading drills, and the Orton-Gillingham methods.
   d. The Reading Recovery approach has been very popular, although evidence about its benefits is being questioned today.
   e. The Corrective Reading Program has generated substantial evidence of effectiveness.
   f. Computer-assisted instruction has begun to develop a body of evidence indicating effectiveness.
   g. Teachers often adopt specific techniques for reading instruction. These include practice to promote fluency, previewing content to encourage understanding, reciprocal teaching, and context training.

13

Teaching Students with Writing Problems

Students who have difficulties with oral language and reading often also have problems with writing. Just as it is important to be able to express oneself clearly in spoken language and to be able to read written language, one should be able to communicate in writing. Without skills in written expression, students cannot do much more than answer orally or mark true-false and multiple-choice questions. A person deficient in writing skills cannot leave an understandable note, compose a letter, complete a job application, or create a poem, play, or story.

Written expression requires skills in three major areas: handwriting, spelling, and composition. Although expression of one's thoughts and feelings may be more important than the mechanical aspects of writing, illegible handwriting, misspellings, grammatical inaccuracies, and poor organization can make it difficult for a reader to understand the meaning of a written piece. Thus, effective writers are skilled enough in these three major areas of written expression to communicate with minimal misunderstanding.

This chapter focuses on each major area of written expression: handwriting, spelling, and composition. Dividing written expression into these categories is useful for discussion purposes, but the areas overlap. Emphasizing their common features is one of the values of thinking about language as a whole, integrated group of competencies. This overlap is important to consider when designing and instituting assessment and intervention programs and techniques. Just as teachers need to coordinate their instruction in spelling, reading, and writing, they should also coordinate their instruction in handwriting, spelling, and composition.

WHAT HANDWRITING PROBLEMS DO STUDENTS EXPERIENCE?

In the past, much of the emphasis in handwriting instruction was on development of a stylish and uniform "hand." Over the years, this emphasis has changed substantially; consider, for example, the differences of style evident in the handwriting of Thomas Jefferson's time and that of today. With the expansion of electronic word-processing equipment and the increasing reliance on keyboarding (typing) skills, there may be even less emphasis on handwriting in the coming years.

Handwriting or penmanship, as it was once called, is a means to an end, a tool. Students who can write legibly and with reasonable speed are not deterred from expressing themselves by weak handwriting skills. Thus, "handwriting is a tool skill which should become routine as rapidly and efficiently as possible" (Herrick, 1961. p. 264). However, handwriting should not be stressed at the expense of other important skills, such as those necessary to speak, listen, read, spell, or compose well.

Sometimes handwriting problems are known as **dysgraphia,** which refers to "partial ability or inability to remember how to make certain alphabet or arithmetic symbols in handwriting" (Jordon, 1977, p. 189; see also Cicci, 1983). Dysgraphia is usually associated with dyslexia in that many who use these medically oriented terms consider both disorders to be the result of psychoneurological disturbance (e.g., McGrady, 1968).

Handwriting has long been an area of interest to those concerned with learning disabilities. Perhaps this is because pupils with writing disabilities produce clearly deviant writing (e.g., scrawling letter formation), thereby providing a tangible product for study. This interest may also reflect our continuing fascination with how variations in physiological or psychological processes can be manifested in physical performance, as in Leonardo da Vinci's "mirror writing," for example.

Problems with Letter Formation

Handwriting problems include malformation of letters, poor spacing, both vertically and horizontally, and extremely slow writing. Everyone occasionally produces some illegible letters, but some students do so frequently enough that understanding what they have written is difficult. In such cases, handwriting would be considered a problem. Also, most children write quite slowly when they are first learning to print or write in cursive. Slow handwriting is a problem, however, when a student's writing speed interferes with his or her other work.

Students sometimes have difficulty simply copying materials from one source to another. Copying material from a chalkboard to a piece of paper is sometimes called **far-point copying.** Its complement is **near-point copying,** which involves copying from a model the student has on the desk. Some children have greater difficulty with far-point copying than near-point copying, perhaps (but not necessarily) due to problems with visual acuity. If they have difficulty with copying, they probably are not adopting useful cognitive strategies for guiding their copying (e.g., not approaching the task systematically).

Most student errors involve a very few letters. Although children make many different mistakes in handwriting, the letters on which errors are most common are *a, e, r,* and *t* (Anderson, 1968). Students form these letters or the connecting strokes incorrectly, and as a result, the letters look like other letters. For example, if a manuscript or cursive *d* is misformed in one way, it looks like *cl.* This and some other handwriting problems are shown in Figure 13.1. All these problems may interfere with other aspects of writing performance.

Students sometimes reverse letters, seeming to substitute one for another (*b* for *d*) or writing a letter backwards (ƨ for *s*). The substituted letter looks like the correct letter, except it is rotated. For example, a student might write "bog" for the word "dog." As noted in Chapter 12, reversal errors are common when children are first learning to read and write. When students continue to reverse letters, it is sometimes taken as an indicator of underlying psychological or physiological disability. However, few students always write a given letter backwards; they do so only sometimes and other times write it correctly. Reversal errors in reading are proportionally no more common in individuals with and without learning disabilities. These facts undermine the contention that reversal errors indicate fundamental learning problems.

Problems with Fluency

Another common handwriting problem for some students with learning disabilities is fluency. Many such students write so slowly and laboriously that they appear to be drawing each letter (Moats, 1983).

Slow and labored handwriting will probably have negative effects on performance in other areas of written expression. Students who write slowly may lose their place more frequently; their slow writing makes it harder—especially for students with memory problems—to remember where they were.

FIGURE 13.1 Samples of Common Handwriting Problems

Manuscript		Cursive	
g	written like oj	a	written like ci
d	written like ol	g	written like cj
n	written like r	d	written like cl
k	written like ti	i	written like e
r	written like v	t	written like l

Source: From *Introduction to Learning Disabilities,* 2nd ed. (p. 238) by D. P. Hallahan, J. M. Kauffman, and J. W. Lloyd, 1985, Upper Saddle River, NJ: Prentice-Hall. Copyright 1985. Reprinted by permission of Allyn & Bacon.

Causes and Effects of Handwriting Problems

Handwriting skills are related to some perceptual and perceptual-motor skills. Young students with handwriting problems have greater difficulties with items requiring them to find a picture of items in the same spatial orientation as shown in a sample, draw poorly when drawing requires crossing from one side of their bodies to the other, and do not benefit as much as other students from practice on handwritinglike tasks (Chapman & Wedell, 1972; Wedell & Home, 1969).

Although IQ is not related to handwriting (Seifert, 1960), spelling apparently is. Students with poor handwriting are likely to lack spelling skills. There are at least two ways in which handwriting may contribute to misspellings. The first is legibility; the second is speed. Handwriting errors may make a word look like another word. Labored writing of letters may cause students to forget the word they are trying to spell or lose their place partway through spelling it.

HOW IS HANDWRITING PERFORMANCE ASSESSED

As discussed in Chapter 4, the three major assessment functions are identification or screening, program planning or diagnosis, and progress monitoring. We discuss each of these briefly. For more information, see texts on assessment methods for special education (Howell, Fox, & Morehead, 1993; Salvia & Hughes, 1990).

Achievement tests commonly used in schools rarely include assessment of handwriting. The original *Test of Written Language* (TOWL) (Hammill & Larsen, 1983) had a handwriting scale, but the current version (Hammill & Larsen, 1996) has no subtest for handwriting. The age of formal devices designed specifically for evaluating handwriting illustrate the decreased emphasis on handwriting; chief among these dedicated instruments are the Ayers (Ayers, 1912) and the Zaner-Bloser scales (Freeman, 1979). On all these instruments, students copy written material. Their copies are compared to standardized samples of writing, and ratings of quality are assigned. Unfortunately, copying does not provide a complete evaluation of handwriting; one should also assess handwriting based on dictation by the teacher and handwriting that students produce on their own.

Experienced teachers can readily recognize poor handwriting, so formal tests are not essential. In fact, testing for spelling and composition often provides samples suitable for at least preliminary evaluation. The examples of handwriting in Figure 13.2 illustrate different degrees of poor handwriting. On the first two examples, the teacher wrote clarifications to help the students.

Which sample has the best letter formation? On which do the letters appear most evenly spaced and aligned? Which has the best overall appearance? Other than letter formation, spacing, and overall appearance, what should a teacher evaluate in handwriting? What other assessments do these handwriting samples suggest? How should teachers evaluate in screening for handwriting problems?

FIGURE 13.2 Three Samples of Young Children's Handwriting

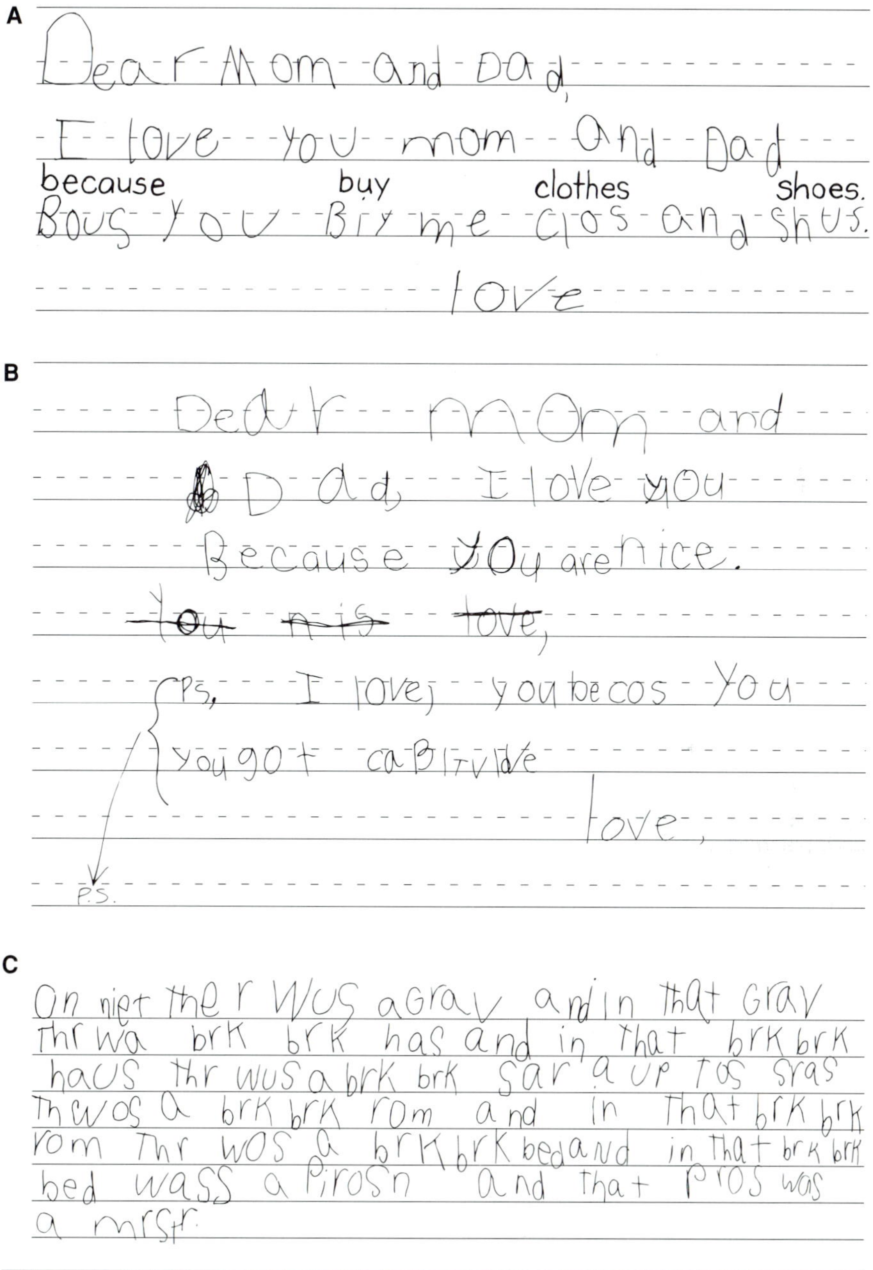

A
Dear Mom and Dad,
I love you mom and Dad
because buy clothes shoes.
Bous you Biy me clos and shus.
love
B
Dear mom and Dad, I love you Because you are nice.
PS, I love you becos you
you got
love,
P.S.
C
On niet ther wus a grav and in that grav

Planning Handwriting Instruction

To plan an instructional program, teachers need to determine which specific letters, types of letters, letter combinations, or other features of handwriting cause individual students difficulty. The *Basic School Skills Inventory—Diagnostic* (Hammill & Leigh, 1983) includes a writing test that assesses aspects of handwriting, including posture and holding a pencil as well as forming letters; the test is norm referenced and includes remedial recommendations.

As with screening, formal diagnostic testing of handwriting is usually unnecessary. Teachers can simply examine samples of students' writing and identify those parts of writing that need further instructional work. To conduct a diagnostic evaluation, a teacher first examines existing samples of a student's writing to judge whether there are general legibility problems (e.g., inconsistent spacing between letters or excessive erasures). Second, the teacher determines whether the sample contains any of the more common types of handwriting errors (refer to Figures 13.1 and 13.2 for examples). Third, the teacher directs the student to produce another handwriting sample (copying from prepared materials) that includes areas not assessed in the first sample or areas that the first assessment has revealed might be problems for the student.

Students' performances on different writing tasks will vary. For example, far-point copying may be more difficult than near-point copying for some students, and both may be easier (or harder) for some students than producing letters when no model is available. Assessment should evaluate these different possibilities. Table 13.1 describes assessment using various writing tasks and gives guidelines for judging accuracy and fluency on them. The activities teachers prescribe should depend on the kinds of mistakes students make.

Monitoring Handwriting Progress

Curriculum-based assessment can be used to evaluate both the legibility and the speed of handwriting. Brief time periods for assessment can be set aside each day. Students can be given probes (short tests designed to assess the specific skill on which they need work) and then asked to write for a specified period of time (perhaps 1 or 2 minutes). The resulting writing samples can be scored for the percentage of letters written legibly (each letter to be judged as either legible or illegible) and the rate of letters written legibly (legible letters per minute). Table 13.1 provides general guidelines for appropriate rates.

Data from progress-monitoring assessments should be placed on graphs or charts to illustrate each student's progress. If more precise scoring is needed for certain aspects of handwriting, each letter can be scored as correct for slant, formation (shape), and ending stroke (Haring, Lovitt, Eaton, & Hansen, 1978). Basic Skill Builders (Beck, Conrad, & Anderson, 1996) includes means for assessing handwriting that conform closely to good practice in monitoring progress.

Students can be taught to evaluate their own progress. The accuracy of their judgments about their writing's legibility can be enhanced by using plastic overlays show-

TABLE 13.1 Guidelines for Assessing Handwriting

Purpose	Directions	Accuracy Standard	Speed Standard
■ Free Writing			
To provide a baseline for evaluating other tasks and for assessing progress	Identify the letters (e.g., alphabet) or words (e.g., names and familiar words) that the student can write readily. Direct the student to write the identified materials repeatedly, as quickly but as neatly as possible.	95–100%	60 characters per minute (cpm); 100 cpm, better
■ Dictation			
To evaluate a student's production of writing when she or he does not know what will come next	Decide whether to test individual letters, words, or phrases. Identify items you are sure the student can write without requiring much thinking (i.e., "known" items); you can use the same item several times in a test. Direct the student to write items as you say them. Watch closely, and, as the student finishes an item, say the next one.	90–100%	70% of standard for free writing
■ Near Copying			
To evaluate a student's production of writing when she or he copies from materials on the desk	1. Familiar: Select highly familiar material for the student to copy. 2. Unfamiliar: Select material the student has not previously seen but that is at about the same difficulty level as in the familiar condition. Compare performances to estimate the contribution of familiarity.	95–100%	75–80% of standard for free writing
■ Far Copying			
To evaluate a student's production of writing when she or he copies from a distant source (e.g., the chalkboard)	1. Familiar: Select highly familiar material for the student to copy. 2. Unfamiliar: Select material the student has not previously seen but that is at about the same difficulty level as in the familiar condition. Compare performances to estimate the contribution of familiarity.	90–100%	75–80% of standard for free writing

ing correctly formed letters or other self-correcting devices (Beck et al., 1996; Jones, Trap, & Cooper, 1977; Stowitschek & Stowitschek, 1979). Self-evaluation improves the handwriting of students with learning disabilities (Kosiewicz, Hallahan, Lloyd, & Graves, 1982; Sweeney, Salva, Cooper, & Talbert-Johnson, 1993). Some commercial products such as Basic Skill Builders (Beck et al., 1996) incorporate self-evaluation to capitalize on its beneficial effects on performance.

Handwriting is an especially good skill to evaluate using portfolio assessment, because the changes in the quality of a student's writing are obvious. Samples of student writing can be kept and compared directly to see whether later efforts are better than earlier ones. Showing such changes to parents can be very helpful in determining whether IEP goals have been achieved. An added advantage of keeping writing samples is that a teacher can evaluate not only handwriting, but also spelling and composition using the same samples.

As already emphasized, a teacher's major concerns about handwriting should be that it is legible and not so slow that production is impaired. To evaluate fluency using portfolios, teachers will need to keep more than just the written products; they will need to add records about the conditions under which the samples were collected, including how long it took students to create the products.

WHAT INTERVENTIONS CAN HELP WITH HANDWRITING DIFFICULTIES?

Teachers regularly confront the question of whether to teach print or cursive handwriting. Those who advocate teaching only printing (e.g., Herrick, 1960; Hildreth, 1960; Templin, 1960; Western, 1977) put forth the following arguments:

1. Printing is more similar to the kind of material students read, making it easier to generalize from one to the other.
2. Printing is learned first and is therefore difficult to unlearn.
3. Printing is more suited to the motor development of young children.
4. Young children's printing is more legible than their cursive writing.
5. Printing is preferred in business and industry.

Others advocate teaching only cursive. The arguments these authorities (e.g., Gillingham & Stillman, 1965; Larson, 1968; Strauss & Lehtinen, 1947) advance include the following:

1. Cursive letters are more difficult to write backward (i.e., reversed).
2. Illegibilities caused by poor letter or word spacing are reduced.
3. Writing cursive is faster.

Research does not show conclusively that a manuscript system is particularly easier to learn than a cursive system or that children write faster in either. In fact, by high school, most students have apparently developed a hybrid writing style that mixes printing and cursive and resembles italics (Duval, 1985). Some authorities contend that special italiclike alphabets are particularly well suited for teaching students with learning disabilities (see Joseph & Mullins, 1970). Probably the best resolution of this matter is to encourage students to use whatever writing system they find comfortable as long as it meets guidelines for speed and legibility.

Developmental Interventions

Traditional handwriting lessons required that students work on near-point copying skills. They practiced forming letters uniformly, neatly, and correctly. Such handwriting lessons are uncommon today.

Many contemporary educators deemphasize handwriting in favor of devoting time to higher-order thinking. Others argue that the advent of technology—particularly use of computers—will mitigate the need for handwriting skill. Given the growing emphasis on teaching fundamental tools, however, lessons on accurate letter formation may return soon. Teachers of students with learning disabilities will need to be prepared to offer adaptations of instruction so their students will not fail under either possible scenario.

Although there is probably little reason to choose one handwriting practice book over another, the application of behavioral principles to handwriting instruction can be helpful. For example, in a program named Write and See, areas of the workbook pages were treated with a chemical so that when students used pens with special ink, the ink and the chemically treated paper interacted. When the students misformed letters, the ink was barely visible. When they formed them correctly, the paper beneath the correct letter strokes turned green. Initially, students traced entire letters, but as the lessons advanced, the cues were gradually made less obvious, and the band within which students had to write for the paper to turn green was narrowed. In this program, accurate responding was automatically reinforced by the changes in ink color, and the reinforcement criteria changed gradually, thus shaping the behavior. Unfortunately, some students with learning disabilities quickly learned that they could obtain the reinforcement by a different means. Instead of tracing the letters, they covered the entire page with the special ink, using the pen like a coloring pen. As they did so, the letters appeared as if by magic.

It is sometimes recommended that young children learning to write use verbal self-guidance; that is, they should tell themselves the stroke sequences as they form letters. For example, while making the printed letter *m,* the child might say, "First, I make a short stick, then I make one hhhuummmp, two hhhuuummmps. There, that's an *m.*" According to Hallahan's theory about the passive learner (Hallahan & Reeve, 1980), this procedure may be particularly helpful for students with learning disabilities. Preliminary research (Hayes, 1980; Hayes & Flower, 1980; Robin, Armel, & O'Leary, 1975) has found small beneficial effects of verbal self-guidance.

Technology

For students in school in the early years of the 21st century, facility with using computers, particularly keyboarding, will be extremely important. One of the questions confronting teachers of students with learning disabilities is whether to teach them keyboarding skills and, if so, by what method.

Following publication of many opinion-based articles, research on keyboarding began to appear in the 1980s. Out of this research came several important findings that teachers should consider regarding keyboarding skills (MacArthur & Graham, 1987; MacArthur & Shneiderman, 1986). Although most students say they prefer using computers to writing by hand (MacArthur & Graham, 1987), when using computers, they

- use the hunt-and-peck method, making them type at only two to ten words per minute
- make errors more frequently when typing than when writing by hand, especially in spacing between words and sentences and in positioning the cursor for deleting text
- do not understand how text on the screen may be reformatted when printed, especially when inserting material near the ends of lines, where they may add unneeded hard returns
- confuse the version of a file in computer memory with the version on the disk, failing to understand that saving a file with a given name will overwrite a file with that same name on the disk
- produce passages that are very similar in length, quality, structure, vocabulary, and other features, regardless of whether they are writing using a computer or by hand

Research clearly shows that students with learning disabilities need instruction in using computers (Margalit & Roth, 1989; Outhred, 1989). For example, students' typing methods and slow rate of composing demand powerful instruction in touch-typing skills. Unless students acquire facility with typing, they will have to devote so much of their time and effort to finding individual letters that they will have little time and effort remaining to devote to creating sensible, coherent, and interesting prose. Similarly, unless they learn rudimentary aspects of computer literacy (e.g., saving a file under a new name), they are likely to be frustrated by mistakes that cause them to lose previous work.

Computer skills will be very important for most students in today's schools. Using computers may help some students overcome some problems (e.g., illegible handwriting), but teachers should expect that they will have to teach students how to use computers. Such instruction is likely to require teachers to adopt or develop powerful techniques (see Graham & MacArthur, 1988). Students with learning disabilities are unlikely to discover how to use keyboards and computers in the absence of strong teaching.

There are many computer-assisted programs for learning keyboarding, some of which are shown in Table 13.2. Teachers report that one of the most substantial impediments to their use of microcomputers is the absence of high-quality software (Okolo, Rieth, & Bahr, 1989). Many keyboarding programs have drawbacks. They usually require that teachers adapt them to suit students with learning disabilities. In help-

TABLE 13.2 Software for Teaching Typing by Touch (Keyboarding)

Product	Ages	Company
Mavis Beacon Teaches Typing	9 to adult	Mindscape
Stickybear Typing	6 to adult	Optimum Resource
Kid Keys	4 to 8	Davidson
Typing Tutor	9 to adult	Simon & Schuster
Mario Teaches Typing	6–10	Brainstorm
Read, Write & Type	6–8	Learning Company
Flash Typing	8–12	Flash Typing
KeyBoard Coach	8–adult	Herzog Research
Type to Learn	7 to adult	Sunburst

ing these students, teachers will have to monitor whether they are following standard practices for typing. For example, do they assume appropriate home-row positions? Are they practicing according to a sensible schedule? As students become more proficient in using a typing program, teachers might adopt a self-monitoring system in which students can ask themselves if they are sitting up straight, keeping their fingers in the home position, curving their fingers, holding their wrists flat, and so forth. For students with learning disabilities, such scaffolding and practice are probably especially important. (See the section on effective strategies in Chapter 3.)

Effective Teaching Procedures

Diverse general recommendations for improving poor handwriting have been advanced. Some suggest that students be given relaxation training (Carter & Synolds, 1974). Others recommend "flipbooks" that make moving models of the strokes for forming letters, much like the simple animations one can produce by flipping pages rapidly (Wright & Wright, 1980). As intriguing as these and other suggestions may be, there is no strong empirical support for using them.

Although handwriting has metacognitive components, it is fundamentally a motor skill. The metacognitive components (planning and monitoring; see Chapter 10) will probably benefit from self-management training. The motoric aspects of handwriting, however, will benefit greatly from practice and reinforcement. Interventions geared to improve handwriting should probably provide copious opportunities for students to practice handwriting (perhaps including multi-sensory components, Massad & Etzel, 1972), receive feedback on its quality, and monitor their own work.

Reinforcement

Behaviorally oriented special educators have repeatedly demonstrated a "near cure" for such handwriting problems as reversals. The procedure is simple: First, when the student writes a target letter, numeral, or word correctly, the teacher provides reinforcement (e.g., praise). Second, when the student writes an item incorrectly, the teacher requires the student to correct it. At least six studies have reported the successful use of this or a similar procedure (Fauke, Burnett, Powers, & Sulzer-Azaroff, 1973; Hasazi & Hasazi, 1972; Lahey, Busemeyer, O'Hara, & Beggs, 1977; Smith & Lovitt, 1973; Stromer, 1975, 1977). The very existence of these studies, let alone their ages, makes it interesting that people continue to see reversals as indicative of learning disabilities.

Self-Instruction Training

Cognitive-behavioral techniques such as self-instruction (Graham, 1982) and self-recording (Blanford & Lloyd, 1987) have also been used extensively for remediating handwriting problems. These techniques have proved effective with both younger students and high school students. For example, adolescents with learning disabilities received specialized instruction in using self-guiding statements and self-correction procedures (Sweeney et al., 1993). The instruction improved their performances markedly, as shown in Figure 13.3.

WHAT SPELLING PROBLEMS DO STUDENTS EXPERIENCE?

Because the English language appears irregular in its spellings, it is difficult to learn to spell. Spelling would be much easier if each phoneme of our language had one and only one grapheme. But that is not the case; there are 251 different spellings for the 44 sounds of English (Hull, 1981), and the language contains many irregularly spelled words. For example, cough, tough, though, and through all end with the same four letters but have different ending pronunciations. Teachers need to know not only how these and other oddities of English spelling work, but also enough about them to help students learn similarities and differences in words. Unfortunately, too few teacher education programs provide sufficient instruction for future teachers to develop a command of the relations between English sounds and their written equivalents (Moats, 1995).

The formal name for the system of representing spoken language in a written form is **orthography,** which comes from the Greek ortho ("straight," "regular," or "correct") and graphy ("process or manner of writing"). Thus, when students learn the orthography of English, they are learning the system for the correct spelling of English.

Spelling requires that a person produce in writing or orally the correct sequence of letters that form a particular word. To do this, a person converts phonemes into graphemes. The phonemes may actually have been heard (as happens when a spelling word is dictated by a teacher), or they may have been covertly produced (as happens when a person spells while writing a poem). Just as grapheme-phoneme correspondence is central to reading, phoneme-grapheme correspondence is central to spelling. Though reading and spelling share many attributes, they differ in important ways. For

FIGURE 13.3 Handwriting Improvement after Specialized Instruction

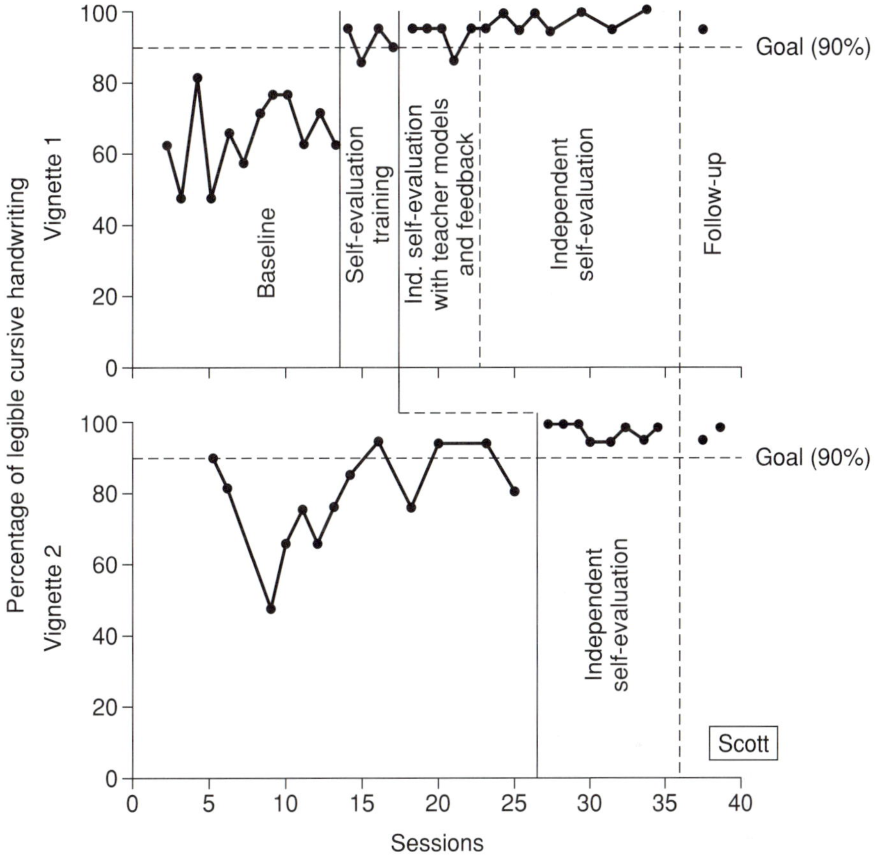

Source: From "Using Self-Evaluation to Improve Difficult-to-Read Handwriting of Secondary Students" by W. J. Sweeney, E. Salva, J. O. Cooper, and C. Talbert-Johnson, 1993, *Journal of Behavioral Education, 3,* p. 436. Copyright 1993 by Journal of Behavioral Education. Reprinted by permission.

example, in the former, students see letters and say sounds, but in the latter, they hear sounds and write letters.

Spellings may also be produced by naming the letters in the correct order. However, spelling aloud is less similar to the usual, or authentic, task in which students must generate spellings while composing. Oral spellings of words are primarily valuable when teaching students word patterns that require similar strategies. Here one can see the divergence between the models of learning disabilities discussed in Chapter 3. Whereas an advocate of a constructivist approach might eschew tasks in which the teacher dictates words and students spell them aloud or write them, an advocate of a task-analytic approach would use just these tasks to provide students intensive practice in applying a strategy to words that conform to a given spelling pattern.

Spelling Errors

Most of our knowledge about spelling problems comes from studies of the kinds of errors people make when they spell. Analyses of misspellings reveal that most errors are phonetically acceptable, made in the middle of words, and involve alterations of a single phoneme (Graham & Miller, 1979).

Figure 13.4 shows the results of a spelling test of a young student with learning disabilities. The words are drawn from the *Wide Range Achievement Test* (Jastak & Jastak, 1978); the correct words are (1) go, (2) cat, (3) in, (4) baby, (5) and, (6) will, (7) make, (8) him, (9) say, (10) cut, (11) cook, (12) light, (13) must, (14) dress, (15) reach, (16) order, (17) watch, and (18) enter. The girl who wrote the words was 8 years old. According to the test manual, her spelling performance was at the sixth month of the first grade; her score was at the tenth percentile. How many mistakes appear to be phonetically acceptable, made in the middle of the words, or show problems with just one phoneme? How many mistakes might simply reflect the quality of the girl's handwriting?

Evidence about changes in the development of spelling skill comes from studies of the spelling errors of normally achieving students (Beers, 1974; Gentry, 1977;

FIGURE 13.4 Spelling Test of a Student with Learning Disabilities

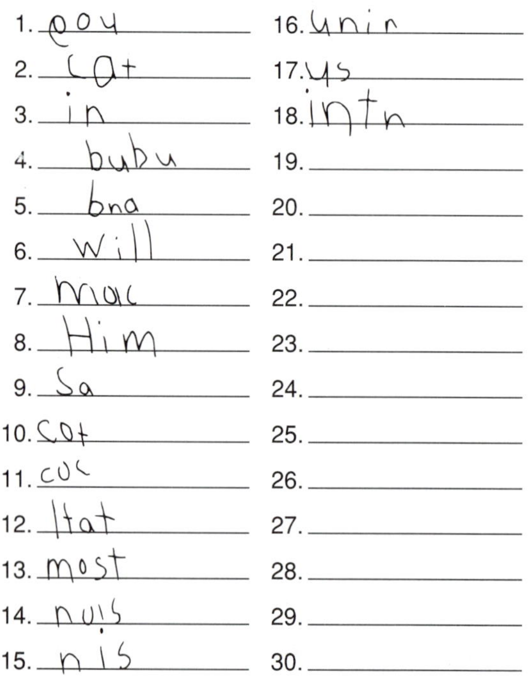
1. eoy
2. cat
3. in
4. bubu
5. bna
6. will
7. mac
8. Him
9. Sa
10. cot
11. cuc
12. ltat
13. most
14. nuis
15. nis
16. unir
17. us
18. intn
19.
20.
21.
22.
23.
24.
25.
26.
27.
28.
29.
30.

Source: From *Introduction to Learning Disabilities,* 2nd ed. (p.246) by D. P. Hallahan, J. M. Kauffman, and J. W Lloyd, 1985, Saddle River, NJ: Prentice-Hall. Copyright 1985 by Prentice-Hall. Reprinted by permission.

Henderson, 1990; Henderson & Beers, 1980; Marsh, Friedman, Welch, & Desberg, 1980; Templeton & Baer, 1992). As children grow, their approach to spelling changes. Initially, they spell words quite simply (e.g., "type" as "TP"). Later, students represent all the phonemes of the word, although they might do so incorrectly (e.g., spelling "type" "TIP," a spelling that reads correctly if the letter *i* "says its name"). This strategy works well as long as the words are regularly pronounced consonant-vowel-consonant words. Still later, students may represent all the sounds and employ some of the conventions of orthography, although they still may not spell correctly (e.g., spelling "type" "TIPE"). By the time they have reached the fifth grade, students have added other, slightly different strategies to the way they approach spelling. They have learned to use additional letters to indicate the pronunciation of parts of words (e.g., using the "silent-e" rule) and appear to work by analogy (e.g., in trying to spell the word "criticize," realizing it has a second *c* because they know the word critic has a second *c*).

The most consistent findings about the spelling of children with learning disabilities come from studies comparing normally achieving students with those who have reading problems (Barron, 1980; Bruck, 1988; Carlisle, 1987; Carpenter, 1983; Carpenter & Miller, 1982; Frith, 1980; Gerber & Hall, 1981; Lennox & Siegel, 1993, 1998; Moats, 1983; Nelson, 1980; Worthy & Invernizzi, 1990). Students with learning disabilities or severe reading problems

- produce unrecognizable spellings
- spell fewer words correctly than do their normally achieving age-mates, even when IQ differences are taken into account
- write words in ways that are more similar to those of younger students and show particular difficulty with morphological structure
- produce spellings that have some phonetic features of the correct spellings
- use spellings that do not include the special markings that show how to pronounce some parts of words
- do not necessarily misspell words by making reversal errors

Indeed, the processes pupils with reading disabilities use to read and spell do not appear to differ qualitatively from those used by nondisabled students. However, older students with reading problems appear to produce errors that are better visual matches for the words than the errors of their peers at the same grade level (Lennox & Siegel, 1998). In general, their characteristic errors are

> best explained by postulating that the dyslexic children do not use their knowledge of sound-spelling correspondences when spelling unfamiliar words. . . . Thus, this difference may reflect performance or strategic factors rather than basic differences in the processes used for spelling. (Bruck, 1988, p. 66)

Those rare students who read well but spell poorly may depend heavily on the syntactic and semantic aspects of print to help them read, but they may have problems using phonology (Frith, 1980). Most of these problems with spelling interact with and have implications for other areas, particularly reading.

Effects of Spelling Problems

Teachers working with students who have substantial spelling problems can expect these students to have difficulties in reading, in part, because of their difficulties with phonemic awareness. Phonemic awareness seems to be important in both the decoding aspect of reading and the encoding aspect of spelling (Hulme & Joshi, 1998). It may also be the result of other related problems yet to be discovered.

Spelling problems may actually hamper handwriting. A student who does not know how to spell a word automatically may experience a delay of the motor activity involved in writing the word. Stopping to think about the spelling of a word disrupts the smooth flow of handwriting or keyboarding. This illustrates the reciprocal nature of many learning problems: Handwriting fluency probably negatively affects spelling, and spelling problems probably negatively affect handwriting. Reciprocal relationships such as these are probably part of the reason learning disabilities are so difficult to correct, part of the reason that simplistic, unidimensional approaches are insufficient.

Students who have trouble spelling words will also have difficulty with composition. They will produce misspellings that make it hard for their readers to understand what they mean. Their writing vocabulary may be limited because they will use only words they are sure they can spell correctly.

HOW IS SPELLING PERFORMANCE ASSESSED?

Assessment is the necessary first step in identifying students with spelling disabilities before interventions can be implemented. For an explanation of ways to assess spelling disabilities, see Howell and Morehead (1987).

Simply scoring spelling words as correct or incorrect is probably the most time-honored way of evaluating spelling. Not all words are equally difficult, however, so more fine-grained means of scoring offer advantages. Teachers should consider counting the number of letters spelled correctly in a word or the number of two-letter sequences spelled correctly. (To use the two-letter sequence system, a teacher looks at the start of the word and counts one correct if it starts with the correct letter, then looks at the first two letters of the word and counts one correct if those two are correct, then looks at the second and third letters and counts one if those are correct, and continues making the decisions about the letters until counting the last letter alone.) Table 13.3 illustrates these strategies, which have been shown to be trustworthy and valuable methods of assessing spelling (Deno, Mirkin, Lowry, & Kuehnle, 1980; Haring et al., 1978). These different ways of scoring are particularly valuable for diagnosing unique needs and monitoring progress. They are less useful for standardized assessments unless one can develop norms.

TABLE 13.3 Comparison of Scoring Systems for Spelling

Word	Student's Spelling	Word Correct	Letters Correct	2-Letter Sequences
cat	cat	1/1	3/3	4/4
cat	kat	0/1	2/3	3/4
skate	scate	0/1	4/5	4/6
misspell	mispell	0/1	7/8	8/9

Standardized Assessment

Most standardized achievement batteries include measures of spelling skills. For example, the *California Achievement Tests 5th Edition* (CTB/Macmillan/McGraw-Hill, 1993), the *Peabody Individual Achievement Test—Revised* (Markwardt, 1989), or PIAT, and the *Weschler Individual Achievement Test,* or WIAT (Psychological Corporation, 1992), all have spelling subtests. Because pupils who have spelling problems are very likely to have low scores on any of these tests, using them makes it possible to identify students with spelling deficits.

Many major achievement tests assess spelling skills by having students select the correct spelling from several choices or indicate whether a spelling is correct or incorrect. Because students' performances on this type of task may differ from their performances when required to produce the correct spellings of words, further testing for spelling skills is usually well advised. When students choose a correct spelling for a word, they may use a different strategy than they use when generating the spelling of that word.

Other achievement batteries require students to write the spellings for words as the examiner dictates them. Examples are the *Metropolitan Achievement Test—7th Edition* (Prescott, Balow, Hogan, & Farr, 1992), the *Wide Range Achievement Test—3* (Wilkinson, 1993), the WIAT, and the *Woodcock-Johnson Psychoeducational Battery—Revised* (Woodcock & Johnson, 1989/1990). Tests that require students to write spellings may seem more difficult, but they test skills that are closer to those required in actual schoolwork.

Some tests that are designed specifically to measure spelling skill may also be useful for screening. For example, the *Test of Written Spelling—3* or TWS—3 (Larsen & Hammill, 1994) provides several scores that allow comparison to norm groups so that a teacher can determine whether and to what extent a student is behind his or her peers. In practice, most teachers who test students to determine whether they are eligible for special education use an individually administered achievement test, such as the *Woodcock-Johnson* or TWS—3, that requires students to write words from dictation.

Planning Spelling Instruction

Planning programs requires information about where to begin instruction, what skill areas need teaching, and so forth. For the purpose of placement, the most useful diagnostic tests are probably those that accompany the spelling program being used. Other methods for diagnosing spelling problems are formal tests, analysis of spelling errors, and informal spelling inventories.

Several formal tests assess different aspects of spelling skill. For example, the TWS—3 is composed of two types of words: those that follow regular spelling patterns (are spelled the way they sound) and those that have irregular spellings. Presumably, if students do well on the regularly spelled words but poorly on the irregularly spelled words, instruction in how to remember some words as wholes would be appropriate.

Some older instruments assess different parts of spelling skill. For example, the *Gates-Russell Spelling Diagnostic Test* (Gates & Russell, 1940) has sections for testing sound-symbol relationships, pronunciation of words, and other areas, as well as skill in spelling words. For students who have difficulty with certain of the subtests but not with others, an instructional plan that emphasizes the subareas on which they need to work would be prepared.

By classifying the words used on other tests, such as the WIAT, teachers can develop preliminary hypotheses about students' needs in spelling. However, such a strategy requires further evaluation of the students' performances, to sample them across types of words. Another time-honored approach is to analyze students' spelling errors.

Error Analysis

Analyzing spelling errors involves looking for consistent patterns in a student's mistakes. One purpose of error analysis is to identify mistaken strategies—to "get inside the head" of a student and determine what is going wrong. Presumably, if teachers can do this, they can prescribe appropriate remedies.

Several methods of analyzing spelling errors have been proposed. One of the most widely known is Boder's (1971a, 1971b) approach to classifying students with reading problems according to their spelling errors. Those whose misspellings vary most from correct spellings are considered "diseidetic," meaning they depend on visual information to produce their spellings. Other students' misspellings are classified as "dysphonetic," meaning they use sound system information to generate their spellings. In practice, dysphonetic misspellings are closer to correct than diseidetic spellings. However, these diagnostic categories appear unreliable, and it is not clear to what extent they actually reflect the instruction students receive (Holmes & Peper, 1977; Lyon, 1983). Indeed, with minor exceptions, the spelling errors students with learning disabilities make are quite similar to those of their nondisabled but younger peers (Bruck, 1988; Worthy & Invernizzi, 1990).

Other approaches to error analysis include recording types of errors, such as where in the word the mistake occurs (Cartwright, 1969; Edgington, 1967). These approaches may have more value than Boder's (1971a, 1971b) because they do not require as much inference and are not based on otherwise unsupported assumptions about subtypes of learners. Also, if students repeatedly make the same types of errors, these error patterns probably form a good basis for monitoring progress. Teachers could record the percentage of time students make the same types of errors and determine whether instruction is appropriately affecting them.

Teachers often base their error analyses on the data they get from informal spelling inventories. Although this is a solid strategy, it must be exercised with caution. As with analyses of students' responses on formal spelling tests, teachers must be certain to sample performance across types of words.

Informal Spelling Inventories

Informal spelling inventories are called informal because they do not have norms and are administered under nonstandard conditions (see Chapter 4). Informal inventories are usually used for clinical rather than psychological reasons.

An informal spelling inventory may be constructed by selecting a sample of words from each level of an available language arts or spelling program. Students can be tested on their spelling of the words from the sample lists, and the level at which they make 20% or more mistakes can be considered their instructional spelling level. However, those who use this approach to diagnosis must be aware that some students may happen to know (or not know) how to spell only those words on the given lists. When placement decisions are made on the basis of an informal spelling inventory, teachers should be certain to use information gained from progress-monitoring tests to adjust the placements as the school year proceeds.

Monitoring Progress in Spelling

Spelling is an area in which the traditional teaching methods come closest to incorporating progress monitoring. Using curriculum-based assessment makes students more aware of their spelling goals and of teacher feedback about progress in spelling (Fuchs, Butterworth, & Fuchs, 1989).

Recording weekly spelling test scores provides teachers with regularly collected data about how well their students are doing in spelling. However, because the lists of words on which the students are tested usually change each week, scores may be at least partially influenced by the difficulty of a particular list. Also, students may be tested on words they already know and not get enough practice on words they do not know. Furthermore, such tests do not assess performance under authentic conditions for spelling, one of the emphases in learning disabilities today.

Another difficulty in using traditional weekly spelling tests to monitor progress is that they do not provide rate-based data that are common in curriculum-based assessment (see Chapter 4). If the teacher or someone else dictates the words to be spelled, some amount of the time it takes to write a word is out of the control of the responding student. Teachers can use a time-limited dictation of about 6–7 seconds to approximate normal rates of spelling words, though this surely must vary on the basis of word length (Shinn, Tindal, & Stein, 1988).

Flow lists (Haring et al., 1978) provide a way to test spelling without depending on weekly lists of different words. A flow list is a spelling list composed of words that an individual student has not mastered; when the student masters a word on the list (i.e., gets it right several times in a row), that word is removed from the flow list, and another word is added. A 50% to 50% ratio of known to unknown words on a list optimally improves spelling of students with learning disabilities. Single- or two-letter scoring systems are particularly valuable for monitoring progress with flow lists.

WHAT INTERVENTIONS HELP STUDENTS' SPELLING DIFFICULTIES?

Even though some of the ability to spell has a genetic component (DeFries, Stevenson, Gillis, & Wadsworth, 1991), spelling ability is not fixed or unchangeable. Spelling performance is affected by many factors and is thus open to instruction.

Some programs for teaching spelling are designed to develop the spelling ability of young children who have not previously been exposed to instruction. As in reading, these are called developmental programs. Other programs are designed to improve the spelling competence of students who have failed to learn to spell well. These are usually called corrective or remedial programs.

Regardless of whether an intervention is designed for teaching beginning or remedial spelling, it should incorporate what research shows are effective practices in spelling instruction. Careful reviews of spelling research have identified many practices that are important for students with learning disabilities (Gordon, Vaughn, & Schumm, 1993, Graham & Miller, 1979; Kerr & Lambert, 1982; McNaughton, Hughes, & Clark, 1994). Table 13.4 describes practices that have been tested with students with learning disabilities and found to be more or less effective.

Developmental Interventions

English orthography is not absolutely consistent. A major controversy in spelling is how much instruction should be devoted to teaching students the regularities of English orthography.

> One of the central issues concerning how spelling should be taught involves the vehicle by which we spell—the writing system. For if, on the one hand, the orthography is regarded as an erratic artifact of its historical development, then the conclusion must inevitably be reached that learning to spell is dependent upon learning the spellings of independent words. On the other hand, if the orthography is regarded as being systematic, then it can be concluded that learning to spell involves learning characteristics of the system which can be generalized to words sharing those characteristics. (Hodges, 1982, p. 285)

Some believe that instruction should not emphasize the relationships between spoken and written English. There are too many rules about converting speech to print

TABLE 13.4 Effective and Ineffective Spelling Instructional Practices

Less Effective	More Effective
Using a memorization approach	Using an approach in which students learn phoneme-grapheme correspondences
Presenting words in sentences or paragraphs	Presenting words in lists
Using the study-test method	Using the test-study-test method
Ignoring errors	Requiring students to practice mistaken words, pointing out (even imitating) mistakes
Presenting extensive lists of words to be learned each week	Using brief lists of only three words per day
Having students devise their own methods of studying	Providing specific strategies for studying, including structured peer tutoring
Treating spelling as an uninteresting and unimportant activity	Rewarding achievement, using spelling games
Having students practice writing words in the air	Having students practice writing words on paper, tracing letter tiles, or typing words on a computer

for children to learn them all. Furthermore, the words that students should be taught in learning to relate spoken language to written language would not be those that are most useful to them. Children rarely use many different words in their writing, so spelling instruction should cover those words they do use.

Others (e.g., Groff, 1979; Hodges, 1982) argue against the notion that students should be taught a core of known words as rote items, even if those words may be the ones they use most frequently in their writing. Despite the apparent irregularities of the spellings of English words, there is a great amount of consistency. The word "cough," although it is irregular, is not spelled "kromp." Depending on which experts one consults, there may be as much as 90% regularity in English spellings (Deverell, 1971; Hanna, Hanna, Hodges, & Erwin, 1966).

Spelling is not simply a matter of writing symbols for the sounds one hears. Sound-symbol spelling gets one started, but the multiple ways a sound can be written in English present problems. For example, the *s* sound can be written with *s* (*s*ent), *c* (*c*ent), or *sc* (*sc*ent), and the first sound in the word "cat" can be written with a *c* (*c*an), *k* (*k*in), *ch* (*ch*ord), or *kh* (*kh*aki). When spelling words, people apparently use not just their knowledge of symbol-sound relationships, but also some knowledge of the probability that certain spellings occur under certain conditions. Furthermore, they apparently use other strategies, such as analogy and, to a lesser extent, simple memory for visual patterns, when spelling words. Particularly important, they use their knowledge of the underlying structure of English. As a consequence, teachers should be prepared to promote flexible use of several different strategies.

To teach efficiently, teachers need to resolve some of this ambiguity for students. One approach is to ignore incorrect spelling of words in young children's writing, allowing them to spell words however they wish. Today in education, allowing children to use their own unique spellings is often referred as "invented spelling" (see Box 13.1).

Another approach to resolving the ambiguity is to build word lists for spelling practice judiciously. Choosing words to be used in teaching spelling is an important step in designing effective spelling instruction. There are several important kinds of words:

- *regular words,* which most closely approximate spelling-to-sound correspondences, such as "cat," "cake," "pinch," "milk," and "run"
- *high-frequency, less regular words,* which, although they approximate spelling-to-sound correspondences in part, are slightly irregular in their orthography, such as "was," "said," and "come"
- *homophonous words,* which require context for the speller to resolve which spelling is correct, such as "there," "their," and "they're"
- *demon words,* which are most often misspelled in English, such as "misspell"

Word lists for spelling should probably incorporate selections from each of these types. Spelling lists based on words that are both frequently used in children's writing and illustrate useful phoneme-grapheme relationships are available (Graham, Harris, & Loynachan, 1994). Learning to spell the words on such lists should help students learn the underlying orthography of English and acquire correct spellings for some words they will use often.

Another important feature of English should be represented in words chosen for spelling instruction. Teaching students building blocks that are slightly larger than sound-symbol relations is one good way to reduce the ambiguity of English orthography. Morphographs are one useful building block (Dixon, 1993). *Morphograph* refers to bases and affixes (prefixes and suffixes) and is based on morphemes (see Chapter 11). The idea behind using morphographs is deceptively simple but extremely powerful.

Let's pretend that you can spell only three morphographs:

Prefix	Base	Suffix
re	cover	ed

You can't make very many words from just these three morphographs: *recover, covered, recovered.* Now let's raise your knowledge from three to seven morphographs:

Prefix	Base	Suffix
re	cover	ed
dis	pute	able
un		

BOX 13.1 ***CURRENT ISSUES***

Invented Spelling

Invented spelling is one of the most controversial topics in education today. It refers to the way that children write words when they have not yet learned correct spellings for them. Examples of invented spellings are "lv" for "love," "cloz" for "clothes," "at" for "eighty," "bi" for "buy," and "frns" for "friends." These are called invented spellings because children develop them on their own, solving the problem of writing by inventing ways to represent words with symbols.

When young children first begin writing, their spelling makes little sense to those who know how to read and spell. Capital letters appear in the middle of words. Letters are misshaped and disproportionately sized. Strings of consonants run together. When one asks a young child what she has written soon after she has written it, however, the child can often point to the "words" and "read" them. Her spellings make very good sense to her. This seems to show what children know about our written language (Rubin & Eberhardt, 1996).

Ideas about invented spelling evolved from research showing how young students' spellings change as they grow older. Research revealed that there was a logic underlying children's spellings. As they grow older, their spellings gradually become closer to the conventional spelling (Beers & Henderson, 1977; Read, 1971). Invented spelling skill appears to predict, in part, later skill in spelling and also whether training in phonological awareness will benefit children (Richgels, 1995; Torgesen & Davis, 1995). Furthermore, when young children receive training in phonemic awareness skills, their invented spellings improve (Tangel & Blachman, 1995).

The heart of the controversy, however, is not whether children invent spellings or whether those who are better at doing so will later do better in reading and writing. The controversy turns on whether teachers of young children should promote invented spellings. Proponents claim that encouraging young students to spell words however they think they should be spelled frees the students from unnecessary concern about correct spelling. They argue that it is more important for young students who are just learning our written language system to learn that writing communicates ideas than it is for them to master the conventional spellings of words. Detractors claim that encouraging children to invent spellings lessens their ability to learn from reading where words are spelled conventionally.

Teachers probably should take a balanced view of invented spelling. Encouraging children to express their ideas freely is important, but so is helping them move toward correct spelling. Teachers who encourage children to write can happily respond to their invented spellings and help them revise their written products so they have correct spellings. Teachers may also use invented spellings as a guide to instruction by matching classroom activities to the spelling level evidenced in children's written work (Invernizzi, Abouzeid, & Gill, 1994).

Take a look at the words you can form when you increase from three to just seven morphgraphs: *recover, recoverable, recovered, unrecoverable, unrecovered, repute, reputable, reputed, disreputable, disrepute, coverable, covered, uncover, uncoverable, uncovered, discover, discoverable, discovered, undiscoverable, undiscovered, disputate, disputable, disputed, indisputable, undisputed,* and so on.

Now let's increase the number of morphographs you can use from 7 to 750. The different combinations they make should give us somewhere in the neighborhood of 12,000 to 15,000 words.

Not bad, considering there's a good chance you can already spell many of the 750 morphographs. (Dixon, 1993, p. 30)

Commercial programs in language arts incorporate spelling instruction. In keeping with tenets of the whole-language philosophy, some programs attempt to coordinate the words students read with those they learn to spell. Others develop spelling independently.

- Spelling Mastery (Dixon, Engelmann, Meier, Steely, & Wells, 1998) is based on systematic teaching of spelling by sounds (a synthetic approach) in the early grades and morphographs in the later grades. It is designed to cover developmental spelling instruction from grades 2 to 6. Spelling Mastery uses the principles of Direct Instruction and coordinates with the Reading Mastery program.
- Open Court Reading and Writing (Open Court, 1989) systematically integrates spelling instruction with reading and writing. Teachers expressly show students individual letters and say the sounds for them. Early in the program, students practice spelling words according to spelling patterns, and later they learn to use more sophisticated strategies.
- Celebrate Reading (Scott, Foresman, 1993) does not stress spelling in the early grades. It introduces different special features (e.g., endings such as -ing and -ed) with each lesson in third grade. In later grades, teachers are to encourage students to proofread their written work.
- Treasury of Literature (Harcourt Brace, 1995) includes early lessons on phonemic awareness and introduces letter-sound correspondences gradually, beginning late in the first grade. In later years, it embeds spelling activities in written expression activities and literature-based reading passages.

Teachers of students with learning disabilities in the primary and elementary grades should study the spelling program used in their students' general education classrooms. It is important to coordinate their work on spelling closely with the instruction delivered there (Kulieke & Jones, 1993). Important adaptations will probably have to include providing for extra practice, making the orthographic relationships among words more explicit (i.e., big ideas), promoting consistent use of effective cognitive strategies, and providing scaffolding.

Remedial Interventions

Many of the same issues that arise in developmental instruction also are apparent in remedial instruction. For example, teachers must decide what words to teach in remedying spelling problems. Using spelling lists composed of words a student has misspelled in his or her compositions does not do much to improve spelling; when students write, they generally choose words they already know how to spell. Thus, this kind of list would not reflect the student's spelling problems. Lists made up of words that many students misspell will be little better because students, especially older ones, vary so much in the words they use. Specially selected word lists probably would not include words that lend themselves to illustrating spelling patterns. Without sufficient examples of spelling patterns, students are unlikely to learn generalized spelling skills (Kerr & Lambert, 1982).

Other practices have empirical support. Chief among these are the ones described in Table 13.4 (Gordon et al., 1993; Graham & Miller, 1979; McNaughton et al., 1994). In addition, researchers have found the following practices helpful with pupils who have learning disabilities (e.g., Anderson-Inman, 1981; Bryant, Drabin, & Gettinger, 1981; Gettinger, Bryant, & Fayne, 1982; McNeish, Heron, & Okyere, 1992; Van Houten & Van Houten, 1991):

- Present only a few spelling words on each day of instruction, and encourage students to break them into morphographs.
- Provide distributed practice (repeat words at different times).
- Teach for generalization by focusing on phonemic spelling patterns (i.e., illustrating the big ideas underlying spelling).
- Maximize the effects of training in one setting to induce transfer to other settings.
- Promote self-correction of spelling words as a means of practicing correct responses.

Technology

Technology has frequently been applied to spelling. In instructional applications, computers have been valuable aids for enhancing spelling skill. For example, computer-assisted spelling practice produces more academic engagement and better achievement than traditional practice using paper and pencil for students with learning disabilities (MacArthur, Haynes, Malouf, & Harris, 1990). Special techniques such as phonological awareness and constant time delay can be adapted to computers and will increase students' spelling performances (Stevens, Blackhurst, & Slaton, 1991; Wise & Olson, 1998).

As a tool for assessing spelling skill, computers have been helpful in some but not all ways. For example, studies have examined the use of computers to administer and score spelling tests (Hasselbring & Crossland, 1982; Varnhagen & Gerber, 1984). Essentially, the computer dictates the spelling words on a test, and the students type their spellings of them. Although administering and scoring the tests by computer took less time, students' answers were sometimes scored improperly, and their scores on the computer-administered versions were lower than when they were administered the tests in the standard format. Similarly, teachers can use computers to help them monitor the progress of students with learning disabilities. Those whose teachers used computers to help monitor their students' progress in spelling had clearer ideas about their goals in spelling and said they were getting better feedback about their progress. However, there were no significant differences between the learning outcomes for these students and others whose teachers had not used computers to supplement their monitoring of progress (Fuchs et al., 1989).

Effective Teaching Procedures

Regardless of the many complexities of spelling, teachers can draw from research about effective practices to guide instruction. Some methods with a long history of use in learning disabilities have preliminary support in research. For example, the Orton-Gillingham methods have produced beneficial effects with students both in elementary schools and in college (Guyer, Banks, & Guyer, 1993; Vickery, Reynolds, & Cochran, 1987). In addition to those practices listed previously (see Tables 13.3, 13.4, and related text), teachers can use the five techniques described in the following sections.

Phonemic Awareness Training

The Auditory Discrimination in Depth program (Lindamood & Lindamood, 1975) illustrates one approach to phonemic awareness training. Based on research examining, among other things, areas of difficulty with phonological tasks (e.g., Calfee, Lindamood, & Lindamood, 1973) and on efforts to identify isolable component skills for reading and spelling (e.g., Calfee, 1977), the Auditory Discrimination in Depth program provides intensive work on phonemic segmentation. Students learn to identify and classify sounds, represent sound segments and syllables using colored blocks, and associate phonemes with graphemes. The program can also be adapted to work with computers (Wise & Olson, 1998). In one study, students with learning disabilities who received instruction based on the Auditory Discrimination in Depth program made greater gains in spelling than did those who received a traditional, intensive reading and spelling program (Kennedy & Bachman, 1993).

Practice Procedures

Behavior analysts have examined several aspects of spelling instruction, and these studies have revealed that many interventions have positive effects on spelling performance. Reinforcing correct spelling—even with access to free time—increases students' spelling accuracy (Lovitt, Guppy, & Blattner, 1969). Another feature that has been studied illustrates the importance of providing adequate practice opportunities. These studies lead to recommendations that teachers

- present daily practice tests on parts of a weekly spelling test before presenting the weekly test itself (Rieth et al., 1974)
- require students to rewrite several times those words they missed on practice tests (Foxx & Jones, 1978; Matson, Esveldt-Dawson, & Kazdin, 1982; Ollendick, Matson, Esveldt-Dawson, & Shapiro, 1980)

- imitate students' errors and then require them to write the words correctly (Gerber, 1986; Kauffman, Hallahan, Haas, Brame, & Boren, 1978)
- present a few unknown words in a list of known spelling words (Cooke, Guzaukas, Pressley, & Kerr, 1993; Neef, Iwata, & Bailey, 1977)
- arrange for tutoring by parents or peers (Broden, Beasley, & Hall, 1978; Harris, Sherman, Henderson, & Harris, 1972)

Some commercial products incorporate various practice procedures that are helpful for students with learning disabilities. Basic Skill Builders (Beck et al., 1996) and Speed Spelling (Proff, 1978) are examples. These programs include features of curriculum-based assessment, such as timing and graphing of student performance, as well.

Time Delay

One technique from the behavioral literature that has been the focus of considerable study is **progressive time delay.** In it, the teacher pauses briefly (3 seconds) after asking a question. If the student responds correctly during the pause, the teacher provides a reward. If the student does not respond (or responds incorrectly), the teacher gives the correct answer but no reward. Gradually, the teacher increases the delay (the duration of the pause). The technique has had beneficial effects when used while students practice spelling, even with a computer (e.g., Stevens et al., 1991; Stevens & Schuster, 1987; Winterling, 1990).

Morphographic Spelling

Morphographic Spelling (Dixon, 1976, 1991) is an intensive, highly structured, teacher-directed remedial spelling program for use with fourth- through twelfth-graders and adults. Students placed in the program are assumed to know the basic spelling skills (sound-symbol relationships, etc.), so the program begins instruction with "morphographs," small units of meaningful writing. Students are taught to spell morphographs and to use five rules for combining them.

After about a year of 20-minute lessons five times a week, they are capable of spelling over 12,000 words. Research reveals that the program is quite effective with students who have been achieving well below their expected levels on spelling (Maggs, McMillan, Patching, & Hawke, 1981). Other research also supports the importance of teaching students morphemic analysis (Darch & Simpson, 1990; Stephens & Hudson, 1984).

Add-A-Word

Add-A-Word is a spelling procedure that uses flow lists (Haring et al., 1978; see also the discussion in Monitoring Progress in Spelling earlier in this chapter). In this approach, teachers create individualized lists and test students on their personal lists each day. When a student demonstrates mastery of a word on the list, it is removed and another one is substituted. Some research (McLaughlin, Reiter, Mabee, & Bryam, 1991; McGuigan, cited in Haring et al., 1978; Pratt-Struthers, Struthers, & Williams,

1983) found that this type of procedure aided in the remediation of spelling problems. Although Add-A-Word is not as effective as Morphographic Spelling, it may be more effective than many other approaches (Lovitt, 1978).

WHAT COMPOSITION PROBLEMS DO STUDENTS EXPERIENCE?

Adequate handwriting and spelling skills are unlikely to enable students with learning disabilities to communicate through writing. Although uncommon, on occasion, teachers may describe a student who writes neatly, spells correctly, and still submits an incomprehensible report. There is more to written expression than spelling and handwriting. Students must also learn to write sensible, orderly prose that is consistent with grammatical conventions.

Composition presents special problems for many students with learning disabilities. It requires development of different ways to represent language than students use when speaking. For example, spoken language uses certain conventions (speaking louder in places, pausing, gesturing, etc.), but written expression uses other conventions (bold or italic type, headings, etc.) to represent these features. Writers do not have the immediate feedback available to speakers, so they must communicate especially clearly. Although writing is like "talk copied down," it requires more than simply transcribing speech.

Children's writing changes as they grow older and more sophisticated. One way to conceptualize writing considers the writer's focus. This focus progressively shifts from (1) the process of writing (handwriting and spelling) to (2) the written product (having written something) to (3) communication with readers (getting across one's message). At this third and most sophisticated level of writing, however, the writer's focus may return to the process. For example, after drafting a poem that expresses a message, the poet may refine the product by focusing on meter or rhyme scheme (Bereiter, 1980).

Initially, children focus on learning and mastering mechanical skills—handwriting and spelling. In later grades, they are given short writing assignments that require them to organize and present their ideas in writing. By high school, students should have mastered the mechanical skills of handwriting, spelling, and grammar so that writing can focus on communicating the idea and refining style.

As students get older, their writing changes. Clear indications of this developmental change can be seen when **T-units** and **type-token ratios** are measured at different ages (see Table 11.8 on p. 314). Comparisons of students' writing at various ages (Hunt, 1977) reveal that older students

- use longer T-units
- are likely to include more ideas in each T-unit
- combine T-units by changing the part of speech of words (Younger students combine them by simply adding "and.")

This last point is important because certain instructional activities can help students use the more mature means of combining sentences. (See the discussion of sentence combining under Developmental Interventions later in this chapter.)

Written expression requires the coordination of many different matters at the same time. Figure 13.5 illustrates the complexity of the task. As it shows, there are many critical features in written products. These not only describe ways to measure performance, but also imply that students need to learn many things to become effective written communicators. Students may have problems in any of these areas.

Few studies of the characteristics of students who have writing disabilities were reported in the early years of the learning disabilities field. Myklebust (1965, 1973) conducted the most extensive early analyses. In his 1973 study, he had pupils write stories about a picture of a little boy playing with dolls and reported that, compared to normally achieving pupils, students identified as having learning disabilities scored lower on measures of total number of words written, words per sentence, syntactic accuracy, and abstraction. Students who had moderate learning disabilities did not differ from their nondisabled peers on gross writing production (numbers of words and sentences), but those who had severe learning disabilities did.

FIGURE 13.5 Components of Written Expression

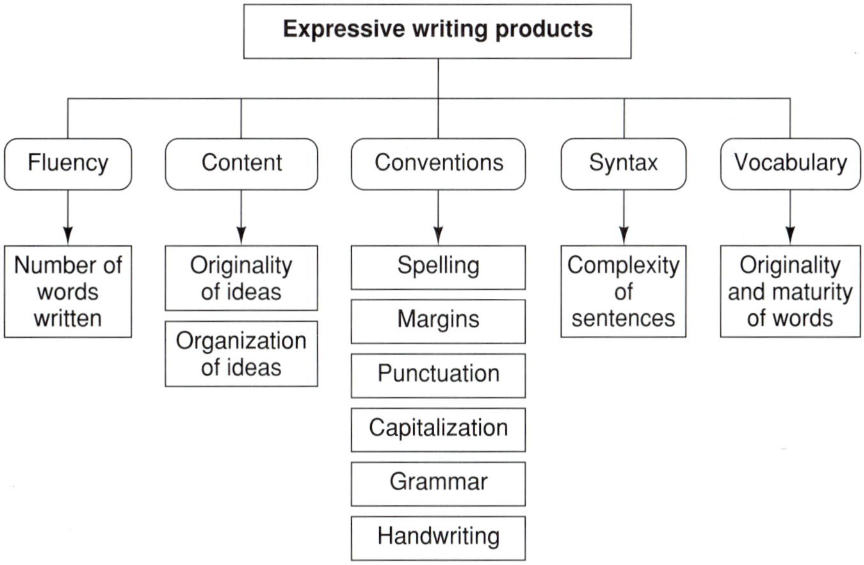

Source: From *Designing Instructional Strategies: The Prevention of Academic Learning Problems* (p. 427) by E. J. Kameenui and D. Simmons, 1990, Columbus, OH: Merrill. Copyright 1990. Reprinted by permission of Prentice-Hall.

More recently, in part because of the growing realization that reading and writing problems are usually connected, the composition skills of students who have learning disabilities and of normally achieving students have been compared more frequently. These studies make clear that students with learning disabilities have substantial problems in written expression that go beyond simply writing shorter passages (Montague, Graves, & Leavell, 1991; Montague, Maddux, & Dereshiwsky, 1990). Although older students use more complex syntax and vocabulary than younger students, regardless of whether they have learning disabilities (Morris & Crump, 1982), students with learning disabilities

- score lower in vocabulary and thematic maturity as well as in word usage, style, and overall writing skill (Poplin, Gray, Larsen, Banikowski, & Mehring, 1980)
- use less complex sentence structures and include fewer types of words (Morris & Crump, 1982; Tindal & Parker, 1991)
- write paragraphs that are less well organized (Englert, Raphael, Anderson, Gregg, & Anthony, 1989; Thomas, Englert, & Gregg, 1987; Tindal & Parker, 1991)
- include fewer ideas in their written products (Englert et al., 1989; Montague et al., 1991)
- write stories that have fewer important components, such as introducing main characters, setting scenes, describing a conflict to be resolved, and so forth (Laughton & Morris, 1989)

Overall these studies imply that pupils with learning disabilities lag behind their nondisabled classmates in many aspects of written expression. The differences are not always consistent, but students with learning disabilities are likely to be weak in both the conventional (e.g., grammar) and the more meaningful aspects of composition (i.e., content). Such students probably will have difficulty with each of the components of written expression shown in Figure 13.5.

Although there is some disagreement in the research about whether students with learning disabilities fall further behind as they get older (Morris & Crump, 1982; Poplin et al., 1980), they are unlikely to catch up with their peers in the absence of powerful instruction. Before providing corrective instruction, teachers must identify students who need it and plan programs for them.

HOW IS COMPOSITION PERFORMANCE ASSESSED?

Powerful assessment of written expression would incorporate ways of evaluating all the features illustrated in Figure 13.5. Such assessment would clearly require several writing samples and careful scoring.

The main reason most widely used general achievement batteries do not require writing samples is that scoring them is time-consuming and unreliable. Thus, there is little hope that general achievement instruments will ever be adequate for screening for writing disabilities. Teachers will have to make an initial judgment of their students' writing and may have to formally identify writing disabilities by administering one of the instruments designed as a diagnostic device.

Screening

Screening for writing disabilities is difficult because many students other than those with learning disabilities write poorly. Broad standardized tests focus on achievement in other areas (e.g., reading and arithmetic) as well, so they often measure only editorial or mechanical skills. For example, the *Metropolitan Achievement Test—7th Edition* (Prescott et al., 1992) has sections on punctuation, capitalization, and word usage, but does not include other measures of writing performance. The *Sequential Tests of Educational Progress* (Educational Testing Service, 1972) and the written expression section of the *Tests of Achievement and Proficiency* (Scannell, Haugh, Schild, & Ulmer, 1978) require students to answer multiple-choice and true-false questions, most of which have to do with mechanics (e.g.. punctuation and capitalization), though some relate to organization and style.

Facility in editing material and answering true-false or multiple-choice questions about written material may be important, but it should not be confused with skill in composing material spontaneously. Better tests of composition require that students provide a sample of their writing. This idea is consistent with today's emphasis on authentic assessment.

Tests specifically designed to assess writing provide more detailed information. For example, the *Test of Written Language* (Hammill & Larsen, 1996) has norms that permit teachers to judge to what extent students' writing corresponds to average. In addition to measuring spelling, it incorporates measures of vocabulary, style, logical sentence formation, facility in combining sentences, competence in mechanics, sentence construction, and overall story quality.

Planning Composition Instruction

Planning instruction also requires more detailed information about students' skills than a teacher gets from broad-focused achievement batteries. The *Picture Story Language Test,* or PSLT (Myklebust, 1965), and the *Test of Written Language,* (Hammill & Larsen, 1996) are two norm-referenced instruments that require students to compose writing samples. On the PSLT, students write a story about a picture of a boy playing. Aspects of the sample (number of words, average number of words per sentence, syntactic correctness, and degree of abstractness) are judged and compared with norms. On the TOWL, some subtests measure correct word usage and style, and students are asked to compose a writing sample about three cartoon panels showing a space adventure. Assessments of the writing sample provide scores for vocabulary,

T-units, and maturity of theme (paragraphing, characterization, beginning-middle-ending structure, etc.). Presumably, students with unusually low scores in any of these areas on either the PSLT or the TOWL should receive remedial instruction in the relevant skills.

Two older models for diagnosis were provided by Poteet (1980) and Weiner (1980a, 1980b). These assessment approaches were designed to evaluate students' writing samples in both mechanics (e.g., grammar) and composition (e.g., meaning). Both systems provide checklists that help the teacher or other evaluator describe the strengths and weaknesses of writing samples. Because they are not based on norms, Poteet's and Weiner's approaches are less formal and depend on careful teacher scrutiny of the samples.

Monitoring Progress in Composition

Progress in composition skills can be easily evaluated by regularly sampling students' writing (Parker, Tindal, & Hasbrouck, 1991). The samples can then be judged to determine whether they represent improvement. Judgments of the samples usually are based on analysis of the given task.

> The task of "writing a paragraph" could be reduced to subtasks comprising "developing the ideational content," "developing paragraph structure," "writing sentences," and "using formal codes." To complete the task analysis, each of these larger components is reduced to subtasks thought to be prerequisite to successful use of each major component of paragraph composition. A component like "using formal codes" may be analyzed into "capitalization" and "punctuation," whereas "writing sentences" may be reduced to "expressing complete thoughts" and "composing sentences. . . ." Developing a progress monitoring system based on a task-analytic approach consists of creating measurement procedures for each of the subtasks that generate data on whether the standard or "criterion" for performance on that task has been met. (Deno, 1997, p. 80)

The resulting task analysis reinforces the importance of the components shown in Figure 13.5. Systems for monitoring increasing facility in these areas would be important in helping teachers adjust instruction to meet individual students' needs.

Teachers can assess improvement in overall quality of writing by simply comparing writing samples taken at different times. Figure 13.6 shows two writing samples from students who had received extensive remedial teaching. Although there are some mistakes in the first sample, the second sample has many more mistakes and many of the characteristics of poor writing discussed in the previous section. Teachers can evaluate the quality of a sample such as the one in part B by noting whether it expresses complete ideas, has complex sentences, is well organized, and includes essential ideas and important components. For example, the second sentence in sample B mixes two different ideas in a disjointed way. The last sentence runs together too many ideas and misrepresents the idea of migration as "going east." Overall, the paragraph omits the important relationship between food and migration. Although these evaluations may seem subjective, in comparison with the sample by the more skillful writer, such evaluations are obvious.

As valuable as overall subjective assessment of a sample is, more formal measures are quite important. For composition, length of T-units, number of "mature" words (Finn, 1977), total number of words, and length of words are useful. The total number of words and the number of mature words used in essays were closely related to students' scores on achievement tests and other measures of writing (Deno, Marston, & Mirkin, 1982). However, these objective measures should be used with caution because a student's writing samples vary greatly and such variation may mask (or provide a false sense of) improvement (Parker et al., 1991).

WHAT INTERVENTIONS HELP STUDENTS WITH COMPOSITION DIFFICULTIES?

Some argue that instruction on the mechanical aspects of writing should be eliminated because it suppresses students' creativity. Although this is an appealing notion, one must be cautious about accepting it too readily. The teaching of writing should certainly encourage people to express the ideas they want to express. But the fundamental aspects of writing must not be disregarded; they are essential to competent, clear communication (Graham & Harris, 1997). Too often we overlook the importance of formal work as a prerequisite to creative products. But jazz musicians know how to play simple scales and other exercises, and the poems of e. e. cummings are creative in part because he knew enough about the conventions of capitalization and punctuation to mock them.

Proponents of whole-language instruction echo the recommendations of popular books such as *Hooked on Books* (Fader & McNeil, 1968) and *Balance the Basics: Let Them Write* (Graves, 1978) by recommending that teachers encourage students to write almost anything (poems, plays, entries in diaries, etc.). Teachers should not try to teach them how to write compositions. The main advantage of this approach is that it provides students with extensive practice opportunities, and practice probably helps them move from the beginning stage of written expression (focus on the process of writing) toward the second stage, when they focus on the product of writing (Bereiter, 1980). However, more specific instruction is usually needed to help students with learning disabilities overcome their deficits in written expression (Graham & Harris, 1997).

Such an approach does not necessarily mean that instruction should be restricted to simple drills on grammatical rules. Even advocates of back-to-basics education (e.g., Fadiman & Howard, 1979) have commented on the unimportance of teaching grammatical rules in the abstract. Programs must teach certain traditional aspects of

FIGURE 13.6 Samples of Student Writing.

A

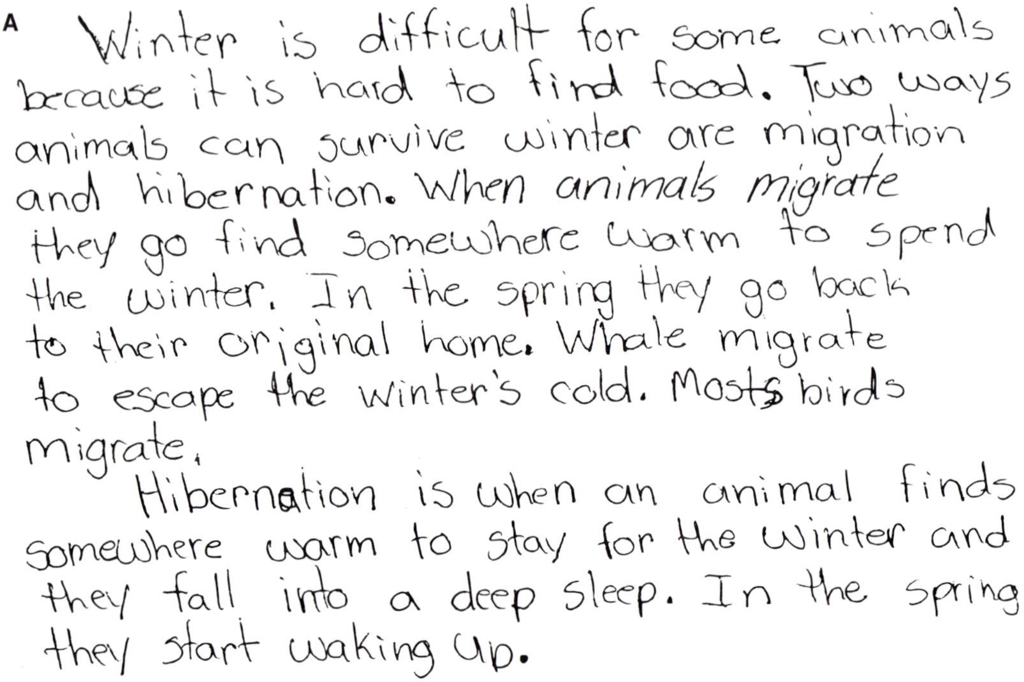

Winter is difficult for some animals because it is hard to find food. Two ways animals can survive winter are migration and hibernation. When animals migrate they go find somewhere warm to spend the winter. In the spring they go back to their original home. Whale migrate to escape the winter's cold. Most~~s~~ birds migrate.

Hibernation is when an animal finds somewhere warm to stay for the winter and they fall into a deep sleep. In the spring they start waking up.

Note: These samples summarize a lesson on how animals adjust to cold and less abundant food. Panel A shows how the summary of a competent writer might look; panel B shows how the work of a less competent writer might look.

Source: Content of summaries from "Exposition: Reading, Writing, and the Metacognitive Knowledge of Learning Disabled Students" by C. S. Englert, T. E. Raphael, L. M. Anderson, S. L. Gregg, and H. M. Anthony, 1989, *Learning Disabilities Research,* 5, pp. 14–15. Copyright 1989 by Division for Learning Disabilities. Reprinted by permission.

grammar (nouns, verbs, etc.) because these are useful in identifying parts of speech when constructing and editing sentences, but mechanics should not overshadow instruction in communicating by writing.

Developmental Interventions

Basal English textbooks include writing exercises designed to teach correct grammar, and there are books of teaching aids and ideas for teachers (e.g., Petty & Bowen, 1967), but few programs have been explicitly designed to teach students writing skills.

FIGURE 13.6 *continued*

B

This is about hibernation and
migration. Different animals that in
the winter the animals go in to a deep
sleep and when it gets warm the animals
wake up. But they have to do a lot of
things to start, Ground hogs have to
dig far in the earth to a warm spot.
Bears have to find a warm place
like in a hole or something lik that.
Whales have to go east and get
to a warm spot and when spot turns
cold they go to the old spot
where they firt was

In lieu of specific directions, many authorities on writing have recommended that students learn to write simply by extensive practice in writing.

Many of the recommendations about developing writing facility echo books that provide general direction to teachers. For example, Sealey, Sealey, and Millmore (1979) describe a program for young children in which they create individual books. The approach begins by having the pupils write labels and captions for pictures they have cut out of magazines or drawn and put in their books. Later the teacher leads them into writing one-sentence descriptions of the pictures or drawings. At the third stage, the children are required to write two-sentence descriptions; here the conventions of punctuation and capitalization are introduced. In the fourth stage, the children write three-sentence or longer descriptions of the pictures; the sentences do not have to relate to one another. At the fifth stage, the children are asked to write thematically. Sealey and colleagues provide numerous activities to aid implementation of their approach.

Other programs provide more explicit directions about instruction. For example, Reasoning and Writing (Engelmann, Arbogast, Davis, Grossen, & Silbert, 1993) includes specific instruction for writing simple sentences, understanding story structure, resolving ambiguities, analyzing sentences, punctuating written materials, editing and revising, correcting unclear sentences, expressing specific concerns, and writing extended critiques. The program is founded on the idea that logical thinking and clear expression are intimately linked. The daily lessons of this program, although very structured and directive, focus on the specific skills that make up coherent written communication.

In some cases, simply having students write more will be sufficient to improve their composition skills (Kraetsch, 1981). However, teachers often demand additional direction. Several broad recommendations about instruction can be made on the basis of research on writing (see Graham, 1982; Hayes & Flower, 1980; Montague et al., 1991; Petty, 1978; Silvermann, Zigmond, Zimmerman, & Vallecorsa, 1981):

- Have students plan what they will write. Planning may range from simply making notes to preparing outlines.
- Have students translate their plans into a written product. Translating should focus mostly on getting a written product, a rough draft.
- Have students edit what they have written. Editing should include reading the product to evaluate whether it communicates what they want to say and improving it. During editing, students might use a checklist to make certain they have followed the conventions of punctuation, capitalization, and grammar. Working with peers and using computers while editing may be beneficial (MacArthur, 1994).

Remedial Interventions

Many of the issues in developmental writing instruction are relevant to remedial instruction, too. As noted, teachers who are working to remedy composition skills will have to coordinate their instruction with the programs used in students' general education classrooms (Kulieke & Jones, 1993).

One remedial intervention developed for students with writing problems or learning disabilities is called Expressive Writing (Englemann & Silbert, 1983). Students are taught how to indent at the beginning of paragraphs, use topic sentences, describe a temporal series of events, and evaluate their own written products for a variety of features (e.g., run-on sentences, capitalization, punctuation, and topic relevance).

Technology

During the 1980s and 1990s, microcomputers had a substantial impact on education, Using them in the classroom has changed the way classes operate (Rieth, Bahr, Polsgrove, Okolo, & Eckert, 1987; Sapona, Lloyd, & Wissick, 1986). Teachers who have used computers are enthusiastic about them (Okolo et al., 1989).

Writing instruction is one of the principal areas in which the influence of computers can be readily seen (MacArthur, 1988). For example, students may spend more time working together, using peer editing procedures, and talking with one another about their work when they use computers for writing. Using computers for writing often requires no special instructional software, but depends primarily on the appropriate application of general teaching principles (MacArthur, 1994; Rieth & Semmel, 1991).

As with any change, there are positive and negative consequences of the computer revolution. Some of the obvious drawbacks to using microcomputers in the classroom are expense, time spent becoming familiar with the computer, and limited access for students (e.g., often only one computer is available per classroom). Another problem that has occasioned teacher complaint is inadequate software, which can frustrate teachers and students.

Teachers working with students who have writing problems may use simple word-processing software such as Bank Street Writer, ClarisWorks, or one of the variants of Microsoft Word. They may also find it useful to teach students how to use speech production features of some programs and computers. For example, many Macintosh computers have built-in speech using many different voices; students can have the computer read their compositions aloud. This can be a very rewarding experience when the student has polished a passage to the point that it makes good sense and is mechanically correct. Some teachers also use specialized software such as Talking Textwriter to promote writing by students with learning disabilities.

Effective Teaching Procedures

Research about effective practices has shown that many other techniques for teaching composition have benefits. These are especially important for students with learning disabilities.

Sentence Combining

Exercises in sentence combining require students to take two related sentences and rewrite them as one. Examples of several such tasks are shown in Table 13.5. Sentence combining has been found to be an effective means of improving students' written compositions (e.g., O'Hare, 1973). There is also evidence that work on sentence combining may benefit students' reading and listening comprehension (Straw & Schreiner, 1982). Perhaps the reason sentence-combining exercises have been found to improve writing is that they help students produce sentences more automatically, thus freeing them to focus on substance rather than mechanics (Flower & Hayes, 1980). However, as Smith (1981) cautioned, sentence combining should not become a decontextualized ritual; rather, it should be taught as a means of composing or editing

TABLE 13.5 Examples of Sentence-Combining Tasks

■ Combine subjects:		
The woman ran the race. The man ran the race.	>	The woman and man ran the race.
Jack went up the hill. Jill went up the hill.	>	Jack and Jill went up the hill.
■ Combine predicates:		
The dog dug a hole. The dog hid the bone.	>	The dog dug a hole and hid the bone.
The kids played basketball. The kids jumped rope.	>	The kids played basketball and jumped rope.
■ Combine with "who" or "which":		
Jim looked at the cat. The cat was asleep.	>	Jim looked at the cat, which was asleep.
The cat looked at Jim. Jim was asleep.	>	The cat looked at Jim, who was asleep.

Source: From *Introduction to Learning Disabilities,* 2nd ed. (p. 256) by D. P. Hallahan, J. M. Kauffman, and J. W. Lloyd, 1985, Upper Saddle River, NJ: Prentice-Hall. Copyright 1985. Reprinted by permission of Allyn & Bacon.

products that communicate what the writer wants them to communicate. A good use of sentence combining, when students have received sufficient training, is to have them use this skill to rewrite and improve their own writing samples.

Reinforcement

Rewarding young students to reinforce writing performance has been studied repeatedly (Brigham, Graubard, & Stans, 1972; Maloney & Hopkins, 1973; Maloney, Jacobson, & Hopkins, 1975). When teachers make reinforcement contingent on writing more words, students write more words. When using more action verbs is rewarded, students use more action verbs in their compositions. ("Run," "swing," and "throw" are action verbs: "think," "are," and "want" are not.) When using a variety of words is reinforced, students write essays that show a wider vocabulary. However, rewarding performance on a certain part of writing may not affect performance on the other parts. Thus, the reward system must result in improvement in many different aspects of composition. Moreover, as effective as reinforcement has been shown to be, it is not a complete teaching program and should be used with other techniques.

Story Grammar

One technique that has gained great currency in helping students with learning disabilities to write better compositions is story grammar. This refers to teaching students the basic components of a story (or essay) and then having them use a skeleton outline as a part of the planning stage in composing their products. Story grammar is sometimes called "procedural facilitation" because it is a strategy that facilitates the procedures of writing.

Although story grammar originated with schema theory (an aspect of the cognitive model of psychology), it has strong task-analytic elements and has been an important part of many cognitive-behavioral interventions. Teaching students how to use story grammar is easy. Suggestions and ideas for using it abound, and research about using story grammar with students with learning disabilities is extensive. Research indicates that this technique helps students produce higher quality written products (Graves, Montague, & Wong, 1990; Montague et al., 1991; Montague & Graves, 1993; Schumm, 1992).

Because of the integrative nature of language arts, teaching students story grammar may also benefit their reading comprehension (see Dimino, Gersten, & Carnine, 1990; Montague et al., 1990; Short & Ryan, 1984). Thus, although there is no one simple solution to a broad range of problems, there are some techniques, such as story grammar, that can be used in slightly different ways to address related problems.

Cognitive-Behavioral Techniques

Advocates of cognitive-behavioral approaches to learning disabilities often recommend that teachers combine components of other methods—story grammar (Martin & Manno, 1995), peer editing (Karegianes, Pascarella, & Pflaum, 1980), and self-evaluation (Harris & Graham, 1985)—when developing instructional programs for improving writing. Box 13.2 describes one successful application of self-evaluation to work with students in a middle school.

Self-evaluation and self-monitoring are particularly effective techniques. When monitoring students' progress in writing, teachers often count the number and different types of words in each essay and plot these counts on graphs. Interestingly, when students receive feedback about these and other features of their compositions, their writing often improves dramatically (Van Houten, Morrison, Jarvis & McDonald, 1974), particularly when they evaluate their own writing (Ballard & Glynn, 1975).

For example, third-graders can learn to check their writing assignments according to specific guidelines. In one study, the self-evaluation procedure required them to count the number of sentences written, words written, and various types of words used and to take other simple measures of their writing. According to these measures, the students assigned themselves points according to a reward system. This combination of self-evaluation and self-reward had positive effects on their writing (Ballard & Glynn, 1975). Similarly, secondary-school students with low achievement scores have

BOX 13.2 *TIPS FOR TEACHING*

Effects of a Check-Off System on Students' Story Compositions

Martin and Manno (1995) examined the effects of a self-management procedure designed to teach three 13- to 14-year-old middle-school boys with learning and behavior problems to improve the completeness (inclusion of identified story elements) and quality (organization and coherence) of their story compositions. The procedure was based on two strategies: teaching the students to plan stories composed in a narrative style and teaching them to monitor the inclusion of elements from the plan with a check-off system. A multiple baseline design was used to assess the effects of the procedure, and a combination of ratings was used to assess the completeness and quality of the students' written work.

The study took place in a resource room, and pictures selected from popular magazines, including *Life, Ebony, National Geographic,* and *Sports Illustrated,* were used to prompt students to write stories. The pictures were first subjected to a social validation procedure with groups of students to ensure that target students would find the pictures interesting enough to write about. In assessing the baseline group, the target students were given two different pictures three times a week and told, "Choose one picture and write the best story you can about it." No other instruction or feedback, apart from the resource room teacher's usual writing instruction, was provided. During intervention training, the students were taught six elements of story grammar (main character, other characters, setting, problem, plan, and ending) and were shown how to plan and write a story using a full-page check-off form. They were asked to pick one of two pictures to write about three times a week and were encouraged to use their check-off forms (see Figure A). The students were taught to write their ideas in the sections titled "Write as I Plan" before beginning to write their stories. They were also taught to check off their planned elements as each element occurred in their stories.

FIGURE A Check-Off Form

	Write as I plan	Check off as I write
Main character		
Other characters		
Setting		
Problem		
Plan (action)		
Ending		

Results indicated that all three students increased their use of story grammar elements after they were taught the self-monitoring procedure. Results for one student are presented in Figure B.

In addition to increasing the number of story elements included in students' written narratives, the researchers also wanted to determine if the overall quality of the students' stories improved. To determine this, they used a system of scoring stories that measured the holistic variables of coherence and organization. Furthermore. they measured atomistic variables (such as total number of words, number of legible words, number of correct word sequences, and words per minute) to determine if increases in any of these variables were related to increases in the overall quality of the students' stories. Results indicated that although coherence did not improve significantly, organization did, along with the overall quality of the stories for all three students. The

BOX 13.2 *continued*

FIGURE B Results of Self-Monitoring for One Student

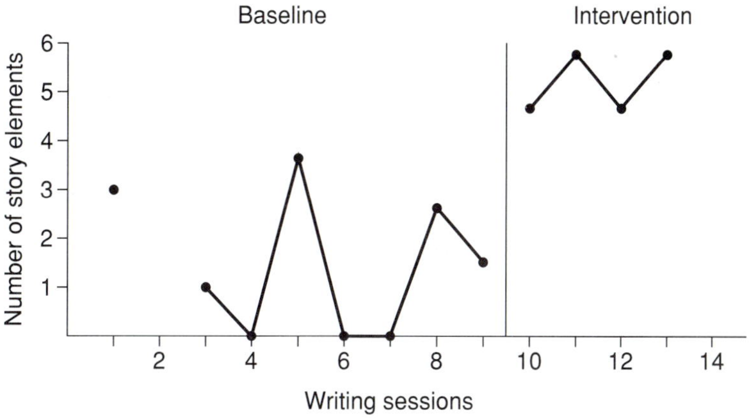

atomistic variables did not increase significantly from baseline to intervention. but there was a moderate relationship between the number of words written and overall story quality (more words written correlated with higher overall quality scores).

Source: From "Use of a Check-Off System to Improve Story Compositions by Middle School Students" by K. F. Martin and C. Manno, 1995, *Journal of Learning Disabilities. 28,* pp. 139–149. Copyright 1995 by PRO-ED. Inc. Reprinted by permission.

learned to use an editing and rating system for evaluating their peers' essays. Later, these students scored higher on a posttest than those whose essays had been edited and rated by teachers.

Self-evaluation and self-monitoring are often incorporated in contemporary interventions for writing. In combination with story grammar and other procedures, cognitive-behavioral instructional techniques form the basis for two broad programs of written expression (Englert & Raphael, 1989; Harris, Graham, & Pressley, 1991). Table 13.6 illustrates one way to teach a self-regulated writing strategy.

Although the stages described in Table 13.6 come from one description (Harris et al., 1991), they are quite similar to what would follow from the other (Englert & Raphael, 1989). Both programs are based on the idea of teaching writing explicitly. By teaching *big ideas* (planning, writing, and editing are fundamental features of writing) and *strategies* (e.g., story grammar or steps in planning), by using *scaffolding* (gradually removing the overt aspects of the procedural facilitation), and by providing extensive practice, these programs illustrate effective teaching for students with learning disabilities (Kameenui & Carnine, 1998).

TABLE 13.6 Self-Regulated Strategy Development: Basic Stages

Stage	Description
Stage 1: *Preskill Development*	Any preskills necessary for understanding, learning, and executing the targeted strategy that are not already in the learner's repertoire are developed.
Stage 2: *Review Current Performance Level*	Instructor and student examine and discuss baseline data and any strategies the student currently uses. Negative or ineffective self-statements or strategies can also be discussed. The significance and potential benefits of the proposed instruction are examined. In addition, commitment to participate as a partner and to attempt the strategies is established, and goals are established in a positive, collaborative manner.
Stage 3: *Discuss the Executive Strategy*	The instructor describes the executive strategy. Then the instructor and student discuss advantages of the strategy as well as how and when to use it.
Stage 4: *Model the Strategy and Self-Instructions*	The instructor or a peer models the strategies to be learned, in context. Instructor and student then discuss the model's performance and the student generates and records his or her own self-instructions to direct the use of the strategy. Instructor and student may also collaborate on any changes that make the strategy more effective.
Stage 5: *Mastery of the Strategy*	The student is required to memorize the steps in the strategy and the self-instructions. Paraphrasing is allowed as long as meaning remains intact.
Stage 6: *Collaborative Practice of Strategy Steps and Self-Instructions*	The student practices the strategy and supporting self-instructions while performing the task. Self-regulation procedure such as goal setting, self-monitoring, or self-reinforcement are discussed, decided on, and used throughout this step. Prompts, interaction, and guidance are faded over practice sessions until the student achieves independent performance. Challenging, proximal goals are determined cooperatively, while criterion levels are gradually increased until the first goal is met. Instructor and student plan for transfer and maintenance of the strategy.
Stage 7: *Independent Performance*	Transition to covert self-instruction is encouraged as the student learns to use the strategy independently. Self-regulation procedures are continued, and plans for transfer and maintenance are implemented. Strategy effectiveness and performance are evaluated collaboratively.

Note: Stages are flexible, recursive, and individualized as necessary; instruction is criterion-based rather than time-based.

Source: From "Cognitive-Behavioral Approaches in Reading and Written Language: Developing Self-Regulated Learners" (p. 437) by K. R. Harris, S. Graham, and M. Pressley, in N. N. Singh and I. L. Beale (Eds.), *Learning Disabilities: Nature, Theory, and Treatment* (pp. 415–451). New York: Springer-Verlag. Copyright 1991 by Springer-Verlag. Reprinted by permission.

Summary

1. What handwriting problems do students with learning disabilities experience?
    a. Handwriting problems include difficulties with letter formation and fluency.
    b. These problems are often associated with other problems, particularly in spelling and composition.

2. How is handwriting performance assessed?
   a. Skills and deficits in handwriting are rarely assessed by using tests. Teachers usually devise less formal, direct measurement methods such as keeping writing samples and administering timed probes.
   b. Teachers can use these informal means of assessment to determine what specific handwriting skills need to be taught.
   c. Teachers need to assess progress in handwriting skills and usually do so by using informal measures.
3. What interventions help students with difficulties in handwriting?
   a. Effective teaching practices in handwriting emphasize lots of practice and feedback.
   b. Today in learning disabilities, teachers must consider how to teach keyboarding skills as well as handwriting.
4. What spelling problems do students with learning disabilities experience?
   a. English orthography is difficult because of the inconsistencies in it.
   b. Students with learning disabilities make spelling mistakes that match words visually, but their errors most often indicate they do not strategically apply spelling-sound knowledge.
   c. Students with spelling problems are very likely to have difficulty with the decoding aspects of reading. They also usually have problems in composition.
5. How is spelling performance assessed?
   a. Most standardized achievement batteries include measures of spelling skills that are scored on whether each word is spelled correctly or incorrectly. These tests are helpful for establishing general ability.
   b. Teachers must have more fine-grained measures of spelling than whether the entire word is spelled correctly. These might include the number of letter sequences within words spelled correctly or the number of important features spelled correctly.
   c. Teachers sometimes analyze spelling errors, looking for consistent patterns in a student's mistakes. Although such analyses may be helpful, classifying a student as a type of learner based on spelling errors has not proved useful.
   d. To monitor progress, teachers need to go beyond recording weekly scores. They should examine students' spelling in their regular written work and use fine-grained measures.
6. What interventions help students with difficulties in spelling?
   a. Spelling in English is made more difficult by the irregularities in the language.
   b. Spelling instruction at either the developmental or remedial level requires that teachers help students learn the alphabetic code for English.
   c. Teachers should teach phonemic awareness skills to students with spelling problems. However, this should not be seen as a complete solution.

d. To encourage students to spell strategically, teachers can teach not just simple sound-symbol spelling, but also the morphological combining forms that enable students to build words from affixes and roots.
e. Spelling instruction is likely to be more effective if it includes only a few spelling words on each day, provides distributed practice, teaches for generalization, and promotes self-correction.

7. What composition problems do students with learning disabilities experience?
   a. Students with learning disabilities have more difficulty than their peers with vocabulary, thematic maturity, word usage, style, sentence complexity, paragraph organization, and incorporation of important elements (e.g., characters, settings).
   b. The problems of students with learning disabilities in other areas (reading, spelling, and handwriting) are related to their difficulties in composition.
8. How is composition performance assessed?
   a. Writing competence is not assessed well by reliance on tests of facility in editing material and answering true-false or multiple-choice questions about written material.
   b. Performance samples, collected repeatedly, provide good material for both diagnosing students' needs and evaluating their progress.
   c. When evaluating students' writing, teachers should include measures of components (e.g., type-token ratios) and content (e.g., story grammar elements), as well as overall judgments.
9. What interventions help students with difficulties in composition?
   a. Teaching of writing should encourage people to express the ideas they want to express, but should not neglect the fundamental aspects of writing.
   b. Developmental instruction should include strategy-laden work on writing simple sentences, understanding story structure, resolving ambiguities, analyzing sentences, punctuating written materials, editing and revising, correcting unclear sentences, expressing specific concerns, and writing extended critiques.
   c. Instruction should encourage students to plan what they will write, generate written products, and edit them.
   d. Technology may help students in composition. Computers can be used to encourage students to outline and edit their work.
   e. Instruction should probably incorporate work on sentence combining and story grammar. Students should receive lots of practice in (and reinforcement for) using these techniques.

14

Teaching Students with Mathematics Problems

In arithmetic and mathematics, students learn not just to compute, but also to reason. They should learn how to solve problems in the sense of situations or tasks. Comprehension of concepts such as number, equality, sets, proportionality, and functional relationships are important aspects of competence in arithmetic and mathematics. Educators also include in arithmetic and mathematics many other skills such as counting money, telling time, and measuring size and weight.

Today there is growing concern about students' deficits in arithmetic and mathematics. National organizations such as the National Council of Teachers of Mathematics have issued strong statements about the need for mathematical competence. Although problems in arithmetic and mathematics once attracted less attention from teachers than those in language arts (Kirk & Elkins, 1975), the increased emphasis today is present in learning disabilities, too. This concern is spurred on by the low levels of achievement for students with learning disabilities (Cawley & Miller, 1989).

Part of the increased attention may be related to increased interest in the cognitive aspects of learning. During the 1980s, extensive research focused on the cognitive aspects of acquisition of arithmetic skills (e.g., Resnick, 1983). Interest in this area has also grown out of the practical experience of teachers revealing that many children with learning disabilities also have problems in arithmetic and mathematics.

HOW DOES MATHEMATICAL KNOWLEDGE DEVELOP NORMALLY?

Some of the most influential approaches to development, based on the work of Piaget (1952), stress the relationship of the concept of conservation to mathematical knowledge and ability. A student is said to have a concept of conservation if she or he understands, for example, that lengths of objects do not change when they are moved or that the amount of a liquid does not change when it is poured into a container of a different size or shape. These general rules of development help one understand mathematical concepts.

In addition to examining general development, one can look at mathematical development more specifically. In what order do children and adolescents acquire concepts and operations? How does a student's approach to arithmetic change with age? Many authors have discussed these transformations and presented developmental theories of children's understanding of mathematical concepts (Carpenter & Moser, 1982; Geary, 1994).

Contemporary theory about mathematical development holds that students match new information with what they already know. Most of what they know about mathematics is intuitive and is often called informal knowledge (Geary, 1994; Ginsberg, 1977, 1997). Formal knowledge, in contrast, is the system of symbols, concepts, procedures, and so forth that form the content of mathematics instruction.

Normally developing young children usually come to school with some informal knowledge. In fact, infants as young as 4 or 5 months of age can discriminate between arrays of two and three objects. By about 18 months, they appear to understand something about numerical order (3 comes after 2). Thus, throughout the preschool years, children learn much about counting and numbers. Twin studies reveal that some mathematics skills are innate (Alarcón, DeFries, Light, & Pennington, 1997), but they are also influenced by the environment. For example, children and parents often play counting games such as "One, two, buckle my shoe. . . ." By age 3 or 4 years, many children actually use number names to identify the number of objects in a group, although they can do so only when the group has a few items (Geary, 1994).

When they arrive at school, many children can use their informal knowledge about numbers and related concepts to solve simple arithmetic problems (Resnick, 1983; Resnick & Ford, 1981). These skills are probably based on a rudimentary understanding of the relationships between counting, numbers, and numerals. The concepts can be represented as a number line, shown in Figure 14.1. The concept of a mental number line holds that each number is conceptually linked to the next higher one in the way that it might be after extensive practice with counting. Each number also is linked to a concept of the number of "things" it represents (as represented by the drawings of dots). Thus, the number line represents children's understanding of the fundamental concepts that numbers occur in order and that numerals are used to represent numbers of objects. As these young children grow more sophisticated, they learn other concepts to go with the mental number line. For example, they learn the related concepts of equality (in the mathematical sense) and correspondence.

Very young children have simple addition skills. By the time they begin to progress through the primary grades, children begin to develop addition concepts further. Regardless of culture, addition skills appear to be based on counting (Geary, 1994). Initially, children employ very simple strategies to add two sets or groups. For example,

FIGURE 14.1 The Mental Number Line Concept

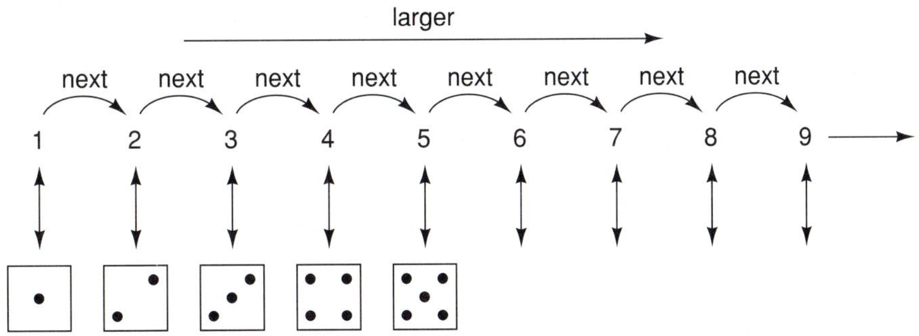

Source: From "A Developmental Theory of Number Understanding" (p. 110) by L. B. Resnick, 1983, in H. Ginsberg (Ed.), *The Development of Mathematical Thinking,* New York: Academic Press. Copyright 1989 by Academic Press. Reprinted by permission.

they count out the objects for one group ("one, two, three"), count out the objects for the second group ("one, two, three, four"), and then physically move the groups together. Once the groups are combined, they count the total ("One, two, three, four, five, six, seven . . . seven eggs! Don't wanna drop 'em.").

In addition to the concept of a number line, primary-school children learn to think about numbers as wholes that are composed of parts. For example, the number 7 may also be thought of as being composed of the numbers 4 and 3, 5 and 2, and 6 and 1. Understanding the part-whole concept of numbers allows school-age children to interpret and solve more sophisticated problems than preschoolers. Some instructional programs—for example, Connecting Math Concepts (Engelmann, Carnine, Engelmann, & Kelly, 1991)—base instruction on simple computation and even on problem solving or mastery of part-whole relationships.

As they develop greater facility with mathematics, children gradually adopt different strategies. For example, for addition, they progress from the counting of manipulatives to more and more efficient strategies, which require fewer cognitive actions. Table 14.1 shows the usual developmental pattern of strategies through which most children go as they become more efficient with addition. Similar patterns also emerge for other forms of computation, such as subtraction (Geary, 1994).

Unfortunately, many educational methods for teaching arithmetic do not conform to the normal development of computational skill. The sequence of development shown in Table 14.1 illustrates this problem. Many education methods encourage young children to work with manipulatives when learning addition. First, they are shown the "counting manipulatives" strategy illustrated in Table 14.1. Next, however, they are required to use the "fact retrieval" strategy shown in Table 14.1. This system of instruction will work well for students who have lots of knowledge of mathematical concepts and competencies with numbers. For students who lack those skills, though, skipping from a counting-manipulatives to a fact-retrieval strategy will probably cause problems.

Another major developmental step in understanding numbers is learning the working of the decimal, or base-10, system. At first, children learn to treat two-digit numbers (e.g., 17) as composed of two parts (10 + 7), then they extend this to other numbers with the requirement that one of the parts must be a multiple of 10 (e.g., 43 is 40 and 3). Handling numbers in this manner, later extended to 100s, 1,000s, and so forth, is sometimes called the concept of **place value.** Development of this concept allows students to perform more complex computations "in their heads" by using strategies related to those they acquired earlier. For example, one can learn to think that 147 + 265 is composed of (100 + 200), (40 + 60), and (7 + 5). These resolve to (300) + (100) + (12), which is 412.

As shown in Table 14.1, older students who solve more difficult problems also gradually adopt more efficient strategies. Their informal knowledge about more sophisticated topics gradually changes as they learn formal mathematics. For example, well before they formally learn rational numbers, they are likely to have informal knowledge about fractions. Most young children can understand the meaning of "half" when it refers to a cookie. However, as they learn more, they understand that the concept of "half" does not stand only for physical relationships. They must learn that the

TABLE 14.1 Commonly Used Addition Strategies

Strategy	Description	Example
■ Simple Addition		
Counting manipulatives	The problem's augend and addend are represented by objects. The objects are then counted, starting from 1.	To solve 2 + 3, two blocks are counted out, then three blocks are counted out, and finally all five blocks are counted.
Counting fingers	The problem's augend and addend are represented by fingers. The fingers are then counted, usually starting from 1.	To solve 2 + 3, two fingers are lifted on the left hand, and three fingers are then lifted on the right hand. The child then moves each finger in succession as he or she counts them.
Verbal counting		
Counting all (sum)	The child counts the augend and addend in succession starting from 1.	To solve 2 + 3, the child counts "1, 2, 3, 4, 5; the answer is 5."
Counting on first	The child states the value of the augend and then counts a number of times equal to the value of the addend.	To solve 2 + 3, the child counts "2, 3, 4, 5; the answer is 5."
Counting on larger (min)	The child states the value of the larger addend and then counts a number of times equal to the value of the smaller addend.	To solve 2 + 3, the child counts "3, 4, 5; the answer is 5."
Derived facts (decomposition)	One of the addends is decomposed into two smaller numbers, so that one of these numbers can be added to the other to produce a sum of 10. The remaining number is then added to 10.	To solve 8 + 7: Step 1. 7 = 5 + 2 Step 2. 8 + 2 = 10 Step 3. 10 + 5 = 15
Fact retrieval	Direct retrieval of basic facts from long-term memory	Retrieving 5 to solve 2 + 3.
■ Complex Addition		
Verbal counting Counting on larger	Same as above	To solve 23 + 2, the child counts "23, 24, 25; the answer is 25."
Regrouping	The addends are decomposed into tens and units values. The tens and units values are summed separately. The two provisional sums are then added together.	To solve 25 + 42: Step 1. 25 = 20 + 5 Step 2. 42 = 40 + 2 Step 3. 20 + 40 = 60 Step 4. 5 + 2 = 7 Step 5. 60 + 7 = 67
Columnar retrieval	The problem is solved by retrieving columnwise sums.	To solve 27 + 38: Step 1. 7 + 8 = 15 Step 2. Note trade (carry) Step 3. 2 + 3 = 5 Step 4. 5 + 1 (from trade) = 6 Step 5. Combined 6 from tens column to 5 from ones column to produce 65

Source: From *Children's Mathematical Development: Research and Practical Applications* (pp. 62–63) by D. C. Geary, 1994, Washington, DC: American Psychological Association. Copyright 1994 by American Psychological Association. Reprinted by permission.

idea of "half" can be applied to "half of the boys that I know" (and that does not require that each boy is cut into two pieces). They learn that the concept of "half" refers to a ratio, a rational number.

More sophisticated concepts in mathematics develop later. Computational skill and conceptual knowledge continue to change with age, although at different rates. Many of the advancements in competence have to do with acquiring and using more sophisticated strategies. Students who do not advance beyond using elementary strategies (e.g., counting manipulatives or counting fingers, as illustrated in Table 14.1) have greater trouble with advanced concepts. For students with learning disabilities, this is a particularly important problem.

Research on the normal development of arithmetic and mathematics knowledge in adolescent students is sparse. Evidence about adult performance indicates that adults retrieve facts and use simple computation strategies to derive arithmetic facts (e.g., Ashcraft, 1982; Groen & Parkman, 1972). Cawley and his associates (e.g., Cawley, Fitzmaurice, Shaw, Kahn, & Bates, 1978, 1979) reported extensively on the problems of secondary-school students with learning disabilities, but these studies were not designed to permit us to infer how skills and concepts develop normally.

WHAT PROBLEMS IN MATHEMATICS DO STUDENTS EXPERIENCE?

Extensive data on the performances of students with learning disabilities on arithmetic and mathematics tasks show great variance (Strang & Rourke, 1985). Thus, just as with reading or writing disabilities, any effort to characterize "the math disabled child" is a mistake—students who have arithmetic and mathematics disabilities are too heterogeneous to constitute a type.

Dyscalculia is the most widely used term for disabilities in arithmetic and mathematics. In general, dyscalculia means inability to calculate. Sometimes the term acalculia is used to refer to complete inability to use mathematical symbols and perform arithmetic computations, and the term dyscalculia is reserved for less severe—but still substantial—problems in arithmetic and mathematics. Developmental dyscalculia in children and youth is distinguished from similar problems experienced by adults who have had severe head injuries.

Regardless of what it is called, difficulty with arithmetic and mathematics is common. Several interested authorities (e.g., Dunlap & House, 1976) have suggested that there are many students with learning disabilities in arithmetic. For example, some studies have indicated that as many as 6% of school-age children have these difficulties (e.g., Badian & Ghublikian, 1983; Kosc, 1974). Teachers say that nearly two out of three of their students need help in arithmetic and mathematics and that more than one in four students receive special education services because of learning disabilities in arithmetic and mathematics (McLeod & Armstrong, 1982). These data are not just a U.S. phenomenon. An epidemiological study of 9- to 10-year-old children in Great Britain revealed that, despite having normal cognitive ability, 1.5% of children had arithmetic problems, and another 2.5% had both arithmetic and reading problems. That is, overall about 4% of the students had arithmetic problems (Lewis, Hitch, & Walker, 1994).

Examinations of the characteristics of pupils served by federally funded demonstration centers in the 1970s (Kirk & Elkins, 1975; Norman & Zigmond, 1980) revealed that many students with learning disabilities have achievement deficits in arithmetic and mathematics. The average mathematics achievement of students was about 75% of what would be expected on the basis of their IQs (Norman & Zigmond, 1980). Although this level of learning efficiency is higher than it was for reading, such inefficiency in learning mathematical skills is significant. Students with learning disabilities who are in the third and fourth grades often score at a first-grade level in arithmetic. Things do not get better later; high school students often score at about the fifth-grade level (Cawley & Miller, 1989). Clearly, the students with such deficits deserve special education.

As a result of these studies, we can reasonably assume that many students referred for services in a program for learning disabilities will need instructional help in arithmetic and mathematics. Thus, problems in these subjects should be considered no less important than problems associated with using spoken and written language. Both types of difficulties indicate a need for especially intensive and extensive educational intervention for students with learning disabilities.

Some students with learning disabilities have problems in both arithmetic and reading. Others have problems in only one area (Lewis et al., 1994). The performance of students who have only mathematics problems differs from that of those who have problems in both reading and mathematics. For example, when tests are timed, students with only mathematics problems make about as many mistakes on simple story and number-fact problems as their peers who have both mathematics and reading problems. However, when tests are untimed, those with only mathematics problems make fewer mistakes and get just about as many problems correct as nondisabled students (Jordon & Montani, 1997).

Problems in Cognitive Development

Students with learning disabilities differ from their peers in cognitive development. Some advocates advance the idea that general or broad cognitive deficits account for these differences. Such an idea contradicts the fundamental concept that "learning disabilities" describes a discrepancy between ability and achievement (see Chapter 1). If general or broad cognitive deficits account for problems in arithmetic and mathematics, then those deficits are more appropriately called mental retardation.

Authorities in learning disabilities have suggested many types of problems that may be associated with disabilities in arithmetic learning. Many of the related difficulties that have been discussed (see Chalfant & Shefflin, 1969; Glennon & Cruickshank,

1981; Kalisiki, 1967) are not directly related to arithmetic performance, but fall into the categories of developmental problems and information-processing disorders. For example, general developmental lags (e.g., difficulty in ordering things by length, weight, size, or time of occurrence or difficulty in outgrowing immature behaviors), perceptual disorders (e.g., difficulties with figure-ground, spatial, temporal, or eye-hand relationships), behavior problems (e.g., perseveration, inattention, and "drive"), and other general characteristics have been attributed to students with arithmetic learning disabilities.

General developmental problems present similar difficulties. Because studies of conservation with students who have learning disabilities yield conflicting results (e.g., Derr, 1985; Finchman, 1979), it is difficult to judge the contribution of problems in conservation to problems in learning arithmetic. Is the general idea of conservation at the heart of students' learning disabilities in arithmetic and mathematics? Probably not. Instead, teachers should consider more specific problems in arithmetic performance.

Neuropsychological studies of students with problems in arithmetic focus primarily on identifying which part of the brain is involved. Some of these individuals are said to have Gerstmann syndrome. Gerstmann syndrome is characterized by confusion of left and right, problems with writing, inability to identify which finger has been touched by touch alone, and arithmetic problems; it is presumed to be caused by damage to the angular gyrus of the dominant hemisphere of the brain (see Chapter 2). However, researchers have not been able to demonstrate that the symptoms consistently occur together and have found that the neurological problem itself may or may not be present in those who have some or even all of the symptoms (Rourke, 1995; Rourke & Conway, 1997).

Problems in Arithmetic Performance

Some of the difficulties identified by authorities as indicative of arithmetic learning disabilities are more directly associated with performance of arithmetic tasks. For example, in their list of behaviors considered characteristic of developmental dyscalculia, Glennon and Cruickshank (1981) included problems with such skills as (1) writing numerals and mathematical symbols correctly, (2) recalling the meanings of symbols and the answers to basic facts, (3) counting, and (4) following the steps in a strategy for solving multistep problems. Difficulties such as these are obviously associated with problems in developing competence in arithmetic.

Performance on Basic Arithmetic Tasks

The most obvious characteristic of pupils with arithmetic and mathematics learning disabilities is that they make mistakes on arithmetic problems. In fact, perhaps the most extensive study in the area of arithmetic and mathematics has been focused on the erroneous answers students give.

Students rarely make random mistakes in answering arithmetic problems. The errors are usually systematic and indicate that students are consistently applying a mistaken strategy to solve the problems (Cox, 1975; Ginsberg, 1977; Lankford, 1972). The analysis of computational errors has a long history (Buswell & John, 1926). Extensive analyses of "bugs," or errors in computation, have also been made by educators and psychologists interested in children's thinking during solution of arithmetic problems (Ashlock, 1994; Brown & Burton, 1978; Young & O'Shea, 1981). Figure 14.2 shows some bugs that might be found in students' answers for various subtraction problems.

FIGURE 14.2 Mistakes Answers to and Strategies for Subtraction Problems

Problem		Mistaken strategy
A.	73 – 44 31	Simply subtract the smaller from the larger number in each column.
B.	93 – 44 50	If the difference is less than zero, write 0 and continue.
C.	8 16 1~~96~~ – 42 1414	Borrow in all cases and write the two-digit difference as if it went in the units place.
D.	236 – 144 112	If the problem does not require borrowing in the first column, do not borrow in any column.
E.	7 13 ~~8~~0~~3~~ – 127 626	Borrow across a zero, without changing it, and subtract zero from the other digit in the column.
F.	7 10 13 ~~803~~ – 127 686	When borrowing across a zero, do not borrow from it in turn.

Source: From *Introduction to Learning Disabilities,* 2nd ed. (p. 272) by D. P. Hallahan, J. M. Kauffman, and J. W. Lloyd, 1985, Upper Saddle River, NJ: Prentice-Hall. Copyright 1985. Reprinted by permission of Allyn & Bacon.

Cognitive research on mathematical difficulties reveals that students with problems have deficits in fact retrieval (Garnett & Fleishner, 1983; Geary, 1994; Goldman, Pellegrino, & Mertz, 1988). These students make more mistakes in giving simple answers in various areas of arithmetic and sometimes recall facts more slowly than their peers. Such fact retrieval problems are probably related to deficits in working memory (see Chapter 10).

Students also make mistakes in applying strategies or procedures (Geary, 1994; Jordon & Montani, 1997). They may not only choose inefficient strategies, but also poorly use those they choose. For example, students with problems are more likely to depend on the counting-all strategy (see Table 14.1), even though it is less efficient than strategies developed later. When they revert to using this strategy, they may also make mistakes in counting, leading to wrong answers.

Difficulties with Story Problems

Difficulties with computation will have obvious effects on whether students can solve story problems correctly. Problems reading the stories will affect performance, too, but students' difficulties with these kinds of tasks are more complex than one would predict because of reading or computation deficits alone.

Certain aspects of story problems make them difficult for many students. For example, story problems given in reverse order and beginning with the missing number (e.g., ones for which an equation might be written in this way: $? - 5 = 3$) were considerably harder than other story problem arrangements (Rosenthal & Resnick, 1974). The difficulties unique to solving story problems by students with learning disabilities have also been investigated (Blankenship & Lovitt, 1976; Trenholme, Larsen, & Parker, 1978). These studies reveal that such students' performances are adversely affected by such features of story problems as (1) presence of extraneous information, (2) use of complex syntactic structures, (3) change of number and type of noun used, and (4) use of verbs such as "purchased" or "bought" rather than "was given." The implication of these findings is not that teachers of students with learning disabilities should avoid assigning problems with these features, but rather that they should teach their students how to solve them.

Students with learning disabilities are vulnerable to inadequate instructional programs and practices. For example, if a program for teaching fractions does not use both proper and improper fractions when demonstrating how to work with fractions, students with learning disabilities are far more likely to make mistakes on problems involving improper fractions (Kelly, Gersten, & Carnine, 1990). The subject of fractions is not the only one where problems are likely to occur. Figure 14.3 illustrates the range of problem areas in which students are likely to have trouble. If instructional practices, including both curriculum and teaching behavior, do not correct for problems in these areas, students with learning disabilities will be most likely to suffer. "Low achieving students are often casualties of curricula that assume too much and teach too little. Difficulties are related to learners' fragile preskills and the subsequent failure of the curriculum to explicitly address those skills" (Kameenui & Simmons, 1990, p. 393).

FIGURE 14.3 Predictable Problems in Mathematics Skill Domain for Students with Learning Disabilities

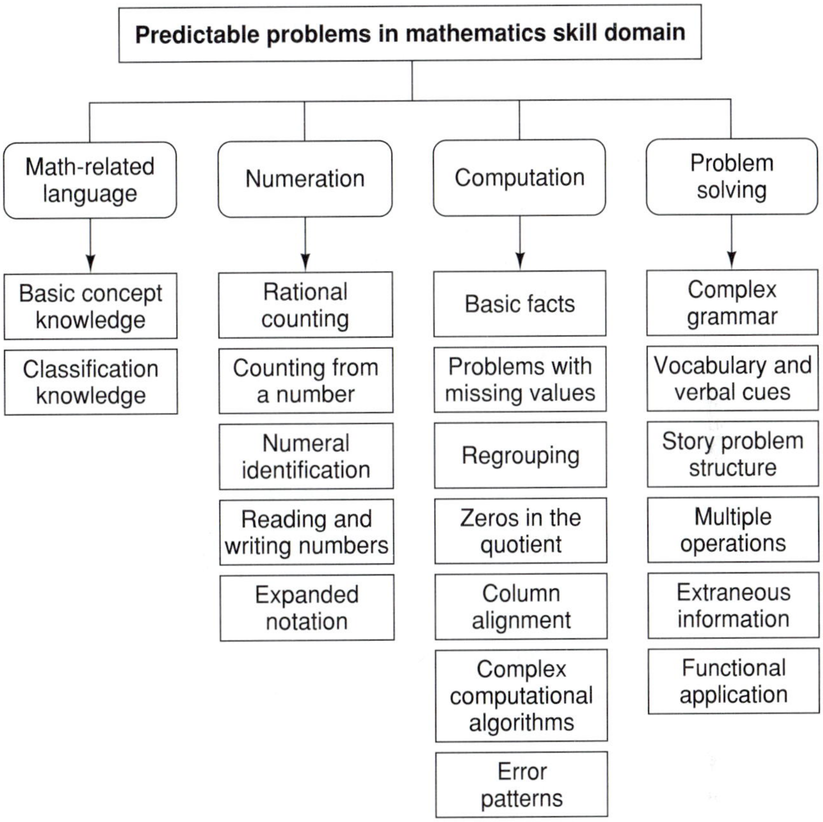

Source: From *Designing Instructional Strategies: The Prevention of Academic Learning Problems* (p. 393) by E. J. Kameenui and D. C. Simmons, 1990, Columbus, OH: Merrill. Copyright 1990 by Merrill Publishing Co. Reprinted by permission.

HOW ARE MATHEMATICS ABILITIES ASSESSED?

Arithmetic and mathematics learning problems are assessed in much the same way as deficits in other areas of academic learning (see Chapter 4). Teachers may make referrals because students appear to be having difficulties, and students may be administered screening tests to determine whether further assessment is needed. Another assessment includes testing used to guide program planning; this form of assessment is designed to help determine what specific arithmetic learning problems students have and what kind of educational program will be needed to remedy them. When remediation is under way, assessment continues in the form of progress monitoring (Bryant & Rivera, 1997).

Unfortunately, most of the work on assessing mathematical competence of students with learning disabilities focuses almost exclusively on computation. Too little work has been done on assessing mathematical concepts. Because knowledge of underlying concepts facilitates mastery of arithmetic computation, students' understanding of concepts is an appropriate area for assessment. Similarly, students' strategies in solving problems are worthy of assessment (Ginsburg, 1991, 1997).

Achievement Tests

To identify students who might need additional services, schools may screen large groups of students in arithmetic and mathematics. As discussed in earlier chapters on academic problems, particularly in Chapter 4, administration of a screening test helps educators decide whether students should be tested further to determine if they have an arithmetic learning problem or, if one is suspected, to confirm it.

Screening usually consists of administering a norm-referenced test that makes it possible to compare the referred student to others of his or her age and grade. When a student is greatly behind age- or grade-mates on arithmetic screening tests, an arithmetic learning disability is suspected. Commonly used screening tests include most of the general achievement batteries—the *California Achievement Test—5th Edition* (Teigs & Clark, 1992), the *Iowa Tests of Basic Skills* (Hieronymus, Lindquist, & Hoover, 1978), the *Metropolitan Achievement Test—7th Edition* (Prescott, Balow, Hogan, & Farr, 1992), and the *Stanford Achievement Test—8th Edition* (Gardner, Rudman, Karlsen, & Merwin, 1988). However, individually administered achievement batteries such as the *Peabody Individual Achievement Test—Revised* (Markwardt, 1989) and the *Woodcock-Johnson Psychoeducational Battery—Revised* (Woodcock & Johnson, 1989/1990), as well as some tests devoted specifically to diagnosing arithmetic and mathematics (discussed in Formal Diagnostic Testing), probably are the instruments most commonly used when identifying students.

Some screening instruments may provide preliminary diagnostic information. For example, the *Metropolitan Achievement Tests* (Prescott et al., 1992) contain two subtests related to arithmetic and mathematics: one that assesses computation skills and one that assesses knowledge of concepts. If a student performs poorly on one of these but not on the other, the difference probably reflects something about his or her difficulties with arithmetic and mathematics. Some authors (e.g., Trembley, Caponiqro, & Gaffrey, 1980) suggest programming based on common achievement tests such as the PIAT and the *Wide Range Achievement Test—3* (Wilkinson, 1993). However, when planning instructional programs, teachers need much more fine-grained assessment measures than tests of this sort offer.

Formal Diagnostic Testing

Diagnostic tests should allow the teacher to determine in which of the many areas of arithmetic and mathematics a student is having difficulties. Table 14.2 identifies some

TABLE 14.2 Areas of Arithmetic and Mathematics Learning

Area	Examples
Basic information	Number-numeral relationships, counting, equality, symbol names
Computation skills	Addition, subtraction, multiplication, division
Problem solving	Writing algorithms for "story problems"
Fractions	Regular, decimals, percentages, renaming, computation using fractions, ratios, proportions, probability
Measurement	Meters and derivatives; inches, feet, miles, etc.; grams and derivatives; ounces, pounds, bushels, pecks, etc.; seconds, minutes
Money	Coin values, equivalencies
Algebra	Linear and quadratic equations
Geometry	Shape names, theorems

Source: From *Introduction to Learning Disabilities,* 2nd ed. (p. 274) by D. P. Hallahan, J. M. Kauffman, and J. W. Lloyd, 1985, Upper Saddle River, NJ: Prentice-Hall. Copyright 1985. Reprinted by permission of Allyn & Bacon.

of these areas and gives examples of them. Diagnostic tests sample from some or all of these.

Key Math Revised: A Diagnostic Inventory of Essential Mathematics (Connolly, 1988) is a very widely used diagnostic instrument for grades kindergarten through 8. Its 14 subtests are arranged into three general areas: content, operations, and applications. The test covers most of the areas of knowledge and skill listed in Table 14.2 and provides different types of scores, ranging from a norm-referenced total test score to scores on individual items that can be used as program-planning aids. An extensive list of instructional objectives corresponding to the items on the test is included, making it easy to program instruction according to a student's performance on the test.

The *Stanford Diagnostic Mathematics Test* (Beatty, Madden, Gardner, & Karlsen, 1984) is another diagnostic instrument. It includes four levels, each designed for administration to a different age group ranging from first grade through high school. Three general areas of skill and knowledge—number system and numeration, computation, and applications—are assessed at each level (these include most of the areas shown in Table 14.2). Because this test can be administered to groups of students, it may also be used as a screening instrument.

Some commercial instruments cover diverse mathematical concepts quite thoroughly. For example, the *Multilevel Academic Survey Test* (Howell, Zucker, & Morehead, 1985) is based on a comprehensive analysis of the concepts that underlie arithmetic and provides a valuable means of identifying areas of difficulty for students. Several other commercially available instruments may be used to diagnose problems in arithmetic and mathematics. *Diagnosis: An Instructional Aid in Mathematics*

(Guzaitis, Carlin, & Juda, 1972) is a system of probes for use with primary- and elementary-school students; items on the probes are based on instructional objectives and are keyed to sections of instructional materials for teachers to use in remediating problems. The *Buswell-John Test* (Buswell & John, 1926) is a test of computation on which students write the answers to many items representing various levels of difficulty for each of the computational operations. The *Diagnostic Mathematics Inventory* (Gessell, 1983) is a test based on instructional objectives in arithmetic and mathematics; the manual provides detailed information about mistaken answers for each item and specific recommendations for remedial activities and materials.

Informal Inventories

Most teachers have students with widely differing skill levels in their classes and must teach each one how to solve different types of problems. Which kinds of mathematics problems are appropriate for each student can be determined by using informal inventories. These inventories can be particularly useful to the teacher of students with learning disabilities.

Informal inventories should include representative examples of different kinds of problems. They may be commercially developed or created by teachers themselves. Many of the diagnostic tests described previously, such as the *Buswell-John Test* (Buswell & John, 1926), do this in a broad way. One important consideration in choosing a commercial informal inventory or creating one is the extent to which it aligns with the curriculum used with the students to be tested. If an informal inventory does not assess the skills the students are expected to acquire, it will not be very helpful in determining what to teach them.

Other informal inventories assess performance in a more detailed way and allow teachers to make precise decisions about planning programs for students. Figure 14.4 shows a placement test for geometry knowledge. Each type of task assessed is associated with a general grade level. The grade levels should not be considered exact or fixed; they simply provide rough guidance about when certain topics might be taught.

Because these tests are designed to assess what a student can do, they are given without time limits or teacher assistance. Their purpose is to allow a teacher to determine what students have learned and what they should be taught next. Teachers can modify inventories such as these so they align with their curricula. Because these inventories are fairly comprehensive, they can even guide curricular decisions (Stein, Silbert, & Carnine, 1997). Stein et al. have provided explicit instructional procedures for teaching each of the skills assessed in the inventories shown in Figure 14.4.

Error Analysis

Analysis of students' mistaken answers has also been suggested as a method for determining what to teach students. (See Figure 14.2 for examples of errors and the faulty algorithms they imply.) Teachers can use instruments such as the *Diagnostic Inventory of Basic Arithmetic Skills* (Enright, 1983). They may also consult books (e.g.,

Ashlock, 1994) that provide extensive examples of students' mistaken answers, interpretations of them, and general suggestions for their remediation. For example, when a student's answers indicate that he or she has failed to "carry," the teacher can employ manipulative aids, such as using bundles of ten sticks and single sticks, drawing boxes in the answer spaces for problems to prompt students to write only one numeral in each column, and playing games requiring the student to trade many chips of lesser value for a single, more valuable chip (Ashlock, 1994).

Monitoring Progress

Some of the assessment instruments described in the preceding section may be readministered to determine if a student is making progress. For example, an achievement test may be given in the fall and spring of each year to assess how much progress students are making. Most formal standardized instruments, however, are not designed to be readministered more than once a year. Also, their analyses are not fine-grained enough to be sensitive to small amounts of student progress. Although some diagnostic instruments allow finer-grained estimates of progress, they do not have enough test items at each level to be readministered frequently. If students take these tests repeatedly, they may begin to answer items correctly, not because they have learned the skills, but because they have become familiar with the items. Furthermore, a formal test often takes over 30 minutes, making frequent testing excessively time-consuming.

One appropriate means for evaluating progress is to assess students' performances on curricular materials. As discussed in Chapter 4, this approach has many advantages, not the least of which is that the teacher learns how well students are doing on the materials they are expected to master. Both computation and problem-solving aspects of mathematics competence can be measured using curriculum-based assessment (Shinn & Hubbard, 1992). Furthermore, a combination of curriculum-based assessment and consultation (e.g., recommendations about using peer tutoring) produces higher arithmetic achievement (Fuchs, Fuchs, Hamlett, & Stecker, 1991). Howell and Morehead (1987) and Howell, Fox, and Morehead (1993) provide detailed information about curriculum-based assessment of arithmetic and mathematics, including valuable suggestions about remedial practices. It is particularly important for teachers to have instructional plans tied to their curriculum-based assessments (Fuchs, Fuchs, Hamlett, Phillips, & Bentz, 1994). For example, one might want to teach students a strategy for taking curriculum-based tests (Whinnery & Fuchs, 1993).

Another appropriate means of overcoming the difficulties of readministering tests is to adopt or create a set of short tests. These short tests, or probes, are similar to curriculum-based assessments in that they are brief (i.e., take only 1 or 2 minutes to administer) and assess actual student performance. They differ from curriculum-based assessment in not being directly linked to the curriculum in use. Probes should include many examples of problems that require specific skills and should be constructed so they can be readministered repeatedly and quickly. Several alternative probes for each type of problem should be created so that different probes can be used

FIGURE 14.4 Instructional Sequence and Assessment Chart

Grade level	*Problem type*	*Performance indicator*
1a	Identify circle.*	Mark each circle with X. 
1b	Identify rectangle.*	Mark each rectangle with X. 
1c	Identify triangle.*	Mark each triangle with X. 
1d	Identify square.*	Mark each square with X. 
1e	Identify interior of closed figure.*	Tell me when I touch the interior of this figure. 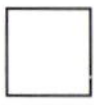
1f	Identify exterior of closed figure.*	Tell me when I touch the exterior of this figure. 
2a	Identify cube.*	Mark each cube with X. 
2b	Identify sphere.*	Mark each sphere with X. 
2c	Identify cone.*	Mark each cone with X. 
2d	Identify the diameter of a circle.*	What is a diameter? Put X on each line that is the diameter of a circle. 

FIGURE 14.4 *continued*

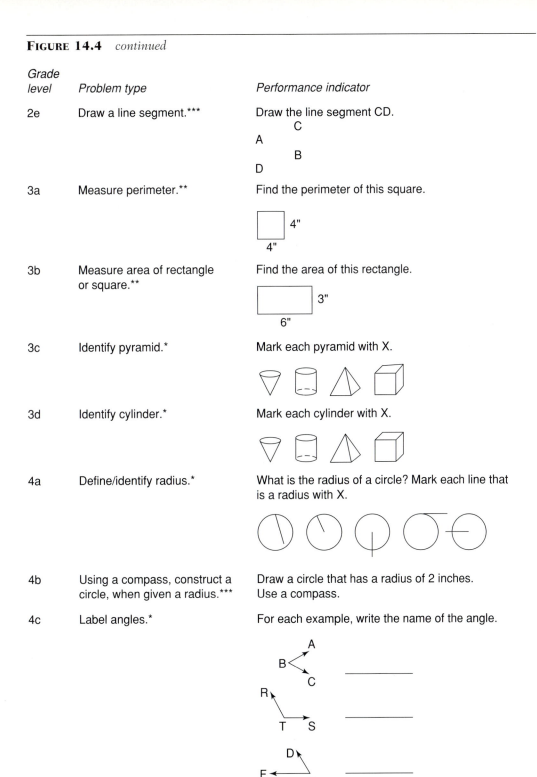

Grade level	*Problem type*	*Performance indicator*
2e	Draw a line segment.***	Draw the line segment CD.

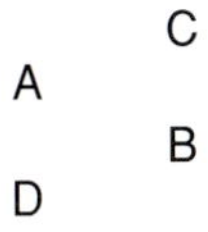

Grade level	*Problem type*	*Performance indicator*
3a	Measure perimeter.**	Find the perimeter of this square.

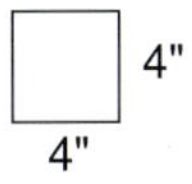

Grade level	*Problem type*	*Performance indicator*
3b	Measure area of rectangle or square.**	Find the area of this rectangle.

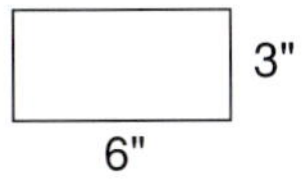

Grade level	*Problem type*	*Performance indicator*
3c	Identify pyramid.*	Mark each pyramid with X.

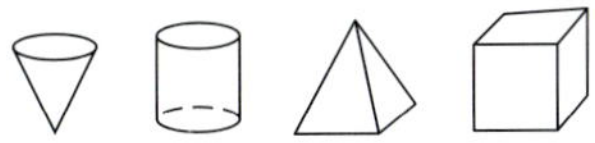

Grade level	*Problem type*	*Performance indicator*
3d	Identify cylinder.*	Mark each cylinder with X.

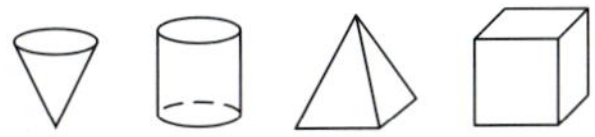

Grade level	*Problem type*	*Performance indicator*
4a	Define/identify radius.*	What is the radius of a circle? Mark each line that is a radius with X.

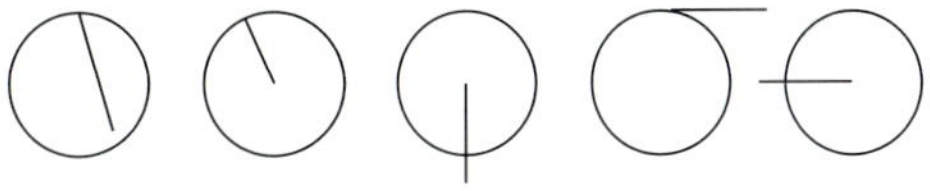

Grade level	*Problem type*	*Performance indicator*
4b	Using a compass, construct a circle, when given a radius.***	Draw a circle that has a radius of 2 inches. Use a compass.
4c	Label angles.*	For each example, write the name of the angle.

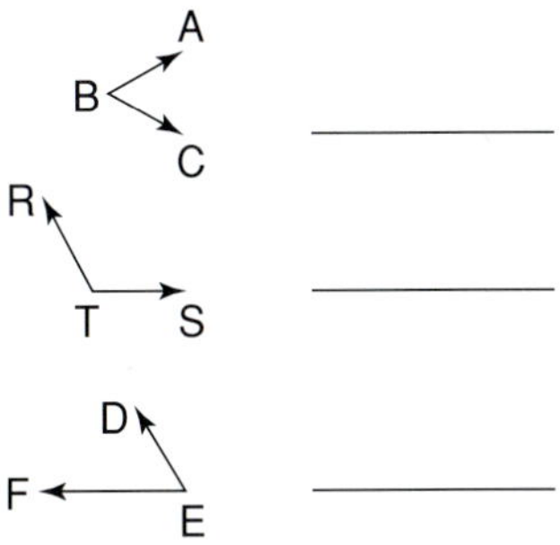

FIGURE 14.4 *continued*

Grade level	*Problem type*	*Performance indicator*
4d	Define degree/measure angles, using a protractor.**	Measure each of the following angles. 
4e	Construct angles, using a protractor.***	Construct the following angles. 90° ________ 45° ________
4f	Define/identify right angle.*	What is a right angle? Circle each right angle. 
4g	Define/identify acute angle.*	What is an acute angle? Circle each acute angle. 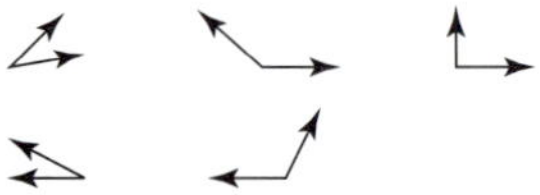
4h	Define/identify obtuse angle.*	What is an obtuse angle? Circle each obtuse angle. 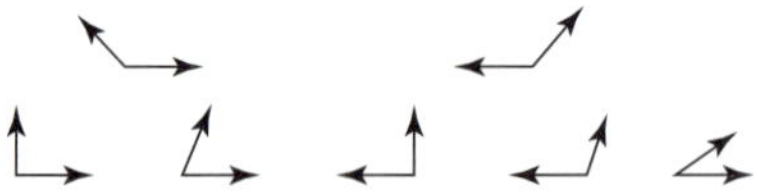
4i	Define/identify right triangle.*	What is a right triangle? Circle each right triangle. 
4j	Define/identify equilateral triangle.*	What is an equilateral triangle? Circle each equilateral triangle. 
4k	Define/identify isosceles triangle.*	What is an isosceles triangle? Circle each isosceles triangle. 
4l	Define/identify scalene triangle.*	What is a scalene triangle? Circle each scalene triangle. 

FIGURE 14.4 *continued*

Grade level	*Problem type*	*Performance indicator*
4m	Identify the following polygons:* pentagon hexagon octagon	Draw a P over the pentagon. Draw an H over the hexagon. Draw an O over the octagon. 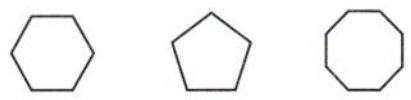
4n	Measure the volume of a cube.**	What is the volume of a figure that is 5 inches long, 3 inches wide, and 6 inches high?
5a	Identify parallel lines.*	Circle each group of parallel lines. 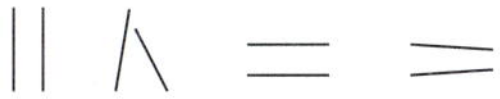
5b	Identify perpendicular lines.*	Circle each group of perpendicular lines. 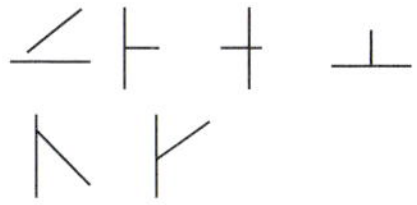
5c	Identify a parallelogram.*	Circle each parallelogram. 

Source: From Designing Effective Mathematics Instruction: A Direct Instruction Approach (3rd ed.) by M. Stein, J. Silbert, and D. Carnine, 1997, Upper Saddle River, NJ: Prentice-Hall. Copyright 1997 by Prentice-Hall, Inc. Reprinted by permission.

rather than repeatedly using the same one. This practice avoids the problem of students learning the answers to the problems used on one probe (see Howell et al., 1993; Howell & Morehead, 1987). Examples of some probes for addition problems are shown in Figure 14.5.

WHAT INTERVENTIONS HELP STUDENTS WITH MATHEMATICS DIFFICULTIES?

Several aspects of instruction have been demonstrated to help arithmetic learning. Effective instruction has several features: "(a) It takes place in groups, (b) it is teacher directed, (c) it is academically focused, and (d) it is individualized" (Stevens &

FIGURE 14.5   Probes for Monitoring Student Progress

add combinations
a-1

5 + 4	0 + 0	1 + 1	4 + 4	3 + 6	4 + 2	0 + 6
4 + 1	1 + 3	4 + 3	1 + 1	5 + 3	2 + 1	2 + 2
2 + 6	4 + 2	0 + 9	5 + 2	3 + 3	4 + 2	4 + 4

add combinations
j-1

7 5 + 8	5 + 63	26 2 + 1	8 + 5	35 2 + 50	3 + 4	14 4 + 30
5 9 + 9	81 + 7	23 42 + 24	43 + 43	7 5 + 7	6 + 0	44 23 + 11
23 42 + 21	9 + 7	9 6 + 8	4 + 84	23 42 + 21	2 + 6	13 15 + 11

add combinations
x-1

6,143 + 87	35 + 468	409 + 3,693	521 + 687	76 + 84
95 + 5,206	98 + 998	8,860 + 978	308 + 997	48 + 96
4,308 + 775	379 + 485	4,322 + 89	897 + 68	59 + 95

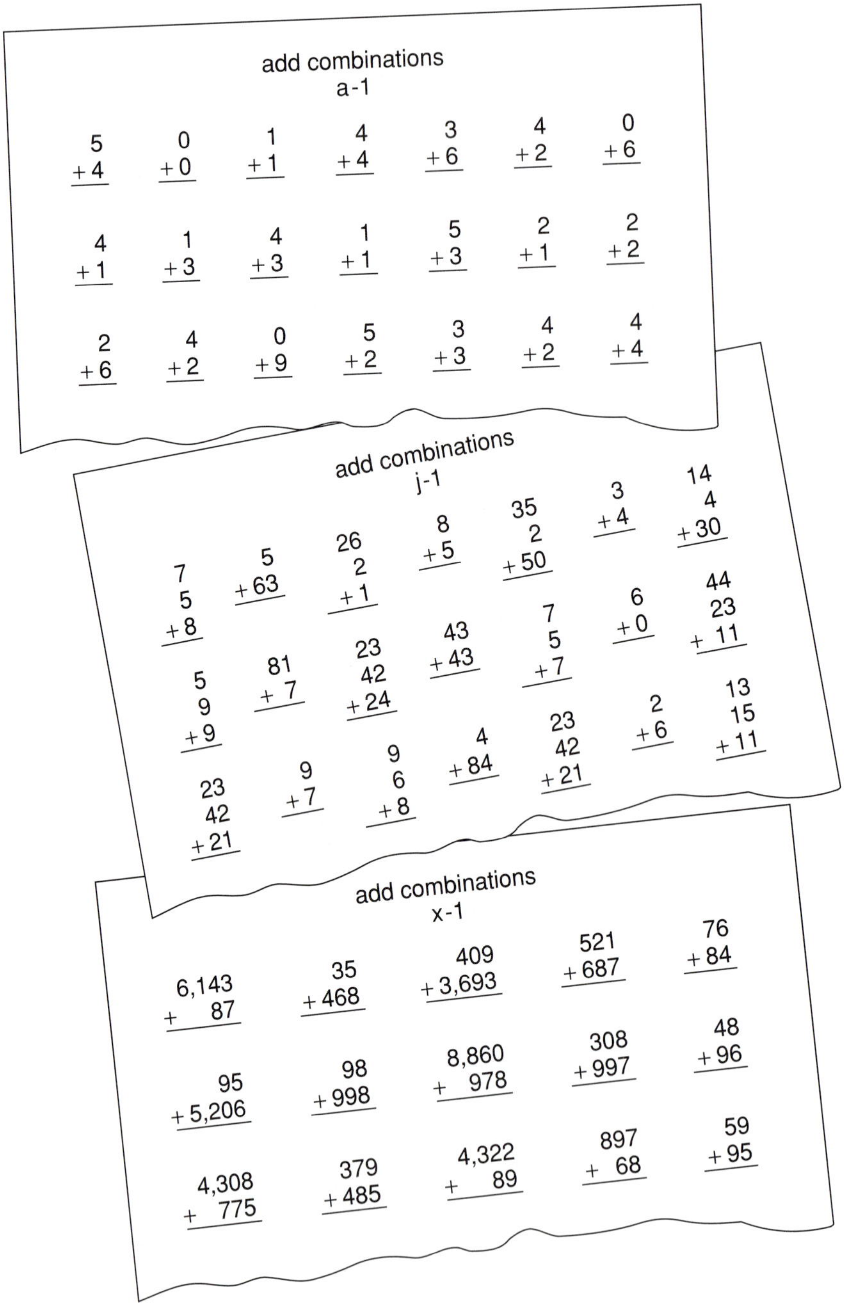

Rosenshine, 1981, p. 1). The Missouri Mathematics Program typifies this approach. It devotes nearly the entire arithmetic period to working on arithmetic problems, provides a daily review, demonstrates new skills, and offers extended opportunities to practice the new skills under individualized teacher supervision and correction. Students using this program learned significantly more than students in traditional programs (Good & Grouws, 1979; Good, Grouws, & Ebmeier, 1983).

Developmental programs rarely are so considerate of students with mathematical problems. For example, in teaching fractions, programs introduce content too rapidly, rarely identify and teach fundamental concepts ("big ideas"), use demonstrations that are convoluted and inefficient, and give students too little chance to practice what the programs are teaching (Carnine, Jitendra, & Silbert, 1997). Given such instruction, students—especially those with learning disabilities—naturally have trouble learning arithmetic and mathematics.

Few teachers have the time to design and implement a program such as the Missouri Mathematics Program on their own. Instead, they must depend on developmental programs adopted by state or local education agencies. Teachers usually must adapt developmental programs to make them suitable for students with learning disabilities. Adaptation requires modifying teaching behaviors (e.g., scheduling plenty of time for arithmetic lessons) as well as instructional programming techniques (e.g., sequencing of lessons). Stein et al. (1997) provide detailed directions about how to make adaptations that result in improved chances of students mastering arithmetic skills and mathematical concepts.

Developmental Interventions

Major publishing companies offer developmental programs in arithmetic and mathematics. Among the most frequently used are Scott, Foresman's Exploring Mathematics (1991), Houghton Mifflin's The Mathematics Experience (1992), and Addison-Wesley's Explorations (1991) series. (From the titles of these programs, one can get an idea of how publishers position their products to stress popular themes; notice the emphasis on "exploration," with a hint of "discovery," in these titles.)

Developmental programs introduce basic skills such as addition, subtraction, multiplication, and division. Most also introduce other important content areas, such as place value, measurement, geometry, and fractions. Despite the many similarities in what they cover, basal programs differ markedly in when they present material. For example, during the first grade, one program may devote a unit to fractions, but others may wait until a later grade to do so.

Connecting Math Concepts (Engelmann et al., 1991) is a basal program designed for use in primary through elementary school and is based on the Direct Instruction model (see Chapter 3). In highly structured lessons involving frequent teacher questions and student answers, students learn fundamental skills for solving mathematical problems. One important feature of this approach is that teachers explicitly teach students strategies to use in solving problems. Another important feature is that basic facts are taught as number families or part-whole relationships (see Figure 14.6). Number families are related sets of numbers:

> Addition and subtraction facts are usually treated as 200 discrete sets of three numbers to be memorized. An alternative organizational structure to teaching facts is to teach them as members of families. This structure prompts important relationships between addition and subtraction, as well as reduces the number of sets to be memorized from 200 to 55. From these 55 number families, all 200 addition and subtraction facts can be quickly derived. (Carnine, 1991, pp. 166–167)

The forerunner of Connecting Math Concepts was DISTAR Arithmetic (Engelmann & Carnine, 1975, 1976). Students whose teachers used DISTAR Arithmetic had higher levels of achievement in arithmetic than those in any of eight other model programs evaluated in one large national study. Not only did the students excel in basic skills such as computation, but they also scored higher on tests of mathematical concepts and problem solving (Abt Associates, 1976, 1977). Similar results have been obtained in comparisons of Connecting Math Concepts with other curricula (Vreeland et al., 1994; Wellington, 1994). Students taught using the DI program not only learn more computation skills, but also learn more concepts.

FIGURE 14.6 Addition and Subtraction Number Family Table

1 1 → 2	1 2 → 3	1 3 → 4	1 4 → 5	1 5 → 6	1 6 → 7	1 7 → 8	1 8 → 9	1 9 → 10	1 10 → 11
	2 2 → 4	2 3 → 5	2 4 → 6	2 5 → 7	2 6 → 8	2 7 → 9	2 8 → 10	2 9 → 11	2 10 → 12
		3 3 → 6	3 4 → 7	3 5 → 8	3 6 → 9	3 7 → 10	3 8 → 11	3 9 → 12	3 10 → 13
			4 4 → 8	4 5 → 9	4 6 → 10	4 7 → 11	4 8 → 12	4 9 → 13	4 10 → 14
				5 5 → 10	5 6 → 11	5 7 → 12	5 8 → 13	5 9 → 14	5 10 → 15
					6 6 → 12	6 7 → 13	6 8 → 14	6 9 → 15	6 10 → 16
						7 7 → 14	7 8 → 15	7 9 → 16	7 10 → 17
							8 8 → 16	8 9 → 17	8 10 → 18
								9 9 → 18	9 10 → 19
									10 10 → 20

Source: From "Increasing the Amount and Quality of Learning through Direct Instruction: Implications for Mathematics" (p. 167) by D. Carnine, in J. W. Lloyd, N. N. Singh, and A. C. Repp (Eds.), *The Regular Education Initiative: Alternative Perspectives on Concepts, Issues, and Models,* 1991, Sycamore, IL: Sycamore. Copyright 1991 by Sycamore Publishing Co. Reprinted by permission.

The Structural Arithmetic program (Stern & Stern, 1971) is designed to develop students' understanding of arithmetic principles by giving them extensive experience with manipulating objects. The program is designed for use in kindergarten through third grade and includes different colored blocks and sticks that represent numbers from 1 to 10. The 1 block is a cube, the 3 stick is the equivalent of laying three 1's in a line, and the 10 is the equivalent of laying ten 1's (or two 5's) in a line. Thus, numerical relationships are represented by different lengths. (Similar blocks are used in other approaches, particularly the Cuisenaire rods advocated by Gattegno, 1963.) Children work with the blocks to discover relationships among numbers; for example, the program includes exercises to help them understand part-whole relationships by showing that the 7 block can be matched by a 6 block and a 1 block, a 4 and a 3, or a 5 and a 2. Although experimental evidence about the effectiveness of Structural Arithmetic is not available, many teachers use this program in working with students who have learning disabilities.

Remedial Interventions

Remedial programs should have the same characteristics as effective developmental programs. Features such as introducing new concepts systematically, providing adequate practice and review, and teaching big ideas are critical (Carnine, Jones, & Dixon, 1994; Kameenui & Carnine, 1998). These features are probably especially important for adolescents with learning disabilities (Jones, Wilson, & Bhojwani, 1997).

The Computational Arithmetic Program, or CAP (Smith & Lovitt, 1982), is designed for use with students who need to learn basic addition, subtraction, multiplication, or division of whole numbers. The program includes directions for monitoring progress, suggestions and materials for reinforcing progress, and an extensive set of carefully sequenced worksheets. It is based on what Smith and Lovitt learned from their research with students who have learning disabilities (Lovitt & Smith, 1974; Smith & Lovitt, 1975, 1976; Smith, Lovitt, & Kidder, 1972).

The Corrective Mathematics program (Engelmann & Carnine, 1981) is composed of several modules, each of which covers a specific area of arithmetic or mathematics skill. These areas include addition, subtraction, multiplication, division, money, and measurement. Scripts for daily lessons are included, and accompanying workbooks provide students with extensive opportunities for practice. Teachers use similar programs, such as Fractions (Engelmann & Steely, 1980) and Ratios and Equations (Engelmann & Steely, 1981), with students who have learning disabilities. Perkins and Cullinan (1984) reported results of a study that revealed that the Fractions program improved the performances of students identified as having learning disabilities.

Technology

Arithmetic and mathematics constitute a popular area for the use of technology. Their regularity and the value of drill and practice in learning computational skills probably contribute to the popularity of using technology in arithmetic instruction. People may also simply associate computers with mathematics and hence consider arithmetic a "natural" area for applying computer technology.

Calculators

One of the first questions many teachers have about technology and arithmetic is whether it is advisable for students to use calculators. Calculators are common in classrooms today and provide many new learning opportunities. For example, some states provide graphing calculators for students so they can learn how to use them to solve problems. Students with disabilities benefit from using calculators in solving computation problems (Horton, Lovitt, & White, 1992). Of course, teachers must teach their students how to use the calculators.

Computer-Assisted Instruction

Teachers who see a natural fit between arithmetic and computers may find some justification for this assumption in evidence concerning drill-and-practice programs. Drill and practice refers to the repeated presentation of and response to a limited number of facts. Although constructivists view drill and practice as undesirable, facility with the automatic retrieval of facts is important in solving problems. Computers can be programmed to provide the practice opportunities many students with learning disabilities need to master basic facts, and such programs have been shown to be an effective medium for helping these students with arithmetic facts (Hasselbring, Goin, & Bransford, 1987, 1988). One current issue about using computer programs is that they may be faulty (see Box 14.1).

Computers can also be used to teach more conceptual arithmetic content. Instructional programs such as Mastering Fractions (Systems Impact, 1986) and Mastering Equations, Roots, and Exponents (Systems Impact, 1988) illustrate the application of technology to learning more than basic facts. Examples of concepts and operations are presented on videodisks, and colorful, animated demonstrations show how, for example, to determine whether a fraction is less than, equal to, or greater than one or how to subtract fractions with unlike denominators. While circulating among the students, the teacher controls the videodisk with a remote control device, and the students answer questions posed by the presenters on video monitors showing the program. As is typical of Direct Instruction programs (see Chapter 3), the questions are rapid, the demonstrations change in subtle but important ways, and the students answer specific questions either chorally or in writing.

The Mastering Fractions program produces substantially greater achievement by students with learning disabilities and those in remedial education than other published instructional programs that cover the same content. In fact, it helps those students master about the same percentage of the objectives for instruction in prealgebra as their peers master in regular education (Grossen & Ewing, 1994; Kelly, Carnine, Gersten, & Grossen, 1986; Lubke, Rogers, & Evans, 1989).

The instructional technology of such programs is more important than the computer technology used in them. Hasselbring, Sherwood, and Bransford (1986) compared the effectiveness of the Mastering Fractions program when it was presented

BOX 14.1 ***TECHNOLOGY***

Technology in Teaching Arithmetic

Arithmetic and mathematics provide excellent opportunities to adopt technology for teaching. Figure A shows a screen from a program designed to help students improve their addition skills by breaking numbers into parts.

Unfortunately, this example also illustrates how a student with learning disabilities might practice faulty strategies and reach mistaken solutions. These students might count the caps and answer "seven." Or then, might add 7 to 25 and answer "32." They might point to 10, say "ten," then point to the 1 and say "eleven," and use 11 as the answer, or add 11 to 25 and get an answer of 36. Or they might get answers of 82 or 86. Because all of these solution strategies are possible but none of them leads to the correct solution (50), students with learning disabilities might have difficulty using such a program.

Students who do not know how to use such software require extensive instruction and supervision so they will not practice mistaken strategies. Teachers should ensure that the directions for using the program anticipate such problems and advise how to avoid them.

Source: From *Pictureware: Addition and Subtraction: A Picture-Based Method for Mastering Basic Math Skills,* by Applied Software Technologies, Acton, MA: Bradford. Copyright 1993 by Applied Software Technologies.

FIGURE A Screen from Computer Program for Improving Addition Skills

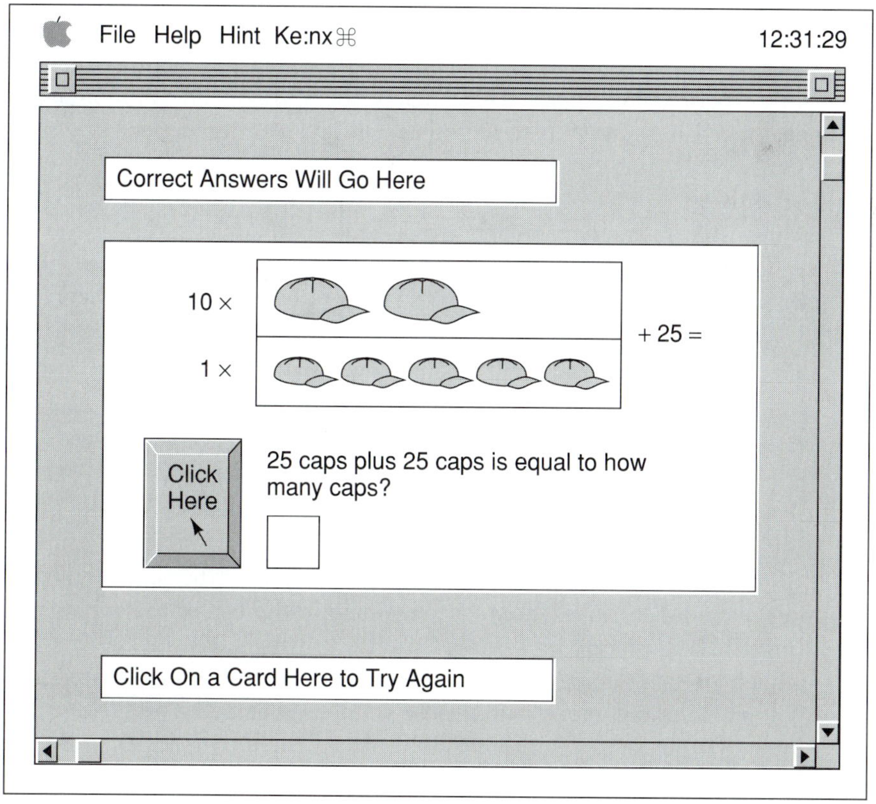

using the videodisk technology to the same program when a teacher presented the lessons according to the scripts but without the colorful animation. Although teachers preferred to use the videodisk version (it was easier for them), student achievement did not differ under the two conditions. Similar results from other studies (e.g., Gleason, Carnine, & Boriero, 1990) support the idea that the means of delivering instruction is not the critical variable in raising the achievement of students with learning disabilities.

Video technology can also be used to simulate an authentic context in which students use mathematics knowledge. For example, Bottge and Hasselbring (1993) used Mastering Fractions to ensure that students knew how to solve problems involving fractions and then compared two further instructional conditions. In one condition, the teacher followed detailed lesson plans to show students how to apply their fraction skills in word problems. In the other condition, the teacher guided students through general problem-solving strategies (particularly, generating a plan for solving a problem) and showed a video that presented a problem and in which information that was useful in solving the problem was embedded but not stated explicitly. Although students in both groups used their fraction skills to solve word problems, the latter group performed better on transfer tasks that required them to notice critical features and organize information in ways that would help them develop solutions.

Effective Teaching Procedures

Many of the techniques recommended for teaching arithmetic and mathematics have little experimental support. Those that do include modeling, reinforcing responses, explicitly teaching students to use strategies, and self-instruction.

Modeling

A mainstay in teaching, modeling may be used in any of several ways:

- The teacher demonstrates for the student (e.g., "Watch me; here's how I do a division problem.").
- The teacher has another student demonstrate (e.g., "Watch Judy; she's going to bisect that line.").
- The teacher simply tells students a factual answer (e.g., "9 plus 5 equals 14.").
- The teacher uses or constructs materials that include demonstrations and leaves these for students to consult while solving problems.

Rivera and Smith (1987) summarized research on the value of modeling in teaching computation skills. In an early example of the use of this technique, Smith and Lovitt (1975) reported a series of studies in which they investigated modeling as a technique for teaching arithmetic skills to boys with learning disabilities. They found that providing a demonstration and a permanent model (a problem with a written solution on the students' arithmetic sheets) resulted in greatly improved performance. Moreover, the students' performance improvements generalized to other problems for which they had received no demonstrations. Modeling can be used not only with simple arithmetic computation (see Rivera & Smith, 1988), but also in correcting procedural errors in complex applications such as algebra (Silver & Smith, 1989).

Reinforcement

Providing reinforcement for correct answers, or reinforcing responses, is another proven method of improving performance. However, arranging reinforcement contingencies for students who do not know how to perform tasks is of little value, as Smith and Lovitt (1976) demonstrated. In other words, it does no good to use rewards to "motivate" students who do not have the skills required to answer arithmetic problems. However, when students do know how to answer problems but do so inaccurately or at too slow a pace, reinforcing accuracy or faster work is an effective way to improve performance (Hasazi & Hasazi, 1972; Smith et al., 1972). Reinforcement does not have to take the form of tangible rewards. Fink and Carnine (1975) found that having students maintain graphs showing their performance had reinforcing effects on their arithmetic progress.

Strategy Training

Strategy training covers a broad range of methods. When teachers model the steps involved in attacking a specific type of arithmetic problem, they usually are modeling a strategy (Cullinan, Lloyd, & Epstein, 1981; Lloyd, 1980; Lloyd & deBettencourt, 1982). In strategy training, a task analysis of a cognitive operation is performed so that the steps leading to the solution can be identified. Then students are taught the skills required by each of the steps. When students have mastered the component skills, they are taught how to put them together in order to attack a given type of problem. Students from preschool to community colleges can benefit from strategy training (Grimm, Bijou, & Parsons, 1973; Montague & Bos, 1986; Smith & Lovitt, 1975; Zawaiza & Gerber, 1993). Mastery of the component skills prior to strategy introduction leads to more rapid learning of the strategy and greater generalization of it to related problems (Carnine, 1980; Kameenui & Carnine, 1988; Lloyd, Saltzman, & Kauffman, 1981).

Today in learning disabilities, strategy training continues to be an important means of teaching arithmetic and mathematics skills. Teachers can help students learn cognitive strategies for representing problems and solving them using modeling, practice, and reinforcement (Montague, 1997). To help students use strategies in many different situations, teachers may ask themselves questions that evaluate application. Table 14.3 shows evaluation questions for strategy training:

Self-Instruction Training

Self-instructional techniques are another potentially effective approach to teaching arithmetic and mathematics. Self-instructional programs have been reported to be successful with learners with disabilities (see Johnston, Whitman, & Johnson, 1981; Whitman & Johnston, 1983). Specific types of self-instruction that have been tested have also shown some promise. For example, when Lovitt and Curtiss (1968) required a boy with learning disabilities to read number sentences aloud (self-verbalization) before writing his answers, they noticed a substantial improvement in his performance.

TABLE 14.3 Evaluation Questions for Strategy Training

Strategy Acquisition	Strategy Application	Strategy Maintenance	Strategy Generalization
■ Can the student recite the strategy from memory and/or paraphrase the strategy (depending on the goal)? ■ Can the student explain or define the terms of the strategy? ■ Does the student understand the rationale for learning the strategy?	■ How does the student's performance on domain-specific tasks (e.g., mathematical word problems, paraphrasing passages) following instruction compare with his or her performance prior to instruction (posttest vs. baseline)? ■ Has the student reached a mastery by achieving a certain preset criterion for acceptable performance? ■ Can the student use the strategy to detect and correct errors (self-monitor performance)?	■ Did the student maintain performance levels on domain-specific tasks over time? ■ Can the student explain how the strategy was used to solve the problem or complete the task? ■ If the student did not maintain performance levels, did a booster session improve performance to mastery level?	■ Did the student use the strategy successfully in other tasks? ■ Did the student use the strategy successfully in other situations or settings? ■ Can the student verbalize his or her rationale for selecting and using the strategy?

Source: From "Cognitive Strategy Instruction in Mathematics for Students with Learning Disabilities" by M. Montague, *Journal of Learning Disabilities,* 1997, *30,* 164–177. Copyright 1997 by PRO-ED, Inc. Reprinted by permission.

Similarly, Parsons (1972) found that requiring a student both to circle the operation sign (e.g., +) and to name it before attempting to solve arithmetic problems produced much better performance than simply having the student circle the sign.

More general self-regulation training also has had beneficial effects on students' performances in arithmetic. For example, Seabaugh and Schumaker (1993) found that having adolescents with learning disabilities actively use aspects of cognitive-behavioral interventions (goal setting, self-monitoring, and self-reinforcement) helped them complete more mathematics assignments.

Self-instructional training often requires that students learn a strategy such as those taught in strategy training. This provides another illustration of how the lines between the models described in Chapter 3 can become blurred. Cognitive-behavioral modification and strategy training share many characteristics (Lloyd, 1980). For example, a teacher might teach students how to guide themselves (self-instruction) through a series of steps to solve problems of a certain sort (task-analytic strategy training). Figure 14.7 illustrates how a student might implement a self-instruction plan to solve the mathematical task of finding equivalent fractions.

FIGURE 14.7 Example of a Solution Algorithm for Finding Equivalent Fractions

Step	Description	Action	
1: Read	Pupil reads problem to him- or herself.	"Let's see . . . um, 9/17ths is equal to how many 102nds?"	$\frac{9}{17} = \frac{?}{102}$
2: Plan	Pupil describes general process to him- or herself.	"Okay, I've got to multiply 9/17ths by some fraction that's the same as 1, and then I can get the number of 102nds that it equals."	$\frac{9}{17} = \frac{?}{102}$
3: Rewrite	Pupil rewrites problem, providing space for work. Note: This step can be completed while performing Step 2.	"Here's my workspace . . . "	$\frac{9}{17}\left(\frac{}{}\right) = \frac{?}{102}$
4: Identify known part	Pupil identifies part of equivalence for which numbers are known.	"Okay, I've got two out of three numbers here (pointing to denominators), so I can start on that part."	$\frac{9}{17}\left(\frac{}{}\right) = \frac{?}{102}$
5: Solve known part	Pupil uses prior knowledge to solve for missing multiplier.	"So, 17 times something equals 102 . . . um . . . I'll just figure that out . . .17 is almost 20, and 20 goes into 100 five times, so I'll try that . . . nope, 17 leftover, so it's 6 times . . . great! It's even."	$\frac{9}{17}\left(\frac{}{}\right) = \frac{?}{102}$; $17\overline{)102}$ = 5, -95, remainder 17
6: Substitute	Pupil uses information derived in Step 5 to complete fraction in equation.	"And that means this (writing) is 6 over 6 . . . which is the same as 1, so . . ."	$\frac{9}{17}\left(\frac{6}{6}\right) = \frac{?}{102}$
7: Derive missing numerator	Pupil solves for missing numerator using information from Step 6.	"Now, I can just multiply these 'cause I've got two out of three and . . . 6 times 9 is 54, sooo. . ."	$\frac{9}{17}\left(\frac{6}{6}\right) = \frac{?}{102}$
8: Read	Pupil reads completed problem.	"9/17ths is equal to 54/102nds."	$\frac{9}{17}\left(\frac{6}{6}\right) = \frac{54}{102}$

Source: From "Effective Mathematics Instruction" by J. W. Lloyd and C. E. Keller, 1989, *Focus on Exceptional Children, 21*(7), pp. 1–10. Copyright 1989 by Love Publishing Co. Reprinted by permission.

Summary

1. How does mathematical knowledge develop normally?
   a. Normally developing children learn many arithmetic operations and mathematical concepts before reaching school age. This is called informal knowledge.
   b. During the school years, a student's knowledge of arithmetic operations and mathematical concepts changes gradually, partially because of aging and partially because of instruction. This is more formal knowledge.
   c. Generally, children progress from using more primitive strategies to using more sophisticated and efficient strategies to solve problems.
   d. Instruction in schools often does not match the progression from primitive to sophisticated strategies.
   e. In difficult situations, even adults fall back to using more primitive strategies for solving problems.
2. What mathematics problems do students with learning disabilities experience?
   a. About 4% to 6% of students with learning disabilities have problems learning arithmetic skills.
   b. Many students with learning disabilities who have problems in arithmetic and mathematics also have problems in reading and related areas in literacy.
   c. Students with learning disabilities in arithmetic and mathematics may have difficulty with computation, problem solving, or both.
   d. For some students with learning disabilities in arithmetic and mathematics, problems are mitigated when tests are not timed.
   e. When solving computational problems, students with difficulties in arithmetic make more mistakes in giving simple answers in various areas of arithmetic and sometimes recall facts more slowly than their peers.
   f. Students with learning disabilities also make mistakes in applying strategies or procedures, choosing inefficient strategies, and choosing poorly.
3. How are mathematics abilities assessed?
   a. Skills and deficits in arithmetic and mathematics are best assessed by using both tests and less formal, direct measurement methods, such as performance samples.
   b. Comprehensive tests of arithmetic and mathematics performance may be used to assess general ability (grade level).
   c. Teachers often use specific tests for more specific arithmetic and mathematics skills areas such as computation in each of the major areas (e.g., addition) and problem solving (e.g., word problems).
   d. Teachers need to be able to assess progress in arithmetic and mathematics skills and usually do so by devising informal measures (e.g., probes to assess speed and accuracy in computation).

4. What interventions help students with difficulties in mathematics?
   a. Choices of instructional methods should be based on whether the methods are effective.
   b. There are benefits to teaching children both fundamental computation skills (adding, subtracting, etc.) and problem-solving skills (e.g., how to think through a problem clearly, set up a strategy for solving it, execute that plan, and monitor its completion).
   c. Specific teaching techniques that have research support are modeling, explicitly teaching students to use strategies, reinforcing responses, and self-instruction.
   d. It's appropriate to teach students with learning disabilities how to use calculators, provided that they know how to compute and solve problems independently.

Glossary

ability-achievement discrepancy the discrepancy between a person's potential for achievement based on intellectual ability and his or her actual achievement

adaptability the amount of flexibility family members display in their interactions with one another

aphasia severe problems in speaking

applied behavior analysis (ABA) the systematic analysis of the observable behavior of learners

assistive technology technology, especially computer software, that helps persons with learning disabilities perform their jobs or learn

attention deficit hyperactivity disorder (ADHD) a condition characterized by severe problems of inattention, hyperactivity, and/or impulsivity; often found in persons with learning disabilities

attribution training training that focuses on getting students to recognize that effort can lead to success

attributions what one thinks are the causes of successes and failures

authentic assessment procedures that are thought to give a more "real" or authentic, useful picture than traditional testing of what the student can and cannot do

axon a long, tubelike extension of the neuron that carries messages to the dendrites of other neurons

basal ganglia a part of the brain (underneath the cortex and behind the frontal lobes) that is responsible for movement; persons with attention deficit hyperactivity disorder may also have problems in this area

behavioral assessment direct, frequent observation and recording of specific target behaviors

behaviorism a theoretical approach that stresses the importance of observing and measuring observable behaviors rather than nonobservable mental events; closely linked to learning theory and environmentalism

brain stem the part of the brain supporting the cerebral cortex and connecting it to the spinal cord; regulates survival reflexes such as respiration and heart rate

Broca's area part of the brain's left frontal lobe associated with the ability to speak

cerebellum the part of the brain below the cerebral cortex next to the brain; regulates several behaviors having to do with movement

cerebral cortex the layer of tissue covering the cerebral hemispheres of the brain; divided into four types of lobes for each hemisphere (frontal, parietal, occipital, and temporal) that regulate motor movements, executive functions, and emotions; bodily sensations and visual perception; visual functions; and attention, memory, and language, respectively

co-teaching a service delivery model in which the general and special educators team up to teach a class together, usually serving a group of students with disabilities and a group without disabilities, who are combined in one class (thus, it is not apparent that the class is "special")

cognition the ability to think and solve problems

cognitive styles the particular approaches individuals use in problem solving (e.g., impulsive or reflective)

cognitive training the techniques and methods that address cognitive, metacognitive, motivational, and attention problems; focuses on changing thought processes

cognitive-behavior modification (CBM) another term for the cognitive-behavioral approach

cohesion the degree to which individual family members are free to act independently

collaborative consultation a service delivery model in which special education teachers do not have classrooms of their own and do not pull students out of their regular classes for special instruction

comorbid conditions two or more conditions (diseases, disabilities) occurring at the same time in a person

compensatory strategies strategies, such as taking more time and rechecking work, that allow individuals to compensate for their disabilities

competence the hidden knowledge of language that nearly all people are presumed to have

computerized axial tomography (CAT-scan) a neuroimaging technique whereby x-rays of the brain are compiled by a computer to produce an overall picture of the brain

constructivism a philosophy of learning that rejects behaviorism and the task-analytic perspective and stresses interrelationships, or the interplay between stages and the mechanisms of change

continuum of alternative placements (CAP) the full range of alternative placements or educational environments ranging from full-time placement in regular classes, with supplementary aids and services, through resource room programs, special self-contained classes, special day and residential schools, and programs provided in hospitals or through home-based instruction

criterion-referenced tests tests designed to measure the extent to which students have mastered specific skills

curriculum-based assessment (CBA) an approach to assessment based on the assumption that learning problems and progress are best measured directly as performance in the curriculum rather than indirectly as test performance related to underlying processes; systematic, frequent, brief samples of the student's performance in the curriculum being taught

curriculum-based measurement (CBM) measurement of student performance based on the assumptions of CBA

decode to receive and understand a message; in oral language or reading, the ability to understand

decoding the aspects of reading that happen as the reader converts the printed words on the page into more familiar spoken or heard language

dendrites treelike projections of the neuron that receive messages from the environment and other neurons

diagnostic-prescriptive teaching an approach to assessment based on the assumption that testing will lead to a "diagnosis" of the underlying difficulty and a prescription for effective instruction

Direct Instruction (DI) a prototypical example of the generic direct instruction (di) that emphasizes logical analysis of instructional communications

direct measurement/instruction theory an approach to assessment based on the assumption that it is most important to measure a student's actual performance on tasks involving academic and social skills

dizygotic twins twins from two different eggs

dyscalculia the inability to perform mathematical calculations

dysgraphia partial ability or inability to remember how to write alphabet or arithmetic symbols by hand

dyslexia severe reading disability

encode to express and send a message; in oral language or writing, the ability to make oneself understood

environmentalism a theoretical approach that posits that what individuals encounter in their environment determines what they learn and how they behave

expansion a means of language acquisition in which an adult enlarges or elaborates (expands) a child's utterances

externalizing behavior antisocial, acting-out behavior

familiality when a condition, such as reading disability, occurs at a greater than chance rate in family relatives

family characteristics descriptive information on the family, including characteristics of the disability, the family, and each family member, as well as special conditions

family functions activities in which families engage to meet their everyday needs

family life cycle the varying stages a family or individual goes through depending on age and stage of development

family systems model a social systems approach that focuses on family characteristics, family interaction, family functions, and family life cycle in explaining individuals' behavior

family-centered models treatment models for families that place the family in control of decision making

far-point copying copying material from a distant source to a piece of paper

fetal alcohol syndrome a syndrome associated with mental retardation, brain damage, anomalies of the face, hyperactivity, and heart failure that affects children of women who drank alcohol excessively when pregnant

field independence–field dependence the degree to which people are influenced by their environment when asked to make decisions on perceptual tasks

flow lists a spelling list made up of words a student has not mastered; when the student masters a word, the word is dropped from the list and another added

free appropriate public education (FAPE) education that is appropriate to the student with disabilities and is free of cost to the parents or guardians of the student

frontal lobes the structures of the cerebral cortex that regulate motor movements and executive functions

functional assessment assessment of factors or events that maintain or trigger certain behaviors in order to devise interventions

functional magnetic resonance imaging (fMRI) an adaptation of the MRI (*see* magnetic resonance imaging) used to detect changes in the brain while it is in an active state that, unlike the PET-scan (*see* PET-scan), does not involve the use of radioactive materials

general education curriculum the curriculum typically offered to nondisabled students

gist comprehension the understanding of the theme of a narrative

heritability the degree to which a condition is genetically transmitted; often estimated by comparing the rate of the condition in monozygotic and dizygotic pairs of twins, one of whom has the condition

holism another term for constructivism

incidental learning learning acquired simply by exposure to the environment

individualized education plan (IEP) a written agreement of educators and parents, required by IDEA, that includes statements about the student's education needs and the special education and related services that will be provided

individualized family service plan (IFSP) a written plan, similar to the IEP, required for preschool children with disabilities; a detailed plan for providing services to meet the needs of the preschool child for special education and related services and for involving the family in these services

Individuals with Disabilities Education Act (IDEA) the federal law governing all aspects of special education (initially enacted in 1975 and reauthorized and amended in 1990 and 1997)

information-processing model another term for the cognitive model

interactive assessment, dynamic assessment a method of assessing how the student uses cues, prompts, and instruction to learn during testing

interim alternative educational setting a setting other than the general education classroom in which the student's special education may be continued

interindividual differences differences between or among individuals (for example, some students with learning disabilities have reading problems, whereas others have math problems)

internalizing behavior social withdrawal, which may include anxiety and depression

intraindividual differences variations within an individual on, for example, psychological, behavioral, or educational measures

lateralization of function refers to the differing roles that the two brain hemispheres play vis-à-vis language, motor movement, and sensory perception (*see* split-brain studies)

learned helplessness the belief that one's efforts will not result in desired outcomes

least restrictive environment (LRE) the least restrictive or most "normal" place in which appropriate education, and the greatest access to the general education curriculum that is compatible with the student's needs and goals can be offered

left and right hemispheres the two cerebral hemispheres of the brain, each of which receives sensory information from and controls movement of the opposite side of the body; in most people, especially right-handers, the left hemisphere is more important for language production and comprehension than the right hemisphere

locus of control the degree to which one views oneself as being controlled by internal or external forces

macroculture a nation or other large social entity with a shared culture

magnetic resonance imaging (MRI) a neuroimaging technique that uses radio waves to produce cross-sectional images of the brain

manifestation determination a meeting of the IEP team and other qualified individuals for the purpose of determining whether a student's misbehavior was related to his or her disability

Matthew effect the idea that the rich get richer while the poor get poorer; for example, in reading, students who develop reading skills early will have an advantage in learning about the world and will, therefore, do better on tests of intelligence

mean the average score; the sum of the scores divided by the number of scores on a test

median the middle score; half the scores are higher and half are lower than the median

mediated learning learning acquired through the training of someone who helps the learner frame a question and focus attention on critical features and who provides feedback and support

metacognition the ability to think about thinking

metacomprehension training a cognitive training method in which students are provided with strategies for thinking about and remembering major points of material they are reading

microculture a smaller group within a larger cultural group having unique values, style, language, dialect, ways of communicating nonverbally, and so forth

minimal brain dysfunction a condition in which a person exhibits fewer pronounced behavioral signs of neurological impairment (e.g., hyperactivity, clumsiness) than persons with verified neurological damage

mnemonic strategies methods for remembering facts or relationships among facts

mnemonics a system for remembering facts and relationships among facts

mode the most frequently obtained score

monozygotic twins twins from the same egg

morphology the system of rules used to construct words and word forms from basic units of meaning that involves the structure of basic meaning

multidisciplinary team (MDT) a team consisting of representatives from the medical, psychological, social, and educational arenas for evaluation for eligibility for special education

near-point copying copying material from a model on one's desk to a piece of paper

neurological dysfunction a condition wherein a person's behavior (e.g., learning, attention, and so forth) is affected by abnormal functioning of the brain; the exact abnormal functioning is as yet poorly understood

neurons brain cells responsible for sending and receiving information

neuropsychological assessment assessment intended to link neurological problems to psychological characteristics

neurotransmitters chemicals secreted by the terminal buttons that transport electrical-chemical messages from the axon to the dendrites of neurons; the particular neurotransmitter secreted helps determine how neurons send and receive messages

nonreferenced tests tests that do not use a normative group or criterion for comparison but focus on the problem-solving strategies used by students in approaching problems

nonverbal learning disabilities disabilities that manifest in problems in math, self-regulation, and particularly in social functioning

normative group *see* standardized scores

norm-referenced tests tests that allow us to measure how a student performed on a test compared to other students comprising a normative sample

occipital lobes the lobes of the cerebral cortex dedicated to various aspects of visual perception

organization a memory strategy involving the clustering of items to be remembered into smaller categories of similar things

orthography the formal name for the system of representing spoken language in written form

parietal lobes the lobes of the cerebral cortex involved in the integration of bodily sensations and visual perceptions

percentile the percentage of the normative group that scored the same or lower

performance both listening and speaking language behavior

phoneme segmentation the separation of words into their parts (sounds)

phonemes the sounds of words

phonological awareness the ability to blend sounds, segment the sounds of words, rhyme, and in other ways manipulate the sounds of spoken words

phonology the system of sounds and sound combinations used according to linguistic rules

place value a developmental step in number conceptualization in which children learn that numbers can be multiples of 10; also called the decimal, or base-10, system

planum temporale a portion of the brain in Wernicke's area in the left temporal lobe that research suggests is affected in persons with dyslexia

positive reinforcement presenting consequences that increase the likelihood that a behavior will be repeated

positron emission tomography (PET-scan) a computerized method for measuring blood flow in the brain; during a cognitive task, a low amount of radioactive dye is injected in the brain; the dye collects into active neurons, indicating which areas of the brain are active

pragmatics the use of language to achieve desired social purposes

precorrection plan a proactive plan for teaching desirable behavior, including statements about the context of misbehavior, expected behavior, modification of the context, rehearsal of the expected behavior, strong reinforcement, prompts, and a monitoring plan

prefrontal lobes the forward part of the frontal lobes that may be implicated in the control of emotions

prereferral strategies instructional or behavior management procedures used by the teacher or a team of teachers prior to referral; prereferral strategies are designed to avert unnecessary referrals for full evaluation for special education

primary prevention prevention designed to keep disabilities from occurring

progressive time delay a teaching practice in which the teacher presents an item, pauses briefly (3 seconds), and then gives the answer; if the student answers correctly during the pause, the teacher provides a reward; the teacher gradually shortens the pause

psychological processes the mental manipulation or interpretation of information perceived through the senses

punishment a consequence that reduces the likelihood that a particular behavior will be performed

range the spread from the lowest to the highest score

reciprocal effects the idea that causation between child and adult behavior can go in either direction

reciprocal teaching a cognitive intervention in which the teacher and student engage in dialogue in order to construct the meaning of text or algorithms; a type of scaffolded instruction

reflectivity-impulsivity the degree to which a person takes time to reflect on alternatives before making a choice

reframing reordering perceptions of a situation so that one can see the positives

rehearsal strategy involving the systematic repetition of the names of items to be remembered

reliable, reliability in measurement, the ability to get the same result again; a dependable measurement

residential school a service delivery model in which students live in dormitories or other residential units, at least during the school week, if not seven days a week, and attend a special school on the campus

resource room a service delivery model in which the special education teacher pulls students into a special class for instruction only in specific areas in which they have difficulties, perhaps for as little as 30 minutes several times a week, perhaps as much as half of each school day

response cost withdrawing rewards or privileges contingent on a particular behavior

scaffolded instruction an instructional technique in which the teacher provides assistance as the student is first learning a task but gradually removes help so that the student can do the task independently

school-home note program a system of communication between teacher and parent in which the teacher evaluates the child's behavior at school on a simple form that goes home to the parent, and the parent then reinforces the child

secondary prevention prevention designed to correct disabilities once they have occurred or to prevent them from getting worse

selective attention the ability to focus on relevant features of a task without being distracted by irrelevant aspects

self-advocacy the ability to act as one's own advocate in explaining learning disabilities and the accommodations they necessitate; this is important for persons with learning disabilities in order for them to succeed, especially in adulthood

self-instruction a cognitive training method in which the teacher and then the student verbalize questions or instructions for performing a task

self-monitoring a cognitive training method in which students are taught to assess and record their progress

semantics the intent and meaning of words and sentences

service delivery model a plan for bringing students, teachers, and instructional methods and materials together; a model of the physical and interpersonal environment required to foster effective teaching and learning

short-term memory the ability to remember information over a few seconds to a minute or two at most

social support systems model a social systems approach that stresses the importance of informal sources of support (i.e., family, friends, neighbors, social clubs, churches)

social systems approach the view that an individual's behavior can best be understood in the context in which it occurs, a significant part of which concerns the family

socially constructed phenomenon an event or concept created by a society to serve certain social purposes; an idea created by and commonly held in a society and used for making social judgments (e.g., democracy, good, disability, giftedness)

soft neurological signs behavioral indicators of neurological dysfunction, such as poor balance, poor visual-perceptual skills, and distractibility; although often present in persons with documented brain injury, these signs do not always mean a person has brain injury or brain dysfunction

soma the cell body, composed of the nucleus and material that supports the functioning of the neuron

sound blending the combining of parts of words (sounds) into the whole word

special day school a service delivery model designed to serve a special student clientele during the entire school day but not before or after school hours

special self-contained class a service delivery model generally thought to be appropriate for students who need a more highly structured and intensive instructional and behavior management program than can be afforded in a regular classroom, usually serving a dozen or fewer students with a special education teacher and a paraprofessional

split-brain studies studies of the effects on patients of a surgical procedure that severs the area between the two hemispheres of the brain; each hemisphere controls movement and receives information from the opposite side of the body; the left hemisphere is more responsible for language production and comprehension than the right hemisphere

standard scores scores depicting how a student performed in comparison to the **normative group**—the group that is assumed to be a representative sample and is used to establish a typical or normal distribution of scores, including a normal range, mean, and percentiles

standardized tests tests with set procedures for administration, objective scoring criteria, and a specific frame of reference for interpreting scores

structuralism another term for constructivism

supported employment model a method that uses job coaches to integrate workers into competitive employment situations

synapse a small gap between the axon and the dendrite

syntax the set of rules that governs how words are put together in combinations and proper order to form sentences

teacher-made tests informal tests constructed by teachers to assess their students' learning

temporal lobes the lobes of the cerebral cortex involved in attention, memory, and language production and reception

teratogens agents that cause abnormal growth or malformation in the fetus

terminal buttons buttonlike structures at the end of the axon that secrete a neurotransmitter into the synapse

tertiary prevention prevention designed to keep the effects of the problem or disability from spreading to other areas of functioning

test-teach-test cycle a cycle of measuring, teaching, and remeasuring in which the teacher tests to identify a problem, uses this information to guide teaching, and then checks progress by measuring again

trait assessment/classification theory an approach to assessment based on the assumption that the most important things to measure are the traits, abilities, cognitive processes, or developmental stages underlying learning disabilities

transition a change in status from behaving primarily as a student to assuming emergent adult roles in the community

T-unit a single main clause and the subordinate clauses that accompany it (used in measuring language development)

type-token ratio the ratio of the number of different words (type) to the total number of words (tokens) in a language sample

valid, validity in measurement, measuring what is intended; a true representation of the ability being assessed

Wernicke's area part of the left temporal lobe associated with the ability to comprehend language

working memory the ability to keep a small amount of information in mind while carrying out further mental operations

zone of proximal development the gap between a child's level of performance when working independently and when helped by an adult

References

Abruscato, J. (1993). Early results and tentative implications from the Vermont Portfolio Project. *Phi Delta Kappan, 74,* 474–477.

Abt Associates. (1976). *Education as experimentation: A planned variation model* (Vol. 3A). Cambridge, MA: Author.

Abt Associates. (1977). *Education as experimentation: A planned variation model* (Vol. 4). Cambridge, MA: Author.

Achenbach, T. M. (1985). *Assessment and taxonomy of child and adolescent psychopathology.* Newbury Park, CA: Sage.

Achenbach, T. M., & Edelbrock, C. S. (1989). Diagnostic, taxonomic, and assessment issues. In T. H. Ollendick & M. Hersen (Eds.), *Handbook of child psychopathology* (2nd ed.). New York: Plenum.

Ackerman, P. T., Dykman, R. A., & Gardner, M Y. (1990). Counting rate, naming rate, phonological sensitivity, and memory span: Major factors in dyslexia. *Journal of Learning Disabilities, 23,* 325–327.

Ackerman, P. T., Peters, J. E., & Dykman, R. A. (1971). Children with specific learning disabilities: WISC profiles. *Journal of Learning Disabilities, 4,* 150–166.

Adams, G., & Engelmann, S. (1996). *Research on Direct Instruction: 25 years beyond DISTAR. Seattle: Educational Achievement Systems.*

Adams, M. J. (1990). *Beginning to read: Thinking and learning about print.* Cambridge, MA: MIT Press.

Adams, M. J., Foorman, B., Beeler, T., & Lundberg, I. (1997). *Phonemic awareness in young children: A classroom curriculum.* Baltimore: Brookes.

Addison-Wesley. (1991). *Explorations.* Menlo Park, CA: Author.

Adelman, H. S., & Taylor, L. (1991). Issues and problems related to the assessment of learning disabilities. In H. L. Swanson (Ed.), *Handbook on the assessment of learning disabilities* (pp. 21–43). Austin, TX: PRO-ED.

Adelman, P. B., & Vogel, S. A. (1990). College graduates with learning disabilities: Employment attainment and career patterns. *Learning Disability Quarterly, 13*(3), 154–166.

Adelman, P. B., & Vogel, S. A. (1993). Issues in the employment of adults with learning disabilities. *Learning Disability Quarterly, 16*(3), 219–232.

Alarcón, M., DeFries, J. C., Light, J. G., & Pennington, B. F. (1997). A twin study of mathematics disability. *Journal of Learning Disabilities, 30,* 617–623.

Alberto, P. A., & Troutman, A. C. (1995). *Applied behavior analysis for teachers* (4th ed.). Columbus, OH: Merrill.

Algozzine, B., Christenson, S., & Ysseldyke, J. E. (1982). Probabilities associated with the referral to placement process. *Teacher Education and Special Education,* 5, 19–23.

Algozzine, B., & Ysseldyke, J. E. (1983). Learning disabilities as a subset of school failure: The oversophistication of a concept. *Exceptional Children,* 50, 242–246.

Alvermann, D., Arrington, H., Bridge, C., Bruce, B., Fountas, I., Farcia, E., Paris, S., Ruiz, N., Schmidt, B., Searfoss, L., & Winogard, P. (1995). *Heath literacy.* Lexington, MA: Heath.

American Academy of Ophthalmology. (1987). Policy statement: Learning disabilities, dyslexia, and vision. *Journal of Learning Disabilities, 20,* 412–413.

American Academy of Ophthalmology. (1997, October 15). *Focus on learning disabilities and vision* [On-line]. Available at http://www.eyenet.org/public/faqs/learn_dis/learn_dis_faq.html.

American Psychiatric Association. (1994). *Diagnostic and statistical manual of mental disorders: DSM-IV* (4th ed.). Washington, DC: Author.

Anderson, D. W. (1968). *Teaching handwriting.* Washington, DC: National Education Association.

Anderson, I. H. (1980). Study strategies and adjunct aids. In P. J. Spiro, B. C. Bruce, & W. F. Brewer (Eds.), *Theoretical issues in reading comprehension* (pp. 483–502). Hillsdale, NJ: Erlbaum.

Anderson, R. C., Hiebert, E. F., Wilkinson, I. A. G., & Scott, J. (1985). *Becoming a nation of readers.* Champaign, IL: National Academy of Education and Center for the Study of Reading.

Anderson-Inman, L. (1981). Transenvironmental programming: Promoting success in the regular classroom by maximizing effect of resource room instruction. *Journal of Special Education Technology, 4*(4), 3–12.

Armstrong, F. D., Seidel, J. F., & Swales, T. P. (1993). Pediatric HIV infection: A neuropsychological and educational challenge. *Journal of Learning Disabilities, 26*(2), 92–103.

Arter, J. A., & Jenkins, J. R. (1977). Examining the benefits and prevalence of modality considerations in special education. *Journal of Special Education, 11,* 281–298.

Artiles, A. J., Csapo, M., & de Lorenzo, E. G. (1995). Special education for students with mild disabilities: A third world perspective. In A. J. Artiles & D. P. Hallahan (Eds.), *Special education in Latin America: Experiences and issues* (pp. 42–58). Westport, CT: Praeger.

Artiles, A. J., Trent, S. C., & Hallahan, D. P. (1995). Special education for children with mild disabilities in Latin America: Issues and prospects. In A. J. Artiles & D. P. Hallahan (Eds.), *Special education in Latin America: Experiences and issues* (pp. 251–283). Westport, CT: Praeger.

Ashbaker, M. H., & Swanson, H. L. (1996). Short-term memory and working memory operations and their contribution to reading in adolescents with and without learning disabilities. *Learning Disabilities Research and Practice, 11,* 206–213.

Ashcraft, M. H. (1982). The development of mental arithmetic: A chronometric approach. *Developmental Review, 2,* 213–236.

Ashlock, R. B. (1994). *Error patterns in computation* (6th ed.). Columbus, OH: Merrill.

Association for Children with Learning Disabilities. (1986). ACLD definition: Specific learning disabilities. *ACLD Newsbriefs,* pp. 15–16.

Aune, E. P., & Johnson, J. M. (1992). Transition takes teamwork! A collaborative model for college-bound students with LD. *Intervention in School and Clinic,* 27(4), 222–227.

Ayers, L. P. (1912). *A score for measuring the quality of handwriting of school children.* New York: Division of Education, Russell Sage Foundation.

Badian, N. A., & Ghublikian, M. (1983). The personal social characteristics of children with poor mathematical computation skills. *Journal of Learning Disabilities, 16,* 154–157.

Baker, E. T., Wang, M. C., & Walberg, H. J. (1994). The effects of inclusion on learning. *Educational Leadership,* 52(4), 33–35.

Baker, L. (1982), An evaluation of the role of metacognitive deficits in learning disabilities. *Topics in Learning and Learning Disabilities,* 2(1), 27–35.

Baker, L., & Anderson, R. I. (1982). Effects of inconsistent information on text processing: Evidence for comprehension monitoring. *Reading Research Quarterly, 17,* 281–294.

Baker, S. K., Kameenui, E. J., Simmons, D. C., & Stahl, S. A. (1994). Beginning reading: Educational tools for diverse learners. *School Psychology Review, 23,* 372–391.

Ball, E. W., & Blachman, B. A. (1988). Phoneme segmentation training: Effect on reading readiness. *Annals of Dyslexia, 38,* 203–225.

Ball, E. W., & Blachman, B. A. (1991). Does phoneme awareness training in kindergarten make a difference in early word recognition and developmental spelling? *Reading Research Quarterly, 26,* 49–66.

Ballard, K. D., & Glynn, T. (1975). Behavioral self-management in story writing with elementary school children. *Journal of Applied Behavior Analysis, 8,* 387–398.

Balow, I. H., Farr, R. C., & Hogan, T. R. (1992). *Metropolitan Achievement Tests (7th ed.): survey battery.* San Antonio, TX: Psychological Corporation.

Bandura, A. (1977). *Social learning theory.* Englewood Cliffs, NJ: Prentice-Hall.

Bandura, A. (1986). *Social foundations of thought and action: A social cognitive theory.* Englewood Cliffs, NJ: Prentice-Hall.

Banks, J. A. (1994). *Multiethnic education: Theory and practice.* (3rd ed.). Boston: Allyn & Bacon.

Barbe, W. B., & Milone, M. N. (1980). Modality. *Instructor, 89,* 44–47.

Barnett, D. W., Macmann, G. M., & Carey, K. T. (1992). Early intervention and the assessment of developmental skills: Challenges and directions. *Topics in Early Childhood Special Education, 12,* 21–43.

Baroody, A. J., & Ginsburg, H. P. (1991). A cognitive approach to assessing the mathematical difficulties of children labeled "learning disabled." In H. L. Swanson (Ed.), *Handbook on the assessment of learning disabilities: Theory, research, and practice* (pp. 177–227). Austin, TX: PRO-ED.

Barron, R. W. (1980). Visual and phonological strategies in reading and spelling. In U. Frith (Ed.), *Cognitive processes in spelling* (pp. 195–213). New York: Academic Press.

Bassett, D. S., Jackson, L., Ferrell, K. A., Luckner, J., Hagerty, P. J., Busesn, T. D., & MacIsaac, D. (1996). Multiple perspectives on inclusive education: Reflections of a university faculty. *Teacher Education and Special Education, 19,* 355–386.

Bateman, B. (1967). Three approaches to diagnosis and educational planning for children with learning disabilities. *Academic Therapy Quarterly, 2,* 215–222.

Bateman, B. (1979). Teaching reading to learning disabled and other hard-to-teach children. In L. Resnick & P. Weaver (Eds.), *Theory and practice of early reading* (Vol. 1, pp. 227-259). Hillsdale, NJ: Erlbaum.

Bateman, B. D. (1965). An educator's view of a diagnostic approach to learning disorders. In J. Hellmuth (Ed.), *Learning disorders* (Vol. 1, pp. 219–239). Seattle, WA: Special Child Publications.

Bateman, B. D. (1971). *The essentials of teaching.* Creswell, OR: Otter Ink Press.

Bateman, B. D. (1992). Learning disabilities: The changing landscape. *Journal of Learning Disabilities, 25,* 29–36.

Bateman, B. D. (1994). Who, how, and where: Special education's issues in perpetuity. *Journal of Special Education, 27,* 509–520.

Bateman, B. D. (1996). *Better IEPS* (2nd ed.). Longmont, CO: Sopris West.

Bateman, B. D., & Chard, D. J. (1995). Legal demands and constraints on placement decisions. In J. M. Kauffman, J. W. Lloyd, D. P. Hallahan, & T. A. Astuto (Eds.), *Issues in educational placement: Students with emotional or behavioral disorders* (pp. 285–316). Hillsdale, NJ: Erlbaum.

Battle, D. E. (1997). Language and communication disorders in culturally and linguistically diverse children. In D. K. Bernstein & E. Tiegerman-Farber (Eds.), *Language and communication disorders in children* (4th ed., pp. 382–409). Boston: Allyn & Bacon.

Baumeister, A. A., Kupstas, F., & Klindworth, L. M. (1990). New morbidity: Implications for prevention of children's disabilities, *Exceptionality, 1,* 1–16.

Baumgartner, D., Bryan, T., Donahue, M., & Nelson, C. (1993). Thanks for asking: Parent comments about homework, tests, and grades. *Exceptionality, 4,* 177–185.

Beale, I. L., & Tippett, L. J. (1992). Remediation of psychological process deficits in learning disabilities. In N. Singh & I. L. Beale (Eds.), *Learning disabilities: Nature, theory, and treatment* (pp. 526 568). New York: Springer-Verlag.

Bear, G. G., & Proctor, W A. (1990). Impact of a full-time integrated program on the achievement of nonhandicapped and mildly handicapped children. *Exceptionality, 1,* 227–238.

Beatty, L. S., Madden, R., Gardner, E. G., & Karlsen, B. (1984). *Stanford Diagnostic Mathematics Test.* New York: Harcourt Brace Jovanovich.

Beck, R., Conrad, D., & Anderson, P. (1996). *Basic skill builders: Helping students become fluent in basic skills.* Longmont, CO: Sopris West.

Becker, W. C. (1977). Teaching reading and language to the disadvantaged: What we have learned from field research. *Harvard Educational Review, 47,* 518–543.

Beers, J. W. (1974). First-grade and second-grade children's developing orthographic concepts of tense and lax vowels (Doctoral dissertation, University of Virginia). *Dissertation Abstracts International, 35,* 49708A.

Beers, J. W., & Henderson, E. H. (1977). A study of developing orthographic concepts among first graders. *Research in the Teaching of English, 2, 133–148.*

Beichtman, J. H., Hood, J., & Inglis, A. (1992). Familial transmission of speech and language impairment: A preliminary investigation. *Canadian Journal of Psychiatry,* 37(3), 151–156.

Bell, R. Q., & Harper, L. V. (1977). *Child effects on adults.* Hillsdale, NJ: Erlbaum.

Benthul, H. F., Anderson, E. A., Utech, A. M., Biggy, M. V., & Bailey, B. L. (1974). *Spell correctly.* Morristown, NJ: Silver Burdett.

Bereiter, C. (1980). Development in writing. In L. W. Gregg & E. R. Steinberg (Eds.), *Cognitive processes in writing* (pp. 73–93). Hillsdale, NJ: Erlbaum.

Bergeron, B. S. (1990). What does the term whole language mean? Constructing a definition from the literature. *Journal of Reading Behavior, 22,* 301–329.

Berko, J. (1958). The child's learning of English morphology, *Word, 14,* 150–177.

Bernstein, D. K., & Tiegerman-Farber, E. (Eds.). (1997). *Language and communication disorders in children* (4th ed.). Boston: Allyn & Bacon.

Bijou, S. W. (1970). What psychology has to offer education—now. *Journal of Applied Behavior Analysis, 3,* 65–71.

Birnie-Selwyn, B., & Guerin, B. (1997). Teaching children to spell: Decreasing consonant cluster errors by eliminating selective stimulus control. *Journal of Applied Behavior Analysis, 30,* 69–91.

Bishop, D. V. M. (1997). Uncommon understanding: Development and disorders of language comprehension in children. Hove, East Sussex, England: Psychology Press.

Blachman, B. A. (1997). Early intervention and phonological awareness: A cautionary tale. In B. A. Blachman (Ed.), *Foundations of reading acquisition and dyslexia: Implications for early intervention* (pp. 409–430). Mahwah, NJ: Erlbaum.

Blackman, S., & Goldstein, K. M. (1982). Cognitive styles and learning disabilities. *Journal of Learning Disabilities, 15,* 106–115.

Blackorby, J., & Wagner, M. (1996). Longitudinal postschool outcomes of youth with disabilities: Findings from the National Longitudinal Transition Study. *Exceptional Children, 62,* 399–413.

Blandford, B. J., & Lloyd, J. W. (1987). Effects of a self-instructional procedure on handwriting. *Journal of Learning Disabilities, 20,* 342–346.

Blankenship, C., & Lovitt, T. C. (1976). Story problems: Merely confusing or downright befuddling? *Journal for Research in Mathematics Education, 7,* 290–298.

Blaylock, G., & Patton, J. R. (1996). Transition and students with learning disabilities: Creating sound futures. *Journal of Learning Disabilities, 29,* 7–16.

Bliesmer, E. R., & Yarborough, B. H. (1965). A comparison of ten different beginning reading programs in first grade. *Phi Delta Kappan, 46,* 500–504.

Bloom, L. (1993). *The transition from infancy to language: Acquiring the power of expression.* New York: Cambridge University Press.

Board of Trustees of the Council for Learning Disabilities. (1986). Use of discrepancy formulas in the identification of learning disabled individuals. *Learning Disability Quarterly* 9(3), 245.

Boder, E. (1971a). Developmental dyslexia: A diagnostic screening procedure based on three characteristic patterns of reading and spelling. In B. Bateman (Ed.), *Learning disorders: Reading* (Vol. 4, pp. 297–342). Seattle, WA: Special Child Publications.

Boder, E. (1971b). Developmental dyslexia: Prevailing diagnostic concepts and a new diagnostic approach. In H. R. Myklebust (Ed.), *Progress in learning disabilities* (Vol. 2, pp. 293–321). New York: Grune & Stratton.

Bond, G. L., & Dykstra, R. (1967). The cooperative research program in first-grade reading instruction. *Reading Research Quarterly,* 2 (4), 5–142.

Boning, R. (1990). *Specific skill series* (4th ed.). Baldwin, NY: Barnell Loft.

Borkowski, J. G. (1992). Metacognitive theory: A framework for teaching literacy, writing, and math skills. *Journal of Learning Disabilities, 25,* 253–257.

Borkowski, J. G., & Burke, J. E. (1996). Theories, models, and measurements of executive functioning: An information processing perspective. In G. R. Lyon & N. A. Krasnegor (Eds.), *Attention, memory, and executive function* (pp. 235–261). Baltimore: Paul H. Brookes.

Borkowski, J. G., Estrada, T. M., Milstead, M., & Hale, C. A. (1989). General problem-solving skills: Relations between metacognitive and strategic processing. *Learning Disability Quarterly, 12,* 57–70.

Borkowski, J. G., Johnston, M. B., & Reid, M. K. (1986). Metacognition, motivation, and the transfer of control processes. In S. J. Ceci (Ed.), *Handbook of cognition, social and neuropsychological aspects of learning disabilities* (Vol. 2, pp. 147–174). Hillsdale, NJ: Erlbaum.

Borkowski, J. G., Wehring, R. S., & Carr, M. (1988). Effects of attributional retraining on strategy-based reading comprehension in learning-disabled students. *Journal of Educational Psychology, 7,* 46–53.

Bos, C. (1982). Getting past decoding: Assisted and repeated readings as remedial methods for learning disabled students. *Topics in Learning and Learning Disabilities, 1* (4), 51–57.

Bos, C. S., & Filip, D. (1982). Comprehension monitoring skills in learning disabled and average students. *Topics in Learning and Learning Disabilities,* 2(1), 79–85.

Bos, C. S., & Vaughn, S. (1994). *Strategies for teaching students with learning and behavior problems.* (3rd ed.). Boston: Allyn & Bacon.

Bottge, B. A., & Hasselbring, T. S. (1993). A comparison of two approaches for teaching complex, authentic mathematics problems to adolescents in remedial math classes. *Exceptional Children, 59,* 556–566.

Bowman, B. T. (1994). The challenge of diversity. *Phi Delta Kappan, 76,* 218–225.

Bradley, L., & Bryant, R. E. (1983). Categorizing sounds and learning to read: A causal connection. *Nature, 303,* 419–421.

Braswell, L., & Kendall, P. C. (1988). Cognitive-behavioral methods with children. In K. S. Dobson (Ed.), *Handbook of cognitive-behavioral therapies* (pp. 167–213). New York: Guilford Press.

Bredekamp, S. (Ed.). (1987). *Developmentally appropriate practice in early childhood programs serving children from birth through age* 8. Washington, DC: National Association for the Education of Young Children.

Brigance, A. H. (1977). *Brigance Diagnostic Inventory of Basic Skills* (2nd ed.). North Billerica, MA: Curriculum Associates.

Brigham, F. J., Scruggs, T. E., & Mastropieri, M. A. (1995). Elaborative maps for enhanced learning of historical information: Uniting spatial, verbal, and imaginal information. *Journal of Special Education, 28,* 440–460.

Brigham, T. H., Graubard, P. S., & Stans, A. (1972). Analysis of the effects of sequential reinforcement contingencies on aspects of composition. *Journal of Applied Behavior Analysis, 5,* 421–429.

Brinckerhoff, L. C. (1996). Making the transition to higher education: Opportunities for student empowerment. *Journal of Learning Disabilities, 29,* 118–136.

Brinckerhoff, L. C., Shaw, S. F., & McGuire, J. M. (1992). Promoting access, accommodations, and independence for college students with learning disabilities. *Journal of Learning Disabilities,* 25(7), 417–429.

Broden, M., Beasley, A., & Hall, R. V. (1978). In class spelling performance: Effects of home tutoring by a parent. *Behavior Modification, 2,* 511–530.

Brody-Hasazi, S., Salembier, G., & Finck, K. (1983). Directions for the 80's: Vocational preparation for secondary mildly handicapped students. *Teaching Exceptional Children, 15*(4), 206–209.

Bronfenbrenner, U. (1979). *The ecology of human development: Experiments by nature and design.* Cambridge, MA: Harvard University Press.

Brooks, J. G., & Brooks, M. (1993). *In search of understanding: The case for constructivist classrooms.* Alexandria, VA: Association for Supervision and Curriculum Development.

Brooks-Gunn, J., & Lewis, M. (1984). Maternal responsivity in interactions with handicapped infants. *Child Development, 55,* 858–868.

Brophy, J., & Good, T. L. (1986). Teacher behavior and student achievement. In M. C. Whittrock (Ed.), *Handbook of research on teaching* (3rd ed., pp. 328–375). New York: Macmillan.

Brotherson, M. J., Berdine, W. H., & Sartini, V. (1993). Transition to adult services: Support for ongoing parent participation. *Remedial and Special Education, 14*(4), 44–51.

Brountas, M. (1987). Whole language really works. *Teaching K-8, 18,* 57–60.

Brown, A. L., & Campione, J. C. (1984). Three faces of transfer: Implications for early competence, individual differences, and instruction. In M. E. Lamb, A. L. Brown, & B. Rogoff (Eds.), *Advances in developmental psychology* (Vol. 3, pp. 143–192). Hillsdale, NJ: Erlbaum.

Brown, C. W. (1991). IFSP implementation in the fourth year of P. L. 99–457: The year of the paradox. *Topics in Early Childhood Special Education, 11,* 1–18.

Brown, D. S., & Gerber, P. J. (1994). Employing people with learning disabilities. In P. J. Gerber & H. B. Reiff (Eds.), *Learning disabilities in adulthood: Persisting problems and evolving issues* (pp. 195–203). Boston: Andover Medical Publishers.

Brown, D. S., Gerber, P. J., & Dowdy, C. (1990). *Pathways to employment for people with learning disabilities: A plan for ac-*

tion. Washington, DC: President's Committee on Employment of People with Disabilities.

Brown, J. S., & Burton, R. B. (1978). Diagnostic models for procedural bugs in basic mathematical skills. *Cognitive Science, 2,* 155–192.

Brown, V., Hammill, D. D., & Wiederholt, J. L. (1995). *Test of Reading Comprehension—3rd Edition.* Austin, TX: PRO-ED.

Bruck, M. (1988). The word recognition and spelling of dyslexic children. *Reading Research Quarterly, 23,* 51–69.

Bruck, M. (1998). Outcomes of adults with childhood histories of dyslexia. In C. Hulme & R. M. Joshi (Eds.), *Reading and spelling: Development and disorders* (pp. 179–200). Mahwah, NJ: Erlbaum.

Bruner, J. S. (1964). Some theorems on instruction illustrated with reference to mathematics. *Sixty-third Yearbook of the National Society for the Study of Education, 63* (Pt. 1), 306–335.

Bruner, J. S., Goodnow, J. J., & Austin, G. A. (1956). *A study of thinking.* New York: Wiley.

Bryan, T. (1991). Social problems and learning disabilities. In B. Y. L. Wong (Ed.), *Learning about learning disabilities* (pp. 195–229). New York: Academic Press.

Bryan, T., Bay, M., Lopez-Reyna, N., & Donahue, M. (1991). Characteristics of students with learning disabilities: A summary of the extant data base and its implications for educational programs. In J. W. Lloyd, N. N. Singh, & A. C. Repp (Eds.), *The regular education initiative: Alternative perspectives on concepts, issues, and models* (pp. 113–131). Sycamore, IL: Sycamore.

Bryan, T., & Donahue, M. (1994, April). *Homework: Perspectives of teachers, parents and students of different class settings.* Paper presented at the Council for Exceptional Children Convention, Denver, CO.

Bryan, T., Nelson, C., & Mathur, S. (1995). Homework: A survey of primary students in regular, resource, and self-contained classrooms. *Learning Disabilities Research and Practice, 10,* 85–90.

Bryan, T. H. (1986). Self-concept and attributions of the learning disabled. *Learning Disabilities Focus, 1,* 8289.

Bryan, T. H., & Pflaum, S. (1978). Social interactions of learning disabled children: A linguistic, social and cognitive analysis. *Learning Disability Quarterly, 1* (3), 70–79.

Bryan, T. H., Wheeler, R., Felcan, J., & Henek, T. (1976). "Come on Dummy": An observational analysis of children's communications. *Journal of Learning Disabilities, 9,* 661–669.

Bryant, B. R., & Rivera, D. P. (1997). Educational assessment of mathematics skills and abilities. *Journal of Learning Disabilities, 30,* 57–68.

Bryant, N. D., Drabin, I. R., & Gettinger, M. (1981). Effects of varying unit size on spelling achievement in learning disabled children. *Journal of Learning Disabilities, 14,* 200–203.

Bryden, M. P., McManus, I. C., & Bulman-Fleming, M. B. (1994). Evaluating the empirical support for the Geschwind-Behan-Galaburda model of cerebral lateralization. *Brain and Cognition, 26,* 103–167.

Buchanan, C. (1967). *Spelling.* Palo Alto, CA: Behavioral Research Laboratories.

Budoff, M. (1987). Measures for assessing learning potential. In C. S. Lidz (Ed.), *Dynamic assessment* (pp. 173–195). New York: Guilford Press.

Bus, A. G., & Kruizenga, T. H. (1989). Diagnostic problem solving behavior of expert practitioners in the field of learning disabilities. *Journal of School Psychology, 27,* 277- 287.

Bush, W., & Giles, M. T. (1977). *Aids to psycholinguistic teaching* (2nd ed.). Columbus, OH: Merrill.

Buswell, G. T., & John, L. (1926). *Diagnostic studies in arithmetic.* Chicago: University of Chicago Press.

Buysse, V., & Bailey, D. B. (1993). Behavioral and developmental outcomes in young children with disabilities in integrated and segregated settings: A review of comparative studies. *Journal of Special Education, 26,* 434–461.

Byers, R. K., & Lord, E. E. (1943). Late effects of lead poisoning on mental development. *American Journal of Diseases of Children, 66,* 471–494.

Byrne, B., & Fielding-Barnsley, R. (1991). Evaluation of a program to teach phonemic awareness to young children. *Journal of Educational Psychology, 83,* 451–455.

Byrne, B., & Fielding-Barnsley, R. (1993). Evaluation of a program to teach phonemic awareness to young children: A 1-year follow-up. *Journal of Educational Psychology, 85,* 104–111.

CTB/Macmillan/McGraw-Hill. (1993). *CAT/5.* Monterey, CA: CTB/McGraw-Hill.

CTB/McGraw-Hill. (1977–1978). *California Achievement Test.* Monterey, CA: Author.

Calfee, R. C. (1977). Assessment of independent reading skills: Basic research and practical applications. In A. S. Reber & D. L., Scarborough (Eds.), *Toward a psychology of reading: The proceedings of the CUNY conferences* (pp. 289–323). Hillsdale, NJ: Erlbaum.

Calfee, R. C., Lindamood, P., & Lindamood, C. (1973). Acoustic-phonetic skills and reading: Kindergarten through twelfth grade. *Journal of Educational Psychology, 64,* 293–298.

Camarata, S., Hughes, C. A., & Ruhl, K. (1988). Mild/moderately behaviorally disordered students: A population at risk for language disorders. *Language, Speech, and Hearing Services in Schools, 19,* 191–200.

Campbell, P. H., Strickland, B., & LaForme, C. (1992). Enhancing parent participation in the Individualized Family Service Plan. *Topics in Early Childhood Special Education, 11,* 112–114.

Campione, J. C., & Brown, A. L. (1987). Linking dynamic assessment with school achievement. In C. S. Lidz (Ed.), *Dynamic assessment* (pp. 82–115). New York: Guilford Press.

Caplan, D. (1992). *Language: Structure, processing, and disorders.* Cambridge, MA: MIT Press.

Caplan, N., Choy, M. H., & Whitmore, J. K. (1992, February). Indochinese refugee families and academic achievement. *Scientific American, 266,* 36–42.

Carbo, M. (1990). Igniting the literacy revolution through reading styles. *Educational Leadership, 48* (2), 26–29.

Cardon, L. R., Smith, S. D., Fulker, D. W., Kimberling, W. J., Pennington, B. F., & DeFries, J. C. (1994, October 14). Quantitative trait locus for reading disability on Chromosome 6. *Science, 266,* 276–279.

Carlberg, C. I., & Kavale, K. (1980). The efficacy of special versus regular class placement for exceptional children: A meta-analysis. *Journal of Special Education 14,* 295–309.

Carlisle, J. F. (1987). The use of morphological knowledge in spelling derived forms by learning-disabled and normal students. *Annals of Dyslexia, 37,* 90–108.

Carlson, J. S., & Wiedl, K. H. (1992). The dynamic assessment of intelligence. In H. C. Haywood & D. Tzuriel (Eds.), *Interactive assessment* (pp. 167–186). New York: Springer-Verlag.

Carlson, N. R. (1994). *Physiology of behavior* (5th ed.). Boston: Allyn & Bacon.

Carnine, D. (1976). Similar sound separation and cumulative introduction in learning letter-sound correspondences. *Journal of Educational Research, 69,* 368–372.

Carnine, D. (1977). Phonics versus look-say: Transfer to new words. *Reading Teacher, 30,* 636–640.

Carnine, D. (1991). Increasing the amount and quality of learning through direct instruction: Implications for mathematics. In J. W. Lloyd, N. N. Singh, & A. C. Repp (Eds.), *The regular education initiative: Alternative perspectives on concepts, issues, and models* (pp. 163–175). Sycamore, IL: Sycamore.

Carnine, D. (1993, December 8). Facts, not fads. *Education Week,* p. 40.

Carnine, D., Jitendra, A. K., & Silbert, J. (1997). A descriptive analysis of mathematics curricular materials from a pedagogical perspective: A case study of fractions. *Remedial and Special Education, 18* (2), 66–81.

Carnine, D., Jones, E. D., & Dixon, R. (1994). Mathematics: Educational tools for diverse learners. *School Psychology Review, 23,* 406–427.

Carnine, D., & Kameenui, E. J. (Eds.). (1992). *Higher order thinking: Designing curriculum for mainstreamed students.* Austin, TX: PRO-ED.

Carnine, D., & Kinder, D. (1985). Teaching low performing students to apply generative and schema strategies to narrative and expository material. *Remedial and Special Education, 6* (1), 20–30.

Carnine, D., Silbert, J., & Kameenui, E. J. (1996). *Direct instruction reading* (3rd ed.). Columbus, OH: Merrill.

Carnine, D. W. (1976). Similar sound separation and cumulative introduction in learning letter-sound correspondences. *Journal of Educational Research, 69,* 368–372.

Carnine, D. W. (1980). Preteaching versus concurrent teaching of the component skills of a multiplication problem-solving strategy. *Journal for Research in Mathematics Education, 11,* 375–379.

Carnine, D. W., Prill, N., & Armstrong, J. (1978). *Teaching slower performing students general case strategies for solving comprehension items.* Eugene: University of Oregon Follow-Through Project.

Carpenter, D. (1983). Spelling error profiles of able and disabled readers. *Journal of Learning Disabilities, 16,* 102–104.

Carpenter, D., & Miller, L. J. (1982). Spelling ability of reading disabled LD students and able readers. *Learning Disability Quarterly, 5,* 65–70.

Carpenter, T. P., & Moser, T. M. (1982). The development of addition and subtraction problem-solving skills. In T. P. Carpenter, J. M. Moser, & T. A. Romberg (Eds.), *Addition and subtraction: A cognitive perspective* (pp. 9–24). Hillsdale, NJ: Erlbaum.

Carran, D. T., & Scott, K. G. (1992). Risk assessment in preschool children: Research implications for the early detection of educational handicaps. *Topics in Early Childhood Special Education, 12,* 196–211.

Carrow, E. (1974). *Carrow Elicited Language Inventory.* Austin, TX: Learning Concepts.

Carrow-Woolfolk, E. (1985). *Test for Auditory Comprehension of Language—Revised Edition.* Chicago: Riverside.

Carrow-Woolfolk, E. (1988). *Theory, assessment, and intervention in language disorders: An integrative approach.* Philadelphia: Grune & Stratton.

Carta, J. J., Atwater, J. B., Schwartz, I. S., & Miller, P. A. (1990). Applications of ecobehavioral analysis to the study of transitions across early education settings. *Education and Treatment of Children, 13,* 298–315.

Carta, J. J., Schwartz, I. S., Atwater, J. B., & McConnell, S. R. (1991). Developmentally appropriate practice: Appraising its usefulness for young children with disabilities. *Topics in Early Childhood Special Education, 11,* 1–20.

Carter, J., & Sugai, G. (1989). Survey on prereferral practices: Responses from state departments of education. *Exceptional Children, 55,* 298–302.

Carter, J. L., & Synolds, D. (1974). Effects of relaxation training upon handwriting quality. *Journal of Learning Disabilities, 7,* 236–238.

Cartwright, G. P. (1969). Written expression and spelling. In R. M. Smith (Ed.), *Teacher diagnosis of educational difficulties* (pp. 95–117). Columbus, OH: Merrill.

Case, L. P., Harris, K. R., & Graham, S. (19921). Improving the mathematical problem-solving skills of students with learning disabilities: Self-regulated strategy development. *Journal of Special Education, 26,* 1–19.

Castellanos, F. X. (1997). Toward a pathophysiology of attention-deficit/hyperactivity disorder. *Clinical Pediatrics, 36,* 381–393.

Catts, J. W (1991). Early identification of reading disabilities. *Topics in Language Disorders, 12,* 1–16.

Cawley, J., & Miller, J. H. (1989). Cross-sectional comparisons of the mathematical performance of children with learning disabilities: Are we on the right track toward comprehensive programming? *Journal of Learning Disabilities, 22,* 250–254, 259.

Cawley, J. F., Fitzmaurice, A. M., Goodstein, H. A., Lepore, A. V., Sedlak, R., & Althaus, V. (1976). *Project MATH.* Tulsa, OK: Educational Development Corporation.

Cawley, J. F., Fitzmaurice, A. M., Shaw, R., Kahn, H., & Bates, H. III. (1978). Mathematics and learning disabled youth: The upper grade levels. *Learning Disability Quarterly, 1* (4), 37–52.

Cawley, J. F., Fitzmaurice, A. M., Shaw, R., Kahn, H., & Bates, H. III. (1979). LD youth and mathematics: A review of characteristics. *Learning Disability Quarterly, 2* (1), 29–44.

Chalfant, J. C. (1985). Identifying learning-disabled students: A summary of the National Task Force report. *Learning Disabilities Focus, 1*(1), 920.

Chalfant, J. C., & Shefflin, M. A. (1969). Central processing-dysfunctions in children: A review of research. (NINDS Monograph No. 9, U.S. Public Health Service Publication No. PH 43–67–61). Washington, DC: U.S. Government Printing Office.

Chall, J. (1967). *Learning to read: The great debate.* San Francisco: McGraw-Hill.

Chall, J. (1983). *Learning to read: The great debate* (rev. ed.). San Francisco: McGraw-Hill.

Chall, J., Roswell, F. E., & Blumenthal, S. H. (1963). Auditory blending ability: A factor in success in beginning reading. *Reading Teacher, 17,* 113–118.

Chandler, L. K. (1993). Steps in preparing for transition: Preschool to kindergarten. *Teaching Exceptional Children,* 25(4), 52–55.

Chapman, L. J., & Wedell, K. (1972). Perceptual-motor abilities and reversal errors in children's handwriting. *Journal of Learning Disabilities, 5,* 321–325.

Children with Attention Deficit Disorders (CHADD). (1992). *CHAAD educators' manual: An in-depth look at attention deficit disorders from an educational perspective.* Plantation, FL: Author.

Children's Defense Fund. (1995). *The state of America's children: Yearbook.* Washington, DC: Author.

Choate, J. S., Enright, B. E., Miller, L. J., Poteet, J. A., & Rakes, T. A. (1995). *Curribulum-based assessment programming* (3rd ed.). Boston: Allyn & Bacon.

Choate, J. S., & Evans, S. S. (1992). Authentic assessment of special learners: Problem or promise? *Preventing School Failure,* 37(1), 69.

Chomsky, C. (1969). *The acquisition of syntax in children from 5 to 10.* Cambridge, MA: MIT Press.

Chomsky, N. A. (1957). *Syntactic structures.* The Hague: Mouton.

Chomsky, N. A. (1959). Review of verbal behavior by B. F. Skinner. *Language, 35,* 26–58.

Chomsky, N. A. (1965). *Aspects of the theory of syntax.* Cambridge, MA: MIT Press.

Cicci, R. (1983). Disorders of written language. In H. R. Myklebust (Ed.), *Progress in learning disabilities* (Vol. 5, pp. 207–232). New York: Grune & Stratton.

Clarizio, H. F., & Phillips, S. E. (1986). Sex bias in the diagnosis of learning disabled students. *Psychology in the Schools, 23*(1), 44–52.

Clay, M. M. (1985). *The early detection of reading difficulties.* Auckland, NZ: Heinemann.

Clay, M. M., & Imlach, R. H. (1971). Juncture, pitch and stress as reading behavior variables. *Journal of Verbal Learning and Verbal Behavior, 10,* 133–139.

Clements, S. D. (1966). *Minimal brain dysfunction in children: Terminology and identification, phase one of a three-phase project.* Washington, DC: U.S. Department of Health, Education, and Welfare.

Clements, S. D. (1970). *Minimal brain dysfunction in children: Educational, medical, and health related services.* Washington, DC: U.S. Public Health Service.

Clements, S. D., & Peters, J. E. (1962). Minimal brain dysfunctions in the school-age child. *Archives of General Psychiatry, 6,* 185–197.

Cohen, A. L., Torgesen, J. K., & Torgesen, J. L. (1988). Improving speed and accuracy of word recognition in reading disabled children: An evaluation of two computer program variations. *Learning Disability Quarterly, 11,* 333–341.

Cohen, S. A. (1971). Dyspedagogia as a cause of reading retardation: Definition and treatment. In B. Bateman (Ed.), *Learning disorders: Vol. 4. Reading* (pp. 269–291). Seattle, WA: Special Child Publications.

Coleman, J. M., McHam, L. A., & Minnett, A. M. (1992). Similarities in the social competencies of learning disabled and low-achieving elementary school children. *Journal of Learning Disabilities, 25,* 671–677.

Coleman, J. M., & Minnett, A. M. (1992). Learning disabilities and social competence: A social ecological perspective. *Exceptional Children, 59,* 234–246.

Coles, G. (1987). *The learning mystique: A critical look at "learning disabilities."* New York: Pantheon.

Colvin, G. (1992). *Managing acting-out behavior* (video lecture and workbook). Eugene, OR: Behavior Associates.

Colvin, G., Sugai, G., & Patching, B. (1993). Pre-correction: An instructional approach for managing predictable problem behaviors. *Intervention in School and Clinic, 28,* 143–150.

Comings, D. E., & Comings, B. G. (1990). A controlled family history study of Tourette's syndrome, I: Attention-deficit hyperactivity disorder and learning disorders. *Journal of Clinical Psychiatry, 51*(7), 275–280.

Conners, C. K. (1969). A teacher rating scale for use in drug studies with children. *American Journal of Psychiatry, 126,* 884–888.

Connolly, A. (1988). *Key Math revised: A diagnostic inventory of essential mathematics.* Circle Pines, MN: American Guidance Service.

Conte, R. (1991). Attention disorders. In B. Y. L. Wong (Ed.), *Learning about learning disabilities* (pp. 55–101). New York: Academic Press.

Content, A., Kolinski, R., Morais, J., & Bertelson, P. (1986). Phonetic segmentation in prereaders: Effect of corrective information. *Journal of Experimental Child Psychology, 42,* 49–72.

Cooke, N. L., Guzaukas, R., Pressley, J. S., & Kerr, K. (1993). Effects of using a ratio of new items to review items during drill and practice: Three experiments. *Education and Treatment of Children, 16,* 213–234.

Cooper, D. H., & Speece, D. L. (1988). A novel methodology for the study of children at risk for school failure. *Journal of Special Education 22,* 186–198.

Cooper, H. M. (1989). *Homework.* White Plains, NY: Longman.

Cooper, H. M., & Hedges, L. V. (1994). *Handbook of research synthesis.* New York: Russell Sage Foundation.

Council for Children with Behavioral Disorders. (1989). Best assessment practices for students with behavioral disorders: Accommodation to cultural diversity and individual differences. *Behavioral Disorders, 14,* 263–278.

Council for Exceptional Children. (1997a). Making assessments of diverse students meaningful. *CEC Today, 4*(4), 1, 9.

Council for Exceptional Children. (1997b). Reading difficulties vs. learning disabilities. *CEC Today, 4*(5), 1, 9, 13.

Council for Learning Disabilities. (1993). Concerns about the full inclusion of students with learning disabilities in regular classrooms. *Learning Disability Quarterly, 16*(2), 126.

Cox, L. S. (1975). Diagnosing and remediating systematic errors in addition and subtraction competitions. *Arithmetic Teacher, 22,* 151–157.

Crockett, J. B., & Kauffman, J. M. (in press). *The least restrictive environment: Its origins and interpretations in special education.* Hillsdale, NJ: Erlbaum.

Cruickshank, W. M. (1977). Guest editorial. *Journal of Learning Disabilities, 10,* 193–194.

Cruickshank, W. M., Bentzen, F. A., Ratzeburg, F. H., & Tannhauser, M. T. (1961). *A teaching method for brain-injured and hyperactive children.* Syracuse, NY: Syracuse University Press.

Cruickshank, W. M., Bice, H. V., & Wallen, N. E. (1957). *Perception and cerebral palsy.* Syracuse, NY. Syracuse University Press.

Cruickshank, W. M., & Hallahan, D. P. (Eds.). (1975a). *Perceptual and learning disabilities in children: Vol. 1: Psychoeducational practices.* Syracuse, NY: Syracuse University Press.

Cruickshank, W. M., & Hallahan, D. P. (Eds.). (1975b). *Perceptual and learning disabilities in children: Vol. 2: Research and theory.* Syracuse, NY: Syracuse University Press.

Cullinan, D., & Epstein, M. H. (1985). Adjustment problems of mildly handicapped and nonhandicapped students. *Remedial and Special Education, 6* (2), 5–11.

Cullinan, D., Lloyd, J., & Epstein, M. H. (1981). Strategy training: A structured approach to arithmetic instruction. *Exceptional Education Quarterly,* 2 (1), 41–49.

Cunningham, A. E. (1990). Explicit versus implicit instruction in phonemic awareness. *Journal of Experimental Child Psychology, 50,* 429–444.

Cyprus Group. (1996). *The think time strategy for schools: Bringing order to the classroom* (video and workbook). Spokane, WA: Author.

Darch, C., & Simpson, R. G. (1990). Effectiveness of visual imagery versus rule-based strategies in teaching spelling to learning disabled students. *Research in Rural Education,* 7(1), 61–70.

Davis, B. G., Silbert, J., Forness, S. R., & Kavale, K. A. (1996). Treating social skill deficits in children with learning disabilities: A meta-analysis of the research. *Learning Disability Quarterly, 19,* 2–13.

deBettencourt, L., Zigmond, N., & Thornton, H. (1989). Follow-up of postsecondary-age rural learning disabled graduates and dropouts. *Exceptional Children,* 56(1), 40–49.

deBettencourt, L. U. (1987). Strategy training: A need for clarification. *Exceptional Children, 54,* 24–30.

DeFries, J. C., Gillis, J. J., & Wadsworth, S. J. (1993). Genes and genders: A twin study of reading disability. In A. M. Galaburda (Ed.), *Dyslexia and development: Neurological aspects of extra-ordinary brains* (pp. 187–204). Cambridge, MA: Harvard University Press.

DeFries, J. C., Stevenson, J., Gillis, J. J., & Wadsworth, S. J. (1991). Genetic etiology of spelling deficits in the Colorado and London twin studies of reading disability. *Reading and*

Writing, 3, Special issue: Genetic and neurological influences on reading disability, 271–283.

de Hirsch, K., Jansky, J., & Langford, W. S. (1966). *Predicting reading failure.* New York: Harper & Row.

DeStefano, L., & Wermuth, T. R. (1992). IDEA (P. L. 101–476): Defining a second generation of transition services. In F. R. Rusch, L. DeStefano, J. Chadsey-Rusch, L. A. Phelps, & E. Szymanski (Eds.), *Transition from school to adult life: Models, linkages, and policy* (pp. 537–549). Sycamore, IL: Sycamore Publishing.

Deitz, D. E. D., & Repp, A. C. (1983). Reducing behavior through reinforcement. *Exceptional Education Quarterly,* 3 (4), 34–46.

Delacato, C. H. (1959). *The treatment and prevention of reading problems.* Springfield, IL: Charles C. Thomas.

Demchak, M. A., & Drinkwater, S. (1992). Preschoolers with severe disabilities: The case against segregation. *Topics in Early Childhood Special Education, 11*(1), 70–83.

de Mesquita, P. B., & Gilliam, W. S. (1994). Differential diagnosis of childhood depression: Using comorbidity and symptom overlap to generate multiple hypotheses. *Child Psychiatry and Human Development, 24,* 157–172.

Denckla, M. B. (1993). The child with developmental disabilities grown up: Adult residua of childhood disorders. *Behavioral Neurology, 1,* 105–125.

Deno, S. L. (1997). Whether thou goest . . . Perspectives on progress monitoring. In J. W. Lloyd, E. J. Kameenui, & D. Chard (Eds.), *Issues in educating students with disabilities* (pp. 77–99). Mahwah, NJ: Erlbaum.

Deno, S. L., Foegen, A., Robinson, S., & Espin, C. (1996). Commentary: Facing the realities of inclusion for students with mild disabilities. *Journal of Special Education,* 30, 345–357.

Deno, S. L., & Fuchs, L. S. (1987). Developing curriculum-based measurement systems for data-based special education problem solving. *Focus on Exceptional Children,* 19(2),1–16.

Deno, S. L., Marston, D., & Mirkin, P. K. (1982). Valid measurement procedures for continuous evaluation of written expression. *Exceptional Children, 48,* 368–371.

Deno, S. L., & Mirkin, P. K. (1977). *Data-based program modification: A manual.* Reston, VA: Council for Exceptional Children.

Deno, S. L., Mirkin, P. K., Lowry, L., & Kuehnle, K. (1980). *Relationships among simple measures of spelling and performance on standardized achievement tests* (Research Report No. 21). Minneapolis: Institute for Research on Learning Disabilities, University of Minnesota.

Derr, A. (1985). Conservation and mathematics achieveiement in the reading disabled child. *Journal of Learning Disabilities, 18,* 333–336.

Deverell, A. F. (1971). The learnable features of English orthography. In B. Bateman (Ed.), *Learning disorders: Reading* (Vol. 4, pp. 129–160). Seattle, WA: Special Child Publications.

DiGangi, S. A., Maag, J. W., & Rutherford, R. B. (1991). Self-graphing of on-task behavior: Enhancing the reactive effects of self-monitoring on on-task behavior and academic performance. *Learning Disability Quarterly, 14,* 221–230.

Dimino, J., Gersten, R., & Carnine, D. (1990). Story grammar: An approach for promoting at-risk secondary students' comprehension of literature. *Elementary School Journal, 91,* 19–32.

Dixon, R. (1976). Morphographic spelling. Chicago: Science Research Associates.

Dixon, R., & Carnine, D. (1994). Ideologies, practices, and their implications for special education. *Journal of Special Education, 28,* 356–367.

Dixon, R., Engelmann, S., Meier, M., Steely, D., & Wells, C. (1980). *Spelling mastery.* New York: SRA/McGraw-Hill.

Dixon, R. C. (1991). The application of sameness analysis to spelling. *Journal of Learning Disabilities, 24,* 285–291, 310.

Dixon. R. C. (1993). *The surefire way to better spelling: A revolutionary new approach to turn poor spellers into pros.* New York: St. Martins.

Dixon, W. E., Matheny, A. P., & Mohr, S. R. (1995). Heredity and environment in phoneme articulation: Hereditary and environmental contributions to articulation proficiency. *Acta Geneticae Medicae et Gemellologiae: Twin Research, 44*(2), 63–73.

Donahue, M. (1986). Phonological constraints on the emergence of two-word utterances. *Journal of Child Language 13,* 209–228.

Donahue, M. (1987). Interactions between linguistic and pragmatic development in learning disabled children: Three views of the state of the union. In S. Rosenberg (Ed.), *Advances in applied psycholinguistics* (Vol. 1, pp. 126–179). Cambridge, England: Cambridge University Press.

Drotar, D., Baskiewicz, A., Irvin, N., Kennell, J., & Klaus, M. (1975). The adaptation of parents to the birth of an infant with a congenital malformation: A hypothetical model. *Pediatrics, 56,* 710–717.

Dunlap, G., dePerczel, M., Clarke, S., Wilson, D., Wright, S., White, R., & Gomez, A. (1994). Choice making to promote adaptive behavior for students with emotional and behavioral challenges. *Journal of Applied Behavior Analysis, 27,* 505–518.

Dunlap, W. P., & House, A. D. (1976). Why can't Johnny compute? *Journal of Learning Disabilities, 4,* 210–214.

Dunn, L. M., & Dunn, L. (1981). *Peabody Picture Vocabulary Test—Revised.* Circle Pines, MN: American Guidance Service.

Dunn, L. M., & Dunn, L. (1997). *Peabody Picture Vocabulary Test—III.* Circle Pines, MN: American Guidance Service.

Dunn, L. M., Smith, J. O., Dunn, L. M., Horton, K. B., & Smith, D. D. (1981). *Peabody Language Development Kits—Revised.* Circle Pines, MN: American Guidance Service.

Dunn, R. (1990). Bias over substance: A critical analysis of Kavale and Forness' report on modality-based instruction. *Exceptional Children, 56,* 352–356.

Dunn, R., Griggs, S. A., Olson, J., Beasley, M., & Gorman, B. S. (1995). Meta-analytic validation of the Dunn and Dunn model of learning style preferences. *Journal of Educational Research, 88,* 353–362.

Dunst, C. J., Johanson, C., Trivette, C. M., & Hamby, D. (1991). Family-oriented early intervention policies and practices: Family-centered or not? *Exceptional Children, 58,* 115–126.

Dunst, C. J., Trivette, C. M., & Deal, A. (1988). *Enabling and empowering families.* Cambridge, MA: Brookline Books.

DuPaul, G. J., Eckert, T. L., & McGoey, K. E. (1997). Interventions for students with attention-deficit/hyperactivity disorder: One size does not fit all. *School Psychology Review, 26,* 369–381.

Dupre, A. P. (1997). Disability and the public schools: The case against "inclusion." *Washington Law Review,* 72 (Whole No. 3).

Durlak, C. M., Rose, E., & Bursuck, W. D. (1994). Preparing high school students with learning disabilities for the transition to postsecondary education: Teaching the skills of self-determination. *Journal of Learning Disabilities,* 27(1), 51–59.

Duval, B. (1985). *Evaluation of eleventh grade students' writing supports teaching italic handwriting* (ERIC Document Reproduction Services No. ED 263 608).

Dykstra, R. (1968a). The effectiveness of code- and meaning-emphasis beginning reading programs. *Reading Teacher, 22,* 17–23.

Dykstra, R. (1968b). Summary of the second-grade phase of the Cooperative Research Program in primary reading instruction. *Reading Research Quarterly, 4,* 49–70.

Dyson, L. L. (1996). The experiences of families of children with learning disabilities: Parental stress, family functioning, and sibling self-concept. *Journal of Learning Disabilities, 29,* 280–286.

Eaton, M. D., & Lovitt, T. C. (1972). Achievement tests vs. direct and daily measurement. In G. Semb (Ed.), *Behavioral analysis and education* (pp. 78–87). Lawrence: University of Kansas.

Edelsky, C. (1991). *Whole language: What is the difference?* Portsmouth, NH: Heinemann.

Edelsky, C., Draper, K., & Smith, K. (1983). Hookin' 'em in at the start of school in a "whole language" classroom. *Anthropology and Education Quarterly, 14,* 257–281.

Edgar, E. (1988). Congregate. *Habilitation News,* 8(3), 6–7.

Edgington, R. (1967). But he spelled them right this morning. *Academic Therapy, 3,* 58–61.

Educational Testing Service. (1972). *Sequential Tests of Educational Progress.* Princeton, NJ: Author.

Edyburn, D. L. (1994). An equation to consider: The portfolio assessment knowledge base + technology = the Grady profile. *ED Forum, 19*(4), 35–38.

Ehri, L. C., & Robbins, C. (1992). Beginners need some decoding skill to read words by analogy. *Reading Research Quarterly, 27,* 13–25.

Eisenson, J. (1972). *Aphasia in children.* New York: Harper & Row.

Engelmann, S. (1967a). Relationship between psychological theories and the act of teaching. *Journal of School Psychology, 5,* 92–100.

Engelmann, S. (1967b). Teaching reading to children with low MAs. *Education and Training of the Mentally Retarded, 2,* 193–201.

Engelmann, S. (1969). *Preventing failure in the primary grades.* Chicago: Science Research Associates.

Engelmann, S. (1997). Theory of mastery and acceleration. In J. W. Lloyd, E. J. Kameenui, & D. Chard (Eds.), *Issues in educating students with disabilities* (pp. 177–195). Mahwah, NJ: Erlbaum.

Engelmann, S., Arbogast, A. B., Davis, K. L. S., Grossen, B., & Silber, J. (1993). *Reasoning and writing.* Chicago: Science Research Associates.

Engelmann, S., Becker, W. C., Hanner, S., & Johnson, G. (1978). *Corrective reading program: Series guide.* Chicago: Science Research Associates.

Engelmann, S., Becker, W. C., Hanner, S., & Johnson, G. (1988). *Corrective reading program Series guide* (rev. ed.). Chicago: Science Research Associates.

Engelmann, S., & Canine, D. W. (1975). *DISTAR arithmetic I* (2nd ed.). Chicago: Science Research Associates.

Engelmann, S., & Canine, D. W. (1976). *DISTAR arithmetic II* (2nd ed.). Chicago: Science Research Associates.

Engelmann, S., & Canine, D. W. (1981). *Corrective Mathematics.* Chicago: Science Research Associates.

Engelmann, S., & Canine, D. W. (1982). *Theory of instruction: Principles and applications.* New York: Irvington.

Engelmann, S., Canine, D., Engelmann, O., & Kelly, B.(1991). *Connecting math concepts.* Chicago: Science Research Associates.

Engelmann, S., Haddox, P., Hanner, S., & Osborn, J. (1978). *Thinking basics: Corrective reading comprehension A.* Chicago: Science Research Associates.

Engelmann, S., & Osborn, J. (1977). *DISTAR Language.* Chicago: Science Research Associates.

Engelmann, S., & Silbert, J. (1983). *Expressive writing.* Tigard, OR: C. C. Publications.

Engelmann, S., & Steely, D. (1980). *Fractions I and II.* Chicago: Science Research Associates.

Engelmann, S., & Steely, D. (1981). *Ratios and equations.* Chicago: Science Research Associates.

Englert, C. S. (1990). Unraveling the mysteries of writing through strategy instruction. In T. Scruggs & B. Y. L. Wong (Eds.), *Intervention research in learning disabilities* (pp. 186–223). New York: Springer-Verlag.

Englert, C. S., & Raphael, T. E. (1989). Developing successful writers through cognitive strategy instruction. In J. E. Brophy (Ed.), *Advances in research on teaching* (Vol. 1., pp. 105–151). Greenwich, CT: JAI Press.

Englert, C. S., Raphael, T. E., Anderson, L. M., Gregg, S. L., & Anthony, H. M. (1989). Exposition: Reading, writing, and the metacognitive knowledge of learning disabled students. *Learning Disabilities Research, 5,* 5–24.

Enright, B. C. (1983). *Diagnostic inventory of basic arithmetic skills.* North Billerica, MA: Curriculum Associates.

Epps, S., Ysseldyke, J. E., & Algozzine, B. (1983). Impact of different definitions of learning disabilities on the number of students identified. *Journal of Psychoeducational Assessment, 1,* 341–352.

Epps, S., Ysseldyke, J. E., & Algozzine, B. (1985). An analysis of the conceptual framework underlying definitions of learning disabilities. *Journal of School Psychology, 23,* 133–144.

Epstein, M. H., Hallahan, D. P., & Kauffman, J. M. (1975). Implications for the reflectivity-impulsivity dimension for special education. *Journal of Special Education, 9,* 1–25.

Epstein, M. H., Polloway, E. A., Foley, R. M., & Patton, J. R. (1993). Homework: A comparison of teachers' and parents' perceptions of the problems experienced by students identified as having behavioral disorders, learning disabilities, or no disabilities. *Remedial and Special Education, 14*(5), 40–50.

Evers, R. B. (1996). The positive force of vocational education: Transition outcomes for youth with learning disabilities. *Journal of Learning Disabilities, 29,* 69–78.

Fabbro, F., & Masutto, C. (1994). An Italian perspective on learning disabilities. *Journal of Learning Disabilities, 27,* 138–141.

Fader, D. N., & McNeil, E. B. (1968). *Hooked on books: Program and proof.* New York: Putnam.

Fadiman, C. A., & Howard, T. (1979). *Empty pages.* Belmont, CA: Fearon Pitman.

Faraone, S. V., Biederman, J., Chen, W. J., Milberger, S., Warburton, R., & Tsuang, M. T. (1995). Genetic heterogeneity in attention-deficit hyperactivity disorder (ADHD): Gender, psychiatric comorbidity, and maternal ADHD. *Journal of Abnormal Psychology, 104,* 334–345.

Faraone, S. V., Biederman, J., Lehman, B. K., Keenan, K., Norman, D., Seidman, L. J., Kolodny, R., Kraus, I., Perrin, J., & Chen, W. J. (1993). Evidence for the independent familial transmission of attention deficit hyperactivity disorder and learning disabilities: Results from a family genetic study. *American Journal of Psychiatry, 150,* 891–895.

Farmer, M. E., Klein, B., & Bryson, S. E. (1992). Computer-assisted reading: Effects of whole-word feedback on fluency and comprehension in readers with severe disabilities. *Remedial and Special Education, 13* (2), 50–60.

Farris, P J., & Kaczmarsh, D. (1988). Whole language, a closer look. *Contemporary Education, 59,* 77–81.

Fauke, J., Burnett, J., Powers, M. A., & Sulzer-Azaroff, B. (1973). Improvement of handwriting and letter recognition skills: A behavior modification procedure. *Journal of Learning Disabilities, 6,* 296–300.

Fayne, H. R. (1981). A comparison of learning disabled adolescents with normal learners on an anaphoric pronominal reference task. *Journal of Learning Disabilities, 14,* 597–599.

Feagans, L., & Applebaum, M. (1986). Validations of language subtypes in learning disabled children. *Journal of Educational Psychology,* 78, 358–364.

Feldman, R. G., & White, R. F. (1992). Lead neurotoxicity and disorders of learning. *Journal of Child Neurology,* 7, 354–359.

Felton, R. H. (1992). Early identification of children at risk for reading disabilities. *Topics in Early Childhood Special Education, 12,* 212–229.

Fernald, G. M. (1943). *Remedial techniques in basic school subjects.* New York: McGraw-Hill.

Feuer, M. J., & Fulton, K. (1993). The many faces of performance assessment. *Phi Delta Kappan, 74,* 478.

Feuerstein, R. (1979). *The dynamic assessment of retarded performers.* Baltimore: University Park Press.

Feuerstein, R. (1980). *Instrumental enrichment: An intervention program for cognitive modifiability.* Baltimore: University Park Press.

Fiedler, W. R., & Feeney, G. (1972). *Inquiring about cities: Studies in geography and economics.* New York: Holt, Rinehart & Winston.

Finchman, F. (1979). Piagetian theory in LD research. *Journal of Learning Disabilities, 12,* 25–31.

Fink, W. T., & Carnine, D. W. (1975). Control of arithmetic errors using informational feedback and graphing. *Journal of Applied Behavior Analysis, 8,* 461. (Abstract)

Finn, P. J. (1977). Computer-aided description of mature word choices in writing. In C. R. Cooper & L. Odell (Eds.), *Evaluating writing: Describing, measuring, judging* (pp. 68–89). Urbana. IL: National Council of Teachers of English.

Fischer, F. W., Liberman, I. Y., & Shankweiler, D. (1978). Reading reversals and developmental dyslexia: A further study. *Cortex, 14,* 496–510.

Flavell, J. H. (1977a). *Cognitive development.* Englewood Cliffs, NJ: Prentice-Hall.

Flavell, J. H. (1977b). Metacognition and cognitive monitoring: A new area of cognitive-developmental inquiry. *American Psychologist, 34,* 906–911.

Flavell, J. H., & Wellman, H. M. (1977). Metamory. In R. V. Kail & J. W. Hagen (Eds.), *Perspectives on the development of memory and cognition* (pp. 3–33). Hillsdale, NJ: Erlbaum.

Fleisher, L. S., & Jenkins, J. R. (1978). Effects of contextualized and decontextualized practice conditions on word recognition. *Learning Disability Quarterly, 1* (3), 39–47.

Flesch, R. (1955). *Why Johnny can't read and what you can do about it.* New York: Harper & Row.

Flesch, R. (1981). *Why Johnny still can't read: A new look at the scandal of our schools.* New York: Harper & Row.

Fletcher, J. M., Francis, D. J., Rourke, B. P., Shaywitz, S. E., & Shaywitz, B. A. (1992). The validity of discrepancy-based definitions of reading disabilities. *Journal of Learning Disabilities,* 25(9), 555–561, 573.

Fletcher, J. M., Shaywitz, S. E., Shankweiler, D. P., Katz, L., Liberman, I. Y., Stuebing, K. K., Francis, D. J., Fowler, A. E., & Shaywitz, B. A. (1994). Cognitive profiles of reading disability: Comparisons of discrepancy and low achievement definitions. *Journal of Educational Psychology, 86,* 6–23.

Flower, L. S., & Hayes, J. R. (1980). The dynamics of composing: Making plans and juggling constraints. In L. W. Gregg & E. R. Steinberg (Eds.), *Cognitive processes in writing* (pp. 31–50). Hillsdale, NJ: Erlbaum.

Flowers, D. L. (1993). Brain basis for dyslexia: A summary of work in progress. *Journal of Learning Disabilities,* 26(9), 575–582.

Flowers, D. L., Wood, F. B., & Naylor, C. E. (1991). Regional cerebral blood flow correlates of language processes in reading disability. *Archives of Neurology, 48,* 637–643.

Foorman, B. R., Francis, D. J., Novy, D. M., & Liberman, D. (1991). How letter-sound instruction mediates progress in first-grade reading and spelling. *Journal of Educational Psychology, 83,* 456–469.

Forness, S. R., & Kavale, K. A. (1988). Psychopharmacologic treatment: A note on classroom effects. *Journal of Learning Disabilities,* 2(1), 144–147.

Forness, S. R., & Kavale, K. A. (1994). Meta-analysis in intervention research: Methods and implications. In J. Rothman & J. Thomas (Eds.), *Intervention research: Effective methods for professional practice* (pp. 117–131). Chicago: Haworth Press.

Forness, S. R., & Kavale, K. A. (1996). Treating social skill deficits in children with learning disabilities: A meta-analysis of the research. *Learning Disability Quarterly, 19,* 2–13.

Forness, S. R., & Kavale, K. A. (1997). Defining emotional or behavioral disorders in school and related services. In J. W. Lloyd, E. J. Kameenui, & D. Chard (Eds.), *Issues in educating students with disabilities* (pp. 45–61). Mahwah, NJ: Erlbaum.

Forness, S. R., Kavale, K. A., Blum, I. M., & Lloyd, J. W. (1997). What works in special education and related services: Using meta-analysis to guide practice. *Teaching Exceptional Children,* 29(6), 4–9.

Forrest, D. L., & Waller, I. G. (1981, April). Reading ability and knowledge of important information. Paper presented at the meeting of the Society for Research in Child Development, Boston.

Fowler, S. A., Schwartz, I., & Atwater, J. (1991). Perspectives on the transition from preschool to kindergarten for children with disabilities and their families. *Exceptional Children,* 58, 136–145.

Foxx, R. M., & Jones, J. R. (1978). A remediation program for increasing the spelling achievement of elementary and junior high school students. *Behavior Modification, 2,* 211–230.

Franklin, B. M. (Ed.) (1987). *Learning disability: Dissenting essays.* London: Falmer Press.

Freeman, F. N. (1979). *Handwriting measuring scale.* Columbus, OH: Zaner-Bloser.

Freeman, T. J., & McLaughlin, T. F. (1984). Effects of a taped-word treatment procedure on learning disabled students' sight-word oral reading. *Learning Disability Quarterly,* 7, 49–54

Fries, C. C. (1963). *Linguistics and reading.* New York: Holt, Rinehart & Winston.

Frisby, C. L., & Braden, J. P. (1992). Feuerstein's dynamic assessment approach: A semantic, logical, and empirical critique. *Journal of Special Education, 26,* 281–301.

Frith, U. (1980). Unexpected spelling problems. In U. Frith (Ed.), *Cognitive processes in spelling* (pp. 495–515). New York: Academic Press.

Frostig, M. (1967). Testing as a basis for educational therapy. *Journal of Special Education, 2,* 15–34.

Frostig, M., & Horne, D. (1964). *The Frostig program for the development of visual perception.* Chicago, Follett.

Frostig, M., Lefever, D. W., & Whittlesey, J. R. B. (1964). *The Marianne Frostig Developmental Test of Visual Perception.* Palo Alto, CA: Consulting Psychologists Press.

Fuchs, D., & Fuchs, L. S. (1994a). Inclusive schools movement and the radicalization of special education reform. *Exceptional Children, 60,* 294–309.

Fuchs, D., & Fuchs, L. S. (1994b). Sometimes separate is better. *Educational Leadership,* 52(4), 22–26.

Fuchs, D., & Fuchs, L. S. (1995a). Special education can work. In J. M. Kauffman, J. W Lloyd, D. P. Hallahan, & T. A. Astuto (Eds.), *Issues in educational placement: Students with emotional and behavioral disorders* (pp. 363–377). Hillsdale, NJ: Erlbaum.

Fuchs, D., & Fuchs, L. S. (1995b). What's "special" about special education? *Phi Delta Kappan, 76,* 522–530.

Fuchs, L. S., Butterworth, J. R., & Fuchs, D. (1989). Effects of ongoing curriculum-based measurement on student awareness of goals and progress. *Education and Treatment of Children, 12,* 63–72.

Fuchs, L. S., & Deno, S. L. (1991). Paradigmatic distinctions between instructionally relevant measurement models. *Exceptional Children, 57,* 488–500.

Fuchs, L. S., & Deno, S. L. (1994). Must instructionally useful performance assessment be based on the curriculum? *Exceptional Children, 61,* 15–24.

Fuchs, L. S., & Fuchs, D. (1986a). Effects of systematic formative evaluation: A meta-analysis. *Exceptional Children, 53,* 199–208.

Fuchs, L. S., & Fuchs, D. (1986b). Curriculum-based assessment of progress toward long-term and short-term goals. *Journal of Special Education, 20,* 69–81.

Fuchs, L. S., Fuchs, D., Hamlett, C. L., & Stecker, P. M. (1991). Effects of curriculum-based measurement and consultation on teacher planning and student achievement. *American Educational Research Journal, 28,* 617–641.

Fuchs, L. S., Fuchs, D., Hamlett, C. L., Phillips, N. B., & Bentz, J. (1994). Classwide curriculum-based measurement: Helping general educators meet the challenge of student diversity. *Exceptional Children, 60,* 518–537.

Fulk, B. M. (1996). The effects of combined strategy and attribution training on LD adolescents' spelling performance. *Exceptionality, 6,* 13–27.

Fulk, B. M., Lohman, D., & Belfiore, P. J. (1997). Effects of integrated picture mnemonics on the letter recognition and letter-sound acquisition of transitional first-grade students with special needs. *Learning Disability Quarterly, 20,* 33–42.

Gagne, R. M. (1970). *The conditions of learning* (2nd ed.). New York: Holt, Rinehart & Winston.

Gajar, A. (1992). Adults with learning disabilities: Current and future research priorities. *Journal of Learning Disabilities,* 25(8), 507–519.

Gajria, M., & Salend, S. J. (1995). Homework practices of students with and without learning disabilities: A comparison. *Journal of Learning Disabilities, 28,* 291–296.

Galaburda, A. M. (1994). Developmental dyslexia and animal studies: At the interface between cognition and neurology. *Cognition, 50,* 133–149.

Galaburda, A. M., & Kemper, T. L. (1979). Cytoarchitectonic abnormalities in developmental dyslexia: A case study. *Annals of Neurology, 6,* 94–100.

Galaburda, A. M., Menard, M. T., & Rosen, G. D. (1994). Evidence for aberrant auditory anatomy in developmental dyslexia. *Proceedings of the National Academy of Science USA, 91,* 8010–8013.

Galaburda, A. M., Sherman, G. F., Rosen, G. D., Aboitiz, F., & Geschwind, N. (1985). Developmental dyslexia: Four consecutive patients with cortical anomalies. *Annals of Neurology, 18,* 222–233.

Galda, L., Cullinan, B. E., & Strickland, D. S. (1997). Language, literacy, and the child (2nd ed.). Ft. Worth, TX: Harcourt Brace.

Gallagher, J. J. (1994). The pull of societal forces on special education. *Journal of Special Education, 27,* 521–530.

Gallagher, W. (1993). *The power of place: How our surroundings shape our thoughts, emotions, and actions.* New York: Poseidon.

Gardner, E. R., Rudman, H. C., Karlsen, B., & Merwin, J. C. (1988). *Stanford Achievement Test—Eighth Edition.* New York: Harcourt Brace Jovanovich.

Gardner, M. F. (1985). *Receptive One-Word Picture Vocabulary Test.* Novato, CA: Academic Therapy.

Gardner, M. F. (1991). *Expressive One-Word Picture Vocabulary Test—Revised.* Novato, CA: Academic Therapy.

Garner, R. (1980). Monitoring of understanding: An investigation of good and poor readers' awareness of induced miscomprehension of text. *Journal of Reading Behavior, 12,* 55- 63.

Garner, R., Alexander, P. A., & Hare, V. C. (1991). Reading comprehension and failure in children. In B. Y. L. Wong (Ed.), *Learning about learning disabilities* (pp. 283–307). New York: Academic Press.

Garnett, K., & Fleischner, J. E. (1983). Automatization and basic fact performance of normal and learning disabled children. *Learning Disability Quarterly, 6,* 223–230.

Gartner, A., & Lipsky, D. K. (1989). *The yoke of special education: How to break it.* Rochester, NY: National Center on Education and the Economy.

Gates, A. I., McKillop, A. S., & Horowitz, E. C. (1981). *Gates-McKillop-Horowitz Reading Diagnostic Tests—Second Edition.* Colchester, VT: Teachers College Press.

Gates, A. I., & Russell, D. (1940). *Gates-Russell Spelling Diagnostic Test.* New York: Columbia University Press.

Gattegno, C. (1963). *For the teaching of elementary mathematics.* Mt. Vernon, NY: Cuisenaire Company of America.

Gazzaniga, M. S., & LeDoux, J. E. (1978). *The integrated mind.* New York: Plenum Press.

Geary, D. C. (1994). *Children's mathematical development: Research and practical applications.* Washington, DC: American Psychological Association.

Gelzheiser, L. M., & Clark, D. B. (1991). Early reading and instruction. In B. Y. L. Wong (Ed.), *Learning about learning disabilities* (pp. 261–281). New York: Academic Press.

Gentry, J. R. (1977). A study of the orthographic strategies of beginning readers (Doctoral dissertation, University of Virginia). *Dissertation Abstracts International, 39,* 4017.

Gerber. M. M. (1986). Generalization of spelling strategies by LD students as a result of contingent imitation/modeling and mastery criteria. *Journal of Learning Disabilities 19,* 530–537.

Gerber, M. M. (1987). Application of cognitive-behavioral training methods to teaching basic skills to mildly handicapped elementary school students. In M. C. Wang, M. C. Reynolds, & H. J. Walberg (Eds.), *Handbook of special education: Research and practice: Vol. 1. Learner characteristics and adaptive education* (pp. 167–186). New York: Pergamon.

Gerber, M. M. (1995). Inclusion at the high-water mark? Some thoughts on Zigmond and Baker's case studies of inclusive educational programs. *Journal of Special Education, 29,* 181–191.

Gerber, M. M., & Hall, R. J. (1981). Development of spelling in learning disabled and normally-achieving children. Unpublished manuscript, Learning Disabilities Research Institute, University of Virginia.

Gerber, M. M., & Semmel, M. I. (1984). Teacher as imperfect test: Reconceptualizing the referral process. *Educational Psychologist, 19,* 137–148.

Gerber, M. M., Semmel, D., & Semmel, M. I. (1994). Computer-based dynamic assessment of multidigit multiplication. *Exceptional Children, 61*(2), 114–115.

Gerber, P. J. (1992). At first glance: Employment for people with learning disabilities at the beginning of the Americans-With-Learning-Disabilities-Act era. *Learning Disability Quarterly, 15*(4), 330–332.

Gerber, P. J., & Reiff, H. B. (1991). *Speaking for themselves: Ethnographic interviews with adults with learning disabilities.* Ann Arbor: University of Michigan Press.

Gerber, P. J., Ginsberg, R., & Reiff, H. B. (1992). Identifying alterable patterns in employment success for highly successful adults with learning disabilities. *Journal of Learning Disabilities, 25*(8), 475–487.

Gerber, P. J., Reiff, H. B., & Ginsberg, R. (1996). Reframing the learning disabilities experience. *Journal of Learning Disabilities, 29,* 98–101,97.

German, D. J. N. (1979). Word-finding skills in children with learning disabilities. *Journal of Learning Disabilities, 12,* 176–181.

Gersten, R., Brengelman, S., & Jiménez, R. (1994). Effective instruction for culturally and linguistically diverse students: A reconceptualization. *Focus on Exceptional Children,* 27(1),1–16.

Gersten, R., & Carnine, D. (1984). On the relationship between auditory-perceptual skills and reading: A response to Kavale's meta-analysis. *Remedial and Special Education,* 5(1), 16–19.

Gersten, R., & Dimino, J. (1993). Visions and revisions: A special education perspective on the whole language controversy. *Remedial and Special Education, 14,* 513.

Gersten, R. M., & Maggs, A. (1982). Teaching the general case to moderately retarded children: Evaluation of a five year project. *Analysis and Intervention in Developmental Disabilities,* 2, 329–343.

Gersten, R. M., White, W. A. T., Falco, R., & Carnine, D. (1982). Teaching basic discriminations to handicapped and nonhandicapped individuals through a dynamic presentation of instructional stimuli. *Analysis and Intervention in Developmental Disabilities,* 2, 305–317.

Geschwind, N., & Behan, P. O. (1984). Laterality, hormones, and immunity. In N. Geschwind & A. M. Galaburda (Eds.), *Cerebral dominance: The biological foundations* (pp. 211–224). Cambridge, MA: Harvard University Press.

Geschwind, N., & Galaburda, A. M. (1985). Cerebral lateralization: Biological mechanisms, associations, and pathology: I. A hypothesis and program for research. *Archives of Neurology, 42*(5), 428–459.

Geschwind N., & Levitsky, W. (1968). Human brain: Left-right asymmetries in temporal speech. *Science, 161,* 186–187.

Gessell, J. (1983). *Diagnostic Mathematics Inventory.* Monterey, CA: CTB/McGraw-Hill.

Gettinger, M. (1993). Effects of invented spelling and direct instruction on spelling performance of second-grade boys. *Journal of Applied Behavior Analysis, 26,* 281–291.

Gettinger, M., Bryant, N. D., & Fayne, H. R. (1982). Designing spelling instruction for learning-disabled children: An emphasis on unit size, distributed practice, and training for transfer. *Journal of Special Education, 16,* 439–448.

Gilger, J. W., Pennington, B. F., & DeFries, J. C. (1992). A twin study of the etiology of comorbidity: Attention-deficit hyperactivity disorder and dyslexia. *Journal of the Academy of Child and Adolescent Psychiatry, 31*(2), 343–348.

Gillingham, A., & Stillman, B. (1965). *Remedial training for children with specific disability in reading, spelling and penmanship* (7th ed.). Cambridge, MA: Educators Publishing Service.

Gilmore, J. V., & Gilmore, E. C. (1968). *Gilmore Oral Reading Test.* New York: Harcourt Brace Jovanovich.

Ginsberg, H. (1977). *Children's arithmetic: The learning process.* New York: Van Nostrand.

Ginsberg, H. P. (1991). A cognitive approach to assessing the mathematical difficulties of children labeled "learning disabled." In H. L. Swanson (Ed.), *Handbook on the assessment of learning disabilities: Theory, research, and practice* (pp. 177–227). Austin, TX: PRO-ED.

Ginsberg, H. P. (1997). Mathematics learning disabilities: A view from developmental psychology. *Journal of Learning Disabilities, 30,* 20–33.

Giorgi, A., Fischer, W. F., & Murray, E. (Eds.). (1975). *Duquesne studies in phenomenological psychology* (Vol. 2). Pittsburgh: Duquesne University Press.

Giorgi, A., Fischer, W. F., & Von Eckartsberg, R. (Eds.) (1971). *Duquesne studies in phenomenological psychology* (Vol. 1). Pittsburgh: Duquesne University Press.

Giorgi, A., Knowles, R., & Smith, D. (Eds.). (1979). *Duquesne studies in phenomenological psychology* (Vol. 3). Pittsburgh: Duquesne University Press.

Glass, G. G. (1971). Perceptual conditioning for decoding: Rationale and method. In B. Bateman (Ed.), *Learning disorders: Vol. 4. Reading* (pp. 75–108). Seattle, WA: Special Child Publications.

Gleason, M., Carnine, D., & Boriero, D. (1990). Improving CAI effectiveness with attention to instructional design in teaching story problems to mildly handicapped students. *Journal of Special Education Technology, 10,* 129–136.

Glennon, V. J., & Cruickshank, W. M. (1981). Teaching mathematics to children and youth with perceptual and cognitive deficits. In V. J. Glennon (Ed.), *The mathematical education of exceptional children and youth: An interdisciplinary approach* (pp. 50–94). Reston, VA: National Council of Teachers of Mathematics.

Goldberger, S., & Kazis, R. (1996). Revitalizing high schools: What the school-to-career movement can contribute. *Phi Delta Kappan, 77,* 547–554.

Goldman, R., Fristoe, M., & Woodcock, R. W. (1970). *Goldman-Fristoe-Woodcock Test of Auditory Discrimination.* Circle Pines, MN: American Guidance Service.

Goldman, S. R., Pellegrino, J. W., & Mertz, D. L. (1988). Extended practice of basic addition facts: Strategy changes in learning disabled students. *Cognition and Instruction, 5,* 223–265.

Goldstein, A. P. (1988). *The Prepare curriculum: Teaching prosocial competencies.* Champaign, IL: Research Press.

Golinkoff, R. M., & Rosinski, R. R. (1976). Decoding, semantic processing, and reading comprehension skill. *Child Development, 47,* 252–258.

Gollnick, D. M., & Chinn, P. C. (1994). *Multicultural education in a pluralistic society* (4th ed.). New York: Macmillan.

Good, T. L., & Grouws, D. A. (1979). The Missouri Mathematics Effectiveness Project: An experimental study in fourth-grade classrooms. *Journal of Educational Psychology, 71,* 355–362.

Good, T. L., Grouws, D. A., & Ebmeier, H. (1983). *Active mathematics teaching.* New York: Longman.

Goodlad, J. I., & Lovitt, T. C. (Eds.). (1993). *Integrating general and special education.* Columbus, OH: Merrill/Macmillan.

Goodman, K. S. (1965). A linguistic study of cues and miscues in reading. *Elementary English, 42,* 639–643.

Goodman, K. S. (1986). *What's whole in whole language: A parent-teacher guide.* Portsmouth, NH: Heinemann.

Gordon, J., Vaughn, S., & Schumm, J. S. (1993). Spelling interventions: A review of literature and implications for instruction for students with learning disabilities. *Learning Disabilities Research and Practice, 8,* 175–181.

Goswami, U. (1991). Learning about spelling sequences: The role of onsets and rimes in analogies in reading. *Child Development, 62,* 1110–1123.

Goswami, U. (1998). Word reading by sight and by analogy. In C. Hulme & R. M. Joshi (Eds.), *Reading and spelling: Development and disorders* (pp. 69–86). Mahwah, NJ: Erlbaum.

Gough, P B. (1972). One second of reading. In J. F. Kavanagh & I. G. Mattingly (Eds.), *Language by ear and by eye: The relationships between speech and reading* (pp. 331–358). Cambridge, MA: MIT Press.

Goyette, C. H., Conners, C. K., & Ulrich, B. F. (1978). Normative data on Revised Conners Parent and Teacher Rating Scales. *Journal of Abnormal Child Psychology, 6,* 221–236.

Graham, S. (1982). Composition research and practice: A unified approach. *Focus on Exceptional Children, 14*(8), 1–16.

Graham, S., & Harris, K. R. (1997). Whole language and process writing: Does one approach fit all? In J. W. Lloyd, E. J. Kameenui, & D. Chard (Eds.), *Issues in educating students with disabilities* (pp. 239–258). Mahwah, NJ: Erlbaum.

Graham, S., Harris, K. R., & Loynachan, C. (1994). The spelling for writing list. *Journal of Learning Disabilities, 27,* 210–214.

Graham, S., Harris, K. R., MacArthur, C., & Schwartz, S. (1991). Writing instruction. In B. Y. L. Wong (Ed.), *Learning about learning disabilities* (pp. 309–343). New York: Academic Press.

Graham, S., & MacArthur, C. (1988). Improving learning disabled students' skills at revising essays produced on a word processor: Self-instructional strategy training. *Journal of Special Education, 22,* 133–152.

Graham, S., & Miller, L. (1979). Spelling research and practice: A unified approach. *Focus on Exceptional Children, 12*(2), 1–16.

Graves, A., Montague, M., & Wong, Y. (1990). The effects of procedural facilitation on the story composition of learning disabled students. *Learning Disabilities Research, 5,* 88–93.

Graves, D. (1978). *Balance the basics: Let them write.* New York: Ford Foundation.

Gray, B., & Ryan, B. (1973). *A language program for the nonlanguage child.* Champaign, IL: Research Press.

Green, R. (1992). "Learning to learn" and the family system: New perspectives on underachievement and learning disorders. In M. J. Fine & C. Carlson (Eds.), *The handbook of family-school intervention: A systems perspective* (pp. 157–174). Boston: Allyn & Bacon.

Green, R. M. (1984). Structuralism and its heuristic implications. *Learning Disability Quarterly, 7,* 359–362.

Greenbaum, B., Graham, S., & Scales, W. (1996). Adults with learning disabilities: Occupational and social status after college. *Journal of Learning Disabilities, 29,* 167–173.

Greene, R. W., Biederman, J., Faraone, S. V., Sienna, M., & Garcia-Jetton, J. (1997). Adolescent outcome of boys with attention-deficit/hyperactivity disorder and social disability: Results from a 4-year longitudinal follow-up study. *Journal of Consulting and Clinical Psychology, 65*, 758–767.

Greenwood, C. R. (1994). Advances in technology-based assessment within special education. *Exceptional Children, 61*, 102–104.

Greer, J. V. (1990). The drug babies. *Exceptional Children, 56*(5), 382–384.

Gresham, F. M., MacMillan, D. L., & Bocian, K. M. (1996). Learning disabilities, low achievement, and mild mental retardation: More alike than different? *Journal of Learning Disabilities, 29*, 570–581.

Griffith, P. L. Klesisu, J. P., & Kromrey, J. D. (1992). The effect of phonemic awareness on the literacy development of first grade children in a traditional or a whole language classroom. *Journal of Reseach in Childhood Educaiton, 6*(2), 85–92.

Grigorenko, E. L., Wood, F. B., Meyer, M. S., Hart, L. A., Speed, W. C., Shuster, A., & Pauls, D. L. (1997). Susceptibility loci for distinct components of developmental dyslexia on Chromosomes 6 and 15. *American Journal of Human Genetics, 60*, 27–39.

Grimm, J. A., Bijou, S. W., & Parsons, J. A. (1973). A problem solving model for teaching remedial arithmetic to handicapped young children. *Journal of Abnormal Child Psychology, 1*, 26–39.

Groen, G. J., & Parkman, J. M. (1972). A chronometric analysis of simple addition. *Psychological Review, 79*, 329–343.

Groff, P. (1979). Phonics for spelling? *Elementary School Journal, 79*, 269–275.

Gross, A. M. (1984). Behavioral interviewing. In T. H. Oliendick & M. Hersen (Eds.), *Child behavioral assessment: Principles and procedures* (pp. 61–79). New York: Pergamon.

Gross-Glenn, K., Duara, R., Barker, W. W., Loewenstein, D., Chang, J., Yoshii, F., Apicella, A. M., Pascal, S., Boothe, T., Sevush, S., Jallad, B. J., Novoa, L., & Lubs, H. A. (1991). Positron emission tomographic studies during serial word-reading by normal and dyslexic adults. *Journal of Clinical and Experimental Neuropsychology*, 13(4), 531–544.

Grossen, B. (1993a). Child-directed teaching methods: A discriminatory practice of Western education. *Effective School Practices, 12*(2), 9–20.

Grossen, B. (1993b). Focus: Heterogeneous grouping and curriculum design. *Effective School Practices, 12*(1),5–8.

Grossen, B., Coulter, G., & Ruggles, B. (1996). Reading recovery: An evaluation of benefits and costs. *Effective School Practices, 15*(3), 6–24.

Grossen, B., & Ewing, S. (1994). Raising mathematical problem-solving performance: Do the NCTM teaching standards help? *Effective School Practices, 13* (2), 79–91.

Grotclushchen, A. K., Borkowski, J. G., & Hale, C. (1991). Strategy instruction is often insufficient: Addressing the interdependency of executive and attributional processes. In T. E. Scruggs & B. Y. L. Wong (Eds.), *Intervention research in learning disabilities* (pp. 81–101). New York: Springer-Verlag.

Gunderson, L. (1997). Whole-language approaches to reading and writing. In S. A. Stahl & D. A. Hayes (Eds.), *Instructional models in reading* (pp. 221–247). Mahwah, NJ: Erlbaum.

Gunter, P. L., & Coutinho, M. J. (in press). Negative reinforcement in classrooms: What we're beginning to learn. *Teacher Education and Special Education*.

Gunter, P. L., Hummel, J. H., & Conroy, M. A. (in press). Increasing correct academic responding: An effective intervention strategy to decrease behavior problems. *Effective School Practices*.

Gurney, D., Gersten, R., Dimino, J., & Carnine, D. (1990). Story grammar: Effective literature instruction for high school students with learning disabilities. *Journal of Learning Disabilities, 23*, 335–342, 348.

Gurren, L., & Hughes, A. (1965). Intensive phonics vs. gradual phonics in beginning reading: A review. *Journal of Educational Research, 58*, 339–346.

Guyer, B. P., Banks, S. R., & Guyer, K. E. (1993). Spelling improvement for college students who are dyslexic. *Annals of Dyslexia, 43*, 186–193.

Guzaitis, J., Carlin, J. A., & Juda, S. (1972). *Diagnosis: An instructional aid in mathematics*. Chicago: Science Research Associates.

Haager, D., & Vaughn, S. (1997). Assessment of social competence in students with learning disabilities. In J. W. Lloyd, E. J. Kameenui, & D. Chard (Eds.), *Issues in educating students with disabilities* (pp. 129–152). Mahwah, NJ: Erlbaum.

Haberlandt, K. (1994). *Cognitive psychology.* Boston: Allyn & Bacon. Hagman, J. O., Wood, F., Buchsbaum, M. S., Tallal, P., Flowers, L., & Katz, W. (1992). Cerebral brain metabolism in adult dyslexic subjects assessed with positron emission tomography during performance of an auditory task. *Archives of Neurology, 49*, 734–739.

Hadden, S., & Fowler, S. A. (1997). Preschool: A new beginning for children and parents. *Teaching Exceptional Children, 30*(1), 36–39.

Hajek, E. (1984). Whole language: Sensible answers to the old problems. *Momentum, 15*, 39–40.

Hall, M. (1981). *Teaching reading as a language experience* (3rd ed.). Columbus, OH: Merrill.

Hallahan, D. P. (1975). Distractibility in the learning disabled child. In W. M. Cruickshank & D. P. Hallahan (Eds.), *Perceptual and learning disabilities in children: Vol. 2. Research and theory* (pp. 195–218). Syracuse, NY. Syracuse University Press.

Hallahan, D. P. (1992). Some thoughts on why the prevalence of learning disabilities has increased. *Journal of Learning Disabilities, 25*(8), 523–528.

Hallahan, D. P., & Cottone, E. A. (1997). Attention deficit hyperactivity disorder. In T. E. Scruggs & M. A. Mastropieri (Eds.), *Advances in learning and behavioral disabilities* (Vol. 1, pp. 27–67). Greenwich, CT: JAI Press.

Hallahan, D. P., & Cruickshank, W. M. (1973). *Psycho-educational foundations of learning disabilities.* Englewood Cliffs, NJ: Prentice-Hall.

Hallahan, D. P., Gajar, A. H., Cohen, S. B., & Tarver, S. G. (1978). Selective attention and locus of control in learning disabled children. *Journal of Learning Disabilities, 4,* 47–52.

Hallahan, D. P., & Kauffman, J. M. (1977). Labels, categories, behaviors: ED, LD, and EMR reconsidered. *Journal of Special Education, 11,* 139–149.

Hallahan, D. P., & Kauffman, J. M. (1994). Toward a culture of disability in the aftermath of Deno and Dunn. *Journal of Special Education, 27,* 496–508.

Hallahan, D. P., & Kauffman, J. M. (1995). From mainstreaming to collaborative consultation. In J. M. Kauffman & D. P. Hallahan (Eds.), *The illusion of full inclusion: A comprehensive critique of a special education bandwagon* (pp. 5–17). Austin, TX: PRO-ED.

Hallahan, D. P., & Kauffman, J. M. (1997). *Exceptional learners: Introduction to special education* (7th ed.). Boston: Allyn & Bacon.

Hallahan, D. P., Kauffman, J. M., & Ball, D. W (1973). Selective attention and cognitive tempo of low achieving and high achieving sixth grade males. *Perceptual and Motor Skills, 36,* 579–583.

Hallahan, D. P., Kauffman, J. M., & Lloyd, J. W. (1985). *Introduction to learning disabilities* (2nd ed.). Englewood Cliffs, NJ: Prentice-Hall.

Hallahan, D. P., Kneedler, R. D., & Lloyd, J. W (1983). Cognitive behavior modification techniques for learning disabled children: Self-instruction and self-monitoring. In J. D. McKinney & L. Feagans (Eds.), *Current topics in learning disabilities* (Vol. 1, pp. 207–244). New York: Ablex.

Hallahan, D. P., Lloyd, J. W., Kosiewicz, M. M., Kauffman, J. M., & Graves, A. W (1979). Self-monitoring of attention as a treatment for a learning disabled boy's off-task behavior. *Learning Disability Quarterly, 2,* 24–32.

Hallahan, D. P., Lloyd, J. W., & Stoller, L. (1982). *Improving attention with self-monitoring: A manual for teachers.* Charlottesville, VA: Learning Disabilities Research Institute.

Hallahan, D. P., & Reeve, R. E. (1980). Selective attention and distractability. In B. K. Keogh (Ed.), *Advances in special education: Vol. 1. Basic constructs and theoretical orientations* (pp. 141–181). Greenwich, CT: JAI Press.

Hallenbeck, B. A., & Kauffman, J. M. (1995). How does observational learning affect the behavior of students with emotional or behavioral disorders? A review of research. *Journal of Special Education, 29,* 45–71.

Hallgren, B. (1950). Specific dyslexia (congenital word blindness): A clinical and genetic study. *Acta Psychiatrica et Neurologica, 65,* 1–279.

Hallowell, E. M., & Ratey, J. J. (1994). *Driven to distraction.* New York: Pantheon.

Halpern, A. S. (1993). Quality of life as a conceptual framework for evaluating transition outcomes. *Exceptional Children,* 59(6), 486–498.

Halpern, A. S. (1994). The transition of youth with disabilities to adult life: A position statement of the Division on Career Development and Transition, the Council for Exceptional Children. *Career Development for Exceptional Individuals, 17,* 115–124.

Hammill, D. D. (1987). Assessing students in the schools. In D. D. Hammill (Ed.), *Assessing the abilities and instructional needs of students* (pp. 5–37). Austin, TX: PRO-ED.

Hammill, D. D. (1990). On defining learning disabilities: An emerging consensus. *Journal of Learning Disabilities, 23*(2), 74–84.

Hammill, D. D., Brown, V., Larsen, S., & Weiderholt, J. L. (1994). *Test of Adolescent Language—3.* Austin, TX: PRO-ED.

Hammill, D. D., & Bryant, B. R. (1991a) *Detroit Tests of Learning Aptitude—Adult.* Austin, TX: PRO-ED.

Hammill, D. D., & Bryant, B. R. (1991b) *Detroit Tests of Learning Aptitude—Primary, Second Edition.* Austin, TX: PRO-ED.

Hammill, D. D., & Bryant, B. R. (1991c). The role of standardized tests in planning academic instruction. In H. L. Swanson (Ed.), *Handbook on the assessment of learning disabilities* (pp. 373–406). Austin, TX: PRO-ED.

Hammill, D. D., & Larsen, S. C. (1974a). The effectiveness of psycholinguistic training. *Exceptional Children, 41,* 514.

Hammill, D. D., & Larsen, S. C. (1974b). The relationship of selected auditory perceptual skills and reading ability. *Journal of Learning Disabilities, 7,* 429–435.

Hammill, D. D., & Larsen, S. C. (1983). *Test of Written Spelling.* Austin, TX: PRO-ED.

Hammill, D. D., & Larsen, S. C. (1996). *Test of Written Language* (3rd ed.). Austin, TX: PRO-ED.

Hammill, D. D., Larsen, S., & McNutt, G. (1977). The effects of spelling instruction: A preliminary study. *Elementary School Journal, 78,* 67–72.

Hammill, D. D., & Leigh, J. E. (1983). *Basic School Skills Inventory—Diagnostic.* Austin, TX: PRO-ED.

Hammill, D. D., Leigh, J. E., McNutt, G., & Larsen, S. C. (1981). A new definition of learning disabilities. *Learning Disability Quarterly, 4,* 336–342.

Hammill, D. D., & Newcomer, P. (1991). *Test of Language Development—3.* Austin, TX: PRO-ED.

Hammill, D. D., & Newcomer, P. L. (1988). *Test of Language Development-2, Intermediate.* Austin, TX: PRO-ED.

Hanley, T. V. (1994). The need for technological advances in assessment related to national education reform. *Exceptional Children, 61,* 222–229.

Hanna, P., Hanna, J., Hodges, R., & Erwin, R., Jr. (1966). *Phoneme-grapheme correspondences as cues to spelling improvement.* Washington, DC: U. S. Government Printing Office.

Hanson, M. J., & Carta, J. J. (1996). Addressing the challenges of families with multiple risks. *Exceptional Children, 62,* 201–212.

Hanson, M. J., & Lynch, E. W. (1992). Family diversity: Implications for policy and practice. *Topics in Early Childhood Special Education, 12,* 283–306.

Harber, J. R. (1980). Auditory perception and reading: Another look. *Learning Disability Quarterly,* 3 (3), 19–29.

Harcourt Brace. (1995). *Treasury of literature.* Orlando: Author.

Haring, K. A., Lovett, D. L., Haney, K. F., Algozzine, B., Smith, D. D., & Clarke, J. (1992). Labeling preschoolers as learning disabled: A cautionary position. *Topics in Early Childhood Special Education, 12*(2), 151–173.

Haring, K. A., Lovett, D. L., & Smith, D. D. (1990). A follow-up of recent special education graduates of learning disabilities programs. *Journal of Learning Disabilities,* 23(2), 108–113.

Haring, N. G. (1968). *Attending and responding.* San Rafael, CA: Dimensions.

Haring, N. G. (1969). *Minimal brain dysfunction in children: Educational, medical and health related services, phase two of a three-phase project.* Washington, DC: U.S. Department of Health, Education, and Welfare.

Haring, N. G., & Hauck, M. (1969). Improved learning conditions in the establishment of reading skills with disabled readers. *Exceptional Children,* 35, 341–351.

Haring, N. G., Lovitt, T. C., Eaton, M. D., & Hansen, C. L. (1978). *The fourth R: Research in the classroom.* Columbus, OH: Merrill.

Haring, N. G., & Phillips, E. L. (1962). *Educating emotionally disturbed children.* New York: McGraw-Hill.

Harris, K. R., & Graham, S. (1985). Improving learning disabled students' composition skills: A self-control strategy training approach. *Learning Disability Quarterly,* 8, 27–36.

Harris, K. R., & Graham, S. (1994). Constructivism: Principles, paradigms, and integration. *Journal of Special Education, 28,* 233–247.

Harris, K. R., Graham, S., & Pressley, M. (1991). Cognitive-behavioral approaches in reading and written language: Developing self-regulated learners. In N. N. Singh & I. L. Beale (Eds.), *Learning disabilities: Nature, theory, and treatment* (pp. 415–451). New York: Springer-Verlag.

Harris, K. R., Graham, S., Reid, R., McElroy, K., & Hamby, R. S. (1994). Self-monitoring of attention versus self-monitoring of performance: Replication and cross-task comparison studies. *Learning Disability Quarterly,* 17, 121–139.

Harris, V. W., Sherman, J. A., Henderson, D. G., & Harris, M. S. (1972). Effects of peer tutoring on the spelling performance of elementary classroom students. In G. Semb (Ed.), *Behavior analysis and education—1972* (pp. 222–231). Lawrence: Department of Human Development, University of Kansas.

Harry, B. (1995). African American families. In B. A. Ford, F. E. Obiakor, & J. M. Patton (Eds.), *Effective education of African American exceptional learners: New perspectives* (pp. 211–233). Austin, TX: PRO-ED.

Hart, B., & Risley, T. (1995). *Meaningful differences in the everyday experiences of young American children.* Baltimore: Paul H. Brooks.

Hasazi, J. E., & Hasazi, S. E. (1972). Effects of teacher attention on digit-reversal behavior in an elementary school child. *Journal of Applied Behavior Analysis,* 5, 157–162.

Hasselbring, T., Sherwood, R., & Bransford, J. (1986). Evaluation of the Mastering Fractions level one instructional videodisc program. Unpublished manuscript, Tennessee Valley Authority.

Hasselbring, T. S., & Crossland, C. L. (1982). Application of microcomputer technology to spelling assessment of learning disabled students. *Learning Disability Quarterly,* 5, 80–82.

Hasselbring, T. S., Goin, L. I., & Bransford, J. (1987). Developing automaticity. *Teaching Exceptional Children, 19,* 30–33.

Hasselbring, T. S., Goin, L. I., & Bransford, J. (1988). Developing math automaticity in learning handicapped children: The role of computerized drill and practice. *Focus on Exceptional Children, 20* (2), 1–7.

Hayes, D. J. (1980). The effect of guiding six-year-old kindergarten and nine-year-old third grade children to verbalize formational strokes upon their ability to reproduce letterlike forms (Doctoral dissertation, University of Virginia). *Dissertation Abstracts International, 41,* 1234A.

Hayes, J. R., & Flower, L. S. (1980). Identifying the organization of writing processes. In L. W. Gregg & E. R. Steinberg (Eds.), *Cognitive processes in writing* (pp. 3–30). Hillsdale, NJ: Erlbaum.

Haywood, H. C. (1992). Interactive assessment: A special issue. *Journal of Special Education, 26,* 233–234.

Hebbeler, K. M., Smith, B. J., & Black, T. L. (1991). Federal early childhood special education policy: A model for the improvement of services for children with disabilities. *Exceptional Children,* 58, 104–112.

Heckelman, R. G. (1969). A neurological impress method of remedial reading. *Academic Therapy, 4,* 277–282.

Hedge, M. N. (1991). *Introduction to communicative disorders.* Austin, TX: PRO-ED.

Hegge, T. G., Kirk, S. A., & Kirk, W. D. (1970). *Remedial reading drills.* Ann Arbor, MI: Wahr.

Henderson, E. H. (1990). *Teaching spelling.* Boston: Houghton Mifflin.

Henderson, E. H., & Beers, J. W. (Eds.). (1980). *Developmental and cognitive aspects of learning to spell: A reflection of word knowledge.* Newark, DE: International Reading Association.

Henker, B., & Whalen, C. K. (1989). Hyperactivity and attention deficits. *American Psychologist, 44,* 216–223.

Herrick, V. E. (1960). Handwriting and children's writing. *Elementary English, 37,* 248–258.

Herrick, V. E. (1961). Manuscript and cursive writing. *Childhood Education, 37,* 264–267.

Heshusius, L. (1989). The Newtonian mechanistic paradigm, special education, and contours of alternatives: An overview. *Journal of Learning Disabilities, 22,* 403–415.

Heshusius, L. (1994). Freeing ourselves from objectivity: Managing subjectivity or turning toward a participation mode of consciousness. *Educational Researcher, 23* (3), 15–22.

Hessler, G., & Kitchen, D. (1980). Language characteristics of a purposive sample of early elementary learning disabled students. *Learning Disability Quarterly,* 3 (3), 36–41.

Hiebert, E. (1994). Reading recovery in the United States: What difference does it make to an age cohort? *Educational Researcher, 23* (9), 15–25.

Hieronymus, A. N., Hoover, H. D., & Lindquist, E. F. (1986). *Iowa Tests of Basic Skills.* Lombard, IL: Riverside Publishing.

Hieronymus, A. N., Lindquist, E. F., & Hoover, H. D. (1978). *Iowa Tests of Basic Skills.* Lombard, IL: Riverside.

Hightower, A. D., & Braden, J. (1991). Prevention. In T. R. Kratochwill & R. J. Morris (Eds.), *The practice of child therapy* (2nd ed., pp. 410–440). New York: Pergamon.

Hildreth, G. (1960). Manuscript writing after 60 years. *Elementary English, 37,* 3–13.

Hildreth, G. H. (1965). Experience-related reading for school beginners. *Elementary English, 42,* 280–284, 298–299.

Hinshelwood, J. (1907). Four cases of congenital word-blindness occurring in the same family. *British Medical Journal, 2,* 1229–1232.

Hinshelwood, J. (1917). *Congenital word blindness.* London: Lewis.

Hodges, R. E. (1982). Research update on the development of spelling ability. *Language Arts, 59,* 284–290.

Hollingsworth, P. M. (1970). An experiment with the impress method of teaching reading. *Reading Teacher, 24,* 112–114.

Holmes, D. L., & Peper, R. J. (1977). An evaluation of the use of spelling error analysis in the diagnosis of reading disabilities. *Child Development, 48,* 1708–1711.

Horner, R. H. (1994). Functional assessment: Contributions and future directions. *Journal of Applied Behavior Analysis, 27,* 401–404.

Horton, S. V., Lovitt, T. C., & White, O. R. (1992). Teaching mathematics to adolescents classified as mentally handicapped: Using calculators to remove the onus. *Remedial and Special Education, 13* (3), 36–61.

Houghton Mifflin. (1992). *The mathematics experience.* Boston: Author.

House, E. R., Glass, G. V., McLean, L. D., & Walker, D. F. (1978). No simple answer: Critique of the Follow Through evaluation. *Harvard Educational Review, 48,* 128–160.

Howe, K. B., & Miramontes, O. B. (1992). *The ethics of special education.* New York: Teachers College Press.

Howell, K. W., & Davidson, M. R. (1997). Aligning teacher thought processes with the curriculum. In J. W. Lloyd, E. J. Kameenui, & D. Chard (Eds.), *Issues in educating students with disabilities* (pp. 101–128). Mahwah, NJ: Erlbaum.

Howell, K. W., Fox, S. L., & Morehead, M. K. (1993). *Curriculum-based evaluation: Teaching and decision making* (2nd ed.). Pacific Grove, CA: Brooks/Cole.

Howell. K. W., Fox, S. L., & Morehead, M. K. (1997). *Curricullum-based evaluation for special and remedial education: A handbook for deciding what to teach* (2nd ed.). Pacific Grove, CA: Brooks/Cole.

Howell, K. W., & Morehead, M. K. (1987). *Curriculum-based evaluation for special and remedial education: A handbook for deciding what to teach.* Columbus, OH: Merrill.

Howell, K. W., Zucker, S. H., & Morehead, M. K. (1985). *MAST: Multilevel Academic Survey Test.* San Antonio, TX: Psychological Corporation.

Hresko, W. (1979). Elicited imitation ability of children from learning disabled and regular classes. *Journal of Learning Disabilities, 12,* 456–461.

Huefner, D. S. (1994). The mainstreaming cases: Tensions and trends for school administrators. *Educational Administration Quarterly,* 30, 27–55.

Huey, E. B. (1908). *The psychology and pedagogy of reading: With a brief review of the history of reading and writing and of methods, texts, and hygiene in reading.* New York: Macmillan.

Hugdahl, K. (1994). The search continues: Causal relationships among dyslexia, anomalous dominance, and immune function. *Brain and Cognition, 26,* 275–280.

Hughes, J. N. (Ed.). (1988). *Cognitive behavior therapy with children in schools.* New York: Pergamon.

Hughes, J. N., & Baker, D. B. (1990). *The clinical child interview.* New York: Guilford Press.

Hull, M. A. (1981). *Phonics for the teacher of reading: Programmed for self-instruction* (3rd ed.). Columbus, OH: Merrill.

Hulme, C. (1988). The implausibility of low-level visual deficits as a cause of children's reading difficulties. *Cognitive Neuropsychology,* 5, 369–374.

Hulme, C., & Joshi, R. M. (Eds.). (1998). *Reading and spelling: Development and disorders.* Mahwah, NJ: Erlbaum.

Hulme, C., & Snowling, M. (1992). Phonological deficit in dyslexia: A "sound" reappraisal of the verbal deficit hypothesis. In N. N. Singh & I. I. Beale (Eds.), *Learning disabilities:*

Nature, theory, and treatment (pp. 270–301). New York: Springer-Verlag.

Humphreys, P., Kaufmann, W. E., & Galaburda, A. M. (1990). Developmental dyslexia in women: Neuropathological findings in three patients. *Annals of Neurology, 28,* 727–738.

Hunt, J. McV. (1961). *Intelligence and experience.* New York: Ronald Press.

Hunt, K. W. (1977). Early blooming and late blooming syntactic structures. In C. R. Cooper & L. Odell (Eds.), *Evaluating writing: Describing, measuring, judging* (pp. 91–104). Urbana, IL: National Council of Teachers of English.

Hurford, D. R., Johnston, M., Nepote, P., Hampton, S., Moore, S., Neal, J., Mueller, A., McGeorge, K., Huff, L., Awad, A., Tatro, C., Juliano, C., & Huffman, D. (1994). Early identification and remediation of phonological processing deficits in first-grade children at risk for reading disabilities. *Journal of Learning Disabilities, 27,* 647–659.

Hurford, D. P., Schauf, J. D., Bunce, L., Blaich, T., & Moore, K. (1994). Early identification of children at risk for reading disabilities. *Journal of Learning Disabilities, 27,* 371–382.

Hynd, G. W., & Semrud-Clikeman, M. (1989). Dyslexia and brain morphology. *Psychological Bulletin, 106,* 447–482.

Iano, R. (1986). The study and development of teaching with implications for the advancement of special education. *Remedial and Special Education,* 7 (5), 50–61.

Idol, L., & Croll, V. (1987). Story mapping training as a means of improving reading comprehension. *Learning Disability Quarterly, 10,* 214–230.

Individuals with Disabilities Education Act (IDEA) Amendments of 1997. Public Law, 105–17.

Inge, K. J., & Tilson, G. (1994). Supported employment: Issues and applications for individuals with learning disabilities. In P. J. Gerber & H. B. Reiff (Eds.), *Learning disabilities in adulthood: Persisting problems and evolving issues* (pp. 179–193). Boston: Andover Medical Publishers.

Inhelder, B., Sinclair, H., & Bovet, M. (1974). *Learning and the development of cognition.* Cambridge, MA: Harvard University Press.

Interagency Committee on Learning Disabilities. (1987). *Learning disabilities: A report to Congress.* Bethesda, MD: National Institutes of Health.

Invernizzi, M., Abouzeid, M., & Gill, J. T. (1994). Using students' invented spellings as a guide for spelling instruction that emphasized word study. *Elementary School Journal, 95, 155–167.*

Invernizzi, M., Meier, J. D., Juel, C., & Swank, L. K. (1997). *PALS II: Phonological awareness and literacy screening.* Charlottesville: University of Virginia.

Irvin, L. K., & Walker, H. M. (1994). Assessing children's social skills using video-based microcomputer technology. *Exceptional Children, 61,* 182–196.

Iversen, S., & Tunmer, W. E. (1993). Phonological processing skills and the Reading Recovery Program. *Journal of Educational Psychology, 85,* 112–126.

Jacobs, A. E., & Hendricks, D. J. (1992). Job accommodations for adults with learning disabilities: Brilliantly disguised opportunities. *Learning Disability Quarterly,* 15(4), 274–285.

Jacobson, R. (1968). *Child language, aphasia, and general sound laws* (A. Keiler, Trans.). The Hague: Mouton. (Original work published 1941)

Jastak, J., & Jastak, S. (1978). *Wide Range Achievement Test.* Wilmington, DE: Guidance Associates.

Jeffrey, W. E., & Samuels, S. J. (1967). Effect of method of reading training on initial learning and transfer. *Journal of Verbal Learning and Verbal Behavior, 6,* 354–358.

Jenkins, J. J., & Palmero, D. S. (1964). Mediation processes and the acquisition of linguistic structure. In U. Bellugi & R. Brown (Eds.), The acquisition of language. *Monographs of the Society for Research in Child Development, 29* (1, Whole No. 92).

Jenkins, J. R., Barksdale, A., & Clinton, L. (1978). Improving reading comprehension and oral reading: Generalization across behaviors, settings, and time. *Journal of Learning Disabilities, 11,* 607–617.

Jenkins, J. R., Jewell, M., Leicester, N., Jenkins, L., & Troutner, N. M. (1991). Development of a school building model for educating students with handicaps and at-risk students in general education classrooms. *Journal of Learning Disabilities, 24,* 311–320.

Jerger, M. A. (1996). Phoneme awareness and the role of the educator. *Intervention in School and Clinic, 32,* 5–13.

Jitendra, A. K., & Kameenui, E. J. (1988). A design of instruction analysis of concept teaching in five basal language programs: Violations from the bottom up. *Journal of Special Education, 22,* 199–219.

Johnson, D. J. (1994). Measurement of listening and speaking. In G. R. Lyon (Ed.), *Frames of reference for the assessment of learning disabilities: New views on measurement issues* (pp. 203–227). Baltimore: Brookes.

Johnson, D. J., & Myklebust, H. R. (1967). *Learning disabilities: Educational principles and practices.* New York: Grune & Stratton.

Johnson, J. E., & Johnson, K. M. (1992). Clarifying the developmental perspective in response to Carta, Schwartz, Atwater, and McConnell. *Topics in Early Childhood Special Education, 12,* 439–457.

Johnston, D., Proctor, W., & Corey, S. (1994). Not a way out: A way in. *Educational Leadership,* 52(4), 46–49.

Johnston, M. B., Whitman, T. L., & Johnson, M. (1981). Teaching addition and subtraction to mentally retarded children: A self-instructional program. *Applied Research in Mental Retardation, 1,* 141–160.

Jones, E. D., Wilson, R., & Bhojwani, S. (1997). Mathematics instruction for secondary students with learning disabilities. *Journal of Learning Disabilities, 30,* 151–163.

Jones, J. C., Trap, J., & Cooper, J. O. (1977). Technical report: Students' self-recording of manuscript letter strokes. *Journal of Applied Behavior Analysis, 10,* 509–514.

Jordon, D. R. (1977). *Dyslexia in the classroom* (2nd ed.). Columbus, OH: Merrill.

Jordon, N. C., & Montani, T. O. (1997). Cognitive arithmetic and problem solving: A comparison of children with specific and general mathematics difficulties. *Journal of Learning Disabilities, 30,* 624–634, 684.

Joseph, F., & Mullins, J. (1970). A script to supplant cursive writing or printing. *Teaching Exceptional Children,* 3(1), 23–32.

Joshi, R. M., Williams, K. A., & Wood, J. R. (1998). Predicting reading comprehension from listening comprehension: Is this the answer to the IQ debate? In C. Hulme & R. M. Joshi (Eds.), *Reading and spelling: Development and disorders* (pp. 319–327). Mahwah, NJ: Erlbaum.

Juel, C. (1988). Learning to read and write: A longitundinal study of fifty-four children from first through fourth grade. *Journal of Educational Psychology, 80,* 437–447.

Juel, C. (1991). Beginning reading. In R. Barr, M. L. Kamil, P. B. Mosenthal, & P. D. Pearson (Eds.), *Handbook of reading research* (Vol. 2, pp. 759–788). New York: Longman.

Juel, C., Griffith, P. L., & Gough, P. B. (1986). Acquisition of literacy: A longitudinal study of children in first and second grade. *Journal of Educational Psychology, 78,* 243–255.

Julian, T., McHenry, P., & McKelvey, M. (1994). Cultural variations in parenting: Perceptions of Caucasian, African-American, Hispanic, and Asian-American parents. *Family Relations, 43,* 30–37.

Kagan, J., Rosman, B. L., Day, D., Albert, J., & Phillips, W. (1964). Information processing in the child: Significance of analytic and reflective attitudes. *Psychological Monographs,* 78(1, Whole No. 578).

Kagan, S. L. (1994a). Early care and education: Beyond the fishbowl. *Phi Delta Kappan, 76,* 184–185.

Kagan, S. L. (1994b). Readying schools for young children: Polemics and priorities. *Phi Delta Kappan, 76,* 226–233.

Kail, R. V., & Leonard, L. B. (1986). *Word-finding abilities in language-impaired children.* Rockville, MD: American Speech-Language-Hearing Association.

Kaliski, L. (1967). Arithmetic and the brain-injured child. In E. C. Frierson & W. B. Babe (Eds.), *Educating children with learning disabilities: Selected readings* (pp. 458–466). New York: Appleton-Century-Crofts.

Kameenui, E., Carnine, D., & Maggs, A. (1980). Instructional procedures for teaching reversible passive voice and clause constructions to three mildly handicapped children. *Exceptional Child,* 27 (1), 29–41.

Kameenui, E. J., & Carnine, D. W. (1998). *Effective teaching strategies that accommodate diverse learners.* Upper Saddle River, NJ: Merrill.

Kameenui, E. J., & Darch, C. B. (1995). *Instructional classroom management: A proactive approach to behavior management.* White Plains, NY: Longman.

Kameenui, E. J., & Simmons, D. C. (1990). *Designing instructional strategies: The prevention of academic learning problems.* Columbus, OH: Merrill.

Kanfer, F. H., & Grimm, L. G. (1977). Behavioral analysis: Selecting target behaviors in the interview. *Behavior Modification, 1,* 7–28.

Kaplan, B. J., & Crawford, S. G. (1994). The G-B-G model: Is there more to consider than handedness? *Brain and Cognition, 26,* 291–299.

Karegianes, M. L., Pascarella, E. T., & Pflaum, S. W. (1980). The effects of peer editing on the writing proficiency of low-achieving tenth grade students. *Journal of Educational Research, 73,* 203–207.

Karlsen, B., & Gardner, E. F. (1995). *Stanford Diagnostic Reading Tests—Fourth Edition.* San Antonio: Psychological Corporation.

Karlsen, B., Madden, R., & Gardner, E. E (1976). *Stanford Diagnostic Reading Test* (rev. ed.). New York: Harcourt Brace Jovanovich.

Karnes, M. (1972). *The GOAL program language development.* Springfield, MA: Milton Bradley.

Kass, C. E. (1966). Psycholinguistic disabilities of children with reading problems. *Exceptional Children, 32,* 533–539.

Katsiyannis, A. (1994). Pre-referral practices: Under Office of Civil Rights scrutiny. *Journal of Developmental and Physical Disabilities, 6,* 73–7.

Katz, L. G. (1994). Perspectives on the quality of early childhood programs. *Phi Delta Kappan, 76,* 200–205.

Katzen, K. (1980). A teacher's view. *Exceptional Children, 48,* 582.

Kauffman, J. M. (1975). Behavior modification. In W. M. Crucikshank & D. P. Hallahan (Eds.), *Perceptual and learning disabilities in children: Vol. 2. Research and theory* (pp. 395–444). Syracuse, NY: Syracuse University Press.

Kauffman, J. M. (1989). The regular education initiative as Reagan-Bush education policy: A trickle-down theory of education of the hard-to-teach. *Journal of Special Education, 23,* 256–278.

Kauffman, J. M. (1990, April). What happens when special education works? The sociopolitical context of research in the 1990s. Paper presented at the annual meeting of the American Educational Research Association, Boston.

Kauffman, J. M. (1992). Foreword, in K. R. Howe & O. B. Miramontes, *The ethics of special education* (pp. xi–xvii). New York: Teachers College Press.

Kauffman, J. M. (1993a). *Characteristics of emotional and behavioral disorders of children and youth* (5th ed.). Columbus, OH: Merrill/Macmillan.

Kauffman, J. M. (1993b). How we might achieve the radical reform of special education. *Exceptional Children, 60*, 6–16.

Kauffman, J. M. (1994). Places of change: Special education's power and identity in an era of educational reform. *Journal of Learning Disabilities, 27*, 610–618.

Kauffman, J. M. (1995). Why we must celebrate a diversity of restrictive environments. *Learning Disabilities Research and Practice, 10* (4), 225–232.

Kauffman, J. M. (1997). *Characteristics of emotional and behavioral disorders of children and youth* (6th ed.). Upper Saddle River, NJ: Prentice-Hall.

Kauffman, J. M., & Hallahan, D. P. (Eds.). (1976). *Teaching children with learning disabilities: Personal perspectives.* Columbus, OH: Merrill.

Kauffman, J. M., & Hallahan, D. P. (Eds.). (1995). *The illusion of full inclusion: A comprehensive critique of a special education bandwagon.* Austin, TX: PRO-ED.

Kauffman, J. M., & Hallahan, D. P. (1997). A diversity of restrictive environments: Placement as a problem of social ecology. In J. W. Lloyd, E. J. Kameenui, & D. Chard (Eds.), *Issues in educating students with disabilities* (pp. 325–342). Hillsdale, NJ: Erlbaum.

Kauffman, J. M., Hallahan, D. P., & Ford-Harris, D. Y. (Eds.). (1998). Disproportional representation of minorities in special education. *Journal of Special Education, 32*, 3.

Kauffman, J. M., Hallahan, D. P., Haas, K., Brame, T., & Boren, R. (1978). Imitating children's errors to improve their spelling performance. *Journal of Learning Disabilities, 11*, 217–222.

Kauffman, J. M., & Lloyd, J. W. (1995). A sense of place: The importance of placement issues in contemporary special education. In J. M. Kauffman, J. W. Lloyd, D. P. Hallahan, & T. A. Astuto (Eds.), *Issues in educational placement: Students with emotional and behavioral disorders* (pp. 3–19). Hillsdale, NJ: Erlbaum.

Kauffman, J. M., Lloyd, J. W., Astuto, T. A., & Hallahan, D. P. (1995). Toward a sense of place for special education in the 21st century. In J. M. Kauffman, J. W. Lloyd, D. P. Hallahan, & T. A. Astuto (Eds.), *Issues in educational placement: Students with emotional and behavioral disorders* (pp. 379–385). Hillsdale, NJ: Erlbaum.

Kauffman, J. M., Mostert, M. P., Trent, S. C., & Hallahan, D. P. (1998). *Managing classroom behavior: A reflective case-based approach.* Boston: Allyn & Bacon.

Kauffman, J. M., & Trent, S. (1991). Issues in service delivery for students with learning disabilities. In B. Y. L. Wong (Ed.), *Learning about learning disabilities* (pp.465–481). Orlando, FL: Academic Press.

Kavale, K. (1981a). Functions of the Illinois Test of Psycholinguistic Abilities (ITPA): Are they trainable? *Exceptional Children, 47*, 496–510.

Kavale, K. (1981b). The relationship between auditory perceptual skills and reading ability: A meta-analysis. *Journal of Learning Disabilities, 14*, 539–546.

Kavale, K. A. (1980). The reasoning abilities of normal and learning disabled readers on measures of reading comprehension. *Learning Disability Quarterly, 3* (4), 34–45.

Kavale, K. A. (1982). The efficacy of stimulant drug treatment for hyperactivity: A meta-analysis. *Journal of Learning Disabilities, 15*, 280–289.

Kavale, K. A. (1988). The long-term consequences of learning disabilities. In M. C. Wang, M. C. Reynolds, & H. J. Walberg (Eds.), *Handbook of special education: Research and practice: Vol. 2. Mildly handicapped conditions.* New York: Pergamon.

Kavale, K. A., & Forness, S. R. (1983). Hyperactivity and diet treatment: A meta-analysis of the Feingold hypothesis. *Journal of Learning Disabilities, 16*, 324–330.

Kavale, K. A., & Forness, S. R. (1985). *The science of learning disabilities.* San Diego, CA: College Hill Press.

Kavale, K. A., & Forness, S. R. (1987a). History, politics, and the general education initiative: Sleeter's reinterpretation of learning disabilities as a case study. *Remedial and Special Education*, 8(5), 6–12.

Kavale, K. A., & Forness, S. R. (1987b). Substance over style: A quantitative synthesis assessing the efficacy of modality testing and teaching. *Exceptional Children, 54*, 228–234.

Kavale, K. A., & Forness, S. R. (1992). History, definition, and diagnosis. In N. N. Singh & I. L. Beale (Eds.), *Learning disabilities: Nature, theory, and treatment* (pp. 3–41). New York: Springer-Verlag.

Kavale, K. A., & Forness, S. R. (1995a). *The nature of learning disabilities.* Hillsdale, NJ: Erlbaum.

Kavale, K. A., & Forness, S. R. (1995b). Social skill deficits and training: A meta-analysis of the research in learning disabilities. In T. E. Scruggs & M. A. Mastropieri (Eds.), *Advances in learning and behavioral disabilities* (pp. 119–160). Greenwich, CT: JAI Press.

Kavale, K. A., & Forness, S. R. (1997). Defining learning disabilities: Consonance and dissonance. In J. W. Lloyd, E. J. Kameenui, & D. Chard (Eds.), *Issues in educating students with disabilities* (pp. 3–25). Mahwah, NJ: Erlbaum.

Kavale, K. A., Fuchs, D., & Scruggs, T. E. (1994). Setting the record straight on learning disability and low achievement: Implications for policymaking. *Learning Disabilities Research and Practice, 9*, 70–77.

Kavale, K. A., & Mattson, P. D. (1983). "One jumped off the balance beam": Meta-analysis of perceptual-motor training. *Journal of Learning Disabilities, 16*, 165–173.

Kavale, K. A., & Mundschenk, N. A. (1991). A critique of assessment methodology. In H. L. Swanson (Ed.), *Handbook on the assessment of learning disabilities* (pp. 407–432). Austin, TX: PRO-ED.

Kazdin, A. E. (1995). *Conduct disorders in childhood and adolescence* (2nd ed.). Thousand Oaks, CA: Sage.

Keller, C. E. (1991). Cognitive-behavioral assessment and intervention. In H. L. Swanson (Ed.), *Handbook on the assessment of learning disabilities: Theory, research, and practice* (pp. 331–349). Austin, TX: PRO-ED.

Kelley, M. L. (1990). *School-home notes: Promoting children's classroom success.* New York: Guilford Press.

Kelley, M. L., & McCain, A. P. (1995). Promoting academic performance in inattentive children. *Behavior Modification, 19,* 357–375.

Kelly, B., Carnine, D., Gersten, R., & Grossen, B. (1986). The effectiveness of videodisc instruction in teaching fractions to learning-disabled and remedial high school students. *Journal of Special Education Technology, 8* (2), 5–17.

Kelly, B. F., Gersten, R., & Carnine, D. (1990). Student error patterns as a function of curriculum design: Teaching fractions to remedial high school students and high school students with learning disabilities. *Journal of Learning Disabilities, 23,* 23–29.

Kendall, P. C., & Cummings, L. (1988). Thought and action in educational interventions: Cognitive-behavioral approaches. In J. C. Witt, S. N. Elliott, & F. M. Gresham (Eds.), *Handbook of behavior therapy in education* (pp. 403–418). New York: Plenum Press.

Kennedy, K. M., & Bachman, J. (1993). Effectiveness of the Lindamood Auditory Discrimination in Depth Program with students with learning disabilities. *Learning Disabilities Research and Practice, 8,* 253–259.

Kenny, D. T., & Chekaluk, E. (1993). Early reading performance: A comparison of teacher-based and test-based assessments. *Journal of Learning Disabilities, 26,* 227–236.

Keogh, B. K., & Becker, L. D. (1973). Early detection of learning problems: Questions, cautions, and guidelines. *Exceptional Children, 40,* 5–11.

Keogh, B. K., & Hall, R. J. (1984). Cognitive training with learning-disabled pupils. In A. W. Meyers & W. E. Craighead (Eds.), *Cognitive behavior therapy with children* (pp. 163–191). New York: Plenum Press.

Keogh, B. K., & Margolis, J. (1976). Learn to labor and wait: Attentional problems of children with learning disorders. *Journal of Learning Disabilities, 9,* 276–286.

Keogh, B. K., & Pelland, M. (1985). Vision training revisited. *Journal of Learning Disabilities, 18,* 228–236.

Keogh, B. K., & Sears, S. (1991). Learning disabilities from a developmental perspective: Early identification and prediction. In B. Y. L. Wong (Ed.), *Learning about learning disabilities* (pp. 485–503). New York: Academic Press.

Keohane, N., Rosaldo, M., & Gelpi, B. (1981). *Feminist theory: A critique of ideology.* Chicago: University of Chicago Press.

Kephart, N. C. (1971). *The slow learner in the classroom* (rev. ed.). Columbus, OH: Merrill.

Kerr, M. M., & Lambert, D. L. (1982). Behavior modification of children's written language. In M. Hersen, R. M. Eisler, & P. M. Miller (Eds.), *Progress in behavior modification* (Vol. 13, pp. 79–108). New York: Academic Press.

Kerr, M. M., & Nelson, C. M. (1998). *Strategies for managing behavior problems in the classroom* (3rd ed.). Upper Saddle River, NJ: Prentice-Hall.

Kinder, D., & Carnine, D. (1991). Direct instruction: What it is and what it is becoming. *Journal of Behavioral Education, 1,* 193–213.

Kirk, S. A. (1962). *Educating exceptional children.* Boston: Houghton Mifflin.

Kirk, S. A. (1963). Behavioral diagnosis and remediation of learning disabilities. In *Proceedings of the conference on exploration into problems of the perceptually handicapped child.* Chicago: Perceptually Handicapped Children.

Kirk, S. A. (1969). Illinois Test of Psycholinguistic Abilities: Its origin and implications. In J. Hellmuth (Ed.), *Learning disorders* (Vol. 3, pp. 395–427). Seattle, WA: Special Child Publications.

Kirk, S. A. (1975). Behavioral diagnosis and remediation of learning disabilities. In S. A. Kirk & J. M. McCarthy (Eds.), *Learning disabilities: Selected ACLD papers* (pp. 7–10). Boston: Houghton Mifflin.

Kirk, S. A. (1976). S. A. Kirk. In D. P. Hallahan & J. M. Kauffman (Eds.), *Teaching children with learning disabilities: Personal perspectives* (pp. 238–269). Columbus, OH: Merrill.

Kirk, S. A., & Elkins, J. (1975). Characteristics of children enrolled in the child service demonstration centers. *Journal of Learning Disabilities, 8,* 630–637.

Kirk, S. A., & Kirk, W. E. (1971). *Psycholinguistic learning disabilities: Diagnosis and remediation.* Urbana: University of Illinois Press.

Kirk, S. A., Kirk, W. E., & Minskoff, E. H. (1985) *Phonic remedial reading lessons.* Novato, CA: Academic Therapy Publishing.

Kirk, S. A., & McCarthy, J. (1962). *Illinois Test of Psycholinguistic Abilities* (Exper. ed.). Urbana: University of Illinois Press.

Kirk, S. A., McCarthy, J., & Kirk, W. E. (1968). *Illinois Test of Psycholinguistic Abilities.* Urbana: University of Illinois Press.

Klausmeier, H. J. (1992). Concept learning and concept teaching. *Educational Psychologist, 27,* 267–286.

Kleiman, G. N. (1975). Speech receding in reading. *Journal of Verbal Learning and Verbal Behavior, 14,* 323–339.

Kleinhammer-Tramill, P. J., Rosenkoetter, S. E., & Tramill, J. L. (1994). Early intervention and secondary/transition services: Harbingers of change in education. *Focus on Exceptional Children, 27*(2), 1–14.

Kline, C. L., & Kline, C. L. (1975). Follow-up study of 216 dyslexic children. *Bulletin of the Orton Society, 25,* 127–144.

Knapczyk, D. R., & Livingston, G. (1974). The effects of prompting question-asking upon on-task and reading comprehension. *Journal of Applied Behavior Analysis, 7,* 115–121.

Kneedler, R. D., & Hallahan, D. P. (1984). Self-monitoring as an attentional strategy for academic tasks with learning disabled children. In B. Gholson & T. Rosenthal (Eds.), *Applications of cognitive development theory* (pp. 243–260). New York: Academic Press.

Kneedler, R. D., & Meese, R. L. (1988). Learning-disabled children. In J. C. Witt, S. N. Elliott, & F. M. Gresham (Eds.), *Handbook of behavior therapy in education* (pp. 601–629). New York: Plenum Press.

Konstantareas, M. M., & Homatidis, S. (1989). Parental perception of learning-disabled children's adjustment problems and related stress. *Journal of Abnormal Child Psychology, 17,* 177–188.

Kosc, L. (1974). Developmental dyscalculia. *Journal of Learning Disabilities, 7,* 164–177.

Kosiewicz, M. M., Hallahan, D. P., Lloyd, J., & Graves, A. W. (1982). Effects of self-instruction and self-correction procedures on handwriting performance. *Learning Disability Quarterly, 5,* 71–78.

Kotsonis, M. E., & Patterson, C. J. (1980). Comprehension-monitoring skills in learning disabled children. *Developmental Psychology, 16,* 541–542.

Kraetsch, G. A. (1981). The effects of oral instructions and training on the expansion of written language. *Learning Disability Quarterly, 4,* 82–90.

Kratochwill, T. R., & McGivern, J. F. (1996). Clinical diagnosis, behavioral assessment, and functional analysis: Examining the connection between assessment and intervention. *School Psychology Review, 25,* 342–355.

Kronick, D. (1990). Holism and empiricism as complementary paradigms. *Journal of Learning Disabilities, 23,* 5–8.

Kulieke, M., & Jones, B. (1993). Cognitive instructional techniques in relation to whole language approaches. *Remedial and Special Education, 14,* 26–29.

Kunzelmann, H. P. (1970). *Precision teaching: An initial training sequence.* Seattle, WA: Special Child Publications.

Kushch, A., Gross-Glenn, K., Jallad, B., Lubs, H., Rabin, M., Feldman, E., & Duara, R. (1993). Temporal lobe surface area measurements on MRI in normal and dyslexic readers. *Neuropsychologia, 31,* 811–821.

LaBerge, D., & Samuels, S. J. (1973). Toward a theory of automatic information processing in reading. *Cognitive Psychology, 6,* 293–33.

Lahey, B. B., Busemeyer, M. K., O'Hara, C., & Beggs, V. E. (1977). Treatment of severe perceptual-motor disorders in children diagnosed as learning disabled. *Behavior Modification, 1,* 123–140.

Lahey, B. B., McNees, M. R., & Brown, C. C. (1973). Modification of deficits in reading for comprehension. *Journal of Applied Behavior Analysis, 6,* 460–475.

Lankford, F. C., Jr. (1972). *Some computational strategies of seventh grade pupils* (Final Report of Project No. 2-C 013, U.S. Department of Health, Education, and Welfare Grant No. OEG-3–72–0035). Charlottesville: Center for Advanced Studies, University of Virginia.

Larsen, J. P., Hoien, T., Lundberg, I., & Odegaard, H. (1990). MRI evaluation of the symmetry of the planum temporale in adolescents with dyslexia. *Brain and Language, 39,* 289–301.

Larsen, S., & Hammill, D. D. (1994). *Test of Written Spelling—3.* Austin, TX: PRO-ED.

Larsen, S., Rogers, D., & Sowell, V. (1976). The use of selected perceptual tests in differentiating between normal and learning disabled children. *Journal of Learning Disabilities, 9,* 85–90.

Larson, C. E. (1968). Teaching beginning writing. *Academic Therapy, 4*(1), 61–66.

Larson, K. A., & Gerber, M. M. (1992). Metacognition. In N. N. Singh & I. L. Beale (Eds.), *Learning disabilities: Nature, theory, and treatment* (pp.126–169). New York: Springer-Verlag.

Laughon, P. (1990). The dynamic assessment of intelligence: A review of three approaches. *School Psychology Review, 19,* 459–470.

Laughton, J., & Morris, N. T. (1989). Story grammar knowledge of learning disabled students. *Learning Disabilities Research, 4,* 87–95.

Learning Disabilities Association of America. (1993). Position paper on full inclusion of all students with learning disabilities in the regular education classroom. *LDA Newsbrief, 28*(2).

Learning Disabilities Council. (1989). *Understanding learning disabilities: A parent guide and workbook.* Richmond, VA: Learning Disabilities, Inc.

Lee, L. (1971). *Northwestern Syntax Screening Test.* Evanston, IL: Northwestern University Press.

Lee, L., Koenigsknecht, R. A., & Mulhern, S. T. (1975). *Interactive language development teaching.* Evanston, IL: Northwestern University Press.

Leete-Guy, L., & Schor, J. B. (1992). *The great American time squeeze: Trends in work and leisure, 1969–1989.* (Briefing paper for the Economic Policy Institute, Washington, DC).

Leinhardt, G., Seewald, A., & Zigmond, N. (1982). Sex and race differences in learning disabilities classrooms. *Journal of Educational Psychology, 74,* 835–845.

Lenchner, O., Gerber, M. M., & Routh, D. K. (1990). Phonological awareness tasks as predicators of decoding ability: Beyond segmentation. *Journal of Learning Disabilities, 23,* 240–247.

Lennox, C., & Siegel, L. S. (1993). Visual and phonological spelling errors in subtypes of children with learning disabilities. *Applied Psycholinguistics, 14,* 473–488.

Lennox, C., & Siegel, L. S. (1998). Phonological and orthographic processes in good and poor spellers. In C. Hulme & R. M. Joshi (Eds.), *Reading and spelling: Development and disorders* (pp. 395–404). Mahwah, NJ: Erlbaum.

Lerner, J. W. (1975). Remedial reading and reading disabilities: Are they the same or different? *Journal of Special Education, 9,* 119–132.

Lerner, J. W., Cousin, R. T., & Richeck, M. (1992). Critical issues in learning disabilities: Whole language learning. *Learning Disabilities Research and Practice, 7,* 226–230.

Levi-Strauss, C. (1963). *Structural anthropology.* New York: Basic Books.

Leviton, A., Bellinger, D., Allred, E. N., Rabinowitz, M., Needleman, H., & Schoenbaum, S. (1993). Pre- and postnatal low-level lead exposure and children's dysfunction in school. *Environmental Research, 60,* 30–43.

Lewis, B. A. (1992). Pedigree analysis of children with phonology disorders. *Journal of Learning Disabilities,* 25(9), 586–597.

Lewis, B. A., & Thompson, L. A. (1992). A study of developmental speech and language disorders in twins. *Journal of Speech and Hearing Research, 35,* 1086–1094.

Lewis, C., Hitch, G. J., & Walker, P. (1994). The prevalence of specific arithmetic difficulties and specific reading difficulties in 9- to 10-year-old boys and girls. *Journal of Child Psychology and Psychiatry and Allied Disciplines, 35,* 283–292.

Liberman, I. Y. (1970). Segmentation of the spoken word and reading acquisition. *Bulletin of the Orton Society,* 23, 65–77.

Liberman, I. Y., & Shankweiler, D. (1979). Speech, the alphabet, and teaching to read. In L. Resnick & R. Weaver (Eds.), *Theory and practice of early reading* (Vol. 2, pp. 109–132). Hillsdale, NJ: Erlbaum.

Liberman, I. Y., & Shankweiler, D. (1991). Phonology and beginning reading: A tutorial. In L. Rieben & C. A. Perfetti (Eds.), *Learning to read: Basic research and its implications* (pp. 3–17). Hillsdale, NJ: Erlbaum.

Linan-Thompson, S., & Jean, R. E. (1997). Completing the parent participation puzzle: Accepting diversity. *Teaching Exceptional Children,* 30(2), 46–50.

Lindamood, C. H., & Lindamood, P. C. (1979). *Lindamood Auditory Conceptualization Test—Revised Edition.* Chicago: Riverside.

Lindamood. C. H., & Lindamood, P. C. (1975). *The A. D. D. program: Auditory Discrimination in Depth.* Hingham, MA: Teaching Resources Corporation.

Lipsky, D. K., & Gartner, A. (1987). Capable of achievement and worthy of respect: Education for handicapped students as if they were full-fledged human beings. *Exceptional Children, 54,* 69–74.

Lipsky, D. K., & Gartner, A. (1991). Restructuring for quality. In J. W. Lloyd, N. N. Singh, & A. C. Repp (Eds.), *The regular education initiative: Alternative perspectives on concepts, issues, and models* (pp. 43–56). Sycamore, IL: Sycamore Press.

Lloyd, J. (1980). Academic instruction and cognitive-behavior modification: The need for attack strategy training. *Exceptional Education Quarterly, 1* (1), 53–63.

Lloyd, J., Cullinan, D., Heins, E. D., & Epstein, M. H. (1980). Direct instruction: Effects on oral and written language comprehension. *Learning Disability Quarterly,* 3 (4), 70–76.

Lloyd, J., Epstein, M. H., & Cullinan, D. (1981). Direct teaching for learning disabilities. In J. Gottlieb & S. S. Strichart (Eds.), *Developmental theory and research in learning disabilities* (pp. 278–309). Baltimore: University Park Press.

Lloyd, J., Saltzman, N. J., & Kauffman, J. M. (1981). Predictable generalization in academic learning as a result of preskills and strategy training. *Learning Disability Quarterly, 4,* 203–216.

Lloyd, J. W. (1984). How shall we individualize instruction—or should we? *Remedial and Special Education,* 5(1), 7–15.

Lloyd, J. W., & Blanford, B. J. (1991). Assessment for instructional planning. In H. L. Swanson (Ed.), *Handbook on the assessment of learning disabilities: Theory, research, and practice* (pp. 45–58). Boston: Little, Brown.

Lloyd, J. W., & deBettencourt, L. U. (1982). *Academic strategy training: A manual for teachers.* Charlottesville: Learning Disabilities Research Institute, University of Virginia.

Lloyd, J. W., Cameron, N. A., & Lloyd, R. A. (1984). Reading assessment. In R. Fox & A. Rotori (Eds.), *Assessment in regular and special education.* (pp. 109–140). Austin, TX: PRO-ED.

Lloyd, J. W., & Keller, C. E. (1989). Effective mathematics instruction. *Focus on Exceptional Children, 21* (7), 1–10.

Lloyd, J. W. & Kauffman, J. M. (1995). Demands of less restrictive placements on classroom teachers. In J. M. Kauffman, J. W. Lloyd, D. P. Hallahan, & T. A. Astuto (Eds.), *Issues in educational placement: Students with emotional and behavioral disorders.* Hillsdale, NJ: Erlbaum.

Lloyd, J. W., Kauffman, J. M., Landrum, T. J., & Roe, D. L. (1991). Why do teachers refer pupils for special education? An analysis of referral records. *Exceptionality, 2,* 115–126.

Lloyd, J. W., Kosiewicz, M. M., & Hallahan, D. R (1982). Reading comprehension: Cognitive training contributions. *School Psychology Review, 11*(3), 5–41.

Lloyd, J. W., & Loper, A. B.(1986). Measurement and evaluation of task-related learning behaviors: Attention to task and metacognition. *School Psychology Review, 15,* 336–345.

Lloyd, J. W., Singh, N. N., & Repp, A. C. (Eds.). (1991). *The regular education initiative: Alternative perspectives on concepts, issues, and models.* Sycamore, IL: Sycamore Press.

Lloyd, J. W., Tankersley, M., & Talbott, E. (1994). Using single-subject research methods to study learning disabilities. In S. Vaughn & C. Bos (Eds.), *Research issues in learning disabilities: Theory methodology assessment, and ethics* (pp. 163–177). New York: Springer-Verlag.

Loeber, R., Green, S. M., Lahey, B. B., Christ, M. A. G., & Frick, P. J. (1992). Developmental sequences in the age of onset of disruptive child behaviors. *Journal of Child and Family Studies, 1,* 21–41.

Lomax, R. G. (1983). Applying structural modeling to some component processes of reading comprehension development. *Journal of Experimental Education, 52,* 33–40.

Loper, A. B., & Murphy, D. M. (1985). Cognitive self-regulatory training for underachieving children. In D. Forrest-Pressley, G. E. MacKinnon, & T. G. Waller (Eds.), *Metacognition, cognition, and human performance* (Vol. 2, pp. 223–265). New York: Plenum Press.

Lopez-Reyna, N. A., & Bay, M. (1997). Enriching assessment using varied assessments for diverse learners. *Teaching Exceptional Children, 29*(4), 33–37.

Lopez-Reyna, N. A., Bay, M., & Patrikakou, E. N. (1996). Use of assessment procedures: Learning disabilities teachers' perspectives. *Diagnostique, 21*(2), 35–49.

Lorenz, L., & Vockell, E. (1979). Using the neurological impress method with learning disabled readers. *Journal of Learning Disabilities, 12,* 420–422.

Lorsbach, T. C., & Frymier, J. (1992). A comparison of learning disabled and nondisabled students on five at-risk factors. *Learning Disabilities Research and Practice, 7,* 137–141.

Lovegrove, W. (1991). The visual deficit hypothesis. In N. N. Singh & I. L. Beale (Eds.), *Learning disabilities: Nature, theory, and treatment* (pp. 246–269). New York: Springer-Verlag.

Lovett, M. W. (1987). A developmental approach to reading disability: Accuracy and speed criteria of normal and deficient reading skill. *Child Development, 58,* 234–260.

Lovitt, T. C. (1967). Assessment of children with learning disabilities. *Exceptional Children, 34,* 233–239.

Lovitt, T. C. (1975). Applied behavior analysis and learning disabilities: Part 1. Characteristics of ABA, general recommendations, and methodological limitations. *Journal of Learning Disabilities, 8,* 432–443.

Lovitt, T. C. (1978). New applications and new techniques in behavior modification. *Journal of Special Education, 12,* 89–93.

Lovitt, T. C. (1991). Behavioral assessment of learning disabilities. In H. L. Swanson (Ed.), *Handbook for the assessment of learning disabilities: Theory, research, and practice* (pp. 95–119). Austin, TX: PRO-ED.

Lovitt, T. C. (1995). *Tactics for teaching.* New York: Merrill.

Lovitt, T. C., & Curtiss, K. A. (1968). Effects of manipulating an antecedent event on mathematics response rate. *Journal of Applied Behavior Analysis, 1,* 329–333.

Lovitt, T. C., & Fantasia, K. (1980). Two approaches to reading program evaluation: A standardized test and direct assessment. *Learning Disability Quarterly, 3*(4), 77–87.

Lovitt, T. C., Guppy, T. E., & Blattner, J. E. (1969). The use of a free time contingency with fourth graders to increase spelling accuracy. *Behavior Research and Therapy, 7,* 151–156.

Lovitt, T. C., & Hansen, C. L. (1976a). Round one: Placing the child in the right reader. *Journal of Learning Disabilities, 9,* 347–353.

Lovitt, T. C., & Hansen. C. L. (1976b). The use of contingent skipping and drilling to improve oral reading and comprehension. *Journal of Learning Disabilities, 9,* 481–487.

Lovitt, T. C., & Smith, D. D. (1974). Using withdrawal of positive reinforcement to alter subtraction performance. *Exceptional Children, 40,* 357–358.

Lovitt, T. C., & Smith, J. O. (1972). Effects of instructions on an individual's verbal behavior. *Exceptional Children, 38,* 685–693.

Lubke, M. M., Rogers, B., & Evans, K. T. (1989). Teaching fractions with videodiscs. *Teaching Exceptional Children, 21,* 55–56.

Lucangeli, D., Galderisi, D., & Cornoldi, C. (1995). Specific and general transfer effects following metamemory training. *Learning Disabilities Research and Practice, 10,* 11–21.

Luecking, R. G., Tilson, G., & Willner, M. (1991). *Corporate employee assistance for workers with learning disabilities.* Rockville, MD: TransCen, Inc.

Lund, K., Foster, G. E., & McCall-Perez, F. C. (1978). The effectiveness of psycholinguistic training: A reevaluation. *Exceptional Children, 44,* 310–319.

Lundberg, I., Frost, J., & Peterson, O. R. (1988). Effects of an extensive program for stimulating phonological awareness in preschool children. *Reading Research Quarterly, 23,* 263–285.

Luria, A. (1961). *The role of speech in the regulation of normal and abnormal behaviors.* New York: Liveright.

Lyon, G. R. (1983). Learning-disabled readers: Indentification of subgroups. In H. R. Myklebust (Ed.), *Progress in learning disabilities* (Vol. 5, pp. 103–133). New York: Grune & Stratton.

Lyon, G. R. (1995). Research initiatives in learning disabilities: Contributions from scientists supported by the National Institute of Children Health and Human Development. *Journal of Child Neurology, 10*(Suppl. 1), 120–126.

Lyon, G. R. (1997, December 28). *Testimony of G. Reid Lyon, Ph.D. on children's literacy.* (On-line). Available at: http://www.apa.org/ppo/lyon.html.

Lyon, G. R., & Flynn, J. M. (1991). Assessing subtypes of learning abilities. In H. L. Swanson (Ed.), *Handbook on the assessment of learning disabilities* (pp. 59–74). Austin, TX: PRO-ED.

Lyon, G. R., Newby, R. E., Recht, D., & Caldwell, J. (1991). Neuropsychology and learning disabilities. In B. Y. L. Wong (Ed.), *Learning about learning disabilities* (pp. 375–406). New York: Academic Press.

Lyon, G. R., & Watson, B. (1981). Empirically derived subgroups of learning disabled readers: Diagnostic characteristics. *Journal of Learning Disabilities, 14,* 256–261.

MacArthur, C. A. (1988). The impact of computers on the writing process. *Exceptional Children, 54,* 536–542.

MacArthur, C. A. (1994). Peers + word processing + strategies = a powerful combination for revising student writing. *Teaching Exceptional Children, 27,* 24–29.

MacArthur, C. A., & Graham, S. (1987). Learning disabled students' composing under three methods of text production: Handwriting, word processing, and dictation. *Journal of Special Education, 21,* 22–42.

MacArthur, C. A., Graham, S., & Schwartz, S. S. (1993). Integrating strategy instruction and word processing into a process approach to writing instruction. *School Psychology Review, 22,* 671–681.

MacArthur, C. A., Haynes, J. A., Malouf, D. B., & Harris, K. R. (1990). Computer assisted instruction with learning disabled students: Achievement, engagement, and other factors that influence achievement. *Journal of Educational Computing Research, 6,* 311–328.

MacArthur, C. A., & Shneiderman, B. (1986). Learning disabled students' difficulties in learning to use a word processor: Implications for instruction and software evaluation. *Journal of Learning Disabilities, 19,* 248–253.

Maccoby, E. E., & Zellner, M. (1970). *Experiments in primary education: Aspects of Follow-Through.* New York: Harcourt Brace Jovanovich.

MacMillan, D. L., Gresham, F. M., Lopez, M. F., & Bocian, K. M. (1996). Comparison of students nominated for prereferral interventions by ethnicity and gender. *Journal of Special Education, 30,* 133–151.

MacMillan, D. L., & Reschly, D. J. (1998). Overrepresentation of minority students: The case for greater specificity or reconsideration of the variables examined. *Journal of Special Education, 32,* 15–24.

MacMillan, D. L., Semmel, M. I., & Gerber, M. M. (1994). The social context of Dunn: Then and now. *Journal of Special Education, 27,* 466–480.

MacMillan, D. L., Widaman, K. F., Balow, I. H., Borthwick-Duffy, S., Hendrick, I. G., & Hemsley, R. E. (1992). Special education students exiting the educational system. *Journal of Special Education, 26*(1), 20–36.

Macmillan Publishing Company. (1987). *Connections.* New York: Author.

Madaus, G., & Kellaghan, T. (1993). The British experience with "authentic" testing. *Phi Delta Kappan, 74,* 458–469.

Madden, N. A., Slavin, R. E., Karweit, N. L., Dolan, L., & Wasik, B. A. (1991). Success for all. *Phi Delta Kappan, 72,* 593–599.

Maggs, A., & Maggs, R. (1979). Review of direct instruction research in Australia. *Journal of Special Education Technology,* 2 (3), 26–34.

Maggs, A., & Morath P. (1976). Effects of direct verbal instruction on intellectual development of institutionalized moderately retarded children: A 2 year study. *Journal of Special Education, 10,* 357–364.

Maggs, A., McMillan, K., Patching, W., & Hawke, H. (1981). Accelerating spelling skills using morphographs. *Educational Psychology, 1,* 49–56.

Mahoney, G., & Robenalt, K. (1986). A comparison of conversational patterns between mothers and their Down syndrome and normal infants. *Journal of the Division for Early Childhood, 10,* 172–180.

Mahoney, M. J. (1974). *Cognition and behavior modification.* Cambridge, MA: Ballinger.

Mallory, B. L. (1992). Is it always appropriate to be developmental? Convergent models for early intervention practice. *Topics in Early Childhood Special Education, 11,* 1–12.

Maloney, J. (1994). A call for placement options. *Educational Leadership,* 52(4), 25.

Maloney, K. B., Jacobson, C. R., & Hopkins, B. L. (1975). An analysis of the effects of lectures, requests, teacher praise, and free time on the creative writing behaviors of third-grade children. In E. Ramp & G. Semb (Eds.), *Behavior analysis: Areas of research and application* (pp. 244–260). Englewood Cliffs, NJ: Prentice-Hall.

Maloney, K. B., & Hopkins, B. L. (1973). The modification of sentence structure and its relationship to subjective judgment of creativity in writing. *Journal of Applied Behavior Analysis, 6,* 425–433.

Mann, L. (1971). Psychometric phrenology and the new faculty psychology. *Journal of Special Education, 5,* 3–14.

Mann, L. (1979). *On the trail of process.* New York: Grune & Stratton.

Mann, L., & Phillips, W. (1967). Fractional practices in special education. *Journal of Special Education, 5,* 3–14.

Mannuzza, S., Klein, R. G., Bessler, A., Malloy, P., & Hynes, M. E. (1997). Educational and occupational outcome of hyperactive boys grown up. *Journal of the Academy of Child and Adolescent Psychiatry, 36,* 1222–1227.

Mannuzza, S., Klein, R. G., Bonagura, N., Malloy, P., Giampino, T. L., & Addalli, K. A. (1991). Hyperactive boys almost grown up, V: Replication of psychiatric status. *Archives of General Psychiatry, 48,* 77–83.

Manset, G., & Semmel, M. I. (1997). Are inclusive programs for students with mild disabilities effective? A comparative review of model programs. *Journal of Special Education, 31,* 155–180.

Mantzicopoulos, P. Y., & Morrison, D. (1994). Early prediction of reading achievement: Exploring the relationship of cognitive and noncognitive measures to inaccurate classifications of at-risk status. *Remedial and Special Education, 15,* 244–251.

Margalit, M., & Almougy, K. (1991). Classroom behavior and family climate in students with learning disabilities and hyperactive behavior. *Journal of Learning Disabilities, 24,* 406–412.

Margalit, M., Raviv, A., & Ankonina, D. B. (1992). Coping and coherence among parents with disabled children. *Journal of Clinical Child Psychology, 21,* 202–209.

Margalit, M., & Roth, Y. B. (1989). Strategic keyboard training and spelling improvement among children with learning disabilities and mental retardation. *Educational Psychology, 9,* 321–329.

Markwardt, F. C. (1989). *Peabody Individual Achievement Test—Revised.* Circle Pines, MN: American Guidance Service.

Marsh, G., Friedman, M., Welch, V., & Desberg, P. (1980). The development of strategies in spelling. In U. Frith (Ed.), *Cognitive processes in spelling* (pp. 339–353). New York: Academic Press.

Marston, D. (1987–1988). The effectiveness of special education: A time series analysis of reading performance in regular and special education settings. *Journal of Special Education, 2*(4), 13–26.

Marston, D. (1996). A comparison of inclusion only, pull-out only, and combined service models for students with mild disabilities. *Journal of Special Education, 30,* 121–132.

Martin, J. (1985). *Reclaiming a conversation: The ideal of the educated woman.* New Haven, CT: Yale University Press.

Martin, K. F., & Manno, C. (1995). Use of a check-off system to improve story compositions by middle school students. *Journal of Learning Disabilities, 28,* 139–149.

Massad, V. I., & Etzel, B. C. (1972). Acquisition of phonetic sounds by preschool children: I. Effects of response and reinforcement frequency; II. Effects of tactile differences in discriminative stimuli. In G. Semb (Ed.), *Behavior analysis and education—1972* (pp. 88–111). Lawrence: Department of Human Development, University of Kansas.

Mastropieri, M. A., & Fulk, B. J. M. (1990). Enhancing academic performance with mnemonic instruction. In T. E. Scruggs & B. Y. L. Wong (Eds.), *Intervention research in learning disabilities* (pp. 102–121). New York: Springer-Verlag.

Mastropieri, M. A., & Scruggs, T. E. (1989). Constructing more meaningful relations: Mnemonic instruction for special populations. *Educational Psychology Review, 1* (2), 83–111.

Mastropieri, M. A., & Scruggs. T. E. (1987). *Effective instruction for special education.* Austin, TX: PRO-ED.

Mastropieri, M. A., & Scruggs, T. E. (1994). *Effective instruction for special education* (2nd ed.). Austin ,TX: PRO-ED.

Mastropieri, M. A., Scruggs, T. E., & Whedon, C. (1997). Using mnemonic strategies to teach information about U.S. presidents: A classroom-based investigation. *Learning Disability Quarterly,* 20, 13–21.

Matheny, N., & Panagos, J. M. (1978). Comparing the effects of articulation and syntax programs on syntax and articulation improvement. *Language, Speech, and Hearing Services in Schools, 9,* 57–61.

Mather, N. (1992). Whole language reading instruction for students with learning disabilities: Caught in the cross fire. *Learning Disabilities Research and Practice, 7,* 87–95.

Mather, N., & Roberts, R. (1994). Learning disabilities: A field in danger of extinction? *Learning Disabilities Research & Practice, 9*(1), 49–58.

Mathes, M. Y., & Bender, W. N. (1997). The effects of self-monitoring on children with attention-deficit/hyperactivity disorder. *Remedial and Special Education, 18,* 121–128.

Matson, J., Esveldt-Dawson, K., & Kazdin, A. E. (1982). Treatment of spelling deficits in mentally retarded children. *Mental Retardation, 20,* 76–81.

Mazurek, K., & Winzer, M. A. (Eds.). (1994). *Comparative studies in special education.* Washington, DC: Gallaudet University Press.

McCain, A. P., & Kelley, A. P. (1994). Improving classroom performance in underachieving adolescents: The additive effects of response cost to a school-home note program. *Child and Family Behavior Therapy, 16,* 27–41.

McDonnell, L. M., McLaughlin, M. J., & Morison, P. (Eds.). (1997). *Educating one and all: Students with disabilities and standards-based reform.* Washington, DC: National Academy Press.

McGrady, H. J., Jr. (1968). Language pathology and learning disabilities. In H. R. Myklebust (Ed.), *Progress in learning disabilities* (Vol. 1, pp. 199–233). New York: Grune & Stratton.

McIntyre, T., & Silva, P. (1992). Culturally diverse childrearing practices: Abusive or just different? *Beyond Behavior, 4,* 8–12.

McKinney, J. D. (1983). Contributions of the institutes for research on learning disabilities. *Exceptional Education Quarterly, 4* (1), 129–144.

McKinney, J. D. (1987). Research on conceptually and empirically derived subtypes of specific learning disabilities. In

M. C. Wang, M. C. Reynolds, & H. J. Walberg (Eds.), *Handbook of special education: Research and practice* (pp. 253–281). New York: Pergamon.

McKinney, J. D., Short, E. J., & Feagans, L. (1985). Academic consequences of perceptual-linguistic subtypes of learning disabled children. *Learning Disabilities Research, 1*(1), 6–17.

McKinney, J. D., & Speece, D. L. (1986). Academic consequences and longitudinal stability of behavioral subtypes of learning disabled children. *Journal of Educational Psychology, 78,* 365–372.

McLaughlin, T. F., Reiter, S. M., Mabee, W. S., & Byram, B. J. (1991). An analysis and replication of the Add-A-Word Spelling Program with mildly handicapped middle school students. *Journal of Behavioral Education, 1,* 413–426.

McLean, M. E., & Odom, S. L. (1993). Practices for young children with and without disabilities: A comparison of DEC and NAEYC identified practices. *Topics in Early Childhood Special Education, 13,* 274–292.

McLeod, T. M., & Armstrong, S. W. (1982). Learning disabilities in mathematics: Skill deficits and remedial approaches at the intermediate and secondary level. *Learning Disability Quarterly, 5,* 305–311.

McNaughton, D., Hughes, C. A., & Clark, K. (1994). Spelling instruction for students with learning disabilities: Implications for research and practice. *Learning Disability Quarterly, 17,* 169–185.

McNeill, D. (1966). Developmental psycholinguistics. In F. Smith & G. A. Miller (Eds.), *The genesis of language: A psycholinguistic approach* (pp. 15–84). Cambridge, MA: MIT Press.

McNeill, D. (1970). The development of language. In P. H. Mussen (Ed.), *Carmichael's manual of child psychology* (Vol. 1, 3rd ed., pp. 1061–1161). New York: Wiley.

McNeish, J., Heron, T. E., & Okyere, B. (1992). Effects of self-correction on the spelling performance of junior high school students with learning disabilities. *Journal of Behavioral Education, 2,* 17–27.

McNutt, C. (1984). A holistic approach to language arts instruction in the resource room. *Learning Disability Quarterly, 7,* 315–320.

McNutt, J. C., & Li, J. C.-Y. (1980). Repetition of time-altered sentences by normal and learning disabled children. *Journal of Learning Disabilities, 13,* 25–29.

Mecham, M., Jex, J. L., & Jones, J. D. (1967). *Utah Test of Language Development.* Salt Lake City, UT: Communication Research Associates.

Meichenbaum, D. (1977). *Cognitive-behavior modification: An integrative approach.* New York: Plenum Press.

Meichenbaum, D. (1981, April). Teaching thinking: A cognitive behavioral approach. Paper presented at the meeting of the Society for Learning Disabilities and Remedial Education, New York.

Meichenbaum, D., & Goodman, J. (1971). Training impulsive children to talk to themselves: A means of developing self-control. *Journal of Abnormal Psychology, 77,* 115–126.

Mellard, D. F., & Hazel, J. S. (1992). Social competencies as a pathway to successful life transitions. *Learning Disability Quarterly, 15*(4), 251–271.

Meltzer, L. (1994). Assessment of learning disabilities: The challenge of evaluating the cognitive strategies and processes underlying learning. In G. R. Lyon (Ed.), *Frames of reference for the assessment of learning disabilities: New views on measurement issues* (pp. 571–606). Baltimore: Paul Brooks.

Meltzer, L., & Reid, D. K. (1994). New direction in the assessment of students with special needs: The shift toward a constructivist perspective. *Journal of Special Education, 28,* 338–345.

Menyuk, P. (1972). *The development of speech.* New York: Bobbs-Merrill.

Mercer, C. D., Forgnone, C., & Wolking, W. D. (1976). Definitions of learning disabilities used in the United States. *Journal of Learning Disabilities, 9,* 376–386.

Mercer, C. D., Jordan, L., Allsopp, D. H., & Mercer, A. R. (1996). Learning disabilities definitions and criteria used by state education departments. *Learning Disability Quarterly, 19,* 217–232.

Mersereau, Y., Glover, M., & Cherland, M. (1989). Dancing on the edge. *Language Arts, 66,* 109–117.

Michaels, C. R., & Lewandowski, L. J. (1990). Psychological adjustment and family functioning of boys with learning disabilities. *Journal of Learning Disabilities, 23,* 446–450.

Michaels, R. J. (1987). Evaluating the college of choice. *Academic Therapy, 22*(5), 485–488.

Midgette, R. E. (1995). Assessment of African American exceptional learners: New strategies and perspectives. In B. A. Ford, F. E. Obiakor, & J. M. Patton (Eds.), *Effective education of African American exceptional learners: New perspectives* (pp. 3–25). Austin, TX: PRO-ED.

Miller, S. P., & Mercer, C. D. (1997). Educational aspects of mathematics disabilities. *Journal of Learning Disabilities, 30,* 57–68.

Milner, B. (1974). Hemispheric specialization: Scope and limits. In F. O. Schmitt & F. G. Worden (Eds.), *The neurosciences: Third study program* (pp. 75–89). Cambridge, MA: MIT Press.

Minder, B., Das-Smaal, E. A., Brand, E. F., & Orlebeke, J. F. (1994). Exposure to lead and specific attentional problems in schoolchildren. *Journal of Learning Disabilities, 27*(6), 393–399.

Minke, K. M., & Scott, M. M. (1993). The development of individualized family service plans: Roles for parents and staff. *Journal of Special Education, 27,* 82–106.

Minskoff, E. H., Wiseman, D. E., & Minskoff, J. G. (1972). *The MWM program for developing language abilities.* Ridgefield, NJ: Educational Performance Association.

Mischel, W. (1973). Toward a cognitive social learning reconceptualization of personality. *Psychological Review, 80,* 252–283.

Moats, L. C. (1983). A comparison of the spelling errors of older dyslexic and second-grade normal children. *Annals of Dyslexia, 33,* 121–140.

Moats, L. C. (1995). The missing foundation in teacher education. *American Educator, 19*(2), 9, 43–51.

Moats, L. C., & Lyon, G. R. (1993). Learning disabilities in the United States: Advocacy, science, and the future of the field. *Journal of Learning Disabilities, 26,* 282–294.

Monroe, M. (1932). *Children who cannot read.* Chicago: University of Chicago Press.

Montague, M. (1997). Cognitive strategy instruction in mathematics for students with learning disabilities. *Journal of Learning Disabilities, 30,* 164–177.

Montague, M., & Bos, C. (1986). The effect of cognitive strategy training on verbal math problem solving performance of learning disabled adolescents. *Journal of Learning Disabilities, 19,* 26–33.

Montague, M., & Graves, A. (1993). Improving students' story writing. *Teaching Exceptional Children, 25,* 36–37.

Montague, M., Graves, A., & Leavell, A. (1991). Planning, procedural facilitation, and narrative composition of junior high students with learning disabilities. *Learning Disabilities Research and Practice, 6,* 219–224.

Montague, M., Maddux, C. D., & Dereshiwsky, M. I. (1990). Story grammar and comprehension and production of narrative prose by students with learning disabilities. *Journal of Learning Disabilities, 23,* 190–197.

Morgan, D. P., & Jenson, W. R. (1988). *Teaching behaviorally disordered students.* Columbus, OH: Merrill/Macmillan.

Morningstar, M. E. (1997). Critical issues in career development and employment preparation for adolescents with disabilities. *Remedial and Special Education, 18,* 307–320.

Morris, N. T., & Crump, W. D. (1982). Syntactic and vocabulary development in the written language of learning disabled and non-learning disabled students at four age levels. *Learning Disability Quarterly, 5,* 163–172.

Morris, R. D., Krawiecki, N. S., Wright, J. A., & Walter, L. W. (1993). Neuropsychological, academic, and adaptive functioning in children who survive in-hospital cardiac arrest and resuscitation. *Journal of Learning Disabilities, 26*(1), 46–51.

Morrison, G. M., & Zetlin, A. (1992). Family profiles of adaptability, cohesion, and communication for learning handicapped and nonhandicapped adolescents. *Journal of Youth and Adolescents, 21,* 225–240.

Mosenthal, R. B. (1989). The whole language approach: Teachers between a rock and a hard place. *Reading Teacher, 42,* 628–629.

Murphy, D. M. (1986). The prevalence of handicapping conditions among juvenile delinquents. *Remedial and Special Education,* 7 (3), 7–17.

Murray, C., Goldstein, D. E., & Edgar, E. (1997). The employment and engagement status of high school graduates with learning disabilities through the first decade after graduation. *Learning Disabilities Research and Practice, 12,* 151–160.

Muter, V. (1998). Phonological awareness: Its nature and its influence over early literacy development. In C. Hulme & R. M. Joshi (Eds.), *Reading and spelling: Development and disorders* (pp. 113–125). Mahwah, NJ: Erlbaum.

Muter, V., Snowling, M., & Taylor, S. (1993). Orthographic analogies and phonological awareness: Their role and significance in early reading development. *Journal of Child Psychology and Psychiatry and Allied Disciplines, 35,* 293–310.

Myers, C. A. (1978). Reviewing the literature on Fernald's technique of remedial reading. *Reading Teacher, 31,* 614–619.

Myklebust, H. R. (1965). *Development and disorders of written language: Vol. 1. Picture Story Language Test.* New York: Grune & Stratton.

Myklebust, H. R. (1973). *Development and disorders of written language: Vol. 2. Studies of normal and exceptional children.* New York: Grune & Stratton.

Myklebust, H. R. (1975). Nonverbal learning disabilities: Assessment and intervention. In H. R. Myklebust (Ed.), *Progress in learning disabilities* (Vol. 3, pp. 85–121). New York: Grune & Stratton.

Myklebust, H. R. (Ed.). (1973). *Progress in learning disabilities.* New York: Grune & Stratton.

Myklebust, H. R., Bannochie, M. N., & Killen, J. R. (1971). Learning disabilities and cognitive processes. In H. R. Myklebust (Ed.), *Progress in learning disabilities* (Vol. 2, pp. 213–251). New York: Grune & Stratton.

National Joint Committee on Learning Disabilities. (1988). Letter to NJCLD member organizations.

National Joint Committee on Learning Disabilities. (1993). A reaction to full inclusion: A reaffirmation of the right of students with learning disabilities to a continuum of services. Austin, TX: Author.

National Joint Committee on Learning Disabilities. (1997, February). *Operationalizing the NJCLD definition of learning disabilities for ongoing assessment in schools: A report from the National Joint Committee on Learning Disabilities.* Austin, TX: PRO-ED.

National Research Council. (1998, March 18). *Preventing reading difficulties in young children.* Washington, DC: National Academy of Sciences (online). Available at http://www2.nas.edu/whatsnew/286a.html.

Neal, C. (1984). The holistic teacher. *Learning Disability Quarterly, 7,* 309–313.

Neef, N., Iwata, B., & Bailey, J. (1977). The effects of known-item interspersal on acquisition and retention of spelling and sightreading words. *Journal of Applied Behavior Analysis, 10,* 738.

Neef, N. A., Shade, D., & Miller, M. S. (1994). Assessing influential dimensions of reinforcers on choice in students with serious emotional disturbance. *Journal of Applied Behavior Analysis, 27,* 575–583.

Neisworth, J. T., & Bagnato, S. J. (1992). The case against intelligence testing in early intervention. *Topics in Early Childhood Special Education, 12,* 1–20.

Nelson, H. E. (1980). Analysis of spelling errors in normal and dyslexic children. In U. Frith (Ed.), *Cognitive process in spelling* (pp. 475–493). London: Academic Press.

Nelson, J. R., Roberts, M., Mather, S., & Rutherford, R. J. (in press). Has public policy exceeded our knowledge base? A review of the functional behavioral assessment literature. *Behavioral Disorders.*

Nelson, N. W. (1998). *Childhood language disorders in context: Infancy through adolescence* (3rd ed). Boston: Allyn & Bacon.

Nelson. N. W. (1993). *Childhood language disorders in context: Infancy through adolescence.* New York: Macmillan.

Newcomer, P. L., & Hammill, D. D. (1977). *Test of Language Development.* Austin, TX: PRO-ED.

Newcomer, P. L., & Hammill, D. D. (1988). *Test of Language Development—2, Primary.* Austin, TX: PRO-ED.

Nicholson, T. (1991). Do children read words better in context or in lists? A classic study revisited. *Journal of Educational Psychology 83,* 444–450.

Noel, M. M. (1980). Referential communication abilities of learning disabled children. *Learning Disability Quarterly, 3* (3), 70–87.

Norman, C., & Zigmond, N. (1980). Characteristics of children labeled and served as learning disabled in school systems affiliated with child service and demonstration centers. *Journal of Learning Disabilities, 13,* 542–547.

Obrzut, J. E., & Bolick, C. A. (1991). Neuropsychological assessment of childhood learning disabilities. In H. L. Swanson (Ed.), *Handbook on the assessment of learning disabilities* (pp. 121–145). Austin, TX: PRO-ED.

Ochoa, S. H., Rivera, B. D., & Ford, L. (1997). An investigation of school psychology training pertaining to bilingual psycho-educational assessment of primarily Hispanic students: Twenty-five years after Diana v. California. *Journal of School Psychology, 35,* 329–349.

Ochoa, S. H., Rivera, B. D., & Powell, M. P. (1997). Factors used to comply with the exclusionary clause with bilingual and limited-English-proficient pupils: Initial guidelines. *Learning Disabilities Research and Practice, 12,* 161–167.

O'Connor, R. E., Jenkins, J. R., & Slocum, T. A. (1995). Transfer among phonological tasks in kindergarten: Essential instructional content. *Journal of Educational Psychology, 57,* 202–217.

O'Connor, R. E., Notari-Syverson, A., & Vadasy, P. F. (1996). Ladders to literacy: The effects of teacher-led phonological activities for kindergarten children with and without disabilities. *Exceptional Children, 63,* 117–130.

O'Hare, F. (1973). *Sentence-combining: Improving student writing without formal grammar instruction.* Urbana, IL: National Council of Teachers of English.

Okolo, C., Rieth, H. J., & Bahr, C. (1989). Microcomputer use in secondary special education: Special education teachers', administrators', and students' perspectives. *Journal of Special Education, 23,* 107–117.

Ollendick, T., Matson, J., Esveldt-Dawson, K., & Shapiro, T. (1980). Increasing spelling achievement: An analysis of treatment procedures utilizing an alternating treatments design. *Journal of Applied Behavior Analysis, 13,* 645–654.

Ollendick, T. H., & Hersen, M. (Eds.). (1984). *Child behavioral assessment: Principles and procedures.* New York: Pergamon.

Olson, R., Wise, B., Conners, F., Rack, J., & Fulker, D. (1989). Specific deficits in component reading and language skills: Genetic and environmental influences. *Journal of Learning Disabilities, 22,* 339–348.

Olympia, D. E., Sheridan, S. M., Jenson, W. R., & Andrews, D. (1994). Using student-managed interventions to increase homework completion and accuracy. *Journal of Applied Behavior Analysis, 27,* 85–99.

Open Court. (1989). *Open Court reading and writing.* LaSalle, IL: Author.

Opp, G. (1994). Historical roots of the field of learning disabilities: Some nineteenth-century German contributions. *Journal of Learning Disabilities,* 27, 10–19.

Ortiz, A. A. (1997). Learning disabilities occurring concomitantly with linguistic differences. *Journal of Learning Disabilities, 30,* 321–332.

Orton, S. T. (1937). *Reading, writing and speech problems in children.* New York: Norton.

Osborne, A. G. (1997). *Legal issues in special education.* Boston: Allyn & Bacon.

Osborne, S. S., Schulte, A. C., & McKinney, J. D. (1991). A longitudinal study of students with learning disabilities in mainstream and resource programs. *Exceptionality, 2,* 81–95.

Osgood, C. E. (1957a). A behavioristic analysis. In J. Bruner (Ed.), *Contemporary approaches to cognition* (pp. 75–117). Cambridge, MA: Harvard University Press.

Osgood, C. E. (1957b). Motivational dynamics of language behavior. In M. R. Jones (Ed.), *Nebraska symposium on motivation* (Vol. 5, pp. 348–424). Lincoln: University of Nebraska Press.

Outhred, L. (1989). Word processing: Its impact on children's writing. *Journal of Learning Disabilities, 22,* 262–263.

Overton, T. (1996). *Assessment in special education: An applied approach* (2nd ed.). Englewood Cliffs, NJ: Prentice-Hall.

Owens, R. E. (1988). *Language development: An introduction.* Columbus, OH: Merrill.

Palinscar, A. S. (1986). Metacognitive strategy instruction. *Exceptional Children, 53,* 118–124.

Palinscar, A. S., & Brown, A. L. (1984). The reciprocal teaching of comprehension fostering and comprehension monitoring activities. *Cognition and Instruction, 1,* 117–175.

Palinscar, A. S., Brown, A. L., & Campione, J. C. (1991). Dynamic assessment. In H. L. Swanson (Ed.), *Handbook on the assessment of learning disabilities* (pp. 75–94). Austin, TX: PRO-ED.

Palincsar, A. S., & Klenk, L. (1992). Fostering literacy learning in supportive contexts. *Journal of Learning Disabilities, 2,* 211–225.

Palincsar, A. S., & Klenk, L. (1993). Broader vision encompassing literacy, learners, and contexts. *Remedial and Special Education, 14,* 19–25.

Paris, S. G., Cross, D. R., & Lipson, M. Y. (1984). Informed strategies for learning: A program to improve children's reading awareness and comprehension. *Journal of Educational Psychology, 72,* 250–256.

Paris, S. G., & Myers, M. (1981). Comprehension monitoring, memory, and study strategies of good and poor readers. *Journal of Reading Behavior, 13,* 5–22.

Parker, R., Tindal, G., & Hasbrouck, J. (1991). Progress monitoring with objective measures of writing performance for students with mild disabilities. *Exceptional Children, 58,* 61–73.

Parmar, R. S., Deluca, C. B., & Janczak, T. M. (1994). Investigations into the relationship between science and language abilities of students with mild disabilities. *Remedial and Special Education, 15* (2), 117–126.

Parsons, J. A. (1972). The reciprocal modification of arithmetic behavior and program development. In G. Semb (Ed.), *Behavior analysis and education—1972* (pp. 185–199). Lawrence: Department of Human Development, University of Kansas.

Pascarella, E. T., & Pflaum, S. W. (1981). The interaction of children's attribution and level of control over error correction in reading instruction. *Journal of Educational Psychology, 73,* 533–540.

Patton, J. (1998). The disproportionate representation of African Americans in special education: Looking behind the curtain for understandings and solutions. *Journal of Special Education, 32,* 25–31.

Pauls, D. L., Leckman, J. F., & Cohen, D. J. (1993). Familial relationship between Gilles de la Tourette's syndrome, attention deficit disorder, learning disabilities, speech disorders, and stuttering. *Journal of the American Academy of Child Adolescent Psychiatry,* 32(5), 1044–1050.

Pearl, R. (1987). Social cognitive factors in learning-disabled children's social problems. In S. J. Ceci (Ed.), *Handbook of cognitive, social, and neuropsychological aspects of learning disabilities.* Mahwah, NJ: Erlbaum.

Pearl, R., & Bay, M. (in press). Psychosocial correlates of learning disabilities. In D. H. Saklofske & V. L. Schwean (Eds.), *Handbook of psychosocial characteristics of exceptional children.* New York: Plenum.

Pearl, R., Donahue, M., & Bryan, T. (1985). The development of tact: Children's strategies for delivering bad news. *Journal of Applied Developmental Psychology, 6,* 141–149.

Pelham, W. E. (1981). Attention deficits in hyperactive and learning-disabled children. *Exceptional Education Quarterly,* 2(3), 13–23.

Pennington, B. F. (1990). Annotation: The genetics of dyslexia. *Journal of Child Psychology and Child Psychiatry, 31*(2), 193–201.

Pennington, B. F. (1995). Genetics of learning disabilities. *Journal of Child Neurology, 10* (Suppl. No. 1), S69-S77.

Pennington, B. F., Gilger, J. W., Olson, R. K., & DeFries, J. C. (1992). The external validity of age-versus-IQ-discrepant definitions of reading disability: Lessons from a twin study. *Journal of Learning Disabilities, 25*(9), 562–573.

Perfetti, C. A. (1991). Representations and awareness in the acquisition of reading competence. In L. Rieben & C. A. Perfetti (Eds.), *Learning to read: Basic research and its implications* (pp. 33–44). Hillsdale, NJ: Erlbaum.

Perfetti, C. A., & Hogoboam, T. (1975). Relationship between single word decoding and reading comprehension skill. *Journal of Educational Psychology, 67,* 461–469.

Perkins, V. L., & Cullinan, D. (1984). Effects of direct instruction intervention for fraction skills. *Education and Treatment of Children, 7,* 109–117.

Petty, W. T. (1978). The writing of young children. In C. R. Cooper & L. Odell (Eds.), *Research on composing: Points of departure* (pp. 73–83). Urbana, IL: National Council of Teachers of English.

Petty, W. T., & Bowen, M. E. (1967). *Slithery snakes and other aids to children's writing.* New York: Appleton-Century-Crofts.

Pfiffner, L. J., & O'Leary, S. G. (1987). The efficacy of all positive management as a function of the prior use of negative consequences. *Journal of Applied Behavior Analysis, 20,* 265–271.

Pfiffner, L. J., Rosen, I. A., & O'Leary, S. G. (1985). The efficacy of an all-positive approach to classroom management. *Journal of Applied Behavior Analysis, 18,* 257–261.

Pflaum, S. W., & Bryan, F. H. (1981). Oral reading behaviors in the learning disabled. *Journal of Educational Research, 73,* 252–258.

Pflaum, S. W., & Pascarella, E. T. (1980). Interactive effects of prior reading achievement and training in context on the reading of learning disabled children. *Reading Research Quarterly, 16,* 138–158.

Pflaum, S. W., Walberg, H. J., Karegianes, M. L., & Rasher, S. R. (1980). Reading instruction: A quantitative synthesis. *Educational Researcher, 9,* 12–18.

Phillips, P. (1990). A self-advocacy plan for high school students with learning disabilities: A comparative case study analysis of students', teachers', and parents' perceptions of program effects. *Journal of Learning Disabilities,* 23(8), 466–471.

Piaget, J. (1952). *The shields conception of number.* New York: Norton. (Original work published 1941)

Piaget, J. (1970). *Structuralism.* New York: Basic Books.

Piaget, J., & Inhelder, B. (1969a). *Memory and intelligence.* New York: Basic Books.

Piaget, J., & Inhelder, B. (1969b). *The psychology of the child.* New York: Basic Books.

Pinel, J. P. J. (1993). *Biopsychology* (2nd ed.). Boston: Allyn & Bacon.

Pinnell, G. S. (1989). Reading recovery: Helping at-risk children learn to read. *Elementary School Journal, 90,* 159–181.

Pinnell, G. S. (1990). Success for low achievers through reading recovery. *Educational Leadership, 48*(1), 17–21.

Polkinghorne, D. (1983). *Methodology for the human sciences systems of inquiry.* Albany: State University of New York Press.

Polloway, E. J., Epstein, M. H., Polloway, C., Patton, J., & Ball, D. (1986). Corrective Reading Program: An analysis of effectiveness with learning disabled and mentally retarded students. *Remedial and Special Education, 7,* 41–47.

Polloway, E. J., Foley, R. M., & Epstein, M. H. (1992). A comparison of the homework problems of students with learning disabilities and nonhandicapped students. *Learning Disabilities Research and Practice, 7,* 203–209.

Poplin, M. S. (1984). Toward an holistic view of persons with learning disabilities. *Learning Disability Quarterly, 7,* 290–294.

Poplin, M. S. (1988a). Holistic/constructivist principles of the teaching/learning process: Implications for the field of learning disabilities. *Journal of Learning Disabilities, 21,* 401–416.

Poplin, M. S. (1988b). The reductionist fallacy in learning disabilities: Replicating the past by reducing the present. *Journal of Learning Disabilities, 21,* 389–400.

Poplin, M. S., Gray, R., Larsen, S., Banikowski, A., & Mehring, R. (1980). A comparison of components of written expression abilities in learning disabled and non-learning disabled students at three grade levels. *Learning Disability Quarterly,* 3(4), 46–53.

Poteet, J. A. (1980). Informal assessment of written expression. *Learning Disability Quarterly,* 3(4), 88–98.

Poteet, J. A., Choate, J. S., & Stewart, S. C. (1993). Performance assessment and special education: Practices and prospects. *Focus on Exceptional Children, 26*(1), 1–20.

Potts, M., & Savino, C. (1968). The relative achievement of first graders under three different reading programs. *Journal of Educational Research, 61,* 447–450.

Powell, S., & Nelson, B. (1997). Effects of choosing academic assignments on a student with attention deficit hyperactivity disorder. *Journal of Applied Behavior Analysis, 30,* 181–183.

Prater, M. A., Joy, R., Chilman, B., Temple, J., & Miller, S. R. (1991). Self-monitoring of on-task behavior by adolescents with learning disabilities. *Learning Disability Quarterly, 14,* 164–177.

Pratt-Struthers, J., Struthers, L., & Williams, R. L. (1983). The effects of the Add-A-Word Spelling Program on spelling accuracy during creative writing. *Education and Treatment of Children, 6,* 277–283.

Prescott, G. A., Balow, I. H., Hogan, T. R., & Farr, R. C. (1992). *Metropolitan Achievement Tests—7th Edition Survey Battery.* New York: Harcourt Brace Jovanovich.

Pressley, M., Hogan, K., Wharton-McDonald, R., Mistretta, J., & Ettenberger, S. (1996). The challenges of instructional scaffolding: The challenges of instruction that supports student thinking. *Learning Disabilities Research and Practice, 11,* 138–146.

Pressley, M., & Rankin, J. (1994). More about whole language methods of reading instruction for students at risk for early reading failure. *Learning Disabilities Research and Practice, 9,* 157–168.

Pressley, M., Symons, S., Snyder, B. L., & Cariglia-Bull, T. (1989). Strategy instruction comes of age. *Learning Disability Quarterly, 12,* 16–30.

Proff, J. (1978). *Speed spelling.* Tigard, OR: C. C. Publications.

Psychological Corporation. (1992). *Weschler Individual Achievement Test.* San Antonio, TX: Harcourt Brace Jovanovich.

Ramey, S. L., & Ramey, C. T (1994). The transition to school: Why the first few years matter for a lifetime. *Phi Delta Kappan, 76,* 194–198.

Rashotte, C. A., & Torgesen, J. K. (1985). Repeated reading and reading fluency in learning disabled children. *Reading Research Quarterly, 20,* 180–188.

Raskind, M. (1993). Assistive technology and adults with learning disabilities: A blueprint for exploration and advancement. *Learning Disability Quarterly, 16*(3), 185–196.

Read, C. (1971). Pre-school children's knowledge of English phonology. *Harvard Educational Review, 41,* 1–34.

Reid, D. K. (1991). Assessment strategies inspired by genetic epistemology. In H. L. Swanson (Ed.), *Handbook on the assessment of learning disabilities: Theory, research, and practice* (pp. 249–263). Austin, TX: PRO-ED.

Reid, D. K. (1993). Another vision of "visions and revisions." *Remedial and Special Education, 14,* 14–16.

Reid, D. K., & Hresko, W. P. (1981). *A cogntive approach to learning disabilities.* New York: McGraw-Hill.

Reid, D. K., Hresko, W. P., & Swanson, H. L. (Eds.) (1996). *Cognitive approaches to learning disabilities* (3rd ed.). Austin, TX: PRO-ED.

Reid, D. K., Knight-Arest, I., & Hresko, W. P. (1981). Cognitive development in learning disabled children. In J. Gottlieb & S. S. Strichart (Eds.), *Developmental theory and research in learning disabilities* (pp. 169–212). Baltimore: University Park Press.

Reid, R. (1996). Research in self-monitoring with students with learning disabilities: The present, the prospects, the pitfalls. *Journal of Learning Disabilities, 29,* 317–331.

Reiff, H. B., Gerber, P. J., & Ginsberg, R. (1993). Definitions of learning disabilities from adults with learning disabilities: The insiders' perspectives. *Learning Disability Quarterly, 16*(2), 114–125.

Reiff, H. B., Gerber, P. J., & Ginsberg, R. (1997). *Exceeding expectations: Successful adults with learning disabilities.* Austin,TX: PRO-ED.

Reis, S. M., Neu, T. W., & McGuire, J. M. (1997). Case studies of high-ability students with learning disabilities who have achieved. *Exceptional Children, 63,* 463–479.

Resnick, L. B. (1970). Relations between perceptual and syntactic control in oral reading. *Journal of Educational Psychology, 61,* 382–385.

Resnick, L. B. (1983). A developmental theory of number understanding. In H. P. Ginsburg (Ed.), *The development of mathematical thinking* (pp. 110–151). New York: Academic Press.

Resnick, L. B. (1988). Teaching mathematics as an ill-structured discipline. In R. I. Charles & E. A. Silver (Eds.), *The teaching and assessment of mathematical problem solving* (pp. 288–315). Hillsdale, NJ: Erlbaum.

Resnick, L. B., & Ford, W. W. (1981). *The psychology of mathematics for instruction.* Hillsdale, NJ: Erlbaum.

Reutzel, D. R., & Hollingsworth. R. M. (1988). Whole language and the practitioner. *Academic Therapy, 23,* 405–416.

Reynolds, C. A., Hewitt, J. K., Erickson, M. T., Silberg, J. L., Rutter, M., Simonoff, E., Meyer, J., & Eaves, L. J. (1996). The genetics of children's oral reading performance. *Journal of Child Psychology & Psychiatry & Allied Disciplines, 37,* 425–434.

Rhode, G., Jenson, W. R., & Reavis, H. K. (1992). *The tough kid book: Practical classroom management strategies.* Longmont, CO: Sopris West.

Riccio, C. A., Gonzalez, J. J., & Hynd, G. W (1994). Attention-deficit hyperactivity disorder (ADHD) and learning disabilities. *Learning Disability Quarterly, 17,* 311–322.

Rice, M. L., & Wexler, K. (1996). Toward tense as a clinical marker of specific language impairment in English-speaking children. *Journal of Speech and Hearing Research, 39,* 1239–1257.

Rich, S. J. (1985). Restoring power to teachers: The impact of "whole language." *Language Arts, 62,* 717–724.

Richards, J. C., Gipe, J. R., & Thompson, B. (1987). Teachers' beliefs about good reading instruction. *Reading Psychology, 8,* 1–6.

Richardson, E., DiBenedetto, B., & Bradley, C. M. (1977). The relationship of sound blending to reading achievement. *Review of Educational Research, 47,* 319–334.

Richardson, E., DiBenedetto, B., Christ, A., & Press, M. (1980). Relationship of auditory and visual skills to reading retardation. *Journal of Learning Disabilities, 13,* 77–82.

Richardson, S. O. (1992). Historical perspectives on dyslexia. *Journal of Learning Disabilities, 25,* 40–47.

Richgels, D. J. (1995). Invented spelling ability and printed word learning in kindergarten. *Reading Research Quarterly, 30,* 96–109.

Rieth, H. J., Axelrod, J., Anderson, R., Hathaway, F., Wood, K., & Fitzgerald, C. (1974). Influence of distributed practice and daily testing on weekly spelling tests. *Journal of Educational Research, 68*(2), 73–77.

Rieth, H. J., Bahr, C., Polsgrove, L., Okolo, C., & Eckert, I. R. (1987). The effects of microcomputers on the secondary special education classroom ecology. *Journal of Special Education Technology, 8*(4), 36–45.

Rieth, H. J., & Semmel, M. I. (1991). Use of computer assisted instruction in the regular classroom. In G. Stoner, M. R. Shinn, & H. M. Walker (Eds.), *Interventions for achievement and behavior problems in regular class settings* (pp. 215–239). Stratford, CT: National Association of School Psychologists.

Rivera, D., & Smith, D. D. (1988). Using a demonstration strategy to teach learning disabled midschool students how to compute long division. *Journal of Learning Disabilities, 21,* 77–81.

Rivera, D., & Smith, D. D. (1987). Influence of modeling on acquisition and maintenance of computational skills A summary of research findings from three sites. *Learning Disability Quarterly, 10,* 69–80.

Roach, E., & Kephart, N. C. (1966). *Pardue perceptual motor survey.* Columbus, OH: Merrill.

Robbins, M., & Glass, G. V. (1969). The Doman-Delacato rationale: A critical analysis. In J. Hellmuth (Ed.), *Educational therapy,* Vol. 2). Seattle, WA: Special Child Publications.

Roberts, M., & Smith, D. D. (1980). The relationship among correct and error oral reading rates and comprehension. *Learning Disability Quarterly,* 3(1), 54–64.

Robin, A. L., Armel, S., & O'Leary, K. D. (1975). The effects of self-instruction on writing deficiencies. *Behavior Therapy, 6,* 178–197.

Robinson, P. W., Newby, T. J., & Ganzell, S. L. (1981). A token system for a class of underachieving hyperactive children. *Journal of Applied Behavior Analysis, 14,* 307–315.

Roffman, A. J., Herzog, J. E., & Wershba-Gershon, P. M. (1994). Helping young adults understand their learning disabilities. *Journal of Learning Disabilities,* 27(7), 413–419.

Rooney, K. (1988). Independent strategies for efficient study. Richmond, VA: J. R. Enterprises.

Rose, T. L. (1984a). Effects of previewing on the oral reading of mainstreamed behaviorally disordered students. *Behavioral Disorders, 10,* 33–39.

Rose, T. L. (1984b) The effects of previewing on retarded learners' oral reading. *Education and Training of the Mentally Retarded, 19,* 49-53.

Rose, T. L. (1984c). The effects of two prepractice procedures on oral reading. *Journal of Learning Disabilities, 17,* 544–548.

Rose, T. L., & Beattie, J. R. (1986). Relative effects of teacher-directed and taped previewing on oral reading. *Learning Disability Quarterly, 9,* 193–199.

Rose, T. L., & Sherry, L. (1984). Relative effects of two previewing procedures on the oral reading performance of learning disabled adolescents. *Learning Disability Quarterly, 7,* 39–44.

Rosenberg, M. S. (1989). The effects of daily homework assignments on the acquisition of basic skills by students with learning disabilities. *Journal of Learning Disabilities, 22,* 314–323.

Rosenberg, M. S. (1997). Learning disabilities occurring concomitantly with other disability and exceptional conditions: Introduction to the series. *Journal of Learning Disabilities, 30,* 242–244.

Rosenshine, B. (1976). Classroom instruction. In N. L. Gage (Ed.), *The psychology of teaching methods: The 75th yearbook of the National Society for the Study of Education* (pp. 335–371). Chicago: University of Chicago Press.

Rosenshine, B. (1997). Advances in research on instruction. In J. W. Lloyd, E. J. Kameenui, & D. Chard (Eds.), *Issues in educating students with disabilities* (pp. 197–220). Mahwah, NJ: Erlbaum.

Rosenshine, B., & Stevens, R. (1986). Teaching functions. In M. C. Wittrock (Ed.), *Handbook of research on teaching* (3rd ed., pp. 376–391). New York: Macmillan.

Rosenthal, D. J., & Resnick, L. B. (1974). Children's solution processes in arithmetic word problems. *Journal of Educational Psychology, 66,* 817–825.

Rosenzweig, M. R. (1966). Environmental complexity, cerebral change, and behavior. *American Psychologist, 21,* 321–332.

Ross, G., Lipper, E. G., & Auld, P. A. M. (1991). Educational status and school-related abilities of very low birth weight premature children. *Pediatrics, 88*(6), 1125–1134.

Roswell, F. G., & Chall, J. C. (1978). *Roswell-Chall Diagnostic Reading Test of Word Analysis Skills* (rev. ed.). New York: Essay Press.

Rourke, B. P. (1989). *Nonverbal learning disabilities: The syndrome and the model.* New York: Guilford.

Rourke, B. P. (Ed.). (1995). *Syndrome of non-verbal learning disabilities: Neurodevelopmental manifestations.* New York: Guilford.

Rourke, B. P., & Conway, J. A. (1997). Disabilities of arithmetic and mathematical reasoning: Perspectives from neurology and neuropsychology. *Journal of Learning Disabilities, 30,* 34–46.

Rourke, B. P., & Tsatsanis, K. D. (1996). Syndrome of nonverbal learning disabilities: Psycholinguistic assets and deficits. *Topics in Language Disorders, 16*(2), 30–44.

Rourke, B. P., Young, G. C., & Leenaars, A. A. (1989). A childhood learning disability that predisposes those afflicted to adolescent and adult depression and suicide risk. *Journal of Learning Disabilities, 22*(3), 169–175.

Rous, B., Hemmeter, M. L., & Schuster, J. (1994). Sequenced transition to education in the public schools: A systems approach to transition planning. *Topics in Early Childhood Special Education, 14,* 374–393.

Rovet, J. F., Ehrlich, R. M., Czuchta, D., & Akler, M. (1993). Psychoeducational characteristics of children and adolescents with insulin-dependent diabetes mellitus. *Journal of Learning Disabilities, 26*(1), 7–22.

Rozin, P., & Gleitman, L. R. (1977). The structure and acquisition of Reading 11: The reading process and the acquisition of the alphabetic principle. In A. S. Reber & D. L. Scarborough (Eds.), *Toward a psychology of reading: The proceedings of the CUNY conferences* (pp. 55–141). Hillsdale, NJ: Erlbaum.

Rubin, H., & Eberhardt, N. C., (1996). Facilitating invented spelling through language analysis instruction: An integrated model. *Reading and Writing: An Interdisciplinary Journal, 8,* 27–43.

Rueckl, J. B., & Dror, I. E. (1994). The effect of orthographic-semantic systematicity on the acquisition of new words. In C. Umilta & M. Moscovitch (Eds.), *Attention and performance: Vol. 15. Conscious and nonconscious information processing* (pp. 571–588). Cambridge, MA: MIT Press.

Rusch, F. R., & Hughes, C. (1990). Historical overview of supported employment. In F. R. Rusch (Ed.), *Supported employment: Models, methods, and issues* (pp. 5–14). Sycamore, IL: Sycamore Publishing.

Rusch, F. R., Rose, T., & Greenwood, C. R. (1988). *Introduction to behavior analysis in special education.* Englewood Cliffs, NJ: Prentice-Hall.

Sabatino, D. A. (1973). Auditory perception: Development, assessment, and intervention. In L. Mann & D. A. Sabatino (Eds.), *First review of special education* (Vol. 1, pp. 49–82). Philadelphia: JSE Press.

Sachs, J. (1989). Communication development in infancy. In J. Gleason (Ed.), *The development of language* (pp. 35–58). Columbus, OH: Merrill.

Sah, A., & Borland, J. (1989). The effects of a structured home plan on the home and school behaviors of gifted learning-disabled students with deficits in organizational skills. *Roeper Review, 12,* 54–57.

Sainato, D. M., & Strain, P. S. (1993). Increasing integration success for preschoolers with disabilities. *Teaching Exceptional Children,* 25(2), 36–37.

Saint-Laurent, L., Glasson, J., & Couture, C. (1997). Parents + children + reading activities = emergent literacy. *Teaching Exceptional Children,* 30(2), 52–56.

Salend, S. J., & Schliff, J. (1989). An examination of the homework practices of teachers of students with learning disabilities. *Journal of Learning Disabilities, 22,* 621–623.

Salend, S. J., & Nowack, M. R. (1988). Effects of peer previewing on LD students' oral reading skills. *Learning Disability Quarterly, 11,* 47–52.

Salend, S. J., & Taylor, L. (1993). Working with families: A cross-cultural perspective. *Remedial and Special Education, 14*(5), 25–32, 39.

Salvia, J., & Hughes, C. A. (1990). *Curriculum-based assessment: Testing what is taught.* New York: Macmillan.

Salvia, J., & Ysseldyke, J. E. (1991). *Assessment* (5th ed.). Boston: Houghton Mifflin.

Salvia, J., & Ysseldyke, J. E. (1998). *Assessment* (7th ed.). Boston: Houghton Mifflin.

Sameroff, A., & McDonough, S. C. (1994). Educational implications of developmental transitions: Revisiting the 5- to 7-year shift. *Phi Delta Kappan, 76,* 188–193.

Samuels, S. J. (1979). The method of repeated readings. *Reading Teacher, 32,* 403–408.

Samuels, S. J. (1981). Some essentials of decoding. *Exceptional Education Quarterly,* 2(1), 11–25.

Sapona, R. H., Lloyd, J. W., & Wissick, C. A. (1986). Microcomputer use in resource rooms with learning-disabled children. *Computers in the Schools,* 2(4), 51–59.

Sarason, S. B. (1949). Psychological problems in mental deficiency. New York: Harper.

Satz, P., & Fletcher, J. M. (1988). Early identification of learning disabled children: An old problem revisited. *Journal of Consulting and Clinical Psychology, 56,* 824–829.

Satz, P., & Morris, R. (1980). Learning disability subtypes: A review. In F. Pirozzolo & M. Wittrock (Eds.), *Neuropsychological and cognitive processes in reading* (pp. 109–141). New York: Academic Press.

Sawyer, D. J. (1987). *Test of awareness of language segments.* Frederick, MD: Aspen.

Sawyer, V., Nelson, J. S., Jayanthi, M., Bursuck, W. D., & Epstein, M. H. (1996). Views of students with learning disabilities of their homework in general education classes: Student interviews. *Learning Disability Quarterly, 19,* 70–85.

Scannell, D. P., Haugh, O. M., Schild, A. H., & Ulmer, G. (1978). *Tests of Achievement and Proficiency.* Boston: Houghton Mifflin.

Schrag, P., & Divoky, D. (1975). *The myth of the hyperactive child.* New York: Pantheon.

Schulte, A. C., Osborne, S. S., & Kauffman, J. M. (1993). Teacher responses to two types of consultative special education services. *Journal of Educational and Psychological Consultation, 4,* 1–27.

Schulte-Korne, G., Deimel, W., Muller, K., Gutenbrunner, C., & Remschmidt, H. (1996). Familial aggregation of spelling disability. *Journal of Child Psychology and Psychiatry, 37,* 817–822.

Schulz, E. (1994, October 5). Beyond behaviorism. *Education Week,* pp. 19–21, 24.

Schulz, J. B. (1987). *Parents and professionals in education.* Boston: Allyn & Bacon.

Schumm, J. S. (1992). Using story grammar with at-risk high school students. *Journal of Reading,* 35, 296.

Schumm, J. S., & Vaughn, S. (1992). Planning for mainstreamed special education students: Perceptions of general classroom teachers. *Exceptionality,* 3, 81–98.

Schumm, J. S., Vaughn, S., Gordon, J., & Rothlein, L. (1994). General education teachers' beliefs, skills, and practices in planning for mainstreamed students with learning disabilities. *Teacher Education and Special Education, 17,* 22–37.

Scott, Foresman. (1993). *Celebrate reading.* Glenview, IL: Author.

Scott, Foresman. (1991). *Exploring mathematics.* Glenview, IL: Author.

Scott, S. (1994). Determining reasonable academic adjustments for college students with learning disabilities. *Journal of Learning Disabilities, 27*(7), 403–412.

Scruggs, T. E., & Mastropieri, M. A. (1992). Classroom applications of mnemonic instruction: Acquisition, maintenance, and generalization. *Exceptional Children, 58,* 219–229.

Seabaugh, G. O., & Schumaker, J. B. (1993). The effects of self-regulation training on the academic productivity of secondary students with learning disabilities. *Journal of Behavioral Education, 4,* 109–133.

Sealey, L., Sealey, N., & Millmore, M. (1979). *Children's writing: An approach for the primary grades.* Newark, DE: International Reading Association.

Sedlak, R., & Weiner, P. (1973). Review of research on the Illinois Test of Psycholinguistic Abilities. In L. Mann & D. A. Sabatino (Eds.), *First review of special education* (Vol. 1, pp. 113–163). Philadelphia: Buttonwood Farms.

Seidenberg, P. L. (1997). Understanding learning disabilities. In D. K. Bernstein & E. Tiegerman-Farber (Eds.), *Language and communication disorders in children* (4th ed., pp. 411–456). Boston: Allyn & Bacon.

Seifert, E. P. (1960). Personal styles of handwriting in grades 6, 7, 8, and 9. *Dissertation Abstracts International, 20*(9), 3581–3582.

Seligman, M., & Darling, R. B. (1989). *Ordinary families, special children: A systems approach to childhood disability.* New York: Guilford.

Seligman, M. E. (1992). *Helplessness: On depression, development and death.* San Francisco: Freeman.

Semel, E. (1970). *Sound-order-sense* (Levels 1–2). Chicago: Follett.

Semel, E. (1976). *Semel auditory processing program.* Chicago: Follett.

Semel, E. M., & Wiig, E. H. (1975). Comprehension of syntactic structures and critical verbal elements by children with learning disabilities. *Journal of Learning Disabilities, 8,* 46–51.

Semel, E. M., & Wiig, E. H. (1981). Semel Auditory Processing Program training effects among children with language-learning disabilities. *Journal of Learning Disabilities, 14,* 192–197.

Semmel, M. I., Gerber, M. M., & MacMillan, D. L. (1994). Twenty-five years after Dunn's article: A legacy of policy analysis research in special education. *Journal of Special Education, 27,* 481–495.

Semrud-Clikeman, M., & Hynd, G. W. (1990). Right hemispheric dysfunction in nonverbal learning disabilities: Social, academic, and adaptive functioning in adults and children. *Psychological Bulletin, 107*(2), 196–209.

Senapati, R., & Hayes, A. (1988). Sibling relationships of handicapped children: A review of conceptual and methodological issues. International *Journal of Behavioral Development, 11,* 89–115.

Shanahan, T., & Barr, R. (1995). Reading recovery: An independent evaluation of the effects of an early instructional intervention for at-risk learners. *Reading Research Quarterly, 30,* 958–996.

Shatz, M., & Gelman, R. (1973). The development of communication skills: Modifications in the speech of young children as a function of the listener. *Monographs of the Society for Research in Child Development, 38* (5, Serial No. 152).

Shaw, S. F., McGuire, J. M., & Brinckerhoff, L. C. (1994). College and university programming. In P. J. Gerber & H. B. Reiff (Eds.), *Learning disabilities in adulthood: Persisting problems and evolving issues* (pp. 141–151). Boston: Andover Medical Publishers.

Shaywitz, B. A., Fletcher, J. M., & Shaywitz, S. E. (1995). Defining and classifying learning disabilities and attention-deficit/hyperactivity disorder. *Journal of Child Neurology, 10* (Supplement), S50-S57.

Shaywitz, S. E., & Shaywitz, B. A. (1987). Attention deficit disorder: Current perspectives. Paper presented at the National Conference on Learning Disabilities, National Institute of Child Health and Human Development (NIH), Bethesda, MD.

Shaywitz, S. E., Shaywitz, B. A., Fletcher, J. M., & Escobar, M. D. (1990). Prevalence of reading disabilities in boys and girls: Results of the Connecticut Longitudinal Study. *Journal of the American Medical Association, 264*(8), 998–1002.

Shaywitz, S. E., Shaywitz, B. A., Pugh, K. R., Fulbright, R. K., Constable, R. T., Mencl, W. E., Shankweiler, D. P., Liberman, A. M., Skudlarski, P., Fletcher, J. M., Katz, L., Marchione, K. E., Lacadie, C., Gatenby, C., & Gore, J. C. (1988). Functional disruption in the organization of the brain for reading dyslexia. *Proceedings of the National Academy of Sciences, 95,* 2636–2641.

Shepard, G., & Koch, C. (1990). Introduction to synaptic circuits. In G. Shepard (Ed.), *The synaptic organization of the brain* (pp. 3–31). London: Oxford University Press.

Shepard, L. A. (1994). The challenges of assessing young children appropriately. *Phi Delta Kappan, 76,* 206–212.

Shinn, M., Tindal, G., & Stein, S. (1988). Curriculum-based measurement and the identification of mildly handicapped students: A review of research. *Professional School Psychology, 3,* 69–85.

Shinn, M. R., & Hubbard, D. D. (1992). Curriculum-based measurement and problem-solving assessment: Basic procedures and outcomes. *Focus on Exceptional Children, 24* (5), 1–20.

Short, E. I., & Ryan, E. B. (1984). Metacognitive differences between skilled and less skilled readers: Remediating deficits through story grammar and attribution training. *Journal of Educational Psychology, 76,* 225–235.

Short, E. J., & Weissberg-Benchell, J. (1989). The triple alliance for learning: Cognition, metacognition, and motivation. In C. B. McCormick, G. E. Miller, & M. Pressley (Eds.), *Cognitive strategy research: From basic research to educational applications* (pp. 33–63). New York: Springer-Verlag.

Siegel, L. S. (1989). IQ is irrelevant to the definition of learning disabilities. *Journal of Learning Disabilities, 22*(8), 469–478, 486.

Siegel, S., & Gaylord-Ross, R. (1991). Factors associated with employment success among youths with learning disabilities. *Journal of Learning Disabilities, 24*(1), 40–47.

Siegel, S., Greener, K., Prieur, J., Robert, M., & Gaylord-Ross, R. (1989). The community vocational training program: Transitions for youths with mild handicaps. *Career Development for Exceptional Individuals, 12*(1), 48–64.

Silbert, J., Carnine, D., & Stein, M. (1988). *Direct instruction mathematics* (2nd ed.). Columbus, OH: Merrill.

Silver, E. A., & Smith, M. S. (1989). Canceling cancellation: The role of worked-out examples in unlearning a procedural error. In C. A. Maher, G. A. Goldin, & R. B. Davis (Eds.), *Proceedings of the eleventh annual meeting of the North American Chapter of the International Group for the Psychology of Mathematics Education* (pp. 40–46). New Brunswick, NJ: Center for Math, Science and Computer Education, Rutgers University.

Silver, E. A., & Smith, M. S. (1990). Research into practice: Teaching mathematics and thinking. *Arithmetic Teacher, 37* (8), 34–37.

Silverman, R., Zigmond, N., Zimmerman, J. M., & Vallecorsa, A. (1981). Improving written expression in learning disabled students. *Topics in Language Disorders, 1*(2), 91–99.

Simmons, D. C., & Kameenui, E. J. (Eds.). (1998). *What reading research tells us about children with diverse learning needs.* Mahwah, NJ: Erlbaum.

Simms, R. B., & Crump, W. D. (1983). Syntactic development in the oral language of learning disabled and normal students at the intermediate and secondary level. *Learning Disability Quarterly, 6,* 155–165.

Sinclair, E. (1993). Early identification of preschoolers with special needs in Head Start. *Topics in Early Childhood Special Education, 13,* 184–201.

Sindelar, P. I., & Deno, S. L. (1979). The effectiveness of resource programming. *Journal of Special Education, 12,* 17–28.

Sindelar, P. T., Monda, L. E., & O'Shea, L. J. (1990). Effects of repeated readings on instructional- and mastery-level readers. *Journal of Educational Research, 83,* 220–226.

Sindelar, R. T., & Stoddard, K. (1991). Teaching reading to mildly disabled students in regular classes. In G. Stoner, M. R. Shinn, & H. M. Walker (Eds.), *Interventions for achievement and behavior problems* (pp. 357–378). Silver Spring, MD: National Association of School Psychologists.

Singer, J. D. (1988). Should special education merge with regular education? *Educational Policy, 2,* 409–424.

Singer, J. D., & Butler, J. A. (1987). The Education of All Handicapped Children Act: Schools as agents of social reform. *Harvard Educational Review, 57,* 125–152.

Skiba, R., & Casey, A. (1985). Interventions for behavior disordered students: A quantitative review and methodological critique. *Behavioral Disorders, 10,* 239–252.

Skinner, B. F. (1953). *Science and human behavior.* New York: Macmillan.

Skinner, B. F. (1957). *Verbal behavior.* Englewood Cliffs, NJ: Prentice-Hall.

Skinner, B. F. (1968). *The technology of teaching.* New York: Appleton-Century-Crofts.

Slaughter, H. (1988). Indirect and direct teaching in a whole language program. *Reading Teacher, 42,* 30–34.

Slavin, R. E., Madden, N. A., Dolan, L. J., & Wasik, B. A. (1994). Roots and wings: Inspiring academic excellence. *Educational Leadership,* 52(3), 10–14.

Sleeter, C. E. (1986). Learning disabilities: The social construction of a special education category. *Exceptional Children,* 53, 46–54.

Slingerland, B. H. (1970). *Slingerland Screening Test for Identifying Children with Specific Language Disability* (2nd ed.). Cambridge, MA: Educators Publishing Service.

Slocum, T. A., O'Connor, R. E., & Jenkins, J. R. (1993). Transfer among phonological manipulation skills. *Journal of Educational Psychology, 85,* 618–630.

Smith, D. D., & Lovitt, T. C. (1973). The educational diagnosis and remediation of written b and d reversal problems: A case study. *Journal of Learning Disabilities, 6,* 356–363.

Smith, D. D., & Lovitt, T. C. (1975). The use of modeling techniques to influence the acquisition of computational arithmetic skills in reading-disabled children. In E. Ramp & G. Semb (Eds.), *Behavior analysis: Areas of research and application* (pp. 283–308). Englewood Cliffs, NJ: Prentice-Hall.

Smith, D. D., & Lovitt, T. C. (1976). The differential effects of reinforcement contingencies on arithmetic performance. *Journal of Learning Disabilities, 9,* 21–29.

Smith, D. D., & Lovitt, T. C. (1982). The Computational Arithmetic Program. Austin, TX: PRO-ED.

Smith, D. D., Lovitt, T. C., & Kidder, J. D. (1972). Using reinforcement contingencies and teaching aids to alter subtraction performance of children with learning disabilities. In G. Semb (Ed.), *Behavior analysis and education* (pp. 342–360).

Lawrence: Department of Human Development, University of Kansas.

Smith, D. D., & Rivera, D. P. (1991). Mathematics. In B. Y. L. Wong (Ed.), *Learning about learning disabilities* (pp. 345–374). New York: Academic Press.

Smith, F. (1977). Making sense of reading—and of reading instruction. *Harvard Educational Review, 47,* 386–395.

Smith, H. D., Baehner, R. L., Carney, T., & Majors, S. J. (1963). The sequelae of pica with and without lead poisoning: A comparison of the sequelae five or more years later. I: Clinical and laboratory observations. *American Journal of Diseases of Children, 105,* 609–616.

Smith, M., & Tarallo, B. (1993, March). The unsettling resettlement of Vietnamese boat people: How are refugees from Southeast Asia adapting to cultural differences in the U.S.? *USA Today,* 121, pp. 27–29.

Smith, S. B., Simmons, D. C., & Kameenui, E. J. (1998). Phonological awareness: Instructional and curricular basics and implications. In D. C. Simmons & E. J. Kameenui, (Eds.), *What reading research tells us about children with diverse learning needs.* Mahwah, NJ: Erlbaum.

Smith, W. (1981). The potential and problems of sentence combining. *English Journal, 70*(6), 79–81.

Snider, V. E. (1992). Learning styles and learning to read: A critique. *Remedial and Special Education, 13* (1), 6–18.

Snider, V. E. (1995). A primer on phonemic awareness: What it is, why it's important, and how to teach it. *School Psychology Review, 24,* 443–455.

Southeastern Community College v. Davis, 422 U.S. 397 (1979).

Speece, D. L., & Cooper, D. H. (1990). Ontogeny of school failure: Classification of first-grade children. *American Educational Research Journal 27,* 119–140.

Speece, D. L., McKinney, J. D., & Appelbaum, M. I. (1985). Classification and validation of behavioral subtypes of learning-disabled children. *Journal of Educational Psychology, 77,* 67–77.

Sperry, R. W. (1964). The great cerebral commissure. *Scientific American, 210,* 42–52.

Spillane, S. A., McGuire, J. M., & Norlander, K. A. (1992). Undergraduate admission policies, practices, and procedures for applicants with learning disabilities. *Journal of Learning Disabilities, 25*(10), 665–670, 677.

Sprick, R. S., & Howard, L. M. (1995). *The teacher's encyclopedia of behavior management.* Longmont, CO: Sopris West.

Staats, A. W. (1968). *Learning, language, and cognition.* New York: Holt, Rinehart & Winston.

Staats, A. W. (1974). Behaviorism and cognitive theory in the study of language: A neopsycholinguistics. In R. L. Schiefelbusch & L. L. Lloyd (Eds.), *Language perspectives: Acquisition, retardation, and intervention* (pp. 615–646). Baltimore: University Park Press.

Stahl, S. A. (1988). Is there evidence to support matching reading styles and initial reading methods? *Phi Delta Kappan, 70,* 317–327.

Stahl, S. A. (1992). Saying the "p" word: Nine guidelines for exemplary phonics instruction. *Reading Teacher 45,* 618–625.

Stahl, S. A., & Miller, R. D. (1989). Whole language and language experience approaches for beginning reading: A quantitative research synthesis. *Review of Educational Research, 59,* 87–116.

Stainback, S., & Stainback, W. (1988). Letter to the editor. *Journal of Learning Disabilities,* 21, 452–453.

Stainback, W., & Stainback, S. (1984). A rationale for the merger of special and regular education. *Exceptional Children, 51,* 102–111.

Stanovich, K. E. (1980). Toward an interactive compensatory model of individual differences in the development of reading fluency. *Reading Research Quarterly, 16,* 32–71.

Stanovich, K. E. (1986a). Cognitive processes and the reading problems of learning disabled children: Evaluating the assumption of specificity. In J. Torgesen & B. Y. L. Wong (Eds.), *Psychological and educational perspectives on learning disabilities* (pp. 87–113). New York: Academic Press.

Stanovich, K. E. (1986b). Matthew effects in reading: Some consequences of individual differences in the acquisition of literacy. *Reading Research Quarterly, 21,* 360–407.

Stanovich, K. E. (1988). Explaining the differences between the dyslexic and the garden-variety poor reader: The phonological-core variable-difference model. *Journal of Learning Disabilities, 21,* 590–612.

Stanovich, K. E. (1989). Has the learning disabilities field lost its intelligence? *Journal of Learning Disabilities, 22,* 465–528.

Stanovich, K. E. (1991). Discrepancy definitions of reading disability: Has intelligence led us astray? *Reading Research Quarterly, 26,* 7–29.

Stanovich, K. E. (1994). Constructivism in reading. *Journal of Special Education, 28,* 259–274.

Stanovich, K. E., Cunningham, A., & Freeman, D. (1984). The relationship between early reading acquisition and word decoding with and without context: A longitudinal study of first grade children. *Journal of Educational Psychology, 76,* 668–677.

Stanovich, K. E., & Siegel, L. S. (1994). Phenotypic performance profile of children with reading disabilities: A regression-based test of the phonological-core variable-difference model. *Journal of Educational Psychology, 86*(1), 24–53.

Starlin, C. (1971). Evaluating progress toward reading proficiency. In B. Bateman (Ed.), *Learning disorders: Vol. 4. Reading* (pp. 389–465). Seattle, WA: Special Child Publications.

Stauffer, R. G. (1980). *The language-experience approach to the teaching of reading* (2nd ed.). New York: Harper & Row.

Stein, C. L., & Goldman. J. (1980). Beginning reading instruction for children with minimal brain dysfunction. *Journal of Learning Disabilities, 13,* 219–222.

Stein, M., & Osborne, J. (1993). Revising the revisions. *Remedial and Special Education, 14,* 17–18.

Stein, M., Silbert, J., & Carnine, D. (1997). *Designing effective mathematics instruction: A Direct Instruction approach* (3rd ed.). Upper Saddle River, NJ: Merrill.

Stephens, R., & Hudson, A. (1984). A comparison of the effects of direct instruction and remedial English classes on the spelling skills of secondary students. *Educational Psychology, 4,* 261–267.

Stephenson, S. (1907). Six cases of congenital word-blindness affecting three generations in one family. *Opthalmoscope, 5,* 482–484.

Stern, C. A., & Stern, M. B. (1971). Children discover arithmetic: *An introduction to structural arithmetic* (Rev. ed.). New York: Harper & Row.

Stevens, K. B., & Schuster, J. W. (1987). Effects of a constant time-delay procedure on the written spelling performance of a reading disabled student. *Learning Disability Quarterly, 10,* 9–16.

Stevens, K. B., Blackhurst, A. E., & Slaton, D. B. (1991). Teaching memorized spelling with a microcomputer: Time delay and computer-assisted instruction. *Journal of Applied Behavior Analysis, 24,* 153–160.

Stevens, R., & Rosenshine, B. (1981). Advances in research on teaching. *Exceptional Education Quarterly,* 2(1), 1–9.

Stevenson, J., Pennington, B. F., Gilger, J. W., DeFries, J. C., & Gillis, J. J. (1993). Hyperactivity and spelling disability: Testing for shared genetic aetiology. *Journal of Child Psychology and Psychiatry,* 34(7), 1137–1152.

Stone, I. F. (1988). *The trial of Socrates.* Boston: Little, Brown.

Stowitschek, C. E., & Stowitschek, J. J. (1979). Evaluating handwriting performance: The student helps the teacher. *Journal of Learning Disabilities, 12,* 203–206.

Strang, J. D., & Rourke, B. P. (1985). Arithmetic disability subtypes: The neuropsychological significance of specific arithmetical impairment in childhood. In B. P. Rourke (Ed.), *Neuorpsychology of learning disabilities: Essentials of subtype analysis* (pp. 167–183). New York: Guilford.

Strauss, A. A., & Kephart, N. C. (1955). *Psychopathology and education of the brain-injured child: Vol. 2. Progress in theory and clinic.* New York: Grune & Stratton.

Strauss, A. A., & Lehtinen, L. (1947). *Psychopathology and education of the brain-injured child.* New York: Grune & Stratton.

Strauss, A. A., & Werner, H. (1942). Disorders of conceptual thinking in the brain-injured child. *Journal of Nervous and Mental Diseases, 96,* 153–172.

Straw, S. B., & Schreiner, R. (1982). The effect of sentence manipulation on subsequent measures of reading and listening comprehension. *Reading Research Quarterly, 17,* 339–352.

Stromer, R. (1975). Modifying letter and number reversals in elementary school children. *Journal of Applied Behavior Analysis, 8,* 211.

Stromer, R. (1977). Remediating academic deficiencies in learning disabled children. *Exceptional Children, 43,* 432–440.

Sullivan, M. (1966). *Sullivan reading program.* Palo Alto, CA: Behavioral Research Labs.

Swank, L. K., Meier, J. D., Invernizzi, M., & Juel, C. L. (1997). *PALS I: Phonological awareness and literacy screening.* Charlottesville: University of Virginia.

Swanson, H. L. (1990). Instruction derived from the strategy deficit model: Overview of principles and procedures. In T. E. Scruggs & B. Y. L. Wong (Eds.), *Intervention research in learning disabilities* (pp. 34–65). New York: Springer-Verlag.

Swanson, H. L. (1991). Introduction: Issues in the assessment of learning disabilities. In H. L. Swanson (Ed.), *Handbook on the assessment of learning disabilities* (pp. 1–19). Austin, TX: PRO-ED.

Swanson, H. L. (1994). Short-term memory and working memory: Do both contribute to our understanding of academic achievement in children and adults with learning disabilities? *Journal of Learning Disabilities, 27,* 34–50.

Swanson, H. L. (Ed.). (1991). *Handbook on the assessment of learning disabilities: Theory, research, and practice.* Boston: Little, Brown.

Swanson, H. L., & Cooney, J. B. (1991). Learning disabilities and memory. In B. Y. L. Wong (Ed.), *Learning about learning disabilities* (pp. 103–127). New York: Academic Press.

Swanson, H. L., & Watson, B. L. (1989). *Educational and psychological assessment of exceptional children: Theories, strategies, and applications* (2nd ed.). Columbus, OH: Merrill.

Swanson, L. (1981). Modification of comprehension deficits in reading disabled children. *Learning Disability Quarterly, 4,* 189–202.

Sweeney, W. J., Salva, E., Cooper, J. O., & Talbert-Johnson, C. (1993). Using self-evaluation to improve difficult-to-read handwriting of secondary students. *Journal of Behavioral Education, 3,* 427–443.

Swicegood, P. (1994). Portfolio-based assessment practices. *Intervention, 30*(1), 6–15.

Symons, S., Snyder, B. L., Cariglia-Bull, T., & Pressley, M. (1989). Why be so optimistic about cognitive strategy instruction? In C. B. McCormick, G. E. Miller, & M. Pressley (Eds.), *Cognitive strategy research: From basic research to educational applications.* New York: Springer-Verlag.

Systems Impact. (1986). *Mastering fractions.* Washington, DC: Author.

Systems Impact. (1988). *Mastering equations, roots, and exponents.* Washington, DC: Author.

Szymanski, E. M. (1994). Transition: Life-span and life-space considerations for empowerment. *Exceptional Children, 60*(5), 402–410.

Talbott, E., Lloyd, J. W., & Tankersley, M. (1994). Effects of reading comprehension interventions for students with learning disabilities. *Learning Disability Quarterly, 17,* 223–232.

Tallal, P., Townsend, J., Curtiss, S., & Wulfeck, B. (1991). Phenotypic profiles of language-impaired children based on genetic/family history. *Brain and Language, 41,* 81–95.

Tangel, D. M. & Blachman, B. A. (1995). Effect of phoneme awareness instruction on the invented spelling of first-grade children: A one-year follow-up. *Journal of Reading Behavior, 27,* 163–185.

Tarver, S. G. (1986). Cognitive behavior modification, direct instruction and holistic approaches to the education of students with learning disabilities. *Journal of Learning Disabilities 19,* 368–375.

Tarver, S. G. (1994). In search of effective instruction. *Effective School Practices, 13*(4), 23–32.

Tarver, S. G., & Dawson, M. M. (1978). Modality preference and the teaching of reading: A review. *Journal of Learning Disabilities, 11,* 17–29.

Tarver, S. G., & Ellsworth, P. S. (1981). Written and oral language for verbal children. In J. M. Kauffman & D. P. Hallahan (Eds.), *Handbook of special education* (pp. 491–511). Englewood Cliffs, NJ: Prentice-Hall.

Tarver, S. G., Hallahan, D. P., Kauffman, J. M., & Ball, D. W. (1976). Verbal rehearsal and selective attention in children with learning disabilities: A developmental lag. *Journal of Experimental Child Psychology, 22,* 375–385.

Taylor, H. G., & Schatschneider, C. (1992). Academic achievement following childhood brain disease: Implications for the concept of learning disabilities. *Journal of Learning Disabilities, 25*(10), 630–638.

Taylor, R. L. (1997). *Assessment of exceptional students: Educational and psychological procedures* (4th ed.). Boston: Allyn & Bacon.

Teigs, E. W., & Clark, W. W. (1992). *The California Achievement Tests—Fifth Edition.* Monterey, CA: CTB/McGraw-Hill.

Templeton, S., & Baer, D. (1992). *Development of orthographic knowledge and the foundations of literacy.* Hillsdale, NJ: Erlbaum.

Templin, E. M. (1960). Research and comment: Handwriting, the neglected R. *Elementary English, 37,* 386–389.

Terwilliger, J. (1997). Semantics, psychometrics, and assessment reform: A close look at "authentic" assessments. *Educational Researcher, 26*(8), 24–27.

Tharp, R. G., & Gallimore, R. (1988). *Rousing minds to life: Teaching, learning, schooling in social context.* New York: Cambridge University Press.

Thomas, B. (1994). Education should be special for all. *Phi Delta Kappan, 75,* 716–717.

Thomas, C. C., Englert, C. S., & Gregg, S. (1987). An analysis of errors and strategies in the expository writing of learning disabled students. *Remedial and Special Education, 8,* 21–30.

Thomas, C. J. (1905). Congenital "word-blindness" and its treatment. *Opthalmoscope, 3,* 380–385.

Thompson, L. (1997). *Children talking: The development of pragmatic competence.* Philadelphia: Multilingual Matters.

Thorp, E. K. (1997). Increasing opportunities for partnership with culturally and linguistically diverse families. *Intervention in School and Clinic, 32,* 261–269.

Thorpe, L., Lafever, D., & Haslund, R. (1963). *SRA Achievement Series.* Chicago: Science Research Associates.

Tilson, G. P., Luecking, R. G., & Donovan, M. R. (1994). Involving employers in transition: The Bridges Model. *Career Development for Exceptional Individuals, 17,* 77–89.

Tindal, G., & Parker, R. (1991). Identifying measures for evaluating written expression. *Learning Disabilities Research and Practice, 6,* 211–218.

Tindal, G. A., & Marston, D. B. (1990). *Classroom-based assessment: Evaluating instructional outcomes.* Columbus, OH: Merrill/Macmillan.

Torgesen, J. K. (1977). The role of nonspecific factors in the task performance of learning disabled children: A theoretical assessment. *Journal of Learning Disabilities, 10,* 27–34.

Torgesen, J. K. (1979). Factors related to poor performance in reading disabled children. *Learning Disability Quarterly, 2,* 17–23.

Torgesen, J. K. (1991). Learning disabilities: Historical and conceptual issues. In B. Y. L. Wong (Ed)., *Learning about learning disabilities* (pp. 3–37). New York: Academic Press.

Torgesen, J. K. (1996). A model of memory from an information processing perspective: The special case of phonological memory. In G. R. Lyon & N. A. Krasnegor (Eds.), *Attention, memory, and executive function* (pp. 157–184). Baltimore: Paul H. Brookes.

Torgesen, J. K., & Bryant, B. (1994). *Test of phonological awareness.* Austin, TX: PRO-ED.

Torgeson, J. K., & Davis, C. (1995). Individual difference variables that predict response to training in phonological awareness. *Journal of Experimental Child Psychology, 63,* 1–21.

Torgesen, J. K., Morgan, S. T., & Davis, C. (1992). Effects of two types of phonological awareness training on word learning in kindergarten children. *Journal of Educational Psychology, 84,* 364–370.

Torgesen, J. K., Waters, M. D., Cohen, A. L., & Torgesen, J. L. (1988). Improving sight-word recognition skills in LD children: An evaluation of three computer program variations. *Learning Disability Quarterly, 11,* 125–132,

Towle, M. (1978). Assessment and remediation of handwriting deficits for children with learning disabilities. *Journal of Learning Disabilities, 11,* 370–377.

Trembley, P., Caponiqro, J., & Gaffrey, V. (1980). Effects of programming from the WRAT and PIAT for students determined to have learning disabilities in arithmetic. *Journal of Learning Disabilities, 13,* 291–293.

Trenholme, B., Larsen, S. C., & Parker, R. (1978). The effects of syntactic complexity upon arithmetic performance. *Learning Disability Quarterly, 1*(4), 80–85.

Tucker, J. (1987). Curriculum-based assessment is not a fad. *Collaborative Educator, 1*(4), 4, 10.

Tuckman, B. W (1988). *Testing for teachers* (2nd ed.). New York: Harcourt, Brace, Jovanovich.

Turnbull, A. P., & Turnbull, H. R. (1990). *Families, professionals, and exceptionality: A special partnership* (2nd ed.). Columbus, OH: Merrill.

Turnbull, A. P., & Turnbull, H. R. (1996). *Familes, professionals, and exceptionality: A special partnership* (3rd ed.). Upper Saddle River, NJ: Prentice-Hall.

U.S. Census Bureau. (1996). Statistical abstract of the United States, 1996. Washington, DC: U.S. Department of Commerce.

U.S. Department of Education. (1992). *Fourteenth annual report to Congress on the implementation of the Individuals with Disabilities Education Act.* Washington, DC: Author.

U.S. Department of Education. (1994). *Sixteenth annual report to Congress on the implementation of the Individuals with Disabilities Education Act.* Washington, DC: Author.

U.S. Department of Education. (1996). *Eighteenth annual report to Congress on the implementation of the Individuals with Disabilities Education Act.* Washington, DC: U.S. Department of Education, Office of Special Education Programs.

U.S. Office of Education. (1968). *First annual report of National Advisory Committee on Handicapped Children.* Washington, DC: U.S. Department of Health, Education, and Welfare.

U.S. Office of Education. (1976, December 29). Proposed rulemaking. *Federal Register, 41,* (230), 52404–52407. Washington, DC: U.S. Government Printing Office.

U.S. Office of Education. (1977, December 29). Assistance to states for education of handicapped children: Procedures for evaluating specific learning disabilities. *Federal Register, 42,* (250), 65082–65085. Washington, DC: U.S. Government Printing Office.

U.S. Senate Committee on Labor and Human Relations. (1993). New challenges for Head Start. (Hearing 103–166). Washington, DC.

van der Lely, H. K. J., & Stollwerck, L. (1996). A grammatical specific language impairment in children: An autosomal dominant inheritance? *Brain and Language, 52,* 484–504.

Van Houten, R., & Van Houten, J. (1991). The effects of breaking new spelling words into small segments on the spelling performance of students with learning disabilities. *Journal of Behavioral Education, 1,* 399–411.

Van Houten, R., Morrison, E., Jarvis, R., & McDonald, M. (1974). The effects of explicit timing and feedback on compositional response rate in elementary school children. *Journal of Applied Behavior Analysis, 7,* 547–555.

van Keulen, J. E., Weddington, G. T., & DeBose, C. E. (1998). *Speech, language, learning, and the African American child.* Boston: Allyn & Bacon.

Vandever, T. R., & Neville, D. D. (1976). Transfer as a result of synthetic and analytic reading instruction. *American Journal of Mental Deficiency, 80,* 498–503.

Varnhagen, S., & Gerber, M. M. (1984). Use of microcomputers for assessment: Reasons to be cautious. *Learning Disability Quarterly, 7,* 266–270.

Vaughn, S., Bos, C., & Schumm, J. S. (1997). *Teaching mainstreamed, diverse, and at-risk students in the general education classroom.* Boston: Allyn & Bacon.

Vaughn, S., Bos, C. S., Harrell, J. E., & Lasky, B. A. (1988). Parent participation in the initial placement/IEP conference ten years after mandated involvement. *Journal of Learning Disabilities, 21,* 82–89.

Vaughn, S., Schumm, J. S., & Arguelles, M. E. (1997). The ABCDEs of co-teaching. *Teaching Exceptional Children, 30*(2), 4–10.

Vaughn, S., Zaragoza, N., Hogan, A., & Walker, J. (1993). A four-year longitudinal investigation of the social skills and behavior problems of students with learning disabilities. *Journal of Learning Disabilities, 26,* 404–412.

Vellutino, E. R. (1977). Alternative conceptualizations of dyslexia: Evidence in support of a verbal-deficit hypothesis. *Harvard Educational Review, 47,* 334–354.

Vellutino, E. R., & Scanlon, D. M. (1987). Phonological coding, phonological awareness, and reading ability: Evidence from a longitudinal and experimental study. *Merrill-Palmer Quarterly, 33,* 321–363.

Vickery, K. S., Reynolds, V. A., & Cochran, S. W. (1987). Multisensory teaching approach for reading, spelling, and handwriting, Orton-Gillingham based curriculum, in a public school setting. *Annals of Dyslexia, 37,* 189–200.

Vogel, S. A. (1974). Syntactic abilities in normal and dyslexic children. *Journal of Learning Disabilities, 7,* 103–109.

Vogel, S. A. (1977). Morphological ability in normal and dyslexic children. *Journal of Learning Disabilities,* 10, 41–49.

Vogel, S. A., & Adelman, P. B. (1992). The success of college students with learning disabilities: Factors related to educational attainment. *Journal of Learning Disabilities, 25*(7), 430–441.

Vreeland, M., Vail. J., Bradley, L., Buetow, C., Cipriano, K., Green, C., Henshaw, P., & Huth, E. (1994). Accelerating cognitive growth: The Edison School math project. *Effective School Practices, 13*(2), 64–69.

Vygotsky, L. (1962). *Thought and language.* New York: Wiley.

Vygotsky, L. (1978). *Mind in society: The development of higher psychological processes.* Cambridge, MA: Harvard University Press.

Wagner, M., Blackorby, J., Cameto, R., Hebbeler, K., & Newman, L. (1993). *The transition experiences of young people with disabilities: A summary of findings from the National Longitudinal Transition Study of special education students.* Menlo Park, CA: SRI International.

Wagner, R. K., & Torgesen, J. K. (1987). The nature of phonological processing and its causal role in the acquisition of reading skills. *Psychological Bulletin, 101,* 192–212.

Wagner, R. K., Torgesen, J. K., & Rashotte, C. A. (1994). Development of reading-related phonological processing abilities: New evidence of bidirectional causality from a latent variable longitudinal study. *Developmental Psychology, 30,* 73–87.

Walker, H. (1983). Application of response cost in school settings: Outcomes, issues, and recommendations. *Exceptional Education Quarterly, 3*(4), 47–55.

Walker, H. M. (1995). *The acting-out child: Coping with classroom disruption.* Longmont, CO: Sopris West.

Walker, H. M., Block-Pedego, A., Todis, B., & Severson, H. (1991). *School Archival Records Search (SARS).* Longmont, CO: Sopris West.

Walker, H. M., Calvin, G., & Ramsey, E. (1995). *Antisocial behavior in school: Strategies and best practices.* Pacific Grove, CA: Brooks/Cole.

Walker, H. M., Kavanagh, K., Stiller, B., Golly, A., Severson, H. H., & Feil, E. G. (in press). First step to success: An early intervention approach for preventing school antisocial behavior. *Journal of Emotional and Behavioral Disorders.*

Walker, H. M., & McConnell, S. (1988). *The Walker-McConnell Scale of Social Competence and School Adjustment: A social skills rating scale for teachers.* Austin, TX: PRO-ED.

Walker, H. M., McConnell, S., Holmes, D., Todis, B., Walker, J., & Golden, N. (1983). *The Walker Social Skills Curriculum: The ACCEPTS program.* Austin, TX: PRO-ED.

Walker, H. M., & Severson, H. H. (1990). *Systematic Screening for Behavior Disorders (SSBD): A multiple gating procedure.* Longmont, CO: Sopris West.

Walker, H. M., Severson, H., Stiller, B., Williams, G., Haring, N., Shinn, M., & Todis, B. (1988). Systematic screening of pupils in the elementary age range at risk for behavior disorders: Development and trial testing of a multiple gating model. *Remedial and Special Education, 9*(3), 8–14.

Wallace, C., Larsen, S. C., & Elksnin, L. K. (1992). *Educational assessment of learning problems: Testing for teaching* (2nd ed.). Boston: Allyn & Bacon.

Wallace, G., & Hammill, D. D. (1994). *Comprehensive Receptive and Expressive Vocabulary Test (CREVT).* Austin, TX: PRO-ED.

Wallach, M. A., & Wallach, L. (1976). *Teaching all children to read.* Chicago: University of Chicago Press.

Warren, S. F., & Yoder, P. J. (1994). Communication and language intervention: Why a constructivist approach is insufficient. *Journal of Special Education, 28,* 248–258.

Watson, D. J. (1989). Defining and describing whole language. *Elementary School Journal, 90,* 129–141.

Waugh, R. (1975). The ITPA: Ballast or bonanza for the school psychologist? *Journal of School Psychology, 13,* 201–208.

Wechsler, D. (1974). *Manual for the Wechsler Intelligence Scale for Children—Revised.* New York: Psychological Corporation.

Wedell, K., & Home, L. E. (1969). Some aspects of perceptual-motor disability in 5-year-old children. *British Journal of Educational Psychology, 39,* 174–182.

Weiner, E. S. (1980a). Diagnostic Evaluation of Writing Skills. *Journal of Learning Disabilities, 13,* 43–48.

Weiner, E. S. (1980b). The Diagnostic Evaluation of Writing Skills (DEWS): Application of DEWS criteria to writing samples. *Learning Disability Quarterly, 3*(2), 54–59.

Weiss, G., & Hechtman, L. T. (1993). *Hyperactive children grown up: ADHD in children, adolescents, and adults* (2nd ed.). New York: Guilford.

Weller, C. (1979). The effects of two language training approaches on syntactical skills of language-deviant children. *Journal of Learning Disabilities, 12,* 470–479.

Wellington, J. (1994). Evaluating a mathematics program for adoption: Connecting math concepts. *Effective School Practices, 13*(2), 70–75

Wepman, J. M. (1958). *Auditory Discrimination Test.* Chicago: Language Research Associates.

Wepman, J. M. (1964). The perceptual basis for learning. In H. A. Robinson (Ed.), *Meeting individual differences in reading* (pp. 25–33). Chicago: University of Chicago Press.

Wepman, J. M. (1973). *Auditory Discrimination Test* (rev. ed.). Chicago: Language Research Associates.

Werner, H., & Strauss, A. A. (1939). Problems and methods of functional analysis in mentally deficient children. *Journal of Abnormal and Social Psychology, 34,* 37–62.

Werner, H., & Strauss, A. A. (1940). Causal factors in low performance. *American Journal of Mental Deficiency, 45,* 213–218.

Werner, H., & Strauss, A. A. (1941). Pathology of figure background relation in the child. *Journal of Abnormal and Social Psychology, 36,* 236–248.

Western, R. D. (1977). The case against cursive script. *Elementary School Journal, 78,* 1–3.

Wethy, C. (1993). Whole language and learners with mild handicaps. In E. L. Meyen, G. A. Vargason, & R. J. Whelan (Eds.), *Educating students with mild disabilities* (pp. 273–294). Denver: Love.

Wexler, K. (1990). Innateness and maturation in linguistic development. *Developmental Psychobiology, 23,* 645–660.

Whinnery, K. W., & Fuchs, L. S. (1993). Effects of goal and test-taking strategies on the computation performance of students with learning disabilities. *Learning Disabilities Research and Practice, 8,* 204–214.

White, W. A. T. (1988). A meta-analysis of the effects of direct instruction in special education. *Education and Treatment of Children, 11,* 364–374.

White, W. J. (1992). The postschool adjustment of persons with learning disabilities: Current status and future projections. *Journal of Learning Disabilities,* 25(7), 448–456.

Whitman, T., Burgio, L., & Johnston, M. B. (1984). Cognitive behavioral interventions with mentally retarded children. In A. W. Meyers & W. E. Craighead (Eds.), *Cognitive behavior therapy with children* (pp. 193–227). New York: Plenum Press.

Whitman, T., & Johnston, M. B. (1983). Teaching addition and subtraction with regrouping to educable mentally retarded children: A group self-instructional training program. *Behavior Therapy, 14,* 127–143.

Wiederholt, J. L. (1974). Historical perspectives on the education of the learning disabled. In L. Mann & D. Sabatino (Eds.), *The second review of special education* (pp. 103–152). Philadelphia: Journal of Special Education Press.

Wiederholt, J. L., & Bryant, B. R. (1992). *Gray Oral Reading Tests—3rd Edition.* Austin, TX: PRO-ED.

Wiggins, G. P. (1993). *Assessing student performance: Exploring the purpose and limits of testing.* San Francisco: Jossey-Bass.

Wiig, E., & Semel, E. (1984). *Language assessment and intervention for the learning disabled* (2nd ed.). Columbus, OH: Merrill.

Wiig, E. H. (1990). Linguistic transitions and learning disabilities: A strategic learning perspective. *Learning Disability Quarterly, 13,* 128–140.

Wiig, E. H., & Roach, M. A. (1975). Immediate recall of semantically varied "sentences" by learning disabled adolescents. *Perceptual and Motor Skills,* 40, 119–125.

Wiig, E. H., & Semel, E. M. (1975). Productive language abilities in learning disabled adolescents. *Journal of Learning Disabilities, 8,* 578–586.

Wiig, E. H., Semel, E. M., & Abele, E. (1981). Perception of ambiguous sentences by learning disabled twelve-year-olds. *Learning Disability Quarterly, 4,* 3–12.

Wiig, E. H., Semel, E. M., & Crouse, M. A. (1973). The use of English morphology by high-risk and learning disabled children. *Journal of Learning Disabilities, 6,* 457–465.

Wilkinson, G. S. (1993). *The Wide Range Achievement Test—III.* Wilmington, DE: Wide Range.

Will, M. (1984). *OSERS programming for the transition of youth with disabilities: Bridges from school to working life.* Washington, DC: U.S. Department of Education, Office of Special Education and Rehabilitative Services.

Williams, J. R. (1977). Building perceptual and cognitive strategies into a reading curriculum. In A. S. Reber & D. L. Scarborough (Eds.), *Toward a psychology of reading: The proceedings of the CUNY conferences* (pp. 257–288). Hillsdale, NJ: Erlbaum.

Williams, J. R. (1980). Teaching decoding with an emphasis on phoneme analysis and phoneme blending. *Journal of Educational Psychology, 72,* 1–15.

Williams, J. R. (1991). The use of schema in research on the problem solving of learning disabled adolescents. In T. E. Scruggs & B. Y. L. Wong (Eds.), *Intervention research in learning disabilities* (pp. 302–321). New York: Springer-Verlag.

Williams, J. R., Brown, L. G., Silverstein, A. K., & deCani, J. S. (1994). An instructional program in comprehension of narrative themes for adolescents with learning disabilities. *Learning Disability Quarterly, 17,* 205–221.

Winterling, V. (1990). The effects of constant time delay, practice in writing or spelling, and reinforcement on sight word recognition in a small group. *Journal of Special Education, 24,* 101–116.

Winzer, M. A. (1993). *The history of special education: From isolation to integration.* Washington, DC: Gallaudet University Press.

Wise, B. W., & Olson, R. K. (1998). Studies of computer-aided remediation for reading disabilities. In C. Hulme & R. M. Joshi (Eds.), *Reading and spelling: Development and disorders* (pp. 473–487). Mahwah, NJ: Erlbaum.

Witkin, H. A., Goodenough, D. R., & Karp, S. A. (1967). Stability of cognitive style from childhood to young adulthood. *Journal of Personality and Social Psychology, 7,* 291–300.

Wolery, M. (1991). Instruction in early childhood special education: "Seeing through a glass darkly . . . Knowing in part." *Exceptional Children, 58,* 127–135.

Wolery, M. (1993). Foreword. *Topics in Early Childhood Special Education, 13,* viii–x.

Wolery, M., Bailey, D. B., & Sugai, G. M. (1988). *Effective teaching: Principles and procedures of applied behavior analysis with exceptional children.* Boston: Allyn & Bacon.

Wolery, M., Bailey, D. B., Jr., & Sugai, G. M. (1988). *Effective teaching: Principles and procedures of applied behavior analysis with exceptional students.* Boston: Allyn and Bacon.

Wolery, M., Holcombe-Ligon, A., Brookfield, J., Huffman, K., Schroeder, C., Martin, C. G., Venn, M. L., Werts, M. G., & Fleming, L. A. (1993). The extent and nature of preschool mainstreaming: A survey of general early educators. *Journal of Special Education, 27,* 222–234.

Wong, B. Y. L. (1982). Understanding the learning disabled student's reading problems: Contributions from cognitive psychology. *Topics in Learning and Learning Disabilities, 1*(4), 43–50.

Wong, B. Y. L. (1985a). Issues in cognitive-behavioral interventions in academic skill areas. *Journal of Abnormal Child Psychology, 13,* 425–441.

Wong, B. Y. L. (1985b). Metacognition and learning disabilities. In D. L. Forrest-Pressley, G. E. MacKinnon, & T. G. Waller (Eds.), *Metacognition, cognition, and human performance* (Vol. 2, pp. 137–180). New York: Academic Press.

Wong, B. Y. L. (1986). Metacognition and special education: A review of a view. *Journal of Special Education, 20,* 9–29.

Wong, B. Y. L. (1991). The relevance of metacognition to learning disabilities. In B. Y. L. Wong (Ed.), *Learning about learning disabilities* (pp. 231–258). New York: Academic Press.

Wong, B. Y L., & Jones, W. (1982). Increasing metacomprehension in learning disabled and normally achieving students through self-questioning training. *Learning Disability Quarterly, 5,* 228–240.

Wong, B. Y. L., & Roadhouse, A. (1978). The Test of Language Development (TOLD): A validation study. *Learning Disability Quarterly, 1*(3), 48–61.

Woodcock, R. W. (1987). *Woodcock Reading Mastery Tests—Revised.* Circle Pines, MN: American Guidance Service.

Woodcock, R. W. (1997). *Woodcock Diagnostic Reading Battery.* Circle Pines, MN: American Guidance Service.

Woodcock, R. W., Clark, C., & Davies, C. (1979). *Peabody rebus reading program.* Circle Pines, MN: American Guidance Service.

Woodcock, R. W., & Johnson, M. B. (1989/1990). *Woodcock-Johnson Psychoeducational Battery—Revised.* Boston: Teaching Resources.

Woodward, J., & Howard, L. (1994). The misconceptions of youth: Errors and their mathematical meaning. *Exceptional Children, 61*(2), 126–127.

Worrall, R. S. (1990). Detecting health fraud in the field of learning disabilities. *Journal of Learning Disabilities, 23,* 207–212.

Worrall, R. S., & Carnine, D. (1994, March). *Lack of professional support undermines teachers and reform—A contrasting perspective from health and engineering.* Unpublished manuscript. National Center to Improve the Tools of Educators, College of Education, University of Oregon, Eugene.

Worthen, B. R. (1993). Critical issues that will determine the future of alternative assessment. *Phi Delta Kappan, 74,* 444–456.

Worthy, M. J., & Invernizzi, M. (1990). Spelling errors of normal and disabled students on achievement levels one through four: Instructional implications. *Annals of Dyslexia, 40,* 138–151.

Wright, C. D., & Wright, J. P. (1980). Handwriting: The effectiveness of copying from moving versus still models. *Journal of Educational Research, 74,* 95–98.

Yell, M. L. (1998). *The law and special education.* Upper Saddle River, NJ: Prentice-Hall.

Yell, M. L., & Shriner, J. G. (1997). The IDEA amendments of 1997: Implications for special and general education teachers, administrators, and teacher trainers. *Focus on Exceptional Children, 30*(1), 1–19.

Yopp, H. K. (1988). The validity and reliability of phonemic awareness tests. *Reading Research Quarterly, 23,* 159–177.

Young, R. M., & O'Shea, T. (1981). Errors in children's subtraction. *Cognitive Science, 5,* 153—177.

Ysseldyke, J. E. (1973). Diagnostic-prescriptive teaching: The search for aptitude-treatment interactions. In L. Mann & D. A. Sabatino (Eds.), *First review of special education* (Vol. 1, pp. 5–32). Philadelphia: JSE Press.

Ysseldyke, J. E., & Christenson, S. L. (1987). Evaluating students' instructional environments. *Remedial and Special Education, 8*(3), 17–24.

Ysseldyke, J. E., Algozzine, B., & Epps, S. (1983). A logical and empirical analysis of current practice in classifying students as handicapped. *Exceptional Children, 50,* 160–166.

Ysseldyke, J. E., Algozzine, B., Shinn, M. R., & McGue, M. (1982). Similarities and differences between low achievers and students classified as learning disabled. *Journal of Special Education, 16,* 73–85.

Ysseldyke, J. E., Algozzine, B., & Thurlow, M. L. (1992). *Critical issues in special education* (2nd ed.). Boston: Houghton Mifflin.

Ysseldyke, J. E., & Salvia, J. A. (1974). Diagnostic prescriptive teaching: Two models. *Exceptional Children, 41,* 181–186.

Ysseldyke, J. E., Thurlow, M., Graden, J., Wesson, C., Algozzine, B., & Deno, S. (1983). Generalizations from five years of research on assessment and decision making: The University of Minnesota Institute. *Exceptional Education Quarterly, 4*(1), 75–93.

Zawaiza, T., & Gerber, M. M. (1993). Effects of explicit instruction on math word-problem solving by community college students with learning disabilities. *Learning Disability Quarterly, 16,* 64–79.

Zigler, E., & Black, K. B. (1989). America's family support movement: Strengths and limitations. *American Journal of Orthopsychiatry, 59,* 6–19.

Zigmond, N. (1990). Rethinking secondary school programs for students with learning disabilities. *Focus on Exceptional Children,* 23(1), 1–22.

Zigmond, N., & Baker, J. M. (1996). Full inclusion for students with learning disabilities: Too much of a good thing? *Theory into Practice,* 35(1), 26–34.

Zigmond, N., Jenkins, J., Fuchs, L., Deno, S., Fuchs, D., Baker, J. N., Jenkins, L., & Couthino, M. (1995). Special education in restructured schools: Findings from three multi-year studies. *Phi Delta Kappan, 76,* 531–540.

Zigmond, N., & Miller, S. E. (1986). Assessment for instructional planning. *Exceptional Children, 52,* 501–509.

Zigmond, N., & Miller, S. E. (1992). Improving high school programs for students with learning disabilities: A matter of substance as well as form. In F. R. Rusch, L. DeStefano, J. Chadsey-Rusch, L. A. Phelps, & E. Szymanski (Eds.), *Transition from school to adult life* (pp. 17–31). Sycamore, IL: Sycamore Publishing.

Zigmond, N., & Thornton, H. (1985). Follow-up of postsecondary age learning disabled graduates and dropouts. *Learning Disabilities Research, 1*(1), 50–55.

Name Index

Subject Index